Digest of Paper

Twenty-Ninth Annual International Symposium on

Fault-Tolerant Computing

Front Cover:

Photo by Joseph Kaski © 1998 (used with permission)

Back Cover (clockwise):

State of Wisconsin Capitol Dome
Photo by Charles R. Kime © 1999

Engineering Mall "Maquina" sculpture at sunset
Photo by Jeff Miller © UW-Madison News & Public Affairs 1995

Memorial Union Terrace lake front and downtown
Photo by Jeff Miller © UW-Madison News & Public Affairs 1996

Digest of Papers

Twenty-Ninth Annual International Symposium on
Fault-Tolerant Computing

June 15-18, 1999

Madison, Wisconsin, USA

Sponsored by

IEEE Computer Society
Technical Committee on Fault-Tolerant Computing

In Cooperation with

IFIP WG 10.4 on Dependable Computing and Fault Tolerance,

Supported by

The Department of Electrical and Computer Engineering of the University of Wisconsin-Madison
The Department of Electrical and Computer Engineering of the University of Iowa
The University of Illinois at Urbana-Champaign
AlliedSignal Inc.
The Madison Section of IEEE
Tandem (Compaq Computer Corp.)
International Business Machines

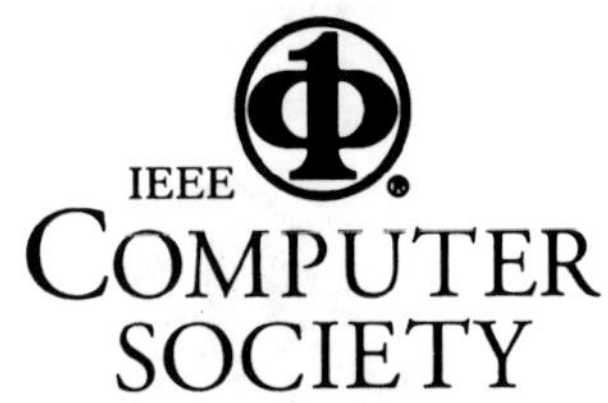

Los Alamitos, California
Washington • Brussels • Tokyo

IEEE Computer Society Order Number PR00213
ISBN 0-7695-0213-X
ISBN 0-7695-0215-6 (microfiche)
ISSN 0731-3071
IEEE Order Plan Catalog Number 99CB36352

Additional copies may be ordered from:

IEEE Computer Society
Customer Service Center
10662 Los Vaqueros Circle
P.O. Box 3014
Los Alamitos, CA 90720-1314
Tel: + 1-714-821-8380
Fax: + 1-714-821-4641
E-mail: cs.books@computer.org

IEEE Service Center
445 Hoes Lane
P.O. Box 1331
Piscataway, NJ 08855-1331
Tel: + 1-732-981-0060
Fax: + 1-732-981-9667
mis.custserv@computer.org

IEEE Computer Society
Asia/Pacific Office
Watanabe Building,
1-4-2 Minami-Aoyama
Minato-ku, Tokyo 107-0062 JAPAN
Tel: + 81-3-3408-3118
Fax: + 81-3-3408-3553
tokyo.ofc@computer.org

Editorial production by Danielle C. Martin

Cover art production by Alex Torres

Printed in the United States of America by The Printing House

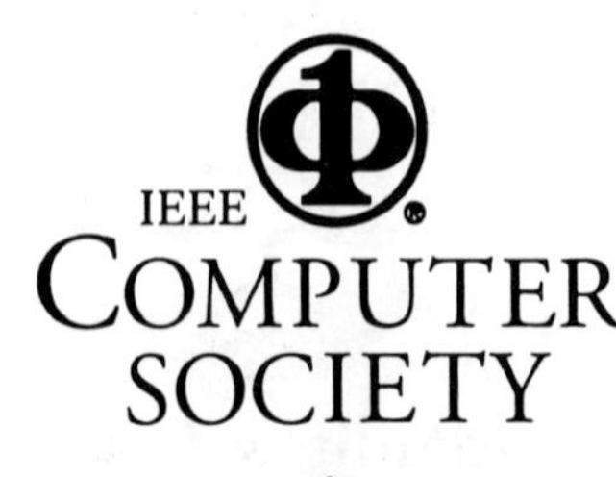

Table of Contents

FTCS-29

Session 3B: Student Papers I

Chair: W. Kent Fuchs, Purdue University, USA

Session 4A: Design of Fault-Tolerant Systems

Chair: David Rennel, University of California at Los Angeles, USA

Session 4B: Networking Issues I

Chair: John Meyer, University of Michigan, USA

Moderator: Ravi K. Iyer, University of Illinois, USA

Organizers: Ravi K. Iyer, University of Illinois, USA
A. Avizienis, University of California at Los Angeles, USA

Panelists: A. Avizienis, University of California at Los Angeles, USA
D. Barron, Compaq
D. Powell, LAAS
H. Levendel, Motorola
J. Samson, Honeywell

Session 6A: Diagnosis and Reconfiguration

Chair: Weiping Shi, University of North Texas, USA

Session 6B: Fast Abstracts I

Presentation of work in progress and late-breaking research results

Session 7A: CORBA and Group Communication

Chair: Richard Buskens, Bell Laboratories, USA

Session 7B: Coding and On-Line Testing

Chair: Hideo Fujiwara, Nara Institute of Science and Technology, Japan

Session 7C: Fast Abstracts II

Presentation of work in progress and late-breaking research results

Session 8A: Software Demonstrations and Practical Experience Reports

Chair: Jeff Zhou, AlliedSignal Inc., USA

Session 8B: Special Seminar: Intrusion Detection 238

Moderator: ***Roy Maxion, Carnegie Mellon University, USA***

Speakers: ***Marc Dacier, IBM Research, Switzerland***
Sami Saydjari, DARPA Information Technology Office, USA

Session 8C: Posters and Round Table

Chair: Nirmal Saxena, Stanford University, USA

Interactive time between students and other participants

Session 9A: Checkpointing II

Chair: Neeraj Suri, Boston University, USA

Session 9B: Testing

Chair: Kozo Kinoshita, Osaka University, Japan

Session 10A: Networking Issues II

Chair: Parmesh Ramanathan, University of Wisconsin at Madison, USA

Session 10B: Student Papers II

Chair: Christian Landrault, LIRMM, France

Session 11A: Dependability Evaluation

Chair: Jean-Claude Laprie, LAAS-CNRS, France

Session 11B: Practical Experience Reports

Chair: Robert Horst, 3ware, Inc., USA

Message from the General Chair

Kewal Saluja

FTCS has returned to Madison after 20 years and the Twenty-Ninth Annual International Symposium on Fault-Tolerant Computing (FTCS-29) is the last such meeting to be held in the 1900's. I am very pleased to welcome all the participants to the doubly-enriching experience of attending the premier conference in Fault-Tolerant Computing in one of the premier cities of the USA.

With the Symposium approaching its 30th Anniversary, what happens next? Taking the optimistic view, I am certain that we will survive the Y2K problem. Our computer systems will withstand the loss of two digits, or should I say, will correctly recover the two digits lost on the changing of the millennium, just as these machines withstood a somewhat similar problem associated with the Dow Index (D10K problem) when it moved from 4 to 5 digits. In any case, this is the time for reflection, as it provides an opportunity to analyze the past and predict what lies ahead.

FTCS content has moved from a heavy hardware emphasis to a more software-oriented emphasis. The general area of fault-tolerance has matured in the sense that many of the concepts and methods that appear in the archives of the Proceedings of the FTCS have either been applied or, in some cases, fallen by the wayside. Nearly all computing systems use some means of checking and achieving fault-tolerance in practice. It is important that we adapt to this change and initiate steps necessary for sustaining innovative achievements in the new millennium.

I believe that involvement of new researchers and practitioners in fault-tolerant computing, including participation in major leadership roles, is essential to sustaining the vitality of FTCS. I am sure that I speak for the organizing committee of the FTCS-29 when I say that long term future of this conference lies with the students of today. As a result we have made special efforts to attract students to this conference. We have strengthened the existing student programs and introduced new programs to encourage student participation. This has been helped by a number of industrial participants, namely Allied Signal, Tandem (Compaq) and IBM. A number of individuals from these organizations have been particularly helpful in achieving this goal.

I was fortunate to have an efficient and dedicated team as the organizing committee of the conference. My thanks to the Program Committee Chairs, Irith and Bill; and the Tutorials Chair, Arun; who were determined to put together an excellent technical and tutorials program. Nitin, the Publicity Chair, has been particularly efficient and helpful in disseminating the conference information. My thanks also to the International Liaison Committee members, and Rick, the Steering Committee Chair, for helping in getting things approved in an expeditious manner. I am especially thankful to my mentor, Sudhakar Reddy, the Student Participation Chair, for I often drew upon his experience and turned to him for help.

Finally, I am especially indebted to the local members of the organizing committee: Chuck — Local Arrangements Chair, Parmesh — Finance and Registration Chair, and Don — Publications Chair, who happily put up with all the demands I placed on them. I am also thankful to their families for they had also to tolerate the excessive demands of this conference. I am particularly thankful to my wife, Neeta, and my children, Sonali and Saurabh, for tolerating my frequent pre-occupation with conference matters.

I thankfully acknowledge the support and resources provided by the Departments of Electrical and Computer Engineering of the University of Wisconsin-Madison, the University of Iowa, the University of Illinois, and the Madison section of the IEEE. Lastly, on behalf of the FTCS-29 Organizing Committee, I express my sincere appreciation to all the participants of this year's symposium for their many contributions.

Message from the Program Co-Chairs

William H. Sanders

Irith Pomeranz

The International Symposium on Fault-Tolerant Computing is the premier forum in computer system dependability. This year's program contains several types of presentations, some of which are being introduced to FTCS for the first time this year. In addition to regular papers, the program contains practical experience reports, software demonstrations, student papers, FastAbstracts, a special seminar, and a panel.

Recognizing the importance of student contributions, we introduce this year a new category of papers called "On-Going Student Research." Papers in this category outline preliminary results and future directions of on-going research carried out by students. The student participation committee, chaired by Sudhakar Reddy, selected 18 out of 24 submissions in this category for presentation at the conference. The selected papers appear in a special proceedings, and are presented in two special sessions at the conference. Another new addition to FTCS this year is the inclusion of a special seminar session. The special seminar takes an in-depth look at an area that is related to dependable computing, but that has not traditionally been represented at the Symposium. This year's special seminar is on intrusion detection; it was organized by Roy Maxion, and is presented by Marc Dacier and Sami Saydjari.

In addition to introducing these two new types of presentations, we continue the tradition begun last year of presenting papers of timely interest as "FastAbstracts." FastAbstracts are intended to be a rapid mechanism for reporting on current work that may be incomplete, to provide a way to introduce new ideas to the FTCS community, and to act as a forum in which positions on controversial issues may be stated. The time between submission and presentation of a FastAbstract is short; abstracts were accepted until several weeks before the conference. Chuck Weinstock, the special submissions chair, coordinated the submission and screening of contributions in this category. Like student papers, FastAbstracts appear in a special proceedings and are presented in special sessions at the Symposium. This year's conference also includes a panel organized by Ravi Iyer and Algirdas Avizienis concerning the use of COTS to design dependable networked systems.

The program also has papers in the more traditional categories of practical experience reports and software demonstrations, as well as regular papers, which constitute the main part of the program. We received 121 submissions in these categories. To carry out the task of selecting the papers in these categories, we held two meetings of the program committee. In the first meeting, held in December in Urbana, Illinois, the program committee assigned the papers to reviewers. Prior to the meeting, 1,729 reviewer assignment suggestions were collected from program committee members via the web. The majority of the reviews were also collected via the web; in all, we collected 544 reviews from 286 reviewers. The paper selection meeting took place in Iowa City, Iowa, in February. Forty-three papers were selected for inclusion in the proceedings, including thirty-five regular papers, five practical experience reports, and three software demonstrations.

We would like to thank the many individuals whose help was crucial in putting together the program. The authors submitted high-quality papers. The reviewers and program committee members provided us with invaluable comments on the papers. The program committee members assigned reviewers and selected the papers included in this proceedings. Sudhakar Reddy chaired the student participation committee, which included W. Kent Fuchs, Miroslaw Malek, and Arun Somani. Chuck Weinstock, the special submissions chair, handled the FastAbstracts. Algirdas Avizienis, Ravi Iyer, and Roy Maxion organized special sessions. Kewal Saluja, the general chair, and Rick Schlichting, the steering committee chair, were always available to provide us with guidance on a variety of issues.

We would also like to thank the many individuals who provided invaluable assistance with administrative matters. Jenny Applequist helped in many ways throughout the process of putting together the program, including developing the web site for the conference, preparing the material for the referee assignment meeting, and helping to design and test the review database (which was based on David Powell's FTCS-26 database). Jim Cramer implemented the database and assisted with its use. Michael Chan created the web interface to the database, and, together with Chuck Weinstock, provided technical support in obtaining and implementing the www.ftcs.org domain name. Carol Eltoft entered the reviews into the database and Doug Eltoft helped with the implementation and use of the database. Michel Cukier, David Daly, Dan Deavours, Jay Doyle, Ramesh Chandra, Jennifer Ren, Paul Rubel, and Aaron Stillman helped with local arrangements for the referee assignment meeting. Carma Kuhl helped with local arrangements for the paper selection meeting.

We hope that you will find many contributions that are of interest to you, and that you will benefit from the papers included in this proceedings.

Irith Pomeranz and William H. Sanders
Program Co-Chairs
Twenty-Ninth Annual International Symposium on Fault-Tolerant Computing

Conference Committee

General Chair

Kewal K. Saluja, *University of Wisconsin at Madison, USA*
saluja@engr.wisc.edu

Program Co-Chairs

Irith Pomeranz, *University of Iowa, USA*
irith@eng.uiowa.edu

William H. Sanders, *University of Illinois at Urbana-Champaign, USA*
whs@crhc.uiuc.edu

Finance and Registration Chair

Parmesh Ramanathan, *University of Wisconsin at Madison, USA*
parmesh@engr.wisc.edu

Publications Chair

Donald L. Dietmeyer, *University of Wisconsin at Madison, USA*
dld@engr.wisc.edu

Local Arrangements Chair

Charles R. Kime, *University of Wisconsin at Madison, USA*
kime@engr.wisc.edu

Publicity Chair

Nitin Vaidya, *Texas A&M University, USA*
vaidya@cs.tamu.edu

Tutorials Chair

Arun Somani, *Iowa State University, USA*
arun@iastate.edu

Student Participation Chair

Sudhakar M. Reddy, *University of Iowa, USA*
reddy@eng.uiowa.edu

Special Submissions Chair

Charles B. Weinstock, *Software Engineering Institute, Carnegie Mellon University, USA*
weinstock@sei.cmu.edu

Ex Officio

Richard D. Schlichting, *University of Arizona, USA*
rick@cs.arizona.edu

International Liaison Committee

Hideo Fujiwara
Michael Nicolaïdis
David Taylor
Yervant Zorian

Program Committee

Jacob A. Abraham, *University of Texas at Austin, USA*
Jean Arlat, *LAAS-CNRS, France*
Algirdas Avizienis, *University of California at Los Angeles, USA*
Bernd Becker, *University of Freiburg, Germany*
Douglas M. Blough, *University of California at Irvine, USA*
Richard W. Buskens, *Bell Laboratories, USA*
Ram Chillarege, *IBM T.J. Watson Research Center, USA*
Joanne Bechta Dugan, *University of Virginia, USA*
Robert Horst, *3ware, Inc., USA*
Yennun Huang, *Bell Laboratories, USA*
Ravi K. Iyer, *University of Illinois, USA*
Farnam Jahanian, *University of Michigan, USA*
Niraj K. Jha, *Princeton University, USA*
Zbigniew Kalbarczyk, *University of Illinois, USA*
Nobuyasu Kanekawa, *Hitachi, Ltd., Japan*
Karama Kanoun, *LAAS-CNRS, France*
Johan Karlsson, *Chalmers University of Technology, Sweden*
Christian Landrault, *LIRMM, France*
Jean-Claude Laprie, *LAAS-CNRS, France*
Henrique Madeira, *Universidade de Coimbra, Portugal*
Miroslaw Malek, *Humboldt-Universität, Germany*
Roy Maxion, *Carnegie Mellon University, USA*
Michele Morganti, *ITALTEL-Central Research Labs, Italy*
Takashi Nanya, *University of Tokyo, Japan*
Janak Patel, *University of Illinois, USA*
David Powell, *LAAS-CNRS, France*
Parmesh Ramanathan, *University of Wisconsin, USA*
Sudhakar M. Reddy, *University of Iowa, USA*
John Rushby, *SRI International, USA*
André Schiper, *École Polytechnique Fédérale de Lausanne, Switzerland*
Weiping Shi, *University of North Texas, USA*
Santosh Shrivastava, *University of Newcastle upon Tyne, UK*
Daniel P. Siewiorek, *Carnegie Mellon University, USA*
Arun Somani, *Iowa State University, USA*
Lorenzo Strigini, *City University, UK*
Neeraj Suri, *Boston University, USA*
Ann Tai, *IA Tech, Inc., USA*
Kishor Trivedi, *Duke University, USA*
Shambhu Upadhyaya, *SUNY at Buffalo, USA*
Nitin H. Vaidya, *Texas A&M University, USA*
Paulo Veríssimo, *University of Lisboa, Portugal*

William C. Carter Award

William C. Carter

The William C. Carter Award is presented annually to recognize an outstanding FTCS submission in the area of dependable computing based on the author's graduate dissertation. The award honors the late William C. Carter, a key figure in the formation and development of the field of dependable computing, and someone who always took the time to encourage, mentor and inspire newcomers to the field. The award is sponsored by the IEEE Technical Committee on Fault-Tolerant Computing (TC-FTC) in cooperation with the IFIP Working Group on Dependable Computing and Fault Tolerance (WG 10.4).

Requirements for the award were announced in the FTCS-29 Call for Papers. To qualify, a paper must have been submitted to FTCS as a regular paper and must have been either single-authored by a graduate student or senior-authored by the student in conjunction with the dissertation advisor or committee member(s). Submissions by former students who are no more than two years past degree completion were also eligible. A paper is self-nominated for the award by certifying on its title page that it has met the requirements for consideration.

All Carter Award submissions accepted to the symposium as regular papers were evaluated by the Carter Award Committee established by the TC-FTC chair. Based on this evaluation, the Committee selected the following winner:

"The Systematic Improvement of Fault Tolerance in the Rio File Cache"

Wee Teck Ng and Peter M. Chen, University of Michigan, USA

Harrison Hagan Schmitt

Harrison Hagan Schmitt

Harrison Hagan Schmitt has the diverse experience of a geologist, pilot, astronaut, administrator, businessman, writer, and U.S. Senator. He studied at Caltech, as a Fulbright Scholar at Oslo, and at Harvard, receiving his Ph.D. in geology in 1964 based on field studies in Norway. As a civilian, Schmitt received Air Force jet pilot wings in 1965 and Navy helicopter wings in 1967.

Selected for the Scientist-Astronaut program in 1965, Schmitt, a native of Silver City, NM, organized the lunar science training for the Apollo Astronauts, managed much of the development of hardware and procedures for lunar surface exploration, and oversaw the final preparation of the Apollo Lunar Module Descent Stage. He was designated Mission Scientist in support of the Apollo 11 mission. After training as back-up Lunar Module Pilot for Apollo 15, Schmitt served in that same capacity on Apollo 17 — the last Apollo mission to the moon. On December 11, 1972, he and Gene Cernan landed in the Valley of Taurus-Littrow as the only scientists and the last of 12 men to step on the Moon.

In 1975, after two years managing NASA's Energy Program Office, Schmitt fulfilled a long-standing personal commitment by entering politics in 1976. He served in the U.S. Senate from 1977 through 1982, representing his home state of New Mexico. Senator Schmitt served on the Senate Commerce, Banking, Appropriations, Intelligence, and Ethics Committees. In his last two years in the Senate, Schmitt was Chairman of the Subcommittee on Science, Technology, and Space and of the Appropriations Subcommittee on Labor, Health and Human Services, and education. He later served on the President's Foreign Intelligence Advisory Committee, the President's Commission on Ethics Law Reform, as Co-Chairman of the International Observer Group for the 1992 Romanian elections, as Vice Chairman of the U.S. delegation to the 1992 World Administrative Radio Conference in Spain, and as chairman of the Technical Advisory Board for the U.S. Army Research Laboratory.

Harrison Schmitt consults, speaks, and writes on policy issues of the future, space, and the American Southwest. He presently serves as Chair of The Annapolis Center (risk assessment evaluation) and holds an appointment as Adjunct Professor in the Department of Engineering, University of Wisconsin, teaching "Resources from Space."

Schmitt's corporate board memberships include Orbital Sciences Corporation, the Draper Laboratory, Annapolis Center, PhDx Systems, Inc., Magplane Technology, Inc., and SVS Inc. He is a founder and serves as Chairman of Interlune Intermars Initiative, Inc., advancing the private sector's acquisition of lunar resources and 3He fusion power.

Schmitt's honors include 1973 Arthur S. Fleming Award, 1973 Distinguished Graduate of Caltech, 1973 Caltech Sherman Fairchild Scholar, NASA Distinguished Service Award, Fellow of the AIAA, Honorary Member of the Norwegian Geographical Society and Geological Association of Canada, 1989 Lovelace Award (space biomedicine), 1989 G.K. Gilbert Award (planetology), and Honorary Fellow of the Geological Society of America, American Institute of Mining, and Geological Society of London. Dr. Schmitt has received several honorary degrees.

Reviewers

Abraham, Jacob A.
Agrawal, Vishwani D.
Altman, Jörn
Alvisi, Lorenzo
Amato, Nancy
Amir, Yair
Arlat, Jean
Avizienis, Algirdas
Avresky, Dimiter R.
Balakrishnan, Meera
Banerjee, Prithviraj
Bartlett, Wendy
Basagni, Stefano
Bearden, Mark
Becker, Bernd
Behnia, Salimeh
Birman, Kenneth
Blough, Douglas M.
Bondavalli, Andrea
Boppana, Vamsi
Bose, Bella
Bowen, Nicholas S.
Bressoud, Thomas C.
Breuer, Mel
Bruck, Jehoshua
Burns, Alan
Buskens, Richard
Campbell, Roy H.
Cao, Y.
Carrasco, Juan
Casimiro, António
Castro, Miguel
Chakrabarty, Krishnendu
Chase, Craig
Chatterjee, Abhijit
Chen, Lan
Chen, Peter
Cheng, Kwang-Ting (Tim)
Chillarege, Ram
Chlamtac, Imrich
Choi, Gwan S.
Chung, Pi-Yu Emerald
Clark, Jeff
Constantinescu, Cristian
Cooper, Robert
Cristian, Flaviu
Cukier, Michel
Dahlgren, Peter
Dal Cin, Mario
Das, Chita R.
Das, Sajal K.
DeLong, Todd
Deswarte, Yves
DeVale, John
Dugan, Joanne Bechta
Dutt, Shantanu
Echtle, Klaus
Ekanadham, Eknath
Elaoud, Moncef
Elgindy, Hossam
Elnozahy, Elmootazbellah
Eschermann, Bernhard
Ezhilchelvan, Paul D.
Fabre, Jean-Charles
Fernsler, Kimberly M.
Fetzer, Christof
Figueras, Joan
Floering, Benjamin
Fuchs, W. Kent
Fujiwara, Eiji
Gaisler, Jiri
Galla, Thomas M.
Galpin, Vashti
Gao, Yuan
Ge, Ge
Ghosh, Indradeep
Gil, Pedro-Joaquin
Greenwood, Garry
Gregori, Enrico
Guerraoui, Rachid
Gupta, Sandeep
Han, Seungjae
Hayes, John P.
Heitmeyer, Constance
Helvik, Bjarne E.
Hiltunen, Matti A.
Holger, Karl
Horst, Robert W.
Hou, Jennifer
Huang, Yennun
Ibach, Peter
Iyer, Ravishankar K.
Jacobson, Doug
Jahanian, Farnam
Jain, Ravi
Jha, Niraj K.
Johnson, David B.
Johnson, Scott
Kaâniche, Mohamed
Kalbarczyk, Zbigniew
Kalyankrishnan, M.
Kandasamy, Nagarajan
Kanekawa, Nobuyasu
Kannan, Sampath
Kanoun, Karama
Karlsson, Johan
Karpovsky, Mark
Kasbekar, Mangesh M.
Kieckhafer, Roger M.
Kim, Hyungwon
Kim, Jae
Kim, Kane H.
Kim, Kee Sup
Kintala, Chandra M.R.
Kitakami, Masato
Koopman, Philip
Kopetz, Hermann
Krishna, C. Mani
Krishna, P.
Kulkarni, Shriram
Kuo, Sy-Yen
Lala, Jay
Landrault, Christian
Landwehr, Carl
Laprie, Jean-Claude
Lee, Kyung T.
Lee, Roger
Levendel, Isaac (Haim)
Leveson, Nancy G.
Liberato, Frank
Lin, Kwei-Jay
Liskov, Barbara
Little, Mark
Liu, Jane W.S.
Liu, Juqiang
Liu, Robin
Liu, Steve
Lo, Jien-Chung
Lombardi, Fabrizio
Lu, Songwu
Madeira, Henrique
Madhavan, Indumath
Mahapatra, Nihar Ranjan
Malan, Rob

Malek, Miroslaw
Manivannan, D.
Marron, Pedro
Marzullo, Keith
Maxion, Roy A.
Maxwell, Peter
Mazumder, Pinaki
Meadows, Catherine
Medidi, Muralidhar
Mehrotra, Sharad
Melhem, Rami
Merritt, Mike
Meyer, John F.
Millinger, Dietmar E.
Mishra, Shivakant
Mohan, G
Morganti, Michele
Moser, Louise E.
Mossé, Daniel
Murakami, Kazutaka
Murthy, C. Siva Ram
Nair, Sukumaran
Nanya, Takashi
Neves, Nuno
Nicolaïdis, Michael
O'Halloran, Colin
Offenberg, Joel
Pallierer, Roman
Pan, Jiantao
Panda, Dhabaleswar
Paradkar, Amit
Partridge, Derek
Patel, Janak H.
Paul, Sanjoy
Peterson, Lena
Piestrak, Stanislaw J.
Plank, James S.
Poledna, Stefan
Popov, Peter
Powell, David
Prakash, Ravi
Prata, Paula
Raghavendra, C. S.
Ramamritham, Krithi
Ramanathan, Parameswaran
Ramani, Srinivasan
Randell, Brian
Rangarajan, Sampath
Rao, Sriram
Ravi, S. S.
Reddy, Sudhakar M.
Redinbo, G. Robert
Rennels, David A.
Robinson, John P.
Rodrigues, Luis E.T.
Romanovsky, Alexander
Rufino, Jose
Rushby, John
Saglietti, Francesca
Saluja, Kewal K.
Sanders, William H.
Sasao, T.
Savir, Jacob
Saxena, Nirmal R.
Schiper, Andre
Schlichting, Richard D.
Scholl, Christoph
Schwarz, Janek
Segall, Zary
Sha, Lui
Shahabuddin, Perwez
Shankar, Mallikarjun
Sharma, Tilak C.
Shen, Jian
Shi, Weiping
Shin, Kang G.
Shrivastava, Santosh K.
Sieh, Volkmar
Siewiorek, Daniel P.
Silva, João Gabriel
Silva, Luis Moura
Simoncini, Luca
Singhal, Mukesh
Sinha, Prasun
Sinha, Purnendu
Sivalingam, Krishna M.
Smith, T. Basil
Somani, Arun K.
Sommer, Siegmar
Sonza Reorda, Matteo
Srinivasan, Balaji
Ssu, Kuo-Feng
Stanton, Jonathan
Stott, David T.
Strigini, Lorenzo
Stunkel, Craig
Su, Chouchin
Sun, Hairong
Suri, Neeraj
Tai, Ann T.
Tallini, Luca
Tang, Dong
Taylor, David J.
Thévenod-Fosse, Pascale
Torin, Jan
Touba, Nur A.
Trivedi, Kishor S.
Tsai, Timothy K.
Tschirpke, Steffen
Tzeng, Nian-Feng
Unsal, Osman
Upadhyaya, Shambhu J.
Vaduvur, Bharghavan
Vaidya, Aniruddja S.
Vaidya, Nitin H.
van Moorsel, Aad
Veríssimo, Paulo
Viega, John
Voas, Jeff
Vogels, Werner
Voges, Udo
Waeselynck, Helene
Wah, Benjamin
Walker, Duncan M.
Walter, Chris J.
Wang, Honge
Wang, Yi-Min
Werner, Matthias
Wheater, Stuart M.
Whisnant, Keith
White, Allan L.
Wolff, Burkhart
Wood, Alan
Wu, Jie
Xie, Wei
Xu, Lihao
Yajnik, Shalini
Yalamanchili, Sudhakar
Yao, Bin
Yum, K.-H.
Zang, Xinyu
Zou, Hengmin

Session 1

Opening Session

Session 2A

Algorithm-Based Fault Tolerance

Chair: Jacob Abraham
The University of Texas at Austin, USA

Algorithm Based Fault Tolerance Versus Result-Checking for Matrix Computations

Paula Prata
Universidade da Beira Interior
Dep. Matemática/Informática
Rua Marquês d'Ávila e Bolama
P- 6200 Covilhã, Portugal
pprata@dei.uc.pt

João Gabriel Silva
Universidade de Coimbra/CISUC
Dep. Eng. Informática
Pinhal de Marrocos
P-3030 Coimbra – Portugal
jgabriel@dei.uc.pt

Abstract[1]

Algorithm Based Fault Tolerance (ABFT) is the collective name of a set of techniques used to determine the correctness of some mathematical calculations. A less well known alternative is called Result Checking (RC) where, contrary to ABFT, results are checked without knowledge of the particular algorithm used to calculate them.

In this paper a comparison is made between the two using some practical implementations of matrix computations. The criteria are performance and memory overhead, ease of use and error coverage. For the latter extensive error injection experiments were made. To the best of our knowledge, this is the first time that RC is validated by fault injection.

We conclude that Result Checking has the important advantage of being independent of the underlying algorithm. It also has generally less performance overhead than ABFT, the two techniques being essentially equivalent in terms of error coverage.

Keywords: Result-checking, ABFT, Fault injection, Error Detection, Matrix operations.

1. Introduction

Algorithm-Based Fault-Tolerance (ABFT) [1] [2] is a very effective error detection technique, applicable to various matrix computations that are central to many scientific and engineering programs. Essentially some additional calculations are added to (mostly linear) matrix transformations, enabling a check at the end that provides very high error coverage with low performance overhead. Besides, ABFT complements very well other low overhead error detection methods, like memory protection and control flow checking [3] [4].

A less well known set of techniques, collectively called Result-Checking (RC) [5], comprises theoretical work on developing low-redundancy checkers to verify the result of various kinds of mathematical functions, including most of those for which ABFT algorithms exist. RC has the attraction of being problem-based, that is, it does not depend on the algorithm used to solve a problem, but only on the mathematical function being calculated.

The idea behind this paper is to compare these two different approaches. We use three different criteria for that comparison.

First we examine the error coverage. Since there is no analytical way of calculating it under realistic fault models, we used our Xception fault injection tool [6] to determine that coverage experimentally. To the best of our knowledge, this is the first time that RC is validated by fault injection.

The second criterion is the overhead, both in performance and in memory usage.

Finally, we consider the ease of use, where essentially the ease of programming is taken into account.

We left out of our comparison one aspect where ABFT would do better than RC, namely fault localization and error recovery, studied extensively e.g. in [7] (RC has no such capability). We did that because fault localization and error recovery are available only for a subset of the ABFT algorithms, and because they are only possible in multiprocessor architectures like systolic arrays, where very good fault containment exists between the several processors involved in the computation. For the more general case where no such fault containment exists or is quite imperfect, these features of ABFT are of little use.

In this way our conclusions make no assumption about the underlying architecture.

The mathematical calculations that we used in our experiments were matrix multiplication and QR factorization, two widely used algorithms for which ABFT and RC techniques are available. A third case study is matrix inversion.

[1] This work was partially supported by the Portuguese Ministério da Ciência e Tecnologia, the European Union through the R&D Unit 326/94 (CISUC) and the project PRAXIS XXI 2/2.1/TIT/1625/95 (PARQUANTUM).

0-7695-0213-X/99 $10.00 © 1999 IEEE

This small set of computations is quite representative, being nuclear in four standard problems of numerical linear algebra: linear systems of equations, least square problems, eigenvalue problems and singular value problems. These are the problems that constitute for instance the Lapack [9] and ScaLapack libraries.

To make our study as impartial as possible, for the ABFT mechanism applied to matrix multiplication and QR factorization we used the source code produced by Chowdhury [7][1], that implements ABFT assuming a single fault model. To study the RC mechanism for those cases, we have eliminated, from that code, the ABFT checkers, and introduced Freivalds' simple checker for matrix multiplication described in [8].

For matrix inversion (using LU decomposition) we used routines from the public domain library LAPACK [9], to illustrate the fact that a very important advantage of RC is its capability to use practical code. In fact, many of the "clean" mathematical algorithms used for the derivation of ABFT algorithms are seldom used in numerical analysis, for performance and stability reasons. Adapting ABFT algorithms to those practical routines is not a trivial task. For the LAPACK routines used in our test case, we only used RC, that can use them as a black box, and did not undertake the lengthy and complex task of deriving some ABFT variation for them.

The main conclusion is that the central advantage of RC is its independence of the underlying algorithm, being able to use real numerical algorithms directly. It also has generally less performance overhead than ABFT, the two techniques being essentially equivalent in terms of error coverage.

The structure of this paper is as follows: in sections 2 and 3 the concepts of ABFT and RC are reviewed and section 4 describes the fault injection process. Sections 5 and 6 describe the experimental evaluation for the problems of matrix multiplication and QR factorization respectively. Section 7 describes the results for matrix inversion and section 8 presents the conclusions.

2. Algorithm based fault tolerance

ABFT was first proposed as a checksum scheme for matrix operations [2]. The input matrices are augmented with an additional checksum row and an additional checksum column. Each element of the checksum column/row is the sum of the elements of the original matrix that are in the same row/column. The augmented matrices are then multiplied using an unchanged multiplication algorithm - in the end, the additional row and column of the result matrix should still be the sum of the elements of the same row or column. If that is not the case, some error occurred. The initial ABFT schemes have been proposed for systolic architectures, [2] [10], and required additional processors to compute the checking operations. In those systems each processor calculates a bounded number of data elements, and the fault model considered assumes that if only one processor at a time fails (single fault assumption), then only a bounded number of output data items could be wrong.

Schemes for general-purpose multiprocessors have also been developed for several numerical algorithms like matrix multiplication, LU and QR decompositions, Fast Fourier Transforms and Iterative solvers for partial differential equations ([11] [1] [12]). These works have considered the following fault-model: The processor that reads in and distributes the data, collects and interprets the results, is assumed to be fault free. It is called the host. The processors that perform the computations (the nodes) are the same that execute the checking operations. Each processor checks the results from another node and not its own results. These nodes may be faulty and may corrupt all the data they possess. Assuming a single fault model, if a faulty processor produces wrong results, its checker processor will detect the fault. If an error only affects the execution of the test, it will signal as faulty the wrong node.

This model has some weak points: A fault may affect the data before the check columns and rows are calculated, or after the results have been verified, but before they are safely stored somewhere, probably in the host's disk. Besides, it may not be realistic to assume a fault free host. To overcome these problems we have recently proposed a technique that complements the fault tolerant capabilities of ABFT, protecting that part of the program that ABFT does not cover, namely input, output and the execution of the test itself. Since the method can be applied to any calculation that is checked by an assertion (like e.g. a Result Checker), we call the general method "Robust Assertions" [13]. We have considered that extension to ABFT in the experiments described in this paper.

Another important issue related to ABFT (and RC) is the rounding error inherent in all floating-point computations, which means that the test made to determine whether there was some error in an ABFT protected computation cannot be exact. A tolerance interval has to be calculated to account for that rounding error. This means that, if a fault produces an error whose magnitude falls inside the tolerance interval, that fault won't be detected, which is probably reasonable since it can be argued that it is not significant. Then the tolerance interval will establish the threshold for what is considered an error and what is not. There are many works on deriving rounding error upper bounds [14]; a simplified error analysis to calculate the tolerance interval at run-time for some ABFT techniques is proposed in [15].

3. Result-checking

It is often easier to check the result of a mathematical function than to compute it. Starting from this idea, some theoretical work has been done in the RC field [5]. The concept of a simple checker for a function f, is presented as [8]: *"a program which, given inputs x and y, returns the correct answer to the question, does f(x)=y?; The checker may be randomized, in which case, for any x and y, it must give the correct answer with high probability over its internal randomization. Moreover, the checker must take asymptotically less time than any possible program for computing f "*. The initial motivation of this work was to assure software-fault tolerance by checking the result, instead of testing the program in a set of random inputs or by a formal proof of correctness. There are checkers proposed for very different areas such as sorting [5], linear transformations [16] and algebraic expressions of trigonometric functions [17].

The result checker that we will experimentally evaluate is Freivalds' simple checker for matrix multiplication described in [18] [8], that can be applied to the three examples used in this paper: matrix multiplication, QR factorization and matrix inversion. Suppose that we want to verify if a computed matrix C is the product of the given matrices A and B. To do that we can check if the product of C with a random vector r is equal to the product of A with B times r, (C×r=?A×(B×r)). When C=A×B, the condition is obviously verified; if C≠A×B, the probability that a random r verifies C×r=A×(B×r) is very small. If we repeat the process for several values of r the probability that it detects an error can be made arbitrarily high. Thus we have an $O(n^3)$ computation (where n is the matrix order) verified by an $O(n^2)$ checker.

There remains the problem of verifying the checker. In [16] it is argued that: checkers are much simpler than the code they check, therefore less likely to have bugs. If the checker fails but the program is correct, there occurs a false alarm that alerts us to an error somewhere. The situation when a checker incorrectly accepts a wrong result is the worst one. The authors claim that correlated errors that lead to such a situation are very unlikely. As to the consequences of hardware faults (or software faults with similar effects), the protection of the checker can be done by the "Robust Assertions" method referred before.

Finally we should note that, like ABFT, RC also has the problem of rounding error.

4. Fault injection

We have evaluated our fault-detection mechanisms with a fault injection tool, called Xception [6], which emulates hardware faults at a very low level. Xception is a software fault injection and environment monitoring tool that can inject transient faults in specific microprocessor functional units such as Floating-point ALU, Integer ALU, Data Bus, Address Bus, General Purpose Registers, Condition Code Register(s), Memory Management Unit and Memory. Each fault affects only one machine instruction and one functional unit at a time.

The system used in this paper is a Parsytec PowerXplorer with 4 PowerPC 601, each with 8 Mbytes of memory, running Parix, a parallel OS similar to UNIX, with a Sun SparcStation as the host. We have distributed the computations over three nodes, with the fourth processor acting as the host.

In all experiments reported in this paper, the faults injected were transient bit flips of one bit, randomly chosen, applied to a randomly selected functional unit in a randomly selected processor, time triggered (i.e. randomly distributed during the program execution time). The fault definition parameters have been exactly the same in all experiments, except for the duration of the program that was adapted for each case. Since our main purpose is to compare ABFT and RC, in this work we only have considered faults in the processing nodes. The "Robust Assertion" [13] technique would handle faults in the host. To classify the outputs we have done a component-wise comparison between the result matrix (which is outputted even when an error was detected) and a reference solution, obtained in a run with no injected fault. The outputs were classified as: *correct output*, *no output* -the program terminates but does not produce any result, *timeout* - no output because of a crash and *wrong output* - at least one matrix element is different from the reference value.

5. Matrix multiplication

Given two matrices A and $B \in \mathbb{R}^{n \times n}$, the usual matrix multiplication algorithm computes each entry c_{ij} of matrix C=A×B as the dot product of A's ith row and B's jth column. In Chowdhury's algorithm [7] [1], the matrix A is distributed block-wise by rows and B is replicated over all processing nodes. Each processor P_i performs the sub-matrix multiplication $C_i=A_i \times B$ using the sequential algorithm described above. At the end, each node sends the result sub-matrices back to the host, which concatenates them.

We have computed the product of two 270-by-270 double precision matrices with random entries chosen in the range (-100, +100). The error bound for that matrix-matrix product was approximately 10^{-8} (this is a component-wise error bound obtained from the expression $|C - C'| \leq \gamma_n |A||B|$, where C' is the computed matrix and $\gamma_n = nu/(1-nu)$, with n=270 and $u=2^{-53}$ [14]). Since this rounding error bound is only an approximation, we did not use it to distinguish just two intervals (below and above), but instead considered two additional small intervals of the size of one order of magnitude, around that central value, to enable a more precise understanding of the results. The considered intervals for the absolute difference between two corresponding elements are then: Maximum difference less than 10^{-9}, maximum difference between 10^{-9} and 10^{-8}, maximum difference between 10^{-8} and 10^{-7}, and maximum difference greater than 10^{-7}. This last group contains the "clearly wrong results".

Another problem that we have faced was that some faults cause Not a Numbers (NaNs) - special codes used in the IEEE floating point format that when compared with anything, including itself, always returns false. Since the original program did not handle them, we had to introduce some additional code to detect them. This acts as an additional error detection method.

5.1 Matrix multiplication with ABFT

We have used the source code available from the work of Chowdhury [7] [1] as described earlier. Because of ABFT, each node additionally calculates the checksum row of their part of the result matrix, and verifies the sub-matrix calculated by its neighbor, in a directed circular cycle. It should be noted that, probably for performance and memory usage reasons, Chowdhury chose not to verify the checksum column, which can have some impact on coverage. In the comparison of the checksum vectors we have used a fixed tolerance of 10^{-8}. This was the minimum value for which we did not get false alarms in the data set used. This experimentally calculated tolerance has the same magnitude of the error bound estimated for the matrix multiplication.

The outcomes of the experiments are shown in table I, following the classification described above. As can be seen only 21 faults (that is approx. 0.2%), that have produced clearly wrong results, were not detected. The study of those cases has shown that 7 faults have been injected in a low-level routine of memory copy, which is called from the communication routines used by our program. In a previous study [13], we have concluded that if we protect the results with a CRC, before sending them to the host, those faults are detected. The other 14 faults have been injected in the line of the source code that performs the dot product of each A's row with each B's column. These faults were mainly injected in the integer unit, and the bit that has been modified was always in the less significant bits of the word. A manual analysis of one undetected wrong result has shown that it corresponds to a situation where two errors in the same column cancel each other. Errors like these could be detected if the checksum column of C would also be verified. We have approx. 2.8% of undetected small errors.

To improve the detection capabilities of ABFT we have implemented a new version of the program adding to the algorithm the checker that verifies the checksum column of C, and protecting the results with a CRC after they were produced, as suggested in [13]. Table II presents the results for this enhanced version of matrix multiplication with ABFT. The percentage of undetected wrong results is now approx. 2.3%. But we have an important qualitative difference. All the clearly wrong results have been detected. This means that the probability of undetected "clearly wrong results" is very low for the fault/error model used. In section 5.3 we present an upper bound confidence limit for the probability of the undetected errors. As can also be seen from the table the number of wrong outputs decreases while the number of correct outputs grows. This is a natural consequence of adding test code.

Matrix mult. with ABFT (checksum row only)		no. of faults	% of total	Undetected	
				no.	%
Correct Output		3944	44.5	-	-
No output		4	0.1	-	-
Timeout		1959	22.1	-	-
Wrong outputs	NaNs	4	0.1	0	0.0
	diff. > 10^{-7}	2605	29.4	21	0.2
	10^{-8}<diff. ≤10^{-7}	82	0.9	0	0.0
	10^{-9}<diff. ≤10^{-8}	66	0.7	52	0.6
	diff. ≤10^{-9}	194	2.2	194	2.2
Total		8858	100.0	267	3.0

Table I - Results of fault injection for matrix multiplication with ABFT (with checksum row only).

Matrix mult. with ABFT (and CRC)		no. of faults	% of total	Undetected	
				no.	%
Correct Output		4029	47.7	-	
No output		7	0.1	-	
Timeout		1813	21.5	-	
Wrong outputs	NaNs	6	0.1	0	0.0
	diff. > 10^{-7}	2303	27.3	0	0.0
	10^{-8}<diff. ≤10^{-7}	60	0.7	0	0.0
	10^{-9}<diff. ≤10^{-8}	54	0.6	30	0.3
	diff. ≤10^{-9}	169	2.0	168	2.0
Total		8441	100.0	198	2.3

Table II - Results for matrix multiplication with ABFT (version with row and column checksums and CRC)

5.2 Matrix multiplication with result-checking

To evaluate the RC mechanism for matrix multiplication we have used the initial program, without fault-detection mechanisms, and added Freivalds' checker, described in section 3, to the code that is executed in the host. After reading the matrices A and B, the host processor also reads a random vector r (with values in the range (-1,1)) that was generated first. Then it computes the two matrix-vector products, B×r and A×(B×r). Matrices A and B are sent to the processing nodes and the program follows as before. The host, after receiving the result matrix C, computes the vector C×r. Finally the component-wise comparison between the two check-vectors, A× (B×r) and C×r, is performed. The tolerance value was 10^{-8}. Again it was the minimum value for which we did not get false alarms in the data set used. First we have implemented the checker using just one random vector. Table III shows the outcomes of the experiments.

As can be seen all the clearly wrong results have been detected. The value of undetected errors is slightly higher than in ABFT cases (approx. 3.1%), including some results with a maximum difference from the reference result, between 10^{-8} and 10^{-7}, (0.3%). We tried to improve this mechanism using two vectors, that is, we checked the result twice with different random vectors.

Table IV shows the outcomes of the experiments, with this second RC version. One random vector r1, with values in the range (-1,1), as the previous one, and a second vector r2, with values in the range (0,5). The undetected wrong results are now approx. 2.7% but there were 4 "clearly wrong results" that were detected only with the second random vector. This shows that small variations in the random vector (we only changed the seed of vector r1 between the two experiments) can have some impact in the coverage of errors close to the rounding error.

Matrix mult. with RC (one random vector)		no. of faults	% of total	Undetected no.	Undetected %
Correct Output		3921	44.2	-	-
No output		13	0.2	-	-
Timeout		1983	22.4	-	-
Wrong outputs	NaNs	11	0.1	0	0.0
	diff. > 10^{-7}	2600	29.3	0	0.0
	10^{-8}<diff. ≤10^{-7}	82	0.9	27	0.3
	10^{-9}<diff. ≤10^{-8}	69	0.8	59	0.7
	diff. ≤10^{-9}	187	2.1	187	2.1
Total		8866	100.0	273	3.1

Table III - Results of fault injection for matrix multiplication with RC (using one random vector).

Matrix mult. with RC (two random vectors)		no. of faults	% of total	Undetected no.	Undetected %
Correct Output		4027	45.17	-	-
No output		14	0.16	-	-
Timeout		1945	21.82	-	-
Wrong outputs	NaNs	5	0.06	0	0.0
	diff. >10^{-7}	2574	28.87	0	0.0
	10^{-8}<diff.≤10^{-7}	67	0.75	2	0.02
	10^{-9}<diff.≤10^{-8}	80	0.89	43	0.48
	diff. ≤10^{-9}	203	2.28	198	2.22
Total		8915	100.0	243	2.72

Table IV - Results of fault injection for matrix multiplication with RC (using two random vectors)

5.3 ABFT Vs result-checking

The error coverage of both mechanisms for matrix multiplication looks very similar. The values of undetected wrong results are summarized in table V. We assume that the injected faults are representative faults that is, the selection probability of each injected fault is equal to its occurrence probability. Then *f/n* is an unbiased estimator for the non-coverage $\overline{C}$ of each mechanism studied (n is the number of injected faults and f the number of undetected faults). An upper 100γ% confidence limit estimator for the non-coverage is given by $\frac{(f+1)F_{2(f+1),2(n-f),\gamma}}{(n+f)+(f+1)F_{2(f+1),2(n-f),\gamma}}$ [19], where $F_{v1,v2,\gamma}$ is the 100γ% percentile point of the F distribution with $v1, v2$ degrees of freedom. The last column of table V presents the upper 99% confidence limit estimates for the non-coverage of each mechanism studied.

Matrix multip. – undetected wrong outputs					
mechanism	injected faults	diff> 10^{-7}	diff≤ 10^{-7}	$\overline{C}$	$\overline{C}^{\uparrow}_{99\%}$
ABFT row ch. only	8858	21	246	3.01%	3.27%
whole ABFT+CRC	**8441**	**0**	**198**	**2.35%**	**2.63%**
RC-1 rand. vect.	8866	0	273	3.08%	3.33%
RC-2 rand. vect.	**8915**	**0**	**243**	**2.72%**	**2.99%**

Table V – Undetected wrong outputs, ABFT Vs RC, for matrix multiplication.

In summary we can say that the final version of ABFT has a fault/error coverage greater than 97.37% and the final version of RC has a fault/error coverage greater than 97.01% with a confidence level of 99%.

ABFT has a slightly better coverage for small errors. This is explained by the fact of that, in the ABFT scheme, each partial test verifies a fraction of the data smaller than in the result-checking test. But then those are almost certainly non-significant errors. For both mechanisms the percentage of undetected small errors will depend on how accurate is the tolerance value used to compare the check vectors. After all we can consider that when a fault detection mechanism does not detect errors of the same magnitude as the rounding error this is not a "real failure" of the fault-detection mechanism. In that case the coverage lower bounds estimates became 99.95% for both mechanisms with a confidence level of 99%.

Comparing the execution time of both fault-detection mechanisms, both are checkers of $O(n^2)$ for a calculation of $O(n^3)$. Then we can expect that the overhead will be negligible for large matrix sizes. But in the ABFT case when we add the test for the second matrix dimension, we are introducing additional communication. Moreover, with the first test (using only the checksum row) we are taking advantage of the row distribution of matrix A, but this is not the case in the second test.

Table VI shows the calculation time overheads for some matrix dimensions. We have excluded the input/output operations from the time measured. We can see that ABFT is superior to RC only in the first version (the one where the second matrix dimension was not tested and the results were not protected). Comparing the versions that have equivalent fault coverage (whole ABFT with CRC and RC with two random vectors) result checking has a clear advantage.

Comparing the memory overheads, initially both checkers have an O(n) overhead. That corresponds to the check vectors. But, in the ABFT case, when we introduce the test for the second matrix dimension, we need to send to each node a copy of the block of A corresponding to the next processor. That means a duplication of the matrix A. In that case the memory overhead for ABFT is $O(n^2/p)$.

Finally, ABFT is much more complex to implement than RC. We have compared the number of lines of code for the unprotected initial program, and the final versions of both ABFT and RC. The overheads are 67% for RC and 104% for the ABFT version. But the main advantage of RC is that it can be used, without modification, with any algorithm of matrix multiplication. ABFT, by design, depends on the particular algorithm used.

Matrix multiplication – calculation overheads						
matrix dim.	base time: second	ABFT-row check.	whole ABFT	whole ABFT+ CRC	RC - 1 rand. vector	RC - 2 rand. vectors
210	2.80	1.4%	14.3%	**18.2%**	2.5%	**4.6%**
300	6.78	1.2%	11.9%	**14.9%**	2.2%	**3.7%**
360	10.8	0.9%	10.8%	**13.1%**	2.0%	**3.5%**

Table VI – Calculation time overheads, ABFT Vs RC, for matrix multiplication.

6. QR factorization

The problem of QR factorization is to decompose an initial matrix A into an upper triangular matrix R and an orthogonal matrix Q, i. e, A=QR.

Chowdhury's parallel algorithm that we use [7], initializes Q as the identity matrix and does a column cyclic data distribution of A and Q. These matrices are successively transformed to obtain R and Q^T respectively, using orthogonal (Householder) transformations. To perform the *k*th update each processor needs the *k*th column of the previously updated matrix A. This column is sent to all processors by its owner, in each iteration.

A component-wise error bound for QR factorization is given by $|A-QR| \leq nr\gamma_{cn}G|A|$, where $\gamma_{cn}=cnu/(1-cnu)$ with c a small integer constant, n is the matrix dimension, r is the number of Householder transformations, and $G = n^{-1}ee^T$, with $e=(1,1,\ldots,1)^T$ [14].

We have got a bound of approx. 10^{-9} for our data, which is quite high because computing the real difference for the data we used $|A - QR|$ we got a maximum error of approx. 10^{-13}. For this case we then decided to use three intervals to classify the errors: the case when the maximum absolute difference to the reference results is less than 10^{-12}, the case when that difference is between 10^{-12} and 10^{-9} and the case when that difference is greater than 10^{-9}.

We used as our test case a 210-by-210 double precision matrix with random entries chosen from (-100, +100). The output is a file with the matrices Q and R.

6.1 QR factorization with ABFT

The ABFT used for QR factorization [7] checks both dimensions of Q and R, and also tests the column that is broadcast in each iteration. As before the nodes are logically configured in a directed cycle. Before sending the final results to the host, the working processors protect their results with a CRC.

The tolerance values used in each test were the minimum values for which we did not get false alarms for the data set used. We also test if any value of the result matrices, Q and R, are NaNs. The results of fault injection experiments are shown in table VII. As can be seen all the faults that lead to results with an error greater than 10^{-12} have been detected.

QR with ABFT (and CRC)		no. of faults	% of total	Undetected no.	Undetected %
Correct Output		4306	48.8	-	-
No output		70	0.8	-	-
Timeout		2550	28.9	-	-
Wrong outputs	NaNs	21	0.2	0	0.0
	diff. $>10^{-9}$	1608	18.2	0	0.0
	$10^{-12}<$diff.$\leq10^{-9}$	117	1.3	0	0.0
	diff. $\leq10^{-12}$	160	1.8	140	1.6
Total		8832	100.0	140	1.6

Table VII - Results for QR factorization with ABFT.

6.2 QR factorization with result-checking

For the RC version, we eliminated from the previous program all the code corresponding to the ABFT, and added Freivalds' checker to the QR factorization. That is, we verify A=Q×R by checking the equality Ax r=Q×(R×r), where r is a random vector. We used two random vectors with entries in the range (-1,1) and (0,1). The tolerance value was 10^{-12}, again calculated in order to eliminate false alarms for the matrix used. Table VIII presents the outcomes for this experiment

The results are similar to those of the ABFT mechanism. As can be seen only one wrong output between 10^{-12} and 10^{-9} and a number of errors smaller than 10^{-12} were not detected.

QR with RC (2 random vectors)		no. of faults	% of total	Undetected	
				no.	%
Correct Output		4332	45.4	-	-
No output		16	0.2	-	-
Timeout		2604	27.3	-	-
Wrong outputs	NaNs	25	0.3	0	0.0
	diff. $>10^{-9}$	2226	23.3	0	0.0
	$10^{-12}<$diff.$\leq 10^{-9}$	139	1.5	1	0.01
	diff. $\leq 10^{-12}$	196	2.0	149	1.56
Total		9538	100.0	150	1.57

Table VIII - Results for QR factorization with RC.

6.3 ABFT Vs result-checking

Comparing the error coverage of both mechanisms for QR factorization, we find similar results. Table IX shows the estimates for the non-coverage of both mechanisms and the corresponding upper 99% confidence limit estimates, calculated as in the matrix multiplication case.

Then ABFT has a fault/error coverage greater than 98.14% and RC has a fault/error coverage greater than 98.16% with a confidence level of 99%. If we consider only errors of magnitude greater than 10^{-12}, which is probably more realistic, we get 99.99% for the coverage lower bound of ABFT and 99.93% for RC, with the same confidence level of 99%.

It is when comparing the execution time of both mechanisms that significant differences begin to appear, because ABFT has a much higher overhead than RC. Table X shows the calculation time overheads for some matrix dimensions. This large difference mainly results from the extra communication introduced by ABFT.

Memory overhead is of O(n) and is similar for both checkers.

Finally, ABFT is again much more complex to implement than RC, and RC is again applicable to a black box routine, while ABFT depends heavily on the particular algorithm and decomposition used.

QR – undetected wrong outputs					
mechanism	injected faults	diff> 10^{-12}	diff≤ 10^{-12}	$\overline{C}$	$\overline{C}^{\uparrow}_{99\%}$
ABFT+CRC	8832	0	140	1.59%	1.86%
RC-2 rand. vec.	9538	1	149	1.57%	1.84%

Table IX – Undetected wrong outputs, ABFT Vs RC, for QR.

QR factorization – calculation overheads			
matrix dim.	base time (second)	ABFT + CRC	RC 2 random vectors
210	5.05	41.58%	1.58%
300	11.83	39.98%	1.44%
360	19.08	34.75%	1.36%

Table X – Calculation time overheads, ABFT Vs RC, for QR.

7. Matrix inversion

Computing the inverse of a matrix A is equivalent to solving the system of linear equations AX=I (where I is the identity matrix). This is usually done by first computing the LU factorization of matrix A where L is a unit lower triangular matrix and U is upper triangular. It is known that the Gaussian elimination used to perform the LU decomposition is unstable unless we use partial or complete pivoting [20]. Introducing ABFT in that algorithm, as is proposed in [21] for systolic architectures, is complex, and the overhead due to the extra communication, needed to check the pivoting operations, will probably be even higher than in the QR case. Moreover, [22] shows, with an example, that the ABFT may not be able to detect faults in the pivoting operations. Besides, since we used here LAPACK routines, the changes needed to introduce ABFT would affect essentially all the routines' code, and would not be trivial at all to do (and thus quite error prone). We did not attempt to do it.

On the other hand, we did implement RC for that particular LAPACK routine, again using Freivalds' checker. This is intended as a very clear demonstration of the most important advantage of RC - its adaptability to already available, highly complex, numerical routines. We verified $A\times A^{-1}=I$ by checking the equality $A\times(A^{-1}xr)=I\times r$, with r a random vector. We should note that computing the inverse is an $O(n^3)$ algorithm. Testing directly $A\times A^{-1}=I$, is an approx. $O(n^3)$ test , while Freivalds' checker is an $O(n^2)$ calculation.

We have used the LAPACK routines DGETRF and DGETRI to compute the inverse of a 200-by-200 double precision matrix with random entries from (-10, +10). The random vector had entries in the range (-1, +1) and the tolerance value was experimentally determined to be 10^{-11} for the data set used. Table XI presents the outcomes for this experiment where we used only one processing node.

The results are quite good even with just one random vector. As can be seen all the wrong results with an error greater than 10^{-11} have been detected and just 2.2% of the faults produced undetected wrong results with an error smaller than 10^{-11}. That means an upper bound for the non-coverage of 2.51% (with 99% of confidence level).

This case shows that RC has a very high coverage even for Gauss elimination with pivoting. In that algorithm, faults that affect some intermediate results used for determining the order of the rows in pivoting, can not be detected by ABFT because these errors do not affect the checksum vectors. This shows that RC, due to its end-to-end nature, is able in this case to verify calculation steps that ABFT does not cover. This means that, although we did not perform that test, we would expect for this algorithm a coverage advantage for RC.

Matrix inversion with RC		no. of faults	% of total	Undetected	
				no.	%
Correct Output		3657	42.8	-	-
No output		12	0.2	-	-
Timeout		2039	23.9	-	-
Wrong outputs	NaNs	46	0.5	0	0.0
	diff. $>10^{-11}$	2488	29.1	0	0.0
	diff. $\leq 10^{-11}$	301	3.5	190	2.2
Total		8543	100.0	190	2.2

Table XI - Results for matrix inversion with RC.

8. Conclusions

In this work we compared RC with ABFT for some common matrix calculations. We tried to establish which has better coverage, lower overhead, greater ease of use and wider applicability. To the best of our knowledge, this is the first time that RC is validated by fault injection.

The main advantage of RC over ABFT is its independence of the underlying algorithm used to calculate some mathematical function. In fact, a complicated practical hurdle to use ABFT is the fact that many of the "clean" mathematical algorithms used for the derivation of ABFT algorithms are seldom used in numerical analysis, for performance and stability reasons. Adapting ABFT algorithms to those practical routines is not a trivial task. Result Checking can use those practical routines unchanged, as we have shown in the Matrix Inversion example. Besides, at least for the cases studied, the number of lines of code needed to implement RC is much smaller than for ABFT.

In terms of performance overhead, the advantage of RC is also clear for the more complex algorithms studied, where the difference can become quite large. In the more simple examples there is no significant difference between the two. No relevant difference was found in memory overhead.

Regarding coverage, RC and ABFT proved to be essentially equivalent, at least for the examples studied. It would be interesting to see RC and ABFT compared for other mathematical calculations.

A general conclusion of this work is that RC is a very promising line of research. It would be very nice to have a kind of library of result checkers for most of the existing numerical algorithms.

References

[1] Chowdhury, A. R. and P. Banerjee, "Algorithm-Based Fault Location and Recovery for Matrix Computations" in FTCS-24, Austin, Texas, 1994, pp. 38-47.

[2] Huang, K.-H. and J. A. Abraham, "Algorithm-Based Fault Tolerance for Matrix Operations", in IEEE Trans. on Comp., vol. C-33 no. 6, 1984, pp. 518-528.

[3] Rela, M., H. Madeira, and J. G. Silva. "Experimental Evaluation of the Fail-Silent Behavior of Programs with Consistency Checks" in FTCS-26, Sendai, Japan, 1996, pp. 394-403.

[4] Silva, J. G., J. Carreira, H. Madeira, D. Costa, and F. Moreira, "Experimental Assessment of Parallel Systems" in FTCS-26, Sendai, Japan, 1996, pp. 415-424.

[5] Blum, M. and S. Kannan, "Designing Programs that Check Their Work", Journal of the Association for Computing Machinery, 42(1), 1995, pp. 269-291.

[6] Carreira, J., H. Madeira, and J. G. Silva, "Xception: A Technique for the Experimental Evaluation of Dependability in Modern Computers", in IEEE Trans. on Software Eng., vol. 24, no. 2, Feb. 1998, pp. 125-135.

[7] Chowdhury, A. R., "Manual and Compiler Assisted Methods for Generating Fault-Tolerant Parallel Programs", Ph.D. Thesis. University of Illinois at Urbana-Champaign, 1995, 127 pages.

[8] Blum, M. and H. Wasserman, "Reflections on The Pentium Division Bug", in IEEE Trans. on Comp., vol. 45, no. 4, April 1996, pp. 385-393.

[9] Anderson, E., Z. Bai, C. Bischof, and e. al., "LAPACK Users' Guide", 1995, SIAM.

[10] Jou, J.-Y. and J. A. Abraham, "Fault-Tolerant Matrix Arithmetic and Signal Processing on Highly Concurrent Computing Structures", in Proc. of the IEEE, vol. 74, no. 5, 1986, pp. 732-741.

[11] Banerjee, P., et al., "Algorithm-Based Fault Tolerance on a Hypercube Multiprocessor", in IEEE Trans. on Comp., vol. 39, no. 9, Sep. 1990, pp. 1132-1144.

[12] Chowdhury, A. R., N. Bellas, and P. Banerjee, "Algorithm-Based Error-Detection Schemes for Iterative Solution of Partial Differential Equations", in IEEE Trans. on Comp., vol. 45, no. 4, April 1996, pp. 394-407.

[13] Silva, J. G., P. Prata, M. Rela, and H. Madeira. "Practical Issues in the Use of ABFT and a New Failure Model" in FTCS-28, Munich, Germany, 1998, pp. 26-35.

[14] Higham, N., "Accuracy and Stability of Numerical Algorithms", SIAM, 1996.

[15] Chowdhury, A. R. and P. Banerjee, "Tolerance Determination for Algorithm-Based Checks Using Simplified Error Analysis Techniques" in FTCS-23, 1993, pp. 290-298.

[16] Wasserman, H. and M. Blum, "Software Reliability via Run-Time Result-Checking", Journal of the ACM, 44(6), 1997, pp. 826-849.

[17] Rubinfeld, R. "Robust functional equations with applications to self-testing / correcting" in 35th IEEE Conference on Foundations of Computer Science, 1994, pp. 288-299.

[18] Rubinfeld, R., "A Mathematical Theory of Self-Checking, Self-Testing and Self-Correcting Programs", PhD Thesis. University of California at Berkeley, 1990, 103 pages.

[19] Powell, D., M. Cukier, and J. Arlat, "On Stratified Sampling for High Coverage Estimations", in 2nd European Dependable Computing Conference, Taormina, Italy, 1996, pp. 37-54.

[20] Golub, G. H. and C. F. V. Loan, "Matrix Computations", Johns Hopkins University Press, Second edition 1989, 642 pages.

[21] Yeh, Y.-M. and T.-Y. Feng, "Algorithm-Based Fault Tolerance for Matrix Inversion with Maximum Pivoting" Journal of Parallel and Distributed Computing, 14, 1992, pp. 373-389.

[22] Boley, D., G. E. Golub, S. Makar, N. Saxena, and E. J. McCluskey, "Floating Point Fault Tolerance with Backward Error Assertions", in IEEE Trans. on Comp., vol. 44, no. 2, Feb. 1995, pp. 302-311.

An Algorithm Based Error Detection Scheme for the Multigrid Algorithm

Amitabh Mishra
Broadband Switching Concept Center
Bell Laboratories - Lucent Technologies
2000 N. Naperville Road, Naperville, IL 60566
mishra@lucent.com

Prithviraj Banerjee
Center for Parallel & Distributed Computing
Northwestern University
2145 Sheridian Road, Evanston, IL 60208-3118
banerjee@ece.nw.edu

Abstract

In this paper an Algorithm Based Error Detection (ABED) scheme is applied to the multigrid algorithm which provides an iterative solution to a system of linear algebraic equations resulting from a finite difference discretization of a Poisson equation. Invariants are created to implement checking in the relaxation, restriction and interpolation operators. Modifications to invariants due to roundoff errors accumulated within the operators which often lead to a situation known as false alarms have been addressed by deriving the expressions for the roundoff errors in the algebraic processes in the operators and correcting the invariants accordingly. ABED encoded multigrid algorithm is shown to be insensitive to the size and the range of the input data, besides providing excellent error coverage at a low latency for floating point, integer and memory errors.

1. Introduction

Algorithm Based Fault Tolerance (ABFT) is a cost effective technique to detect and correct errors caused by permanent or transient failures in the hardware. This technique has already been applied to numerical algorithms e.g. matrix multiplications, LU factorizations etc. [1], [2]; the fast Fourier transforms [3], [4], QR factorization [5], singular value decomposition [6] etc. running on array processors. Later the same set of problems were resolved using parallel algorithms [7], [8] running on general-purpose multiprocessors.

The ABFT technique is known as ABED (algorithm based error detection) when applied only for the detection of errors. The ABED technique provides fault tolerance by preserving an invariant before the start and at the end of all computations in an algorithm. It can also preserve an invariant during the computations by slightly modifying the algorithm. Lack of preservation of the invariant during the course of the algorithm signals presence of errors in the computation due to faults. Since most of these computations are performed on computers which have finite precision, sometimes invariants are not preserved because of roundoff errors in the computation of the invariant and in the algorithm, and the ABFT technique can signal presence of faults even in the absence of any actual hardware faults. This situation is known as false alarms. Invariant computations, therefore should be corrected for roundoff errors to eliminate or minimize the false alarms by using some kind of tolerance.

It has been shown that methods which compute tolerance using error analysis of the algebraic manipulations in the algorithm are superior to other methods [9]. The error analysis provides upper bounds of roundoff errors which can occur in the computation of an expression on a machine with finite precision. The invariants when modified by adding the computed value of the roundoff error accumulated in an algorithm totally solves the problem of false alarms for any data set of any magnitude or dimension.

While there has been significant activity in the area of algorithm based error detection for the numerical algorithms running on array or multiple processors, a special class of numerical algorithms especially those dealing with the iterative solution of algebraic equations have not been pursued in the literature until recently. Very recently an algorithm based error detection scheme using error analysis has been applied to the successive overrelaxation algorithm to iteratively solve the Laplace's equation on a two dimensional grid [10]. Also, a short version of the present paper discussed how ABED encodings could be applied to a multigrid algorithm [13].

This paper presents details of a low cost ABED multigrid algorithm for the iterative solution of linear algebraic equations resulting from a finite difference discretization of a Poisson equation in two dimensions. We use error analysis to derive expressions for the upper bound of roundoff errors in the multigrid algorithm which are then used to modify the invariants in the checking step.

This paper has been organized as follows. We first present a basic multigrid algorithm which has been used for ABED encodings. The multigrid algorithm with checking is subsequently presented along with the derivations of error expressions for relaxation, restriction and

0-7695-0213-X/99 $10.00 © 1999 IEEE

interpolation. Algorithms for relaxation and restriction with individual checks are also given. Finally results for error coverages and time overhead for the ABED encoded multigrid algorithm computed on a SUN Sparcserver 2000, a shared memory symmetric multiprocessor (SMP) are presented.

2. The Multigrid Algorithm

The multigrid method is basically an iterative method which attempts to exploit the presence of an inherent continuous problem in reaching a discrete solution. For the sake of simplicity we present it for a two dimensional solution of a Poisson equation

$$\frac{\partial^2 u}{\partial x^2} + \frac{\partial^2 u}{\partial y^2} = f \qquad 1$$

on a domain Ω subject to boundary conditions such that $u = 0$ on the boundary. The finite difference discretization of equation (1) gives

$$(A^1 u^1)_{jk} = h^{-2}(u^1_{j+1,k} + u^1_{j-1,k} + u^1_{j,k+1} + u^1_{j,k-1} - 4u^1_{jk}) \qquad 2$$

where $h = \frac{1}{(M+1)}$ and M is the odd number of interior nodes in the discretization in both x and y directions. The superscript 1 refers to the grid. The total number of nodes N including boundary conditions are: $N = (M + 2)**2$ Thus for a N noded problem equation (2) can be written as matrix equation:

$$A^1 u^1 = f^1 \qquad 3$$

2.1 The Algorithm

The most simple multigrid algorithm is called a coarse grid correction algorithm. This name comes from the use of a coarse grid with mesh spacing $2*h$ to correct an approximate solution on the fine (mesh spacing h) grid. Here is the precise description of a coarse grid correction algorithm that uses only one auxiliary grid [14].

Let $G^1(.,.)$ denote a relaxation process on the fine grid. Let R^2_1 (restriction) denote a mapping from grid functions on the fine grid to grid functions on the coarse grid. Let I^1_2 (interpolation) denote a mapping from functions on the coarse grid to the functions on the fine grid. Let A^2 be the matrix which is obtained by discretizing the differential equation on the coarse grid. The algorithm can now be given as :

1. Choose an initial guess u^1
2. Do ν relaxation steps: for $k = 1, \nu$
   $u^1 \leftarrow G^1(u^1 f^1)$
3. Transfer residual to coarse grid: $r^1 = f^1 - A^1 u^1$; and let $r^2 = R^2_1 r^1$
4. Solution Process on Coarse grid: solve $A^2 e^2 = r^2$
5. Interpolation to the fine grid and solution update: $u^1 = u^1 + I^1_2 e^2$
6. Stopping test:
   $||e^2||_2 = [\sum_{i=1}^{i=M} |e^2_i|]^{1/2}$
   If $||e^2_2|| \le \varepsilon$; *stop else goto step* 2

The steps and some of the terms used in the algorithm are explained in the following.

2.1.1 Step I & II: In step I, an initial guess to the solution is chosen which is further relaxed in step II. The relaxation process typically consists of a few steps of some convergent iterative process on the fine grid which yields an acceptable solution, if iterated long enough. Such a process might be a Jacobi method, a Gauss Seidel, variants of Gauss Seidel, Successive Overrelaxation (SOR) or any other method. The most common iterative process is the Jacobi method which can be summarized as:

```
for (k = 0; k<= 2; k++ ) {
  for ( i = 1; i <= n; i++ )
    for ( j = 1; j <= n; j++ )
```

$$u^{(1)}_{i,j} = \frac{1}{4}(u^0_{i,j-1} + u^0_{i,j+1} + u^0_{i-1,j} + u^0_{i+1,j} - h^2 f_{i,j}); \qquad 4$$

}

In equation (4), the subscript denotes the grid, and the superscript denotes the iteration count. For the multigrid method only a few Jacobi iterations (1 to 3) are sufficient. The preparatory work for step III is done in step II, where we compute the error in the solution by defining it as:

$$e^1 = \bar{u} - u^1 \qquad 5$$

where $\bar{u}$ is the exact solution of the discrete equations. Premultiplying equation (5) by A^1 gives us:

$$\begin{aligned} A^1 e^1 &= A^1 \bar{u} - A^1 u^1 \\ &= f^1 - A^1 u^1 = r^1 \end{aligned} \qquad 6$$

where r^1 is the residual vector. Equation (6), therefore provides another alternative to solving the original matrix problem.

2.1.2 Step III & IV: In this phase the residue is transferred onto a coarse grid and then equation (6) is solved. The coarse grid has many fewer nodes than the finer grid. In general 1/2 as many as in one dimension, 1/4 in two dimension, and 1/8 in three dimensions. Therefore, the work required to solve the system of equations (6) is much less than that on the fine grid.

For a one dimensional problem, the simple restriction operator can be given by equation (7)

$$R_1^2 r_j^1 = (r^1)_{2j} \qquad 7$$

which transfers the even subscripted residual values from a fine grid to a coarse grid. Alternatively a weighted restriction operator can also be defined by equation (8) for a one dimensional mesh as depicted by Fig. 1,

$$(R_1^2 r^1)_j = 1/4(r^1)_{2j-1} + 1/2(r^1)_{2j} + 1/4(r^1)_{2j+1} \qquad 8$$

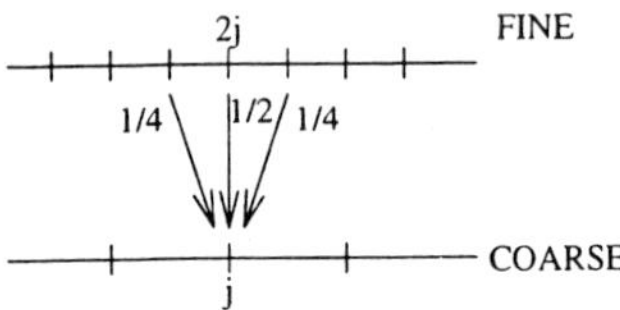

Figure 1 - Weighted Restriction in 1 - Dimension

which can be extended to equation (9) for a two dimensional grid. Equation (9) can be shown pictorially by Figure 2.

$$(R_1^2 r^1)_{j,k} = 1/2(\, r_{2j,2k}^1\,) + 1/8(r_{2j-1,2k}^1 + r_{2j+1,2k}^1 + r_{2j,2k-1}^1 + r_{2j,2k+1}^1) \qquad 9$$

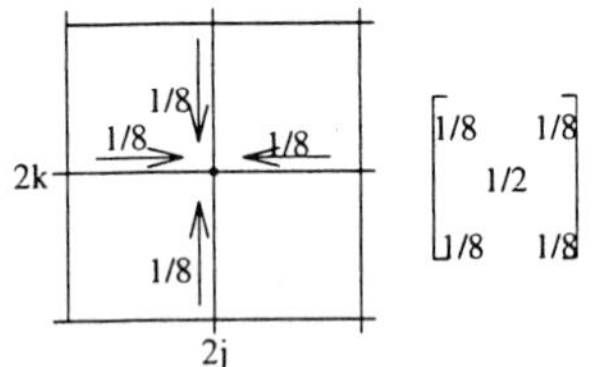

Figure 2 - Weighted Restriction in Two Dimensions

In step IV, a system of linear algebraic equations

$$A^2 e^2 = r^2 \qquad 10$$

is solved. Any suitable method for solving a system of equations, direct or iterative can be chosen.

2.1.3 Step V - Interpolation: In this phase a computed solution of equation (10) on the coarse grid is interpolated to all points of the fine grid by a linear interpolation operator I_2^1 defined below by equation (11)

$$(I_2^1 e^2)_{jk} = \begin{cases} e_{p,m}^2 & \text{if} j = 2p,\ k = 2m \\ \frac{1}{2}(e_{p,m-1}^2 + e_{p,m}^2) & \text{if} j = 2p, k = 2m-1 \\ \frac{1}{2}(e_{p-1,m}^2 + e_{p,m}^2) & \text{if} j = p-1, k = 2m \\ \frac{1}{4}(e_{p-1,m-1}^2 + e_{p-1,m}^2 + e_{p,m-1}^2 + e_{p,m}^2) & \text{if} j = 2p-1, k = 2m-1 \end{cases} \qquad 11$$

and then updating the approximate solution u on the fine grid according to equation (12). Figure 3 depicts the interpolation on a two dimensional grid.

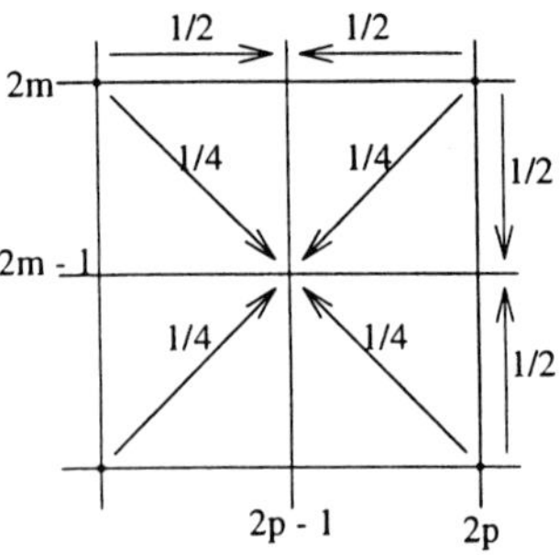

Figure 3 - Interpolation in Two Dimensions

The hope is that the interpolated $I_2^1 e^2$ is sufficiently close to the exact error e^1 thus the updating process on the fine grid will significantly

$$u^1 = u^1 + I_2^1 e^2 \qquad 12$$

improve the quality of the solution.

2.1.4 Step VI: In this step a convergence criterion is applied to the solution vector on the fine grid and the algorithm is stopped if the criterion is met. Otherwise the algorithm is restarted from step II.

3. The Multigrid Algorithm with Checking

In this section we develop checkings for three basic operators namely relaxation, restriction, and interpolation.

3.1 Jacobi Relaxation with Checks

We have chosen the Jacobi method for relaxation in the multigrid algorithm because of its simplicity. The Jacobi relaxation begins with some initial guess u^1 and then follows the algorithm described earlier.

The checks for Jacobi can be developed by looking at equation (4) which is the summation of five terms on the right hand side over $1 \le i,j \le n$. Lets denote $s0$, $s1$, $s2$, $s3$, $s4$, and $s5$ as sums of $u[i][j]$, $u[i][j-1]$, $u[i][j+1]$, $u[i-1][j]$, $u[i+1][j]$ and $f[i][j]$ over both the indices $1 \le i,j \le n$. A checking based on the linearity property requires that a checksum is to be maintained by summing over both the indices for each of the terms in equation (4) which requires $5n^2$ operations. $s1$ through $s4$ have been shown to be summed at the cost of $2n$ operations [9] by using $s0=0$, a very reasonable choice. $s5$ which sums the source terms will have an operation count of zero if we are solving a Laplace's equation and can have an upper bound of $O(N)$ for a Poisson equation as a very few nodes have sources associated with them.

Also, $s5$ remains constant because neither h nor $f(i,j)$ change during the relaxation loop. We have,

$$s0 = \sum_{i=1}^{n} \sum_{j=1}^{n} u[i][j]$$

$$s1 = s0 + \sum_{i=1}^{n} [\ u[i][0] - u[i][n]]$$

Similarly,

$$s2 = s0 + \sum_{i=1}^{n} u[i][n+1] - u[i][1]$$

$$s3 = s0 + \sum_{j=1}^{n} u[0][j] - u[n][j]$$

$$s4 = s0 + \sum_{j=1}^{n} [u[n+1][j] - u[1][j]]$$

$$s5 = h^2 \sum_{i=1}^{m} \sum_{j=1}^{m} f[i][j] \qquad 13$$

here m denotes the total number of nodes which have non-zero source terms. The Jacobi relaxation algorithm with checks can be written as:

3.1.1 Algorithm

```
s0 = s5 = 0;
for (i=1; i <= m; i++)
for (j=1; j <= m; j++)
s5 = s5 + (-h **2 )*f[i][j];
for(k=0; k<=iter; k++)
{
        s4 = s3 = s2 = s1 = s0;
        for (i=1; i <= n; i++)
    {
                s1 = u[i][0] - u[i][n] + s0;
                s2 = u[i][n+1] - u[i][1] + s2;
    }

    for(j=1; j<= n; j++)
    {
        s3 = u[0][j] - u[n][j] + s3;
        s4 = u[n+1][j] - u[1][j] + s4;
        }

for(i=1; i<= n; i++)
for(j=1; j<= n; j++)
t[i][j] = 0.25*[ u[i][j-1] + u[i][j+1] + u[i-1][j] + u[i+1][j]
        - (h**2)* f[i][j]];
s0 = 0.25*[ s1 + s2 + s3 + s4 + s5 ];
for(i=1; i <= n; i++)
for(j=1; j <= n; j++)
u[i][j] = t[i][j];
}
```

Figure 5 - Relaxation - Jacobi Algorithm with Checking

If there are no errors, $s0$ and the sum of $u[i][j]$ over $1 \le i,j \le n$ will be equal and can be used for error detection, assuming no roundoff, or that the roundoff errors have the same magnitude in both the terms hence they cancel each other. Thus, $s0$ and the sum of $u[i][j]$ can be used as invariants for fault detection.

3.1.2 Error Bound Expressions: The roundoff error accumulation in $u[i][j]$ and $s0$ are going to be different because of the way each of these are computed i.e. in the number of steps as well as the differences in the expressions themselves. A proper tolerance value for checking thus can only be arrived if we derive the expressions for the upper bounds of the error accumulated due to roundoff in each of the terms. Error bound derivations for the iterative solution of Laplace's equation using the SOR algorithm are given in [9], [10], which are extended here for a Jacobi solution to a Poisson equation. The global error in the Jacobi algorithm is computed for each iteration by accumulating the local errors in each of the variables which affect the invariants and then adding these up to global errors of the previous iteration. Thus at the end of the iteration, the invariants are available for error detection.

In the following, we shall provide the derivations of the error expressions for the algorithm given in Fig. 5.

The algebraic expressions which we need to analyze for roundoff errors for the Jacobi relaxation are of two types:

$$(I) \quad a = d + b + c$$

$$(II) \quad a = K\,[c + d + e + f - Ng]$$

Here lower case letters and upper case letters are denoting variables and constants respectively. We denote by notation $|err(a)|$ the upper bound on the absolute error associated with a variable a which results due to a floating point operation on a. We can write therefore for a variable v,

$$|\bar{v}| \le |v| + |err(v)| \qquad 14$$

knowing that any floating point operation $z = fl(x \oplus y)$ results in an error $err(z) = (x+y)\delta$, where $|\delta| \le \varepsilon = 2^{-t}$ for a t digit mantissa [11].

Now we shall derive the error expression for (I). Rewriting (I) using the notation of equation (14)

$$\bar{a} = fl(\bar{d} + \bar{b} + \bar{c})$$

Let us denote,

$$t_1 = fl(\bar{d} + \bar{b}) = (\bar{d} + \bar{b})(1 + \delta_1)$$

so $\bar{a} = fl(t_1 + \bar{c}) = (t_1 + \bar{c})(1 + \delta_2)$

Now substituting for t_1 in the expression for $\bar{a}$, and replacing $|\delta_i| = \varepsilon$, we get

$$\bar{a} = (\bar{d} + \bar{b} + \bar{c}) + 2(\bar{d} + \bar{b})\varepsilon + \bar{c}\varepsilon$$

$$|\bar{a}| \le [\ |\bar{d} + \bar{b} + \bar{c}| + (\ 2|\bar{d}| + 2|\bar{b}| + |\bar{c}|)\varepsilon]$$

Now upon substitution $|\bar{a}| \leq |a| + |err(a)|$ in the above expression, we get

$$|a|+|err(a)|\leq(|d|+|b|+|c|)+|err(d)+err(b)+err(c)|$$
$$+2(|d|+|err(d)|+|b|+|err(b)|)\varepsilon+(|\bar{c}|+|err(c)|)\varepsilon$$

Since, $|a| = |d| + |b| + |c|$, we get

$$|err(a)|\leq|err(d)+err(b)+err(c)|+(2|d|+2|b|+|c|)\varepsilon \qquad 15$$

upon ignoring the second order terms.

Now we shall derive a similar expression for (II). Rewriting (II) using the notation of equation (14):

$$\bar{a} = fl[K(\bar{c} + \bar{d} + \bar{e} + \bar{f} - N\bar{g})]$$

Denoting (i) $t_3 = fl(\bar{c} + \bar{d} + \bar{e} + \bar{f})$, (ii) $t_2 = fl(\bar{c} + \bar{d} + \bar{e} + \bar{f} - N\bar{g})$, and (iii) $t_1 = fl(Kt_2)$, and following the steps of *I*, the error in *a* is given by:

$$err(a) \leq K[(|5c| + |5d| + |4e| + |3f| + |3Ng|]\varepsilon \qquad 16$$
$$+ K[|err(c)| + |err(d)| + |err(e)| + |err(f)| + |err(g)|]$$

Please refer to [12] for the complete derivation.

3.1.3 Jacobi Relaxation with Checks - Algorithm: We will now modify the algorithm given in Fig. 5 by introducing the expressions derived earlier for rounding errors in the invariants. The modified algorithm is given in Fig. 6 below. The terms *erru*, *errs*0 – *errs*5 denote the errors in the variables u, $s0 - s5$ respectively. Variable $fs0$ contains the summation of $u[i][j]$, $1 \leq i,j \leq n$, and $errfs0$ contains the floating point error accumulated while computing $fs0$. All other terms in the algorithm are self explanatory.

```
s0 = erru = errs0 = 0.0;
for (k = 0; k < iter; k ++)
{
        s5 = s4 = s3 = s2 = s1 = s0;
        errs5 = errs4 = errs3 = errs2 = errs1 = errs0;
}

for(i =1; i <=n; i ++)
{
        s1 = u[i][0] - u[i][n] + s1;
        s2 = u[i][n+1] - u[i][1] + s2;
        errs1 = 2*(u[i][0] + u[i][n]) + s1 + errs1;
        errs2 = 2*(u[i][n+1] + u[i][1]) + s2 + errs2;
}

for(j=1;j<=n;j++)
{
        s3 = u[0][j] - u[n][j] + s3;
        s4 = u[n+1][j] - u[1][j] + s4;
        errs3 = 2*(u[0][j] + u[n][j]) + s3 + errs3;
        errs4 = 2*(u[n+1][j] - u[1][j]) + s4 + errs4;
}
for(i=1; i<=n; i++)
for(j=1; j<=n; j++)
{
        t[i][j] = 0.25*[u[i][j-1] + u[i][j] + u[i-1][j] + u[i+1][j]
                - (h**2)*f[i][j];
        s5 = s5 + (h**2)*f[i][j];
        errs5 = errs5 + s5 + (h**2)*f[i][j];
}
s0 = 0.25*[s1 + s2 + s3 + s4 + s5 ];
erru = 0.25*[5s1 + 5s2 + 4s3 + 3s4 + 4s5 ];
errs0 = 0.25*[errs1 + errs2 + errs3 + errs4 + errs5] + errs0;
for(i=1;i<=n; i++)
for(j=1;j<=n; j++)
{
        u[i][j] = t[i][j];
}
errfs0 = fs0 = 0;
for( i = 1; i <= n; i++)
for( j = 1; j <= n; j++)
{
        fs0 = fs0 + u[i][j];
        errfs0 = fs0 + errfs0 + u[i][j];
}
if(abs(s0-fs0) > (errfs0 + erru + errs0)*epsilon )
error_is_detected;
}
```

Figure 6 - Jacobi Relaxation with Checks - Algorithm

In order to make the Jacobi algorithm with checks more readable and consistent with the algorithm presented in Figure 5, we have used double subscripted notations for $u[i][j]$ and $t[i][j]$. However, a pair (i,j) representing a node on the grid can be uniquely replaced by a single subscripted index *l*, where $1 \leq l \leq n$, as there are only *N* nodes on the fine grid. With this substitution, some of the double for loops in the algorithm can be replaced by a single for loop in the actual implementation.

3.2 Restriction with Checks

For the equations governing the restriction given in Section 2, we shall define invariants which can be used for error detection for the restriction operator. Since the residual on each of the nodes on the fine grid is known, the sum of residual on the entire grid can be maintained as one invariant. This can be done at the beginning of the restriction.

Let *csf* (Checksum on fine grid) denote the sum of residuals on the fine grid given as:

$$csf = \sum_{i=1}^{N} r_i \qquad 17$$

where *N* is the number of nodes. Please note that nodes which are unconstrained are the ones which contribute to the *csf*. The boundary nodes do not contribute anything to *csf* because residual is zero at these nodes. Now we use the restriction operator given by equation (9) to project the residual on to the coarse grid. We define another invariant *csr* (Checksum on coarse grid)

$$csr = \sum_{i=1}^{N} rr_i \quad 18$$

on the coarse grid. The auxiliary vector rr_i contains the projected residual given by $(R_1^2 r^1)$ for the entire fine grid. In the absence of roundoff errors both invariants are equal i.e.

$$csr = csf \quad 19$$

and can be used for error detection. The restriction operation with checking is accomplished in $O(N)$ operations.

3.2.1 Error Analysis: The algebraic expression for the restriction operator given by equation (9) can be represented as:

$$a = Kb + M(c + d + e + f) \quad 20$$

and the floating point error in computing a can be given as

$$err(a) = [2Kb + M(|5c| + |5d| + |4e| + |3f|)]\varepsilon \quad 21$$

Please refer [12] for the proof.

The algorithm for restriction with checking is given below. Here variables *err_csf* and *err_csr* denote the roundoff errors

3.2.2 Restriction with Checks - Algorithm

```
/*initialize*/
err_csf = 0.0; /*error in invariant csf*/
err_csr = 0.0; /*error in invariant csr*/
err_a = 0.0; /*error in a*/
{
for (i=1; i<=n; i++)
{           csf = csf + r(i);
            csr = csr + rr(i);
            err_csf = err_csf + csf*epsilon;
            err_csr = err_csr + csr*epsilon;
}
/*computing the err(a)*/
for(i=1; i<=node_coarse; i++)
err_a = err_a + 0.5*b[i] + 0.125*( c[i] + d[i] + e[i] + f[i]);
err_a = err_a*epsilon;
/*checking*/
if(abs(csf - csr) > err_a + err_csf + err_csr) error_is_detected;
}
```

3.3 Interpolation

The error obtained by solving $A^1 e^1 = r^1$ on the coarse grid is projected on the fine grid by the interpolation operator given by equation (11). In this section we derive the error expressions for the error accumulated in the interpolation operator,

For error analysis we are dealing with the equations of the following types in the interpolation:

$$\begin{aligned}(i)\ & a = a \\ (ii)\ & a = M(b + c) \\ (iii)\ & a = M(c + d + e + f)\end{aligned} \quad 22$$

The first equation is an assignment operation, and (ii) is the subset of (iii) so from the roundoff perspective we will concentrate on (iii) .

The roundoff error in the computation of $a = M(c + d + e + f)$ is given by:

$$err(a) \le M[|5c| + |5d| + |4e| + |3f|]\varepsilon \quad 23$$

Please refer [12] for the proof.

3.3.1 Construction of Invariants: Let S be the sum of errors on each of the nodes on the coarse grid i.e

$$S = \sum_i y_i \quad 24$$

Let x_i 's be the errors projected on the nodes on the fine grid which were not on the coarse grid, computed using the formulas given in the multigrid algorithm. Then let

$$T = \sum_i y_i + \sum_i x_i = S + Q \quad 25$$

We create an auxiliary vector (checksum_auxiliary) denoted by P which stores the error on each of the nodes on the fine grid, modified by the normalizing constant $K = \frac{S}{T}$ given by

$$P = K \sum_{i=1}^{kfree} e_i \quad 26$$

Here *kfree* denotes number of unconstrained nodes on the fine grid. In the absence of roundoff errors, S and P should be equal. The operation count for the interpolation operator with checking is still $O(N)$.

The algorithm for the Interpolation operator with checking can be constructed in a manner similar to restriction and relaxation. A complete algorithm, however is given in [12].

4. Experimental Results

The target hardware chosen for running the multigrid algorithm with ABFT is a Sun Sparcserver 2000 with four processors. Each of the processor had a Superscalar Sparc version 8 architecture with 36 Kbytes of on chip cache, 2

MBytes of cache and 64 Mbytes of memory. The parallel multigrid algorithm was implemented using the multithreaded library on the SUNs. In this section the error coverage results under simulated fault conditions and the timing overhead are presented.

4.1 Error Coverage

The error coverage is defined to be percentage of all hardware injected errors that are detected by the error detection scheme regardless of the magnitude of the error. The Significant Error Coverage (SEC), on the other hand, is the coverage achieved when the error introduced in an element causes its value to change by 0.1%.We used an error injection methodology similar to [8] where word level and bit level errors were injected in software. While error coverage is studied for several types of transient and permanent faults e.g.

1. Floating Point Computation Error - Bit and Word Levels
2. Integer Computation Error - Bit and Word Levels
3. Errors in Memory Access

only the transient bit level errors for floating point addition scenario have been analyzed in more detail, because this type of errors have been shown to have the least amount of coverage. For the transient bit level errors two scenarios have been considered. In the first scenario the magnitude of data is varied in the algorithm, and in the second case the number of unknowns *N* were varied while keeping the underlying geometry of the problem the same.

Table 1 Error coverage

Data Range	Error Coverage	SEC
0.1	76	98
1	77	99
10	77	99
100	76	99
1000	76	99
10000	77	99

Table 1 summarizes the results of error coverage and the significant error coverage for transient bit level errors for floating point additions for a data range varying between 0.1 and 10,000. The data range was simulated by assigning boundary conditions within the specified range. For example a geometrical domain discretized by the N number of variables was solved with the boundary conditions assigned to 0.1. Again the same problem was solved on the same model with same number of nodes with boundary conditions set to 1.0, and so on. It is evident from the results contained in Table 1 that the algorithm is insensitive to the magnitude of data for the entire data range.

Not a single case of false alarm was noticed while running the multigrid algorithm with different data sizes. This is due to the fact that the present algorithm uses the tolerance bound computed using error analysis.

The second column gives the error coverage under this scenario. The error coverage is virtually constant around 76% for varying data range. The significant error coverage is around 98-99%.

Table 2 Error Coverage

Matrix Dimension	Error Coverage	SEC
144	81	98
289	81	98
484	79	98
729	81	98
1024	81	98
1369	81	98

Table 2 contains results of another set of experiments in which we vary the size of the problem i.e. number of variables *N*, while keeping the same domain and the same boundary conditions.

In this case also not a single case of false alarm was noted when the *N* was varied from 144 to 1369. The error coverage varied between 79-81%. The significant error coverage remained very high at 98%.

The error coverage for all other fault types injected in the multigrid algorithm, e.g. word level errors, memory access errors, and integer adder errors was found to be 100%.

4.2 Timing Overhead

The overhead due to checking is plotted against the problem size *N* in Fig. 9. The overhead has been obtained by computing the multigrid solution to an acceptable convergence criteria with no fault tolerance for a problem with *N* nodes i.e. no checking, and then rerunning the same program with checking. The difference in the elapsed times for the two runs gives the overhead due to checking. This experiment was repeated with increasing *N*. The percentage overhead which is around 40% for *N* equal to 200 to becoming approximately 5% when *N* was 1024.

It is one of the goals of the ABED algorithms that checking based on any types of encodings should incur a minimum overhead. The checkings implemented for the multigrid algorithm meet this goal as illustrated by Fig 9.

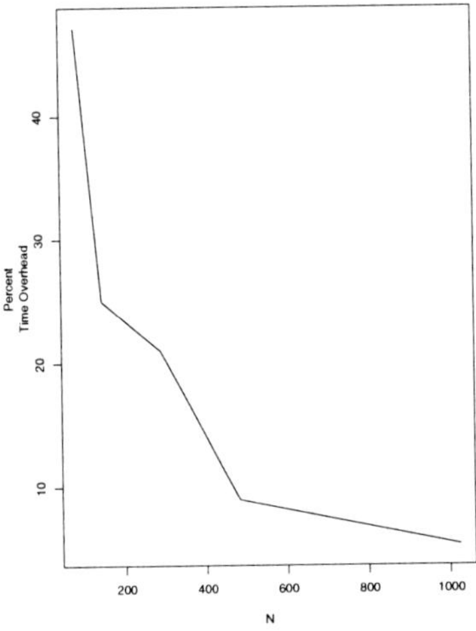

Figure 9 - Variation of Overhead vs. N

Multigrid algorithm computes the solution of N unknowns in approximately $O(N^2)$ operations while all the checking operations implemented in relaxation, restriction and interpolation run in $O(N)$ time. Therefore as N increases, the overhead due to checking starts to decrease and ultimately for a large N it becomes almost negligible.

5. Conclusions

In this paper the algorithm based error detection scheme has been applied to a multigrid algorithm which iteratively solves systems of linear algebraic equations. We have developed invariants for checking for a Jacobi relaxation for a Poisson equation by modifying the successive overrelaxation algorithm, and developed invariants for restriction and interpolation. We have derived the error expressions for the roundoff errors in the algebraic processes for the three operators in the multigrid namely relaxation, restriction, and interpolation individually and modified the invariants for checking by taking into account the accumulated roundoff errors. Our results suggest that the multigrid algorithm with checking provides error detection at low costs (less than 5% for a 1000 unknowns), excellent error coverage (98-100%) for floating point arithmetic in the presence of permanent bit and word errors. The implemented algorithm is insensitive to the data range and the data size and reports no false alarms.

6. References

[1] K. H. Huang and J. A. Abraham, "Algorithm based fault tolerance for matrix operations", IEEE Trans. Comput., Vol. C-33, pp. 518-528, June 1984.

[2] J. Y. Jou and J. A. Abraham, "Fault tolerant matrix operations on multiple processor systems using weighted checksum", SPIE Proceedings, Vol. 495, August 1984.

[3] Y. -H. Choi and M. Malek, "A fault tolerant fft processor", IEEE Trans. Comput., vol. 37, pp. 617-621, May 1988.

[4] J. Y. Jou and J. A. Abraham, "Fault tolerant FFT networks", IEEE Trans. Comput., vol. 37, pp. 548-561, May 1988.

[5] A. L. N. Reddy and P. Banerjee, "Algorithm-based fault detection for signal processing applications", IEEE Trans. Comput., Vol. 39, pp. 1304-1308, October 1990.

[6] C. -Y. Chen and J. A. Abraham, "Fault-tolerant systems for the computation of eigenvalues and singular values", in Proc. SPIE Conf., pp. 228-237, Aug. 1986.

[7] V. Balasubramaniam and P. Banerjee, "Tradeoffs in the design of efficient algorithm based error detection schemes for hypercube multiprocessors", IEEE Trans. Softw. Eng., Vol. 16, pp. 183-194, February 1990.

[8] P. Banerjee, J. T. Rahmeh, C. Stunkel, V. S. Nair, K. Roy, V. Balasubramaniam, and J. A. Abraham, "Algorithm-based fault tolerance on a hypercube multiprocessor", IEEE Trans. Comput., Vol. 39, pp. 1132-1145, Sept. 1990.

[9] A. Roy-Chowdhury and P. Banerjee, "Tolerance determination for algorithm based checks using simplified error analysis", Proc. FTCS - 93, Toulouse, France, June 1993.

[10] A. Roy-Chowdhury, N. Bellas, & P. Banerjee, "Algorithm based error detection schemes for iterative solution of partial differential equations", IEEE Trans. on Comput., Vol. 45, pp. 394-407, April 1996.

[11] J. H. Wilkinson, "The Algebraic eigenvalue problem", Oxford: Clarendon Press, 1965.

[12] A. Mishra, " A Fault Tolerant Parallel Multigrid Algorithm", M. S. Thesis, University of Illinois, Urbana-Champaign, Dec. 1995.

[13] A. Mishra, and P. Banerjee, " A Fault Tolerant Parallel Multigrid Algorithm", Proc. of PDCS -98 , Chicago, Illinois, pp. 282-289. Aug. 98.

[14] William L. Briggs, "A multigrid tutorial", SIAM, 1987.

Session 2B

Operating Systems

Chair: Nirmal Saxena
Stanford University, USA

MetaKernels and Fault Containment Wrappers

Frédéric Salles, Manuel Rodríguez, Jean-Charles Fabre and Jean Arlat

LAAS-CNRS

7, Avenue du Colonel Roche

31077 Toulouse cedex 4 - France

E-mail: {salles, rodriguez, fabre, arlat}@laas.fr

Abstract

This paper addresses the problem of using COTS microkernels in dependable systems. Because they are not developed with this aim, their behavior in the presence of faults is a main concern to system designers. We propose a novel approach to contain the effect of both external and internal faults that may affect their behavior. As microkernels can be decomposed into simple components, modeling of their expected behavior in the absence of faults is most often possible, which allows for the easy definition of dynamic predicates. For an efficient implementation of fault containment wrappers checking for these predicates, we introduce the notion of MetaKernel to reify the information required for implementing the predicates and to reflect appropriate actions. This approach is exemplified on a case study using an open version of the Chorus microkernel. MAFALDA, a software-implemented fault injection tool, is used to illustrate the benefits procured by the proposed wrappers.

1 Introduction

The use of COTS (Commercial Off-The-Shelf) software components in the design and the implementation of computer systems offers a very attractive solution for several reasons, such as reduced cost and time to market, rapid integration of new technology, etc. This trend also impacts the development of dependable systems, often supporting safety-critical applications. Among the various COTS software components that can be considered, clearly COTS operating systems (OSs) kernels occupy a central position: their development is complex, long and costly and the upper layers including (safety-critical) applications rely on their correct behavior.

Can we rely on COTS OSs for building dependable systems? Clearly, system designers need some additional inputs regarding the quality of service of the candidate component, especially from a dependability perspective to support their decision whether to actually incorporate it. Because COTS development process does not often consider the de facto standards of the target application domain, the available design and validation documents are rather weak. Accordingly, the confidence level for making such a decision can be significantly improved by experimental evaluation. This has led to several studies aiming at evaluating the robustness of conventional operating systems with respect to erroneous invocations (e.g., see [1]). The idea is to simulate faulty accesses to the operating system functions and analyze their behavior. As the microkernel technology is now the current practice for structuring OSs, recent work has considered the assessment of such basic components by fault injection [2].

These studies reveal the weaknesses of the built-in error detection mechanisms. The results also expose some decisions made during the design and/or the implementation of COTS OSs. Such information on the behavior in the presence of faults is of high interest, in particular regarding microkernels, since the upper layer software (i.e., OS functions/services) relies on this basic component. Clearly, any conventional COTS OS (or microkernel) cannot be used as is for developing highly dependable systems. Conversely, to take advantage of the advances in operating system technology, system designers/integrators can no longer bypass their consideration in system development. Defining a methodology and complementary techniques for improving the confidence in the OS software is thus a key issue.

Understanding the behavior of a general-purpose OS is very difficult, and because last generation operating systems are developed as middleware on top of a microkernel, we claim that this problem must be tackled rather at the microkernel level. For dependable systems, a specific middleware must be designed and implemented to provide services to handle fault tolerance. Whatever solution for implementing the middleware, the confidence placed in a given microkernel instance must be as high as possible. Furthermore, because a given microkernel instance can be unique, i.e., customized for a given OS, this confidence cannot be based on statistical data obtained from the deployment of the target microkernel.

The paper is organized as follows. Section 2, motivates our work by analyzing briefly results obtained by several studies that evaluated the robustness of COTS OSs and microkernels. Most of these results show that the observed behavior in the presence of faults is often non-satisfactory. Section 3 proposes to improve this behavior by adding consistency checks based on the modeling of microkernel functional classes. These consistency checks are the basis for the definition of the fault containment wrappers described in Section 4. The implementation of the wrappers is based on the notion of reflective component. Section 5 presents and discusses the results obtained by fault injection into an instance of the Chorus microkernel, without and with wrappers. Section 6 provides some concluding remarks.

0-7695-0213-X/99 $10.00 © 1999 IEEE

2 Problem statement and related work

The current practice for the assessment of COTS software is to use fault injection techniques, in particular *SoftWare-Implemented Fault Injection* (SWIFI) [3].

The work reported in [4] compares the robustness of 10 off-the-shelf POSIX-compliant operating systems using the BALLISTA tool. The basic idea is to corrupt system calls parameters (using pre-defined wrong values) and observe the output. In summary, the results show that between 42% and 63% of the POSIX functions fail on the considered candidates, exhibiting several types of failure. In some cases, these tests have led to a catastrophic failure of the system.

FINE [5] is a fault injection tool developed for the assessment of dependability properties of the SunOS 4.1.2 kernel with respect to both software and hardware faults. The main result is that most of activated software faults lead to the failure of the kernel (automatic reboot). This work reveals also that a lot of errors due to physical faults (on the bus or in the data segments of the kernel) are not detected by internal error detection mechanisms and propagate to the application level leading one or several applications to fail. A similar result has been observed in [6].

Our recent work [2], targeting the Chorus ClassiX r3.1 microkernel, shows similar effects. We not only observed system crashes but also error propagation to the application level, which is the most severe case from our viewpoint. Actually, the ideal situation would be that either (i) the error is detected, and an error status is reported or an exception raised to the application level, or (ii) no error propagates to upper layers and the application just hangs. In the first case, application dependent strategies can be implemented, for instance, trying to procure a fail-silent behavior (e.g., see [7]).

Experiments with BALLISTA, FINE, MAFALDA and others using specific or randomly injected faults can lead to unexpected failures of the system and/or the applications. The analysis of the results show that, in some cases, the application failure is very subtle (not only a crash) and may have a very bad impact on the system/application outputs. The assessment of the error detection mechanisms, a better understanding of the failure modes, even a more predictable behavior in the presence of faults, are key issues for using COTS OS in dependable systems. These issues are the main motivation for the development of fault containment wrappers considered in the sequel of the paper.

3 Modeling kernel classes

After a brief introduction of the concept of wrapper, we present the notion of predicate as an invariant relation on the model of a given functional class. The definition of predicates is then exemplified on two typical classes: (i) synchronization by semaphores and (ii) scheduling of tasks.

3.1 Principles and wrappers

Trying to detect all possible faults leading to the corruption of upper layer software is a difficult issue and certainly impossible as far as COTS software is considered. Anyway, preventing faults to impact the upper layers can only be achieved by external mechanisms. This claim leads to the notion of wrapper, originally introduced for security concerns [8].

The incorporation of defense through wrapping in order to check component's functionality, was described in [9] regarding off-the-shelf application software. The author distinguishes both input and output wrappers. The former prevent certain inputs from reaching the component and can been seen as filters of some syntactically incorrect invocation pattern (see also [1]). The later must check the output to ensure it meets certain constraints before releasing it.

This paper develops the idea of wrappers that verify consistency constraints at a semantic level. Such constraint verification usually relies on the notion of executable assertions (e.g., see [10-11]). Here, we use a model of the expected behavior of the executive functional classes. Both inputs and outputs impact the behavioral model on which constraints are verified at runtime. The possibility of establishing in practice such a model depends on (i) the complexity of the target component and (ii) the level of abstraction needed to obtain a realistic model. Modeling all functional classes is almost impossible for a general-purpose COTS OS. However, this is reachable for a COTS microkernel, as it is composed of a small number of functional classes (e.g., synchronization, scheduling, memory), whose specifications are easy to understand and thus amenable to modeling their expected behavior in the absence of faults.

3.2 Predicates definition and examples

Predicates are defined to assert the correct behavior of a single class. This consists, whenever possible, in defining in a formal way the correct behavior of a functional class, invoked by some primitives of the executive software.

It is worth noting that, although independent from a semantic viewpoint, the classes are linked together and interact. For instance, a thread suspended when requesting a semaphore handled by the synchronization class leads to the activation of a different thread by the scheduling class. The activation of one primitive may thus have an impact on the behavior of a companion class. Thus, although predicates can be defined independently, they must be verified altogether at runtime for the above reason.

Predicates are complementary to the error detection mechanisms already provided by the COTS executive. A predicate characterizes the consistency of the results produced (output parameters) and modified internal data, according to the given input parameters and the internal state before the invocation. The violation of a predicate will be thus interpreted as a faulty behavior of the corresponding class of objects.

Three major criteria have to be accounted for in the definition of predicates: (i) ability to define (model) the semantics of the functional class considered, (ii) appropriate abstract level of their definition to master the complexity; and (ii) observability — to a limited extent — of the internal state of the executive. Some microkernel mechanisms can be analyzed on the basis of their specifications, i.e., a logical expression or a model of their correct behavior. In most cases, some access to internal data is needed. These two aspects are illustrated in the next subsections.

3.2.1 Synchronization

We illustrate here on synchronization mechanisms (semaphores), how predicates can be derived from the specifications of a class of objects handled by the microkernel. A semaphore *s* corresponds to an integer value *s.val* and a process queue denoted *s.queue*. Three main primitives are provided to the applications: Init *I(s)*, Get *P(s)*, and Release *V(s)*.

The semaphore s is initialized by a first value denoted *init_value* (i.e., the initial number of available tokens). Let *#P(s)* (resp. *#V(s)*) be the total number of calls to the *P(s)* and *V(s)* primitives. The invariant property that can be derived from the definition of *P(s)* and *V(s)* is:

$$s.val = init\_value - \#P(s) + \#V(s)$$

This property is obviously true at initialization time (since *s.val* = *init_value*) and must be kept true for any number of invocations to *P(s)* and *V(s)*. Then, denoting *#Suspended(s)* the number of threads in *s.queue*:

$$\#Suspended(s) = max(0, -s.val)$$

The interpretation of this relation is as follows. If *s.val* is negative, then there are –*s.val* threads suspended in *s.queue*. When $s.val \geq 0$, then *s.queue* is empty. Accordingly, the predicate can be defined as:

$$[s.val = init\_value - \#P(s) + \#V(s)] \wedge [\#Suspended(s) = max(0, -s.val)] \quad (1)$$

This predicate can be assessed after the execution of the *P(s)* and *V(s)* primitives, provided the number of suspended threads is accessible. For example, in the case of the Chorus microkernel, some semaphores data structures are located in the application address space (user space) even though the *s.queue* is located in the microkernel address space. This means that the size of the *s.queue*, must be visible to execute the predicate of expression (1).

3.2.2 Scheduling

The problem of modeling a scheduling policy or of defining formal specification of a scheduling policy is an important issue in the design of real-time microkernels [12-14]. Nevertheless, this concern is out of the scope of our work: our objective is limited to the detection of any violation of the scheduling of the tasks that may be caused by an error. Accordingly, the model considered here is voluntarily simple.

Task scheduling can be expressed informally in the following way: the scheduler is responsible for electing the first task (thread) among existing tasks ready to run, according to a given policy. Depending on the policy, the first task ready to run is the task with the highest priority (rate monotonic scheduling) or the task with the earliest deadline (EDF policy), etc. Such rules can be easily described as predicates provided some internal data and events of the scheduler component are accessible. The example considered in this subsection is based on the priority-based FIFO preemptive scheduling policy. The behavior of the corresponding scheduler can be modeled as illustrated in Figure 1.

Newly created tasks can be put either in the *Stopped* state or in the *Ready_to_run* state. A stopped task becomes ready to run when the `start` operation is executed by another task. A task returns to stopped state when either itself or a different task executes the `stop` operation. In this case, the running task is a *Ready_to_run* task with the higher priority. All tasks with the same priority level are scheduled on a FIFO basis. The running task (denoted a) can change the priority of a *Ready_to_run* task or delay it. This delay operation can be used to release the CPU for another task at the same priority level (`NoDelay` in this case). Alternatively, a task can be put in the waiting state. Such a transition may be due to a blocking operation on a semaphore object, a voluntary suspension for a given delay or a blocking receive. Conversely, a task resumes to the *Ready_to_run* state when either (i) a release operation is performed on a semaphore object, (ii) the delay has expired or (iii) an event related to the reception of a message has been observed. The last two cases correspond to an asynchronous event related purely to an external input.

All the transitions in this model are related either to a primitive of the scheduler itself or a primitive of a companion class within the microkernel. From an object-oriented viewpoint, several objects are responsible for the evolution of the task queues handled by the microkernel. The scheduler object provides the following external primitives to handle threads: `Create`, `Start`, `Stop`, `Delay`, `PrioritySet` and `Delete`. Some internal functions are also available to control the thread behavior: `Wait`, `Signal` and also `PrioritySet`. A semaphore object has two primitives `SemP` and `SemV`. The `MessageQueue` object has two primitives `Send` and `Receive`. A `TimeOut` object has a `TimeoutSet` internal function to initialize a timer and the `OneClockTick` activated by the real-time clock and responsible for timers management. Each of these primitives and internal functions leads to a transition within the scheduling state diagram.

The considered predicates perform consistency checks on the scheduler behavior. Let *P_Sched(•)* be the predicate defining the selection process of the current running task among all the candidate tasks. Under a FIFO preemptive policy, such a predicate states that "the running task *a* is always the first one of the highest priority level in the *Ready_to_run* queue *R*." This will simply be denoted: *P_Sched(R,a)*.

It is clear that checks based on such a predicate cannot ensure that the behavior of the tasks handled by the microkernel is correct. For instance, a given task may block forever on a semaphore or wait for a message that never arrives. The verification of the transition from *waiting* state to *ready_to_run* state is possible only when a message is

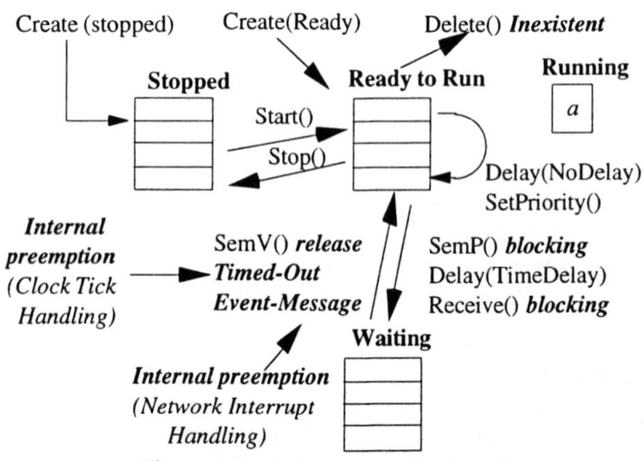

Figure 1. A simple scheduler model

received by a task or when a semaphore is released. Another example is a stopped task that is never re-activated. In most cases, such situations relate to either a fault in a companion component (e.g., lost message) or a wrong design of the application. Handling these situations would require modeling and simulating the whole application to be able to reveal the corresponding design faults. This would involve verifying application-dependent safety and liveness properties.

Regarding the microkernel behavior, the predicates verify that the activation of a primitive or a given event leads to the appropriate transition in the scheduling state diagram. As an example, the post-condition after a `SemV(S)` can be:

$$t \notin W(s) \wedge t \in R \wedge P\_Sched(R,a) \quad (2)$$

where $W(s)$ is the queue of tasks waiting on semaphore s and t denotes the first task blocked on s. All predicates are based on the same model, since in most cases a transition corresponds to a task t leaving a given queue and entering another one. The predicate *P_Sched* of expression (2) must always hold right after a transition occurs. Similarly, the expiration of a delay involves the verification of the following predicate:

$$t \notin Wd \wedge t \in R \wedge P\_Sched(R,a) \quad (3)$$

where Wd is the queue of tasks waiting on a delay and t is the task whose delay has just expired.

Similar predicates are defined for all primitives and events in the state diagram of Figure 1. The implementation of these predicates assumes an access to the descriptor of the running task and to several queues used in the microkernel.

3.3 Discussion

The definition of predicates depends on the ability to formally specify the behavior of objects managed by the microkernel. We showed how this was achievable for semaphores and scheduling policies. A cost/efficiency trade-off exists between predicates based on a very detailed modeling (that would be very difficult to develop) and simpler predicates corresponding to a higher modeling level (but, that might not be as efficient).

However, for many other functional classes, such a formal specification can seldom be obtained, particular for the memory or communication management classes. Two distinct options are possible. One may want to define a model of the memory management policy or of the basic communication protocols. This activity may be very tedious and the resulting model questionable. The second option is more pragmatic. It is based on operational consistency checks such as acceptance or validity checks. For instance, an allocated memory segment must be entirely accessible (i.e., no bus error observed when reading or writing any of its bytes) as a result of the primitive call.

4 Fault containment wrappers

Verifying the predicates as runtime assertions often requires high levels of observability and controllability. Such properties are of course not provided by off-the-shelf microkernels, which are thus often considered as black-box components. This is why we introduce the notion of reflective component, so as to reach the observability and controllability levels required for the implementation of the predicates.

4.1 Principles

The improvement of the behavior of a COTS microkernel with respect to fault containment relies on the verification of the predicates defined in Section 3.2. The implementation is based on wrappers. The wrapping approach consists in (i) trapping every API primitive, (ii) checking the validity of the call, (iii) executing the primitive if allowed, and (iv) checking the consistency of the results for each class of primitives. Then, an extended error status can be reported to the application software, if needed. In some cases, a corrective or emergency action (e.g., placing the system in a safe state) can also be performed by the wrapper itself.

The main problem for the implementation of such wrappers is to access the microkernel internal information identified in the definition of the predicates. Indeed, the identified data structures — e.g., see expressions (1),(2),(3) — must be visible by the wrapper. Since elaborating on the source code is not a satisfactory solution for the customer, we have added a specific module to the microkernel that is responsible for exhibiting such required information. Moreover, as the wrapper may be used to perform some corrective actions, this module enables the behavior of the microkernel to be modified when a faulty situation has been signaled. Here comes the notion of *reflective microkernel.*

4.2 Reflection and MetaKernels

This notion of making explicit at upper layers structural and behavioral aspect of the COTS microkernel leads to the notion of *reflective* component. Reflection [15] is the process by which internal aspects of a component can be observed and controlled outside from the component. Reflection distinguishes two levels, the baselevel and the metalevel (Fig. 2).

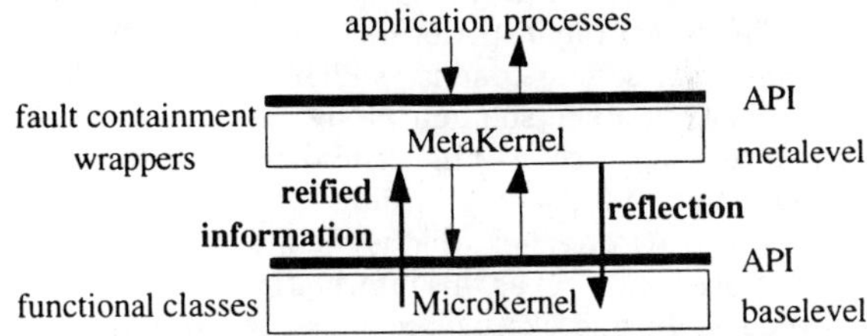

Figure 2. Reflection concepts and microkernels

Information is provided from the base level to the metalevel and becomes metalevel data (reification process). Such data correspond to an abstraction – a model – of the baselevel behavior and structure. The metalevel handles this metainformation and is able to control and update the baselevel (reflection process). Thus, any change in the metainformation is reflected to the baselevel. In our case, the baselevel is the microkernel and the metalevel is called *MetaKernel.*

The notion of *MetaKernel* provides an attractive framework for the verification of various properties on the microkernel itself. It is a form of encapsulation, but in a more powerful approach, since more static and dynamic aspects of the encapsulated component can be handled.

In Figure 2 one can also understand the difference between a conventional and a reflective implementation of a wrapper. Conventional wrappers only intercept calls to the kernel; thus, consistency checks apply only to information available

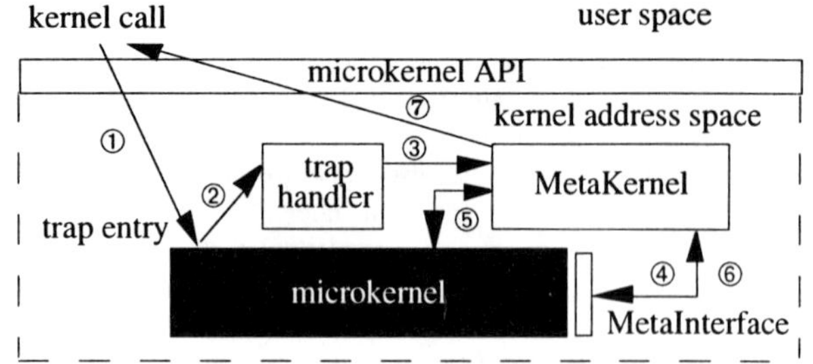

1. Kernel call - 2. Call trap - 3. MetaKernel invocation - 4. Pre-execution actions - 5. Execution of the call - 6. Post-execution actions - 7. Call return

Figure 3. Implementing a MetaKernel on a "black-box" COTS microkernel

at the interface. By providing more information to the metalevel about the behavior and the internal state of the component, the reflective approach would enable more complex situations to be handled.

4.3 Implementation issues

The *MetaKernel* is responsible for (i) intercepting and filtering systems calls and some internal functions, and (ii) running predicates when a system call is performed. Any kernel call enter the microkernel through a trap mechanism. This trap is intercepted by inserting break points and activating an handler routine rerouting the call to the *MetaKernel.* The verification of the predicates and the execution of the primitive are performed by the *MetaKernel.* Such an interception is thus binary compliant.

To be able to verify the predicates, the *MetaKernel* accesses internal information into the microkernel. The implementation of the predicate for the semaphore objects, for instance, requires internal information such as semaphore queues. This access can be performed directly into the microkernel when the source code is available. Nevertheless, we advocate here another solution to bypass the problem of obtaining the source code of the candidate microkernel. The idea is to identify precisely, according to the predicates to be verified by the *MetaKernel,* what is the internal information that is required. As soon as this information is specified, one has to request the microkernel provider a *MetaInterface* able to access and control this information. This approach is illustrated in Figure 3.

According to the predicates examples of Section 3.2, we can define the *MetaKernel* interface (simplified) as shown on Figure 4-a. From a dynamic viewpoint (see Figure 4-b), the trap handler intercepts a system call and diverts it to the *MetaKernel,* invoking `Meta-KernelCall` with the corresponding parameters. Within this method the analysis, mainly based on the evaluation of the predicate, is carried out (pre- and post-execution actions) and the actual call to the kernel can be performed using `Meta-HandleKernelCall` with the relevant parameters. The `FailStop` method enables the *MetaKernel* to stop the microkernel when a critical situation is detected.

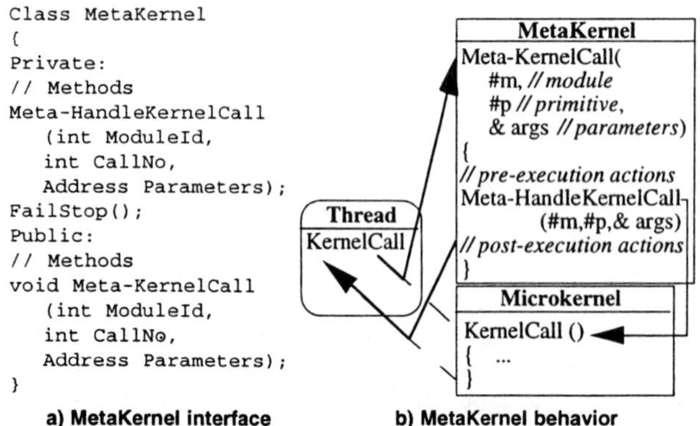

Figure 4. MetaKernel interface and behavior

The metainformation required for the evaluation of the previously defined predicates corresponds to several attributes of the *MetaKernel* and can easily be defined, as shown below.

```
Class SemQueue
{public:
   GetLength(KnSem);
   GetNext(KnSem);
   GetFirst(KnSem);
   IsIn(KnSem,ThId);
} Semqueue;

Class SchedQueue
{public:
   GetNextRR()
   GetFirstRR()
   IsInRR(ThId);
} Schedqueue;

Class DelayedQueue
{public:
   IsInDQ(ThId);
} Delayedqueue;

Class MessageWaitingQueue
{public:
   IsInAnyMWQ(ThId);
} Messagewaitingqueue;

Class ThreadsContextQueue
{public:
   GetThreadContext(ThId);
   GetNextThread();
} Threadcontextqueue;
```

Examples of private attributes of the *MetaKernel* class are the following: `Semqueue`, `Schedqueue`, `Delayedqueue`, `Messagewaitingqueue`, `Threadcontextqueue`. The *MetaInterface* is defined by the list of methods belonging to these classes. More details can be found in [16].

5 Case study

After a brief description of the target microkernel, this section presents the main characteristics of the tool (MAFALDA) used to carry out the fault injection experiments. The results obtained are then reported and discussed.

5.1 Chorus ClassiX r3

The Chorus ClassiX microkernel [17-18] is an open version of earlier versions of this microkernel [19]. It is composed of various internal modules given below:

Core (COR): set of primitives for the management of threads and actors (Chorus multi-threaded processes) and hardware related basic functions (e.g., interrupts, timers, traps, MMU).

Synchronization (SYN): set of primitives for the management and the use of semaphores, mutexes, event-flags, etc.

Memory Management (MEM): set of primitives for the management and the use of memory segments and regions including functions for flat memory, protected address spaces management policies, etc.

Scheduling (SCH): various off-the-shelf schedulers are available including priority-based FIFO preemptive scheduling or with fixed quanta, Unix Time-Sharing or Real-Time policies, etc. This module does not directly provide visible primitives, but it handles running threads and actors and is thus indirectly activated by the creation of threads and actors.

Communication (COM): set of primitives for local and remote message passing.

A customized microkernel can be generated from the available off-the-shelf internal modules. Some of them can be user-defined (e.g., a specific scheduler) and used during the generation of a given microkernel instance. Users can thus specialize the microkernel for a given application context. The microkernel and the application processes have separate address spaces; the microkernel runs in supervisor mode while application processes (normally) run in user mode.

The fault injection experiments have been performed on the following configuration of Chorus ClassiX r3: a standard module handling semaphores (SYN), a protected address space memory management module (MEM), a priority-based FIFO preemptive scheduler (SCH) and a standard module for local and remote communications (COM).

5.2 MAFALDA

5.2.1 Basic principles

MAFALDA (*Microkernel Assessment by Fault injection AnaLysis for Design Aid*), is a SWIFI tool based on a "classical" architecture that integrates three sets of components: components that form the workload to activate the various microkernel functional classes (modules), components that perform fault injection either at the interface or within the microkernel address space, and components monitoring the experiments and devoted to result analysis. A more complete description of MAFALDA can be found in [2].

The fault models supported by MAFALDA correspond to two types of fault injection: the corruption of the input parameters of a primitive call and the corruption of the microkernel address space. In each case, a single microkernel module is targeted: a randomly selected bit is flipped either in a randomly selected parameter of a module, or in a randomly selected byte in the address space of a module. As in Xception [6], MAFALDA uses processor debugging facilities to inject either permanent or transient faults. This also enables monitoring of the activation of the faults and limits the interference with the target executive. This technique is thus less intrusive than using software traps. MAFALDA uses both spatial triggers (the fault is injected when execution flow accesses a specified memory location either for instruction fetch or for data read/write access) and temporal triggers (a programmable delay governs the time between the starting of the application and the fault injection instant.)

5.2.2 Experiment description

During a fault injection experiment, application processes (one for each microkernel module) are executed concurrently. Results are collected and compared to those of a fault-free run to check whether any application process was corrupted.

Outcomes can be identified at three different levels. The first level corresponds to errors detected either by the microkernel error detection mechanisms, namely error status and exception, or by the added wrappers. The next level corresponds to internal failures (e.g., system hang, kernel debugger). The last level concerns wrong application behavior or results, in short "application failure", or "application hang".

5.3 Experimental results

In this section, we present and discuss the results obtained when applying MAFALDA on the Chorus ClassiX instance, both without and with wrappers. The main goal is to assess, with the help of MAFALDA, the improvement of the error detection coverage provided by the two wrapper mechanisms introduced in Section 4. This comparison is based on results we previously obtained when analyzing the faulty behavior of the microkernel without wrapper mechanisms [2]. In the sequel, we present in turn the results obtained for the synchronization (SYN) and task scheduling (SCH) modules.

5.3.1 Synchronization module

The results obtained when subjecting the microkernel to faulty synchronization input parameters are very striking: from roughly 1000 experiments, 87% led to an application failure; this is actually the most severe case. Indeed, this means that the errors remained undetected, and propagated to the upper layers of the system, making applications behave in a faulty way. The remaining 13% of experiments relate to errors injected into an unused field of an input parameter; accordingly, they had no impact at all (no observation).

Repeating the same injection campaign with the SYN wrapper, showed that the wrapper was able to detect all the propagated errors before any application failure.

The results observed when subjecting the microkernel to transient faults affecting the code segment are shown on Figure 5 (for Fig. 5-a,b,c the target is the SYN module, while for Fig. 5-d,e, the target is the SCH module). Figure 5-a depicts the results obtained without wrapper. Out of the 3000 errors injected, 9% led to an application failure, 7.4% provoked either application or system hangs, while about 41% of the errors were successfully detected by the microkernel. Still, an important percentage of the experiments (28.5%) did not lead to any observation. Higher rates of non-significant experiments are usually reported (e.g., see [5]). Indeed, MAFALDA permits one to select only experiments for which the faulted memory word is actually accessed. Three main possible reasons can be identified for such experiments: (i) long error latency (at least longer than the duration of the experiment), (ii) injection in unused fields (data structures or instruction format), or (iii) production of "equivalent mutations" causing no deviation from the normal execution (e.g., corruption of an arithmetic operation or conditional jump leading to a similar operation or condition).

The same experiments were carried out with the SYN wrapper. The results are shown in Figure 5-b. The SYN wrapper significantly reduces the percentage of application failures (from 9.0% to 2.2%). Although important, this result shows that the SYN wrapper is unable to prevent all the errors from propagating to the application level. A closer examination of these 66 (2.2%) residual application failures showed that most of them were scheduling related problems (e.g., threads mixed up in an incorrect way). The SYN wrapper is not designed to handle such a kind of faulty behavior. We then decided to carry out the same fault injection campaign using both the SYN and SCH wrappers. The corresponding results obtained are shown in Figure 5-c. Now, only 0.5% of the injected errors remain undetected. Table 1 summarizes the percentages of application failures for the various experimental configurations previously described.

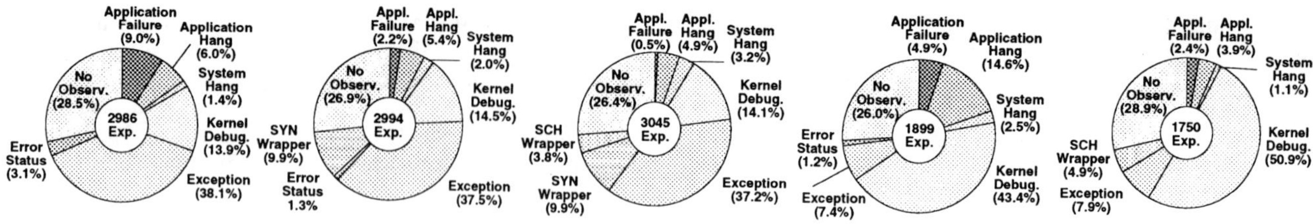

a) standard SYN mod. b) SYN mod. and wrapper c) SYN mod. + SYN & SCH wrap. d) standard SCH mod. e) SCH mod. and wrapper

Figure 5. Distribution of errors - parameter injection

The model of the synchronization functional class developed by the SYN wrapper is efficient enough to keep applications from misbehaving when faulty parameters are delivered to the microkernel. This is why no further experiments were carried out using both wrappers in this case. However, synchronization requests may impact scheduling; errors affecting the SYN module can thus propagate to the SCH module. The results obtained when combining the use of both SYN and SCH wrappers support this analysis. Although we did not analyze yet in details the 15 (0.5%) residual cases of application failure, the restriction to a small number of failures makes such a detailed analysis readily feasible. Furthermore, it is expected that such an analysis will provide useful insights according to several complementary viewpoints: (i) on the design and implementation of the microkernel (microkernel provider viewpoint), (ii) on the design and the implementation of upper layers (system integrator viewpoint), and as well (iii) on further development of the wrappers (our viewpoint).

5.3.2 Task scheduling module

We now concentrate on the study of the behavior in presence of faults of the code segment of the SCH module. The related results are shown in Figure 5-d. About 4.9% of the errors led to an application failure, 14.6% to an application hang, 2.5% provoked the hang of the system, and 52% of the remaining errors were successfully detected by the microkernel: most errors are detected by mechanisms internal to the microkernel rather than hardware mechanisms. While 43.4% activate the Kernel Debugger, only 7.4% raise an Exception. The activation of the Kernel Debugger means that the microkernel has detected a critical error and deliberately put the system into a safe state, by freezing the microkernel.

The same fault injection campaign using the scheduling wrapper gives the results of Figure 5-e. The use of the wrapper reduces the percentage of application failures to 2.3%. In addition, the application and system hangs are reduced to 3.9% and 1.1%, respectively. As an illustration of the role of the SCH wrapper, let us consider the following examples of faulty situations it successfully handled and notified:

- A thread newly created, awoken, or changing priority has not been correctly inserted (or not inserted at all) in the ready-to-run queue.
- The running thread is not preempted either (i) upon reception of a message by a waiting thread with higher priority, or (ii) upon expiration of a time-out that should wake-up a delayed higher priority thread.
- A thread performing a blocking action on a mutex semaphore is not removed from the ready-to-run queue.
- The elected thread has not the highest priority of all threads in the ready-to-run queue.
- The impact of the SCH wrapper on the percentages of failures and hangs observed for the injection experiments affecting the SCH module is summarized in Table 2.

Further analysis of the 41 (2.4%) residual application failures showed that the corresponding erroneous situations were definitely out of reach of the proposed simple scheduling wrapper: i.e., they provoked errors significantly departing from a mere incorrect ordering of the threads. Thanks to a detailed analysis of these error situations, we are able categorize them into four classes. Interestingly, one class gathers about half of them, while the other are almost evenly distributed among the three remaining classes. The distribution of the residual application failures within these four classes along with a brief description of the corresponding error situation are given below:

a) 21 failures are provoked by wrong priority information returned by the microkernel, leading the requesting applications to no longer behave correctly.
b) 7 failures are related to asynchronous events (e.g., arrival of a message or the expiration of a time-out) which are not correctly handled by the microkernel.
c) 7 failures correspond to the hang of all the threads in the same application, without neither any previous violation of the ordering of the threads nor failure of the application.
d) 6 failures result from the modification of the execution flow of the applications, without any previous violation of any ordering property.

These observations set new grounds for the development of improved wrappers. In particular, a scheduling wrapper tailored to deal with the real time specification of the microkernel should be able to avoid failures of class c). Improving the trapping of asynchronous events should enable failures of class b) to be avoided, while wrappers specially designed to control the application behavior are mandatory to avoid failures of classes a) and d).

Table 1. Distribution of failures (SYN module)

Injection	Standard mod.	SYN wrapper	SYN & SCH wrap.
Parameter	87%	0%	—
Microkernel	9%	2.2%	0.5%

Table 2. Impact of the SCH wrapper (SCH module)

Module	Application Failure	Application Hang	System Hang	Total
Standard	4.9%	14.6%	2.5%	22%
SCH wrapper	2.3%	3.9%	1.1%	7.3%

6 Conclusion

The development of dependable systems is today often based on a middleware running on top of COTS OSs. The definition and the implementation of error processing and fault treatment mechanisms integrated into the middleware rely on several assumptions. In most distributed fault-tolerant systems implementing generic fault tolerance strategies, the fail silence of the nodes is assumed. For safety critical applications, error-processing strategies are more application dependent and aim to place the system in a safe state. In this case, all errors affecting the nodes must be reported to the application level. Ensuring a high coverage for these assumptions is thus a very important issue.

Because most COTS OSs are imperfect and cannot always confine errors (due to either faulty requests from applications, or internal software and hardware faults), the need for fault containment wrappers is mandatory. This paper proposed a new approach to tackle this problem by modeling the expected behavior of operating system functions. This modeling is possible when OS functions are simple which is readily the case when considering microkernels. Indeed, microkernels are today the basis for the development of specialized OSs and other dedicated middleware, either general-purpose or more domain dependent. This technology is of course appealing for implementing middlewares for fault tolerance.

The definition and implementation of fault containment wrappers was illustrated on two sensitive functional classes of a COTS microkernel and, as shown by the experimental results obtained, proved to be very efficient. The implementation of these wrappers was based on a reflective approach supports the good observability and commandability necessary for implementing the defined dynamic predicates. This approach is very attractive since it enables implementing fault containment wrappers on microkernels, without requiring to have access to the source code, yet, at the expense of obtaining the implementation of the *MetaInterface* from the microkernel provider. The *MetaInterface* is defined according to the predicates that must be evaluated at runtime. When the source code is available, this interface can also be implemented by the system integrator. Clearly, the development of safety critical real-time systems requires access to the source code. As demonstrated in [20], one has to quantify from a timing viewpoint blocking times upper limits within the microkernel.

The results obtained in the various experiments we have conducted show however that some faults are not contained by the proposed wrappers. The efficiency of the underlying predicates depends on the modeling level of their definition. Clearly, as far as real-time microkernels are concerned, the predicates definition must take into account temporal aspects in a more explicit way; this is one of our main objective for future work. Also, the activation profile of the microkernel could have an impact on the observed results. Various activation profiles from different application fields will be considered in the next future together with various configurations of the microkernel itself. Finally, similar experiments will be performed on several microkernel candidates.

Acknowledgments: This work was partially supported by ESPRIT Project 20072, Design for Validation (DeVa). Manuel Rodríguez is currently supported by Thomson-CSF (SRTI SYSTEM) in the framework of the Laboratory for Dependability Engineering (LIS). LIS is a Cooperative Laboratory between Aerospatiale Aéronautique, Électricité de France, Matra Marconi Space France, Technicatome, Thomson-CSF and LAAS-CNRS. We would like to thank Scott Hazelhurst for his reading that help us produce the final manuscript.

References

[1] P. Koopman, J. Sung, C. Dingman, D. Siewiorek and T. Marz, "Comparing Operating Systems using Robustness Benchmarks", *Proc. IEEE SRDS-16*, Durham, NC, USA, 1997, pp. 72-79.

[2] J.-C. Fabre, F. Salles, M. Rodríguez and J. Arlat, "Assessment of COTS Microkernels by Fault Injection", *Proc. IFIP DCCA-7*, San Jose, California, USA, 1999, pp. 19-38.

[3] M.-C. Hsueh, T. Tsai and R. Iyer, "Fault Injection Techniques and Tools", Computer, vol. 30, pp. 75-82, April 1997.

[4] N. P. Kropp, P. J. Koopman, D. P. Siewiorek, "Automated Robustness Testing of Off-The-Shelf Software Components", *Proc. IEEE FTCS-28*, Munich, Germany, 1998, pp. 230-239.

[5] W. Kao, R. K. Iyer, D. Tang, "FINE: A Fault Injection and Monitoring Environment for Tracing the UNIX System Behavior under Faults", *IEEE Tr. Soft. Eng.*, vol. 19, pp. 1105-1118, 1993.

[6] J. Carreira, H. Madeira, J. G. Silva, "Xception: A Technique for the Experimental Evaluation of Dependability in Modern Computers", *IEEE Tr. Soft. Eng.*, vol. 24, pp. 125-136, 1998.

[7] D. Powell, G. Bonn, D. Seaton, P. Veríssimo, F. Waeselynck, "The Delta-4 Approach to Dependability in Open Distributed Computing Systems", *Proc. IEEE FTCS-18*, Tokyo, Japan, 1988, pp. 246-251 .

[8] W. Cheswick, S. Bellovin, *Firewalls and Internet Security: Repelling the Willy Hacker*, Addison Wesley Eds, ISBN 0-201-63357-4, 1994, 306 p.

[9] J. Voas, "Certifying Off-The-Shelf Software Components", *IEEE Computer*, vol. 31, pp. 53-59, June 1998.

[10] A. Mahmood, D. M. Andrews, E. J. McCluskey, "Executable Assertions and Flight Software", *Proc. 6th AIAA/IEEE Digital Avionics Syst. Conf.*, (Baltimore, MD, USA), pp.346-351, 1984.

[11] C. Rabéjac, J.-P. Blanquart, J.-P. Queille, "Executable Assertions and Timed Traces for On-Line Software Error Detection", *Proc. IEEE FTCS-26*, (Sendai, Japan), pp.138-147, IEEE CS Press, 1996.

[12] N. C. Audsley, A. Burns, R. Davis, K. Tindell, A. J. Wellings, "Fixed Priority Pre-emptive Scheduling: An Historical Perspective", J. of Real-Time Systems, vol. 8, pp. 173-198, 1995.

[13] A. Burns, A. J. Wellings, Scheduling Analysis for GUARDS, ESPRIT Project 20716 GUARDS Rep. D1A4 A0 7013 B, 1996.

[14] J. Lehoczky, "Real-Time Queueing Network Theory", *Proc. IEEE RTSS'97*, San Francisco, CA, USA, 1997, pp. 220-229.

[15] P. Maes, "Concepts and Experiments in Computational Reflection", *Proc. OOPSLA'87*, 1987, pp. 147-155.

[16] F. Salles, "Dependability of Microkernel-based Operating Systems: Failure Mode Analysis and Fault Containment", Ph.D. Dissertation, Université Paul Sabatier, Toulouse, France (in French, available from LAAS-CNRS, Toulouse, France).

[17] Chorus, "Chorus/ClassiX r3.1b for ix86 - Product Description", Technical Report CS/TR-96-221.1, Chorus Systems, 1996.

[18] Chorus, "Chorus/ClassiX r3 - Technical Overview", Technical Report CS/TR-96-119.8, Chorus Systems, 1996.

[19] M. Rozier et al., "Overview of the CHORUS Distributed Operating Systems", Tech. Rep. CS/TR-90-25.1, Chorus Systems, 1991.

[20] N. Audsley, A. Wellings, "Analysing APEX Applications", *Proc. IEEE RTSS'96*, Washington, DC, USA, 1996, pp. 39-44.

Comparing the Robustness of POSIX Operating Systems

Philip Koopman & John DeVale
Department of Electrical and Computer Engineering &
Institute for Complex Engineered Systems
Carnegie Mellon University, Pittsburgh, Pennsylvania, USA
koopman@cmu.edu jdevale@ece.cmu.edu

Abstract

Critical system designers are turning to off-the-shelf operating system (OS) software to reduce costs and time-to-market. Unfortunately, general-purpose OSes do not always respond to exceptional conditions robustly, either accepting exceptional values without complaint, or suffering abnormal task termination. Even though direct measurement is impractical, this paper uses a multi-version comparison technique to reveal a 6% to 19% normalized rate at which exceptional parameter values cause no error report in commercial POSIX OS implementations. Additionally, 168 functions across 13 OSes are compared to reveal common mode robustness failures. While the best single OS has a 12.6% robustness failure rate for system calls, 3.8% of failures are common across all 13 OSes examined. However, combining C library calls with system calls increases these rates to 29.5% for the best single OS and 17.0% for common mode failures. These results suggest that OS implementations are not completely diverse, and that C library functions are both less diverse and less robust than system calls.

1. Introduction

The robustness of the operating system (OS) Application Programming Interface (API) is becoming increasingly important. Cost and time-to-market constraints are pressuring even critical-system developers to use off-the-shelf commercial OS software. While many of these OSes are generally considered robust, the Ballista testing system has produced results showing that commercial OSes have a significant robustness failure rate for single procedure calls with exceptional parameter values at the task level, and even a few readily reproducible catastrophic failure modes [13].

This paper compares the results of multiple OS implementations to increase the understanding of their robustness failure modes and, in particular, instances in which they fail to detect exceptional input parameter values. Additionally, a large set of test data on multiple implementions of the same API offers a unique chance to explore the issue of quantifying large-scale software diversity, albeit only of exception handling characteristics.

First, a multi-version comparison of Ballista testing results is used to identify so-called Silent robustness failures in fifteen OSes. A Silent failure is one in which a function call produces no indication of an error when fed exceptional parameter values when, in fact, such an indication should be produced to implement robust behavior. These failures cannot otherwise be measured without a behavioral specification. Additional results presented include using a similar technique to "distill" non-exceptional test cases from the Ballista combinational testing approach, and a listing of the data types most often correlated with robustness failures.

Next, N-way comparisons of different OS robustness testing results are used to measure software diversity from the point of view of robust exception handling. While actually implementing a system with an N-version OS seems impractical, the results of this comparison give the first large-scale experimental results for understanding the level of software diversity that is likely to be found in commercial products (again, limited to exception handling characteristics). The results of comparing thirteen OS implementations (two OSes had to be eliminated to maximize usable comparison data) show that OS implementations are not entirely diverse, and that an assumption of failure independence seems less unreasonable for OS system calls than for C library functions.

2. Background

This paper takes concepts from the field of N-version software fault tolerance and combines them with results from a scalable robustness testing methodology. It then assesses OS robustness failures and the inherent diversity of multiple version techniques on one type of large software system.

0-7695-0213-X/99 $10.00 © 1999 IEEE

2.1. N-version software

N-version software involves using *N* different versions of programs implementing the same specification for building robust, fault-tolerant software [1][2]. Generally these systems use an idea similar to N-version modular hardware redundancy, basing actions upon a majority vote taken of several software versions to determine which output values are correct. Numerous experiments have been performed to study N-version software effectiveness in several mission critical areas, most notably in the aerospace industry [3][5][15]. Variations on this theme have been successfully implemented in safety critical industrial systems such as the Airbus flight control system, NASA's Space Shuttle, and railway control systems.

As an example, a large research effort involving fault tolerant software controls for a NASA avionics system involved five independent teams of developers chosen from various universities [8]. They carefully constructed a specification and performed several levels of testing on the developing software, which upon completion averaged approximately 2500 lines of Pascal code. Detailed analysis was performed on the collected data in a later study, and found that less than 20% of the faults detected could be classified as similar[17]. Further, the study concluded that after certification testing this number dropped significantly, and had eliminated all specification faults.

Another study suggests that an assumption of failure independence based on diversity may not be universally possible [4][9][10], but these results are controversial [3][11][17]. More importantly, such studies are inherently limited by the high cost of software development, making it prohibitively expensive to conduct full-scale N-version software studies in general. So, it is reasonable to ask an assumption of multi-version diversity scales to systems having a million lines of code, but in general undertaking a parallel development effort of that magnitude is impractical.

Fortunately, there are a some commercially developed, full-size systems built to standard Application Programming Interfaces (APIs). These systems can be tested to determine the relative independence of failures. The problem of evaluating multiple version effectiveness can thus be reduced to one of finding a test suite which is economical to develop, and yet has not already been used by software vendors for defect removal. This paper uses such results for robustness failures found by the Ballista robustness testing system applied to POSIX [7] OS implementations.

2.2. Ballista testing methodology

In brief, the Ballista testing methodology involves automatically generating combinations of exceptional and valid parameter values to be used in calling software modules. The results of these calls are examined to determine whether the module detected and notified the calling program of an error, the task abnormally terminated, the task hung, or whether the entire system crashed. A detailed discussion of test case generation can be found in a previous paper [13], but the general test methodology is summarized below.

Ballista operates at the level of single function calls to create repeatable, simple tests that nonetheless uncover robustness failures. In each *test case*, a single software Module under Test (or *MuT*) is called a single time to determine whether it is robust when called with a particular set of parameter values. These parameter values, or *test values*, are drawn from pools of normal and exceptional values based on the data type of each argument passed to the MuT. A test case therefore consists of the name of the MuT and a tuple of test values that are passed as parameters (*i.e.*, a test case is a procedure call of the form: *MuT_name(test_value1, test_value2, ...)*) . Thus, the general approach to Ballista testing is to test the robustness of a single call to a MuT for a single tuple of test values, and then repeat this process for multiple test cases that each have different combinations of both valid and invalid test values. While actual tests are performed in batches for efficiency, in practice virtually all test results have been found to be reproducible in isolation.

The Ballista test harness categorizes the test results according to the CRASH severity scale [12]:

- **Catastrophic** failures occur when the entire OS becomes corrupted or the machine crashes or reboots. In other words, this is a complete system crash.
- **Restart** failures occur when a function call to an OS function never returns, resulting in a task that has "hung" and must be terminated by force.
- **Abort** failures tend to be the most prevalent, and result in abnormal termination (a "core dump") of a task caused by a signal generated within the MuT.
- **Silent** failures occur when an OS returns no indication of error on an exceptional operation which clearly cannot be performed (for example, writing to a read-only file), and which should in fact produce an error report in a robust system. This is not to be confused with the problem of non-diagnosable experiments due to limited observability, because the error reporting mechanism is fully observable, and is observed to falsely indicate "no error" (this is an application-centric rather than OS-centric view).
- **Hindering** failures occur when an incorrect error code is returned from a MuT, which could make it more difficult to execute appropriate error recovery. These failures have been observed in practice, but are beyond the

scope of this paper.

There are two additional possible outcomes of executing a test case. A test case might return with an error code that is appropriate for invalid parameters forming the test case. This is a case in which the test case passes – in other words, generating an error code is the correct response. Additionally, in some tests the MuT legitimately returns no error code and successfully completes the desired operation. This happens when the parameters in the test case happen to be all valid (a non-exceptional test case), or when it is unreasonable to expect the OS to detect an exceptional situation (such as pointing to an invalid address in the same memory page as a valid address).

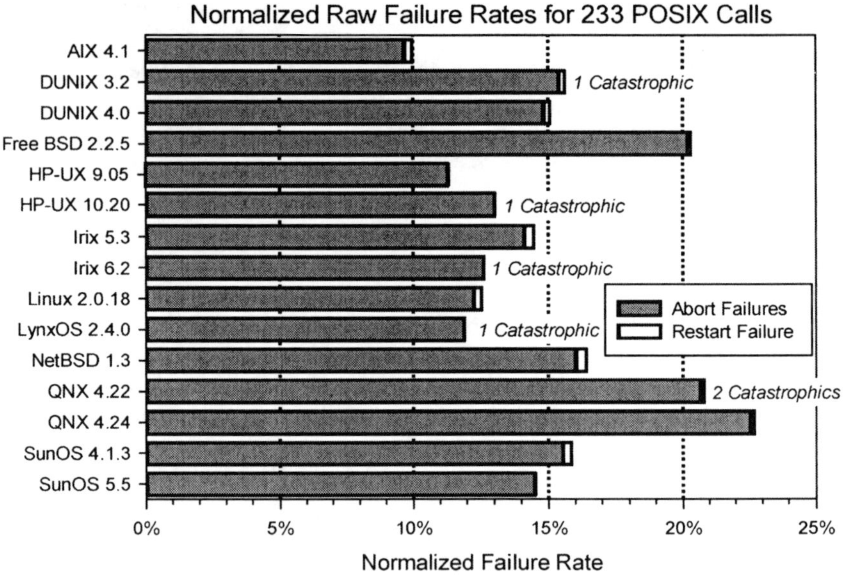

Normalized Raw Failure Rates for 233 POSIX Calls

AIX 4.1
DUNIX 3.2 — 1 Catastrophic
DUNIX 4.0
Free BSD 2.2.5
HP-UX 9.05
HP-UX 10.20 — 1 Catastrophic
Irix 5.3
Irix 6.2 — 1 Catastrophic
Linux 2.0.18
LynxOS 2.4.0 — 1 Catastrophic
NetBSD 1.3
QNX 4.22 — 2 Catastrophics
QNX 4.24
SunOS 4.1.3
SunOS 5.5

Abort Failures
Restart Failure

0% 5% 10% 15% 20% 25%

Normalized Failure Rate

Figure 1. Raw robustness tests on 15 POSIX operating systems reveal a significant Abort failure rate and several Catastrophic failures.

3. OS test data

Fifteen OS implementations from ten vendors were tested with Ballista, yielding a total of 1,074,782 data points on up to 233 selected POSIX functions and system calls (most systems did not support all tested calls, and thus not all tests were run on every OS). The compilers and libraries used to generate the test suite were those provided by the OS vendor. In the case of FreeBSD, NetBSD, Linux, and LynxOS, this meant that GNU C version 2.7.2.3 and the GNU C libraries were used to build the test suite. A summary of robustness failure rates is shown in Figure 1, in which an average failure rate is computed by normalizing the failure rate as a proportion of failed test cases for each function, and then taking a uniformly weighted arithmetic mean across all supported functions. (For a particular application, a weighted mean per an operational profile might be desirable, but the results presented here are generic for the API rather than any particular system.) Test execution took approximately three to eight hours per system.

There were six function/OS pairs that resulted in entire operating system crashes (either automatic reboots or system hangs). As an example of these Catastrophic failures, Irix 6.2 crashes and requires a manual hardware reset when executing the call:

```
munmap(malloc((1<<30+1)),MAXINT);
```

Restart failures were relatively scarce, but present in all but two operating systems. Abort failures were common, indicating that in all operating systems it is relatively straightforward to elicit a core dump from an instruction within a function or system call. A check was made to ensure that Abort failures were not due to corruption of stack values and subsequent corruption/misdirection of calling program operation.

A particular point of interest was that previously reported results were subject to criticism by OS vendors because in several cases the latest available OS version had not been tested. However, when a newer version was tested there was not necessarily an improvement in robustness (*e.g.*, for HP-UX and QNX). Additionally, Figure 1 reports results for DUNIX 4.0B with no Catastrophic failures. However, on DUNIX 4.0D a catastrophic failure sprang into existence due to an apparent change in the aio_raw library for the call:

```
mprotect(malloc((1<<29)+1),65537,0);.
```

There are, however, some questions left unanswered by the data in Figure 1. For example, the designers of FreeBSD have told us that they intentionally generate Abort failures as their preferred error reporting mechanism, and suggested it was possible they look bad by comparison because other OS implementations might instead suffer from elevated levels of Silent failures. (The merits of the FreeBSD strategy involve a debate about the desire to make errors highly visible during development *vs.* a desire to perform fine-grain error recovery once an application is fielded, but that is beyond the scope of this discussion.) For example, this might mean that AIX looks better than it really is because address 0 is readable without exception, leading to the possibility of elevated Silent failure rates for NULL pointer dereferencing. Therefore, it was important to determine Silent failure rates even though they could not be directly measured.

4. Data analysis via multi-version comparison

The scalability of the Ballista testing approach hinges on not needing to know the functional specification of a MuT, so that the same combinations of parameter values can be used to test any function taking a given tuple of data types. In the general case, this results in having no way to deal with tests that pass with no indication of error – they could either be non-exceptional test cases (in which all parameter values fall within normal, expected ranges) or Silent failures, depending on the actual functionality of the MuT. However, the availability of a number of operating systems with a standardized API permits estimating and refining robustness failure rates using a variation of multiple version software voting.

There have been many efforts to define and evaluate various multiple version voting algorithms and schemes (*e.g.*, [6][14][16]). Most of these focus on resolving problems with the existing standard voting techniques. Of particular concern is how separate algorithmic approaches might induce different round-off errors, leading to separate correct, but different, answers.

When applying voting techniques to the domain of software robustness, we benefit from our studied disinterest in the functional correctness of the output. Thus, robustness testing results are only concerned with whether parameter values were in fact exceptional, whether exceptional values were detected, and whether at least one of *N* OS versions responded to exceptional values gracefully, but *not* to whether the function performed as specified (which is obviously important, but is more properly the subject of traditional software testing). Thus, for our purposes, it suffices if *at least one* of *N* versions performs exception detection and returns gracefully, so we use a one-of-N *comparison* strategy rather than requiring an M-of-N majority voting scheme. For example, if any OS version reports an exception condition, it is assumed that all versions should have detected that exception (false alarm rates are discussed shortly).

4.1. Elimination of non-exceptional tests

Ballista uses combinations of exceptional and non-exceptional parameter values to do testing. Partly this is to avoid correct detection of exceptional values for one parameter from masking exceptions that might otherwise go unnoticed on other parameters. But, also, partly this is a side-effect of scalable testing in which all functions are tested with parameter values that may be exceptional for only some functions (for example, a read-only file is exceptional for a write function, but not for a read function tested with the same parameter values).

N-way comparisons were used to identify and prune non-exceptional test cases from the data set. The comparisons assumed that any test case in which all operating systems returned with no indication of error were in fact non-exceptional tests (or, were exceptional tests which could not reasonably be expected to be detected on current computer systems). In all, 129,731 non-exceptional tests were removed across all 15 operating systems. Figure 2 shows the adjusted failure rates after removing non-exceptional tests.

Hand sampling of several dozen removed test cases indicated that all of them were indeed non-exceptional, thus suggesting a low rate of false screenings. While there is the possibility that exceptional test cases slipped passed this screening, it seems unlikely that the number involved would materially affect the results.

4.2. An estimation of Silent failure rates

Once the non-exceptional tests were removed, a different variation on multi-version software comparison was used to detect Silent Failures. The heuristic used was that if at least one OS returns an error code, then all other operating systems should either return an error code or

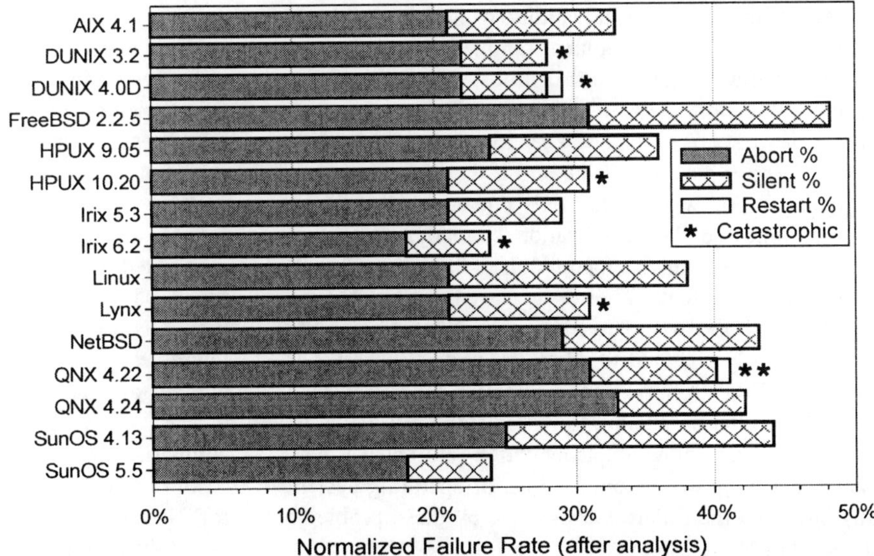

Figure 2. Multi-version comparisons eliminate the effects from non-exceptional tests and permit estimating Silent failure rates.

suffer some form of robustness failure (typically an Abort failure). As an example, when attempting to compute the logarithm of zero, AIX, HPUX-10, and both versions of QNX failed to return an error code, whereas other operating systems tested did report an error code. This indicated that AIX, HPUX-10, and QNX had suffered Silent robustness failures.

Of course, the heuristic of detection based on a single OS reporting an error code is not a completely accurate mechanism. Manual random sampling of several dozen results indicated that approximately 80% of detected test cases were actually Silent failures. Of the 20% of test cases that were false alarms:

- 28% were due to POSIX permitting discretion in how to handle an exceptional situation. For example, `mprotect()` is permitted, but not required, to return an error if the address of memory space does not fall on a page boundary.
- 21% were due to bugs in C library floating point routines returning false error codes. For example, Irix 5.3 returns an error for `tan(-1.0)` instead of the correct result of -1.557408. Two instances were found that are likely due to overflow of intermediate results -- HPUX 9 returns an error code for `fmod(DBL_MAX, PI)` and QNX 4.24 returns an error for `ldexp(e, 33)`.
- 9% were due to a filesystem bug in QNX 4.22, which incorrectly returned errors for filenames having embedded spaces.
- The remaining 42% were instances in which it was not obvious whether an error code could reasonably be required; this was mainly a concern when passing a pointer to a structure containing garbage data, where some operating systems (such as SunOS 4.1.3) apparently checked the data for validity, while others did not.

Classifying the Silent failures sampled revealed some additional software defects that manifested in unusual, but specified, situations. For instance, POSIX requires `int fdatasynch(int filedes)` to return the `EBADF` error if `filedes` is not valid, and if the file is not open for write [7]. Yet when tested, only one operating system, Irix 6.2, followed the specification correctly. All other operating systems which supported the `fdatasynch` call did not indicate that an error occurred. POSIX also specifically allows writes to files past `EOF`, requiring the file length to be updated to allow the write [7]; however only FreeBSD, Linux, and SunOS 4.1.3 returned successfully after an attempt to write data to a file past its `EOF`, while every other implementation returned `EBADF`. Manual checking of random samples of operating system calls indicated the failure rates caused by these problems ranged from 1% to 3% overall.

A second approach was attempted for detecting Silent failures based on voting successful returns against Abort failures in functions for which no error codes were returned. To our surprise this was only somewhat effective at identifying Silent failures, but did turn out to be a fruitful way to reveal software defects. A relatively small number (37,434) of test cases generated an Abort failure for some operating systems, but successfully completed for all other operating systems. A randomly sampled hand analysis indicated that this detection mechanism was incorrect approximately 50% of the time.

Part of the high false alarm rate for this second approach was due to differing orders for checking arguments among the various operating systems. For example, writing zero bytes from a NULL pointer memory location might Abort if a byte is fetched from memory before checking remaining length to transfer, or return successfully if length is checked before touching memory.

The other part of the false alarm rate was apparently due to programming errors in floating point libraries. For instance, FreeBSD suffered an Abort failure on both `fabs(DBL_MAX)` and `fabs(-DBL_MAX)`.

Figure 2 shows the aggregate results of Silent failures from multiple version comparisons with error codes (weighted at 80%) plus Silent failures from multiple version comparisons with only Abort failures (weighted at 50%). These results are obviously approximated, but do indicate that Silent errors can be prevalent. With respect to the earlier discussion of potential AIX Silent errors, it was found that error checking in other areas apparently made up for lack of error detection on NULL pointer reads, giving it a Silent failure rate comparable to several other systems, including FreeBSD.

5. Multi-version comparison of OS diversity

An additional use for multi-version comparison techniques is in attempting to quantify the diversity among OS implementations with respect to exception handling robustness. Analysis in this section was performed on a subset of the robustness testing data: 40,619 tests cases on each of 13 operating systems, for a total of 528,047 test results in all. Two OSes (QNX 4.22 and Irix 5.3) were eliminated because they did not support many of the functions supported by other OSes, and similarly many functions were eliminated because they were supported by few OSes. The selected OSes and functions maximize the number of usable test cases constrained by a requirement of every test case being supported by all OSes used in the comparisons.

In Figure 3, the horizontal axis indicates the value of N for N-way comparisons, from N=1 (data points for 13 possibilities, one for each single OS) through intermediate values such as 6 (depicting all combinations of 13 OSes taken 6 at a time), to a single data point for 13-way OS

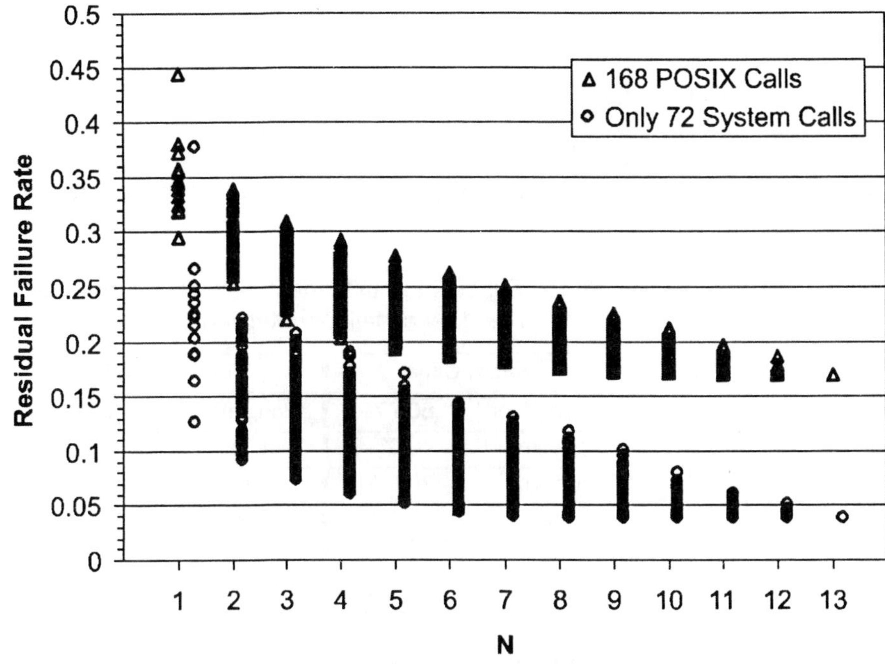

Figure 3. Multi-version comparisons of all combinations of *N* OS implementations reveal wide variations in robustness failure rates and exception handling diversity.

comparisons. For each value of N there are two sets of data: triangles for all 168 calls, and circles for the subset of 72 system calls (excluding C library calls). The data points for most values of N blend together, but the result is one that shows the span of effectiveness for various combinations, with the lowest point being the lowest possible robustness failure rate for the best possible *hypothetical* combination of N OS versions executed back-to-back (maximum available diversity), and the highest point being the worst one could do by hypothetically picking the set of N OS versions with the highest degree of robustness failure overlap (minimum available diversity).

Thus, in Figure 3 the height of any particular data point measures the robustness failure rate not detected by *any* of the N OS implementations for that point. The span of points for a particular *N* value indicates the difference in diversity among combinations (least diverse being the highest). The general difference between triangles and circles indicates differences between aggregate POSIX calls and a system-call-only subset of the POSIX API. Finally, the downward trend in failure rates as N increases indicates the additional diversity added by each additional OS considered in a pool of N OS implementations (*i.e.*, removing additional common mode failures for a hypothetical composite exception detection system).

From Figure 3, one can see that system calls are generally far more robust than C library calls (except for the N=1 point for QNX 4.24 at 37.8% robustness failure rate), especially taking into account that the triangle points are for aggregate behavior of 169 functions that also includes the data for the 72 system calls.

For both C library functions and system calls there is a significant span of robustness failure rates up through moderately high values of N, as well as a noticeable decrease in the lowest possible residual failure rate for increasing N. These trends indicate that an increasing amount of diversity in exception handling robustness is available for increasing N. Or, put another way, Figure 3 suggests that careful selection of *N* OS implementations reduces the common mode robustness failures observed as *N* increases. Furthermore, which *N* OS implementations one selects dramatically affects the degree of common mode failure observed.

To a degree, one might expect a wide spread of residual failure rates due to the fact that BSD and System V Unix implementations have significantly diverged, and that Linux was specifically developed from scratch to avoid licensing entanglements. In fact, the data for system calls suggest that a half-dozen implementations have evolved significant diversity from each other with respect to system calls (the bottom-most circle decreases in residual failure rate significantly through about *N*=6). Similarly, the fact that the GNU C libraries and BSD-based libraries were independently developed helped provide diversity.

However, the potential bad news from a diversity point of view is that no *two* OS implementations approach the system call diversity of all 13 OS implementations. Suppose that one were to, in the best case, select the two most diverse OS implementations (AIX and FreeBSD, which also appeared in personal correspondence to have the most extreme views as to what constituted robustness). If one were to make that selection with the intent of avoiding all common-mode OS exception handling failures among multiple machines running the same application software, one would only achieve a 9.7% common mode failure exposure for system calls and a 25.4% exposure for all calls tested, assuming equal weighting among all functions. And, if one were to pick any two other OS implementations, the common mode failure exposure would be higher. Selecting the best four or five or six OS implementations improves the situation to a degree, but becomes increasingly impractical in a real installation.

An additional conclusion from Figure 3 and other analysis we have performed is that a significant fraction of Abort failures come from C library calls, and tend to be correlated among OS versions. This is perhaps not a surprise considering that these calls, most notably the string handling routines, are notoriously susceptible to memory over-run and pointer value problems, and have an API definition that does not specifically encourage robustness. Similarly it is not unreasonable to conjecture that C library code has been shared and redistributed largely unchanged, since most OS vendors concentrate on porting an OS to their hardware and optimizing performance of system calls rather than the C library functions. Nonetheless, if one were to presume a high degree of implementation diversity simply because C libraries were (presumed to be) independently developed and came from independent vendors, one would be mistaken from an exception-handling perspective.

5.1. Frequent sources of robustness failure

Given that robustness failures are prevalent, what might be fixed to improve them? Source code to most of the operating systems tested was not available, and manual examination of available source code to search for root causes of robustness failures is impractical with such a large set of experimental data. Therefore, the best that can be presented is a list of data values that are highly correlated with robustness failures (Table 1) and functions that have high robustness failure rates even after 13-way failure detection comparisons are applied (Table 2).

Table 1: Data types most commonly associated with abort robustness failures for 15 operating systems.

Data Value	Percent associated with robustness failures
Invalid file pointers (excluding NULL)	94.0%
NULL file pointers	82.5%
Invalid buffer pointers (excluding NULL)	49.8%
NULL buffer pointers	46.0%
MININT integers	44.3%
MAXINT integers	36.3%

Table 1 shows that NULL and invalid pointer values are the most common causes of Abort failures, which is probably no great surprise. However, minimum and maximum integer values also seem to be correlated with robustness failures, which was not an obvious outcome.

Table 2 shows the sigjmp/longjmp pair high on the robustness failure rate list for both system calls and C library calls. Note that Table 2 deals with residual failure rates after comparisons, and so represents failures that no OS dealt with gracefully. Beyond that, string functions and math functions appear on the C library list, but are not the only culprits.

Table 2: Functions with highest residual failure rates after 13-way failure detection voting.

System Calls		C Library Calls	
siglongjmp	66.7%	longjmp	100%
sigsetjmp	40.0%	strcpy	50%
ctermid	20.0%	atan	44.4%
closedir	14.3%	frexp	40.0%
readdir	14.3%	modf	40.0%
getenv	13.3%	setjmp	40.0%
getgrnam	12.5%	sprintf	39.8%
getpwnam	12.5%	strftime	33.3%
getgrnam	12.5%	strncat	29.2%
getcwd	12.5%	strcat	28.1%
creat	11.1%	printf	25%
execlp	11.1%	strncpy	23.3%
execvp	11.1%	fabs	22.2%
sigaddset	8.2%	tan	22.2%

6. Conclusions

This paper documents the use of multi-version software comparison techniques in analyzing a set of large, mature, commercially available software systems. In terms of robustness assessment, the multi-version approach permitted identifying Silent failures (failure to indicate the occurrance of an exceptional condition when one could have been indicated) with a reasonable degree of accuracy, but without need to create functional specifications for all 233 functions tested. The result was the discovery of a normalized Silent robustness failure rate of 6% to 19% for single-OS tests. Additionally, a multi-version comparison approach permitted screening out the non-exceptional tests generated by Ballista robustness testing. An additional, unexpected, result was finding some bugs (software defects with respect to required POSIX functionality) on POSIX-certified, commercial operating systems.

A second approach to using multi-version software comparisons produced measurements of the diversity of POSIX operating systems. In particular, measurements were made for the residual robustness failure rate that would remain if one were to (hypothetically) combine the most graceful exception handling abilities of every one of *N* different OS implementations, with the value of *N* ranging from one to thirteen. The results were that the core set of 78 system calls tested were moderately robust and diverse, but not perfectly so. This result suggests that system calls have a reasonable level of software diversity for multiple version purposes, or alternately that a developer combining techniques already in existing OS implementations into a single OS might possibly (barring technical hurdles) improve the robustness that single OS. However, selecting any *pair* of OS implementations did not seem to result in the highest possible degree of implementation diversity.

The results for multi-version assessment of C library calls were less promising. C library calls appear to be significantly less robust on average than OS system calls, and additionally do not appear to be highly diverse in implementation. This finding means that presuming that C library implementations are diverse simply because they come from different vendors or have been independently developed is probably not a good idea.

Although the data presented here do not purport to apply to functional correctness, they do suggest that commercial off-the-shelf software developed to a particular API might possibly lack diversity, at least with respect to exception handling. It seems very likely that some of this lack of diversity is due to the design of the API itself, but it is difficult to believe that this is the only factor at work.

The detailed source data used in preparing this paper are available at http://www.ices.cmu.edu/ballista

7. Acknowledgment

This research was sponsored by DARPA contract DABT63-96-C-0064, the Ballista project.

8. References

[1] Avizienis, A., "The N-version approach to fault-tolerant software", *IEEE Trans. on Software Engineering*, vol.SE-11, no.12, 1985, p. 1491-501.

[2] Avizienis, A., Gunningberg, P., Kelly, J.P.J., Stringini, L., Traverse, P.J., Tso, K.S., Voges, U., "The UCLA DEDIX System: A Distributed Testbed for Multiple-Version Software", *15th Fault Tolerant Computing Symp.*, 1985, p. 126-134.

[3] Avizienis, A., Lyu, M., Schutz, W., "In Search of Effective Diversity: A Six-Language Study of Fault-Tolerant Flight Control Software," *18th Intl. Symp. on Fault Tolerant Computing*, 1988.

[4] Brilliant, S.S., Knight, J.C., Leveson, N.G., "Analysis of Faults in an N-Version Software Experiment", *IEEE Trans. on Software Engineering*, vol. 16, no. 2, 1990, pp. 238-47.

[5] Chen, L., Avizienis, A., "N-Version Programming : A Fault Tolerance Approach to Reliability of Software Operation," *The Eighth Intl. Symp. on Fault Tolerant Computing*, 1978.

[6] Gersting, J.L., Nist, R.L., Roberts, D.B., Van Valkenburg, R.L., "A Comparison of Voting Algorithms for N-Version Programming," *Proceedings of the twenty-fourth Annual Hawaii Intl. Conference on System Sciences*, vol. 2, 1991, pp. 253-62.

[7] *IEEE Standard for Information Technology - Portable Operating System Interface (POSIX) Part 1: System Application Program Interface (API) Amendment 1: Realtime Extension [C Language]* , IEEE Std 1003.1b-1993, IEEE Computer Society, 1994.

[8] Kelly, J.P., Eckhardt, D.E., Vouk, M.A., McAllister, D.F., Caglayan, A.K., "A Large scale Second Generation Experiment in Multi-Version Software: Description and Early Results," *Eighteenth Intl. Syposium on Fault Tolerant Computing*, 1988.

[9] Knight J.C., Leveson, N.G., St. Jean L.D., "A large scale experiment in N-version programming", *15th Fault Tolerant Computing Symp.*, 1985, 135-139

[10] Knight Leveson, "An empricial suty of failure probabilities in multi-version software", *16th Intl. Fault Tolerant Computing Symp.*, 1986, 165-170

[11]Knight, J.C., Leveson, N.G., "A reply to the criticisms of the Knight and Leveson experiment", *SIGSOFT Software Engineering Notes*, vol. 15, no.1, 1990, p. 24-35.

[12] Koopman, P., Sung, J., Dingman, C., Siewiorek, D. & Marz, T., "Comparing Operating Systems Using Robustness Benchmarks", *Proceedings Symp. on Reliable and Distributed Systems*, Durham, NC, Oct. 22-24 1997, pp. 72-79.

[13] Kropp, N., Koopman, P. & Siewiorek, D., "Automated Robustness Testing of Off-the-Shelf Software Components", *28th Fault Tolerant Computing Symp.*, June 23-25, 1998.

[14] Lorczak, P.R., Caglayan, A.K., Eckhardt, D.E., "A Theoretical Investigation of Generalized Voters for Redundant Systems," *19th Intl. Symp. on Fault Tolerant Computing*, 1989.

[15] Lyu, M.R., "Software Reliability Measurements in N-Version Software Execution Environment," *Proceedings of the Third Intl. Symp. on Software Reliability and Engineering*, 1992.

[16] McAllister, D.F., Sun, C., Vouk, M.A., "Reliability of Voting in Fault-Tolerant Software Systems for Small Output-Spaces," *IEEE Trans. on Reliability*, vol. 39, no. 5, 1990, pp. 524-34.

[17] Vouk, M.A., McAllister, D.F., Caglayan, A.K., Walker, J.L., Eckhardt, D.E., "Analysis of Faults Detected in a Large-Scale Multi-Version Software Development Experiment," *Proceedings of the Ninth Digital Avionics Systems Conference*, 1990.

Session 3A

Checkpointing I

Chair: Henrique Santos Madeira
Universidade de Coimbra, Portugal

Multiprocessor Architecture Using an Audit Trail for Fault Tolerance

Dwight Sunada[1], David Glasco[2], and Michael Flynn[1]

[1]Computer Systems Laboratory
Stanford University
Stanford, California 94305
dwight@cs.stanford.edu
flynn@umunhum.stanford.edu

[2]Austin Research Laboratory
International Business Machines, Inc.
Austin, Texas 78758
dglasco@us.ibm.com

Abstract

In order to deploy a tightly-coupled multiprocessor (TCMP) in the commercial world, the TCMP must be fault tolerant. Researchers have designed various checkpointing algorithms to implement fault tolerance in a TCMP. To date, these algorithms fall into 2 principal classes, where processors can be checkpoint dependent on each other. We introduce a new apparatus and algorithm that represents a 3rd class of checkpointing scheme. Our algorithm is distributed recoverable shared memory with logs (DRSM-L) and is the first of its kind for TCMPs. DRSM-L has the desirable property that a processor can establish a checkpoint or roll back to the last checkpoint in a manner that is independent of any other processor. In this paper, we describe DRSM-L and present results indicating its performance.

I. Introduction

A tightly-coupled multiprocessor (TCMP) is a multiprocessor where specialized hardware maintains the image of a single shared memory. In order to deploy a TCMP in the commercial world, the TCMP must be fault tolerant. The dominant method of fault tolerance is roll-back recovery and has 2 principal aspects. First, a processor establishes an occasional checkpoint, a consistent state of the system. Second, if a processor encounters a fault, the processor rolls back to the last checkpoint and commences execution from the state saved in that checkpoint. The first aspect, the establishment of checkpoints, is the more important one as it is a cost that the TCMP regularly experiences even if no fault arises. The second aspect, the actual rolling-back, is less important as faults tend to occur infrequently. Hence, much of the research in roll-back recovery for TCMPs has focused on developing efficient algorithms for establishing checkpoints. This paper presents the first apparatus and algorithm enabling a processor to perform roll-back or checkpoint establishment in a way that is independent of any other processor in a TCMP. Our algorithm is called distributed recoverable shared memory with logs (DRSM-L).

II. Background

Throughout our discussion, we assume that a memory block and the highest-level-cache line are identical in size and that the TCMP uses a write-back cache policy. To minimize the cost of the system, we assume that it can hold only 1 level of checkpoint.

Under these assumptions for a TCMP, a dependency can arise when 2 processors, "P" and "Q", access the same memory block. Two types of processor interaction cause dependencies to arise.

1. <u>**write–read**</u>: A write by "P" precedes a read by "Q".
   roll-back dependency: P -> Q checkpoint dependency: Q -> P
2. <u>**write–write**</u>: A write by "P" precedes a write by "Q".
   roll-back dependency: P <-> Q checkpoint dependency: P <-> Q

For a write-read interaction, if "P" rolls back to the last checkpoint, then "Q" must also roll back to the last checkpoint. If "Q" establishes a checkpoint, then "P" must also establish a checkpoint. For a write-write interaction, if one processor rolls back to the last checkpoint or establishes a new checkpoint, then the other processor must roll back to its last checkpoint or establish a new checkpoint, respectively [13].

The current schemes for establishing checkpoints in TCMPs fall into 2 major categories: tightly synchronized method (TSM) and loosely synchronized method (LSM) [13]. Wu proposes a TSM-type algorithm [16]. If a checkpoint dependency arises between any 2 processors, the processor supplying the dirty data must immediately establish a checkpoint. Both Ahmed [2] and Hunt [6] have done work related to research by Wu.

An example of a LSM-type algorithm is one presented by Banatre [3]. If a checkpoint dependency arises, the TCMP simply records the dependency without requiring the immediate establishment of a checkpoint. At some time in the future, if a processor establishes a checkpoint, that processor must query the records of dependencies to determine all other processors that must establish a checkpoint as well. Hence, a LSM-type algorithm is more flexible than a TSM-type algorithm in terms of when checkpoints must be established.

There exists a 3rd category of checkpointing algorithms: unsynchronized method (USM) [13]. In a USM-type algorithm, a processor can establish a checkpoint (or roll back to the last checkpoint) without regard to any other processor. Some USM-type algorithms [10][14] exist for a loosely-coupled multiprocessor like a network of workstations, but until now, such algorithms did not exist for TCMPs. In this paper, we present DRSM-L, the first USM-type algorithm for a TCMP.

III. Assumptions

The TCMP into which we shall incorporate DRSM-L is a multi-node multiprocessor like that shown in Figure 2. Each node has a processor module and a memory module. The nodes are connected by a high-speed dedicated network. We assume the following.

1. The processor module is not fault tolerant but is fail-safe. We can use double-modular redundancy to quickly detect whether the output of a processor module is faulty <u>before</u> the output is emitted from the processor module.
2. The TCMP suffers at most a single point of failure.
3. The network and each memory module is fault tolerant.

0-7695-0213-X/99 $10.00 © 1999 IEEE

4. The virtual machine monitor (VMM) is fault-tolerance aware. Specifically, if communication occurs between a processor and the environment outside of the TCMP, then the VMM will invoke the processor to establish a checkpoint.

The first 3 assumptions are commonly found in research papers proposing checkpointing algorithms for a TCMP. Under the 4th assumption, the TCMP views the OS as simply another user application running on top of the VMM [4]. It enables us to run any non-fault-tolerant OS while the entire TCMP remains fault-tolerant.

IV. DRSM-L

A. Apparatus

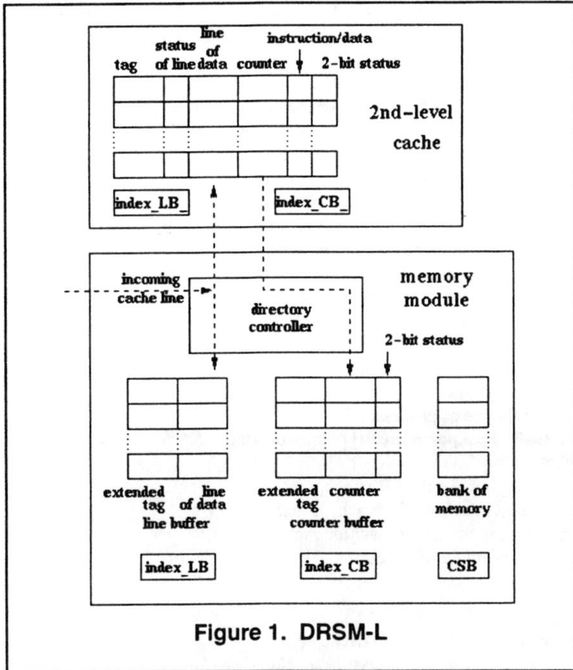

Figure 1. DRSM-L

DRSM-L is an apparatus and algorithm that enables the TCMP to recover from a failure of the processor module. Figure 1 illustrates the apparatus of DRSM-L. Each line of the 2nd-level cache has the traditional fields: tag, status (SHARED, EXCLUSIVE, and INVALID) of line, and line of data. Each line has 3 additional fields: counter, instruction/data flag (IDF), and 2-bit status flag (SF). The SF assumes any 1 of 4 values: "N" (no event), "R" (remote read), "E" (ejection), "V" (counter overflow). The cache also has 2 index registers that mirror 2 index registers in the local memory module.

The local memory module has the traditional directory controller and bank of memory. The module also has a line buffer and a counter buffer. Each buffer has an index register ("index_LB" or "index_CB") pointing at the next free entry. There is also a checkpoint-state buffer (CSB).

In the following discussion, we assume that the TCMP (1) prohibits self-modifying code and (2) requires instructions and regular data to reside in separate memory blocks (i. e. cache lines). If a cache line contains instructions, then the IDF is 0; if the line contains data, then the IDF is 1. DRSM-L uses only regular data to build an audit trail.

B. Algorithm

The general operation of DRSM-L is the following. The directory controller stores each incoming memory block (of regular data) destined for the 2nd-level cache into the next entry (at which the "index_LB" points) in the line buffer and, concurrently, forwards the memory block to the cache. Each data-access hitting on a 2nd-level-cache line causes its counter to increment; the counter records the number of accesses between consecutive events. When a cache-coherence event like (1) a write-back due to a dirty read by a remote processor or (2) an ejection (i. e. eviction/invalidation) occurs on a 2nd-level-cache line, the cache sends a reply to the local directory controller and, concurrently, forwards the counter to it in the reply. The directory controller installs the counter into the counter buffer. Saving (1) the incoming memory block into the line buffer and (2) the counter into the counter buffer incurs no additional delay since these events occur in parallel with the usual activities of (1) forwarding the memory block from the directory controller to the 2nd-level cache and (2) maintaining cache coherence, respectively. The contents of the line buffer and the counter buffer constitute an audit trail of incoming memory blocks and cache-coherence events that occurred since the last checkpoint.

A recovery logic circuit (RLC) in each memory module periodically sends "Are you alive?" messages to the processor. If it does not respond within a timeout period, then the RLC concludes that a fault has occurred. The RLC resets the local processor if the fault is transient or the processor in the spare processor module if the fault is permanent. Then, the processor performs recovery by resuming execution from the state saved in the last checkpoint. On each 2nd-level-cache miss, the VMM installs the next matching memory block from the line buffer into the appropriate cache line and also installs the next matching counter and SF from the counter buffer into that same cache line. Each data-access hitting on a 2nd-level-cache line causes its counter to decrement; once it underflows, the VMM simulates the cache-coherence event indicated by the SF.

Finally, a processor establishes a checkpoint when (1) the line buffer overflows, (3) the counter buffer overflows, (3) a timer expires, or (4) communication occurs between a processor and the environment outside of the TCMP. Establishing a checkpoint empties the 2 buffers.

Below, we use C-like code to precisely describe how the DRSM-L (1) fills the line buffer and counter buffer in the normal mode of execution, (2) rolls the processor back to the last checkpoint after encountering a fault, (3) uses the audit trail to satisfy data-access misses and to simulate cache-coherence events, and (4) establishes a checkpoint. In our code, we refer to the 2nd-level cache as simply "cache". Due to limitations on space, we present only the key aspects of the full algorithmic description in [13].

explanatory notes

States of cache line are INVALID, SHARED, and EXCLUSIVE.
Number of entries in line buffer is 8192.
Number of entries in counter buffer is 8192.
Extended tag is tag appended with index of specific cache line into which memory block is installed.
Width of counter is 32 bits.

execution mode: normal

switch (*event*) { /* events in cache */

```
  data_write_has_upgrade_miss_in_cache_data_line: {  ;  }
  data_access_misses_in_cache_data_line: {
    if (index_LB_ == 0x2000) establish_checkpoint();  }
  data_access_hits_in_cache_data_line: {
    if (cache_line.counter == 0x0FFFFFFFF) {
      if (index_CB_ == 0x2000) {
        establish_checkpoint();  }
      else {
        index_CB_++;
        log_counter_into_counter_buffer(cache_line, "V");  }  }
    else {
      cache_line.counter++;  }  }
  evict_cache_line:
  invalidate_cache_line: {
    if (index_CB_ == 0x2000) {
      establish_checkpoint();  }
    else {
      index_CB_++;
      log_counter_into_counter_buffer(cache_line, "E");  }  }
  remotely_read_local_dirty_cache_line: {
    if (index_CB_ == 0x2000) {
      establish_checkpoint();  }
    else {
      index_CB_++;
      log_counter_into_counter_buffer(cache_line, "R");  }  }
  timer_expires:
  communication_between_cpu_and_environment_
                              outside_TCMP_occurs: {
    establish_checkpoint();  }
  default: {
    do nothing special;  }  }

switch (event) {  /*  events in directory controller  */
  memory_block_arrives: {
    if (original access is data access) {
      log_memory_block_into_line_buffer();
      install_memory_block_into_cache_data_line();  }
    else {
      install_memory_block_into_cache_instruction_line();  }  }
  default: {  do nothing special;  }  }

log_memory_block_into_line_buffer() {
  line_buffer[index_LB].extended_tag <=
                        extended_tag(memory_block);
  line_buffer[index_LB].line_of_data <= data(memory_block);
  index_LB++;  }
log_counter_into_counter_buffer(cache_line, event) {
  counter_buffer[index_CB].extended_tag <=
                        extended_tag(cache_line);
  counter_buffer[index_CB].counter <= cache_line.counter;
  counter_buffer[index_CB].SF <= event;
  index_CB++;  }
install_memory_block_into_cache_instruction_line() {
  cache_line.IDF <= 0;  cache_line.counter <= 0;
  set tag, status_of_line, and line_of_data of cache_line;}
install_memory_block_into_cache_data_line() {
  index_LB_++;  cache_line.IDF <= 1;  cache_line.counter <= 0;
  set tag, status_of_line, and line_of_data of cache_line;}
```

fault detection and roll-back

```
if (RLC detects fault in processor module) {
  if (fault == permanent) {
    replace processor module with spare module;
    reset spare processor module, invalidating all entries
      in both 1st-level cache and 2nd-level cache;  }
  else {
    reset processor module, invalidating all entries
      in both 1st-level cache and 2nd-level cache;  }
  trap to virtual machine monitor;
  query all memory modules to find lost cache-coherence messages;
  negatively acknowledge all cache-coherence messages
    until recovery is complete;
  if (CSB.CF == PERMANENT_CHECKPOINT_IS_ACTIVE) {
    complete_permanent_checkpoint();
    i <= CSB.toggle_flag;
    if (CSB.checkpoint_area[i].status !=
            PERMANENT_CHECKPOINT_AREA) {
      i = 1 - CSB.toggle_flag;  }
    load internal state of processor
      from CSB.checkpoint_area[i].processor_state;
    for (each cache_line in cache) {
      load cache_line from CSB.checkpoint_area[i].cache;
      cache_line.counter <= 0;  }
    return from trap to virtual machine monitor;
    exit and resume normal execution;  }
  if (CSB.CF == TENTATIVE_CHECKPOINT_IS_ACTIVE) {
    i <= 1 - CSB.toggle_flag;  CSB.checkpoint_area[i].status <= NULL;
    CSB.CF <= CHECKPOINT_IS_NOT_ACTIVE;
    discard tentative checkpoint;  }
  read all valid entries from line buffer;
  group all entries according to cache index but, for each
    cache index, maintain the temporal order in which the
    entries were originally inserted into the line buffer;
  place grouped entries into sorted_line_buffer;
  read all valid entries from counter buffer;
  group all entries according to cache index but, for each
    cache index, maintain the temporal order in which the
    entries were originally inserted into the counter buffer;
  place grouped entries into sorted_counter_buffer;
  i <= CSB.toggle_flag;
  if (CSB.checkpoint_area[i].status !=
          PERMANENT_CHECKPOINT_AREA) {
    i = 1 - CSB.toggle_flag;  }
  load internal state of processor
    from CSB.checkpoint_area[i].processor_state;
  for (each cache_line in cache) {
    load cache_line from CSB.checkpoint_area[i].cache;
    cache_line.counter <= 0;  cache_line.SF <= "V";  }
  return from trap to virtual machine monitor;
  enter recovery mode of execution;  }
```

execution mode: recovery

```
switch (event) {  /*  events in cache  */
  data_write_has_upgrade_miss_in_cache_data_line: {
    cache_line.status_of_line <= EXCLUSIVE;  }
  data_access_misses_in_cache_data_line: {
    trap to virtual machine monitor;
    cache_line <= available_cache_line();
    get_entry_from_sorted_line_buffer(cache_line)
    get_entry_from_sorted_counter_buffer(cache_line);
    return from trap to virtual machine monitor;
    exit_recovery_upon_completion();  }
  data_access_hits_in_cache_data_line: {
    switch (cache_line.SF) {
      "N":  {  cache_line.counter <= 0;  }
      "E":  {
        if (cache_line.counter != 0) {
          cache_line.counter--;  }
        else {
          trap to virtual machine monitor;
          cache_line.status_of_line <= INVALID;
          get_entry_from_sorted_line_buffer(cache_line);
          get_entry_from_sorted_counter_buffer(cache_line);
          return from trap to virtual machine monitor;  }  }
      "R":  {
        if (cache_line.counter != 0) {
          cache_line.counter--;  }
        else {
```

```
            trap to virtual machine monitor;
            cache_line.status_of_line <= SHARED;
            get_entry_from_sorted_counter_buffer(cache_line);
            return from trap to virtual machine monitor;  }  }
        "V": {
          if (cache_line.counter != 0) {
            cache_line.counter--;  }
          else {
            trap to virtual machine monitor;
            get_entry_from_sorted_counter_buffer(cache_line);
            return from trap to virtual machine monitor;  }  }  }
      exit_recovery_upon_completion();  }
  default: {  exit_recovery_upon_completion();  }  }

switch (event) {  /*  events in directory controller  */
memory_block_arrives: {
    if (original access is data access) {  ;  }
    else {
      install_memory_block_into_cache_instruction_line();  }  }
default: {
    do nothing special;  }  }

get_entry_from_sorted_line_buffer(cache_line) {
  get next matching entry from sorted_line_buffer;
  cache_line.tag <= tag(sorted_line_buffer[entry].extended_tag);
  if (data-access == write) {
    cache_line.status_of_line <= EXCLUSIVE;  }
  else {
    cache_line.status_of_line <= SHARED;  }
  cache_line.line_of_data <=
              sorted_line_buffer[entry].line_of_data;  }
get_entry_from_sorted_counter_buffer(cache_line) {
  get next matching entry from sorted_counter_buffer;
  if (no matching counter) {
    cache_line.counter <= 0;
    cache_line.IDF <= 1;  cache_line.SF <= "N";  }
  else {
    cache_line.counter <= sorted_counter_buffer[entry].counter;
    cache_line.IDF <= 1;
    cache_line.SF <= sorted_counter_buffer[entry].SF;  }  }
exit_recovery_upon_completion() {
  if ((sorted_counter_buffer has no entry where SF is "E"
       or "R") && (counters in all valid cache data lines
       where SF is "E" or "R" are 0)) {
    for (each valid cache_line in cache) {
      switch (cache_line.SF) {
        "E":  {  cache_line.status_of_line <= INVALID;  }
        "R":  {  cache_line.status_of_line <= SHARED;  }
        default:  {  ;  }  }  }
    establish_checkpoint();
    write_back_and_invalidate_cache_lines();
    exit recovery and resume normal execution;  }
  else {  ;  }  }
```

checkpoint establishment

```
establish_checkpoint() {
  CSB.CF <= TENTATIVE_CHECKPOINT_IS_ACTIVE;
  wait until all pending memory accesses are completed
                              or negatively acknowledged;
  negatively acknowledge all cache-coherence messages
                              until checkpoint is established;
  establish_tentative_checkpoint();
  CSB.CF <=  PERMANENT_CHECKPOINT_IS_ACTIVE;
  establish_permanent_checkpoint();
  CSB.CF <= CHECKPOINT_IS_NOT_ACTIVE;  }
establish_tentative_checkpoint() {
  i <= 1 - CSB.toggle_flag;
  save tag, status_of_line, line_of_data, and IDF of all
        cache lines into CSB.checkpoint_area[i].cache;
  save internal state of processor
        into CSB.checkpoint_area[i].processor_state;
  CSB.checkpoint_area[i].status <=
        TENTATIVE_CHECKPOINT_AREA;  }
establish_permanent_checkpoint() {
  index_LB_ <= 0;  index_CB_ <= 0;
  index_LB <= 0;  index_CB <= 0;
  for (each cache_line in cache) {  cache_line.counter <= 0;  }
  i <= CSB.toggle_flag;
  CSB.checkpoint_area[i].status <= NULL;
  i <= 1 - CSB.toggle_flag;
  CSB.checkpoint_area[i].status <=
        PERMANENT_CHECKPOINT_AREA;
  CSB.toggle_flag <= i;  }
```

V. Hardware and Software Issues

For a given amount of silicon area from which we can build the line buffer and counter buffer, the optimal size of each is one that minimizes the number of checkpoints. The optimal size of each buffer is one where

optimum ratio = E[CB] / E[LB] = R[CB] / R[LB]. (equation #1)

"E[CB] " and "E[LB]" are the number of entries in the counter buffer and the line buffer, respectively. "R[CB]" and "R[LB]" are the rates at which the counter buffer and the line buffer, respectively, fill [13].

On the software side, the description of the above algorithm applies to a single thread of a single process running on a processor in a TCMP. In order to deal with multiple threads and processes, the DRSM-L must direct a processor, "P", to establish a checkpoint just after "P" switches context (and before "P" sends any dirty data to the rest of the TCMP).

Establishing a checkpoint at each context switch will not cause appreciable deterioration in performance. Establishing a checkpoint involves mainly saving the 2nd-level-cache and processor state into the CSB and, hence, costs about 41 microseconds for a 8192-line cache of a 200 megahertz processor. The fastest context-switch time (of a thread) is approximately 8 microseconds, scaled for a 200 megahertz SPARC processor from the results by Narlikar [9]. The checkpoint time and the context-switch time have roughly the same order of magnitude.

VI. Simulation Methodology

A. Multiprocessor Simulator

We evaluated DRSM-L by simulating its operation within a multiprocessor simulator. Figure 2 illustrates its base TCMP. The model of the memory system and the network is the NUMA model packaged with the SimOS simulator [5]. Instead of SimOS, we use ABSS to simulate the processors and to drive the NUMA model [11]. The delays through the components in figure 2 have values that are typical for a processor running at 200 megahertz and are listed in [13]. Below are the other parameters.

base parameters

processor = SPARC V7 @ 200 megahertz
cache policy = write-back
memory model = sequential consistency
1st-level instruction cache = 32 kilobytes with 4-way set associativity, 2 states (INVALID, SHARED), 64-byte line

1st-level data cache = 32 kilobytes with 4-way set associativity, 3 states (INVALID, SHARED, EXCLUSIVE), 64-byte line
2nd-level cache = 1 megabyte with 4-way set associativity, 3 states (INVALID, SHARED, EXCLUSIVE), 128-byte line

DRSM-L parameters

width of counter = 32 bits
line buffer = 8192 entries
counter buffer = 8192 entries
timer = expiration per 20 million cycles

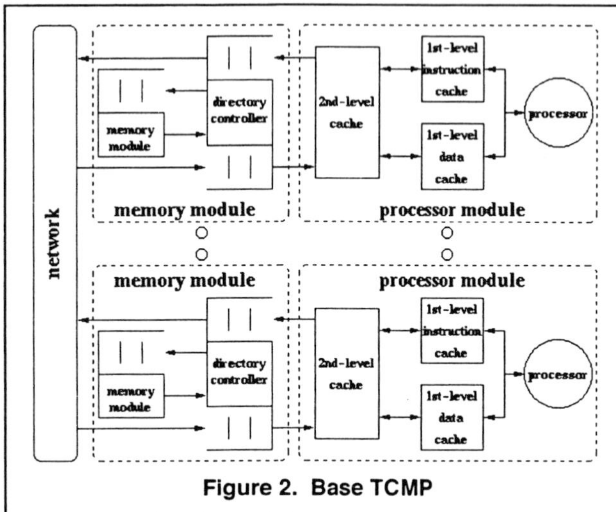

Figure 2. Base TCMP

B. Benchmarks

We run 6 benchmarks -- Cholesky, FFT, LU, ocean, radix, and water -- from the SPLASH2 suite [15] . Cholesky factors a sparse matrix. FFT performs a fast Fourier transform. LU factors a dense matrix. Ocean simulates eddy and boundary currents in oceans. Radix performs a radix sort. Finally, water evaluates the forces and potentials as they change over time among water molecules.

These benchmarks have 2 common characteristics. First, the working set of each benchmark fits within our large 2nd-level cache. Second, these benchmarks represent a scientific workload. They are useful in representing a wide variety of memory-access patterns but do virtually no communication with the environment outside of the TCMP. So, a checkpoint triggered by communication between a processor and the environment outside of the TCMP does not occur. We note that regardless of the event triggering a checkpoint, the procedure for establishing one remains the same, so we can still evaluate the performance of our algorithms even if checkpoints are triggered by a smaller set of events.

C. LSM-type Apparatus and Algorithm

In order to compare the performance of DRSM-L (as a USM-type algorithm) against a LSM-type algorithm, we introduce DRSM. It is a recently developed LSM-type algorithm and is an extension of recoverable shared memory (RSM) developed by Banatre[3]. Figure 3 illustrates only the key structures of DRSM for a 3-processor configuration.

We very briefly describe how DRSM works. Bank #1 of memory holds the working data (and tentative checkpoint), and bank #2 holds the permanent checkpoint. The dependency matrix records checkpoint dependencies that can arise when 2 processors access the same memory block in the memory module. If a processor, "P", wishes to establish a checkpoint, the DRSM recursively queries all the dependency matrices and identifies all processors that are dependent on "P". Then, "P" and all its dependent processors establish a checkpoint. A processor establishes a checkpoint by saving the processor state into the local memory module and by writing all dirty 2nd-level-cache lines back into main memory (i. e. bank #1).

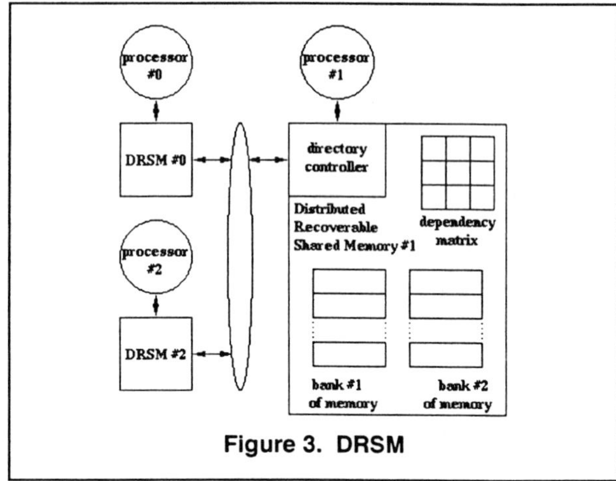

Figure 3. DRSM

The establishment of a checkpoint is triggered by only 2 events: (1) expiration of a timer and (2) communication between a processor and the environment outside of the TCMP.

The DRSM described here differs from the DRSM in prior work [13] in regards to only 1 aspect. In the current DRSM, bank #2 always holds the permanent checkpoint, but in the prior DRSM, bank #2 alternates between holding permanent-checkpoint data and holding working data. The extra functionality in the prior DRSM proved unnecessary, so we removed the functionality and simplified the hardware.

VII. Results and Analysis

A. Overall Performance of Benchmarks

Due to space limitations, we focus on 2 representative benchmarks: Cholesky and ocean. (The full set of results appears in [13].) Figure 5 shows their performance on the base TCMP, the TCMP with DRSM, and the TCMP with DRSM-L. We set the number of processors to 8, 16, and 32. We decompose the execution time into 5 categories: non-idle time of the processor, the instruction stall, the lock stall, the data stall, and the barrier stall. In general, the performance of DRSM-L exceeds the performance of DRSM.

For ocean, the barrier stall and the lock stall increase substantially as the number of processors increases from 8 to 32 processors because ocean, unlike Cholesky, has (1) several locks within global barriers and (2) global locks. All processors compete for these locks, causing hot spots to arise.

B. Checkpoints and Checkpoint Data

Table 2 shows statistics about the rate at which DRSM-L establishes checkpoints. Each application has 4 rows of statistics. The 1st row indicates the total number of checkpoints established per processor. Checkpoints in DRSM-L are triggered by effectively 3 events: (1) timer expiration, (2) line-buffer overflow, and (3) counter-buffer overflow. The checkpoints attributed to each trigger appear in the 2nd row of statistics. For example, the 2nd row for Cholesky running on an 8-processor TCMP has "(9.62 + 0.12 + 0.62)". The number of checkpoints due to timer expiration, line-buffer overflow, and counter-buffer overflow are 9.62, 0.12, and 0.62, respectively.

The remaining 2 rows show the time consumed by checkpoint establishment. The 3rd row shows the number of cycles for which a processor is stalled in establishing the number of checkpoints in the 2nd row. Each number within parentheses in the 3rd row indicates a fraction of 10,000 cycles. The 4th row shows the percentage (of the total execution time of the benchmark) represented by the number of cycles in the 3rd row. For example, during the execution of the Cholesky benchmark by the 8-processor TCMP, a processor consumed 81,890 cycles in establishing 9.62 timer-triggered checkpoints. The 81,890 cycles is 0.03977 % of the total number of cycles needed to execute Cholesky.

The data for DRSM-L indicates that the 8192-entry line buffer and the 8192-entry counter buffer are adequately large. They overflow infrequently and, hence, trigger the establishment of checkpoints only infrequently. Based on the number of bits of storage, the size of the combination of the line buffer and the counter buffer is close to the size of the 2nd-level cache.

Table 3 shows statistics about the rate at which DRSM establishes checkpoints. The checkpoints in table 2 are triggered by the expiration of the timer.

Table 4 shows statistics about the amount of data written into the line buffer and counter buffer. Each row has 3 consecutive numbers enclosed within parentheses. The 1st number is the number of entries written into the line buffer. The 2nd number is the number of entries written into the counter buffer. The 3rd number is the ratio of the 2nd number to the 1st number. This ratio is the optimum ratio, according to equation #1.

For DRSM-L with 8, 16, and 32 processors, the ratios represented by the 3rd numbers are concentrated in the range of [0.62, 0.94], [0.69, 0.89], and [0.61, 0.89], respectively, excluding 3 atypical extrema (i.e. 0.42, 0.41, and 0.41). That the ratios are concentrated in a somewhat narrow band over several different applications is opportune. We can then select the average ratio (according to a geometric average) to determine the relative sizes of the line buffer and counter buffer, and this average ratio shall yield good system performance across all the benchmarks. The geometric averages of the ratios within the bands of [0.62, 0.94], [0.69, 0.89], and [0.61, 0.89] are 0.79, 0.80, and 0.79, respectively. Our selected ratio of 1.0 -- ratio of 8192 entries in the counter buffer to 8192 entries in the line buffer -- is slightly larger than these 3 geometric averages.

C. Performance Impact of Checkpoints

When a processor establishes checkpoints, 2 types of interference can degrade its performance in both DRSM and DRSM-L. First, the processor wastes time in actually establishing a checkpoint. Second, establishing a checkpoint causes certain resources to be unavailable; a processor attempting to access them receives a negative acknowledgment. For example, when a processor, "P", establishes a checkpoint, "P" negatively acknowledges cache-coherence messages (like invalidations) indirectly sent from other processors.

A processor in DRSM also suffers a 3rd type of interference. During the establishment of a checkpoint, "P" converts much dirty data (in state EXCLUSIVE) in the 2nd-level cache into clean data (in state SHARED) by writing it back into main memory. After "P" resumes execution after establishing the checkpoint, "P" wastes time in submitting many upgrade requests to memory in order to convert clean data (which was dirty prior to the checkpoint) back into dirty data so that "P" can resume writing into it.

Table 5 shows the negative acknowledgments (NAKs) and upgrade misses generated by the base TCMP, the TCMP with DRSM, and the TCMP with DRSM-L. For each of the benchmarks, the 1st row shows the number of NAKs; the impact of the 2nd type of interference is the increase in NAKs over that of the base TCMP. The 2nd row shows the number of upgrade misses; the impact of the 3rd type of interference is the increase in upgrade misses over that of the base TCMP. (A processor in DRSM-L does not suffer the 3rd type of interference.) For DRSM, the large increase in the number of upgrade misses is a major reason that DRSM performs worse than DRSM-L.

D. DRSM Versus DRSM-L

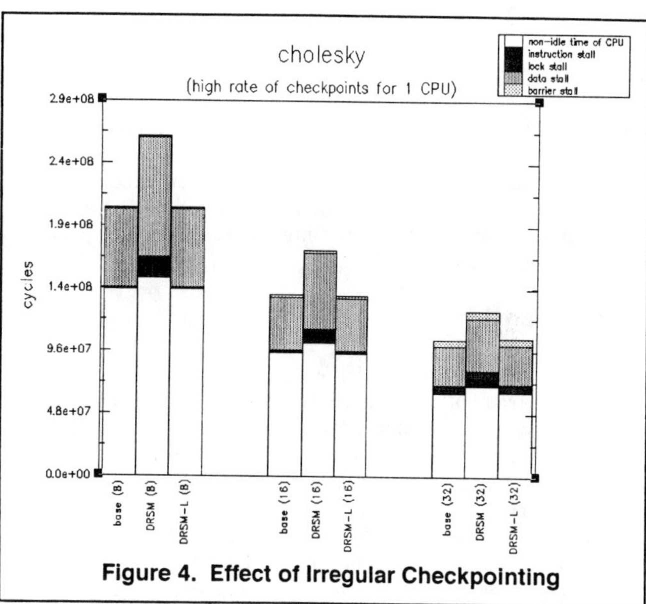

Figure 4. Effect of Irregular Checkpointing

DRSM-L has an inherent advantage over DRSM. DRSM-L enables a processor, "P", to establish a checkpoint without regard to any other processor. By contrast, in a system with DRSM, if "P" establishes a checkpoint, then all processors that are checkpoint dependent on "P" must also establish a checkpoint. Suppose that "P" tends to establish checkpoints at a much higher rate than the other processors. If the TCMP uses DRSM, then checkpoint dependencies between "P" and the other processors tend to cause the other processors to establish checkpoints at a high rate, degrading the performance of the TCMP. On the other hand, if the TCMP uses DRSM-L, the high rate of checkpoints by "P" does not cause the other processors to establish checkpoints at a high rate. Hence, DRSM-L has an inherent performance advantage over DRSM.

To quantitatively demonstrate this performance advantage, we increase the rate at which processor #3 in our TCMP establishes checkpoints. We set the timer of processor #3 to expire after each interval of 2 million cycles, but we keep the current timer interval of 20 million cycles for the other processors. In other words, we increase, by a factor of 10, the rate at which processor #3 tends to establish timer-triggered checkpoints.

	DRSM	DRSM-L	
8 CPUs	(120; 92.9)	(103; 9.6)	checkpoints
16 CPUs	(80; 68.8)	(68; 6.9)	checkpoints
32 CPUs	(58; 50.4)	(51; 5.1)	checkpoints

Table 1. Timer-triggered Checkpoints: (number for processor #3; average for other processors)

We focus on Cholesky. Figure 4 shows the overall results. (For DRSM, expiration of a timer is effectively the only event that triggers establishing a checkpoint.) In figure 5, DRSM-L runs about 9.09%, 6.13%, or 4.77% faster than DRSM for a TCMP with 8, 16, or 32 processors, respectively. In figure 4, DRSM-L runs about 26.75%, 25.00%, or 19.28% faster than DRSM for a TCMP with 8, 16, or 32 processors, respectively. DRSM performs much worse then DRSM-L in figure 4. To obtain insight into the extent to which checkpoint dependencies cause a high rate of checkpointing by one processor to impact other processors, we introduce a lumped parameter that is the average number of timer-triggered checkpoints across all processors except processor #3. Table 1 shows the values for this new parameter. Each row has 2 sets of numbers. In each set, the 1st number is the number of timer-triggered checkpoints established by processor #3, and the 2nd number is the average number of timer-triggered checkpoints across all processors except processor #3. Clearly, due to the checkpoint dependencies that are in DRSM, the high rate of establishing checkpoints by processor #3 causes all the other processors to establish checkpoints at almost the same high rate. Hence, DRSM performs much worse than DRSM-L.

VIII. Related Work

Alewine proposes a read buffer that is similar to the line buffer. The read buffer saves the data read from a register file; after the processor encounters a fault, the register file restores its original state from the read buffer [1]. This technique provides fast roll-back but assumes that the read buffer is not affected by faults in another part of the processor.

Also, Janssens analyzes the performance of TSM-type and LSM-type algorithms in an insightful study [8]. It focuses exclusively on bus-based systems. By contrast, we focus on TCMPs created from more general networks, using directories to maintain the coherence of the caches.

The methods of establishing checkpoints in a TCMP are somewhat similar to methods in a loosely-coupled multiprocessor (LCMP) like a network of workstations, where software maintains the image of a single shared memory. An example of a TSM-type algorithm for a LCMP is another checkpointing scheme proposed by Wu[17]. An example of a LSM-type algorithm is the one proposed by Janakiraman[7]. The logging schemes proposed by Richard[10] and Suri[14] are examples of USM-type algorithms.

IX. Conclusion

We conclude that DRSM-L is a good checkpointing apparatus and algorithm for a TCMP. DRSM-L is the first USM-type algorithm for a TCMP. Unlike current algorithms, DRSM-L allows independent establishment of a checkpoint and independent roll-back from a fault and, hence, is much more scalable than DRSM. DRSM-L performs much better than DRSM. Also, DRSM-L is substantially cheaper to implement than DRSM. For example, DRSM-L requires only a single bank of memory, but both DRSM and RSM [3] require 2 banks of memory.

X. References

1. N. Alewine, S. Chen, et. al., "Compiler-Assisted Multiple Instruction Rollback Recovery Using a Read Buffer", "IEEE Transactions on Computers", vol. 44, no. 9, pp. 1096-1107, September 1995.
2. R. E. Ahmed, R. C. Frazier, et. al., "Cache-Aided Rollback Error Recovery (CARER) Algorithms for Shared-Memory Multiprocessor Systems", Proceedings of the 20th International Symposium on Fault-Tolerant Computing Systems, pp. 82-88, 1990.
3. M. Banatre, A. Gefflaut, et. al., "An Architecture for Tolerating Processor Failures in Shared-Memory Multiprocessors", "IEEE Transactions on Computers", vol. 45, no. 10, pp. 1101-1115, October 1996.
4. E. Bugnion, S. Devine, et. al., "Disco: running commodity operating systems on scalable multiprocessors", "ACM Transactions on Computer Systems", vol. 15, no. 4, pp. 412-447, November 1997.
5. S. Herrod, M. Rosenblum, et. al., "The SimOS Simulation Environment", Stanford University, pp. 1-31, February 1997.
6. D. B. Hunt and P. N. Marinos, "A General Purpose Cache-Aided Rollback Error Recovery (CARER) Technique", Proceedings of the 17th International Symposium on Fault-Tolerant Computing Systems, pp. 170-175, 1987.
7. G. Janakiraman and Y. Tamir, "Coordinated Checkpointing-Rollback Error Recovery for Distributed Shared Memory Multicomputers", In Proceedings of the 13th Symposium on Reliable Distributed Systems, pp. 42-51, October 1994.
8. B. Janssens and W. K. Fuchs, "The Performance of Cache-Based Error Recovery in Multiprocessors", "IEEE Transactions on Parallel and Distributed Systems", vol. 5, no. 10, pp. 1033-1043, October 1994.
9. G. J. Narlikar and G. E. Blelloch, "Pthreads for Dynamic and Irregular Parallelism", Proceedings of Supercomputing 98: High Performance Networking and Computing, November 1998.
10. G. Richard III and M. Singhal, "Using Logging and Asynchronous Checkpointing to Implement Recoverable Distributed Shared Memory", Proceedings of the 12th Symposium on Reliable Distributed Systems, pp. 58-67, October 1993.
11. D. Sunada, D. Glasco, M. Flynn, "ABSS v2.0: a SPARC Simulator", Proceedings of the Eighth Workshop on Synthesis and System Integration of Mixed Technologies , pp. 143 - 149, October 1998.
12. D. Sunada, D. Glasco, M. Flynn, "Hardware-assisted Algorithms for Checkpoints", technical report: csl-tr-98-756, Stanford University, pp. 1-38, July 1998.
13. D. Sunada, D. Glasco, M. Flynn, "Novel Checkpointing Algorithm for Fault Tolerance on a Tightly-Coupled Multiprocessor", technical report: csl-tr-99-776, Stanford University, pp. 1-50, January 1999.
14. G. Suri, B. Janssens, et. al., "Reduced Overhead Logging for Rollback Recovery in Distributed Shared Memory", Proceedings of the 25th International Symposium on Fault-Tolerant Computing Systems, pp. 279-288, 1995.
15. S. C. Woo, M. Ohara, E. Torrie, J. Singh, A. Gupta, "The SPLASH-2 Programs: Characterization and Methodological Considerations", Proceedings of the 22nd Annual International Symposium on Computer Architecture, pp. 24 - 36, June 1995.
16. K. Wu, W. Fuchs, et. al., "Error Recovery in Shared Memory Multiprocessors Using Private Caches", "IEEE Transactions on Parallel and Distributed Systems", vol. 1, no. 2, pp. 231-240, April 1990.
17. K. Wu and W. Fuchs, "Recoverable Distributed Shared Virtual Memory", "IEEE Transactions on Computers", vol. 39, no. 4, pp. 460-469, April 1990.

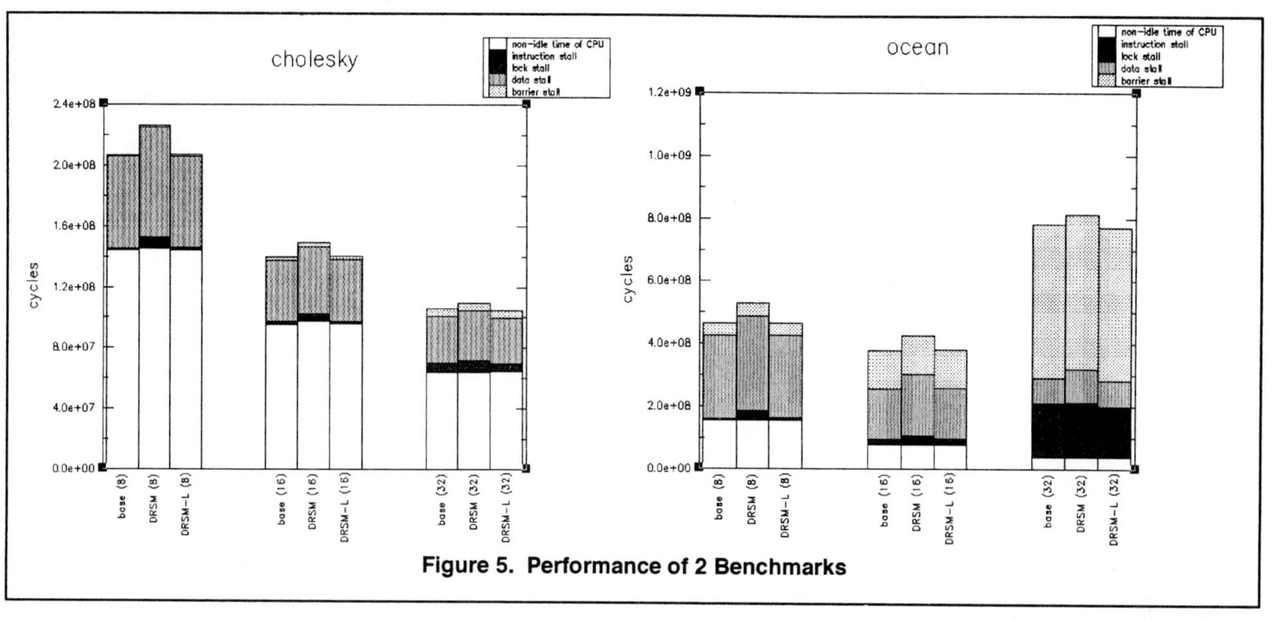

Figure 5. Performance of 2 Benchmarks

	8-processor TCMP	16-processor TCMP	32-processor TCMP	
Cholesky	10.38	7.00	5.19	checkpoints
	(9.62 + 0.12 + 0.62)	(6.94 + 0.00 + 0.06)	(5.03 + 0.12 + 0.03)	(please see text)
	(8.189 + 0.106 + 0.532)	(5.902 + 0.000 + 0.055)	(4.281 + 0.106 + 0.027)	x 1e+4 cycles
	(3.977 + 0.052 + 0.258)	(4.229 + 0.000 + 0.040)	(4.109 + 0.102 + 0.026)	x 0.01 % of run time
ocean	22.38	18.19	37.25	checkpoints
	(21.38 + 0.25 + 0.75)	(18.19 + 0.00 + 0.00)	(37.25 + 0.00 + 0.00)	(please see text)
	(18.186 + 0.213 + 0.682)	(15.474 + 0.000 + 0.000)	(31.692 + 0.000 + 0.000)	x 1e+4 cycles
	(3.903 + 0.046 + 0.146)	(4.045 + 0.000 + 0.000)	(4.098 + 0.000 + 0.000)	x 0.01 % of run time

Table 2. Checkpoints for DRSM-L

	8-processor TCMP	16-processor TCMP	32-processor TCMP	
Cholesky	11.00	8.00	6.00	checkpoints
	(7.530)	(3.447)	(2.039)	x 1e+6 cycles
	(3.353)	(2.327)	(1.868)	% of run time
ocean	24.00	20.00	39.00	checkpoints
	(31.227)	(17.650)	(10.910)	x 1e+6 cycles
	(5.871)	(4.117)	(1.338)	% of run time

Table 3. Checkpoints for DRSM

	8-processor TCMP	16-processor TCMP	32-processor TCMP
Cholesky	(35559; 28548; 0.80)	(24420; 16946; 0.69)	(18822; 11469; 0.61)
FFT	(8782; 6335; 0.72)	(4602; 3155; 0.69)	(2680; 1882; 0.70)
LU	(10571; 4475; 0.42)	(6794; 2813; 0.41)	(5293; 2147; 0.41)
ocean	(124516; 116525; 0.94)	(61962; 54849; 0.89)	(39862; 35659; 0.89)
radix	(8389; 5223; 0.62)	(12267; 10375; 0.85)	(10379; 8968; 0.86)
water	(4893; 3976; 0.81)	(5123; 4326; 0.84)	(4508; 3874; 0.86)

Table 4. Audit-Trail Data (entries in line buffer; entries in counter buffer; ratio)

	8 processors			16 processors			32 processors			
	base	DRSM	DRSM-L	base	DRSM	DRSM-L	base	DRSM	DRSM-L	
Cholesky	127	148	148	331	334	340	736	768	665	negative ack.'s
	9036	22662	9078	4954	9533	4938	3268	5447	3285	upgrade misses
ocean	6222	6404	6347	15936	16624	16480	50931	51009	50128	negative ack.'s
	41021	75475	40980	28386	61812	28430	14449	38453	14511	upgrade misses

Table 5. Negative Acknowledgments and Upgrade Misses for DRSM-L

Egida: An Extensible Toolkit For Low-overhead Fault-Tolerance

Sriram Rao* Lorenzo Alvisi* Harrick M. Vin†
Department of Computer Sciences
The University of Texas at Austin
Taylor Hall 2.124, Austin, Texas 78712-1188, USA.

Abstract

We discuss the design and implementation of Egida, an object-oriented toolkit designed to support transparent rollback-recovery. Egida exports a simple specification language that can be used to express arbitrary rollback recovery protocols. From this specification, Egida automatically synthesizes an implementation of the specified protocol by gluing together the appropriate objects from an available library of "building blocks". Egida is extensible and facilitates rapid implementation of rollback recovery protocols with minimal programming effort. We have integrated Egida with the MPICH implementation of the MPI standard. Existing MPI applications can take advantage of Egida without any modifications: fault-tolerance is achieved transparently—all that is needed is a simple re-link of the MPI application with Egida.

1 Introduction

Building reliable distributed application is complex. Application developers not only have to worry about the intricacies of their applications, but also have to understand the subtleties of distributed fault-tolerance. Over the past decade, toolkits such as Horus [22], and Transis [8] have addressed this issue by providing higher level primitives for implementing fault-tolerant broadcasting and group communication. These primitives are well-suited for implementing fault-tolerance protocols based on active replication, desirable for mission-critical applications that require the highest degree of availability and the capability to tolerate arbitrary failures.

As distributed computing becomes commonplace, however, a growing number of non mission-critical applications are emerging. For instance, parallel scientific applications that used to be run on supercomputers can be executed on a distributed cluster of servers. For these applications, fault-tolerance is highly desirable, but only if it can be provided with low-overhead in terms of dedicated resources and execution time. Log-based rollback recovery protocols—such as checkpointing and message logging—provide an attractive low-overhead solution for building non-critical distributed applications that can tolerate crash failures.

In this paper, we discuss the design and implementation of *Egida*, an object-oriented toolkit designed to support transparent rollback recovery for low-overhead fault-tolerance. Rather than providing monolithic implementations of a set of protocols, we build Egida around a library of objects that implement a set of functionalities that are at the core of all log-based rollback recovery protocols and define a grammar for configuring protocols from the library of objects. Our approach has several advantages. First, it promotes extensibility and flexibility by allowing multiple implementations of each of the core functionalities. Second, it facilitates rapid implementation of rollback recovery protocols with minimal programming effort by gluing together objects from the available library of building blocks. This enables application developers to experiment with different protocols and then use the one that closely matches the requirements of their application. Finally, Egida enables designers of fault-tolerance protocols to develop new rollback recovery protocols by combining different implementations of the core functionalities in novel ways.

Egida shares some of the design goals of other frameworks—such as OTEC [20] and RENEW [18]—for implementing rollback recovery protocols. Egida is unique in that it allows rollback recovery protocols to be configured from basic building blocks. This approach is similar to the one used in other systems—for instance, in Adaptive [23] and xkernel [13] for networking protocols, and in Horus [22] and Cactus [11] for distributed computing and group membership protocols.

We have integrated Egida with the MPICH implementation of the Message Passing Interface (MPI) standard [25]. This enables existing MPI applications to take advantage of Egida without any modifications. Conversely, the performance of rollback recovery protocols can now be evaluated using a large set of demanding applications.

This paper is organized as follows. In Section 2, we provide a brief overview of log-based rollback recovery protocols. In Section 3, we identify the set functionalities that are at the core of all log-based rollback recovery protocols, and present a grammar for synthesizing these protocols from its core components. Section 4 describes the architecture of Egida. Section 5 describes the implementation of Egida and its integration with the MPICH library [10]. Section 6 presents the related work, and finally, Section 7 summarizes our contributions.

*These authors supported in part by the National Science Foundation (CAREER award CCR-9734185, Research Infrastructure Award CDA-9734185, and DARPA/SPAWAR grant N66001-98-8911).

†This author supported in part by an AT&T Foundation Award, IBM Faculty Development Award, Intel, the National Science Foundation (CAREER award CCR-9624757, and Research Infrastructure Award CDA-9624082), Lucent Bell Laboratories, NASA, Mitsubishi Electric Research Laboratories (MERL), and Sun Microsystems Inc.

2 Flavors of Log-based Rollback Recovery

Log-based rollback recovery protocols—such as checkpointing and message logging—provide a low-overhead solution for building distributed applications that tolerate crash failures. These protocols come in several flavors. Checkpoints can be independent, coordinated, or induced by specific patterns of communication. Logging can be pessimistic, optimistic, or causal. Pessimistic protocols [3, 28] allow processes to communicate only from recoverable states. These protocols enforce this condition by synchronously logging to stable storage any information critical for recovery before letting processes communicate. Optimistic protocols (for instance, [7, 14, 27]) allow processes to communicate with other processes even from states that are not yet recoverable. These protocols guarantee that these states will eventually become recoverable, but only if no failures occur. Failures may indeed render some states permanently unrecoverable, forcing the rollback of any process that depends on such states. Causal protocols [2, 9] weaken the condition imposed by pessimistic protocols and allow the possibility that a state from which a process communicates may become unrecoverable because of a failure, but only if no correct process depends on that state. This is enforced by appending to all communication the information necessary to recover the state from which the communication originates. This information is replicated in the volatile memory of the processes that causally depend [15] on the originating state. Hence, causal protocols never roll back correct processes, but do not require synchronous writes to stable storage.

3 Deconstructing Log-Based Rollback-Recovery Protocols

The diversity of rollback-recovery protocols reflects the heterogeneity in the requirements of applications. For instance, applications that don't interact frequently with the external environment and can tolerate rollback of correct processes may use checkpointing or optimistic protocols. Pessimistic and causal protocols are better suited for applications in which communication with the environment is frequent and rollbacks are unacceptable; pessimistic protocols are preferred when fast and simple recovery is required. Applications that instead demand minimal overhead during failure-free executions would use causal or optimistic protocols. A closer look at these protocols, however, reveals that behind this diversity lies a simple event-driven structure that all these protocols share and that all protocols are interested in the same set of "relevant" events. In this section we identify such events and present a language that can be used to specify a protocol in terms of which actions it takes in response to each of these events.

3.1 Log-based Rollback-Recovery Protocols as Event-Driven Programs

There are five types of events that are relevant to all rollback recovery protocols. These are: (1) non-deterministic events, (2) dependency-generating events, (3) output-commit events, (4) checkpointing events, and (5) failure-detection events.

1. **Non-deterministic events**: A non-deterministic event is an event whose outcome may change for different executions of the same program. For example, a message deliver event is often non-deterministic since its outcome depends on many factors, including process scheduling, routing, and flow control. Thus, a recovering process may not produce the same run upon recovery even if the same set of messages are sent to it.

   If a non-deterministic event cannot be replayed during the recovery of a process, all correct processes whose state depends on that unrecoverable event must be rolled back. These processes are called *orphans*. The information necessary to reproduce the results of the non-deterministic events is called the event's *determinant*. Restoring the system to a consistent state while limiting the extent of rollbacks depends on the ability of the rollback-recovery protocol to replay the determinants of the non-deterministic events executed by the failed processes before crashing. Hence, determinants must be saved to stable storage so that they are available during recovery. In practice, different protocols choose different ways to log determinants and rely on different implementations of stable storage.

2. **Dependency-generating events**: These events can increase the number of processes that depend on the non-deterministic events executed by a process. For example, in message-passing applications, a message-send event is a dependency-generating event since it can create dependencies between non-deterministic events executed by the sender and the state of the receiver. If the sender fails and any of those non-deterministic events is unrecoverable, then the receiver becomes an orphan.

   To enable orphan detection and appropriate rollback, rollback recovery protocols typically append to application messages information that tracks these dependencies—logging protocols piggyback logical clocks [15] or vector clocks [17] and checkpointing protocols piggyback an index that records the number of checkpoints taken by a process. In addition, to speedup the replay of non-deterministic events, it may be desirable to log some information on executing a dependency-generating event. For instance, in sender-based message-logging protocols processes log the content of each message they send.

3. **Output-commit events**: These events can make the external environment depend on the non-deterministic events executed by a process.

   Since it is not reasonable to expect the external environment to roll back in response to a process crash, log-based rollback recovery protocols invoke *output commit* procedures that write synchronously to stable storage the determinants of all non-deterministic events that precede the communication with the external environment, thus making them recoverable. Depending on how determinants are logged, this procedure may require coordination among processes.

4. **Checkpointing events**: These events instruct the protocols to write to stable storage the state of one or more processes. These event can either be transparent to the application (e.g. a signal from a timer indicating that some pre-determined time has elapsed since the last checkpoint) or be explicitly driven by the application.

   Checkpoints can be coordinated, independent, or communication induced. Processes may checkpoint their state incrementally, and checkpoints can be saved to stable storage either synchronously or asynchronously.

5. **Failure-detection events**: These events are generated on detecting the failure of one or more processes.

In response to these events, faulty processes must be restarted, restored to a previously checkpointed state and rolled forward. In turn, correct orphan processes may need to be detected and rolled back. Different protocols implement different strategies to collect the determinants to be replayed during recovery and to detect and rollback orphans.

Implementing a specific protocol therefore amounts to selecting the set of actions performed in response to each relevant event. We now show how a simple language can be used to specify these choices. In Section 4 we show how protocols can be automatically synthesized starting from these specifications.

3.2 Specifying Design Choices in Rollback-Recovery Protocols

Figure 1 shows a simple language that can be used to specify rollback-recovery protocols. The language reflects the discussion of the previous section. A protocol is defined in terms the actions it takes in response to non-deterministic events, dependency generating events, output commit events, checkpointing events and failure-detection events. To define a protocol completely, it is necessary to instantiate a set of variables which specify, for instance, the set of non-deterministic events, the form of their determinant, the implementation of stable storage, etc. Figure 2 shows a set of representative instantiations of these variables used in several existing protocols.

Figure 3 illustrates how the language can be used to specify Damani and Garg's optimistic protocol [7], a hybrid protocol we have recently developed that combines causal logging with asynchronous receiver-based logging to stable storage in order to speed up crash recovery [21]. Our language, however, can be used for more than just specifying existing recovery protocols. Once deconstructing rollback-recovery protocols becomes possible, it is then easy to reassemble the fundamental components in novel ways to implement new protocols. An example is given in Figure 4(b), which shows a specification of a sender-based pessimistic message-logging protocol that tolerates f concurrent failures and implements stable storage by replicating data in the volatile memory of processes. In this protocol, which to our knowledge has not appeared in the literature, a process executing a non-deterministic event broadcasts the corresponding determinant to the other processes and does not send any application message until it has received at least f acknowledgments to its broadcast. This protocol is a variant of Strom, Bacon, and Yemini's sender-based pessimistic protocol [28], whose specification is shown in Figure 4(a).

4 The Architecture of Egida

Figure 1 defines the structure of log-based rollback recovery protocols, while the variables in Figure 2 identify the building blocks which when incorporated into the protocol structure yield different rollback recovery protocols. Egida instantiates these building blocks in a modular, object-oriented architecture. We begin this section by describing the functionality of each module and the interfaces it exports. We then explain how these modules are invoked in response to events and how they can be composed to synthesize rollback-recovery protocols.

4.1 Module Definitions and Interfaces

Egida defines the following modules:

EventHandler: Handles the five types of relevant events defined in Section 3. The methods exported by this module are event-dependent.

Determinant: Creates the determinants for each non-deterministic event. It exports a single method, *CreateDeterminant*.

HowToOutputCommit: Determines how to save the information necessary to recover the system to the state in which an output commit event is executed. It exports a single method, *OutputCommit*.

LogEventDeterminant: Saves the determinants of non-deterministic events to stable storage. It exports four methods: (1) *Log*, (2) *Retrieve*, (3) *Flush*, and (4) *GarbageCollect*.

LogEventInfo: Logs data associated with an event. It exports the same interfaces as the **LogEventDeterminant** module.

HowToLog: Determines how logged information is accessed. It exports two methods, *Read* and *Write*.

WhereToLog: Directs requests for accessing the logs to the appropriate form of storage. It exports the same methods as **HowToLog**.

StableStorage: Implements stable storage for determinants and data associated with an event. It also exports two methods, *Read* and *Write*.

VolatileStorage: Implements volatile storage for determinants and data associated with an event. It exports the same methods as **StableStorage**.

PiggybackLogging: Piggybacks onto application messages the information necessary to track dependencies among process states and, in the case of causal logging, appends the non-stable determinants logged by the message sender. It also processes, and if appropriate logs the piggybacked information. This module exports two methods: *GetPiggyback* and *ProcessPiggyback*.

PiggybackCheckpointing: Piggybacks the information necessary to track the dependencies among checkpoints. It also processes piggybacked information, and if appropriate triggers a checkpoint. It exports the same methods as **PiggybackLogging**.

Checkpoint: Implements the checkpointing protocol. It exports two methods, *TakeCheckpoint* and *RestoreFromCheckpoint*.

HowToCheckpoint: Determines how the checkpoint information is accessed. It exports two methods, *Read* and *Write*.

CollectDeterminants: Collects determinants during recovery. It exports a single method, *RetrieveDeterminants*.

OrphanDetection: Implements the protocol for orphan detection. It exports a single method, *DetectOrphans*.

4.2 Module Invocation

Figure 5 shows the function call graph for the modules introduced in Section 4.1. In addition to the modules discussed in Section 4.1, it shows four other modules:

1. An **API** module that intercepts application-level calls to relevant events and invokes the appropriate handler exported by the **EventHandler**.

Protocol	:=	⟨non-det-event-stmt⟩* ⟨output-commit-event-stmt⟩* ⟨dep-gen-event-stmt⟩* ⟨ckpt-stmt⟩$_{opt}$ ⟨recovery-stmt⟩$_{opt}$
⟨non-det-event-stmt⟩	:=	⟨event⟩ : *determinant* : ⟨determinant-structure⟩ (*Log* ⟨event-info-list⟩ ⟨how-to-log⟩ *on* ⟨stable-storage⟩)$_{opt}$
⟨output-commit-event-stmt⟩	:=	⟨output-commit-proto⟩ *output commit on* ⟨event-list⟩
⟨event-list⟩	:=	⟨event⟩ | ⟨event⟩, ⟨event-list⟩
⟨dep-gen-event-stmt⟩	:=	⟨event⟩ : ⟨piggyback-stmt⟩ | ⟨logging-stmt⟩ | ⟨piggyback-stmt⟩⟨logging-stmt⟩
⟨logging-stmt⟩	:=	*Log* ⟨event-info-list⟩ ⟨how-to-log⟩ *on* ⟨where-to-log⟩
⟨event-info-list⟩	:=	⟨event-info⟩ | ⟨event-info⟩, ⟨event-info-list⟩
⟨piggyback-stmt⟩	:=	*Piggyback* ⟨pb-value-list⟩
⟨pb-value-list⟩	:=	⟨pb-value⟩ | ⟨pb-value⟩, ⟨pb-value-list⟩
⟨ckpt-stmt⟩	:=	⟨ckpt-proto⟩ *checkpoint* ⟨how-to-ckpt⟩ *on* ⟨stable-storage⟩ *Implementation* : ⟨ckpt-impl⟩
⟨recovery-stmt⟩	:=	⟨recovery-get-det-stmt⟩$_{opt}$ ⟨orphan-detection-stmt⟩$_{opt}$ ⟨rollback-stmt⟩$_{opt}$
⟨recovery-get-det-stmt⟩	:=	*Protocol to retrieve determinants* : ⟨recovery-get-det-proto⟩
⟨orphan-detection-stmt⟩	:=	*Protocol to detect orphans* : ⟨orphan-detection-proto⟩
⟨rollback-stmt⟩	:=	*On rollback* : ⟨rb-logging-stmt⟩ | ⟨rb-ckpt-stmt⟩
⟨rb-logging-stmt⟩	:=	*Log* ⟨event-info-list⟩ *on* ⟨stable-storage⟩
⟨rb-ckpt-stmt⟩	:=	*Take independent checkpoint on* ⟨stable-storage⟩

Figure 1 : A grammar for specifying rollback-recovery protocols. In the grammar, we use the following notational convention: ⟨x⟩ means that x is a production rule, ⟨y⟩ means that y is a variable that has to be mapped to a specific value, ⟨z⟩$_{opt}$ means that ⟨z⟩ is an optional statement, and *a* means that *a* is a keyword

2. A Timer module that enables Egida to specify the intervals at which timer interrupts need to be generated to perform periodic actions, such as checkpointing and flushing of volatile logs to stable storage.

3. A FailureDetector module that implements a protocol for detecting process crashes and triggers the appropriate recovery mechanisms through the EventHandler.

4. A Network module that invokes a method of EventHandler to process incoming messages.

To illustrate the interactions among Egida's module, we present two examples that show how this dependency graph is traversed in response to specific events.

Example 1 *Handling a Send event for a causal logging protocol (*see [2]*):*
The API module intercepts the Send event and invokes the corresponding handler in EventHandler. The handler in this example performs three tasks: (1) it saves in a volatile log kept by sender the content of the message being sent; (2) it retrieves the set of non-stable determinants from the log kept by the server; (3) it piggybacks these determinants on the application message and sends the message to the destination.

1. To save the content of the message in the sender's volatile log, the handler invokes the *Log* method of LogEventInfo. *Log* in turn invokes the *Write* method of HowToLog, which invokes the *Write* of WhereToLog, which finally invokes the *Write* method exported by VolatileStorage.

2. To obtain the determinants to piggyback, the handler invokes the *GetPiggyback* method of PiggybackLogging. This method identifies the non-stable determinants and invokes the *Retrieve* method of LogEventDeterminant. *Retrieve* in turn invokes the *Read* method of HowToLog, which invokes the *Read* of WhereToLog, which finally invokes the *Read* of VolatileStorage and, if necessary, of StableStorage. These methods return the requested determinants which are then passed up through the call chain back to *GetPiggyback*.

3. The event handler then piggybacks the determinants to the application message and invokes the send function in the transport layer. ■

Example 2 *Handling a Send event to the external environment for the optimistic protocol of Damani and Garg (*see [7]*):*
The API module intercepts the send event and invokes the corresponding handler in EventHandler. The handler in this example invokes the output commit procedure prior to sending the message. The output commit procedure in turn performs two tasks: (1) it flushes to stable storage the determinants of all the non-deterministic events executed by the process prior to the send to the external environment, thereby making them recoverable; and (2) it initiates a coordinated output commit operation to ensure that all the

⟨event⟩ := send | receive | read | write
⟨determinant-structure⟩ := {source, sesn, dest, desn}
⟨output-commit-proto⟩ := independent | co-ordinated
⟨event-info⟩ := determinant | message
⟨how-to-log⟩ := synchronously | asynchronously
⟨where-to-log⟩ := ⟨stable-storage⟩ | ⟨volatile-storage⟩
⟨volatile-storage⟩ := local disk | volatile memory of self
⟨stable-storage⟩ := local disk | NFS disk | volatile memory of processes
⟨pb-value⟩ := determinants(, ⟨dependency matrix | stability matrix | stability vector⟩)$_{opt}$ |
vector clock | logical clock | checkpoint counter
⟨ckpt-proto⟩ := independent | co-ordinated | communication-induced
⟨how-to-ckpt⟩ := synchronously | asynchronously
⟨ckpt-impl⟩ := full | incremental
⟨recovery-get-det-proto⟩ := centralized | distributed
⟨orphan-detection-proto⟩ := broadcast logical clock | exchange vector clock

Figure 2 : Representative instantiations for the variables defined in the grammar shown in Figure 1.

/* comment: ⟨non-det-event-stmt⟩ */
receive:
determinant : {source, sesn, dest, desn}
Log determinant, data asynchronously on NFS disk

{comment: ⟨output-commmit-event-stmt⟩}
Co-ordinated output commit on write

/* comment: ⟨dep-gen-event-stmt⟩ */
send:
Piggyback vector clock

/* comment: ⟨recovery-stmt⟩ */
Protocol to detect orphans : broadcast logical clock
On rollback: Log determinant, message on NFS disk

(a)

/* comment: ⟨non-det-event-stmt⟩ */
receive:
determinant : {source, sesn, dest, desn}
Log determinant, data asynchronously on NFS disk

/* comment: ⟨dep-gen-event-stmt⟩ */
send:
Piggyback determinants
Log message synchronously on volatile memory of self

/* comment: ⟨recovery-stmt⟩ */
Protocol to retrieve determinants : centralized

(b)

Figure 3 : Example specifications of existing protocols: (a) Damani and Garg's optimistic message logging protocol and (b) hybrid causal message logging protocol

/* comment: ⟨non-det-event-stmt⟩ */
receive:
determinant : {source, sesn, dest, desn}
Log determinant synchronously on NFS disk

/*comment: ⟨dep-gen-event-stmt⟩} */
send:
Log message synchronously on volatile memory of self

/* comment: ⟨ckpt-stmt⟩} */
Independent checkpoint asynchronously on NFS disk
Implementation : incremental

(a)

/* comment: ⟨non-det-event-stmt⟩ */
receive:
determinant : {source, sesn, dest, desn}
Log determinant synchronously on volatile memory of processes

/* comment: ⟨dep-gen-event-stmt⟩ */
send:
Log message synchronously on volatile memory of self

/* comment: ⟨ckpt-stmt⟩ */
Independent checkpoint asynchronously on NFS disk
Implementation : incremental

(b)

Figure 4 : Specification of (a) Strom, Bacon, and Yemini's sender-based pessimistic message logging protocol and (b) a novel sender-based pessimistic protocol

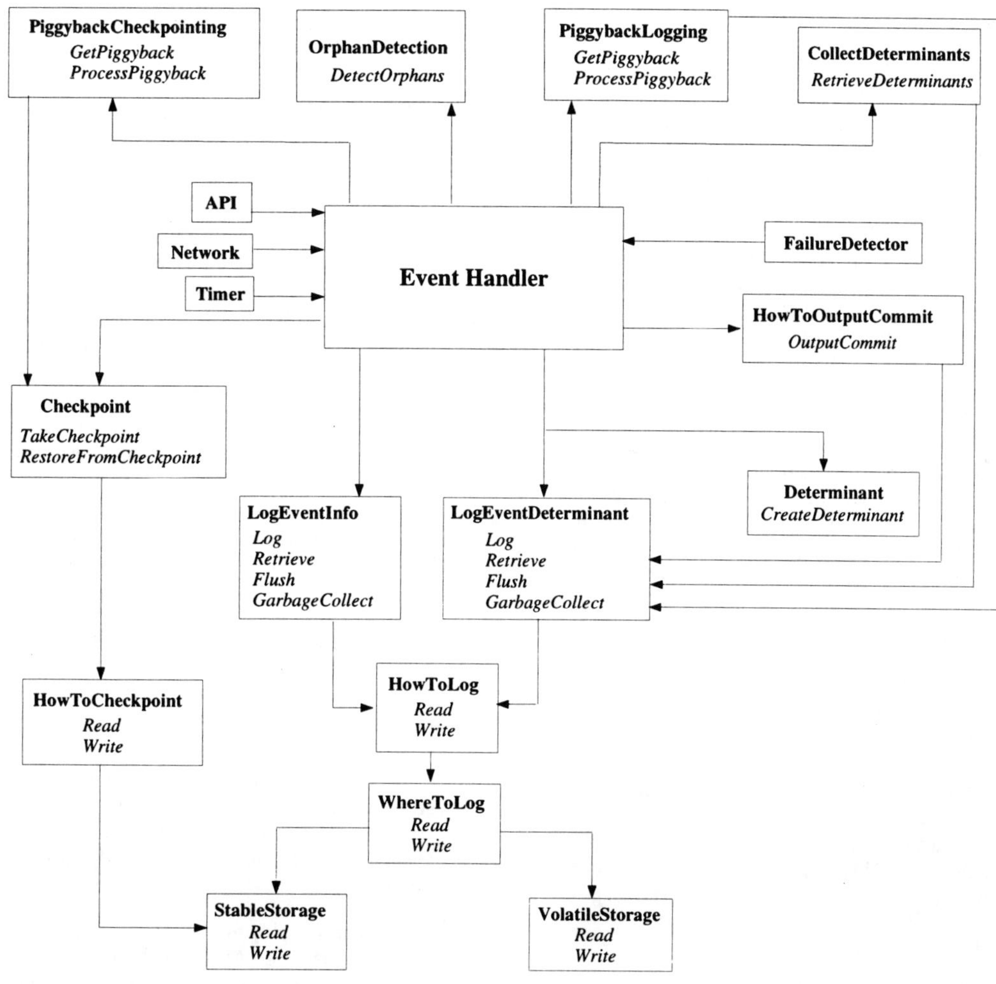

Figure 5 : The architecture of Egida

non-deterministic events that causally precede the send are recoverable.

1. To perform output commit, the handler invokes the *OutputCommit* method of HowToOutputCommit. The *OutputCommit* methods performs the following two tasks:
   (a) To perform a local output commit, *OutputCommit* invokes the *Flush* method of LogEventDeterminant. *Flush* then invokes the *Write* method of HowToLog, which invokes the *Write* of WhereToLog, which finally invokes the *Write* method exported by StableStorage.
   (b) To perform a co-ordinated output commit, *OutputCommit* broadcasts a message requesting an output commit. On receiving this message, the Network module invokes the appropriate handler in EventHandler, which in turn invokes the *OutputCommit* method of HowToOutputCommit[1]. The *OutputCommit* method then invokes the same sequence of methods as in (a).
2. The handler sends the application message to the external environment. ■

[1]Note that the *OutputCommit* method exported by the instance of the HowToOutputCommit module invoked by the handler for processing network messages performs only a local output commit.

4.3 Synthesizing Protocols through Module Composition

Egida allows the co-existence of multiple implementations for each of the modules introduced in Section 4.1. Hence, to synthesize a protocol, one must select a specific implementation of each module. Egida maintains a binding between the values for the variables on the left hand side of Figure 2 and their corresponding implementations. Therefore, synthesizing a protocol requires processing the specification along with this binding information to initialize the modules to their appropriate implementations. It is easy to extend Egida to recognize new implementations of modules; as more implementations of a module functionality become available, the specification language can be extended by simply (1) adding a new value to the right hand side of the corresponding variable in Figure 2, and (2) registering with Egida the binding between the new value and its corresponding implementation.

5 Implementation and Experience

Egida contains multiple implementations for each module introduced in Section 4.1. Each module is defined as a C++ class. The classes we have implemented so far correspond to the values on the right hand side of Figure 2.

To make Egida available to a large number of applications, we have integrated Egida with MPICH [10], a freely available, portable implementation of the MPI (Message Passing Interface) standard 1.1. MPICH has a two-layer architecture: the upper layer exports MPI's application programming interface (API), while the lower layer contains platform-specific message-passing libraries. For our testbed environment consisting of a network of workstations connected by an Ethernet, MPICH's lower layer is implemented using the p4 library [4].

To integrate Egida with MPICH, we replaced in the MPICH's upper layer all the send and receive calls to p4 with corresponding calls to Egida's API; modules in Egida in turn invoke the message passing operations of p4. We had to make two modifications to p4. First, we enhanced p4 to enable transfer of data from non-contiguous buffers. This was necessary to avoid a potential data copy that may occur when the information piggybacked by Egida has to be prepended to an MPICH message. Second, we modified p4 to handle socket errors that occur whenever processes fail and to allow a recovering process to establish socket connections with the surviving processes. For detecting failures and automatically re-starting crashed processes, in Egida, we have implemented a watchdog [12] for each application process. Our implementation provides transparent fault-tolerance to MPI applications—only a simple re-link of the application with Egida and our modified MPICH library is necessary.

We have used Egida to study the performance of rollback recovery protocols with a set of NAS [6] benchmarks. The results of our experimental evaluation are described elsewhere [1, 21].

6 Related Work

The literature contains several systems that have been designed to provide transparent fault-tolerance using rollback-recovery. They include libckpt [19], Fail-safe PVM [16], MIST [5], Co-check [26], Manetho [9] and libft [12]. As opposed to Egida, however, these systems are designed to support only a specific checkpointing or message-logging protocol.

Egida's emphasis on code reusability and extensibility is also present in the recently-introduced OTEC simulator [20]. OTEC's object-oriented design provides some degree of code reusability and can be used to compare the performance of different checkpointing protocols, but only through simulations (for example, varying message rates and checkpoint sizes). The run-time system for rollback-recovery that is closest to Egida in terms of extensibility is RENEW [18], a system that provides a framework for implementing and evaluating different checkpointing protocols. Egida is unique in allowing implementations of protocols to be automatically synthesized from reusable components. The specification language exported by Egida identifies key properties of rollback recovery protocols, simplifying their understanding, while hiding the tedium of combining the various properties to implement a complete protocol.

Egida's architecture, is similar to the one used in other systems—for instance, in Adaptive [23] and xkernel [13] for networking protocols, in Horus [22] and Cactus [11] for distributed computing and group membership protocols, and in COMERA [29] and Quarterware [24] for communications middleware. However, to our knowledge, Egida is the first application of this approach to rollback recovery protocols.

7 Concluding Remarks

We have presented the design and implementation of *Egida*, an object-oriented toolkit designed to support transparent rollback recovery. Egida exports a simple specification language that can be used to express arbitrary rollback recovery protocols. From this specification, Egida authomatically synthesizes an implementation of the specified protocol by glueing together the appropriate objects from an available library of "building blocks".

We have implemented a prototype of Egida and integrated it with the MPICH implementation of the Message Passing Interface (MPI) standard. Through Egida, MPI applications can be made fault-tolerant without any modifications. Conversely, Egida allows to study the robustness and performance of different rollback-recovery protocols with respect to a large set of demanding applications.

Our early experience with the prototype suggests that Egida is extensible, flexible, and facilitates rapid implementations of rollback-recovery protocols with minimal programming effort. We expect that the design of Egida will evolve as we gain more experience specifying and implementing different rollback recovery protocols.

References

[1] L. Alvisi, E. N. Elnozahy, S. Rao, S. A. Husain, and A. De Mel. An Analysis of Communication-induced Checkpointing. In *Proceedings of the IEEE Fault-Tolerant Computing Symposium (FTCS-29)*, Madison, WI, June 1999.

[2] L. Alvisi, B. Hoppe, and K. Marzullo. Nonblocking and Orphan-Free Message Logging Protocols. In *Proceedings of the 23rd Fault-Tolerant Computing Symposium*, pages 145–154, June 1993.

[3] A. Borg, J. Baumbach, and S. Glazer. A message system supporting fault tolerance. In *Proceedings of the Symposium on Operating Systems Principles*, pages 90–99. ACM SIGOPS, October 1983.

[4] R. Butler and E. Lusk. Monitors, Message, and Clusters: the p4 Parallel Programming System.

[5] J. Casas, D. Clark, P. Galbiati, R. Konuru, S. Otto, R. Prouty, and J. Walpole. MIST: PVM with transparent migration and checkpointing. In *3rd Annual PVM Users' Group Meeting*, Pittsburgh, PA, May 1995.

[6] NASA Ames Research Center. NAS Parallel Benchmarks. http://science.nas.nasa.gov/Software/NPB/, 1997.

[7] O. P. Damani and V. K. Garg. How to Recover Efficiently and Asynchronously when Optimism Fails. In *Proceedings of the 16th International Conference on Distributed Computing Systems*, pages 108–115, 1996.

[8] D. Dolev and D. Malki. The Transis Approach to High Availability Cluster Communication. *Communications of the ACM*, 39(4), April 1996.

[9] E. N. Elnozahy and W. Zwaenepoel. Manetho: Transparent rollback-recovery with low overhead, limited rollback and fast output commit. *IEEE Transactions on Computers*, 41(5):526–531, May 1992.

[10] William D. Gropp and Ewing Lusk. *User's Guide for* `mpich`*, a Portable Implementation of MPI*. Mathematics and Computer Science Division, Argonne National Laboratory, 1996. ANL-96/6.

[11] M. A. Hiltunen and R. D. Schlichting. A Configurable Membership Service. *IEEE Transactions on Computers*, 47(5):573—586, May 1998.

[12] Y. Huang and C. Kintala. Software Implemented Fault Tolerance: Technologies and Experience. In *Proceedings of the IEEE Fault-Tolerant Computing Symposium*, pages 2–9, 1993.

[13] N. C. Hutchinson and L. L. Peterson. The x-Kernel: An architecture for implementing network protocols. *IEEE Transactions on Software Engineering*, 17(1):64–76, January 1991.

[14] D. B. Johnson and W. Zwaenepoel. Recovery in Distributed Systems Using Optimistic Message Logging and Checkpointing. *Journal of Algorithms*, 11:462–491, 1990.

[15] L. Lamport. Time, Clocks, and the Ordering of Events in a Distributed System. *Communications of the ACM*, 21(7):558–565, July 1978.

[16] J. Leon, A. L. Ficher, and P. Steenkiste. Fail-safe PVM: A portable package for distributed programming with transparent recovery. Technical Report CMU-CS-93-124, School of Computer Science, Carnegie Mellon University, February 1993.

[17] F. Mattern. Virtual Time and Global States of Distributed Systems. In M. Cosnard et. al., editor, *Parallel and Distributed Algorithms*, pages 215–226. Elsevir Science Publishers B. V., 1989.

[18] N. Neves and W. K. Fuchs. RENEW: A Tool for Fast and Efficient Implementation of Checkpoint Protocols. In *Proceedings of the 28th IEEE Fault-Tolerant Computing Symposium (FTCS)*, Munich, Germany, June 1998.

[19] J. S. Plank, M. Beck, G. Kingsley, and K. Li. Libckpt:Transparent checkpointing under Unix. In *Proceedings of the USENIX Technical Conference*, pages 213–224, January 1995.

[20] B. Ramamurthy, S. J. Upadhyaya, and R. K. Iyer. An Object-Oriented Testbed for the Evaluation of Checkpointing and Recovery Systems. In *Proceedings of the 27th IEEE Fault-Tolerant Computing Symposium*, pages 194–203, June 1997.

[21] S. Rao, L. Alvisi, and H. Vin. The Cost of Recovery in Message Logging Protocols. Technical Report 99-12, University of Texas at Austin, March 1999.

[22] R. Van Renesse, T. Hickey, and K. Birman. Design and Performance of Horus: A Lightweight Group Communications System. Technical Report TR94-1442, Cornell University Computer Science Department, August 1994.

[23] D. Schmidt, D. Box, and T. Suda. Adaptive: A Dynamically Assembled Protocol Transformation, Integration, and Evaluation Environment. *Concurrency: Practice and Experience*, 5(4):269—286, June 1993.

[24] A. Singhai, A. Sane, and R. Campbell. Quarterware for Middleware. In *Proceedings of the International Conference on Distributed Computing and Systems (ICDCS'98)*, pages 192—201, Amsterdam, Holland, May 1998.

[25] M. Snir, S. Otto, S. Huss-Lederman, D. Walker, and J. Dongarra. *MPI: The Complete Reference*. Scientific and Engineering Computation Series. The MIT Press, Cambridge, MA, 1996.

[26] G. Stellner. CoCheck: Checkpointing and process migration for MPI. In *Proceedings of the International Parallel Processing Symposium*, pages 526–531, April 1996.

[27] R. B. Strom and S. Yemeni. Optimistic recovery in distributed systems. *ACM Transactions on Computer Systems*, 3(3):204–226, April 1985.

[28] R. E. Strom, D. F. Bacon, and S. A. Yemini. Volatile Logging in n-Fault-Tolerant Distributed Systems. In *Proceedings of the Eighteenth Annual International Symposium on Fault-Tolerant Computing*, pages 44–49, 1988.

[29] Y. M. Wang and W. J. Lee. COMERA: COM Extensible Remoting Architecture. In *Proceedings of the 4th Conference on Object Oriented Technologies and Systems (COOTS)*, April 1998.

Incremental Messages: Micro-Kernel Services for Flexible and Efficient Management of Replicated Data

Carlos Pérez
Dpt. de Informática y Electrónica
Universitat de València
C/ Doctor Moliner, 50
E-46100 Burjassot SPAIN
carlos.perez@uv.es

Germán Fabregat
Dpt. de Informática
Universitat Jaume I
Campus del Riu Sec
E-12071 Castellón SPAIN
fabregat@inf.uji.es

R.J. Martínez & G. Martín
Institut de Robótica
Universitat de València
Polígono de la Coma S/N
E-46980 Paterna SPAIN
rafael.martinez@uv.es
gregorio.martin@uv.es

Abstract

Incremental messages have been designed to efficiently and flexibly manage replicated copies of critical data. We describe this new type of messages and show how applications benefit from an extended message passing interface which provides support for creating, updating and recovering data copies, combining the advantages of both kernel and user-level approaches. The paper describes the interface offered to applications, its functionality, and how it can be used to implement traditional fault-tolerance mechanisms such as passive replicas, checkpointing and recovery. A fault-tolerant transactional service that exploits the advantages of incremental messages is also presented. Furthermore, the paper presents details about the implementation of incremental messages in VSTa, a micro-kernel based operating system, and the first experimental results obtained.

1. Introduction

Checkpointing and rollback recovery have been traditionally used to tolerate errors, taking advantage of the natural redundancy that distributed systems have. Considerable research efforts have been addressed to reduce as much as possible the inevitable overhead that this technique introduces. Two complementary ways of reducing checkpointing overhead are to optimize checkpointing code, and to reduce the amount of data that has to be included in every checkpoint. Researchers have applied both of them following two different approaches. The first one consists in including checkpointing code in the operating system kernel and employing memory mapping techniques (such as copy-on-write or incremental checkpointing) to make it efficient [1, 2]. The second approach is to implement checkpointing services as user-level routines, which can then be tailored to copy only the critical data of the application [3, 4, 5]. Although both approaches are complementary, there is no implementation that combines their advantages, since current operating system kernels do not provide suitable support for implementing checkpointing and rollback recovery at the application layer. As it is suggested in [6], incremental and concurrent checkpointing, which are effective methods of reducing the overhead of checkpointing, should be provided by the operating system kernel.

In this scenario, our work has focused on the design of a reduced set of services that can be incorporated to operating system kernels to provide satisfactory support for user-level checkpointing and recovery [7]. These services have been designed specifically for micro-kernels, because they (micro-kernels) enforce modular design, appropriated for highly dependable systems [8, 9], and because most of current distributed operating systems are based on the micro-kernel concept, with classical operating system services provided by user-level processes. (Chorus [10], Amoeba [11] and Mach [12] are good examples of it.) Even when traditional kernels are used, numerous distributed services are nevertheless implemented by user-level code.

In this paper, this new set of kernel services —which we have called "Incremental Operations" after incremental checkpointing— are introduced. All of them are based on the same basic mechanism and therefore the increment to the kernel size and complexity is small. At the same time, these services are versatile enough to support the implementation of different user-directed checkpointing and recovery algorithms, as well as other fault-tolerant mechanisms as passive replicas or transactional services. It is worth noting that incremental operations are designed for versatility, and not for transparency, since traditional kernel checkpointing services are appropriate for this purpose.

The outline of the paper is as follows. Sections 2 and 3 describe Incremental Operations, focusing on their functionality and their implementation, respectively. Then, section 4 shows several examples of how they can be used to

0-7695-0213-X/99 $10.00

develop fault-tolerant applications. Section 5 presents the first experimental results obtained after the implementation of these services in VSTa [13], a micro-kernel based operating system. Finally, conclusions of the work and future research directions are presented in Section 6.

2. Incremental Operations

Incremental Operations offer to upper layers' processes tighter control over both their own address space and the address space of other processes. This is achieved using the support of the memory management unit (MMU); facilitating efficient management of replicated information. In addition, they follow the inter-processes message-passing model, thus easing the implementation of fault-tolerance techniques based on that model.

2.1. Incremental Messages

Incremental Messages (IMs) share with traditional messages the function of transferring data from the sender's to the receiver's address space. However, they have been designed to update data copies maintained by different processes. For this reason, they present two unique features: (1) only those pages from the virtual memory region specified by the sender that have been modified since the last IM are transferred to the receiver, and (2) the destination of the message is an existing virtual memory region of the receiver's address space, which contains a copy of the sender's one. Both sender (P1 in Figure 1) and receiver (P2) must reside in the same node, and the effect of sending an IM on their address spaces is depicted in Figure 1. Initially, P2 holds a back-up of P1's critical data that is updated with the modified pages from P1.

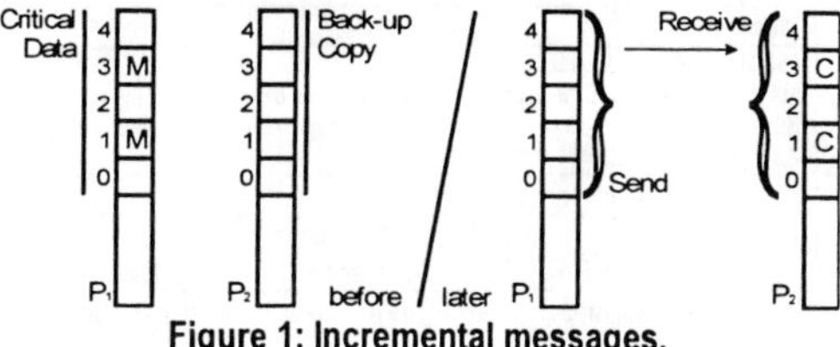

Figure 1: Incremental messages.

IMs are a simple and efficient mean to update data copies maintained in the same node that the critical data they back-up. They are easy to use because to update a back-up copy (or copies), the process holding the primary copy of critical data just has to send an IM to the process (or processes) holding the back-up copy (or copies). They are efficient because only critical data that have been modified have to be transmitted. This efficiency can yet be increased if COW is used.

2.2. Other Incremental Operations

The same micro-kernel mechanism that is needed to implement IMs can be used to provide support for other fault-tolerance mechanisms. The following subsections describe these derived services.

2.2.1. Negative Incremental Messages (NIMs). NIMs have been designed to allow a process to simply and efficiently discard the changes made in the critical data since the previous IM. Their use, clearly oriented to perform efficient rollbacks, is described in the next paragraph.

As in the example of Figure 1, let us assume that P1 has a working copy of the critical data, while P2 holds its back-up. If P1 decides to discard the changes made on its data, comprising only pages 1 and 3 in the figure, it sends an IM with the *negative* option to P2. The micro-kernel does not include the modified pages in the message, but an indication of these pages. P2 then receives the message and identifies it as a NIM, using its contents as a map to select the pages to be returned to P1. A second message is sent back from P2 to P1 using the *map* option (with send) to indicate to the micro-kernel that the pages specified by the map must be included in the IM (instead of those modified by P2, as it would happen with a normal IM). When P1 receives this last message, the micro-kernel replaces the modified pages 1 and 3 with those sent by P2, thus effectively discarding the changes P1 had made.

2.2.2. Packed Incremental Message (PIM). A PIM is a compact representation of the information present in an IM. In addition to the actual pages to be transferred, a PIM contains a special header called 'map', which specifies the contents of the original IM. The map contains the starting address and length of the source region, as well as a list of the pages included in the message.

The main objective of PIMs is to improve the management of IMs by processes that do not hold a copy of the sender's critical data, such as intermediate processes between sender and receiver, or processes handling secondary storage. As an example of how PIMs ease efficient handling of IMs by intermediate processes, Figure 2 shows the case of inter-node communication.

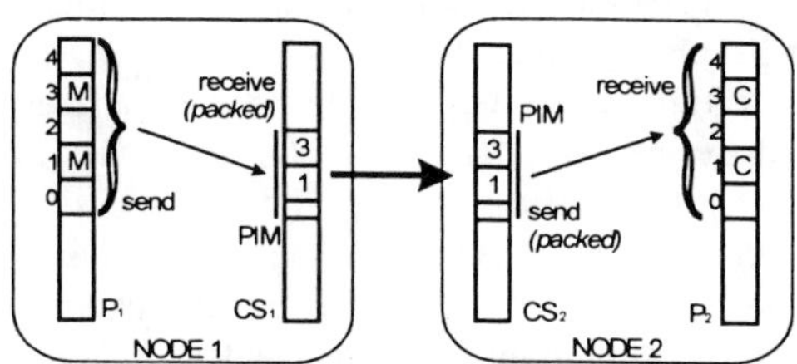

Figure 2: Transferring IMs between nodes using PIMs.

As Figure 2 illustrates, IM packing and unpacking is carried out when the *packed* option is used with send and/or receive. If this option is used when receiving an IM, the micro-kernel adds a new memory region to the virtual address space of the receiver, mapping the whole PIM (both the map and the pages it contains) as a consecutive range of logical addresses. The effect of using the *packed* option when sending an IM is that the micro-kernel interprets the virtual memory region as a PIM (instead of building the IM with the modified pages of the region). If the message is not received with this option, then the pages included in the IM substitute their counterparts in the receiver's address space, just as it happened with IMs. If the *packed* option is used, then the IM is received as a PIM, as it has just been described before. Finally, when the *packed* option is used when both sending and receiving the IM, the data is copied from the sender's to the receiver's address space as a conventional message.

2.2.3. Incremental Copy (IC). This service is designed to manage replicated data when both original and copy reside on the same address space. Its basic operation is the same as that of IM, except that it transfers data between two memory regions of the same process. As with IMs, a Negative Incremental Copy (NIC) has also been defined to allow simple and efficient rollback.

2.3. Header Management

Although IMs have been designed to support the management of replicated data, other requirements of fault-tolerant applications should also be considered. In particular, when using modular redundancy, tasks such as voting, selection or reordering of messages are performed either by library code at senders or receivers, or by intermediate processes [14, 5, 15, 2, 16]. Hence, it is important that IMs can be handled efficiently by these intermediate agents. Furthermore, reordering of messages by library code is not possible with IMs as they have been described so far, since the data copy is updated when the message is received.

To cope with these requirements, the *receive* primitive includes the possibility of receiving only message headers while out-of-line data [18] are placed in an auxiliary queue managed by the micro-kernel (which offers appropriate services to let processes access the contents of messages in the queue: *map*, *forward* and *delete*). The information present in this header can vary from one implementation to another, but should include the in-line data of the message and the list of pages included in it.

This feature, in addition to support the management of intermediate messages, is a mean for error detection and confinement (see subsection 4.1.) and, in the case of using intermediate agents to handle messages, it avoids mapping out-of-line data, thus gaining in performance and protecting them against errors in intermediate agents.

2.4. Management of Multiple Destinations

When several copies of critical data are to be hold, (because more than one simultaneous fault must be tolerated, for example) not all of the copies are to be updated simultaneously. (See subsection 4.2.) So that IMs can be used in these cases, the micro-kernel should keep track of modified pages with regard to every possible destination of IMs (where each copy is maintained). This requires that the concept of "modified bit" (as it is provided by MMUs) be extended into a bitmap managed by the micro-kernel. From this point on, we would refer to this bitmap as "the modified bitmap", after "modified bit". Each element of this bitmap represents the state of the page (modified or not) regarding one possible destination of IMs.

Since user-level code must be able to establish when each copy must be updated, Incremental Operations include a parameter, called *incremental destination.* The micro-kernel uses this parameter to find out which element of the modified bitmap should be considered to establish the set of modified pages.

3. Implementation Issues

Despite the versatility of IMs, the interface that needs to be provided to applications is very compact because IMs are just an extension to the standard message-passing interface. Apart from header management and incremental copy, the whole set of services described in section 2 has been implemented in the micro-kernel based VSTa operating system [13], integrating IMs into its original message-passing interface.

3.1. Basic Interface

The interface can be better described in terms of a basic message passing interface, comprising only the services *receive(src, msg)* and *send(dest, msg)*. Here, *src* and *dst* are any valid source and destination in the existing OS, and *msg*, for the purpose of exchanging IMs, must include the following fields: *flags*, *data*, *map* and *msgid.* The meaning of this fields depends on the operation (*send* or *receive*) and the type of IM being exchanged. Tables 1 and 2 describe these fields for both operations.

Table 1: Message fields when sending an IM.

Field	Meaning
flags	Establishes sending mode. Valid flags are: **MAP**: sender includes the list of pages, which should be included in the message. **NEG**: only the map must be included in the message, no pages must be actually transferred. **PACKED**: *data* is a PIM
idst	Incremental destination (see subsection 2.4).
data: va, len	Virtual address, *va*, and length, *len*, of source memory area. It must point at the critical data area if PACKED is not set, and to a PIM otherwise.
map: va, len	It must point at a map of pages (usually obtained from a previous NIM).

Table 2: Message fields when receiving an IM.

Field	Meaning
flags	Establishes receiving mode. Valid flags are: **PACKED**: IM must be packed at reception. **HEADER**: Only IM's map must be mapped onto the receiver's address space. **SRCVA**: Use virtual address from source. The kernel updates this field to signal the receiver the type of IM received, setting NEG when appropriate.
data: va, len	If no flag is set, it must point to the memory area where updates must be applied. When SRCVA is set, the kernel returns the *va* and *len* included in the IM, pointing at the memory area where updates have been applied. When PACKED (or HEADER) is set, the kernel returns the initial address that the receiver can use to access the PIM (or IM's map), and its length. If the IM is a NIM (flag NEG set by the sender), then the kernel returns the address of the IM's map as above.
msgid	When HEADER is set, the kernel returns an identifier that lets the receiver invoke operations on the message while it is in the auxiliary queue. (See subsection 2.2.3.)

3.2. Integration into VSTa's interface

VSTa's message passing interface is client-server oriented, providing three basic services: *msg_send*, *msg_receive* and *msg_reply*.[1] Clients can control data flow by means of the M_READ flag. When set, the client will receive data provided by the server in its call to *msg_reply*; otherwise, data sent by the client will be transferred to the server at *msg_receive*. (Since VSTa's interface is connection oriented, it provides appropriate additional services for handling connections, which need not be modified for supporting IMs.)

For IM exchange, the arguments that clients and servers must provide when invoking *msg_send*, *msg_receive* and *msg_reply* depend on the information flow. If a client does not set M_READ when invoking *msg_send*, then it is acting as the sender and the meaning the fields of the message are those of Table 1. However, if it sets M_READ, then those of Table 2 apply. In any case, both client and servers must set M_INCR to flag the kernel that they are sending or waiting for an IM.

In subsection 2.2, where NIMs are introduced, it is described how to exchange NIMs using two messages: the first one to request the modified pages and the second, the reply, with the requested pages. With our implementation of IMs on VSTa, only one client-server interaction is needed to exchange a NIM. The client sets NEG and M_READ in *msg_send*. Then the server receives, by means of *msg_receive*, the map of modified pages (and an indication that the IM is negative, as it is described in Table 2) and sends the requested pages in the reply, setting MAP in the call to *msg_reply*.

One of our aims when integrating IMs into VSTa was to permit that any server could receive both normal and incremental messages from the same port. We have achieved this objective providing the necessary automatic conversions when client and server do not agree on the type of message being exchanged. The R process, which is described in subsection 4.4, exemplifies this point.

3.3. Dirty Bit Management

When extending VSTa's message passing interface to support IMs, one important problem that we have addressed has been how to share the MMU's dirty bit with existing kernel modules. The solution should let the kernel maintain several independent copies of this bit per page, so that each page could be sent to several different destinations at different rates (see the discussion about management of multiple destinations in subsection 2.4).

To cope with these requirements, for each page the kernel maintains V, a bitmap of length N with each bit representing one potential destination for IMs (incremental destination). Besides, one more bit is kept for each page, which we will call D', which is the traditional dirty bit maintained to flag if the page needs to be written to disk in case of being stolen. Finally, let us call D the MMU's dirty bit. The algorithm used is as follows:

When a page is the source of an incremental operation, the kernel:

1. If D is set, it sets both D' and every bit in V, and then clears D.
2. Checks V_i (being i the incremental destination for the operation) and, if it is set, includes the page in the operation. Then, it clears V_i.

When a page is the destination for an incremental operation, the kernel sets every bit in V (because it has changed and, therefore, should be included in the next incremental operation) and clears D. D' should be set only if it should be written to disk in case of being stolen.[2]

When the kernel steals a page:

1. Checks D. If it is set, then it sets both D' and every V bit. Then clears D.
2. Checks D'. If it is set, then writes the page to disk and clears D'.

4. Using Incremental Operations

Incremental Operations are a useful tool for the implementation of fault-tolerant applications. The following subsections show how they can be used in different situations, easing the design of several fault-tolerance mechanisms and improving their performance.

4.1. Error Detection and Confinement

It has been outlined how Incremental Operations offer features that can be utilized to increase the reliability of applications. These features can be used by user-mode layers when applications have special dependability requirements.

As it will be shown, the possibility of receiving the header of a message before its contents are mapped onto the receiver's address space is an efficient way to detect sender errors and confine their effects. If the receiver has information regarding the set of pages the sender has permission to modify, the information included in an IM header can then be used to detect errors that have caused the process to write on an unexpected page. Experimental evaluation of standard error detection and confinement mechanisms shows that the checks performed by the MMU when translating logical addresses are very effective to maintain the fail-silent behavior in computers without error masking [19].

[1] Actually, there is another service, *msg_error*, which can be used by server processes to flag error conditions to their clients and, therefore, it can be considered as an special case of *msg_reply* for our discussion.

[2] We have implemented IMs for zero-fill-on-demand virtual memory regions. Therefore, if the source page was not filled yet we just mark the destination as not valid, not swapped, not modified; so that it be filled (with zeroes) when it be referenced.

The example illustrated in Figure 3 shows an application consisting of two processes that concurrently access their private copy of the same data using a distributed mutual exclusion algorithm to avoid non-consistent accesses. Header management (see subsection 2.2.3) lets the receiver detect errors in the sender before they are propagated to its (the receiver's) address space.

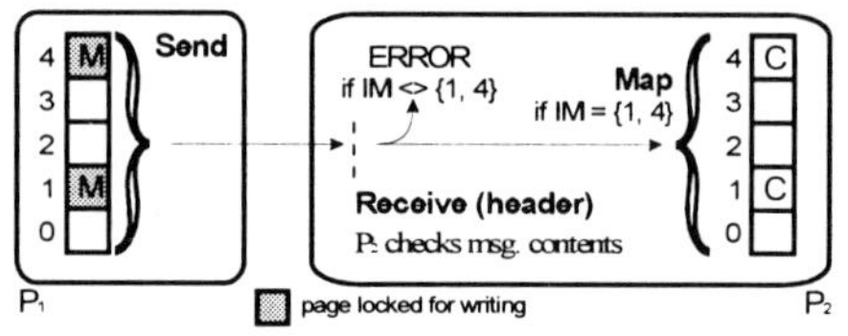

Figure 3: Using the possibility of obtaining only the header of an IM to improve error detection and confinement.

4.2. FT Services Through Server Groups

Another example that demonstrates the effectiveness of IMs to build fault-tolerant applications is the implementation of fault-tolerant services through loosely coupled server groups, following the description given in [3]. There, each group includes a primary server that interacts with clients and periodically updates the state of the remaining processes in the group.

IMs allow the simple and efficient implementation of that technique. To update the state of several replicas the primary server has only to send an IM to each of them, relying on the management of multiple destinations by the micro-kernel. Replicas should only use the receive service to keep their copies up to date. The use of IM guarantees that only modified pages are sent in each message, thus reducing the amount of actual data transferred as the frequency of the updates increases. Therefore, the use of IMs allows keeping the replicas closer to the service state, reducing the time required for recovering after failure of the primary server.

The primary server may update each replica with different periodicity. To accomplish this, it just have to use one different *incremental destination* (see subsection 2.4) for each replica. Figure 4 shows an example with a primary server and two replicas (0 and 1) associated (by the primary server) to incremental destinations 0 and 1. Each page of the server is depicted with its state ('M' meaning modified and '-' not modified) regarding both incremental destinations (to simplify the figure, only these two elements of the "modified vector" are shown). The micro-kernel keeps this information updated transparently to higher system layers. The primary server has just sent an IM to replica 0 and so no page is modified regarding this destination. At the same time, the log kept by replica 0 is empty. On the other hand, replica 1 has several entries in the log, and thus several pages of the primary server are modified regarding destination 1.

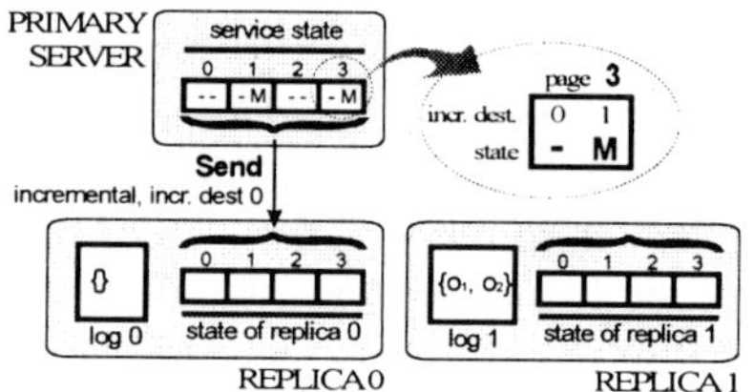

Figure 4: FT through loosely coupled server groups.

4.3. Transactional Services

The versatility and efficiency of Incremental Operations have been also demonstrated by means of the implementation of a transactional file server, that allowed us to obtain some of the first experimental results, which are shown in the following section. This subsection describes the implementation of transactional services [17] based on incremental operations.

The structure of the fault-tolerant transactional service is depicted in Figure 5, for two ongoing transactions. Data regions holding critical data are shown in dark gray. Region D holds service state, D_R is a back-up copy of D, and $C_W{}^i$ is the working copy of D for transaction i. The service is provided by several cooperating processes. Process TS keeps the original data copy (D) and coordinates the transactions; process R acts a back-up server to TS and a set of T_i processes (one per transaction) interact directly with the clients of the service. Each T_i process uses the services provided by TS to coordinate the operations of its transaction with those from other T_i processes.

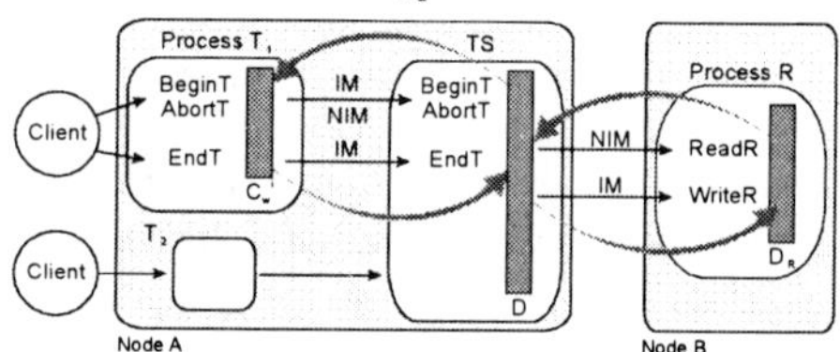

Figure 5: Structure of the service for two concurrent transactions.

When a client connected to a T_i process starts a transaction (service *BeginT* of T_i), $C_W{}^i$ is updated from D through an IM from TS to T_i. During transaction i, all operations are performed (by T_i on client's behalf) on this working copy ($C_W{}^i$). If the transaction is to be committed (service *EndT*), D is updated through an IM from T_i to TS. However, if it has to be aborted, changes to $C_W{}^i$ are discarded by means of a negative IM (NIM) from TS to T_i. To achieve fault-tolerance, TS keeps D_R updated using the services provided by the back-up server process (R). When the service is started, TS sends an initialization request to R, causing that D contents be copied into D_R. From then on, TS sends an IM to R (service *WriteR*) each time a T_i process invokes TS's service to commit the transaction. Only when D and D_R have been updated, R sends back an acknowledgment to T_i. If the transaction is to be aborted, no interaction between TS and R occurs, as D (and thus D_R) is not modified.

Although this service supports concurrency, we have deliberately omitted details about concurrency control algorithms. The reason for this is that the proposed structure is not dependent on the algorithm used, supporting both optimistic and pessimistic approaches.

4.4. Detailed IM Programming Example

In this subsection, we show in detail process R, which has just been described as part of the fault-tolerant transactional service. This process holds a back-up copy of critical data for one client process at a time. Figure 6 shows its main loop, where client messages are received and processed. In the picture, connection-oriented message handling has been omitted because it is not significant to illustrate IM programming. Error handling has also been omitted to simplify the example.

When the client starts, it should invoke FS_OPEN (sending a normal message with FS_OPEN in *msg.m_op*). As a result, process R prepares a new memory region (invoking *mmap*), which will then be used to keep the copy of client's critical data. Please note that the server invokes *msg_receive* with the M_INCR flag cleared until the back-up region is created. From this point on, the server sets M_INCR and specifies as destination for IMs the newly created memory region. The client can update the back-up copy sending an IM with FS_WRITE in *msg.m_op*. To satisfy this request, the server just has to reply to the client, because the back-up copy is updated by the kernel at message reception. Otherwise, the client can discard the changes made to the original data just sending a negative IM. Then, the server receives a new memory region whose address and length are contained in *msg.m_seg[SEG_PGS]* (the values provided by the server to the kernel when invoking *msg_receive* are simply discarded by the kernel, as a new region —with its own virtual address range— is begin provided to the server). To satisfy the request, the server just has to fill *msg.m_seg[SEG_MAP]* and *msg.m_seg[SEG_PGS]* with appropriate values (the map is the new region and the source data pages are those of the back-up region created at FS_OPEN) and then invoke *msg_reply* with flags M_INCR|M_MAP. After replying, the server discards the region holding the map, which is no longer needed.

```
port_t rootport;          /* Port for incoming msgs. */
void *datap = NULL;       /* Start addr. of back-up region */
uint datapgs = 0;         /* Region size (in pages) */

static void bkup_main()
{
        struct msg msg;
        void *map;

loop:
        if (IMs are welcome) {
                /* IM: set destination for FS_WRITE */
                msg.m_nseg = 1;
                msg.m_seg[SEG_PGS].s_buf = datap;
                msg.m_seg[SEG_PGS].s_buflen = ptob(datapgs);
        }
        imsg_receive(rootport, &msg,
                        (IMs are welcome)? M_INCR : 0);

        switch (msg.m_op & M_OPMSK) {
...
        case FS_OPEN: /* m_arg = sz. of crit. data */
                datapgs = msg.m_arg;
                datap = (void *)mmap(0, ptob(datapgs),
                                PROT_READ|PROT_WRITE,
                                MAP_ANON|MAP_PCOW, 0, 0);

                /* Empty answer to client */
                msg.m_nseg = msg.m_arg = msg.m_arg1 = 0;
                msg_reply(msg.m_sender, &msg);
                break;
        case FS_WRITE:              /* Incr. message */
                /* Empty message to client */
                msg.m_nseg = msg.m_arg = msg.m_arg1 = 0;
                msg_reply(msg.m_sender, &msg);
                break;
        case FS_READ:               /* NEG Incr. message */
                /* Client sends us MAP in PGS */
                msg.m_seg[SEG_MAP] = msg.m_seg[SEG_PGS];
                map = msg.m_seg[SEG_MAP].s_buf;

                /* Return to him what he just asked for */
                msg.m_seg[SEG_PGS].s_buf = datap;
                msg.m_seg[SEG_PGS].s_buflen = ptob(datapgs);
                msg.m_nseg = 2;
                imsg_reply(msg.m_sender, &msg, M_INCR|M_MAP);

                /* Free map region */
                munmap(map, 0);
                break;
...
        }
        goto loop;
}
```

Figure 6: Detailed specification of R process.

This example shows how easily IMs can be used to provide back-up and recovery of critical data at user-level. Although process R could be extended to support more than one client simultaneously, each one using several back-up regions, back-up and recovery is simpler to implement when critical data is kept in one memory region. The simplest approach is to modify existing dynamic memory management routines, so that the application can transparently use standard services, such as *malloc* or *free*. This is the approach we followed in the initial phases of implementation to build applications to test IM services.

5. Experimental Results

The first experimental results obtained after implementing IMs show that Incremental Operations can be used in real applications. However, we do not claim to have a particularly efficient implementation of IMs. Previous published results from other researchers [1, 6] prove that incremental and copy-on-write techniques significantly improve performance, and the strength of IMs is to offer these kernel-level techniques to application designers, which can use IMs to selectively create, update and recover critical data copies. Therefore, applications such as the transactional service where only some pages are modified between updates and where critical data is only a part of the process' address space, should show significant performance gains when using IMs. Still, IMs are not well suited to applications which modify most of their critical data pages between messages, and which should better use other IPC mechanisms.

The experiments reported in this section have been performed with processes residing on the same node, a PC with an Intel 486DX2-66 with 16MBytes of RAM and 216MB of swap on an IDE Hard Disk, with 1.92 ms as average seek time, and 1210 KB/s of transfer rate.

5.1. IM Analysis

This experiment has been performed with two processes. The main one holds the working copy of the data, and performs controlled writes on randomly selected pages. The second is an R process as described in the previous section that just waits for IMs to arrive and then processes them immediately. For each size, 50 IM were sent. Between two messages, the main process modifies the specified number of randomly selected pages. Figure 7 shows the mean IM transfer time of IMs versus the size of the memory region. For sizes smaller than 3000 pages, the cost strongly increases as the size decreases. The unexpected behavior (we expected a small increment as the size increased) is caused by blocking due to synchronization among IM services and the page stealing process.[3] When the size of the region is small, blocking is more frequent. On the other hand, from 3000 pages onwards, the cost increase is due mainly to the fact that as the region grows there are more page misses.

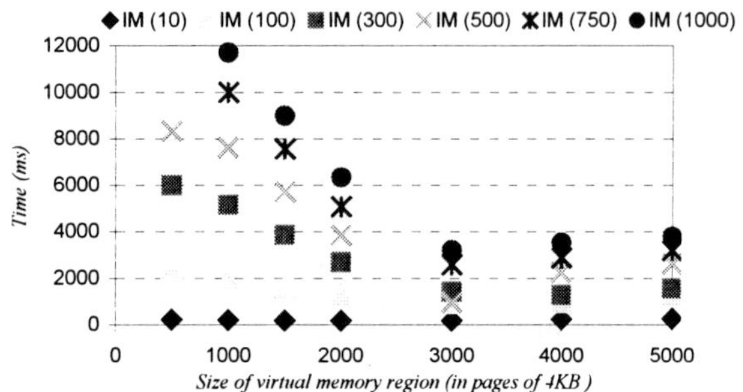

Figure 7: Temporal cost of IMs versus size of VM regions for 10, 100, 300, 500, 750 and 1000 modified pages.

This experiment shows the relevance of synchronization delays, and suggests that IMs should be considered as an integral part of the virtual memory management. For example, in our implementation, a page remains locked while it is being filled or written back to disk. This means that the IM send routine should block if it needs to access the modified page bitmap (see subsection 3.3). However, if a richer blocking mechanism were used, disk transfers would not need to block IM routines, since they (disk transfers) do not alter the modified bitmap for the page.

5.2. Checkpointing Analysis

The overhead that checkpointing implemented using IMs produces on an intensive computing application has been measured on a program that multiplies 615x615-integer matrices. Both matrices reside on a file; the program reads them, performs the product and then writes the result back to disk. Six different checkpointing techniques have been analyzed (see Table 3), which have been implemented by library code that uses IMs. Table 4 shows the results of these tests. Checkpoints have been established 11 times during the execution, which means one every 50 s.

Table 3: Checkpointing techniques used.

N.	Description
0	No checkpointing.
1	Incremental to memory. An IM is sent to the back-up R process.
2	Incremental to disk, synchronous. An IM is sent to a back-up process, which receives it packed and uses the map to update a back-up file. Then it acknowledges the sender.
3	Incremental to disk, asynchronous. As in the previous one, but the acknowledgment is sent before the file is updated.
4	Packed to disk, synchronous. As in method 2, but writing the raw PIM to a new file.
5	Packed to disk, asynchronous. As the previous one, but async.
6	Non incremental to disk. The whole result matrix is written to a file.

Table 4: Temporal cost of checkpointing (CP) using IMs.
"run. t" stands for total execution time, "ov" for overhead, "t" for mean time to establish one CP and "sz" for CP size.

Method	run. t (s)	ov (s)	ov (%)	t (s)	sz (MB)
0	547,9				
1	548,6	0,7	0,1	0,03	0,39
2	566,9	19,1	3,5	1,71	0,39
3	566,6	18,8	3,4	0,05	0,39
4	557,3	9,4	1,7	0,73	0,39
5	556,3	8,5	1,5	0,02	0,39
6	572,3	24,4	4,4	2,04	1,71

It can be noted how, compared to method 6, IMs significantly reduce the overhead due to checkpointing, and this reduction is more important when PIMs are used. It should be noted the high performance that can be obtained when the back-up copy remains in memory (method 1). It is also worth to stand out that methods 2 and 3 incur in an overhead similar to that of method 6. This is caused by the high number of messages exchanged as every modified page is sent to disk in a separate write operation (each one generates one message from process R to the file server, one from the file server to the disk server, and the necessary replies).

These results are similar to those reported in [6] for the same application when user-directed checkpointing is used. Nevertheless, both experiments are not directly comparable since there are significant differences between them, such as the operating system structure (Unix versus VSTa, which is a micro-kernel), or the place where checkpoints are saved (NFS imported file system versus in-memory or local file system).

5.3. Transactional File System

To show how incremental operations are easy to use for implementing fault tolerant applications, a small transactional file server has been implemented. The user has access from the command line to three basic operations, StartT, EndT and AbortT, which cause the client process to invoke these operations on the server. With this structure, off-the-shelf utilities (such as text editors, compilers, or file management utilities) can benefit from the fact of being used inside transactions, and thus their effects be discarded or confirmed as required.

[3] Note that even when only 100 pages are modified between two consecutive IMs, as pages are selected randomly and 50 IMs are sent for each region size, page stealing and page fault treatment are intensive, because with 16MB of RAM there are only 4096 pages available, and they must be shared with the OS kernel and system servers.

The transactional file server has been implemented following the concurrent transactional service described in subsection 4.3. This structure requires: (1) that data are stored in one virtual memory region, and (2) that the smallest unit to be assigned to a file is a page (because concurrency is managed at page level).

A new file system, called *cfs*, which satisfies these requirements, has been implemented on VSTa [20]. Measures have been carried out with a storage region of 5000 pages of 4 KB. Table 5 shows the results of performance comparison among the transactional file server (*ctfs*), the file system implemented on VSTa (*cfs*), the standard temporal file server of VSTa (*tmpfs*) and the FAT (MS-DOS) file system of VSTa. As the table shows, *ctfs* offers similar performance to *cfs* and *tmpfs*, which are memory-based, and much better performance than FAT, which is disk-based.

Table 5: Comparison of "ctfs" versus "cfs", "tmpfs" and "FAT".

(Times expressed in ms.)

Operation	Size	ctfs	cfs	tmpfs	FAT
Read	512 B	1,1	1,6	1,6	26,8
	64 KB	48	60,6	59,4	105
	1 MB	736	967	949	1977
Write	512 B	0,89	2,0	2,1	28,5
	64 KB	38,8	64,2	60,3	57,7
	1 MB	616	986	912	1853

6. Conclusions and Future Work

This paper proposes Incremental Messages (IM), a new type of kernel services designed to efficiently and flexibly manage replicated copies of critical data. These services combine the advantages of both kernel and user-level approaches to checkpointing and recovery. As kernel mechanisms do, IMs take advantage of having direct access to the memory management unit, providing efficient transfer of data by means of concurrent and incremental copying. At the same time, the proposed interface is flexible enough to let user-level applications establish which data must be copied and when, permitting that only critical data be copied.

As section 4 describes, passive replicates, user-level checkpointing and transactional services can be implemented easily and efficiently using IMs. Furthermore, error detection and confinement can also be increased by fully exploiting the proposed interface. Hence, IMs are a valuable tool to support the development of fault-tolerant applications, justifying the cost of including them in a micro-kernel.

The first experimental results obtained following the implementation of IMs on VSTa suggest that the current IM implementation is efficient enough to build practical fault-tolerant applications. However, they also show that the efficiency of these services strongly depends on the design of the virtual memory subsystem and, specially, on the paging strategy. Consequently, to fully exploit the performance improvement that IMs should offer, they should be accounted for as an integral part of the virtual memory management design. This is a limitation of the current implementation, which should be addressed in future works.

References

[1] J.S. Plank, "Efficient checkpointing on MIMD architectures", *PhD Thesis*, Dep. of CS, University of Princeton, June 1993.

[2] E.N. Elnozahy, "Manetho: Fault-Tolerance in Distributed Systems Using Rollback-Recovery and Process Replication", *PhD Thesis*, Rice University, October 1993.

[3] F. Cristian, B. Dancey, and J. Dehn, "Fault-Tolerance in the Advanced Automation System", *In Proc. of the 20th FTCS*, June 1990, pp. 6-17.

[4] Y. Huang, and C. Kintala, "Software Implemented Fault Tolerance: Technologies and Experience", *In Proc. of the 23rd FTCS*, June 1993, pp. 2-9.

[5] D. Powell, "Distributed Fault Tolerance: Lessons from Delta-4", *IEEE Micro*, February 1994, pp. 36-47.

[6] J. S. Plank, M. Beck, et al., "Libckpt: Transparent Checkpointing under Unix", *USENIX Winter 1995 Technical Conference*, January 1995, pp. 213-223.

[7] C. Pérez, G. Fabregat, et al., "Micro-Kernel support for Fault-Tolerant Application Development on Distributed Systems", *In Digest of FastAbstracts: FTCS-28*, IEEE CS, June 1998, pp. 43-44.

[8] V. Abrossimov, F. Herrmann, et al., "Fast Error Recovery in CHORUS/OS: The Hot-Restart Technology", *CSI-T4-96-34 Technical Report, Chorus Systems, Inc.*, August 1996.

[9] J. Lipkis, and M. Rozier, "Fault Tolerance Enablers in the CHORUS Microkernel", *Hardware and Software Architectures for Fault Tolerance*, Lecture Notes in Computer Science nº 774, Springer-Verlag, 1994, pp. 182-190.

[10] M. Rozier, V. Abrossimov, et al., "Overview of the Chorus Distributed Operating System", *USENIX Micro-kernels and Other Kernel Architectures Workshop Proc.*, April 1992, pp. 39-69.

[11] R. van Renesse, and A.S. Tanenbaum, "Short Overview of Amoeba", *USENIX Micro-kernels and Other Kernel Architectures Workshop Proc.*, April 1992, pp. 1-10.

[12] D.L. Black, D.B. Golub, et al., "Microkernel Operating System Architecture and Mach", *USENIX Micro-kernels and Other Kernel Architectures Workshop Proc.*, April 1992, pp. 11-30.

[13] A. Valencia, "An Overview of the VSTa Microkernel", URL:*http://bodhi.zendo.com/vsta/vsta_intro.html.*

[14] S. Levi, and A.K. Agrawala, "Fault Tolerant System Design", *McGraw-Hill*, 1994.

[15] J.-C. Laprie, J. Arlat, et al., "Definition and Analysis of Hardware-and-Software Fault-Tolerant Architectures", *Predictably Dependable Computing Systems*, Basic Research Series, Springer, 1995, pp. 103-122.

[16] G. Deconinck, J. Vounckx, et al., "Survey of Checkpointing and Rollback Techniques", *Project ESPRIT 6731 (FTMPS) Technical Report*, June 1993.

[17] G. Coulouris, J. Dollimore, and T. Kindberg, "Distributed Systems. Concepts and Design", *Addison-Wesley*, 2nd edition, 1996.

[18] R. Draves, "A Revised IPC Interface", *USENIX Mach Workshop Proc.*, October 1990, pp. 101-122.

[19] H. Madeira, and J.G. Silva, "Experimental Evaluation of the Fail-Silent Behavior in Computers Without Error Masking", *In Proc. of the 24th FTCS*, June 1994, pp.350-359.

[20] C. Pérez, "Aportaciones a los Entornos de Desarrollo de Aplicaciones Tolerantes a Fallos", *PhD Thesis*, Dpto. de Informática y Electrónica, Universitat de València, February 1998.

Session 3B

Student Papers I

Chair: W. Kent Fuchs
Purdue University, USA

Session 4A

Design of Fault-Tolerant Systems

Chair: David Rennel
University of California at Los Angeles, USA

Rigorous Development of a Safety-Critical System Based on Coordinated Atomic Actions

J. Xu, B. Randell, A. Romanovsky, R.J. Stroud, and A.F. Zorzo*
University of Newcastle upon Tyne, NE1 7RU, UK

E. Canver and F. von Henke
University of Ulm, D-89069 Ulm, Germany

Abstract

This paper describes our experience using coordinated atomic (CA) actions as a system structuring tool to design and validate a sophisticated control system for a complex industrial application that has high reliability and safety requirements. Our study is based on the "Fault-Tolerant Production Cell", which represents a manufacturing process involving redundant mechanical devices (provided in order to enable continued production in the presence of machine faults). The challenge posed by the model specification is to design a control system that maintains specified safety and liveness properties even in the presence of a large number and variety of device and sensor failures. We discuss in this paper: i) a design for a control program that uses CA actions to deal with both safety-related and fault tolerance concerns, and ii) the formal verification of this design based on the use of model-checking. We found that CA action structuring facilitated both the design and verification tasks by enabling the various safety problems (e.g. clashes of moving machinery) to be treated independently. The formal verification activity was performed in parallel with the design activity: the interaction between them resulted in a combined exercise in "design for validation".

Key Words — Concurrency, coordinated atomic (CA) actions, exception handling, object orientation, formal verification, model checking, reactive systems, reliability and safety.

1: Introduction

The goal of this work is to investigate a rigorous approach to the development of safety-critical applications, in particular to examine the feasibility of using coordinated atomic (CA) actions [11] as a structuring tool to design a realistically-detailed fault-tolerant control system, and then to use model-checking to debug, improve, and verify the design formally.

A production cell model, based on a metal-processing plant in Karlsruhe, Germany, was first created by the FZI (Forschungszentrum Informatik) in 1993 [4] in order to evaluate different formal methods and to explore their practicability for industrial applications. Since then, this original case study, Production Cell I, has attracted wide attention and has been investigated by over 35 different research groups. In 1996, the FZI presented the specification of an extended model, called the "Fault-Tolerant Production Cell" or Production Cell II [6]. This second model exposes more and richer issues related to failures and fault tolerance. Because devices, sensors and actuators can fail, the required control program is necessarily much more complex than the program for the original, non-fault-tolerant production cell.

This paper is organized as follows. Following a brief description of the CA action concept and Production Cell II, Section 3 presents an analysis of the cell's possible failures. Section 4 describes a design of a control system. Sections 5 and 6 describe the formal validation of this design. Section 7 concludes the paper.

2: CA Actions and Production Cell II

Real-world applications often give rise to complex concurrent and interacting activities. An effective mechanism is required for controlling and coordinating such activities. Due to their complexity, concurrent and distributed systems are also very prone to faults and errors. The CA action scheme [11] is motivated by the need to deal with general and complicated fault situations that occur in many real-world applications.

A CA action is a mechanism for coordinating multi-threaded interactions and ensuring consistent access to objects in the presence of concurrency and potential faults. CA actions can be regarded as providing a programming discipline for nested multi-threaded transactions [2] that in addition provides very general exception handling provisions. They augment any fault tolerance that is provided by the underlying transaction system by providing means for dealing with i) unmasked hardware and software faults that have been reported to the application level to deal with, and/or ii) application-level failure situations that have to be responded to.

The concurrent execution threads participating in a given CA action enter and leave the action synchronously. Within the CA action, operations on objects can be performed cooperatively by *roles* executing in parallel. To cooperate in a CA action a group of concurrent threads must

* Present address: Dept. of Computer Science, University of Durham.

0-7695-0213-X/99 $10.00 © 1999 IEEE

come together and agree to perform each role of the action, with each thread undertaking a different role. Inside a CA action, some or all of its roles can be involved in further (nested) CA actions. If an error is detected within a CA action, appropriate recovery measures must be invoked cooperatively, by all the roles, in order to reach some mutually consistent conclusion.

Figure 1 shows an example in which two concurrent threads enter a CA action in order to play the corresponding roles. Within the CA action the two concurrent roles communicate with each other and manipulate the external objects cooperatively in pursuit of some common goal. However, during the execution of the CA action, an exception `e` is raised by one of the roles. The other role is then informed of the exception and both roles transfer control to their respective exception handlers `H1` and `H2` for this particular exception, which then attempt to perform forward error recovery. The effects of erroneous operations on external objects are repaired, if possible, by putting the objects into new correct states so that the CA action is able to exit with an acceptable outcome. The two threads leave the CA action synchronously at the end of the action.

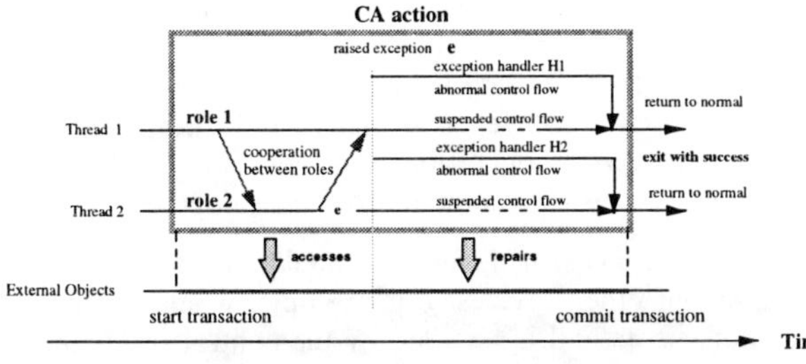

Figure 1 Example of a CA Action.

In general, the desired effect of performing a CA action is specified by an *acceptance test*. The effect only becomes visible if the test is passed. The test allows both a normal outcome and one or more exceptional (or degraded) outcomes, with each exceptional outcome signalling a specified exception to the surrounding environment. The CA action is considered to have failed if the action does not succeed in passing the test, or roles of the action do not agree about the outcome of the action. In either case, it is necessary to try to undo potential effects of the CA action and signal an `abort` exception to the environment. If the CA action is unable to satisfy the "all-or-nothing" property (e.g. because the undo fails), then a `failure` exception must be signalled to the surrounding environment. Ideally, the execution of a CA action will only produce one of the following outputs: a normal outcome, an exceptional outcome, an `abort` exception, or a `failure` exception.

Production Cell II consists of six devices: two conveyor belts (a feed belt and a deposit belt), an elevating rotary table, two presses and a rotary robot that has two orthogonal extendible arms equipped with electromagnets (see Figure 2). These devices are associated with a set of sensors that provide useful information to a "controller", and a set of actuators via which the controller can exercise control over the whole system. The task of the cell is to get a metal blank from its "environment" via the feed belt, transform it into a forged plate by using a press, and then return it to the environment via the deposit belt. More precisely, the production cycle for each blank is: i) if the traffic light for insertion shows green, a blank may be added, e.g. by the blank supplier, to the feed belt, ii) the feed belt conveys the blank to the table, iii) the table rotates and rises to the position where the magnets of the robot are able to grip the blank, iv) arm 1 of the robot picks the blank up and places it into an unoccupied press, v) the chosen press forges the blank, vi) arm 2 of the robot removes the forged plate from the press and places it on the deposit belt, and vii) if the traffic light is green, the plate may be carried to the environment.

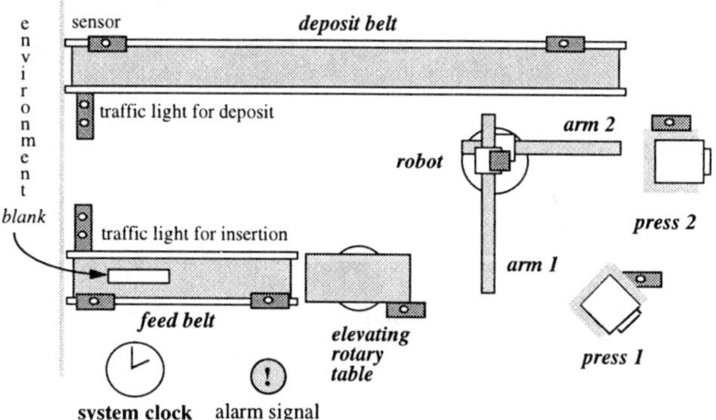

Figure 2 Fault-Tolerant Production Cell (Top View).

Basic System Requirements

A correct controller or control program must satisfy certain requirements specified by the Fault-Tolerant Production Cell model, namely:

Safety: i) device mobility must be restricted, ii) device collisions must be prevented, iii) blanks must not be dropped outside safe areas (i.e. feed belt, table, press, and deposit belt), and iv) sufficient distance must be maintained between blanks.

Liveness: Any blank put into the cell via the feed belt must eventually leave the cell via the deposit belt and must have been forged by one of the presses; this property must still hold if one of the two presses fails.

Failure Detection and Continuous Service: When any of a large number of defined failures occurs, it must be detected and unless it just concerns one of the presses the system must be stopped in a safe state. After recovery from the failure, which typically would require action by the user of the cell, the system should be able to resume operations starting from this safe state. Similarly, after a failed press has been repaired, it should be able to resume its contributions to the production process. (Certain safety requirements can no longer be met if some special failures occur, e.g. a blank is dropped outside safe areas, but other safety properties must still be guaranteed.)

Clock, Stop Watches and Alarm Signals

The Fault-Tolerant Production Cell model provides a global system clock that gives the current time at any instant. Based on this system clock, a control program can implement several stop watches supervising individual processes, e.g. the movement of the feed belt. The model also provides an alarm signal mechanism for reporting component failures to the user of the cell. The control program is required to switch on the alarm whenever a failure is detected — it is switched off by the user when the failed device has been repaired.

3: Failure Definitions and Analysis

The major assumptions made in the Fault-Tolerant Production Cell model, as defined by FZI, are:

1) The system clock, two traffic lights, and the alarm signal mechanism are fault-free and do not fail.
2) Values of sensors, actuators and clocks are always transmitted correctly without any loss or error.
3) No failure can cause devices to exceed certain limiting positions; in the worst case devices are stopped automatically.
4) All sensor failures are indicated by sensor values.
5) All actuator failures will cause devices to stop.

For a given device, we classify possible failures into: i) sensor failures, ii) actuator failures, and iii) lost or stuck blanks. We also show how a failure can be detected by sensors, actuators, stop watches, singly or in combination. In many cases certain different types of failure cannot be distinguished using just the on-line information available. We therefore discuss failure detection only, and assume that fault diagnosis and subsequent device repair are performed off-line. Due to limitations of space, we illustrate the analysis that we performed by treating just the case of a single failure of a press; for a complete treatment, see [12].

Sensor Failures: There are four sensors associated with each press, one reporting whether a blank is in the press (called *blank sensor*), and others reporting press positions. A failure of the blank sensor can be detected by checking whether a robot arm has transferred a blank to or from the press. The failure of a sensor that reports press positions can be detected by using a stop watch to measure the moving time of the press and by checking other sensor values on press positions.

Actuator Failures: Failure modes for the actuators that move the lower part of a press include: no response (i.e. cannot move), and a moving press unexpected stopping, which can be detected by checking values of the press position sensors and values of stop watches.

Stuck or Lost Blank: This failure can be detected only by checking the value of the sensor that reports whether a blank is in a press.

In order to detect various failures of sensors and actuators as well as lost blanks, appropriate detection measures must be incorporated into the control software. Assertion statements are a common form of failure detection measure. For example, after the control program has sent a control command to the robot and asked the robot to drop a blank into press 1, the value of the sensor that reports a blank in the press must be checked by an assertion. If the sensor returns 0, indicating that no blank is in press 1, then an appropriate exception must be raised.

There are several possibilities that could have caused this exception: i) the blank might have been lost, ii) arm 1 of the robot might have failed to drop the blank, and iii) the sensor of press 1 might have failed to report that the blank has been dropped into the press. Unfortunately, our analysis showed that distinguishing these failures from each other at run-time is extremely difficult. In most cases, if a failure occurs and thus an exception is raised, the cell will simply have to be stopped in a safe state, if at all possible, for the user to deal with.

Failures of sensors that report press positions and failures of the press actuator can be detected by assertion statements and identified unambiguously with the aid of stopwatches. Such failures must be reported to the user through the alarm. However, because Production Cell II has two presses, normal operations can be maintained using a single press, albeit with some performance degradation.

A device or sensor failure should not affect normal operations of other devices. For example, when a failure of the robot occurs and is handled by the control program, the deposit belt should still deliver an already forged blank, if there is one, to the blank consumer. In the following, we will demonstrate how CA actions can confine damage and failures effectively, and minimize the impact of component failures on the entire cell.

4: Design of a Control Program

The main characteristics of our design are the way it separates safety, functionality, and efficiency concerns among a set of CA actions, which thus can be designed, and validated, independently of each other, and of the set of device/sensor-controllers that dynamically determine the order in which the CA actions are executed at run-time. In particular, the safety requirements are satisfied at the level of CA actions, while the other requirements are met by the device/sensor-controllers. There is a detailed discussion in [13] as to how these design decision were made and why we used actions to enclose the interaction between certain devices in our control program developed for Production Cell I. Our design for Production Cell II follows a similar strategy. It includes 12 main CA actions; each action controls one step of the blank processing and typically involves passing a blank between two devices. Any device can move only within a CA action.

There are six concurrent execution threads in the control program, corresponding to the six devices, each of which threads basically performs a simple endless loop. All device movements are performed within CA actions, and the devices involved in each action are switched off before the action is left, so that when not under the control of an action each device is stationary. Two additional threads model activities in the environment: *BlankSupplier*, and *BlankConsumer*. Note that *FeedBelt* is responsible for controlling the traffic light that indicates when another blank can be inserted, while *BlankConsumer* is responsible for controlling the light for deposit. A blank is designed as an external object with respect to the top-level CA actions. Usually, one role of a CA action takes the blank as an input argument, and the device corresponding to this role passes it to another role which returns it as an output argument. Figure 3 portrays the 12 related CA actions as overlays on the FZI simulator diagram [6].

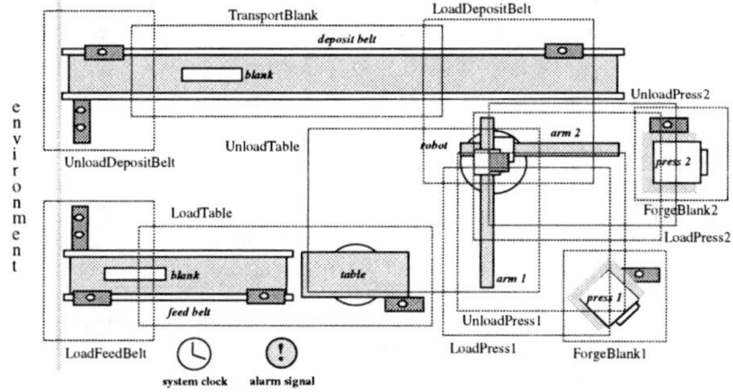

Figure 3 CA Actions That Control Production Cell II.

Each device-controller (i.e. an execution thread) is responsible for dynamically specifying the sequence of actions that the device will participate in. For example, the *robot* thread can skip all the CA actions related to one of the presses if this press has failed. An intersection between CA actions in Figure 3, e.g. between `TransportBlank` and `LoadDepositBelt`, represents the fact that those CA actions cannot be executed in parallel. The mutual exclusion feature of CA actions guarantees that a blank or a device cannot be involved in more than one action at a time so that neither blanks nor devices can collide. Even if the actions that devices participate in are invoked in the wrong order, the result will be at worst a safe deadlock.

4.1: Design of CA Actions

Our design assumes that an action will begin only if its pre-conditions are valid, and that if no exception is raised during the execution of an action then its post-conditions will hold (though this could, if so wished, be checked using an acceptance test). For a given action, these conditions are used to ensure that the execution of that action will not violate in any way the system requirements given in Section 3, especially those related to safety and fault tolerance. Due to limitations of space, we take just the action `LoadPress1` as an example.

CA action `LoadPress1`

pre-conditions	*post-conditions*
robot off	Robot off
Blank on arm 1	No blank on arm 1
Both arms retracted	Both arms retracted
Robot at one of the defined angles	Robot angle: arm 1 towards press 1
press 1 off	Press 1 off
no blank in press 1	Blank in press 1
press 1 in bottom position	press 1 in middle position

Values of the related sensors or states of the related actuators that can be used to check these conditions are identified in our detailed design to facilitate the actual implementation of a control program (see [12]).

Figure 4 illustrates the interactions (themselves involving nested CA actions) between the participating threads within the `LoadPress1` action. This action has four roles: `Robot`, `Press1`, `RobotSensor`, and `Press1Sensor`, and represents the co-operation that arranges for arm 1 of the robot to drop a blank into press 1.

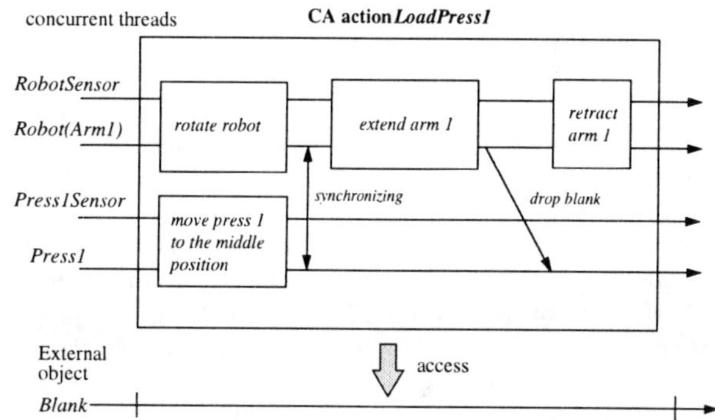

Figure 4 CA Action `LoadPress1`.

Action `LoadPress1` is described below using the COALA notation, which was developed for the formal specification of CA actions [10]. Our Java implementation of the control program is based on a set of pre-defined templates for CA actions that can be used to implement CA action designs specified in COALA.

```
CAA LoadPress1;
Interface
  Use
    MetalBlank;
  Roles
    Robot: blankType, robotActuator;
    Press1: blankType, press1Actuator;
    RobotSensor: arm1ExtensionSensor, ...;
    Press1Sensor: blankSensor, ...;
  Exceptions
    Press1Failure, Arm1Failure1, ...;
                         ;;exceptions to signal
Body
  Use CAA
                     ;;specify nested actions
    RotateRobot, MovePress1toMiddle, ...;
  Object
    robotPress1Channel: Channel;
                     ;;shared local objects
  Exceptions
    press1_failure, blank_sensor_failure, ...;
                     ;;internal exceptions
```

```
  Handlers
    press1_handler, blank_sensor_handler, ...;
  Resolution
    press1_failure -> press1_handler, ...;
                         ;;exception resolution graph
  Role Robot(...);
  Role Press1(...);
  ... ... ... ...
End LoadPress1;
```

The exceptions declared in the **Interface** part of an action are those that can be signalled to the enclosing action. The roles of an action can signal an exception directly but must guarantee that the exception that is signalled has been agreed by all the roles of that action. In the case of abortion or failure, the CA action support mechanism will enforce the abortion and signal the appropriate exception, either `abort` or `failure`, to the enclosing action. When multiple exceptions are raised within an action, the CA action support mechanism controls the execution of a resolution algorithm based on an exception resolution graph declared in the **Resolution** part. After a resolving exception is identified, the corresponding handler declared in the **Handlers** part will be invoked (see Section 4.3).

An exception handler will attempt to bring the system back to normal. If it is successful, the CA action will end with a normal outcome. However, in most situations the handler can only provide some degraded service, i.e. an exceptional outcome, and must signal the corresponding exception. Again, in the case of abortion or failure, the CA action support mechanism will take control. If a further exception is raised during the execution of an exception handler, control is transferred to the CA action support mechanism immediately and the action must either abort or signal a `failure` exception.

4.2: Dealing with Component Failures

We first investigate situations involving single faults, i.e. we assume that *only one component failure can occur before the system is brought if necessary to a safe stop, and the component is repaired.* During the execution of a CA action, if a failure (of a component involved in this CA action) occurs and is detected by an assertion statement or an acceptance test, a corresponding exception will be raised within the action by one of its roles. The exception is propagated immediately to the other roles of the action and all roles then transfer control to their exception handlers for this exception so that they can attempt to perform appropriate error recovery. In most cases when a component failure takes place in the cell, it is not possible to recover completely from the error and the *normal* post-conditions of the action can no longer be satisfied. Thus, exceptional post-conditions with respect to various given failures must be defined to specify the exceptional outcomes of an action.

By way of example, we outline the basic requirements for the handlers of two different exceptions:

Handler for the Press 1 Failure: The `LoadPress1` action performs forward error recovery by moving the robot to an appropriate position so that it will be able to put the unforged blank, which is still on arm 1, into press 2 once the press is available.

Handler for the Rotary Sensor or Motor Failure: (In this case, action `LoadPress1` fails to rotate the robot to the intended position.) The action will simply use backward error recovery to attempt to move the robot back to its initial position and rotate it again. If the failure persists, the action will produce an exceptional outcome as defined below.

For the `LoadPress1` action, we identify seven exceptional outcomes and corresponding exceptional post-conditions (see [12]). By way of example, the following table illustrates the exceptional outcome when press 1 fails. Different exceptional outcomes may lead to different states of the production cell. For example, the exceptional outcome caused by just a press 1 failure corresponds to the situation where the production cell continues with only one operational press. On the other hand, since the blank sensor is a redundant component of the cell, if both presses are still operational its failure merely requires a report to be made to the user of the cell. However, the other five outcomes will have to stop the entire cell in a safe state.

exception to signal	*Exceptional post-conditions*
press 1 failure	robot off
	Blank on arm 1
	Both arms retracted
	Robot angle: arm 1 towards press 2
	press 1 off
	no blank in press 1

By means of such analyses, given the way in which CA actions enable the different failure situations to be treated independently of each other, the design of the actual set of handlers for the various exceptional outcomes of each of the 12 top-level CA actions becomes rather straightforward – full details can be found in [12].

4.3: Dealing with Concurrent Failures

In the interests of simplicity, we assume that *only two failures may occur within the same time interval before the system is stopped and the related components repaired.* Some concurrent failures can be covered implicitly by the corresponding single failure situation. Others may need different handling and require separate post conditions. The following table shows post-conditions for an example pair of concurrent failures:

exception to signal	*Exceptional post-conditions*
(rotary sensor or motor failure) & press 1 failure	robot off
	Blank on arm 1
	Both arms retracted
	press 1 off
	No blank in press 1

The failure of the robot's rotary sensor or motor can be detected automatically and indicated by a special sensor value. However, the returned sensor value does not indicate which component, i.e. the sensor or the motor, actually failed. This causes difficulty in performing effective error recovery. In such circumstances the control program is designed simply to bring the system to a stop in a safe state, so that off-line diagnosis can be performed.

For each (enclosing or nested) action, various exceptions are defined based on failure analysis and an exception graph for resolving concurrent exceptions is defined. For example, the `LoadPress1` action may give rise to exceptions such as `pr1_failure` (press 1 failure), `b_sensor_failure` (blank sensor failure), `arm1_failure1` (blank lost), `arm1_failure2` (cannot drop the blank), etc.

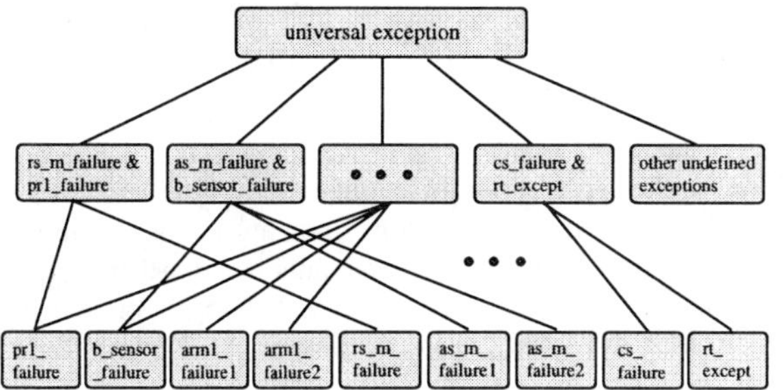

Figure 5 Exception Graph for CA Action `LoadPress1`.

An exception graph for this action is shown in Figure 5. For example, if both press 1 and the robot rotation motor fail simultaneously, this exception graph will be searched and the resolving exception `rs_m_failure & pr1_failure` will be raised instead of the individual exceptions `rs_m_failure` and `pr1_ failure`, so that a suitable handler for this particular situation can be invoked. Any undefined exception pairs will not be resolved and will simply lead to the raising of the `universal` exception. (The handler for the `universal` exception is responsible for stopping the system and leaving the cell in a pre-defined safe state, if possible.)

4.4: Design of Device-Controllers

Device/sensor-controllers are used to determine dynamically the order in which the CA actions are executed. Eight controllers are designed: `FeedBelt`, `Table`, `Robot`, `Press1`, `Press2`, `DepositBelt`, `Supplier`, and `Consumer`. Two queue objects are defined in order to improve the flexibility of operations of both the robot and the deposit belt: `robotQueue` and `depositBeltQueue`. The `Press1` controller is shown below as a simple example:

```
Press1Controller:
  loop forever {
        robotQueue.put(PRESS1_FREE)
        -- put message in robotQueue
        LoadPress1.Press(plate)
        -- activate action LoadPress1
        ForgeBlank1.Press(plate)
        -- activate action ForgeBlank1
        robotQueue.put(FORGED_PLATE_IN_PRESS1)
        -- put message in robotQueue
        UnloadPress1.Press(plate)
        -- activate action UnloadPress1 }
```

5: Validating Properties of the Cell

We had earlier developed a general scheme for formalizing CA action-based designs of finite systems as state transition systems specifically for the purpose of checking system properties such as liveness, safety and fault tolerance [1]. This general approach assumes that a set of controlling processes is defined together with a set of CA actions that are utilized by the controllers, and enables the system behaviour to be formalized in terms of its operations on the global objects in the system that are external to all CA actions.

The state transition system corresponding to a CA action-based design is characterized by its (global) state-space, a set of initial states and a `next-state` relation. The global state-space is composed from the global objects and the state-spaces of the CA actions, representing the kind of outcome – normal or exceptional – produced by each CA action and encoding whether its roles are idle or activated. The initial states are supposed to satisfy two kinds of properties: i) any application specific requirements that need to be considered, and ii) the requirement that initially all roles should be idle and no exception should have been signalled.

The `next-state` relation defines the computation paths that are possible in the system. This corresponds essentially to four kinds of activities that may occur in the system: i) a controlling process may call and thus invoke a role from a CA action, thereby activating it, ii) if all roles of a CA action have been activated, the CA action may be executed according to its interface specification given in terms of pre- and post-conditions for both normal and exceptional outcomes, iii) after a CA action has been executed, a return is issued from its roles to the corresponding controlling processes that called them, and iv) a controlling process may execute an (internal) action in which no CA action is involved.

Due to the atomicity of CA actions and since internal actions of controlling processes are independent from each other, it is sufficient to view only interleaving occurrences of state transitions. Thus we have modelled the `next-state` relation to encode the interleaving semantics. We have used SMV [8] to represent the state transition system so obtained. (The technical details of representing a CA action-based design in SMV and the properties of a system in CTL were described in [1].)

Model-checking is a technique for analyzing whether a given set of behavioural properties is satisfied by a given model. It is similar to exhaustive testing of a finite instance, and it produces a counterexample whenever a property is violated. We have model-checked a significant proportion of the safety, liveness, and fault-tolerance requirements for the Production Cell II case study. The properties are expressed in terms of CTL formulae over the transition system for the CA action-based design formalized in SMV. CTL allows several temporal modalities to be used for expressing properties over the behaviour of a system; we have mainly used the `AG` ("henceforth") operator for expressing properties that are to hold in all reachable states and the `AF` ("eventually") operator for expressing properties that are expected to eventually hold along all execution paths.

We are mainly concerned with fault-tolerance requirements which express properties over the behaviour of a system despite the occurrence of an equipment failure. These may include safety and liveness properties. If `tolerable` is a formula describing states where there are no faults, or only those faults that are supposed to be tolerated by the system, and if `P` expresses some desired property, then formula

```
AG (tolerable -> P)
```

expresses that along each execution path property `P` is valid if faults that occur are tolerable ones, i.e. `P` is treated as a (conditional) safety property. Similarly for liveness: the formula

```
AF (tolerable -> P)
```

expresses that along each execution path either a state satisfying `P` will be reached or a non-tolerable fault will occur. This means that `P` will eventually become true along each path where at most tolerable faults occur, i.e. `P` is treated as a (conditional) liveness property.

We illustrate this scheme for formalizing properties with the main fault-tolerance requirement, i.e. the "continuous service requirement" which states that the system will continue to operate in a degraded manner, even if one of the presses fails. Such failures are signalled by the CA action `LoadPress1` as `press1_failure` or `b_sensor_failure`. The property encoding the continuous service requirement expresses that if a `press1_failure` or a `b_sensor_failure` occurs, then any blank in other devices of Production Cell II or blanks inserted afterwards will be processed and arrive on the deposit belt unless another failure occurs later. This is formalized here for a blank with name `id1` on the feed belt:

"If a press1 related failure occurs ..."

```
AG (loadpress1.signal in
    { press1_failure, b_sensor_failure } ->
```

" then a blank (named `id1`) on the feed belt ..."

```
AG (blank_on_feed_belt.id = id1 ->
```

"will eventually, if only tolerable failures occur, ..."

```
AF ((loadpress1.signal in { normal,
         press1_failure, b_sensor_failure })
```

"arrive on the deposit belt"

```
-> blank_on_end_deposit_belt.id = id1)))
```

We have produced two SMV specifications for the CA action-based design of Production Cell II, a full model and an abstraction of the full model. Both are generic with respect to the number of blanks that may appear in the system concurrently. The full model contains 1251 lines of SMV code, and the abstracted model has 1079 lines of code. The potential state space of the full model is about 10^{34}, whereas the size of the abstracted model is about 10^{26}. These models were instantiated with the number of blanks, and actual model-checking was performed on those instanced on a Sun Sparc Ultra-II platform. The full model produced no result for three or more blanks after one week of computation, whereas the abstracted model responded in all possible situations within about 15 hours.

6: Design for Validation

The analysis of properties of Production Cell II was carried out in parallel with the development of its CA action-based design. Model-checking helped us to find several flaws in early versions of the design. By analyzing the causes for failed proofs of the required properties, we have been able to derive corresponding solutions. The flaws we found affected both the fault tolerance and the coordination aspects of the CA action design of the cell. The results from the formal analysis have directly contributed to refining and improving our design.

To take just one example, we identified a problem that affected the order in which the robot interacts with the devices around it. The problem does not occur in the single blank instance of our model and thus it is hard to detect by just reviewing the specification text. If two blanks are in the system then the robot could manoeuvre itself into a situation from which no further activities were possible. Such "critical" sequences of actions can be derived from counter-example paths generated by the model-checker. The counter-example also helps in finding solutions to the detected problem: we dealt with this particular problem by enabling the occurrence of the next appropriate actions after such critical sequences. This was done by appropriately weakening the preconditions of the actions to be executed next

7: Conclusions

Unlike the first Production Cell model, in the "Fault-Tolerant Production Cell" failures of electro-mechanical components are of major concern. This requires a control program that is much more complex than the program developed for the original cell, though it follows the same general strategy, i.e. using CA actions where there are safety-critical interactions. In order to develop the required control program, we have conducted an analysis of possible component failures and identified the various ways of detecting these failures. We have used the results of this analysis to guide the design of a system employing what is in fact a very sophisticated exception handling scheme, capable of dealing appropriately even with concurrent occurrences of any of the wide variety of possible failures defined in the FZI.

We have implemented our control system using a Java implementation of a distributed CA action support scheme [12]. (This scheme makes use of the nested multi-threaded transaction facilities provided by the Arjuna transaction support system [9].) During the testing phase and the demonstration of our implementation, all injected device or sensor failures were caught successfully and handled immediately by our control program. Even a previously unknown software bug in the original FZI simulator was also detected by the acceptance test of a CA action and recovered by the retry operation associated with the action. We are now in the stage of collecting experimental data for further dependability and performance-related evaluation.

As a result of the experience we have gained during the process of formalizing and designing this control software, we feel that we now have a much fuller understanding of CA actions and the design issues involved in their implementation. It was very pleasing to confirm that the much more complex requirements of Production Cell II could be satisfied by what was in fact a straightforward though large extension of the approach we had used in Production Cell I [13]. This again enabled all the dependability (and especially the safety) related aspects of the problem to be solved very directly using just the CA action mechanism, despite the need to add very extensive exception handling strategies. It was also pleasing to confirm that the CA action structuring greatly aided not just the design but also the validation of the control program, in this case by model-checking.

In light of the fact that the original Production Cell was the subject of extensive studies using various formal approaches, we should emphasize that to the best of our knowledge our work represents the first and so far only complete formal analysis and validation of a design for the much more complex and realistic Production Cell II. The work in [7] describes a system design for Production Cell II that focuses just on a dynamic and transparent reconfiguration scheme that preserves safety properties. Our design is essentially different, and focuses mainly on cooperation between devices during both normal execution and the process of exception handling. A Formal Risk Analysis approach was developed in [5] for analyzing the run-time behaviour of Production Cell II, and studying how various sensor and actuator faults could affect both system reliability and safety. However, their analysis is not complete, and only uses the elevating rotary table of the Production Cell as an example. In contrast, our analysis is much more comprehensive and complete, including the classification of various failures and the identification of possible failures related to every device in the cell. This analysis leads further to the design of a complete control system and an actual, workable implementation.

The design style we have been using was one that we arrived at through very specific consideration of the problems raised by the Production Cell examples. We now realize that a more methodical and general means of arriving at the design of CA action-based programs is possible, as well as being highly desirable [3].

Acknowledgements

This work was supported by the ESPRIT Long Term Research Project 20072 on "Design for Validation" (DeVa).

References

[1] E. Canver, D. Schwier, A. Romanovsky and J. Xu, "Formal Verification of CAA-based Designs: The Fault-Tolerant Production Cell," 3rd Year Report, *ESPRIT Research Project on Design for Validation*, pp.229-258, Nov. 1998.

[2] S.J. Caughey, M.C. Little and S.K. Shrivastava, "Checked Transactions in an Asynchronous Message Passing Environment," in *1st Intl. Symp. OO RT Distr. Computing*, Kyoto, pp. 222-229, April 1998.

[3] R. DeLemos and A. Romanovsky, "Co-ordinated Atomic Actions in Modelling Object Co-operation," in *1st Intl. Symp. OO RT Distr. Computing*, Kyoto, pp.152-161, April 1998.

[4] C. Lewerentz and T. Lindner. *Formal Development of Reactive Systems: Case Study "Production Cell"*, Springer, 1995.

[5] P. Liggesmeyer and M. Rothfelder, "Improving System Reliability with Automatic Fault Tree Generation," in *28th Int. Symp. Fault-Tolerant Computing*, Germany, pp.90-99, June 1998.

[6] A. Lötzbeyer, "Task Description of a Fault-Tolerant Production Cell," version 1.6, available from *http://www.fzi.de/ prost/projects /korsys/korsys.html*, 1996.

[7] G. Matos and E. White, "Application of Dynamic Reconfiguration in the Design of Fault-Tolerant Production Cell," in *4th Intl. Conf. Configurable Distr. Systems*, Maryland, USA, pp.2-9, 1998.

[8] K.L. McMillan, "Symbolic Model Checking," PhD thesis, Carnegie Mellon University, Kluwer Academic Publishers, 1993.

[9] G.D. Parrington, S.K. Shrivastava, S.M. Wheater and M.C. Little, "The Design and Implementation of Arjuna," *USENIX Computing Systems Journal*, vol.8, no.3, 1995.

[10] J. Vachon, D. Buchs, M. Buffo, G.D.M. Serugendo, B. Randell, A. Romanovsky, R.J. Stroud, and J. Xu, "COALA - A Formal Language for Coordinated Atomic Actions," 3rd Year Report, *ESPRIT Research Project on Design for Validation*, Oct. 1998.

[11] J. Xu, B. Randell, A. Romanovsky, C. Rubira, R.J. Stroud and Z. Wu, "Fault Tolerance in Concurrent Object-Oriented Software through Co-ordinated Error Recovery," In *25th Int. Symp. Fault-Tolerant Computing*, Pasadena, pp.499-508, June 1995.

[12] J. Xu, A. Romanovsky, A. Zorzo, B. Randell, R.J. Stroud and E. Canver, "Developing Control Software for Production Cell II: Failure Analysis and System Design Using CA Actions," 3rd Year Report, *ESPRIT Research Project on Design for Validation*, pp.167-188, Nov. 1998.

[13] A.F. Zorzo, A. Romanovsky, J. Xu, B. Randell. R.J. Stroud, and I.S. Welch, "Using Co-ordinated Atomic Actions to Design Complex Safety-Critical Systems: The Production Cell Case Study," 3rd Year Report, *ESPRIT Research Project on Design for Validation*, pp.139-166, Nov. 1998 (also to appear in *Software — Practice & Experience*.)

The Systematic Improvement of Fault Tolerance in the Rio File Cache

Wee Teck Ng and Peter M. Chen
Computer Science and Engineering Division
Department of Electrical Engineering and Computer Science
University of Michigan
{weeteck,pmchen}@eecs.umich.edu
http://www.eecs.umich.edu/Rio

Abstract

Fault injection is typically used to characterize failures and to validate and compare fault-tolerant mechanisms. However, fault injection is rarely used for all these purposes to guide the design and implementation of a fault-tolerant system. We present a systematic and quantitative approach for using software-implemented fault injection to guide the design and implementation of a fault-tolerant system. Our system design goal is to build a write-back file cache on Intel PCs that is as reliable as a write-through file cache. We follow an iterative approach to improve robustness in the presence of operating system errors. In each iteration, we measure the reliability of the system, analyze the fault symptoms that lead to data corruption, and apply fault-tolerant mechanisms that address the fault symptoms. Our initial system is 13 times less reliable than a write-through file cache. The result of several iterations is a design that is both more reliable (1.9% vs. 3.1% corruption rate) and 5-9 times as fast as a write-through file cache.

1 Introduction

Software-implemented fault injection (SWIFI) is a common technique in the fault-tolerant community [12]. Software fault injection can be used for many purposes, such as comparing the robustness of different systems [24, 29, 16], understanding how systems behave during a fault [8, 4, 15], and validating fault-tolerant mechanisms [3, 11, 21, 6]. However, there are very few case studies that use fault injection for all three of these purposes to guide the design and implementation of a fault-tolerant system.

In this paper, we present a systematic approach for using software-implemented fault injection to guide the design and implementation of a fault-tolerant system, focusing on the file system and file cache modules of the FreeBSD operating system. Our system design goal is to enable data in memory to survive operating system crashes as reliably as data on disk. Specifically, we want to build a software file cache that leaves dirty file data in memory (a write-back file cache), yet loses file data as seldomly as if it wrote data immediately to disk (a write-through file cache). Normal write-back file caches are very fast but are much less reliable than write-through caches. For example, the default write-back file cache in FreeBSD loses data during 39% of operating system crashes, while a write-through file cache loses data during 3% of the crashes. Write-back file caches are less reliable because they are often unable to write dirty file data to disk during a crash.

We follow an iterative approach to improve the robustness of a write-back file cache in the presence of operating system errors. In each iteration, we measure the reliability of the system, analyze the fault symptoms that lead to data corruption, and apply fault-tolerant mechanisms that address the fault symptoms. The result of several iterations is a design that improves reliability by a factor of 21. The resulting write-back file cache is both more reliable (1.9% vs. 3.1% corruption rate) and 5-9 times as fast as a write-through file cache.

This paper makes two main contributions:

- We describe the design and implementation of a reliable write-back file cache on Intel PCs. We call this the *Rio file cache* (Rio stands for RAM I/O). An earlier study showed how to implement a write-back file cache on Digital Alpha workstations that is as robust against software errors as a write-through file cache [7]. The earlier study uses *warm reboot*, which writes file cache data to disk during reboot. Unfortunately, warm reboot relies on several Alpha-specific hardware features, such as a reset button that does not erase memory. In this paper, we use a new software technique called *safe sync* that writes dirty file cache data reliably to disk during the last stage of a crash. Safe sync requires no hardware support and can be used on a wide variety of platforms.
- We present a detailed case study of using software fault injection to systematically improve the robustness of a large software system through several iterations. A key feature of our methodology is using quantitative data to guide the design and implementation of the system. At each iteration, we use fault injection to evaluate the reliability of our design, identify vulnerabilities, and provide quantitative results that help select techniques to address these vulnerabilities. We find that several design iterations are needed to reach our reliability goal, because the first iteration may introduce new bugs or leave secondary vulnerabilities hidden. Another feature of our methodology is that we use fault injection to remove faults on real systems, unlike prior simulation-based fault removal studies [12]. Since we inject faults into real systems, we can accurately characterize the system failure process and fault propagation without the

0-7695-0213-X/99 $10.00 © 1999 IEEE

performance overheads of simulation-based tools.

2 Experimental Methodology

Our experiments are performed on PCs running the FreeBSD 2.2.7 operating system [18]. Each PC has an Intel Pentium processor, 128 MB of memory, a 2 GB IDE hard drive, and the Phoenix 4.0 BIOS. We quantify reliability for a design by injecting various faults into a running operating system, letting it crash and reboot, and measuring how frequently the file system is corrupted. *Corruption rate* is the fraction of crashes that corrupt file data. The following sections describe the faults we inject into the operating system, how we inject faults, and how we detect file system corruption.

2.1 Description of Faults

This section describes the types of faults we inject into the operating system. Our primary goal in designing our fault model is to generate a *wide variety* of operating system crashes. Our models are derived from studies of commercial operating systems and databases [27, 26, 17] and from prior models used in fault-injection studies [4, 15, 14, 7]. The faults we inject range from low-level hardware faults such as flipping bits in memory to high-level software faults such as memory allocation errors. We concentrate on software faults because studies have shown that software has become the dominant cause of system outages [10]. We classify injected faults into three categories: bit flips, low-level software faults, and high-level software faults.

The first category of faults flips random bits in the kernel's address space [4, 14]. We target three areas of the kernel's address space: the *text*, *heap*, and *stack*. These faults are easy to inject, and they cause a variety of different crashes. They are the least realistic of our bugs, however. It is difficult to relate a bit flip with a specific error in programming, and most hardware bit flips would be caught by parity on the data or address bus.

The second category of fault changes individual instructions in the kernel text segment. These faults are intended to approximate the assembly-level manifestation of real C-level programming errors [15]. We corrupt assignment statements by changing the *source* or *destination* register. We corrupt conditional constructs by deleting *branches*. We also delete *random instructions* (both branch and non-branch).

The last and most extensive category of faults imitate specific programming errors in the operating system [26]. These are targeted more at specific programming errors than the previous fault category. We inject an *initialization* fault by deleting instructions responsible for initializing a variable at the start of a procedure [15, 17]. We inject *pointer* corruption by corrupting the addressing bytes of instructions which access operands in memory [26, 17]. We either flip a bit within the addressing-form specifier byte (ModR/M) or the scale, index or base (SIB) byte following the instruction opcode [2]. We do not corrupt the stack pointer registers (i.e. *esp* and *ebp* registers) as these are used to access local variables instead of as a pointer variable. We inject an *allocation management* fault by modifying the kernel's malloc procedure to occasionally free the newly allocated block of memory after a delay of 0-64 ms. Malloc is set to inject this error every 1000-4000 times it is called; this fault occurs approximately every 10 seconds on our system. We inject a *copy overrun* fault by modifying the kernel's data copy procedures to occasionally increase the number of bytes they copies. The length of the overrun is distributed as follows: 50% corrupt one byte; 44% corrupt 2-1024 bytes; 6% corrupt 2-4 KB. This distribution was chosen by starting with the data gathered in [26] and modifying it according to our specific platform and experience. The copy routines are set to inject this error every 1000-4000 times it is called; this fault occurs approximately every 5 seconds on our system. We inject *off-by-one* errors by changing conditions such as > to >=, < to <=, and so on. We mimic common *synchronization* errors by randomly causing the procedures that acquire/free a lock to return without acquiring/freeing the lock. We inject *memory leaks* by modifying free() to occasionally return without freeing the block of memory. We inject *interface errors* by corrupting one of the arguments passed to a procedure.

We collect data on 100 crashes (each using a different random seed) for each of the 15 fault types above for each of the five designs in this paper—this represents about 8 machine-months of continuous operating system crashes. Fault injection cannot mimic the exact behavior of all real-world operating system crashes. However, the wide variety of faults we inject (15 types), the random nature of the faults, and the sheer number of crashes we performed (7500) give us confidence that our experiments cover a wide range of real-world crashes.

2.2 Injecting Faults

Our fault injection tool uses object-code modification to inject bugs into the kernel text. It is embedded into the kernel and, when triggered, will select an instruction in the kernel text and corrupt it. Some fault types, such as memory leaks, are implemented by modifying the relevant kernel routines (e.g. malloc) to occasionally fail when the fault is triggered. The fault trigger and injection location within the kernel text are determined by a random seed. We do not inject fault into the recovery and fault-tolerant code we added into the system.

Unless otherwise stated, we inject 10 faults for each run to increase the chance of triggering a fault. Most crashes occur within 10 seconds from the time the fault was injected. If a fault does not crash the operating system after fifteen minutes, we restart the system and discard the run; this happens about 40% of the time. Note that faults that leave the system running will corrupt data on disk for both write-back and write through file caches, so these runs do not change the relative reliability between file caches.

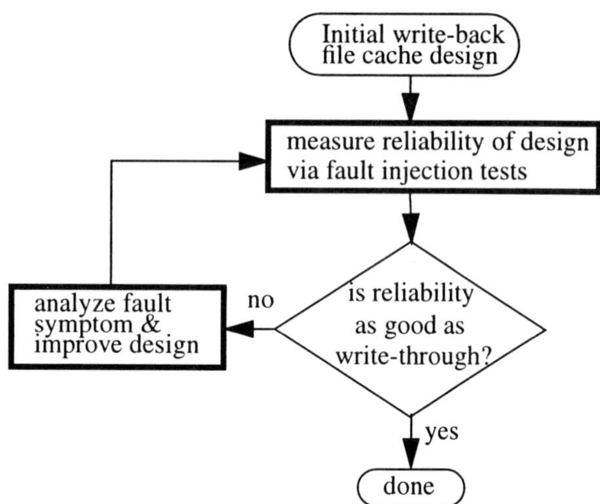

Figure 1: Design Process. The bold boxes represent the stages that use fault injection data to guide the design process.

2.3 Detecting Corruption after a Crash

We run a repeatable, synthetic workload called *memTest* to detect file system corruption. *memTest* generates a repeatable stream of file and directory creations, deletions, reads, and writes, reaching a maximum file set size of 128 MB. Actions and data in *memTest* are controlled by a pseudo-random number generator. After each iteration, *memTest* records its progress in a status file on a network disk that is not affected by the fault injection experiments. After the system crashes, we reboot the system and run *memTest* until it reaches the point when the system crashed. This reconstructs the correct contents of the test directory at the time of the crash, and we then compare the reconstructed, correct contents with the rebooted file system. The experiments are controlled by a host connected to each test system via a serial link. The control host logs relevant data (crash latencies, fault symptoms, etc.) for subsequent analysis.

3 Design Process

We follow an iterative approach, as described in [23], to improve the robustness of a write-back file cache in the presence of operating system errors (Figure 1). In each iteration, we measure the reliability of the system using the approach described in Section 2, analyze the fault symptoms that lead to data corruption, and apply fault-tolerant mechanisms that address the fault symptoms. We use software fault injection at each stage to provide quantitative data to help guide our design. For example, we evaluate the reliability of our system quantitatively to decide if it meets our design goal. We also use the data collected during fault injection to analyze and fix faults. Note that we do not merely fix the faults we ourselves have injected. Rather, we use the bugs we inject to reveal categories of faults, then we fix the entire category.

Our goal is to make Rio (our write-back file cache) as reliable as a write-through file cache. Write-through file caches are considered very reliable against software crashes because they propagate data immediately to disk, and disks are not easily corrupted by operating system crashes [25, 28, 7]. We configure FreeBSD to use a write-through file cache, then measure the corruption rate to be 3.1% using the method described in Section 2. That is, 3.1% of the crashes corrupt some data in the file system. Table 1 summarizes the corruption rate by fault category of all our designs in this paper.

Fault Type	Write-Thru File Cache	Write-Back File Caches			
		Default FreeBSD Sync	Basic Safe Sync	Enhanced Safe Sync	BIOS Safe Sync
text	3	51	7	5	2
stack	0	3	3	2	0
heap	5	28	8	3	1
initialization	10	45	9	7	4
delete random inst.	4	43	8	2	4
dest. reg.	4	42	9	5	2
source reg.	4	43	10	3	1
delete branch	4	51	14	4	5
pointer	3	38	5	4	2
allocation	0	100	5	0	0
copy overrun	4	36	1	3	2
synchronization	0	3	1	0	0
off-by-one	4	59	16	9	3
mem. leak	0	0	0	0	0
interface	1	47	8	3	2
Total of 1500	**46 (3.1%)**	**589 (39%)**	**104 (6.9%)**	**50 (3.3%)**	**28 (1.9%)**

Table 1: Comparing Reliability. This table shows how often each type of fault corrupts data for a write-through file cache (our reliability target) and the four designs for a reliable write-back file cache.

4 Design Iterations

This section describes the four design iterations we went through to arrive at the final system. Each subsection (4.1-4.4) describes the write-back file cache used in a design iteration, presents results from the fault-injection tests on that design, then analyzes the results to select techniques to fix the revealed fault categories.

In all our designs, we modify the FreeBSD file cache in two ways to be a pure write-back file cache. First, FreeBSD normally writes dirty file data to disk every 30 seconds or when a full file block is written. We disable this reliability-induced write-back, so the system only writes data back to disk when dirty blocks are replaced in the file cache. Second, FreeBSD normally limits the amount of dirty file cache data to 10% of available system memory. We increase this limit by allowing dirty file data to migrate from the file cache to the virtual memory system, as is done in memory-mapped file systems [5].

4.1 Design Iteration 1: Default FreeBSD Sync

4.1.1 Design

We start the design process with the default sync used in FreeBSD. Sync refers to the routine that writes dirty file-cache data to disk during a crash. FreeBSD's default sync routine examines all blocks in the file cache and writes dirty blocks to disk using normal file system routines.

4.1.2 Results and Analysis

Unfortunately, the default FreeBSD sync is not very robust during operating system crashes. As shown in Table 1, 39% of crashes corrupted some file system data when using the default FreeBSD sync. This corruption rate is 13 times as high as that of a write-through file cache.

We next examine the corrupted runs in greater detail, focusing on where the faults are injected into the system and how the system crashes. We determine how the system crashes by looking at the crash messages and tracing fault propagation with the aid of the FreeBSD kernel debugger. Our fault-injection tool helps by printing the kernel routine name and location of corrupted code. We use this information to divide the fault symptoms into categories:

- *Hang before sync*: Most data corruptions occur because the system hangs and fails to call the sync routine. Many workstations have a reset key that allows the user to drop the system into the console prompt. The user can then issue a sync command directly or initiate recovery using a user-written routine. But most PCs do not have such a feature, and those that are equipped with a reset switch typically erase memory (including dirty file cache data).
- *Page fault during sync*: Sync often fails because it encounters a page fault while trying to write dirty file cache data to disk. The page fault occurs when the operating system accesses unmapped data or mapped data with the wrong permission settings. It can also happen when the code is invalid or unmapped. The FreeBSD sync routine uses many different kernel routines and data structures (e.g. mounted file system list, vnode data structures, buffer hash list), so this fault is quite common.
- *Buffer locked during sync*: FreeBSD's sync routine obeys the locking protocol used during normal operation. It does not write to disk any file cache blocks that are locked, so data in these blocks are lost.
- *Double fault*: The Pentium processor calls a double-fault handler if it detects an exception while servicing a prior exception [2]. The processor will reset and abandon sync if another exception occurs when the double fault handler is being serviced.
- *File system errors*: Our tool may inject faults into any part of the kernel. Faults that are injected into file system routines often cause data corruption. For example, the file system's write routine might be changed to write to the wrong part of the file. We do not attempt to fix this fault symptom because the write-through file cache is also susceptible to these errors.
- *Device Timeout*: Sync sometimes fails because it experiences repeated device timeouts when writing to the hard drive.
- *Unknown*: A few data corruptions are due to unknown causes. For these corruptions, the sync routine appears to be successful, and the injected bugs appear to be benign. We do not attempt to overcome this problem because of the lack of information and the low frequency of this fault symptom.

Fault Symptom	# of Corruptions	Solutions Used in the Next Design (Section 4.2.1)
hang before sync	268 (17.9%)	software reset key
page fault during sync	163 (10.9%)	registry, safe sync
buffer locked during sync	89 (5.9%)	registry, safe sync
double fault	39 (2.6%)	disable interrupt in safe sync
file system error	25 (1.7%)	
device timeout	3 (0.2%)	
unknown	2 (0.1%)	
Total of 1500	**589 (39.3%)**	

Table 2: Fault Symptoms for Default FreeBSD Sync.

Table 2 summarizes the categories of fault symptoms and some potential solutions we developed (discussed in the next section) to reduce the vulnerability of the system to that fault symptom.

4.2 Design Iteration 2: Basic Safe Sync

4.2.1 Design

A write-back file cache must do two steps to write dirty data back to disk during a crash. First, the system must transfer control to the sync routine. Second, the sync routine must write dirty file data successfully to disk. Most of the corruptions experienced using the default FreeBSD sync fail one of these two steps. *Hang before sync* fails to transfer control to the sync routine during a crash. Most of the other fault symptoms transfer control to sync but experience an error during sync.

We address errors in these two steps separately. First, we must make it more likely that the system will successfully transfer control to the sync routine during a crash. To fix *hang before sync*, we use a software reset key that calls sync when pressed. We modify the low-level keyboard interrupt handler of FreeBSD to call sync whenever it detects a certain key sequence (e.g. control-alt-delete). This addresses the dominant fault symptom in Table 2.

Second, we must make it more likely that the sync routine, once called, will write dirty file data successfully to disk. Default FreeBSD sync fails this step because it depends on many parts of the kernel. The default FreeBSD sync calls many routines and uses many different data structures. Sync fails if *any* of the routines or data structures are corrupted. To make sync more robust, we must minimize the scope of the system that it depends on.

To minimize data dependencies, we implement informational redundancy [13] by creating a new data structure called the *registry*. The registry contains all information needed to find, identify, and write all file cache blocks. For each block in the file cache, the registry contains the physical memory address, file ID (device number and inode number), file offset, and size. The registry allows sync to operate without using previously needed kernel data structures, such as file system and disk allocation data. The registry is wired in memory to reduce the likelihood of page faults during sync. Registry information changes relatively infrequently during normal operation, so the overhead of maintaining it is low.

We replace FreeBSD's default sync routine with a new routine (called *safe sync*) that uses the registry when writing data to disk. Safe sync examines all valid entries in the registry and writes dirty file cache data directly to disk. By using information in the registry, safe sync does not depend on normal file system routines or data structures. Safe sync also takes additional precautions to increase its chances of success. First, safe sync operates below the locking protocol to avoid being stymied by a locked buffer. Second, safe sync disables interrupts to reduce the likelihood of double faults while writing to disk.

In addition to adding the registry and using a new sync routine, we also use the virtual memory system to protect file cache data from wild stores [7]. We turn off the write-permission bits in the page table for file cache pages, causing the system to generate protection violations for unauthorized stores. File cache procedures must enable the write-permission bit in the page table before writing a page and disable writes afterwards.

4.2.2 Results and Analysis

Fault injection tests on the new design show substantial improvement over the default FreeBSD sync. Table 1 shows that the new design has a corruption rate of 6.9%, which is six times better than the default FreeBSD sync. However, it still has twice as many corruptions as a write-through file cache. Table 3 breaks down the fault symptoms for our current design. The fault symptoms are very similar to those in Table 2, but the corruption rates are reduced significantly due to the fault-tolerant measures introduced in Section 4.2.1. We analyze the fault symptoms from this design to see how we can make safe sync more robust in the next iteration:

Fault Symptom	# of Corruptions	Solutions Used in the Next Design (Section 4.3.1)
hang before sync	45 (3.0%)	watchdog timer, no print
file system error	24 (1.6%)	
page fault during sync	18 (1.2%)	read-only text, private stack, restore segment registers
data corruption	11 (0.7%)	fix VM protection
double fault	4 (0.3%)	private stack
device timeout	2 (0.1%)	
Total of 1500	**104 (6.9%)**	

Table 3: Fault Symptoms for Basic Safe Sync.

- *Hang before sync*: Table 3 shows that the reset button reduces the corruption rates substantially from the default FreeBSD sync (from 17.9% to 3.0%). We examine the remaining cases and the keyboard interrupt handler to determine what causes the reset key to fail. The dominant reason is that FreeBSD sometimes masks keyboard interrupts. If the system hangs while keyboard interrupts are masked, the reset key will not transfer control to safe sync. To fix this, we add a watchdog timer to the system timer interrupt handler [13]. The system timer interrupt handler watches for pending keyboard interrupts and calls safe sync if the keyboard interrupt does not get serviced for a long time. For five of the corruptions, the fault was injected into the terminal output routine, and safe sync failed when it tried to print some debugging information. We fix this fault by disabling debugging print statements during safe sync.
- *File system error*: Again, we do not attempt to fix this fault symptom because the write-through file cache is also susceptible to these errors. Note that the corruption rate for file system errors is similar between Table 2 and Table 3. The slight differences are due to the non-determinism inherent to testing a complex, timing-dependent system.
- *Page fault during sync*: This fault symptom occurs for a variety of reasons, and we develop a variety of solutions to fix it. For example, some faults corrupt the Intel segment registers that are used by some instructions in safe sync. To fix this error, we can re-initialize the segment registers to their correct value at the beginning of safe sync. Other faults cause wild stores to write over kernel code. To fix this error, we can map the kernel code as read-only (of course, our fault injector can still modify kernel code).
- *Data corruption*: Some faults corrupted data in the file cache before crashing the system. For these runs, safe sync completed successfully but wrote out the corrupted data. While investigating the source of this corruption, we uncovered a bug in FreeBSD's protection code that sometimes allowed wild stores to overwrite the file cache and kernel code.
- *Double fault*: This bug occurs when part of the stack segment is unmapped by the injected fault but the TLB is not invalidated. The system will continue to function until the stack pointer advances beyond the valid page in the TLB, and encounter multiple page faults when it tries to fault in subsequent pages from the bogus stack. To fix this, we pre-allocate a stack for safe sync during

Fault Symptom	# of Corruptions	Solutions Used in the Next Design (Section 4.4.1)
hang before sync	21 (1.4%)	BIOS I/O, real-mode addressing
file system error	20 (1.3%)	
page fault during sync	4 (0.3%)	real-mode addressing
device timeout	3 (0.2%)	BIOS I/O
data corruption	2 (0.1%)	
Total of 1500	**50 (3.3%)**	

Table 4: Fault Symptoms For Enhanced Safe Sync.

bootup and wire it in memory. Safe sync's first action is to switch to this private stack.

4.3 Design Iteration 3: Enhanced Safe Sync

4.3.1 Design

Our next design improves on the basic safe sync design from the last iteration using the fixes suggested in Section 4.2.2. First, we add a watchdog timer to call safe sync if the system hangs with keyboard interrupts disabled. Second, we disable print statements during safe sync to remove dependencies on the print routines. Third, we re-initialize the segment registers to their proper value. Fourth, we map the kernel code as read-only and fix a bug in FreeBSD's protection code. Finally, we switch to a pre-allocated, wired stack at the beginning of safe sync to remove dependencies on the system stack.

4.3.2 Results and Analysis

We conduct fault injection tests on the new design and find that it has a corruption rate of 3.3%, versus 6.9% for the basic safe sync design of iteration 2. Enhanced safe sync is nearly as reliable as a write-through file cache. Table 4 breaks down the fault symptoms of our current design.

There are two basic dependencies remaining in our system. First, all kernel code, including safe sync, runs in virtual-addressing mode with paging enabled [2], which uses virtual addresses to access code and data. Because safe sync accesses virtual addresses, it depends on the FreeBSD virtual memory code and data (such as the doubly linked address map entries [20]). To fix this dependency, we must configure the processor to use physical addresses during safe sync.

Second, safe sync uses the low-level kernel device drivers to write data to disk. The FreeBSD disk device drivers are quite complex, and there is no simple disk device driver routine to initialize the device driver state or reset the hard drive and disk controller card. Our safe sync code can thus hang or timeout whenever it access the disk. To remove this dependency, we must bypass the complex device driver for a simpler disk interface.

4.4 Design Iteration 4: BIOS Safe Sync

4.4.1 Design

In our final design, we want to remove dependencies on the virtual memory system and device drivers. We remove dependencies on the virtual memory system by switching the processor to use physical addresses [2]. We remove dependencies on the kernel device drivers by using the BIOS interface to the disk [9]. BIOS (Basic Input/Output Service) routines are implemented in the firmware of the I/O controller. Both physical addressing and BIOS routines have limited features and are used normally to load the operating system from disk during system boot. Modern operating systems like FreeBSD use virtual addressing and replace the BIOS with their own device drivers.

Our final design replaces the safe sync code used in design iteration 3. The new safe sync procedure is summarized below (the full source code is available at http://www.eecs.umich.edu/Rio):

- *Part 1: Initial setup*: we followed the instructions outlined in Section 8.8.1 of [2], which includes setting up a linearly mapped segments for data and code, setting the global (code/data) and interrupt descriptor table registers for real-mode operation, and making a long jump to the real-mode switch code.
- *Part 2: Mode switching*: the real-mode switch code disables paging, loads the segment registers with real-mode segments, and clears the paging enable bit before making a jump to the real-mode safe sync code. This jump brings the processor to real-mode operation.
- *Part 3: Real-mode setup*: BIOS safe sync begins by initializing the remaining segment registers, setting the interrupt controllers to real-mode operation [1], and initializing the video console and disk controller using the BIOS interface [9]. The rest of BIOS safe sync is fairly straightforward and is generated from the C version of enhanced safe sync. We modify the resulting assembly code by adding address/data overrides [2] and using a large data segment (i.e. big real-mode [22]) to access data beyond the first 1 MB of memory. During sync, we copy the file cache data into the lower 1 MB of memory because the BIOS disk interface uses 16-bit segment addressing.

Part 1 of BIOS safe sync is a C function and can be invoked directly by the FreeBSD kernel. The rest of BIOS safe sync code is written in assembly and is not accessible to the FreeBSD kernel, because it resides in unmapped physical memory pages that are hidden from the FreeBSD page allocator.

4.4.2 Results and Analysis

We conduct fault injection tests on our BIOS safe sync. Table 5 breaks down the fault symptoms for our latest design. The overall corruption rate is 1.9%, which is 40% more reliable than a write-through file cache. We speculate that Rio is able to achieve higher reliability than a write-through file cache because the virtual memory protection

Fault Symptom	# of Corruptions	Possible Solutions
file system errors	17 (1.1%)	
hang before sync	5 (0.3%)	hardware reset
data corruption	4 (0.3%)	
device timeout	2 (0.1%)	warm reboot
Total of 1500	**28 (1.9%)**	

Table 5: Fault Symptoms For BIOS Safe Sync.

File System	cp+rm	Andrew
UFS	54.0 seconds	1.9 seconds
write-through file cache	186.3 seconds	6.7 seconds
write-back file cache (Rio)	**19.9 seconds**	**1.3 seconds**

Table 6: Performance Comparison. All performance measurements were made on a PC with a 400 MHz Pentium-II processor, 128 MB of 100 MHz SDRAM, and a IBM DCAS-34330W SCSI disk (with the disk write-cache enabled).

described in Section 4.2.1 can protect the file cache (and thus indirectly protect the disk) from wild stores.

It may be possible to improve upon BIOS safe sync by adding a hardware reset key and modifying the PC firmware and motherboard to not initialize memory on reset/reboot. This would allow the system to do a complete reset, then to perform a warm reboot as was done in [7]. Doing so should fix the remaining hangs before sync and device timeouts, but it would incur significant system cost.

5 Discussion

We would like to address the scalability, portability, and cost of our design approach.

- *Scalability*: Our target system is fairly representative of a medium-size software development project. The relevant operating system code (file system, VM, interrupt, etc.) spans approximately 40 files and 20,000 lines of code. We added 3 files and 2000 lines of code. The development effort took one man-year. This includes the substantial time it took to understand FreeBSD and the Intel PC architecture (microarchitecture, assembly language, system BIOS). Since our experimental setup was fully automated and we had sufficient machines to run the experiments in parallel, most of our time was devoted to uncovering fault symptoms and debugging code. The analysis process was largely manual, though we wrote several tools to expedite this process. Our design approach is applicable to many software development projects as long as there are enough resources to perform the fault injection experiments and sufficient expertise to implement the fault-tolerant mechanisms.
- *Portability*: We demonstrated our design methodology on FreeBSD running on Intel PCs. We have also tried this approach on a limited scale when implementing a reliable write-back file cache on Digital Alpha workstations [7] and the Postgres database [19]. We are confident that our approach is portable to other systems.
- *Cost*: Our design took four iterations, requiring 8 machine-months of testing. We tackled the dominant fault symptoms in the first iteration, with diminishing returns on successive iterations. Using software fault injection provided quantitative data on when our system reached our reliability goal. For example, we could have stopped after enhanced safe sync, because its corruption rate was statistically indistinguishable from a write-through file cache. Choosing a reliability goal is a tradeoff between design cost and application requirements.

6 Performance

Table 6 compares the performance of our reliable write-back file cache (Rio) with different Unix file systems (UFS), each providing different guarantees on when data is made permanent. UFS is the default FreeBSD Unix file system. It writes data asynchronously to disk when 64 KB of data has been collected, when the user writes non-sequentially, or when the update daemon flushes dirty file data (once every 30 seconds). UFS writes metadata synchronously to disk to enforce ordering constraints. The write-through file cache writes data and metadata synchronously to disk. The last row shows the performance of the Rio write-back file cache.

We run two workloads, cp+rm and Andrew. cp+rm recursively copies then removes the FreeBSD source tree (23 MB). Andrew models a software development workload. All results represent an average of 20 runs.

Table 6 shows that our Rio file cache prototype is 5-9 times as fast as a write-through file cache. It is also 1.5-2.7 times as fast as the standard Unix file system. Rio is roughly equivalent in reliability to a write-through file cache. Both Rio and a write-through file cache are more reliable than standard UFS. UFS loses up to 30 seconds of data on a crash, while Rio and a write-through file cache typically lose no data on a crash.

7 Conclusions

We have presented a systematic and quantitative approach for using software-implemented fault injection to guide the design and implementation of a fault-tolerant system. Our goal was to build a write-back file cache on Intel PCs that was as reliable as a write-through file cache. We followed an iterative approach to improve the robustness of a write-back file cache in the presence of operating system errors. In each iteration, we measured the reliability of the system, analyzed the fault symptoms that led to data corruption, and applied fault-tolerant mechanisms that addressed the fault symptoms. The result of several iterations was a design that improved reliability by a factor of 21. The resulting write-back file cache is both more reliable (1.9% vs. 3.1% corruption rate) and 5-9 times as fast as a write-through file cache.

8 Acknowledgments

This research was supported in part by NSF grant MIP-9521386 and Intel Technology for Education 2000. Peter Chen was also supported by an NSF CAREER Award (MIP-9624869).

9 References

[1] *Intel 82371AB PCI ISA IDE Xcelerator (PIIX4) Datasheet.* Intel Corporation, 1997.

[2] *Intel Architecture Software Developer's Manual: Volume 1-3.* Intel Corporation, 1997.

[3] Jean Arlat, Martine Aguera, Louis Amat, Yves Crouzet, Jean-Charles Fabre, Jean-Claude Laprie, Eliane Martins, and David Powell. Fault Injection for Dependability Validation: A Methodology and Some Applications. *IEEE Transactions on Software Engineering*, 16(2):166–182, February 1990.

[4] James H. Barton, Edward W. Czeck, Zary Z. Segall, and Daniel P. Siewiorek. Fault injection experiments using FIAT. *IEEE Transactions on Computers*, 39(4):575–582, April 1990.

[5] A. Bensoussan, C.T. Clingen, and R.C. Daley. The Multics Virtual Memory: Concepts and Design. *Communications of the ACM*, 15(5):308–318, May 1972.

[6] Joao Carreira, Henrique Madeira, and Joao Gabriel Silva. Xception: A Technique for the Experimental Evaluation of Dependability in Modern Computers. *IEEE Transactions on Software Engineering*, 24(2):125–136, February 1998.

[7] Peter M. Chen, Wee Teck Ng, Subhachandra Chandra, Christopher M. Aycock, Gurushankar Rajamani, and David Lowell. The Rio File Cache: Surviving Operating System Crashes. In *Proceedings of the 1996 International Conference on Architectural Support for Programming Languages and Operating Systems (ASPLOS)*, pages 74–83, October 1996.

[8] R. Chillarege and N. S. Bowen. Understanding Large System Failure–A Fault Injection Experiment. In *Proceedings of the 1989 International Symposium on Fault-Tolerant Computing (FTCS)*, pages 356–363, 1989.

[9] Frank Van Gilluwe. *The Undocumented PC: A Programmer's Guide to I/O, CPUs, and Fixed Memory Areas.* Addison-Wesley Developer Press, 1997.

[10] Jim Gray. A Census of Tandem System Availability between 1985 and 1990. *IEEE Transactions on Reliability*, 39(4), October 1990.

[11] John Hudak, Byung-Hoon Suh, Dan Siewiorek, and Zary Segall. Evaluation and Comparison of Fault-Tolerant Software Techniques. *IEEE Transactions on Reliability*, 42(2), June 1993.

[12] Ravishankar K. Iyer. Experimental Evaluation. In *Proceedings of the 1995 International Symposium on Fault-Tolerant Computing*, pages 115–132, July 1995.

[13] Barry W. Johnson. *Design and Analysis of Fault-Tolerant Digital Systems.* Addison-Wesley Publishing Co., 1989.

[14] Ghani A. Kanawati, Nasser A. Kanawati, and Jacob A. Abraham. FERRARI: A Flexible Software-Based Fault and Error Injection System. *IEEE Transactions on Computers*, 44(2):248–260, February 1995.

[15] Wei-Lun Kao, Ravishankar K. Iyer, and Dong Tang. FINE: A Fault Injection and Monitoring Environment for Tracing the UNIX System Behavior under Faults. *IEEE Transactions on Software Engineering*, 19(11):1105–1118, November 1993.

[16] Nathan P. Kropp, Philip J. Koopman, and Daniel P. Siewiorek. Automated Robustness Testing of Off-the_shelf Software Components. In *Proceedings of the 1998 Symposium on Fault-Tolerant Computing (FTCS)*, June 1998.

[17] Inhwan Lee and Ravishankar K. Iyer. Faults, Symptoms, and Software Fault Tolerance in the Tandem GUARDIAN Operating System. In *Proceedings of the 1993 International Symposium on Fault-Tolerant Computing (FTCS)*, pages 20–29, 1993.

[18] Marshall Kirk McKusick, Keith Bostic, Michael J. Karels, and John S. Quarterman. *The Design and Implementation of the 4.4BSD Operating System.* Addison-Wesley Publishing Company, 1996.

[19] Wee Teck Ng and Peter M. Chen. Integrating Reliable Memory in Databases. In *Proceedings of the 1997 International Conference on Very Large Data Bases (VLDB)*, pages 76–85, August 1997.

[20] Richard F. Rashid, Jr. Avadis Tevanian, Michael Young, David Golub, Robert Baron, David Black, Jr. William J. Bolosky, and Jonathan Chew. Machine-Independent Virtual Memory Management for Paged Uniprocessor and Multiprocessor Architectures. *IEEE Transactions on Computers*, 37(8):896–908, August 1988.

[21] Mario Zenha Rela, Henrique Madeira, and Joao G. Silva. Experimental Evaluation of the Fail-Silent Behavior in Programs with Consistency Checks. In *Proceedings of the 1996 Symposium on Fault-Tolerant Computing (FTCS)*, June 1996.

[22] Tom Shanley. *Protected Mode Software Architecture.* Addison-Wesley Developer Press, 1996.

[23] Daniel P. Siewiorek. *Reliable Computer Systems: Design and Evaluation.* A K Peters, 1998.

[24] Daniel P. Siewiorek, John J. Hudak, Byung-Hoon Suh, and Zary Segal. Development of a Benchmark to Measure System Robustness. In *Proceedings of the 1993 International Symposium on Fault-Tolerant Computing*, pages 88–97, June 1993.

[25] Abraham Silberschatz and Peter B. Galvin. *Operating System Concepts.* Addison-Wesley, 1994.

[26] Mark Sullivan and R. Chillarege. Software Defects and Their Impact on System Availability–A Study of Field Failures in Operating Systems. In *Proceedings of the 1991 International Symposium on Fault-Tolerant Computing*, June 1991.

[27] Mark Sullivan and Ram Chillarege. A Comparison of Software Defects in Database Management Systems and Operating Systems. In *Proceedings of the 1992 International Symposium on Fault-Tolerant Computing*, pages 475–484, July 1992.

[28] Andrew S. Tanenbaum. *Distributed Operating Systems.* Prentice-Hall, 1995.

[29] Timothy K. Tsai, Ravishankar K. Iyer, and Doug Jewett. An Approach towards Benchmarking of Fault-Tolerant Commercial Systems. In *Proceedings of the 1996 Symposium on Fault-Tolerant Computing (FTCS)*, June 1996.

AR-SMT: A Microarchitectural Approach to Fault Tolerance in Microprocessors

Eric Rotenberg
Computer Sciences Department
University of Wisconsin - Madison
ericro@cs.wisc.edu

Abstract

This paper speculates that technology trends pose new challenges for fault tolerance in microprocessors. Specifically, severely reduced design tolerances implied by gigaherz clock rates may result in frequent and arbitrary transient faults. We suggest that existing fault-tolerant techniques -- system-level, gate-level, or component-specific approaches -- are either too costly for general purpose computing, overly intrusive to the design, or insufficient for covering arbitrary logic faults. An approach in which the microarchitecture itself provides fault tolerance is required.

We propose a new time redundancy fault-tolerant approach in which a program is duplicated and the two redundant programs simultaneously run on the processor. The technique exploits several significant microarchitectural trends to provide broad coverage of transient faults and restricted coverage of permanent faults. These trends are simultaneous multithreading, control flow and data flow prediction, *and* hierarchical processors -- *all of which are intended for higher performance, but which can be easily leveraged for the specified fault tolerance goals. The overhead for achieving fault tolerance is low, both in terms of performance and changes to the existing microarchitecture. Detailed simulations of five of the SPEC95 benchmarks show that executing two redundant programs on the fault-tolerant microarchitecture takes only 10% to 30% longer than running a single version of the program.*

1. Introduction

The commercial success of general purpose computers, from personal computers to servers and multiprocessors, can be attributed to the proliferation of high performance single-chip microprocessors. Both *technology advances* -- circuit speed and density improvements -- and *microarchitecture innovations* -- exploiting the parallelism inherent in sequential programs -- fuel the rapid growth in microprocessor performance that sustains general purpose computing. And interestingly, both technology and microarchitectural trends have implications to microprocessor fault tolerance.

Technology-driven performance improvements will inevitably pose new challenges for fault tolerance in microprocessors [1,2]. In particular, there may come a time when clock rates and densities are so high that the chip is prone to *frequent, arbitrary transient faults* [2]. High clock rate designs require (1) small voltage swings for fast switching and power considerations, and (2) widespread use of high performance, but relatively undisciplined, circuit design techniques, e.g. dynamic logic. This combination is problematic because dynamic logic is susceptible to noise and crosstalk, and low voltage levels at charged nodes only make it more so. Pushing the technology envelope may even compromise conservative, static circuit designs, due to *reduced tolerances in general* (consider, for example, the difficulty in managing clock skew in gigaherz chips).

Specialized fault-tolerant techniques, such as error correcting codes (ECC) for on-chip memories [3] and Recomputing with Shifted Operands (RESO) for ALUs [4,5], do not adequately cover arbitrary logic faults characteristic of this environment. And while self-checking logic techniques [6,7] can provide general coverage, chip area and performance goals may preclude applying self-checking logic globally (for example, integrating self-checking into the design methodology and cell libraries). Finally, system-level fault tolerance, in the form of redundant processors, is perhaps too costly for small general purpose computers.

Therefore, we propose a *microarchitecture-based fault-tolerant approach*. That is, instead of perpetuating the rigid separation between computer architecture and fault tolerance, broad coverage of transient faults, with low to moderate performance impact, can be achieved by exploiting microarchitectural techniques -- techniques that are already incorporated in the microprocessor for performance reasons.

In this paper, we propose and evaluate a time redundancy fault-tolerant approach called *Active-stream/Redundant-stream Simultaneous Multithreading*, or AR-SMT. AR-SMT exploits several recent microarchitectural trends to provide low-overhead, broad coverage of transient faults, and restricted coverage of some permanent faults.

1.1. AR-SMT time redundancy

Time redundancy is a fault-tolerant technique in which a computation is performed multiple times on the same hardware [4,8]. This technique is cheaper than other fault-tolerant solutions that use some form of hardware redundancy, because it does not replicate hardware. Of course, simple time redundancy can only detect transient faults that are present during one or more of the redundant computations, but not all of them. Frequent and relatively short-lived transient faults are the primary focus of this paper, and therefore time redundancy is a viable approach. (However, detection of long-lived transient faults and some permanent faults are also addressed in our proposal.)

The disadvantage of time redundancy is the performance degradation caused by repetition of tasks. In a general purpose computer, full programs are the tasks to be performed. If we assume 2x redundancy, *program-level time redundancy* effectively doubles the execution time of a program because the same program is run twice back-to-back, as shown in Figure 1(a).

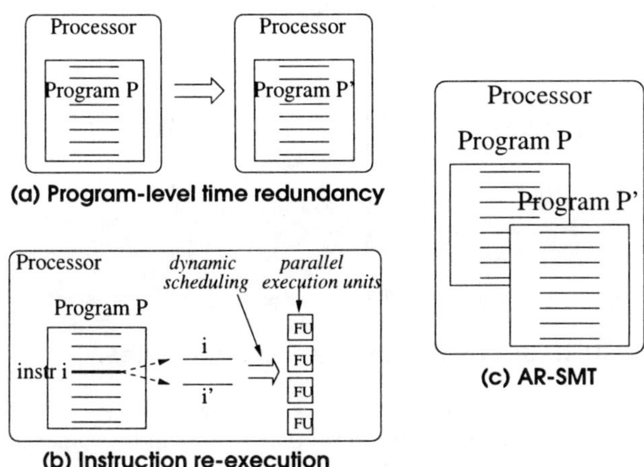

FIGURE 1. Time redundancy techniques.

Instruction re-execution [5] addresses the performance degradation caused by time redundancy. With instruction re-execution, the program is not explicitly duplicated. Rather, when an instruction reaches the execution stage of the processor pipeline, two copies of the instruction are formed and issued to the execution units (Figure 1(b)). Because instructions are duplicated within the processor itself, the processor has flexible control over the scheduling of redundant computations. Dynamic scheduling logic combined with a highly parallel execution core allows the processor to "scavenge" idle execution cycles and execution units to perform the redundant computations. This is possible because there are not always enough independent operations in the program to fully utilize the parallel resources. That is, *dynamically scheduled superscalar processors* [9] are designed for the irregularity of instruction-level parallelism in ordinary, sequential programs, and consequently the peak parallelism supported by the microarchitecture is greater than sustained parallelism of programs.

The downside of instruction re-execution is that it provides limited hardware coverage. Only a *single stage* of a complex processor pipeline is conceptually duplicated: the functional units, i.e. ALUs. In modern superscalar processors, this comprises only a fraction of the overall complexity of the chip.

AR-SMT combines the full processor coverage of program-level time redundancy with the performance advantages of instruction re-execution. In AR-SMT, *two explicit copies of the program run concurrently on the same processor resources*, as shown in Figure 1(c). The two copies are treated as completely independent programs, each having its own state or program context. Consequently, as with program-level time redundancy, the entire pipeline of the processor is conceptually duplicated, providing broad coverage of the chip. The performance advantages of instruction re-execution are retained, however, due to the concurrent sharing of processor resources by the two program threads. This technique is made possible by a recent microarchitecture innovation called *simultaneous multithreading (SMT)* [10,11]. SMT leverages the fine-grain scheduling flexibility and highly parallel microarchitecture of superscalar processors. As we mentioned before, often there are phases of a single program that do not fully utilize the microarchitecture, so sharing the processor resources among multiple programs will increase overall utilization. Improved utilization reduces the total time required to execute all program threads, despite possibly slowing down single thread performance. In AR-SMT, half of the program threads happen to be duplicates for detecting transient faults.

AR-SMT is an example of exploiting the microarchitecture, in this case simultaneous multithreading, to achieve fault tolerance. In the following two sections, we first describe the basic mechanisms behind AR-SMT, and then point out other microarchitecture trends that are exploited for (1) reducing the performance overhead of time redundancy even further and (2) improving fault coverage.

1.2. Basic operation of AR-SMT

Figure 2 shows an abstraction of AR-SMT. The solid arrow represents the dynamic instruction stream of the original program thread, called the *active stream* (A-stream). As instructions from the A-stream are fetched and executed, and their results committed to the program's state, the results of each instruction are also pushed onto a FIFO queue called the *Delay Buffer*. Results include modifications to the program counter (PC) by branches and any modifications to both registers and memory.

A second *redundant instruction stream* (R-stream), represented with a dashed arrow in Figure 2, lags behind the A-stream by no more than the length of the Delay Buffer. The A-stream and R-stream are simultaneously processed using the existing SMT microarchitecture. As the R-stream is fetched and executed, its committed results are compared to those in the Delay Buffer. A fault is detected if the comparison fails, and furthermore, the committed state of the R-stream can be used as a checkpoint for recovery.

The Delay Buffer ensures time redundancy: the A-stream and R-stream copies of an instruction are executed at different times, in general providing good transient fault coverage. A fault may cause an error in the A-stream, the R-stream, or both. An error in the A-stream is detected after some delay through the Delay Buffer. An error in the R-stream is detected before committing the first affected instruction. A fault may induce errors in both streams, in which case only the R-stream plays a role in detection.

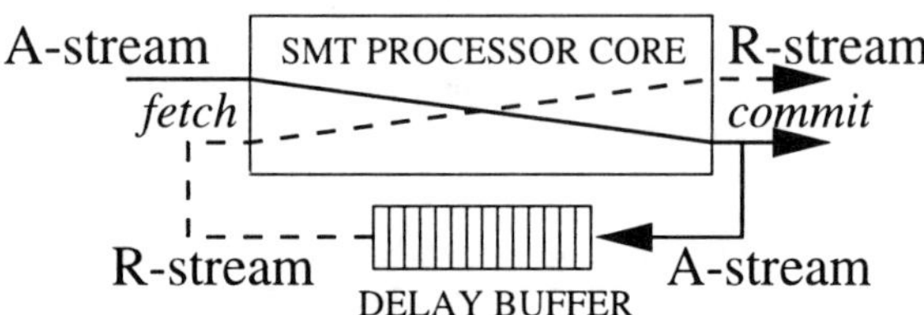

FIGURE 2. High level view of AR-SMT.

1.3. Exploiting other microarchitecture trends

The AR-SMT model exploits simultaneous multithreading to implement time redundancy. We now describe two additional microarchitectural trends that can be leveraged for both higher performance and improved fault tolerance.

1.3.1. Improved performance through control and data "prediction". The order in which instructions may execute is dictated by *data dependences* and *control dependences* among instructions. If instruction *i* produces a value that is used by instruction *j*, *j* cannot execute until *i* completes. This is called a data dependence. Likewise, branch instructions introduce control dependences: the next instructions to be fetched after a branch instruction depends on the outcome of the branch instruction.

High performance processors attempt to execute multiple instructions in parallel each cycle. Unfortunately, *instruction-level parallelism* is limited or obscured by both control and data dependences in the program. Consider the sequence of five instructions shown in Figure 3(a). Instructions i2 through i4 all have a data dependence with an immediately preceding instruction, which means they must execute serially as shown in Figure 3(b). Furthermore, although instruction i5 has no data dependences, it can not be fetched until the outcome of branch i4 is known. The control dependence with i4 is a severe performance penalty because it both serializes execution *and* exposes some number of cycles to fetch instruction i5 into the processor, labeled in the diagram as "pipeline latency".

Control dependences are typically alleviated with branch prediction [12,13]: the outcomes of branches can be predicted with high accuracy based on the previous history of branch outcomes. Branch prediction allows the processor to fetch instructions ahead of the execution pipeline, so i5 can execute as early as cycle 1 if the branch i4 is predicted to be taken, as shown in Figure 3(c).

More recently, researchers have even suggested predicting data values [14,15,16]. At instruction fetch time, the source operands of instructions are predicted. In this way, they do not have to wait for values from their producer instructions -- instructions may execute in parallel under the assumption that the predicted values are correct. In Figure 3(c), values for r1, r2, and r3 are predicted, so instructions i1 through i4 may execute in parallel during cycle 1. In cycle 2, the computed results produced during cycle 1 are used to *validate* the predicted values for r1, r2, and r3 (special recovery actions are required in the event of mispredictions [14,17]).

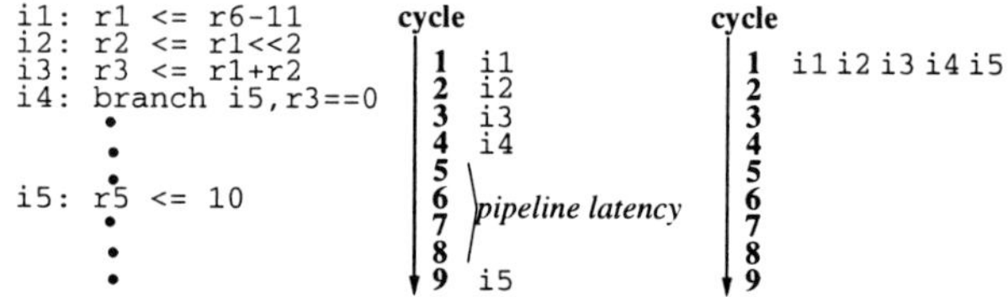

(a) program segment (b) base schedule (c) with prediction

FIGURE 3. Control and data dependences.

With both control and data prediction, the processor exposes more instruction-level parallelism and speeds execution of the program. AR-SMT can exploit this same concept to minimize the execution time of the R-stream, because *the Delay Buffer contains data and control information from the first run of the program* (i.e. results from the A-stream). The state in the Delay Buffer provides the R-stream with *perfect* control and data flow prediction: instructions can execute essentially free from all control and data dependences. Note that this does not reduce fault coverage of the processor in any way, since instructions still pass through all stages of the pipeline. They simply pass through the pipeline quicker.

Furthermore, *the hardware used for validating data and control predictions is in fact the hardware for detecting faults.* Normally, predictions are compared with computed results to detect mispredictions. In the case of the R-stream, these comparators validate so-called "predictions" obtained from the A-stream against values computed by the R-stream. If the validation fails, then a transient fault must have occurred in either stream.

In summary, existing prediction techniques can be leveraged to reduce the overhead of time redundancy, both in terms of performance and hardware: "predictions" from the Delay Buffer speed execution of the R-stream, and existing validation hardware is used for fault detection logic.

1.3.2. Improved fault tolerance through hierarchy and replication. In the search for ever-increasing amounts of instruction-level parallelism, high performance processors have become exceedingly complex. There has been a recent interest among researchers to reduce complexity by dividing up large, centralized structures and wide datapaths [18,19,20,21,17]. By reducing complexity in an intelligent way, a high clock rate can be achieved without sacrificing the exploitation of instruction-level parallelism.

Complexity can be reduced through hierarchy [21]. Instead of having one large processing structure work on, say, 128 or 256 individual instructions at a time, 8 smaller processing elements can each work on 16 or 32 instructions.

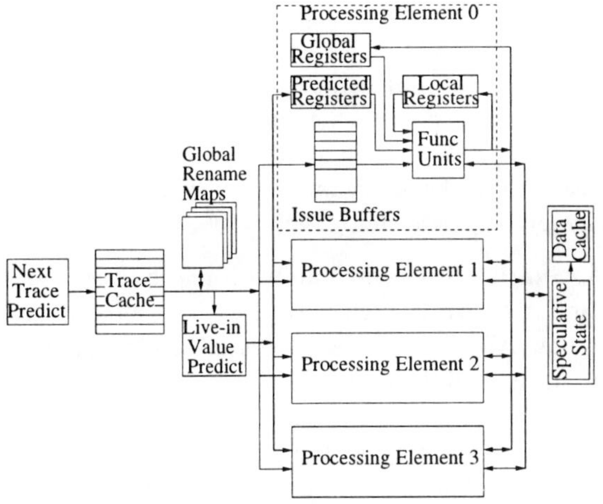

FIGURE 4. A trace processor [17].

A *trace processor* [17], shown in Figure 4, is one example of a hierarchical microarchitecture. It dynamically partitions the instruction stream into larger units of work called *traces*. A trace is a dynamic sequence of instructions; typical trace lengths are 16 or 32 instructions, and there can be any number of branches within a trace. Traces are considered the fundamental unit of work, and the processor is organized as such. In particular, the execution resources are distributed among multiple processing elements (PEs), each PE resembling a moderate-sized superscalar processor. Traces are explicitly predicted and fetched as a unit (i.e. trace prediction instead of individual branch prediction), and subsequently dispatched to a PE. Each PE is allocated a single trace to execute. Inter-trace data dependences are predicted to enhance the parallel processing of traces.

It is beyond the scope of this paper to discuss the complexity and performance advantages of trace processors: suffice it to say that sequencing and executing the program at the higher level of traces is potentially more efficient than processing instructions individually. However, we can point out one particular advantage this microarchitecture offers for AR-SMT: *the replicated PEs inherently provide a coarse level of hardware redundancy.* We propose detecting permanent faults within PEs by guaranteeing that a trace in the A-stream and its corresponding redundant trace in the R-stream execute on different PEs. This requires storing a few extra bits of information per trace in the Delay Buffer to indicate which PE executed the trace. Furthermore, the PE allocation constraint imposed on the R-stream does not degrade performance with respect to arbitrary allocation. If only one PE is currently free, but it cannot be used by the R-stream because it is the same PE on which the trace first executed, then the *next* PE to become available is guaranteed to be a different PE; meanwhile, the A-stream can make use of the available PE.

The coarse level of hardware redundancy is especially appealing for *re-configuring* the trace processor in the event of a permanent PE fault. It is easier to remove a PE from the resource pool than to remove an individual instruction buffer from among hundreds of closely-integrated buffers. The small number of PEs and the fact that PEs are relatively isolated from each other (modularity) makes re-configuration conceptually simple.

1.4. Related work

A spectrum of time redundancy techniques is presented in [22]. The key realization is that all time redundancy approaches essentially duplicate the program and they differ only in the granularity at which redundant computation is *interleaved.* This paper is the culmination of that earlier research.

Recently and independently, the Stanford ROAR project [23] proposed *Dependable Adaptive Computing Systems.* The architecture is composed of a general purpose computer and a reconfigurable FPGA coprocessor, and encompasses at least three significant concepts. First, the use of redundant but *diverse* modules significantly increases dependability during common-mode failures and, furthermore, the reconfigurable coprocessor is an ideal platform for synthesizing diverse modules. Second, the FPGA can be reconfigured down to the gate level, so recovery from failures does not require swapping in large spare modules. Third, SMT is suggested for achieving low-overhead fault tolerance. [23] is an overview of the ROAR project and, consequently, a fault-tolerant SMT implementation is not put forth and evaluation is based on analytical estimates and a compression algorithm multithreaded by hand.

2. AR-SMT implementation issues

In this section key implementation issues are presented. Section 2.1 reviews SMT hardware techniques. Where SMT policy decisions are required, we describe how these policies are tailored to AR-SMT. Section 2.2 discusses new issues that arise because the dynamically created R-stream is not a true software context, requiring minor operating system and hardware support.

2.1. Implementing SMT

Most of the design is derived from work on simultaneous multithreaded machines [10,11]. The techniques are well established and understood, and recent research shows that SMT can be incorporated into existing high performance processors rather seamlessly. The following discussion focuses on two important aspects of any SMT machine: (1) separating register and memory state of multiple threads, and (2) sharing critical processor resources.

2.1.1. Handling register values from multiple threads. Each thread must be provided its own register state, and register dependences in one thread must not interfere with register dependences in another thread. The approach in [11] leverages *register renaming* to transparently and flexibly share a single, large physical register file among multiple threads.

Register renaming overcomes the limitation of having too few general-purpose registers in the instruction-set architecture (e.g. 32). Typically, the processor provides many more *physical registers* so that multiple writes to the same logical register can be assigned unique physical registers. This allows the writes, and their dependent instruction chains, to proceed independently and in parallel. A *register map* maintains the most current mapping of logical to physical registers.

In SMT, there is still a single, large physical register file but each thread has its own register map. The separate maps guarantee the same logical register in two different threads are mapped to two different physical registers.

The approach in [11] has two advantages. First, the most complex part of the processor -- the instruction issue mechanism -- is unchanged. The fact that instructions from multiple threads co-exist in the processor is transparent to the instruction issue and register forwarding logic because it uses physical register specifiers, and renaming ensures the physical registers of various threads do not overlap. Second, managing a shared centralized register file instead of dedicated per-thread register files allows some threads to use more registers than other threads. Section 3.2 shows the R-stream requires fewer resources than the A-stream.

2.1.2. Handling memory values from multiple threads. The *memory disambiguation unit* is the mechanism for enforcing data dependences through memory. It ensures that a load gets its data from the last store to the same memory address. The disambiguation hardware consists of load and store buffers to track all outstanding memory operations, and logic to detect loads and stores having the same memory address. Like the register file, this buffering is shared among the SMT threads, i.e. loads and stores from multiple threads co-exist in the disambiguation unit.

As with register dependences, memory dependences from different threads must not interfere with each other. Thus, memory addresses must be augmented with a *thread identifier* if disambiguation is based on virtual addresses. The same virtual address used by two different threads is distinguishable using the thread id. Thread ids need not be stored in the data cache, however, if physical tags are used.

2.1.3. Concerning instruction fetch for the R-stream. Conventional SMT requires multiple program counters (PCs), one for each of the threads. Furthermore, branch predictor structures must be shared by multiple threads for predicting control flow.

AR-SMT also requires multiple program counters, but the control flow predictor does not have to be shared between the A-stream and R-stream. Recall that the PCs of retired A-stream instructions are stored in the Delay Buffer, in a sense providing control flow predictions for the R-stream. Therefore, the control flow predictor structures are dedicated to the A-stream: predictor accuracy and complexity remain unaffected.

2.1.4. Sharing processor bandwidth. The trace processor pipeline is shown in Figure 5. At each pipeline stage, we show how AR-SMT shares processor bandwidth between the A-stream and the R-stream. Some parts of the pipeline are *time-shared* and others are *space-shared.* Time-shared means in any given cycle, the pipeline stage is consumed entirely by one thread. Space-shared means every cycle a fraction of the bandwidth is allocated to both threads.

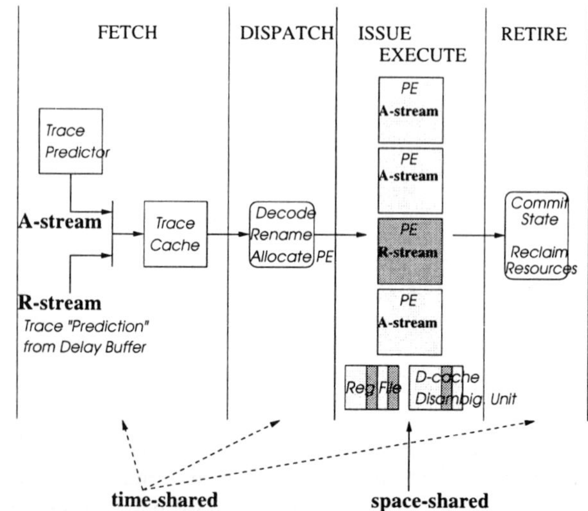

FIGURE 5. How threads share pipeline stages.

The instruction fetch/dispatch pipeline is time-shared due to the nature of traces. Traces are fetched and dispatched as an *indivisible unit*, at a rate of 1 per cycle. Clearly, this bandwidth cannot be split and shared between two threads -- traces belong to one thread or the other.

Likewise, traces are retired from the processor at the rate of 1 per cycle. Retirement is essentially the dual of dispatch in that resources are reclaimed, e.g. the PE, physical registers, load/store buffers, etc. Therefore, the retire stage is also time-shared.

Of course, execution resources are space-shared. In trace processors, the unit of space-sharing is a PE. For example, Figure 5 shows 3 PEs allocated to the A-stream and 1 PE allocated to the R-stream.

An important design decision is how to allocate bandwidth to multiple threads to minimize overall execution time. For pure SMT, many sophisticated policies are possible [11]. Adaptive heuristics allocate bandwidth dynamically based on control prediction accuracies, amount of instruction-level parallelism exhibited by each thread, etc.

For AR-SMT, however, there is significantly less scheduling flexibility because the A-stream and R-stream are tightly coupled via the Delay Buffer. More specifically, (1) the R-stream cannot run ahead of the A-stream and (2) the A-stream can only run ahead of the R-stream by an amount equal to the length of the Delay Buffer. It is not clear how much added benefit an SMT-like algorithm can yield over a simple scheduler given these constraints; clearly this is an area that demands further study.

The AR-SMT scheduling rules are consequently trivial. The rules are based on keeping the Delay Buffer full and only involve arbitration for the fetch/dispatch and retirement stages.

1. **Fetch/dispatch pipeline arbitration.** If the Delay Buffer is full, the R-stream is given priority to access the fetch/dispatch pipeline.
2. **Retirement stage arbitration**: If the Delay Buffer is not full, the A-stream has priority to retire a trace.

These rules cause deadlock if it were not for the following definition of "full" in rule #1: the Delay Buffer is considered full when the number of free entries left (in terms of traces) is equal to the number of PEs in the trace processor. Thus, there is always room to drain the A-stream from the PEs into the Delay Buffer, in turn allowing the R-stream to proceed.

2.2. New issues and operating system support

AR-SMT introduces new issues that do not arise with pure SMT. The R-stream is not a true software context. It is created on the fly by hardware and the operating system (O/S) is unaware of it. Yet the R-stream must maintain a separate physical memory image from the A-stream and exceptional conditions must be properly handled.

2.2.1. Maintaining a separate memory image. The R-stream, because it is delayed with respect to the A-stream, needs a separate memory image (just as there is a separate register "image" in the physical register file). A simple solution is proposed here.

- The O/S, when allocating a physical page to a virtual page in the A-stream context, will actually allocate two contiguous physical pages. The first is for the A-stream to use, and the second is for the R-stream to use. In this way, there is still the appearance of a single address space with a single set of protections, but simple redundancy is added to the address space.
- Address translations are placed in the Delay Buffer for use by the R-stream. This is the only virtual address translation mechanism for the R-stream because no page table entries are explicitly managed on its behalf. Addresses are translated by taking the original translation and adding 1 to it.

Another solution is to make the O/S aware of the R-stream as a true context (pure SMT).

2.2.2. Exceptions, traps, and context switches. Exceptions, traps, and context switches are handled by synchronizing the A-stream and R-stream. When any such condition is reached in the A-stream, the A-stream stalls until the Delay Buffer completely empties. At this point the two contexts are identical and the R-stream is terminated. Now only the A-stream is serviced, swapped out, etc., which is required if the operating system has no knowledge of the redundant thread. When resuming after a context switch (or upon starting the program in general), the O/S must guarantee that the duplicated pages have the same state. This is required for the R-stream to function properly.

2.2.3. Real time I/O support. The method of synchronizing the A-stream and R-stream may not support critical I/O applications in which real time constraints must be met. One solution is to include the synchronization delay in real time guarantees.

3. Performance evaluation

3.1. Simulation environment

A detailed, fully execution-driven simulator of a trace processor [17] was modified to support AR-SMT time redundancy. The simulator was developed using the *simplescalar* simulation platform [24]. This platform uses a MIPS-like instruction set and a gcc-based compiler to create binaries.

The simulator only measures performance of the microarchitecture. *Fault coverage is not evaluated.* It is beyond the scope of this paper to characterize transient faults in future microprocessors, and then develop and simulate a fault model based on this characterization. This is left for future work.

Trace processor hardware parameters are not tabulated here due to space limitations but can be found in [22][17]. The parameters most relevant to this paper are as follows.

- The maximum trace length is 16 instructions. Traces are terminated only at indirect jumps/calls and returns.
- Depending on the experiment, the trace processor consists of 4 or 8 PEs.
- Each PE can issue up to 4 instructions per cycle.
- Results are presented for only two threads sharing the trace processor, the A-stream and the R-stream.

Five of the SPEC95 integer benchmarks (Table 1) were simulated to completion.

TABLE 1. SPEC95 integer benchmarks used.

benchmark	input dataset	dynamic instruction count
compress	400000 e 2231	104 million
gcc	-O3 genrecog.i	117 million
go	9 9	133 million
ijpeg	vigo.ppm	166 million
xlisp	queens 7	202 million

3.2. Results

Two trace processor configurations were simulated, one with 4 processing elements and one with 8 processing elements. Figure 6 shows AR-SMT execution time *normalized with respect to the execution time of a single thread.* With 4 PEs, executing two redundant programs with AR-SMT takes only 12% to 29% longer than executing one program; with 8 PEs, it takes only 5% to 27% longer. This is much better than the 100% overhead of program-level time redundancy.

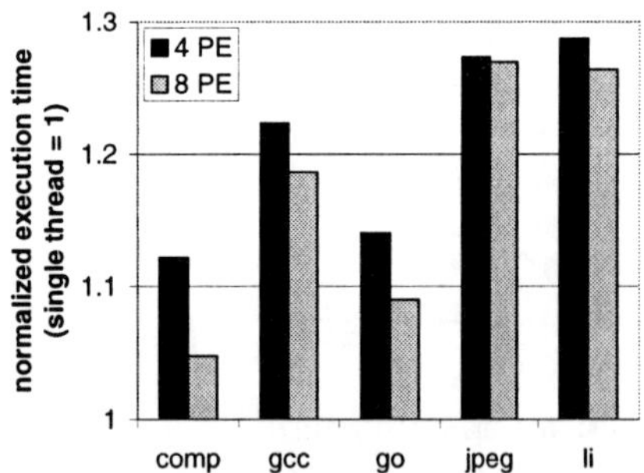

FIGURE 6. AR-SMT execution time normalized to the execution time of a single thread.

Two factors contribute to the good performance of AR-SMT. First, general purpose programs do not fully utilize the peak bandwidth of high performance processors. SMT exploits this by sharing processor bandwidth among multiple threads. Second, the R-stream requires a significantly lower fraction of the processor bandwidth because it executes faster than the A-stream -- the R-stream has the benefit of knowing in advance all control flow changes and data values.

This second point is clearly demonstrated in Figure 7, which shows the utilization of PEs by both the R-stream and A-stream, measured for the *gcc* benchmark running on an 8 PE trace processor. The graph shows the fraction of all cycles that 0 PEs are used, 1 PE is used, 2 PEs are used, etc. As expected, the R-stream utilizes much fewer PEs than the A-stream. Although the total number of traces executed by both streams is identical, R-stream traces are serviced much faster due to perfect control and data flow information. The vertical lines superimposed on the graph show average utilization for both streams. On average, only 1.5 processing elements are in use by the R-stream.

Notice the average utilizations do not add up to 8. This is because the A-stream "squashes" all traces after a mispredicted branch, and one or more PEs will be idle until they are dispatched new traces.

Two other conclusions can be drawn from Figure 6. First, the overhead of AR-SMT is greater for benchmarks that have higher instruction-level parallelism, namely *gcc*, *li*, and *jpeg*. These benchmarks have high trace prediction accuracy, and as a result the A-stream makes good utilization of the trace processor. Therefore, taking resources away from the A-stream has a larger impact relative to less predictable benchmarks (*go*, *compress*).

Second, the overhead of AR-SMT is always lower with 8 PEs than with 4 PEs. Adding more PEs yields diminishing returns for single thread performance, so the additional PEs can be used relatively uncontested by the R-stream. This is particularly true for benchmarks with poor trace prediction accuracy -- *compress* and *go* show a significant drop in AR-SMT overhead with 8 PEs. On the other hand, the A-streams in *li* and *jpeg* utilize 8 PEs and 4 PEs equally well.

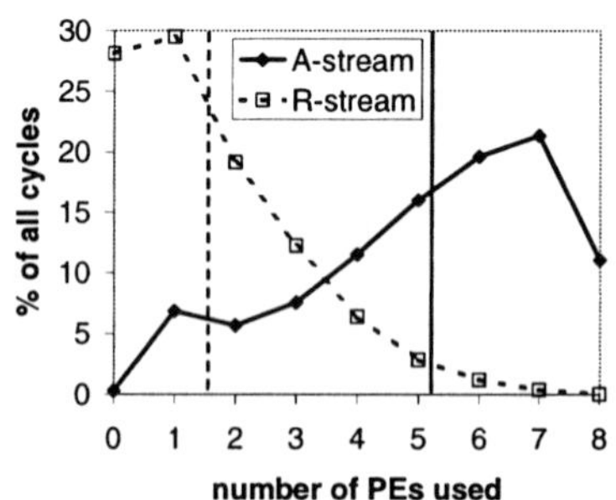

FIGURE 7. PE utilization (*gcc*, 8 PEs).

4. Summary

Both technology and microarchitecture trends have interesting implications for fault tolerance in future high performance microprocessors. On the one hand, technology-driven performance improvements potentially expose microprocessors to a new fault environment, one in which severely reduced tolerances result in frequent transient faults throughout the chip. On the other hand, microarchitecture trends can provide an overall solution for this new fault environment.

AR-SMT is the microarchitecture-based fault-tolerant solution put forth in this paper. Its development can be summarized as follows.

- AR-SMT is a time redundancy technique that combines the broad coverage of program-level time redundancy with the high performance and fast fault detection/recovery capability of instruction re-execution. It achieves this by creating two separate programs (like program-level redundancy) and running both programs simultaneously (like instruction re-execution).
- AR-SMT leverages three important microarchitecture trends -- advances that are likely to be implemented in future microprocessors for high performance and management of complexity. The primary mechanism, simultaneous multithreading, allows the active and redundant streams to co-exist within the processor and thus better utilize resources. Control flow and data flow prediction concepts are applied to speed execution of the redundant stream, and also exploit existing prediction-validation hardware for detecting faults. Hierarchical processors are organized around large, replicated processing elements; this coarse hardware redundancy is exploited to detect permanent faults and dynamically reconfigure the processor to work around the faults.
- Detailed simulations show that AR-SMT increases execution time by only 10% to 30% over a single thread. The low overhead is attributed to improved utilization of the highly parallel microprocessor and use of control/data flow information from the active thread to speed execution of the redundant thread.

Acknowledgements

Kewal Saluja is gratefully acknowledged for his constant encouragement.

References

[1] D. P. Siewiorek. Niche successes to ubiquitous invisibility: Fault-tolerant computing past, present, and future. *25th Fault-Tolerant Computing Symp.*, pages 26–33, June 1995.

[2] P. I. Rubinfeld. Virtual roundtable on the challenges and trends in processor design: Managing problems at high speeds. *Computer*, 31(1):47–48, Jan 1998.

[3] C. L. Chen and M. Y. Hsiao. Error-correcting codes for semiconductor memory applications: A state of the art review. In *Reliable Computer Systems - Design and Evaluation*, pages 771–786, Digital Press, 2nd edition, 1992.

[4] J. H. Patel and L. Y. Fung. Concurrent error detection in alu's by recomputing with shifted operands. *IEEE Trans. on Computers*, C-31(7):589–595, July 1982.

[5] G. Sohi, M. Franklin, and K. Saluja. A study of time-redundant fault tolerance techniques for high-performance pipelined computers. *19th Fault-Tolerant Computing Symp.*, pages 436–443, June 1989.

[6] N. K. Jha and J. A. Abraham. Techniques for efficient mos implementation of totally self-checking checkers. *15th Fault-Tolerant Computing Symp.*, pages 430–435, June 1985.

[7] N. Kanopoulos, D. Pantzartzis, and F. R. Bartram. Design of self-checking circuits using dcvs logic: A case study. *IEEE Trans. on Computers*, 41(7):891–896, July 1992.

[8] B. W. Johnson. Fault-tolerant microprocessor-based systems. *IEEE Micro*, pages 6–21, Dec 1984.

[9] J. E. Smith and G. S. Sohi. The microarchitecture of superscalar processors. *Proc. IEEE*, 83(12):1609–24, Dec 1995.

[10] D. Tullsen, S. Eggers, and H. Levy. Simultaneous multithreading: Maximizing on-chip parallelism. *22nd Intl. Symp. on Computer Architecture*, pages 392–403, June 1995.

[11] D. Tullsen, S. Eggers, J. Emer, H. Levy, J. Lo, and R. Stamm. Exploiting choice: Instruction fetch and issue on an implementable simultaneous multithreading processor. *23rd Intl. Symp. on Computer Architecture*, pages 191–202, May 1996.

[12] J. E. Smith. A study of branch prediction strategies. *8th Symp. on Computer Architecture*, pages 135–148, May 1981.

[13] T.-Y. Yeh and Y. N. Patt. Alternative implementations of two-level adaptive branch prediction. *19th Intl. Symp. on Computer Architecture*, May 1992.

[14] M. Lipasti. *Value Locality and Speculative Execution.* PhD thesis, Carnegie Mellon University, April 1997.

[15] Y. Sazeides, S. Vassiliadis, and J. E. Smith. The performance potential of data dependence speculation and collapsing. *29th Intl. Symp. on Microarchitecture*, pages 238–247, Dec 1996.

[16] F. Gabbay and A. Mendelson. Speculative execution based on value prediction. Technical Report 1080, Technion - Israel Institute of Technology, EE Dept., Nov 1996.

[17] E. Rotenberg, Q. Jacobson, Y. Sazeides, and J. Smith. Trace processors. *30th Intl. Symp. on Microarchitecture*, Dec 1997.

[18] M. Franklin and G. S. Sohi. The expandable split window paradigm for exploiting fine-grain parallelism. *19th Intl. Symp. on Computer Architecture*, May 1992.

[19] G. S. Sohi, S. Breach, and T. N. Vijaykumar. Multiscalar processors. *22nd Intl. Symp. on Computer Architecture*, pages 414–425, June 1995.

[20] S. Vajapeyam and T. Mitra. Improving superscalar instruction dispatch and issue by exploiting dynamic code sequences. *24th Intl. Symp. on Comp. Architecture*, pages 1–12, June 1997.

[21] J. Smith and S. Vajapeyam. Trace processors: Moving to fourth-generation microarchitectures. *IEEE Computer, Billion-Transistor Architectures*, Sep 1997.

[22] E. Rotenberg. Ar-smt: Coarse-grain time redundancy for high performance general purpose processors. *Univ. of Wisc. Course Project (ECE753), http://www.cs.wisc.edu/~ericro/course_projects/course_projects.html*, May 1998.

[23] N. Saxena and E. McCluskey. Dependable adaptive computing systems – the roar project. *Intl. Conf. on Systems, Man, and Cybernetics*, pages 2172–2177, Oct 1998.

[24] D. Burger, T. Austin, and S. Bennett. Evaluating future microprocessors: The simplescalar toolset. Technical Report CS-TR-96-1308, Univ. of Wisconsin, CS Dept., July 1996.

Session 4B

Networking Issues I

Chair: John Meyer
University of Michigan, USA

Routing and Wavelength Assignment for Establishing Dependable Connections in WDM Networks

G. Mohan C. Siva Ram Murthy
Department of Computer Science and Engineering
Indian Institute of Technology, Madras - 600 036, INDIA
{gmohan@pdc.,murthy@}iitm.ernet.in

Abstract

This paper considers the problem of establishing dependable connections (D-connections) for fast failure recovery in wavelength-routed wavelength-division multiplexed (WDM) networks with dynamic traffic demand. A D-connection is realized by a primary lightpath and one or more backup lightpaths. Real time applications usually require timeliness and fault-tolerance. It is not a difficult task to guarantee timely delivery of messages in WDM networks, as a lightpath with its entire bandwidth is dedicated to an application. However, providing fault-tolerance is an important issue to be solved in these networks. In this paper, we focus on backup multiplexing based primary-backup lightpath routing in WDM networks. We present different methods to assign wavelengths to backup lightpaths, for a given primary lightpath. They are broadly classified into primary dependent backup wavelength assignment(PDBWA) and primary independent backup wavelength assignment (PIBWA) schemes. The PDBWA is further classified into PDBWA-S and PDBWA-D, depending on whether the wavelength of the backup lightpath is the same as that of the primary lightpath or not. All the above methods differ in their computational complexity and performance. To improve fairness among the connections with and without fault-tolerant requirements, we propose a method called backup threshold. We conduct extensive simulation experiments to study the performance of the proposed methods.

Keywords: Wavelength division multiplexing, failure recovery, D-connections, primary and backup lightpaths.

1. Introduction

Wavelength-division multiplexed (WDM) networks are a viable solution to emerging applications, such as supercomputer visualization and medical imaging, which need to provide high data transmission rate, low error rate, and minimal propagation delay to a large number of users. All-optical networks employing wavelength division multiplexing and wavelength routing are a promising candidate for future WANs. These networks offer the advantages of wavelength reuse and scalability and thus suitable for WANs. A *lightpath* is an 'optical communication path' between two nodes, established by allocating the same wavelength throughout the route of the transmitted data [1]. A lightpath is uniquely identified by a wavelength and a physical path. The requirement that the same wavelength must be used on all the links along the selected path is known as the *wavelength continuity constraint.* This constraint is unique to the WDM networks. Two lightpaths can use the same fiber link, if and only if they use different wavelengths. If two nodes are connected by a lightpath, a message can be sent from one node to the other without requiring any buffering and electro-optical conversion at the intermediate nodes. In other words, a message is transmitted in one (light)hop from the source to the destination. The networks supporting such message communication are called *single-(light)hop WDM networks.* The problem of establishing lightpaths with the objective of minimization of the required number of wavelengths or minimization of the lightpath blocking probability for a fixed number of wavelengths is termed as the *lightpath establishment* problem (LE) [1]. For these, the establishment is either static (SLE), where a set of lightpaths is given priori, or dynamic (DLE), where lightpaths are established and terminated on-the-fly [1]. A good routing and wavelength assignment (RWA) algorithm is critically important to improve the performance of wavelength-routed WDM networks. Several heuristic methods for the RWA problem are available in the literature [1, 2, 3, 4].

In this paper, we consider WDM networks with dynamic traffic conditions. Every physical link is assumed to have a fixed number of wavelengths and minimizing the blocking probability of connections is the primary objective of our study. When a new connection request arrives, an appropriate route and wavelength constituting a lightpath is chosen to satisfy the request. Certain applications such as real-time applications require timeliness and fault-tolerance for data communication. In single-(light)hop WDM networks with dynamic traffic demand, a connection corresponds to a lightpath and the entire bandwidth of a lightpath is available to an application. In other words, the wavelength on the links of a lightpath is used by a single application and not shared by any other application. Therefore, guaranteeing timeliness in WDM networks is trivial. However, the fault-tolerant requirement is an important issue to be solved in these networks. Throughout this paper, we use the term WDM networks to mean single-(light)hop WDM networks.

The fault-tolerant routing problem for the dynamic traffic has been earlier addressed for non-WDM networks such as ATM networks. Some of the existing approaches for fault-tolerant routing have been surveyed and a pre-routing scheme based on *backup-path multiplexing* has been proposed in [5]. When a link or node fails, all the connections currently using this link or node fail. The methods for recovering from the failure can be broadly classified into reactive and pro-active methods. The reactive method is the simplest way of recovering from failures. In this method, when the existing connection fails, a new connection which does not use failed components is selected and established if available. This has an advantage of low overhead in the absence of failures. However, this does not guarantee successful recovery, as the attempt to establish a new connection may fail due to resource shortage at the time of failure recovery. Also, in case of distributed implementation, contention among simultaneous recovery attempts for different failed connections may require several retries to succeed, thus resulting in increased network traffic and service resumption time. To overcome the above difficulties, pro-active methods can be employed. In the *end-to-end detouring* pro-active method, a backup connection is established between two end nodes of a primary connection. The backup connection takes over the role of the primary connection when it fails. Each backup connection reserves its own spare resources, so that there will be no conflict between recovery attempts. Since the backup connection is established before the failures actually occur, one can use it immediately upon occurrence of a failure to the primary, without the time-consuming connection re-establishment process. Hence, the failure recovery delay of this pro-active method is much smaller leading to fast recovery. However, this method reserves excessive resources. In [5], a resource sharing technique, called *backup multiplexing* has been proposed to minimize the spare resources required on a link. It reserves only a small fraction of link-resources needed for all backup connections traversing the link. This method is used to establish dependable connections in an efficient way in terms of amount of spare resources. A dependable connection (a D-connection for short) consists of a primary connection and one or more backup connections. Each backup connection remains as a cold standby until it is activated. The idea behind the backup multiplexing is that two backup connections can share the resource on a link, if their corresponding primary connections do not fail simultaneously. This happens when they do not share any link.

In [6], some mechanisms to detect and isolate faults such as fiber cuts and router failures have been presented. The problem of fault-tolerant design of WDM networks has been addressed in [7, 8] for the static traffic demand. Here, a set of connection requests is given apriori and lightpaths are assigned for them. For every active lightpath, a set of backup lightpaths is predetermined to handle all possible fault occurrences. The objective of these design algorithms is to minimize the required spare resources such as wavelengths and fibers in order to incorporate fault tolerance. These algorithms can afford to be computationally expensive as they are run off line at the design stage itself. Some dynamic algorithms for fault-tolerant routing in WDM networks have been recently proposed in [9, 10]. These algorithms use distributed protocols to find routes avoiding the faulty components. Basically, these algorithms are 'reactive' in nature, which find a new route after the occurrence of component failures. Our work concerns with fault-tolerant routing in WDM networks with dynamic traffic demand. The dynamic routing schemes must use simpler and faster algorithms. This is because, in a dynamic traffic environment short-lived connections are setup and torn down frequently.

A connection can be either dependable, requiring fault-tolerance or non-dependable without any fault-tolerant requirement. In response to a request for a dependable connection, a D-connection is established, which consists of a primary lightpath and one or more backup lightpaths. We consider the single-link failure scenario and therefore, one backup lightpath is sufficient for a D- connection. In response to a request for a non-dependable connection (ND-connection for short), a single lightpath is established. We propose different wavelength assignment methods for establishing D-connections. Basically we use backup multiplexing based primary-backup lightpath routing in order to improve the network performance (or equivalently reducing the blocking probability of connections). Backup multiplexing in WDM networks is different from that in non-WDM networks due to the unique features such as wavelength continuity constraint and exclusive use of the entire bandwidth of a lightpath by a single application.

The proposed methods are classified into primary dependent backup wavelength assignment(PDBWA) and primary independent backup wavelength assignment (PIBWA) methods. In the PDBWA method, there is a relationship between the wavelengths of the primary and backup lightpaths. The wavelength of a backup lightpath is uniquely determined by that of the primary lightpath and vice versa. In the PIBWA method, there is no restriction on choosing the wavelengths for the primary and backup lightpaths. The wavelengths are chosen so as to minimize certain cost function. The PDBWA is further classified into PDBWA-S and PDBWA-D, depending on whether the wavelength of the backup lightpath is the same as that of the primary lightpath or not. All the above methods differ in their computational complexity and performance.

While backup multiplexing improves the performance of D-connections, it may lead to poor performance of ND-connections. A routing scheme which effectively uses backup multiplexing will tend to multiplex more and more number of backup lightpaths on a wavelength of a link. Therefore, backup multiplexing may become unfair to ND-connections. To improve the performance of ND-connections without any significant degradation of the performance of D-connections, we propose a method called, *backup threshold*. By using this method, for an appropriate value of a threshold parameter, we can achieve a desired level of tradeoff between the performance of D-connections and ND-connections.

2. Routing Strategy

Our schemes basically use alternate routing method. For every pair of source and destination, a set of K alternative routes (also referred to as candidate routes) are precomputed off-line. Let H be the hop length of the longest candidate route. The candidate routes for a source-destination pair are chosen to be link-disjoint to incorporate fault-tolerance. The routes for a source-destination pair are kept in the non-decreasing order of their hop length. A WDM network with N nodes and W wavelengths per fiber can be thought of as a network with W parallel layers each corresponding to a wavelength. In graphical representation, it is a graph with W subgraphs each corresponding to a wavelength. Every physical link in the network has W wavelength channels. Throughout this paper, we use the term 'link' to refer to a 'physical link' and 'wlink' to refer to a 'wavelength channel on a physical link'. Therefore, a link is said to consist of W wlinks. We use R_p and R_b to denote the candidate route used as a primary and backup, respectively. Similarly, w_p and w_b denote the wavelength used by a primary and backup lightpath, respectively. The pair $< R_p, w_p >$ denotes a primary lightpath L_p and the pair $< R_b, w_b >$ denotes a backup lightpath L_b. A D-connection is realized by a primary-backup lightpath pair, denoted by $< L_p, L_b >$.

When a new request arrives for a ND-connection between a source-destination pair $< s, d >$, a lightpath is to be chosen to satisfy the request. Every candidate route for the pair $< s, d >$ is searched in that order on every wavelength and the cost is computed using a cost function. The candidate route and wavelength pair with the least cost is chosen and the lightpath is assigned to the request for data communication. For a ND-connection, only a primary lightpath L_p is required. We use a cost function C_p to find the cost of a primary lightpath. The cost of a primary lightpath is defined as the number of wlinks used by it. It is to be noted that only a free wlink can be used by L_p. In a dynamic traffic environment, this cost function is expected to improve the performance, as using less number of wlinks by a lightpath will leave more number of wlinks that can be used by the connection requests arriving later.

When a new request arrives for a D-connection between a source-destination pair $< s, d >$, a primary-backup lightpath pair $< L_p, L_b >$ is to be chosen to satisfy the request. It is chosen such that the cost of $< L_p, L_b >$ is minimum. The cost of the primary lightpath L_p is the number of hops or wlinks used by it. It is to be noted that only a free wlink can be used by L_p. The cost of a backup lightpath L_b for a given primary lightpath L_p is defined as the number of free wlinks used by it. If a wlink is not free and currently used by some primary lightpath (of a D-connection or a ND-connection), then it can not be used by L_b. If a wlink is not free and currently used by a set of backup lightpaths S, then it can be used by L_b with no extra cost, if and only if its primary route R_p is link-disjoint with the primary route of each and every backup lightpath in the set S. If a wlink is free, it can be used by L_b with the cost value equal to 1. The cost function for a backup lightpath, denoted by C_b tries to minimize the additional free wlinks required to be used at that instant of time. Intuitively, it leaves more wlinks for use by the requests which will arrive later, thus improving the network performance. The cost of a D-connection using the primary-backup lightpath pair $< L_p, L_b >$ is given by

$$C_D(L_p, L_b) = C_p(L_p) + C_b(L_b, L_p);$$

Our objective is to find a primary-backup lightpath pair whose C_D is minimum. We give below the pseudo-code for the primary and backup cost functions, C_p and C_b.

```
Function C_p(L_p)
Begin
        cost ← 0;
        For every wlink w_l of L_p do
                cost ← cost + PrimaryCost(w_l)
        Return(cost)
End.

Function C_b(L_b, L_p)
Begin
        cost ← 0;
        For every wlink w_l of L_b do
        cost ← cost + BackupCost(w_l, R_p)
        Return(cost)
End.
```

3. Wavelength Assignment Methods

In this section, we present and analyze different wavelength assignment methods. These methods differ in their complexity and performance. In the previous section, we defined the cost functions for computing the cost of primary and backup lightpaths. It is to be noted that the cost of a wlink on a primary lightpath, computed by PrimaryCost(w_l) depends only of the current status of the wlink and requires constant time. However, the cost of a wlink on a backup lightpath, computed by BackupCost(w_l, R_p) depends not only on the status of the wlink but also on the primary route of this D-connection and the primary routes of all the D-connections whose backup routes are multiplexed on this wlink. Therefore, the computation of BackupCost(w_l, R_p) has complexity depending upon the wavelength assignment method and the data structures used.

3.1. PDBWA-S Method and its Complexity

In this method, in response to a request for a D-connection, a primary and backup lightpath on the same wavelength are chosen. Since there is a restriction on choosing the wavelength, it may not yield the best performance. For example, there may arise a situation wherein there exist wavelength-continuous routes for the primary on one wavelength and for the backup on some other wavelength, but there are no wavelength-continuous routes available on the same wavelength for the primary and backup. In such a case, the request will be rejected by this method. Similarly, there may arise a situation, wherein a pair of lightpaths with higher cost is chosen, degrading the network performance. In spite of these disadvantages, this method has several advantages. First, it is simpler having less computational complexity. Second, it does not require any additional storage to decide if two backup routes could be multiplexed on a wlink or not. Third, upon occurrence of a failure, when the backup lightpath is activated, its end nodes need not tune to new wavelengths.

First, we consider the case where the adjacent nodes in a network are connected by only one simplex link. From the constraints of the wavelength-routed WDM networks, it is clear that two primary routes on the same wavelength must be link-disjoint. Therefore, if some backup routes are multiplexed on some wlink, then a new backup route can always be multiplexed on it without needing any procedure to check if its primary route is link-disjoint with the primary routes of the already multiplexed backup routes. Now we describe the procedure to choose the least cost pair of lightpaths for establishing a D-connection for the pair $< s, d >$. Consider a wavelength i. There are K candidate routes for $< s, d >$ and hence K possible lightpaths. For every lightpath, compute C_p and C_b. This can be done in $O(KH)$ time units. Choose a lightpath L_p whose C_p is minimum. Then among the lightpaths other than L_p, choose a lightpath L_b whose C_b is minimum. It is easy to verify that the pair $< L_p, L_b >$ has the minimum C_D value. This procedure is repeated for each of the W wavelengths to choose the minimum cost lightpath pair. The complexity of the PDBWA-S method is therefore $O(KHW)$. We now formally prove the claim that the pair of lightpaths on a wavelength chosen by the above method has the minimum C_D value.
It is to be noted that for a lightpath L, if $C_p(L)$ is finite, then $C_b(L)$ is equal to $C_p(L)$.
Let $< L_1, L_2 >$ be the pair chosen by the above method. Let $C_p(L_1)$ be c_1 and $C_b(L_2)$ be c_2.
Assume that there exists some other pair $< L_3, L_4 >$ with a lesser cost than $< L_1, L_2 >$. Let $C_p(L_3)$ be c_3 and $C_b(L_4)$ be c_4.
By way of working of the algorithm we make the following arguments.
(1) cost of any backup lightpath $\geq \min(c_1, c_2)$.
(2) If L_3 is the same as L_1, the claim follows immediately.Therefore, consider the case where L_3 is different from L_1.
(3) $c_3 \geq c_1$
(4) Since L_3 is also a potential backup lightpath L_2, it follows that $c_3 \geq c_2$
(5) From (3) and (4), it follows that $c_3 \geq max(c_1, c_2)$
(6) From (1) it follows that $c_4 \geq \min(c_1, c_2)$.
(7) From (5) and (6) it follows that $c_3 + c_4 \geq c_1 + c_2$. Therefore, the cost of $< L_3, L_4 >$ can not be less than that of $< L_1, L_2 >$.
Hence, our claim is correct.

Now we consider the case where the adjacent nodes in a network are connected by only one duplex link which is realized by a pair of simplex links in opposite directions. It is to be noted that when a link failure occurs both the simplex links will fail. Therefore, unlike the case addressed in the last paragraph, a primary lightpath shares links with other primary lightpaths traversing any opposite simplex link of any of its links. A primary lightpath with H hops can overlap with a maximum of H other primary lightpaths. Now consider a wavelength i. There are K possible primary lightpaths. Process the primary lightpaths one by one. Consider a primary lightpath L_p with some finite cost. Disable the wlinks of the backup lightpaths of every other primary lightpath which overlaps with L_p. This requires $O(H^2)$ time units. For this primary lightpath, choose the least cost backup lightpath. While computing C_b of a backup lightpath, the cost of a wlink on it is computed as follows: If the wlink is free its cost is 1. If it is disabled its cost is infinity. Otherwise its cost is 0, implying that it can be multiplexed with other backup routes on the wlink. This requires $O(KH)$ time units. Similarly, for every other primary lightpath, choose the least cost backup lightpath. Repeat this for each of the W wavelengths to choose the minimum cost lightpath pair to satisfy the connection request. The overall complexity of the PDBWA-S method for this case of duplex links thus becomes $O((KH^2 + K^2H)W)$.

3.2. PDBWA-D Method and its Complexity

This method has all the advantages of that of PDBWA-S method except that when the backup lightpath is activated, the end nodes need to tune to the new wavelength. It also suffers from the drawback of poor performance like the PDBWA-S method due to the restriction on the wavelength usage. Here, although the wavelengths of the primary and backup lightpaths are related to each other, they are different. Say for example, for any primary lightpath on wavelength i, the backup lightpath must be on wavelength $i + 1$.

Now consider the simplex link case. Here also, two backup lightpaths can always be multiplexed on a wlink as their primary lightpaths are automatically link-disjoint. However, we need to choose the best backup lightpath for each of the primary lightpaths separately. The complexity of this method becomes $O(K^2HW)$. In the case of duplex links, similar procedure as that of PDBWA-S can be adopted. The complexity of the PDBWA-D method for the case of duplex links is therefore $O((KH^2 + K^2H)W)$.

3.3. PIBWA Method and its Complexity

This method does not impose any restriction on the use of wavelength for the primary and backup lightpaths. Therefore, we can choose the best possible primary-backup lightpath pair to satisfy a D-connection request. This method has the advantage of better network performance in terms of the blocking probability of the connections. However, it has some disadvantages. First, it is computationally more complex. Second, it requires additional data structures to keep information which would help to determine the cost of a wlink on a backup lightpath for a given primary lightpath.

It uses a two dimensional array called conflict[][] for every pair of wlink and link. If l_w denotes a wlink on some wavelength and l denotes a link then conflict[l_w][l] signifies that there exists a D-connection whose backup lightpath uses l_w and whose primary lightpath uses l. Whenever a D-connection is established, the information about the conflict between each of the wlinks on its backup lightpath with each of the links on its primary lightpath is registered by updating entries in conflict[][] array. When this D-connection terminates, the above updation is undone.

Now consider a wavelength i. There are K possible primary lightpaths. Process the primary lightpaths one by one. Find a minimum cost backup lightpath on any wavelength for each of these primary lightpaths. Consider a primary lightpath L_p with some finite cost. There are K-1 possible backup routes each on one of W possible wavelengths. Therefore, for this L_p there are (K-1)W possible backup lightpaths. To compute C_b of a backup lightpath for the given primary lightpath L_p, we need to find the cost of each of the wlinks on the backup lightpath. If the wlink is free, then its cost is 1. If it is in conflict with L_p, its cost is infinity, otherwise it is 0. A wlink is said to be in conflict with a primary lightpath, if there exists at least one link on the primary lightpath with which this wlink is in conflict. To decide if a wlink is in conflict with a primary lightpath, it requires $O(H)$ time units. Therefore, for a given primary lightpath on a given wavelength, choosing the best lightpath on any wavelength will require $O(KH^2W)$ time units. We need to process every primary lightpath on every wavelength to determine the minimum cost primary-backup lightpath pair to satisfy the connection request. The overall complexity of the PIBWA method thus becomes $O(K^2H^2W^2)$. Although theoretically the worst-case value for K and H could be N-1, in practice these values are low only. Therefore, the actual running time will be low and acceptable.

4. Backup Threshold Method

Any algorithm which effectively makes use of *backup multiplexing* will improve the performance of D-connection traffic. In practice, a network has a mixed traffic. Some applications have fault-tolerant requirement, while others do not. Therefore, at any instant of time both the D-connection and ND-connection traffic co-exist in a network. While backup multiplexing improves the performance of D-connections, it may lead to poor performance of ND-connections. Any wlink used by a primary lightpath will be released as soon as the corresponding connection terminates. Once a wlink is released, it can be either used by a D-connection or ND-connection in future. On the other hand, a wlink on which a set of backup lightpaths are multiplexed will be released only when all the corresponding D-connections terminate. In a dynamic traffic environment, it is highly probable that a wlink is continuously held by some backup lightpaths. This may benefit new D-connections as they can use this wlink for their backup. But, this would prevent ND-connections from using this wlink for a longer time, thus degrading their performance. It will not be wrong to state that, better the performance of D-connections, poorer the performance of ND-connections. The PDBWA-S method tries to pack the lightpaths tightly onto some wavelengths leaving other wavelengths free. Therefore, when the D-connection traffic is higher (when compared to the ND-traffic), it accepts more number of D-connections (when compared to the PDBWA-D method). As a result, PDBWA-S yields better performance for D-traffic and poorer performance for ND-traffic.

To improve the performance of ND-connections without any significant degradation of the performance of D-connections, we propose a method called, *backup threshold*. By using this method, for an appropriate value of a threshold parameter, we can achieve a desired level of tradeoff between the performance of D-connections and ND-connections. This method fixes a threshold value (say T) for the backup lightpaths on a physical link. At any instant of time, it allows only a maximum of T wlinks on a link to have backup lightpaths multiplexed. This will keep more wlinks on a link free which could be used by ND-connections or primary lightpaths of D-connections. A low value for the threshold will result in better performance of ND-connections. Increasing the value of the threshold will improve the performance of D-connections and degrade the performance of ND-connections. An appropriate value for the threshold can be fixed to achieve the desired level of tradeoff between the performance of the D-connections and ND-connections. This method has a shortcoming. If the ND-connection traffic is low and we have chosen a low threshold, then it may so happen that some of the wlinks are not utilized. Similarly, if the ND-connection traffic is high and we have chosen a high threshold, then the performance of ND-connections may degrade as more wlinks are likely to be held by backup lightpaths of D-connections. This shortcoming of poor utilization of wavelength channels can be overcome if the threshold value is adjusted adaptively depending upon the traffic load and performance of the D-connections and ND-connections.

5. Performance Study

We evaluate the effectiveness of the proposed methods by extensive simulation. The simulation networks considered are the 21-node ARPA-2 network with 26 duplex links and 16-node TORUS network with 32 duplex links. While the connectivity of the ARPA-2 network is low, that of the torus network is relatively high. The connection requests arrive at a node as a Poisson process with exponentially distributed holding time with unit mean. Every node is equally likely to be the destination node. The experiments are run for sufficiently longer time and repeated several times to obtain the results with 95% confidence level. We considered an integrated environment wherein connections with fault-tolerant requirement (D-connections) and connections with no fault-tolerant requirement (ND-connections) co-exist. We considered different cases each with a different ratio of D-connection traffic and ND-connection traffic. Due to space limitations we present results for the ratios 100:0 and 50:50 only.

Fig. 1 shows the performance of D-connections in torus network for different traffic loading per node. The percentage of D-connection traffic generated at a node is 100%. Fig. 2 shows the performance for the ARPA-2 network. The curves show the usefulness of the backup multiplexing technique. Compared to the method with no backup multiplexing (NO_BM), all the proposed methods perform better. Among the proposed methods, PIBWA method performs better than the PDBWA methods. The PDBWA-S method performs slightly better than PDBWA-D method as PDBWA-S method tends to pack the connections onto some wavelengths, leaving more wavelength-continuous routes available for the future connection requests. A similar trend can be observed for the ARPA-2 network also. However, due to the dense connectivity, the performance of the methods in case of the torus network is better than that of the ARPA-2 network.

Fig. 3 shows the performance of D-connections in torus network for different traffic loading per node. The percentage of D-connection traffic generated at a node is 50%. Fig. 4 shows the performance for the ARPA-2 network. In this case also, the curves show the usefulness of backup multiplexing. It can be observed from the curves that the performance of the PDBWA methods move away from that of PIBWA method towards that of the NO_BM method. The reason is the following. The PDBWA methods do not fully exploit the benefits of backup multiplexing due to the restriction imposed on the wavelength usage by the primary and backup lightpaths. This results in acceptance of more ND-connection requests which will lead to rejection of more D-connection requests. This benefit enjoyed by the ND-connection traffic when PDBWA methods are used are clear from the Fig. 5 and Fig. 6. The performance of ND-connection traffic is plotted in Fig. 5 and Fig. 6 for the torus and ARPA-2 network, respectively. It can be observed that the PIBWA method performs poorly for the ND-connection traffic, for the same reason explained in the previous section.

From the above figures, we can observe that the better the performance of the D-connection traffic poorer the performance of the ND-connection traffic. The PIBWA method results in higher acceptance ratio of D-connection requests, but at the same time results in higher rejection ratio of ND-connection requests. The performance of PIBWA method using backup threshold is plotted in Fig. 7 and Fig. 8 for the ARPA-2 network. Similar trends were observed for the torus network. The threshold values chosen are 2,3, and 4. As expected, decreasing the threshold value, improves the performance of ND-connections and degrades the performance of D-connections.

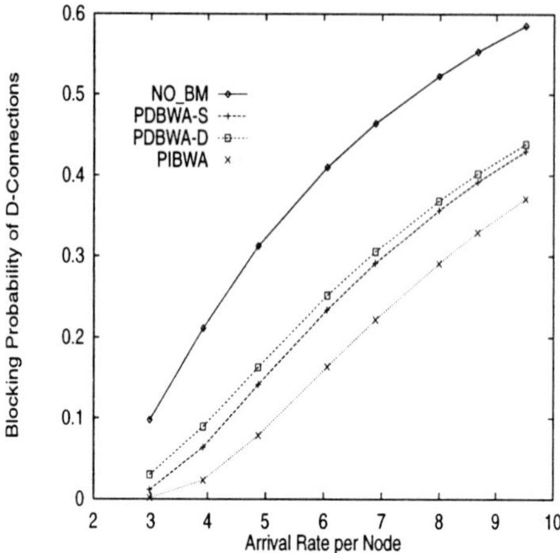

Figure 1. Performance of D-connections for different traffic loading per node for the torus network. The D-connection traffic is 100%.

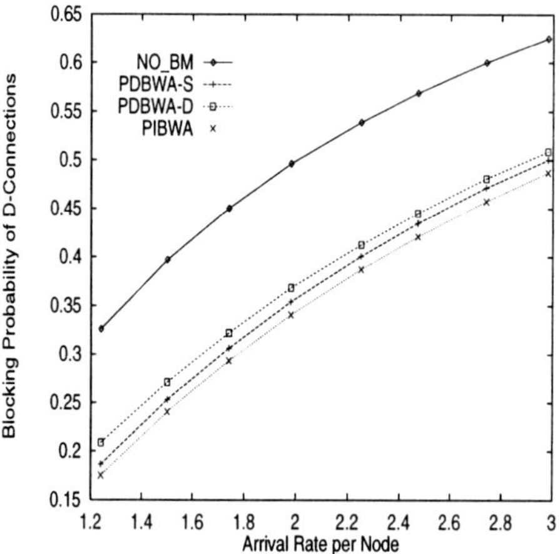

Figure 2. Performance of D-connections for different traffic loading per node for the ARPA-2 network. The D-connection traffic is 100%.

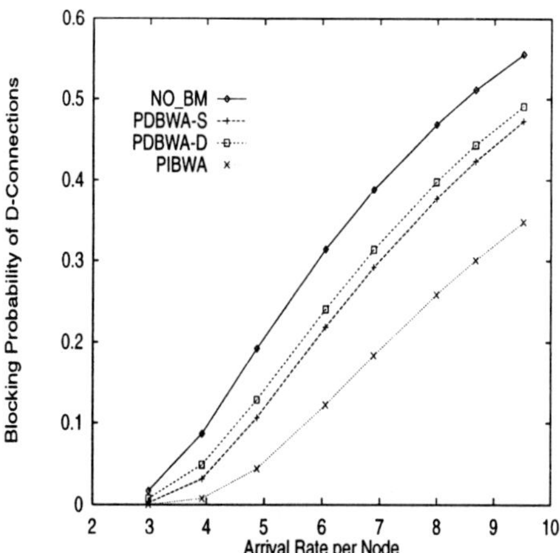

Figure 3. Performance of D-connections for different traffic loading per node for the torus network. The D-connection traffic is 50%.

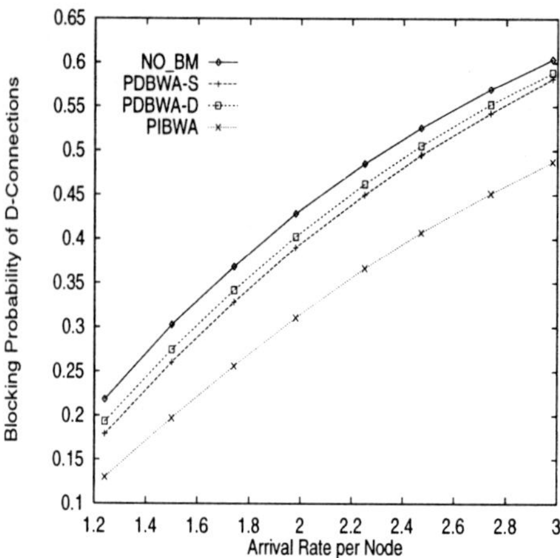

Figure 4. Performance of D-connections for different traffic loading per node for the ARPA-2 network. The D-connection traffic is 50%.

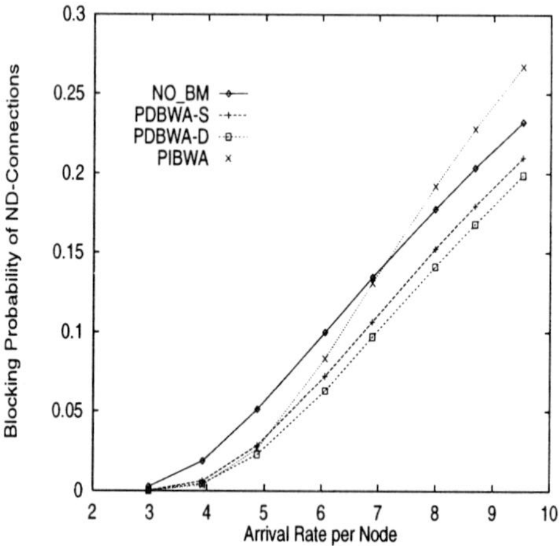

Figure 5. Performance of ND-connections for different traffic loading per node for the torus network. The D-connection traffic is 50%.

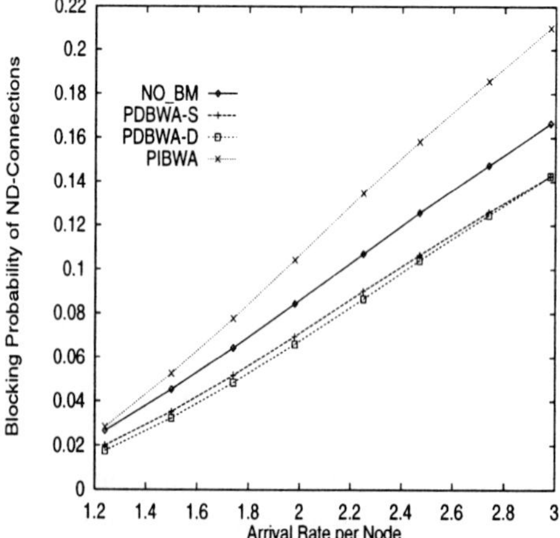

Figure 6. Performance of ND-connections for different traffic loading per node for the ARPA-2 network. The D-connection traffic is 50%.

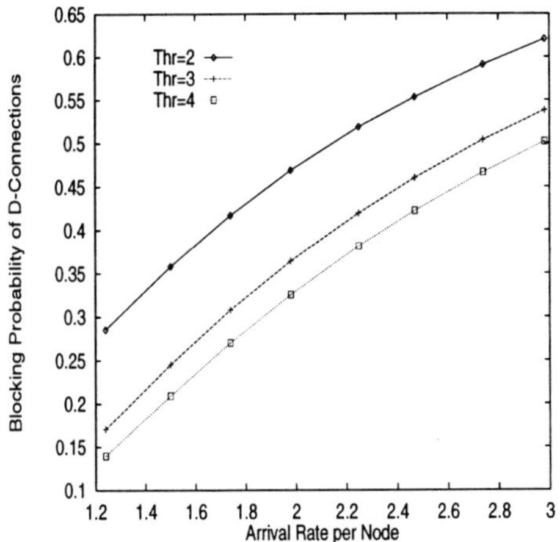

Figure 7. Performance of D-connections for different threshold values for the ARPA-2 network. The D-connection traffic is 50%.

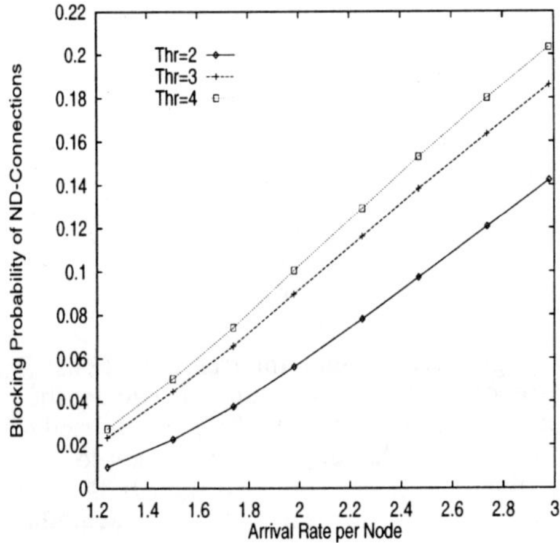

Figure 8. Performance of ND-connections for different threshold values for the ARPA-2 network. The D-connection traffic is 50%.

6. Conclusions

In this paper, we addressed the problem of dynamically establishing primary-backup lightpaths for dependable connections in wavelength-routed WDM networks. We proposed different methods for the pro-active fault-tolerant routing problem. These methods differ in their complexity and performance. All the proposed methods use *backup multiplexing* technique to efficiently use the wavelength channels and thus improving the network performance. All the methods were evaluated through extensive simulation experiments on different networks with different connectivity. In order to improve fairness, we proposed *backup threshold* method and was experimentally evaluated. While it performs well, an adaptive algorithm, which dynamically adjusts the threshold value depending on the network traffic and their performance, could efficiently utilize the wavelength channels.

References

[1] I. Chlamtac, A. Ganz, and G. Karmi, "Lightpath Communications: An Approach to High Bandwidth Optical WANs", IEEE Transactions on Communications, vol. 40, no. 7, pp. 1171-1182, July 1992.

[2] R. Ramaswami and K.N. Sivarajan, "Routing and Wavelength Assignment in All-Optical Networks", IEEE/ACM Transactions on Networking, vol. 3. no. 5, pp. 489-500, October 1995.

[3] D. Banerjee and B. Mukherjee, "A Practical Approach for Routing and Wavelength Assignment in Large Wavelength Routed Optical Networks", IEEE Journal on Selected Areas in Communications, vol. 14, no. 5, pp. 903-908, June 1996.

[4] A. Mokhtar and M. Azizoglu, " Adaptive Wavelength Routing in All-Optical Networks", IEEE/ACM Transactions on Networking, vol. 6, no. 2, pp. 197-206, April 1998.

[5] S. Han and K.G. Shin, "Efficient Spare Resource Allocation for Fast Restoration of Real-Time Channels from Network Component Failures", In Proc. of Real-Time Systems Symposium, RTSS, 1997.

[6] C.S. Li and R. Ramaswami, "Automatic Fault Detection, Isolation, and Recovery in Transparent All-Optical Networks", IEEE/OSA Journal of Lightwave Technology, vol. 15, no. 10, pp. 1784-1793, October 1997.

[7] N. Nagatsu, S. Okamoto, and K. Sato, "Optical Path Cross-Connect System Scale Evaluation Using Path Accommodation Design for Restricted Wavelength Multiplexing", IEEE Journal on Selected Areas in Communications, vol. 14, no. 5, pp. 893-902, June 1996.

[8] M. Alanyali and E. Ayanoglu, "Provisioning Algorithms for WDM Optical Networks", In Proc. of INFOCOM'98, pp. 910-918, 1998.

[9] R. Ramaswami and A. Segall, " Distributed Network Control for Wavelength Routed Optical Networks", In Proc. of INFOCOM'96, 1996.

[10] S. Bandyopadhyay, A. Sengupta, and A. Jaekel, "Fault-tolerant Routing Scheme for All-Optical Networks", In Proc. of SPIE Conference on All-Optical Communication Systems, 1998.

Interference Robust TCP*

Bhaskar Maruthi
Cisco Systems
San Jose, CA
maruthi@cisco.com

Arun K. Somani
Dept. of Elect. and Comp. Eng.
Iowa State University
Ames, IA 50011
arun@iastate.edu

Murat Azizoglu
Dept. of Elect. Eng.
Univ. of Washington
Seattle, WA 98195
aziz@ee.washington.edu

Abstract: *With the exception of the Fast Retransmit and Recovery algorithms, Transmission Control Protocol (TCP) assumes congestion to be the only source of packet loss. When wireless networks experience packet loss due to interference or any other error, congestion control algorithms in TCP are triggered. Unnecessary and incorrect usage of congestion control algorithms results in a high performance penalty. We analyze and present results describing the unsuitability of congestion control algorithms in TCP when packets are lost due to interference. We then present Interference Robust TCP (IR-TCP), which is a transport layer protocol that improves the transport layer performance as compared to TCP in the presence of lossy links such as those in wireless networks. IR-TCP is interference aware and uses the interference information from the link layer for its recovery procedure. IR-TCP is backward compatible and does not affect performance during normal operation or congestion, while providing significant performance improvement during interference. We present experimental implementation of IR-TCP and the measurement of the performance improvement relative to TCP.*

1 Introduction

There has been a considerable increase in the popularity and utility for Wireless Networks (WN) in the recent past [1] due to availability of fast and economical laptop computers. Communication devices [1] connect the computing devices to each other and/or a wired backbone at LAN speeds thereby achieving a wireless extension to the Internet. As a result, there has been accelerated interest in the research community to alleviate bottlenecks in WNs and improve their performance. An important research issue, concerning transport protocols, is the unsuitability of TCP in handling packet loss due to interference[1].

Flow and congestion control algorithms in TCP are relatively inefficient when the underlying physical medium is wireless and experiences interference. This is because of fundamental assumptions that packet loss are only congestion related. Congestion control algorithms identify the presence of congestion using measures of delay in the reception of an acknowledgment (ACK) for a packet transmitted. In the event of a timeout, which is defined as a failure of the arrival of an ACK within the expected time, a congestion control algorithm is invoked. This algorithm reduces the transmission rate (through closing the transmission window) and the retransmission rate (through binary exponential backoff of retransmission timer), and measure the transmission capacity of the end-to-end path again. When interference causes packet loss and timeouts, congestion control algorithms fall out of place, as there is no congestion and the only result is wastage of bandwidth due to the reduction in transmission rates[2].

A satisfactory solution to interference problems in WNs should involve tightly coupled mechanisms for each of the protocol layers. Interaction between layers should not degrade performance. Backward compatibility with existing software is also a very desirable aspect as hosts on the Internet often interact with heterogeneous network hardware and software. It would not be realistic to expect a rehaul of the existing infrastructure to support mobility.

In this paper, we present interference robust TCP (IR-TCP), a protocol that provides such a solution at the transport layer to problems experienced by TCP when used over WNs or any other medium that experiences packet loss due to reasons other than congestion only. It detects the interference information at the link layer and makes it available to TCP for its recovery procedure.

2 TCP and Interference

Transmission Control Protocol (TCP) [2] is a connection oriented protocol that provides a reliable data stream to the layers above. We discuss some aspects of TCP that affect its performance under certain specific conditions. It is necessary to explain our work.

Application data sent to TCP is broken into *segments* before being sent to IP. Segments are sequenced by segment numbers. Reliability in data can be compromised by three events: data corruption, data loss, and reordering of data. TCP maintains a timer (retransmission timer) to measure the delay in receiving an acknowledgment (ACK) from the receiver for a transmitted segment. When an ACK does not arrive within an estimated time interval, the corresponding segment is assumed to be lost and is retransmitted. TCP also manages out-of-order arrival of its segments transmitted as IP datagrams.

*This research was supported in part by the NSF under grants NCR 9628165 and NCR 9796318 and by Nicholas Professorship at Iowa State University.

[1] Interference is used here as a generic term to describe a source, other than congestion, of packet corruption or loss.

[2] Transmission in general, refers here to both transmission and retransmission of packets or ACKs. The difference shall be explicitly stated when required.

0-7695-0213-X/99 $10.00 © 1999 IEEE

2.1 Flow and Congestion Control

Flow control is the procedure of handling the mismatch in processing and buffering capacities between a receiver and a transmitter to best utilize the bandwidth provided by the transmission medium. A sliding window protocol is used by TCP to achieve flow control.

A receiving host, during connection setup phase informs the transmitting host its buffer capacity relating to the "maximum" number of packets that can be outstanding (unacknowledged) at any given time. This is the receiver window size, $rwnd$. The transmitter maintains a sliding window whose current size, wnd, is an estimate of how many packets can be transmitted to the network without waiting for an ACK. An upper bound on wnd is $rwnd$.

The bandwidth-delay product of the path is a rough approximation of the *capacity of the pipe*. The round-trip time (RTT) is estimated by measuring the delay between a segment transmission and the arrival of its ACK. Congestion is a condition of severe delay caused by an overload of datagrams at the switching points (e.g., at gateways) resulting in dropping of packets. A sender reacts to delay and packet loss by retransmitting the affected packets. This adds to congestion which can then grow quickly, resulting in what is now known as a congestion collapse. An intuitive and correct way to react to congestion is to reduce the transmission rate. A receiver may also transmit a duplicate acknowledgment (DACK) if it detects that an original ACK is lost or a packet is received more than once (due to retransmission).

Slow Start and Congestion Avoidance. *Slow Start* (SS) algorithm in TCP sets the window size to zero and measures unknown capacity of the pipe when starting or restarting connections. In every iteration, the window size is doubled reaching the estimate of delay bandwidth product. It is a currently required implementation in TCP [2].

Congestion in the network is detected by a timeout or a DACK. In this case the pipe capacity estimate in the previous iteration is stored in the variable *ssthresh*. This estimate is a rough indication of the pipe capacity and is hence used as a threshold until which slow start has to be performed when the pipe capacity is re-measured later. Beyond a window size of *ssthresh* an additive increase in window size is adopted. This algorithm is called *Congestion Avoidance* (CA). Another variable *cwnd* is used to store a running estimate of the window size as governed by congestion. It can be easily seen that $wnd = \min(cwnd, rwnd)$. Upon detection of congestion through timeout (strong indication of congestion) or a DACK (weak indication of congestion), half of current $cwnd$ is stored in $ssthresh$ to force congestion avoidance. A justification for this 50% reduction factor is given in [4]. This is the *multiplicative decrease* part of the congestion control algorithm. Additionally, if congestion is indicated by a timeout, $cwnd$ is set to one segment size, forcing slow start.

Round Trip Time Measurements. A smoothened RTT estimator (R) which uses a low pass filter is given by,

$$R \leftarrow \alpha R + (1 - \alpha)M$$

where α is a smoothing factor with the recommended value of 0.9 and M is the current measured value of delay. [2] recommends the retransmission timeout value (RTO) to be set to $RTO = R\beta$ where β is a delay variance factor with a recommended value of 2. [3] details the problems with this approach, pointing out that it cannot react to wide fluctuations in RTT, causing unnecessary retransmissions.

Karn's Algorithm and Timer Backoff. An ACK received after the retransmission(s) of a packet can belong to either the original transmission or the secondary transmission(s). This is the *retransmission ambiguity problem.* Karn's algorithm [5] suggests postponing the use of updated RTO until an ACK for a segment that has been transmitted only once has arrived.

If TCP ignores ACKs from retransmitted segments, it will never update its estimate and the cycle will continue. To accommodate such failures, a timer backoff strategy is used in which the round trip timeout value is exponentially increased on every timeout.

$$RTO \leftarrow \gamma RTO.$$

Typically, γ is 2 (which is binary exponential backoff).

Fast Retransmit and Fast Recovery. In *Fast Retransmission and Recovery* (FRR) [6] when the number of DACKs received for a particular transmission exceeds a threshold (typically 3), TCP-*Reno* retransmits the lost packet and the window is reduced by a factor of two instead of being closed to one. Further, in order to prevent a burst of packets from being transmitted when the retransmission is finally acknowledged, new packets are transmitted with each DACK while performing congestion avoidance. FRR fails when a contiguous number of packets greater than wnd is lost. If the loss rate is higher than one packet per RTT, throughput will degrade at the product of the loss rate and bandwidth delay product.

2.2 Interference Problems

Interference may occur in bursts of varying lengths. Let us suppose that there is interference at the transmitter. In this case the Signal to Noise Ratio (SNR) at the transmitter is too low for the correct decoding of ACKs and DACKs that are being transmitted by the receiver, and this causes timeouts at the transmitter. Timeouts result in the following actions.

- Binary timer exponential backoff, which reduces the retransmission rate quickly, resulting in heavy throughput loss.
- The assumption of congestion in the network invalidates all window measurements and SS is forcibly invoked by setting $cwnd$ to one segment size.
- $ssthresh$ is reduced to half the current $cwnd$ under the assumption that the preceding value of pipe capacity was correct. This means that when we restart, we would use SS only until the window size, $cwnd$, reaches half of the current window size. We would have to adopt linear increase in window size (congestion avoidance) thereafter.

In WNs, latency in handoffs could be large owing to delay in handing over connections and routing inconsistencies. This results in packet loss and timeouts, an effect exactly similar to the effect of interference.

3 Related Work

The proposed solutions in literature to improve transport layer performance on wireless links can be classified into two groups: End to End (ETE) and Split Connection (SC). In ETE schemes, receivers convey packet loss information using a Selective Acknowledgment (SACK) [7] or an Explicit Loss Notification (ELN) of local interference to senders avoiding unnecessary retransmission of packets which are not affected by interference. SC schemes, such as, Indirect-TCP (I-TCP) [8] and the Snoop protocol [9], attempt to isolate losses in wireless networks by splitting the connection into two components, a wired connection and wireless connection. Retransmissions for losses in the WN are done at a proxy host, normally the *base station* which marks the transition from the wired to the wireless connection, thereby preventing end-to-end retransmissions. The transport layer proxy incurs processing overhead as the packets have to pass through the four protocol layers twice.

We propose a method to add awareness of interference to TCP. This is similar to the proposal in [11] with an effort to *detect* the presence of interference in a wireless network and use it to control the transport layer functionalities. This is an important difference between our proposal and other efforts that either assume interference over congestion [10], or provide solutions that do not directly involve transport layer functionality [8, 9, 12]. We develop algorithms that use the knowledge of interference to tune the flow and congestion control algorithms, and various window parameters to better react to interference. We also add an active receiver component that helps in faster recovery from the interference.

4 Solution Methodology

An effective scheme to counter interference at the transport layer is to make it interference-aware and modify its flow and congestion control algorithms. Moreover, an accurate decision about the presence of interference is as important as the early and correct detection of congestion. We describe one mechanism to detect and measure interference and develop our transport layer protocol (IR-TCP). Note that more research in effective mechanisms to clearly identify interference are needed.

4.1 Detection of Interference

When a receiver[3] is unable to extract data from the radio waves that it is monitoring (possibly due to low SNR), we say that it is experiencing interference. This results in data corruption or a complete loss of data.

For example, in some wireless networks, the WN interface card is run by a driver software that reads and writes packets from and to the RAM on the card. The driver software performs error detection and some housekeeping functions before passing the packet on to the IP layer through a buffering mechanism. After the IP processing is completed, the packet is handed to TCP through another buffer. In such a set up, there are at least two methods to detect the presence of interference.

- *Monitor integrity of data.* This works when interference causes data corruption. If the Cyclic Redundancy Check (CRC) performed at the link layer for the received frame fails, there is a high probability that there is interference at the receiver. This method of detection relies on the reception on data and hence fails when the interference is strong enough to wipe out the signal.

- *Monitor SNR.* Measuring SNR at the receiver is an appropriate and accurate method to detect interference and works even in the case of signal wipes out. By probing the interface card with device control commands, it is possible to obtain instances of SNR as seen by the receiver. The receiver has a reference signal power level to which it compares the received signal strength and noise level.

A combination of both schemes would add more confidence to the decision, but SNR measurement is more efficient as drops in connectivity (blackouts) due to severe interference, hand-offs and out-of-range instances are more frequent than data corruption. Let I_{CRC} be the event of interference detection due to the first scheme and I_{SNR} the event of detection due to SNR measure falling below a threshold SNR_{min}. Further define S to be a variable indicating the state of the channel, with a value of 1 implying the presence of interference and a 0 implying the lack of detected interference. Summarizing,

$I_{CRC} = I_{SNR} = 0$; [Initialize before sampling]
if $(SNR < SNR_{min})$ $\{ I_{SNR} = 1 \}$;
if (CRC failed) $\{ I_{CRC} = 1 \}$;
$S = I_{SNR} || I_{CRC}$;

4.2 Link and Transport Layer Interaction

Congestion can occur anywhere in the path between the sender and the receiver and has to be detected through end-to-end measurements such as the estimate of round trip delay. The requirement of an end-to-end detection scheme justifies the placement of the scheme in the transport layer. Interference is a local phenomenon and has to be detected at the receiver/transmitter site. The interference detection scheme that we describe here is placed in the link layer and hence, the information on interference has to be passed on to the transport layer. The transport and link layer communicate through a kernel interface.

5 IR-TCP

IR-TCP is an interference aware transport layer that detects the presence of interference while also being congestion aware. Some researchers do not believe that this is a good practice. However, it is our strong belief that without such mechanisms performance cannot be achieved. IR-TCP employs algorithms that improve recovery from interference and overall performance during interference. It also prevents the inappropriate usage of congestion control algorithms when there is interference and not congestion in the path. In the following, we assume that the two ends are asynchronous in terms of experiencing interference.

5.1 Pipe Snapshot Algorithm

The bandwidth of the logical bit pipe between the sender and the receiver is affected by the processing delays, buffering delays, transmission and propagation delays over the entire

[3] In this context, a receiver is the wireless network interface card. This is not to be confused with a "receiver" in the TCP end-to-end notation.

path between the sender and the receiver. Flow and congestion control algorithms measure this varying bandwidth on the occurrence of the events (timeouts, ACK, DACK) we previously described. When the channel is under interference, these events either don't occur (ACKs/DACKs don't arrive) or hold invalid measurements. For example, packet loss, and not congestion in the network, causes timeouts. In regular TCP, a timeout is caused when the observed round trip time is substantially different from RTT. TCP tries to re-measure the pipe capacity in such an instance.

Measurements of the pipe capacity during interference are incorrect. Accordingly, we use a snapshot of the pipe capacity represented in terms of $cwnd$, $ssthresh$ and wnd until a valid measurement can be obtained. Due to the sliding window scheme and the loss of ACKs, the window closes after a window worth of transmission and retransmissions take place. Thus we prevent incorrect measurements during interference and hand over the saved parameters to TCP after the interference period.

5.2 Aggressive Retransmission Algorithm

It is also necessary that we recover from interference as soon as possible once the interference is over. The arrival of an ACK or a DACK marks the beginning of the recovery. The rate at which ACKs/DACKs are arriving at the transmitter is approximately equal to the rate at which retransmission is taking place. Hence, recovery rate is directly proportional to the rate of retransmissions during interference. In the absence of a current measure we assume that the bandwidth available to our connection has not changed during interference and retransmit with a fixed rate that corresponds to the bandwidth delay measurement just before interference. This is the maximum possible recovery rate that can be employed.

The retransmissions to counter interference could occur either at the transport layer or at the link layer. A link layer retransmission scheme should be designed to work in harmony with the retransmission schemes of the transport layer. [13] describes the problems in employing two independent retransmission schemes in the same protocol stack. Layer interactions cause errors in measurement of pipe bandwidth. *Aggressive Retransmission* employs a transport layer retransmission and does not suffer from the defects of layer interaction as in the case of multi-layer retransmission scheme. Interference is detected by monitoring the channel state either at a predetermined rate or on the occurrence of a timeout. A successful transmission marks the termination of interference.

5.3 Active Receiver Algorithm

TCP receivers send ACKs/DACKs only upon the arrival of a packet. If interference were to cause packet loss at the receiver, the receivers would consider it as an end of transmission and would not react. Meanwhile, the sender may experience timeouts and reduces its retransmission rate, resulting in slow recovery after interference.

We, therefore, propose an *active receiver* that retransmits DACKs during interference which are placed about RTT/2 time apart. This is the minimum required rate to prevent the sender from employing binary timer exponential backoff. Presence of interference means that packets either arrive in error and are discarded at the link layer, or it is not possible to decode packets with the current signal level. During the presence of interference at the receiver, *Active Receiver* algorithm transmits DACKs at a fixed rate. All of these DACKs correspond to the last successful segment that was received before interference. The algorithm terminates once interference has subsided, which is indicated by the successful arrival of a packet or the channel state measurement. The effect of this algorithm, like the previous ones, is to increase the recovery rate. Further, if the sender is using TCP-*Reno*, fast retransmission is triggered after the required minimum number of DACKs have arrived.

5.4 Congestion and Interference

What happens when congestion and interference occur simultaneously is another question of importance. Detection of interference at either the sender or the receiver causes the algorithms to maintain transmission rates at a level that would have been optimal before the onset of congestion. Such rates could be detrimental if there were congestion in the network. Hence, we introduce a soft limit to the number of times, or the total contiguous amount of time, for which the algorithms can be executed. After this limit has been exceeded, the algorithms are disabled and TCP reacts to congestion in an appropriate manner. This allows recovery using interference procedure for some time and then the algorithm switches to normal congestion recovery algorithm. The goal is to make best use of the two strategies.

- $MAX\_BACKOFFS$ is the maximum number of *Aggressive Retransmission* performed. The corresponding time duration is $MAX\_BACKOFFS * RTT$.
- $MAX\_RETRANS$ is the maximum number of times the *Active Receiver* algorithm is executed. The maximum time duration for which this algorithm is continually executed is $MAX\_RETRANS * RTT/2$.

6 Implementation of IR-TCP

The implementation of IR-TCP is backward compatible with the existing TCP stack and the design is modular. This section contains a brief discussion of these implementation and design aspects.

In a layered protocol, layers in the stack have well defined Service Access Points (SAP) and should communicate only through these SAPs for utilizing and providing services to their neighboring layers. Such communication is normally vertical, implying that *layer n* can communicate only with *layers (n+1)* and *(n-1)*. This is achieved through encapsulation[4] of data. Vertical communication ensures a phase lock, like a pipeline, in the time-based functioning of the different layers.

When the transport layer needs information about the characteristics of the physical layer or the layers below it for performance improvement, it is necessary that they communicate, and they can if they do not violate the purpose of vertical communication. In our implementation, we have defined a kernel interface through which the link layer informs IR-TCP about the state of the underlying channel.

In our implementation only during interference, IR-TCP uses the modified set of algorithms to work in the interference mode. Otherwise the algorithms work under the regular TCP protocol framework and hence can talk to other machines running a TCP stack. In fact, in all our experiments, one of the two machines runs a regular stack while

[4] The header and data of *layer n* become the payload for *layer (n+1)*.

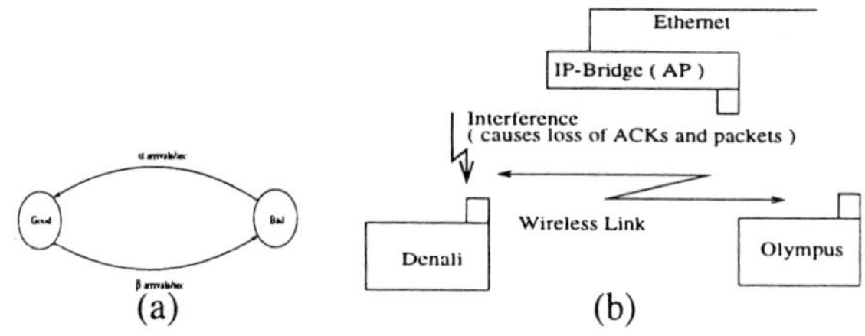

Figure 1: (a) Two state Markov chain used to model interference, and (b) Experimental setup

the other has an IR-TCP stack. The error model is embedded in the wireless driver. These models have been verified using an actual implementation. A kernel interface has been designed for communication between IR-TCP and the driver. The driver updates a channel state variable, WV_CH_STATE, and IR-TCP reads the value of this variable when it requires to know the channel state. A *Channel Test Timer* (CTT) is employed at the receiver whose call-back function samples the channel state. The implementation of the algorithms can be summarized as follows.

- On timeout at the sender,

  if (WV_CH_STATE = Interference)
  {*Pipe Snapshot*;
  Aggressive Retransmission;};
  else {*Congestion Control*};

- On CTT expiry at the receiver,

  if (WV_CH_STATE = Interference) {Send DACK};

7 Experimentation Results

It is difficult to produce a real and controlled interference environment. Therefore, in our experimental setup, we have embedded an interference model into the wireless driver module that simulates various interference probabilities. In this section, we first describe the system setup for experimentation and explain the experiments and results.

7.1 Interference Model

We used a two state Markov chain model to simulate the interference at the channel, under which we measure and study performance improvement provided by IR-TCP.

Figure 1a shows the two state Markov model. *Good* and *Bad* are two states that the channel can be in. When the channel is *Good*, there is no interference, and when the channel state is *Bad*, the channel is experiencing interference. A host cannot receive packets when the channel is in the *Bad* state. Independent Poisson processes generate *Good* and *Bad* events with rates α and β respectively. *Good* and *Bad* events mark the beginning of *Good* and *Bad* states. A burst of interference starts with the arrival of a *Bad* event and ends with the arrival of the first *Good* event after this *Bad* event. The steady-state probabilities of the *Good* and *Bad* states can be controlled by changing the arrival rates α and β. $\pi_g = \alpha/(\alpha + \beta)$ is the probability that the channel is in *Good* state.

7.2 Testbed Setup

Our testbed contains a wireless LAN (WLAN) connected to an Ethernet through a wired to wireless IP bridge (Figure 1b. Two mobile hosts, Denali and Olympus, are laptops with wireless interface cards. The laptops are Intel Pentium machines (133MHz; 32MB RAM). Olympus runs a kernel with the regular TCP stack. There are two kernels in Denali. One with a regular TCP stack and the other with IR-TCP. The wireless driver in Denali contains the interference model and provides for varying probabilities of the *Good* state.

All measurements are obtained from real experiments conducted on this network. During these measurements, the WLAN is disconnected from the Ethernet to prevent traffic from the Ethernet entering the WLAN. The primary parameter for measuring performance improvement was application layer throughput or equivalently the throughput offered by TCP and IR-TCP. We used *ttcp* to measure throughput and *tcpdump* to further analyze the mechanics of TCP and IR-TCP.

7.3 Throughput Measurement

Delivered throughput is experimentally measured using ttcp for TCP and IR-TCP between two mobile hosts (MHs) under varying probabilities of the *Good* state. The duration of transmission is at least the time period of 100 cycles through the *Good* and *Bad* states[5]. For a given probability of good state, the arrival rates of the *Good* and *Bad* events can be scaled. Hence, the experiment can be repeated with scaled rates of arrival as described in Section 7.4.

Figure 2a shows the improvement in throughput when interference occurs at the transmitter and ACKs are getting lost. The theoretical maximum throughput, deliverable by an ideal transport mechanism, when there is no interference is around 1.2 Mbits/sec after accounting for transfer of header data and implementation overheads. This is the throughput what the application layer would see. The dotted lines in all throughput measurement is the maximum achievable throughput with an ideal transport mechanism.

- With the probability of *Good* state close to 0.5, the *Good* and *Bad* states are almost of equal duration with the mean arrival rate of 3.33 events/sec. When timeouts occur in TCP, the retransmission rate quickly drops, and most of the *Good* states are completely missed when the retransmission rate is sufficiently low. With *Aggressive Retransmission* in IR-TCP, the *Good* states are utilized more effectively.

- There is a sharp drop in throughput in TCP around low π_g regions, while for most part IR-TCP exhibits a linear drop in throughput. The removal of the exponential component from the backoff algorithm (binary exponential backoff) and removal of exponential reduction in window size (halving *ssthresh*) are primarily responsible for this behavior.

- When $\pi_g \approx 0.5$, SS dominates most of the *Good* periods and with frequent occurrence of timeouts, the window never grows to a considerable length. *Pipe Snapshot* saves the window size during interference allowing it to grow as if there were no interference.

[5]The number of bytes transferred during one instance varied from 0.6MB to 180MB.

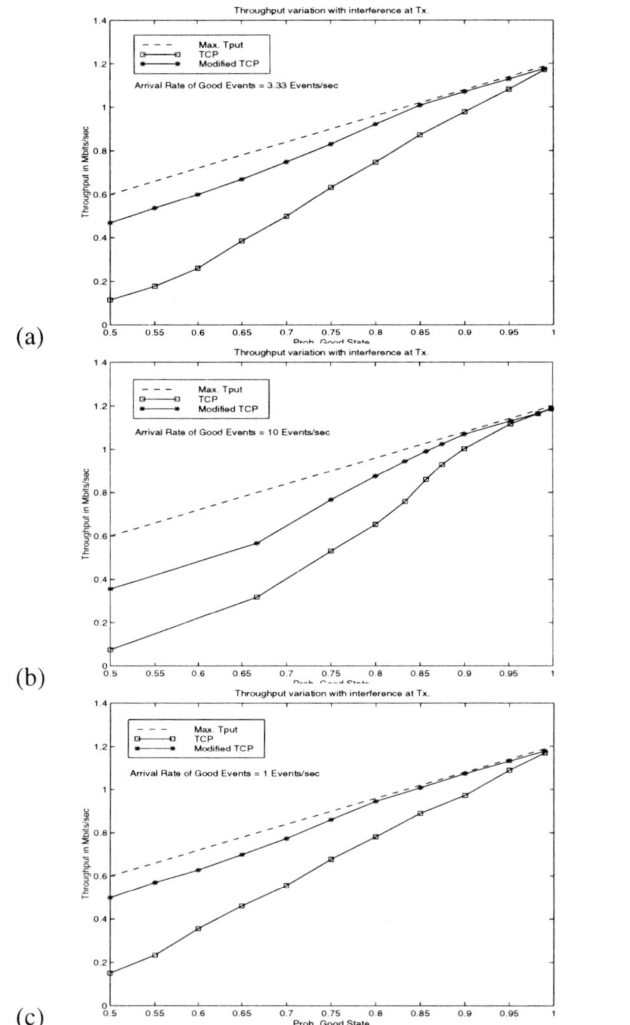

Figure 2: Throughput Measurement: Interference at the Transmitter: (a) Causes loss of ACKs and DACKs. (b) Shorter duration of Good events (α is a constant and β is varied to vary π_g). (c) High arrival rates for a given π_g.

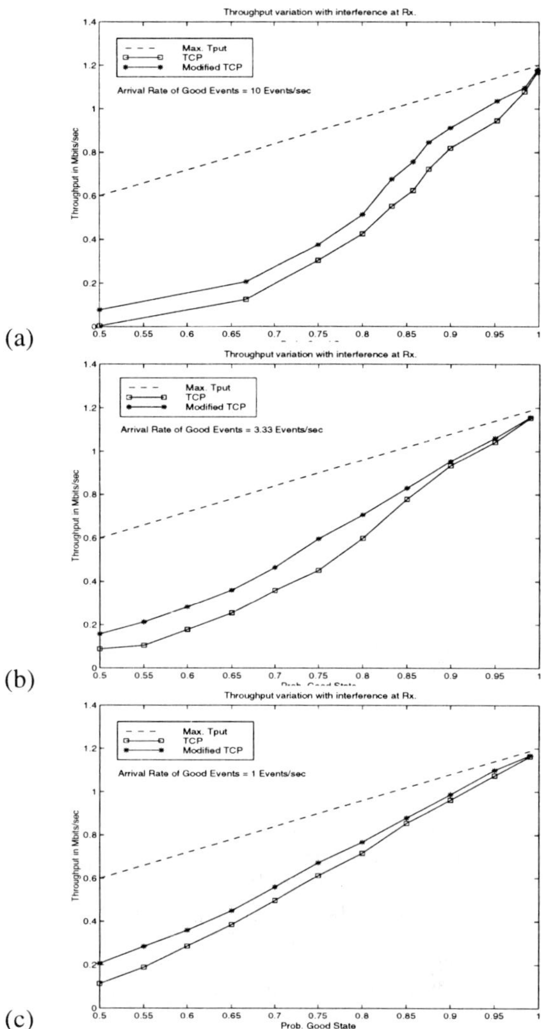

Figure 3: Throughput Measurement: Interference at the Receiver: (a) Causes packet loss at high arrival rates for a given π_g. (b) Moderate arrival rate of events. (c) Low arrival rate of events.

- The difference in throughput between the theoretical maximum and IR-TCP is mostly due to non-negligible recovery time and system overheads.
- As π_g increases, the *Good* periods are longer in duration and there is a smaller number of interference bursts within a given period of time. This accounts for the curves representing both TCP and IR-TCP being closer to the limiting curve than at lower π_g.

Figures 2b and 2c depict results from the first experiment with arrival rates of the events scaled up and down respectively. With high rate of arrivals (Figure 2c) the performance is lower due to the proportionally higher time occupied by the exponential algorithms. Figure 2c represents throughput measurements with relatively low rate of channel state transitions. The curves are almost linear because of the relatively lower time occupied by the exponential algorithms. The improvement in throughput at lower π_g is high, primarily due to differences between exponential backoff and *Aggressive Retransmission*. Maximum window size was mostly around 6 in our LAN environment, and hence there was relatively smaller improvement due to *Pipe Snapshot*. High bandwidth delay product paths would show more improvement.

In the case of interference at the receiver the recovery rate is determined by the retransmission rate at the transmitter. The results for the same three cases as for the transmitter are shown in Figures 3a, 3b, and 3c, respectively. An *Active Receiver* maintains a constant retransmission rate at the sender. The effect of transmission rates is not as dominant as in case of interference at the sender because DACKs do not always cause retransmission. The improvement offered by IR-TCP is higher with interference at the transmitter as TCP follows a cumulative ACK scheme. Loosing an ACK can sometimes be compensated by the arrival of the next ACK in time.

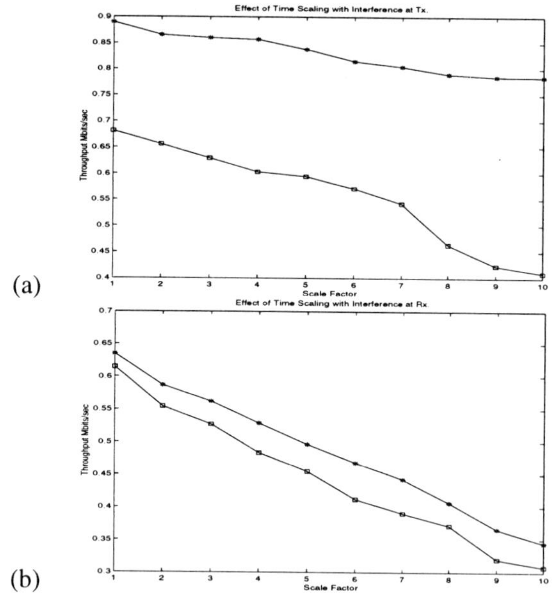

(a)

(b)

Figure 4: Effect of Time Scaling for $\pi_g = 0.5$: Interference at the (a) transmitter causes ACK/DACK loss; and (b) receiver is causing packet loss.

7.4 Time Scaling

There were noticeable variations in results observed amongst the above experiments with different arrival rates of the *Good* and *Bad* events. We study this phenomenon by scaling both the *Good* and *Bad* arrival rates by a factor K with π_g remaining a constant. The ratio of the mean of *Good* and *Bad* periods is the same, but the periods are inversely proportional to K. Therefore, we are scaling time for channel state variations while keeping the time scale of the TCP mechanism a constant.

Measurements made in this experiment are shown in Figures 4a and 4b. With shorter *Good* and *Bad* states, corresponding to higher K, there is an increased chance of missing out the *Good* states. This is why IR-TCP offers higher improvement in throughput at higher values of K. In other words, performance under a given recovery rate drops with an increase in K. For a given RTO, recovery rate drops sharply with larger K in TCP while it is almost constant in IR-TCP because of *Aggressive Retransmission*. Again, the results of this behavior are not as dominant with interference at receiver (Figure 4b) as they are with interference at transmitter.

7.5 Packet Level Observation

In this section we present observations at the packet level from outputs of *tcpdump*. Figures 5a and 5b are time traces of data packet transmissions. The binary exponential backoff of RTO values appears on the first plot. RTO value around the region marked with 2 is as high as 15 seconds, which is approximately 75% of the time required for the entire transmission in the case of IR-TCP (plot2). Note that the time scales for the plots are different. The slope of the dark sections in both the plots, which correspond to transmission during *Good* periods, roughly equals 1.2Mbits/sec. This experiment was conducted with $\pi_g = 0.5$. An ideal transport layer with zero recovery time would transmit useful data 50% of the time. TCP in this experiment transmits useful data about 10% of the time and IR-TCP transmits useful data about 40% of the time. Between TCP and IR-TCP, 30% of *Good* time is lost due to inadequate retransmission rates. The throughput corresponding to these statistics are 0.48 Mbits/sec for IR-TCP and 0.12 Mbits/sec for TCP. Thus our modifications result in an improvement[6] by a factor of 4.

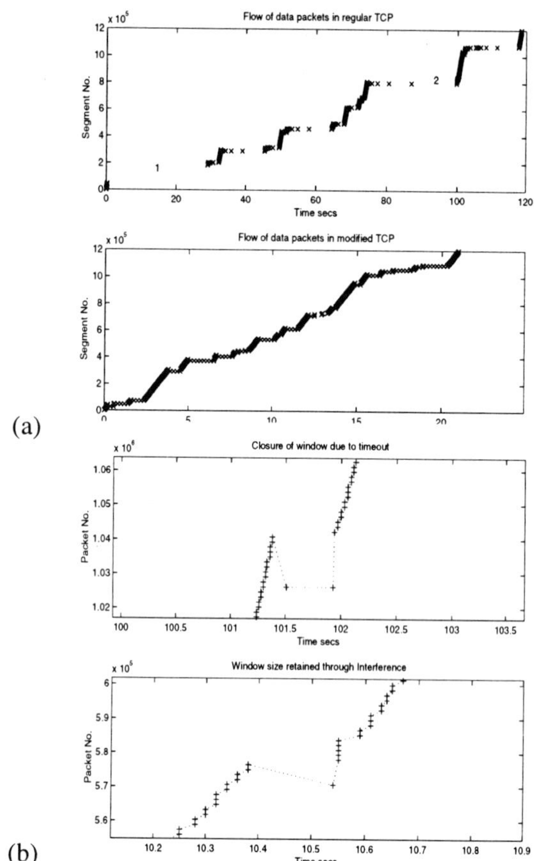

(a)

(b)

Figure 5: (a) "tcpdump" analysis of TCP and IR-TCP: Segment numbers are plotted against transmission times. Each cross mark represents the transmission of a segment. (b) Packet Level Observation: A zoom-in on data transmission trace is shown. A 1.2 MB transfer was used. Each "+" marks the transmission of a packet. The beginning of retransmission appear as dotted line segments with negative slope. Horizontal lines represent retransmission and lines with positive slope mark progressive transmission. The first plot is from TCP and the second from IR-TCP.

The discussion in the previous paragraph focussed on improvements provided by *Aggressive Retransmission*. However, the throughput improvement is also due to the *Pipe Snapshot* algorithm and this partially accounts for the higher factor of increase in throughput observed in the experiment than that calculated by taking only the retransmission

[6] A good instance from IR-TCP and a bad instance from TCP have been used in this experiment for visual clarity. The factor of improvement in this experiment is about 6.

schemes into account. Figure 5b is a zoom-in on the time trace. Vertical stacking of horizontal lines correspond to packet transmissions at the same time[7]. The packet transmission around 101.5 in the first plot is a retransmission. The number of outstanding packets is exactly the window size[8]. This is approximately the number of horizontal dashes above the dash representing the retransmitted packet and before the timeout. Hence, the window size at the point where interference occurred, causing a timeout, was 11. Timeout caused the window to close. The window has to grow again using SS after a successful retransmission detects the end of interference. In the second plot, which is from IR-TCP, a window size of 5 is saved by the *Pipe Snapshot* algorithm. Transmission resumes with the window size that was calculated just before interference. This appears as 5 vertically stacked dashes after the first successful retransmission.

The experimental results show substantial improvement in the throughput with IR-TCP. The improvement in throughput is higher when π_g is low. Low probability of *Good* state corresponds to severe interference. The algorithms show higher improvement when there are long bursts of interference. The improvements are also consistent and at no stage was the throughput observed with IR-TCP lower than the throughput observed with TCP.

8 Conclusions and Future Work

We have studied the problem of unsuitability of TCP for networks whose links experience packet loss due to interference. Starting with an explanation of congestion and flow control in TCP, we have shown how the assumptions under which these algorithms function fail when wireless media experiences interference. We have proposed IR-TCP that addresses specific problems in TCP, with regard to performance during interference. The algorithms collectively improve the throughput while working within the framework of TCP semantics.

As the first of a two step solution, we proposed a scheme of detecting the presence of interference. SNR is a good measure for detecting interference. We showed how this channel state information can be conveyed to the transport layer.

We discussed the issue of optimal recovery rate and presented an optimal recovery rate under our *Aggressive Retransmission* algorithm. We addressed the issue of aggravating congestion by disabling the exponential backoff in retransmission rate. The *Active Receiver* algorithm was presented as a counterpart solution to inadequate recovery rate when interference affects a receiver. We studied and showed that the window size variations in response to occurrence of interference is the reason for performance degradation. *Pipe Snapshot* algorithm has been presented as a solution to this problem.

We presented the results of experiments that demonstrate the improvement in performance offered by the algorithms. Throughput measurements under varying interference situations were made using a real network implementation of the solution. We also studied the effects of scaling time to project the observations of the behavior of our algorithms. Finally, a packet transmission versus time analysis was presented to exhibit a snapshot of the algorithms in action.

The algorithms we propose in this work are steps towards a better solution. However, there are avenues for improvement of the algorithms. The effects of the algorithms when interference and congestion occur simultaneously needs to be further studied. The manner in which fast retransmission and recovery, propagation delays and RTT interact with IR-TCP needs to be further investigated. Finally, IR-TCP uses the channel state when a timeout occurs. How frequently should the driver update this channel state information is an issue. For example, it should be done at least twice the rate at which interference can occur, if the rate can be predicted. We are currently experimenting with an actual hardware set up where noise can be introduced by mixing it in the modem's transmitted signal. The initial results from the hardware experiments verifies the results of simulation experiments reported here in this. The complete results will be reported later on.

[7]Clock accuracy is limited and packet transmission times cluster.

[8]The number of horizontal dashes vertically stacked should not be mistaken for the window size.

References

[1] K. Mann. Up in the air: wireless LAN technology. In *Network Computing.*, volume 6, no.5, pages 26–28, May. 1997.

[2] Postel.J.B. Transmission control protocol. In *RFC 793*, Sept. 1981.

[3] V. Jacobson. Congestion avoidance and control. In *ACM SIGCOMM.*, Aug. 1988.

[4] V. Jacobson. Re: Your congestion control scheme. In *end2end interest mailing list*, Nov. 1987.

[5] P. Karnand C. Partridge. Improving round-trip time estimates in reliable transport protocols. In *ACM Transactions on Computer Systems.*, volume 9, no.4, pages 364–373, Nov. 1991.

[6] V. Jacobson. Modified TCP congestion avoidance algorithm. In *end2end interest mailing list*, Apr. 1990.

[7] M. Mathis J. Mahdavi S. Floyd and A. Romanov. TCP selective acknowledgments options. Internet draft. In *draft-IETF-tcplw-sack-00.txt.*, Jan. 1996.

[8] A. V. Bakre, B. R. Badrinath. Implementation and performance evaluation of indirect TCP. In *IEEE Transactions on Computers.*, volume 46, no.3, pages 260–278, Mar. 1997.

[9] H. Balakrishnan, V.N. Padmanabhan, S. Seshan, and R.H. Katz. A comparison of mechanisms for improving TCP performance over wireless links. In *Proceedings ACM SIGCOMM*, 1996.

[10] R. Dube, C. D. Rais, and S. K. Tripathi. Improving NFS performance over wireless links. In *IEEE Transactions on Computers*, volume 46, no.3, pages 290–298, Mar. 1997.

[11] R. C. Durst and G. J. Miller. TCP Extensions for Space Communications. In *ACM/IEEE Mobicom 1996*, pages 15–26, November 1996.

[12] R. Caceres and L. Iftode. Improving the performance of reliable transport protocols in mobile computing environments. In *IEEE JSAC*, volume 13, no.5, Jun. 1995.

[13] A. DeSimone, M. Chuah, and Y. On-Ching. Throughput performance of transport-layer protocols over wireless LANS. In *IEEE in Houston. GLOBECOM '93.*, volume 1, pages 542–549, Dec. 1993.

Effect of Failures on Optimal Location Management Algorithms *

Govind Krishnamurthi Arun K. Somani
Department of Electrical and Computer Engineering
Iowa State University, Ames, IA 50011
Phone: (515) 294-0941, Fax: (515) 294-8432
e-mail: govindk@andes.ee.iastate.edu, arun@iastate.edu

Abstract: *The current IS-41 standard PCS architecture uses a centralized database, the Home Location Register (HLR), to store service and location information of each mobile registered in the PCS network. However, this is a single point of failure, therefore distributed database architectures have been proposed as possible architectures for future mobile networks. The performance of such architectures improves when the load on the databases is balanced. Though distributed architectures offer increased fault tolerance, they suffer from increased query delay (number of databases to be queried to retrieve the required information). The query delay further increases in the presence of database failures. In this paper, we derive bounds for the performance of load balanced location management algorithms in the presence of database failures for three standard performance metrics, worst-case query delay, average query delay, and call blocking probability. A load balanced algorithm tolerating database failures is presented, and its performance measured using the same performance metrics. A robust parallel location management algorithm which queries databases in parallel is then presented, and we derive expressions for the average query delay for the algorithm in presence of failures.*

Keywords: PCS networks, database failures, robust load balancing, query delay, call blocking probability

1 Introduction

Cellular communication technology has advanced rapidly in the last decade with significant developments in the capabilities of mobile networks. Future Personal Communications Services (PCS) networks, will be capable of providing different types of services to a large population. A large amount of research activities is presently various design problems in PCS networks. In this paper we focus on one of the problems, namely the Location Management Problem.

In PCS networks, a location tracking mechanism is needed to locate the position of the mobile hosts[1] in order to establish connections. Current methods require a mobile to report its location to the network using different criteria [1]. The network stores the location of the mobile in location information databases (LIDs) and this information is retrieved during call delivery. When a LID fails, calls may have to be dropped as the location information of mobiles registered in the LID is unavailable. The failure of some of these databases, therefore, negatively affects the performance of the network.

The IS-41 and GSM standards ([2] and [3]) use a two level hierarchy of such LIDs, a global Home Location Register (HLR), and a local Visitor Location Register (VLR) to store the location information of mobiles. When the databases fail, calls are dropped as the called mobiles cannot be located, thus reducing the Quality of Service (QoS) provided by the network. A centralized database is a single point of failure. Also, as the number of mobiles increase in the system the load on the databases is also a factor which decides the call setup-time of the network. A distributed LID architecture for PCS networks is therefore preferred. Though a distributed architecture alleviates the drawbacks of a centralized architecture, it suffers from higher query delay as several databases may have to be queried before locating the called mobiles location information. Location management/call delivery protocols also have to take into account the possibility of database/network failures at the time of an update or query. Presence of failed LIDs also increases the average query delay of the network.

The rest of the paper is organized as follows. In Section 2, we present the system model assumed in this paper. Some related research in location management is presented in Section 3. Performance bounds to three standard metrics, namely worst-case query delay, average query delay and call blocking probability, are derived in Section 4. In Section 5, we describe a load balanced location management algorithm which is optimal with respect to the performance metrics defined before when the network is fault free. We extend the algorithm to accommodate failures and we measure the performance of the algorithm. We analyze the effect of faults on the average query delay of parallel querying algorithms in Section 6. We conclude the paper in Section 7.

2 System Model

Most PCS networks use a cellular architecture for bandwidth efficiency [1]. In this architecture, each cell has a base station to which the mobiles of the cell communicate through a wireless link. A set of base stations is controlled by a Base Station Controller (BSC). The primary function

*This research was supported in part by the David C. Nicholas Professorship of Electrical and Computer Engineering at Iowa State University. The authors wish to acknowledge the initial discussions had with Stefano Chessa, Ph.D. Candidate, University of Pisa, Italy, in developing portions of Section 6.

[1] We refer to mobile hosts as mobiles in the rest of the paper.

0-7695-0213-X/99 $10.00 © 1999 IEEE

of a BSC is to manage the radio resources of its base stations, by performing hand-offs and by allocating radio channels. Each BSC is connected to a Mobile Switching Center (MSC) through a wired network. A MSC typically provides switching functions and coordinates location registration and call delivery. The MSC has access to the location information databases in the network, which are used to store location and service information for each registered mobile of the PCS network. Several distributed architectures can be found in the literature. A distributed database architecture provides fault tolerance, scalability and modularity, at the expense of increased control traffic and connection delay. In this paper we assume the logical setup for the general distributed LID architecture shown in Figure 1. There are n databases with identical storage and access capabilities. These databases are connected to each other and to the MSCs through a wired network[2]. We assume a fail-stop model for LID/link failures in the network.

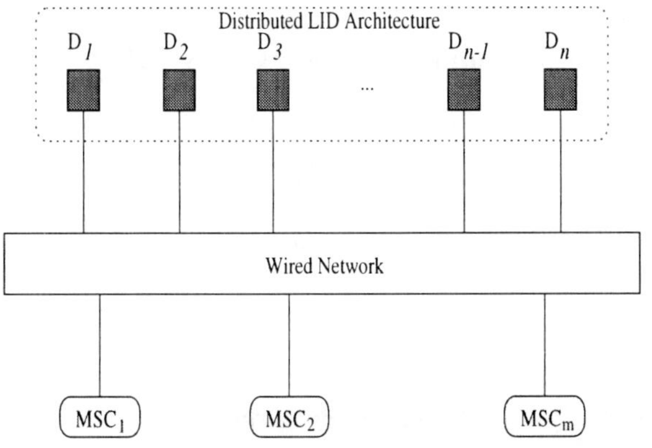

Figure 1. A distributed location database architecture

2.1 Distributed Location Update and Query Protocols

When a mobile leaves a LA and enters another LA, it initiates a Location Update (LU) message. This message updates the position of the mobile in k of the n LIDs. Here k is the replication factor which is chosen to achieve a trade-off between the query delay and the storage costs. When a mobile places a call for another mobile, the MSC checks whether the called mobile is in its LA. This is done by querying a local database or cache if such a database/cache is available. If the called mobile is not in the same LA, the MSC queries the LIDs for the location of the called mobile. Once it receives the information, the MSC routes the call.

3 Previous Work

Several schemes for location management in PCS networks have been developed in the literature. A review of some of these schemes can be found in [1]. In [4], load balancing in quorum systems is discussed and some necessary and sufficient conditions for perfect balancing are given. In [5], a load balancing location management protocol is proposed, in which n databases are partitioned into subsets of cardinality of $2\sqrt{n} - 1$. These subsets are chosen such that any pair of subsets have at least one common database. Upon receiving a location update request, the MSC uses a hash function in selecting a subset for update. Upon receiving a call delivery request, the MSC uses the hash function choose a subset for query. The construction of the subsets guarantees that the MSC is able to find a database with the desired location information.

In [6], a "crumbling walls" approach [7] is used to determine the updated databases. In this work, apart from a dedicated set of location databases, several general purpose servers are used for a variety of tasks including location management. [6] shows that in most load cases the cardinality of the update databases varies between $\log n - \log(\log n)$ and $n/\log n$. One drawback of this scheme is its reliance on the existence of general purpose servers which can be used at times of high load.

A dynamic load balanced location management algorithm which is optimal with respect to average query delay, worst-case query delay and call blocking probability is presented in [8]

The algorithms in [5], [6] and [8] achieve load balance in both updates as well as queries. However, they assume the network to be fault free.

Database recovery issues are addressed in [9] and [10]. However, these research efforts work in the framework of the IS-41 architecture and do not address the issue of query delay in the presence of failures in a distributed database framework, that we propose to do in the rest of this paper.

4 Performance Bounds

In this section we analyze the performance of load balanced location management algorithms in the presence of faults using three standard performance metrics, namely, worst-case query delay, average query delay, and call blocking probability. The metric worst-case query delay refers to the maximum number of LIDs the query algorithm has to query to locate the called mobile's location information. Average query delay similarly, denotes the average number of LIDs queried. Real life networks may have an upper bound on the number of queries possible after which the call is dropped. This performance of algorithms is measured by the third metric. We now define the quantities that will be used in the analysis.

- Let n be the number of LIDs in the system. Let the databases be labeled as $D_1, D_2, \ldots, D_n$.
- Let the replication factor k be the number of databases a mobile's location information is updated in.
- Let X_i be a binary random variable indicating whether D_i has the location information of a given mobile. We define the storage vector as $\mathbf{X} = (X_1, X_2, \ldots, X_n)$.
- Let $\pi = (\pi_1, \pi_2, \ldots, \pi_n)$ be the query order of the databases for accessing the location information of a given mobile. π is a permutation of $\{1, 2, \cdots, n\}$, and D_{π_j} is the jth database to be queried if the location information has not been found in $D_{\pi_1}, D_{\pi_2}, \ldots, D_{\pi_{j-1}}$

[2] In some networks, local databases associated with MSCs may also be present. We do not consider such local databases in this paper.

(while this implies a sequential search, the databases could be searched in parallel).

- Let Y_i be the binary random variable indicating whether the ith queried database has the required information, i.e. $Y_i = X_{\pi_i}$.
- Let there be t LID failures in the system, $0 \leq t < k$. The probability that any database is failed is given by $\frac{t}{n}$. The failures can be either LID failures or link failures which manifest themselves as LID failures, as the LID which is connected by the link is unreachable. We assume that the queried LID being failed or alive, does not have any effect on whether the LID has the required information, i.e., we assume probabilistic independence of "failure" and the "updated LID" events.
- Let T denote the number of queries to find the location information. We refer to T as the *query delay*. It is implicitly assumed that each database query results in a constant time delay, which is normalized to unity.

From the above definitions, the storage vector is a random binary n-vector with Hamming weight k, i.e. $\sum_{i=1}^{n} X_i = k$. Since $\mathbf{Y} = (Y_1, Y_2, \ldots, Y_n)$ is a permutation of the storage vector $\mathbf{X}$, $\mathbf{Y}$ is also a binary n-vector with Hamming weight k. The query delay can be written as

$$T = \min\{i : Y_i = 1\}.$$

A load balanced update mechanism must satisfy $E[X_i] = E[X_j]$, for all i, j. In conjunction with the Hamming weight constraint, this implies that

$$P(X_i = 1) = \frac{k}{n} \qquad i = 1, 2, \ldots, n. \tag{1}$$

Since $\mathbf{Y}$ is a permutation of $\mathbf{X}$, in the fault free case we have

$$P(Y_i = 1) \quad = \quad \frac{k}{n} \qquad i = 1, 2, \ldots, n \tag{2}$$

Note that a location update algorithm may be viewed as a probability distribution on the storage vector $\mathbf{X}$, while a query vector is a probability distribution on π. Thus a load balanced update must satisfy the condition given in (1) on the marginal (Bernoulli) distribution. The theorem below provides a lower bound to the maximum value of the query delay T.

4.1 Lower Bound to Worst-Case Query Delay

In this section, we obtain a lower bound to the worst-case query delay for any load balanced location algorithm in the presence of t faults.

Theorem 1: *For any load balanced algorithm and any query algorithm, if j is an integer such that $P(T > j) = 0$ and there are t LID failures in the network, then $j \geq \lceil \frac{n^2}{k(n-t)} \rceil$.*

Proof: The event that a LID is failed and the event having the required information are independent. The probability of a LID being failed is $\frac{t}{n}$. Let j be an integer such that $P(T > j) = 0$. Then

$$P(\sum_{i=1}^{j} Y_i \geq 1) = 1\,. \tag{3}$$

The event in (3), is the union of the events $\{Y_i = 1\}$, $i = 1, 2, \ldots, j$. Then by union bound

$$1 \;\leq\; \sum_{i=1}^{j} P(Y_i = 1) = \frac{jk(n-t)}{n^2} \tag{4}$$

where we have also used (2) and the independence notion of the failed LID and LID with information events. The result follows from the last inequality, and observing that j is a positive integer. ■

4.2 Lower Bound to Average Query Delay

In this section, we obtain a lower bound to the expected value of the query delay for any load balanced algorithm, in the presence of t faults. We again make use of the independence between the failed LIDs and the LIDs with the information about the called mobile.

Theorem 2: *Given (n, k), the average query delay E[T], for a load balanced location management algorithm in the presence of t failures satisfies $E[T] \geq \frac{1}{2}(\zeta + 1)(1 + \frac{\nu}{n^2})$, where $\zeta = \lfloor \frac{n^2}{k(n-t)} \rfloor$ and $\nu = n^2 - k(n-t)\zeta$.*

Proof: Let $p_j = P(T = j)$, the probability that the query algorithm finds the information in the jth query, $j = 1, 2, \ldots, n$. We have

$$\begin{aligned} p_j &= P(\sum_{i=1}^{j-1} Y_i = 0, (Y_j = 1, \text{LID not failed})) \\ &\leq P(Y_i = 1, \text{LID not failed}) \\ &= \frac{(n-t)k}{n^2} \end{aligned}$$

for any load balanced algorithm, in the presence of t failures. We now construct the following linear program in the variables $(p_1, p_2, \ldots, p_n)$.

$$\begin{aligned} \Theta \;=\; & \min \textstyle\sum_{j=1}^{n} j p_j \\ & \text{subject to} \\ & 0 \leq p_j \leq \tfrac{(n-t)k}{n^2} \qquad j = 1, 2, \ldots, n \\ & \textstyle\sum_{j=1}^{n} p_j = 1\,. \end{aligned}$$

The objective function is minimized by the probability distribution

$$\begin{aligned} p_j &= \frac{(n-t)k}{n^2} \qquad j = 1\,,\, 2, \ldots, \zeta \\ p_j &= \frac{\nu}{n^2} \qquad j = \zeta + 1 \\ p_j &= 0 \qquad j > \zeta + 1 \end{aligned}$$

with the resulting value

$$\Theta = \frac{1}{2}(\zeta + 1)\left(1 + \frac{\nu}{n^2}\right) . \quad (5)$$

Since $E[T] \geq \Theta$ for any load-balancing algorithm, the result is established. ■

4.3 Lower Bound to Call Blocking Probability

In a large PCS network supporting real-time traffic, it may not be acceptable to have large delays in establishing connections. In such a situation, it may be necessary to block a connection request once the query delay has exceeded a certain threshold m. We now obtain a lower bound to the call blocking probability P_B with any load balanced location management algorithm, in the presence of t faults.

Theorem 3: *For any load-balanced location management algorithm, with a query delay threshold r, the blocking probability P_B satisfies*

$$P_B \geq \left(1 - \frac{r(n-t)k}{n^2}\right)^+$$

where t is the number of faults in the network and $a^+ = \max(0, a)$.

Proof: We use the upper bounds on the delay distribution that were found in the proof of Theorem 2 to obtain

$$\begin{aligned} P_B &= P(T > r) \\ &= 1 - \sum_{j=1}^{r} p_i \\ &\geq 1 - \frac{r(n-t)k}{n^2} . \end{aligned} \quad (6)$$

■

Note that the lower bound is nontrivial only if $r \leq \lfloor \frac{n^2}{k(n-t)} \rfloor$.

5 Fault Tolerant Load Balanced Location Management

Location management algorithms in mobile networks are used to update the location information of mobiles in LIDs and the LIDs are queried during call delivery. Failed LIDs during call delivery could lead to calls being blocked. Intermediate link failures can also manifest themselves as LID failures. The location management process therefore, has to be robust to tolerate these failures. In [8], a dynamic location management algorithm is presented. The algorithm is load balanced and is shown to be optimal with respect to worst-case query delay, average query delay and call blocking probability in the absence of database failures ($t = 0$). We adapt the algorithm to accommodate failures in the network. We then analyze the performance of this robust algorithm in the presence of database failures and compare the results with the bounds derived in Section 4.

5.1 Robust Location Management

In this section, we extend the query and update strategies of [8], to accommodate database failures.

Robust Update Strategy: The robust update strategy differs from the update strategy described in [8], in the way the updates are handled when a LID chosen for update is failed or unreachable. We adopt the following approach. The update mapping (the LIDs to be updated) is generated as described in [8]. If some of the LIDs thus chosen for update are failed, a fresh update mapping is generated. This approach assumes that a usable mapping will be found soon. This is true when the number of failures t is low when compared to k and n. This approach ensures that k LIDs are successfully updated, i.e. k replicas of the location information of the mobile generating the location update, are available for the query algorithm, given the prevailing failed set of LIDs. However, if a usable update mapping cannot be generated, i.e. the number of failures in the system is very high, we use the approach described in [10]. Here, the MSC retries the update periodically, with the retry period decided based on the activity of the mobile. These retries are continued until the LID registers the update. A similar approach can be adopted when deleting information from a failed LID. The robust update strategy is shown in Table 1.

Table 1. Pseudo-code for Robust Update Strategy

```
Update(m_i : mobile id);
   γ1 : integer;
   count : integer;
   n : integer; /* Number of Databases */
   k : integer; /* Replication Factor */
   DO_UPDATE : integer; /* LIDs chosen are not failed */
   β : integer;
begin
 β = n − k⌊n/k⌋;
  γ1 := prev_starting_database; /*from mobile or search */
  DELETE old information from databases;
  If LID failed retry until DELETE successful;
   while     DO_UPDATE = 0;
    γ1 := uniform_random[1, n]; /*new starting database */
    if(all LIDs for this γ1 are functional)
      DO_UPDATE = 1 && break;
   done;
    if(DO_UPDATE == 0) /*Fault free mapping unavailable */
      Choose the best mapping and use that as γ1;
    count := 0;
    while count ≤ k − β
      UPDATE D_(γ1⊕(count*⌊n/k⌋));
      count := count + 1;
    done;
    count := 1;
    while count ≤ β
      UPDATE D_(γ1⊕(k−β)⌊n/k⌋⊕(count*⌈n/k⌉));
      count := count + 1;
    done;
end
```

The approach of generating useable mappings, also assumes that the LIDs are not failed for long durations of time. If the failure period is high, then it might be a better approach to use the retry strategy described in [10], and use the first generated update mapping. This is because LIDs which are not failed, but which are part of a set of LIDs in which there are one or more failed LIDs (unuseable mapping) will neverbe used for the duration of the failure.

Table 2. Pseudo-code for Robust Query Strategy

```
Query(m_i : mobile id);
    π1 : integer;
    count : integer;
    n : integer; /* Number of Databases */
    k : integer; /* Replication Factor */
begin
  π1 := uniform_random[1,n]; /* 1st db queried */
  count = 0;
  while count < n
    if (info in D_{π1⊕count})
      return info;
    else
      count := count + 1;
  done;
  return no information found;
end
```

Robust Query Strategy: The first LID D_i is chosen at random. Successive LIDs $D_{i\oplus 1}, D_{i\oplus 2}, \ldots$ are queried till the required information is retrieved. To save on network traffic we assume that a LID responds to a query only if it has the required location information. It is however interesting to note that even if a LID does send a negative response when it does not have the desired information, the query delay is not reduced. This is because, the replication factor k for the queried mobile is not known to the querying MSC. To make the replication factor of every mobile registered in network known to every MSC in the system is very expensive as the status of the mobile can change very often, thus leading to increased network traffic. The robust query strategy is illustrated in Table 2.

5.2 Performance Analysis of the Robust Algorithm

The robust load balanced algorithm is shown to be load-balanced in the absence of faults [8]. Given a set of t faults, $1 \leq t \leq n$, the load is not balanced. This is because, the updated LID "next"to a failed LID on the logical ring of LIDs $D_1, D_2, \ldots, D_n$, with the required information receives more load than other updated LIDs which are not adjacent to a failed LID with information, as it receives its share of queries as well as the queries to the LID which is failed. But this is a specific instance. If we assume that failures distribute uniformly among the LIDs over time, the algorithm is still balanced on the average.

In the presence of failures, a random query strategy in which queried LIDs are chosen at random, might seem a better approach. However, the average as well as the worst-case delay of such a strategy can be shown to be larger than the robust algorithm even in the absence of failures [8]. We now analyze the performance of the robust algorithm proposed, in terms of worst-case, average query delay and call blocking probability.

Proposition 1: *For a given (n, k), the worst-case query delay for proposed algorithm in the presence of t failed LIDs is*

$$T_{max} = \begin{cases} (t+1)\lceil \frac{n}{k} \rceil & t < \beta \\ \beta\lceil \frac{n}{k} \rceil + (t+1-\beta)\lfloor \frac{n}{k} \rfloor & \beta \leq t < k-1 \\ n & t \geq k-1 \end{cases}$$

Proof: The query algorithm picks a LID at random and queries successive LIDs until the required information is found. The maximum number of queries is needed is when t successive LIDs with information LIDs are failed and the query strategy starts in the segment before the first of these failed LIDs. The worst-case number of queries is made when the maximum number of segments of size $\lceil \frac{n}{k} \rceil$ are queried. Observing that for a given (n, k), there are β updated LIDs separated by $\lceil \frac{n}{k} \rceil$ LIDs and $k - \beta$ updated LIDs separated by $\lfloor \frac{n}{k} \rfloor$ LIDs we have

$$T_{max} = \begin{cases} (t+1)\lceil \frac{n}{k} \rceil & t < \beta \\ \beta\lceil \frac{n}{k} \rceil + (t+1-\beta)\lfloor \frac{n}{k} \rfloor & \beta \leq t < k-1 \end{cases}$$

When $t = k - 1$, the worst-case delay is n. The worst-case query delay occurs when $k - 1$ LIDs with information are failed, and the query algorithm queries all these failed LIDs. Using similar reasoning, when $t \geq k$, the worst-case query delay is n. ■

In Figure 2, we illustrate the worst-case query delay in a network with 12 LIDs and the replication factor for the queried mobile being 4. D_1, D_3, D_7 and D_{10} have the required location information. Assume that at the time of query D_4 and D_7 are not reachable/failed. The maximum number of queries needed in this case is when the starting LID for query is D_2. The number of queries needed in this case (worst-case) is 9.

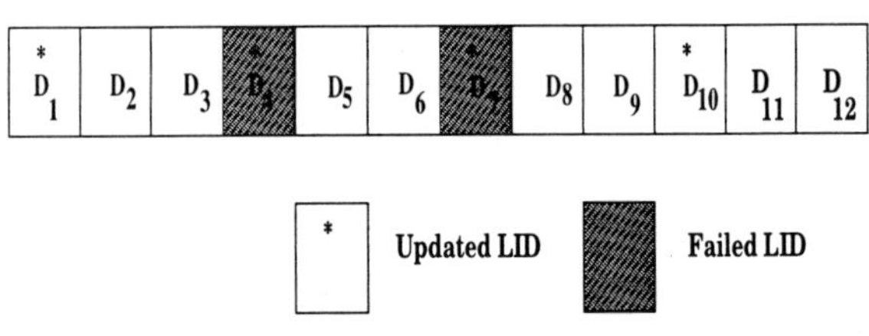

Figure 2. Example to illustrate the worst-case query delay with n = 12, k =4, t = 2.

In Figure 3, we compare the worst-case query delays of the robust algorithm, an ideal algorithm which achieves the worst-case delay described in Theorem 1, and a random algorithm in which each LID chosen for query is picked at random. When using this fully random query strategy, the worst-case number of queries is $n - (k - t) + 1$. From the figure, we see that when the failures are low, the robust algorithm performs comparably with the optimal algorithm. When number of concurrent failures in the system is very high then the worst-case query delay of the robust algorithm is much higher than that achieved by the ideal algorithm. However, it is important to note that such an ideal algorithm might not exist. The robust algorithm performs significantly better than the random algorithm in all failure scenarios.

If the failed set of LIDs contains the LIDs with information, the query algorithm fails to retrieve the information. We analyze this case later in this section.

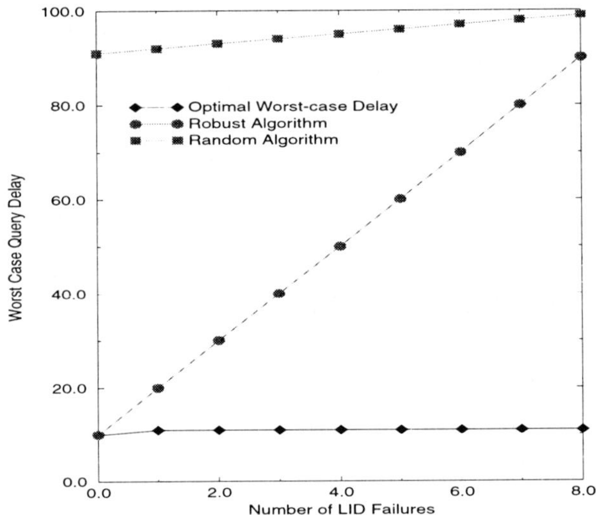

Figure 3. Worst-case query Delay Comparison: n = 100, k = 10, $0 \leq t \leq k-2$

Proposition 2: *For a given (n, k), the average query delay for the proposed algorithm in the presence of t $(0 \leq t < k)$ failed LIDs is $\frac{1}{2}(\alpha+1)(1+\frac{\beta}{n}) + \sum_{m=0}^{t} \frac{\binom{n-(m+1)}{t-m}}{\binom{n}{t}} \frac{mn}{k}$, where α and β are as defined before, and m is the number of "successive" LIDs with information queried, that are failed.*

Proof: Let D_i be the first LID to be queried. If the required information is not available in D_i, $D_{i\oplus 1}, D_{i\oplus 2}, \ldots$ are queried until the information is found. From the description of the update strategy, it can be seen that the number of LIDs the query algorithm queries depends on the number of "successive" LIDs with information the algorithm encounters. Let the first m $(0 \leq m \leq t)$ LIDs with information that are queried be failed. The distance between "successive" updated LIDs is $\lceil \frac{n}{k} \rceil$ or $\lfloor \frac{n}{k} \rfloor$ with probability $\frac{\beta}{k}$ and $1 - \frac{\beta}{k}$ respectively. The expected number of LIDs queried is therefore, $m(\alpha + \frac{\beta}{k}) = \frac{mn}{k}$. Let ϵ be the random variable denoting the number of LIDs queried before the first failed LID with information. The expected value of ϵ is $\frac{1}{2}(\alpha+1)(1+\frac{\beta}{n})$. The probability that the query algorithm queries m successive LIDs with information that are failed, is $\frac{\binom{n-(m+1)}{t-m}}{\binom{n}{t}}$. Observing that the probability that we start in the segment before the first of these m failures is $\frac{1}{k}$, and that there k LIDs where this string of m failed LIDs can begin, we have the expected number of queries as

$$\frac{1}{2}(\alpha+1)(1+\frac{\beta}{n}) + \sum_{m=0}^{t} \frac{\binom{n-(m+1)}{t-m}}{\binom{n}{t}} \frac{mn}{k}. \quad (7)$$

■

Figure 4 compares the average query delay of the robust algorithm with an ideal algorithm which achieves the query delay presented in Section 4. We see that the performance of the robust algorithm is comparable to the optimal bound in all failure scenarios.

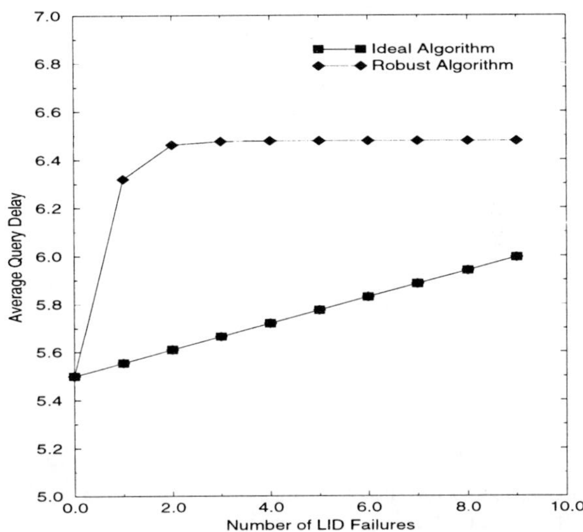

Figure 4. Average Query Delay Comparison: n = 100, k = 10, $0 \leq t < 10$

Call Blocking Probability: The robust algorithm is shown to be optimal with respect to call blocking probability [8], when there are no failed LIDs, i.e., t = 0. In this section we simulate the performance of the algorithm in the presence of failed LIDs. The simulation was performed on SUN Ultra 1 machines running Solaris 2.5.1 and Solaris 2.6. We assumed a population of 10000 mobiles in the system. We also assume that the replication factor for all the mobiles is the same. When each query is made to locate a mobile's location information, we generate a faulty set of t LIDs. The query algorithm then queries the LIDs for the information and the query delay is measured. If the query delay exceeds the maximum prescribed query delay, the call is dropped. The call blocking probability is thus measured over the course of a large number of trials. We present below the results of two such simulations. In [11] it is shown, that the optimal value for the replication factor is $O(\sqrt{n})$. We therefore fix k as 10 in the examples described below.

In Table 3, the performance of the robust algorithm is compared with an ideal algorithm which achieves the lower bound for call blocking probability described in Section 4, for the case when the maximum number of queries acceptable is 10, and $n = 100$, $k = 10$ and $0 \leq t \leq 9$. In Table 4, we compare the two algorithms when the maximum acceptable query delay of 6 is lower than $\lceil \frac{n}{k} \rceil$ of 10. From Tables 3 and 4, it is clear that the robust algorithm achieves the optimal call blocking probability bound described in Theorem 3. An interesting observation here is that, even though the worst-case query delay of the robust algorithm is higher than the bound derived in Theorem 1, the call blocking probability bound derived in Theorem 3 is being achieved for the test cases. This can be explained as follows. The probability that a large number of failed LIDs with information are queried as n and k increase with respect to t becomes very insignificant, hence making it possible to achieve the bound.

Table 3. Call blocking probabilities: n = 100, k = 10, max. query delay = 10, $0 \leq t \leq 9$

No. of Failures t	Optimal Bound	Robust Algo
0	0.0	0.0
1	0.01	0.01
2	0.02	0.02
3	0.03	0.03
4	0.04	0.04
5	0.05	0.05
6	0.06	0.06
7	0.07	0.07
8	0.08	0.08
9	0.09	0.09

Table 4. Call blocking probabilities: n = 100, k = 10, max. query delay = 6, $0 \leq t \leq 9$

No. of Failures t	Optimal Bound	Robust Algo
0	0.40	0.40
1	0.41	0.41
2	0.41	0.41
3	0.42	0.42
4	0.42	0.42
5	0.42	0.43
6	0.44	0.44
7	0.44	0.44
8	0.45	0.45
9	0.45	0.45

As mentioned before when $k \leq t \leq n$, i.e., there are more number of failures than updates for the queried mobile, there is a chance that the required information is not found and the call is blocked. The probability of calls being blocked due to the information not being found is

$$\frac{\binom{n-k}{t-k}}{\binom{n}{t}}. \tag{8}$$

5.3 Recovery of LIDs after a failure

Once a LID becomes functional after a failure, due to the mobility of the mobiles its contents might not reflect the current position of its registered mobiles. In [10], a fast recovery protocol is presented in which nodes like the MSC are used in the recovery process We can use a similar approach for LID recovery in the robust location management protocols described in Section 5.1.

6 Robust Load Balanced Parallel Querying Algorithms

In [11], a parallel querying load balanced location management algorithm is presented. In this scheme, the mobile population is partitioned into *active* and *relaxed* (less active) mobiles based on their activity. The location information of *active* mobiles is replicated in k_1 LIDs and *relaxed* mobiles are updated in k_2 LIDs, with $k_1 > k_2$. The update strategy in [11] is similar to the strategy of [8]. The query strategy is as follows. On receiving a request to locate a mobile, the MSC assumes that the called mobile is a *active* mobile and queries $\lceil \frac{n}{k_1} \rceil$ successive LIDs $(D_i, D_{i\oplus 1}, \ldots, D_{i\oplus \lceil \frac{n}{k_1} \rceil})$ in parallel, with the first of these LIDs chosen at random. If the called mobile is *active* then it is located in one round of parallel queries. If the called mobile is *relaxed*, then there is a chance that the called mobile is not located in one round of queries. Such mobiles are found in a second round of queries in which LIDs $D_{i\oplus \lceil \frac{n}{k_1} \rceil \oplus 1}, \ldots, D_{i\oplus \lceil \frac{n}{k_2} \rceil}$ are queried in parallel.

This algorithm can be extended to accommodate LID failures using the same strategy described in Section 5.1. In the modified version, the querying algorithm queries $\lceil \frac{n}{k_1} \rceil$ LIDs in parallel in the first round, $\lceil \frac{n}{k_1} \rceil - \lceil \frac{n}{k_2} \rceil$ LIDs in the second round. If the required information is not found, $\lceil \frac{n}{k_2} \rceil$ LIDs are queried in parallel in subsequent rounds, until the desired location information is found. The only communication assumed between the MSC and queried LID is an ACK if the required information is present in the LID. Therefore, an absence of a response from a LID could imply a failed/unreachable LID with/without information or the lack of the desired information. We therefore use $\lceil \frac{n}{k_2} \rceil$ parallel queries in subsequent rounds to increase the chance that called mobile is found irrespective of the mobile's activity state. This pseudo-code of the robust parallel query algorithm is illustrated in Table 5. In the next section we analyze the average number of rounds of parallel queries required by the robust parallel querying algorithm to locate *active* and *relaxed* mobiles.

Table 5. Robust Parallel Query procedure

ParallelQuery(m_i : mobile id);
  π_1 : **integer**;
  count : **integer**;
  n : integer; /* Number of Databases */
  k_1, k_2 : integer; /* Replication Factors */
begin
  π_1 := uniform_random[1,n]; /* starting LID for 1st round */
  count = 1;
  ifQuery_in_parallel($\pi_1, \ldots, \pi_{1\oplus \lceil \frac{n}{k_1} \rceil}$)
    return mobile information; information found */
  else
  ifQueryParallel($\pi_{1\oplus \lceil \frac{n}{k_1} \rceil \oplus 1}, \ldots, \pi_{1\oplus \lceil \frac{n}{k_2} \rceil}$)
    return mobile information; /*information found */
  else
    while(count $< k_2 - 1$)
    ifQueryParallel($\pi_{1\oplus (count) \lceil \frac{n}{k_2} \rceil \oplus 1}, \ldots, \pi_{1\oplus (count+1) \lceil \frac{n}{k_2} \rceil}$))
    return mobile information;
    count := count + 1;
    done;
end

6.1 Average Number of Rounds for the Querying Algorithm

In this section, we evaluate the average number of rounds required by the robust parallel query algorithm (RPQA) in the presence of t failed/unreachable LIDs. We denote the average number of rounds for a *relaxed* mobile and *active* mobile by E_t^r and E_t^a respectively. As described in the previous section, a *relaxed* (*active*) mobile's location information is replicated in k_2 (k_1) LIDs.

In the first two rounds the RPQA queries a total of $\lceil \frac{n}{k_2} \rceil$ LIDs, and in subsequent rounds $\lceil \frac{n}{k_2} \rceil$ LIDs are queried per round. To calculate the average number of rounds to locate the information of a *relaxed* mobile, consider an algorithm A, which queries $\lceil \frac{n}{k_2} \rceil$ in every round. The RPQA will need at most one more round of queries to locate the mobile, as the first two rounds query in the RPQA covers $\lceil \frac{n}{k_2} \rceil$ LIDs, which are covered by one round of queries by algorithm A. Therefore, if E_A is the average number of rounds needed by algorithm A to locate a *relaxed* mobile, we have

$$\begin{aligned} E_t^r &\leq 1 + E_A \\ &= 1 + \sum_{m=0}^{t} \frac{m\binom{n-(m+1)}{t-m}}{\binom{n}{t}} \end{aligned} \tag{9}$$

where m is the number of successive failed LIDs with the required location information queried.

Similarly, if E_B is the average number of rounds of an algorithm B, which queries $\lceil \frac{n}{k_1} \rceil$ every round, the average number of rounds needed to locate the information of a *active* mobile in the presence of $t < k_1$ failures for the RPQA is

$$\begin{aligned} E_t^a &\leq 1 + \frac{\lceil \frac{n}{k_2} \rceil}{\lceil \frac{n}{k_1} \rceil} E_B \\ &= 1 + \frac{\lceil \frac{n}{k_1} \rceil}{\lceil \frac{n}{k_2} \rceil} \sum_{m=0}^{t} \frac{m\binom{n-(m+1)}{t-m}}{\binom{n}{t}} \end{aligned} \tag{10}$$

7 Conclusions

Efficient management of location information is an important aspect to consider in the design of future mobile networks, especially since the number of mobiles in the network is poised to increase at a high rate in the near future. We have established fundamental bounds to the performance of load-balanced distributed location management algorithms in presence of database and link failures in terms of three important performance metrics. We then presented a load balanced location management algorithm and studied its performance in the presence of faults. An appealing feature of the proposed solution is that it balances the storage and query load at all times in a real-time environment. We showed that the algorithm performs better than a totally random query algorithm for the worst-case query metric. We then presented a robust parallel querying load balanced algorithm and studied its performance in the presence of faults.

The determination of the replication factor needs to take into consideration the relative costs of storage and query delay, fault tolerance, and possibly other factors. The cost minimization approach can be extended to include the other design constraints, such as the frequency of updates and queries a database is allowed to participate in. We have normalized the cost of accessing any LID to unity. Fault tolerant load balanced location management algorithms without this same cost restriction is an open problem.

References

[1] I. F. Akyildiz, J. S. M. Ho, "On Location Management for Personal Communication Networks", *IEEE Communications Magazine*, vol. 34, no. 9, pp. 138-145, September 1996.

[2] EIA/TIA, "Cellular Radio Telecommunications Intersystems Operation, PN-2991", November 1995.

[3] M. Mouly, M.-B. Pautet, "The GSM System for Mobile Communications", M. Mouly, 49 rue Louise Bruneau, Palaiseau, France, 1992.

[4] R. Holzman, Y. Marcus, D. Peleg, "Load Balancing in Quorum Systems", *SIAM Journal of Discrete Mathematics*, vol. 10, no. 2, pp. 223-245, May 1997.

[5] R. Prakash, M. Singhal, "A Dynamic Approach to Location Management in Mobile Computing Systems", in Proceedings of the *8th International Conference on Software Engineering and Knowledge Engineering (SEKE'96)*, Lake Tahoe, Nevada, pp. 488-495, June 10-12, 1996.

[6] R. Prakash, Z. Haas, M. Singhal, "Load-Balanced Location Management for Mobile Systems using Dynamic Hashing and Quorums", *Technical Report UTDCS-05-97*, University of Texas at Dallas, October 1997.

[7] D. Peleg, A. Wool, "Crumbling Walls: A Class of Practical and Efficient Quorum Systems", in Proceedings of the *14th ACM Symposium on Principles of Distributed Computing*, pp. 120-129, Ottawa, August 1995.

[8] G. Krishnamurthi, M. Azizoğlu, A. K. Somani, "Optimal Location Management Algorithms for Mobile Networks", in Proceedings of the *Fourth Annual ACM/IEEE International Conference on Mobile Computing and Networking*, pp. 223-232, Dallas, October 1998.

[9] ETSI/TC-SMG, "Digital cellular telecommunications system; Restoration procedures", Version 5.0.0, *GSM Technical Specification (GSM 03.07)*, ETSI, Nov. 1996.

[10] G. Krishnamurthi, S. Chessa, A. K. Somani, "Fast Recovery Protocols for Database and Link Failures in Mobile Networks", in Proceedings of the *Seventh Annual International Conference on Computer Communications and Networking*, pp. 32-39, Lafayette, October 1998.

[11] G. Krishnamurthi, S. Chessa, A. K. Somani, "Optimal Replication of Location Information in Mobile Networks", in Proceedings of the *International Conference on Communications*, Vancouver B.C., June 1999.

Session 5

Panel on Using COTS to Design Dependable Networked Systems

Moderator:
Ravi K. Iyer, University of Illinois, USA

Organizers:
Ravi K. Iyer, University of Illinois, USA
A. Avizienis, University of California at Los Angeles, USA

Panelists:
A. Avizienis, University of California at Los Angeles, USA
D. Barron, Compaq
D. Powell, LAAS
H. Levendel, Motorola
J. Samson, Honeywell

COTS Hardware and Software in High-Availability Systems

Chairs:

Ravi K. Iyer
Center for Reliable & High-Performance Computing
Coordinated Science Laboratory
University of Illinois at Urbana-Champaign
1308 W. Main St., Urbana, IL 61801
iyer@crhc.uiuc.edu

A. Avizienis
Computer Science Department
4731 Boelter Hall
University of California, Los Angeles
Los Angeles, CA 90024-1596
aviz@cs.ucla.edu

Panelists: A. Avizienis (UCLA), D. Barron (Compaq), D. Powell (LAAS), H. Levendel (Motorola), J. Samson (Honeywell)

The desire to use commercial, off-the-shelf (COTS) components is prevalent throughout industry, the DoD, and NASA. The potential benefits of using COTS are many, including reduced development time for systems and the availability and maturity of many commercial tools and operating systems. However, use of COTS products is also fraught with pitfalls and dangers. One of these is the highly volatile and competitive nature of commercial product development. What is available commercially today may be gone tomorrow if economics or a change in business focus so dictate. But there are other issues as well. Because COTS products offer features geared to succeed in the commercial marketplace, they can bring undesirable burdens into some life and mission critical application domains, such as space-borne computing. On the other hand, devices useful in developing of high performance (low-power) laptop PCs might also benefit such applications. There is also the question of defining COTS. Is it an entire processing system, or does it just refer to the specific component (e.g., processor)?

Engineering practice seems to suggest that as-is COTS components rarely meet requirements of fault-tolerant systems but, they rarely totally fail to meet the requirements. Rather, COTS components usually require some modification to meet requirements. The issue is, once a component is modified, is it still COTS? What COTS advantages have been lost? Another issue is the expense of licensing and hardening COTS products. COTS vendors are known to have changed, and will probably continue to change, device fabrication processes without notice. As a result, satisfactory parts characterization for highly reliable and fault-tolerant applications may become extremely difficult.

Currently, while COTS processors offer high performance, they also exhibit post-production design faults. For example, errata reports published by Intel describe 68 design faults uncovered in Pentium II from May 1997 to November 1998. Consequently, designers of highly dependable systems must find ways to guarantee that the known design errors in a microprocessor will not lead to system failure.

Use of COTS does however have great potential benefit in the area of network computing systems, where a range of commercial and scientific applications must coexist, each potentially requiring a different level of availability and reliability. In such an environment, it is not cost-effective to provide dedicated hardware-based fault tolerance to each application, nor is it cost-effective to rewrite each application to take advantage of the fault tolerance incorporated in a distributed network through specialized software. Therefore, it could be very effective to find ways to achieve high dependability for COTS applications running on COTS hardware.

A good example of research in this direction is the Remote Exploration and Experimentation (REE) Project undertaken by the Jet Propulsion Laboratory (JPL) and NASA. The key objective of REE is to design and develop a computing architecture suitable for space applications. The architecture is to offer software-implemented fault tolerance for executing NASA applications (e.g., distributed, computation-intensive image processing applications) while employing, to the extent possible, COTS technologies.

Since experience suggests that COTS alone cannot provide high availability, what techniques (in hardware or in software) can be used to facilitate the development of COTS-based, highly dependable systems? Some commercial systems (Microsoft Wolfpack or Sun Microsystems Ultra Enterprise Cluster) do address the issue of providing high-availability services, but these proprietary cluster systems do not scale to networks with large numbers of nodes. A small set of real implementations (e.g., Guards, Chameleon, AQuA, Piranha) are starting to provide insight into how we can design and implement high-availability networked systems using COTS.

Some of the issues this panel will address include (1) the effect of processor bugs on the design of highly dependable systems, (2) COTS versus radiation hard components, (3) use of COTS to build highly available enterprise computing systems, and (4) new research issues in designing COTS-based high availability network systems.

0-7695-0213-X/99 $10.00 © 1999 IEEE

Session 6A

Diagnosis and Reconfiguration

Chair: Weiping Shi
University of North Texas, USA

Efficient Network-Flow Based Techniques for Dynamic Fault Reconfiguration in FPGAs*

NIHAR R. MAHAPATRA
mahapatr@cse.buffalo.edu
Department of Computer Science & Engineering
State University of New York at Buffalo
Buffalo, NY 14260-2000

SHANTANU DUTT
dutt@eecs.uic.edu
Department of Electrical Eng. & Computer Sc.
University of Illinois at Chicago
Chicago, IL 60607-7053

Abstract

In this paper, we consider a "dynamic" node covering framework for incorporating fault tolerance in SRAM-based segmented array FPGAs with spare row(s) and/or column(s) of cells. Two types of designs are considered: one that can support only node-disjoint (and hence nonintersecting) rectilinear reconfiguration paths, and the other that can support edge-disjoint (and hence possibly intersecting) rectilinear reconfiguration paths. The advantage of this approach is that reconfiguration paths are determined dynamically depending upon the actual set of faults and track segments are used as required, thus resulting in higher reconfigurability and lower track overheads compared to previously proposed "static" approaches. We provide optimal network-flow based reconfiguration algorithms for both of our designs and present and analyze a technique for speeding up these algorithms, depending upon the fault size, by as much as 20 *times. Finally, we present reconfigurability results for our FPGA designs that show much better fault tolerance for them compared to previous approaches—the reconfigurability of the edge-disjoint design is 90% or better and 100% most of the time, which implies near-optimal spare-cell utilization.*

1 Introduction

Field programmable gate arrays (FPGAs) consist of a large array of programmable cell or logic blocks (CLBs) and interconnects that can be reconfigured to implement a wide variety of application logic. They are commonly used for the development of prototype systems and their early introduction to market and also as emulators to verify and test designs. An important criterion in the design of FPGAs is *fault tolerance*, which is the ability to retain full or partial functionality in the presence of CLB or interconnect faults that arise during fabrication or operation. Being able to tolerate fabrication faults means higher yield and lower costs for the manufacturer. Tolerance for operational faults translates into higher reliability and reduced downtime for the user.

*S. Dutt was supported partly by a grant from Xilinx Corp. and partly by Darpa Grant # F33615-98-C-1318.

Two different approaches have been used to provide fault tolerance in FPGAs. The first is to reroute the user's circuit to avoid faulty cells and/or interconnects, using spares or other unused cells instead [5, 8, 9, 10, 11]. Requiring the layout tools to perform a new routing for every fault places a heavy burden on the user, who must also keep track of all the different routings possible on different chips for a given circuit design. The other approach, adding spare rows and/or columns of cells, is intended for reconfiguration at the factory, making the technique transparent to the user. To reconfigure around a faulty row, fuses are burned at the factory such that non-faulty rows are remapped to include the spare row. For the faulty row to be transparent, it is necessary to maintain the original connectivity between the rows on either side of the faulty one. One method of doing this is to employ longer wiring segments in the vertical channels, but then extra *tracks* must be added to these channels to retain the original routing flexibility [6].

Of the previous work done in this area, the method of interest to this research is the *node covering* method for cell fault tolerance [3]. The model of FPGA considered is shown in Fig. 1 and consists of an $n_1 \times n_2$ rectangular array of CLBs. Wiring tracks run along channels between adjacent rows and columns of CLBs to support routing of nets connecting different CLBs. In a *single-spare row (1S-R) design*, there is an additional row of spare CLBs at the bottom of the array—the spare in column j is denoted $s^b_{*,j}$, where "b" stands for "bottom"; a *single-spare column (1S-C) design* is defined similarly with the spare column to the right. A *single-spare row-column (1S-RC) design* has a spare row of CLBs at the bottom and a spare column of CLBs to the right. Finally, a *double-spare row-column (2S-RC)* design has spares on all four sides as in Fig. 1. The spare CLBs and the unused track segments provide the necessary reconfiguration capability for the array.

In the node-covering method, a faulty FPGA is reconfigured by finding for each fault a *covering sequence*, which is an ordered sequence of CLBs beginning with the faulty CLB and ending in a spare CLB such that each CLB re-

0-7695-0213-X/99 $10.00 © 1999 IEEE

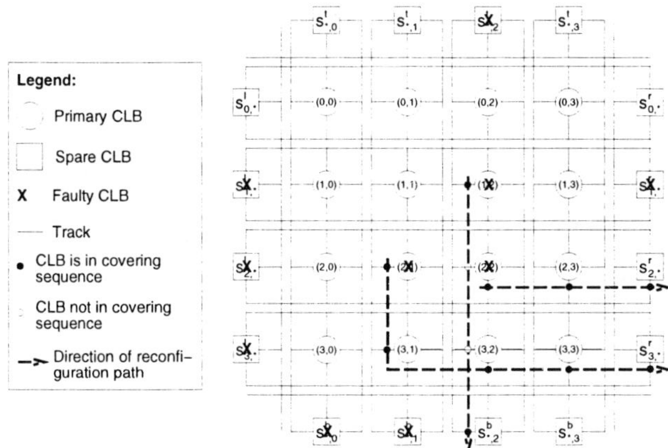

Figure 1: FPGA reconfiguration model showing reconfiguration paths for faults $(1,2)$, $(2,1)$, and $(2,2)$.

places or "covers" the preceding CLB in the sequence by taking over its functionality as well as connectivity. A CLB v_2 that covers another CLB v_1 needs to connect to nets originally connected to v_1, and this is accomplished by using track segments adjoining intermediate CLBs on a path from v_1 to v_2 called the *covering path.* A *reconfiguration path* for a fault u is a path from u to a spare through a superset of CLBs in its covering sequence obtained by concatenating all covering paths between consecutive CLBs in the covering sequence. For example, in Fig. 1, the covering sequence for fault $(1,2)$ is $((1,2), s^b_{*,2})$, while the corresponding reconfiguration path is $\langle(1,2),(2,2),(3,2),s^b_{*,2}\rangle$. Since in the above model a CLB can cover another CLB only via the track segments adjoining intervening CLBs, reconfiguration paths always consist of adjacent CLBs and hence are *continuous.* Covering sequences, on the other hand, may be *discontinuous*—this is the case in the above example in which CLBs $(2,2)$ and $(3,2)$ are *skipped* in $(1,2)$'s reconfiguration path.

In the *static node-covering* method, reconfiguration paths for faults are predetermined and are independent of the set of faults [3]. For instance, in a 1S-C FPGA, reconfiguration paths go straight to the spare CLB on the right and only one fault per row can be tolerated—similar to the reconfiguration path for fault $(2,2)$ in Fig. 1. A *cover* cell that replaces a *dependent* cell must be able to duplicate the functionality of the latter. In an FPGA, all cells are identical, so configuration data for the dependent cell can simply be transposed to the cover cell. The cover cell must also be able to duplicate the connectivity of the dependent cell with respect to the rest of the array. This is accomplished by ensuring that each net connected to a cell through a channel segment also includes the corresponding channel segment—a *cover segment*—bordering the cover cell (see Figs. 2(a) and (b)). Cover segments are included in a net in one of two ways. First, segments in the net may already be in positions to act as covers. In case the above condition does not hold, additional segments, termed *reserved segments* (RSs), should be attached to the net to provide covers. Essentially, segments are reserved to act as covers at all branch points of the circuit netlist. Thus this method requires neither the factory nor the user to generate new routing maps to reconfigure around faulty cells or wiring, as is required by [5, 8, 9, 10, 11]. Instead, the original configuration data can be reused. Also, no explicit additional tracks are needed in the channels in order to avoid the loss of connection flexibility seen in [6]. The additional wiring segments used to support reconfiguration paths cause a track overhead in the routing—for a number of benchmark circuits, the track overhead is found to be 34% [3]. This results in retaining total functionality with reduced routability or total routability with reduced functionality.

To retain total functionality with as little overhead as possible, a *dynamic node-covering* method was proposed in [13]. In this method, reconfiguration paths are dynamically determined depending upon the fault set and RS insertions are made only along channels where reconfiguration paths pass. This results in higher reconfigurability and lower overhead. Two types of dynamic designs are considered: *node-disjoint* and *edge-disjoint* FT FPGA designs. In the first type, only node-disjoint rectilinear reconfiguration paths can be supported. Thus in Fig. 1, reconfiguration paths for faults $(2,1)$ and $(2,2)$ can both be supported—note that the reconfiguration path for $(2,1)$ shown in Fig. 1 can not be supported in the static node-covering method since it is bent. However, reconfiguration paths for $(1,2)$ and $(2,2)$ and/or $(2,1)$ can not be supported in the node-disjoint dynamic-FT method, since the former intersects the latter two. The second type of FPGA design can support any set of edge-disjoint rectilinear reconfiguration paths, and hence can support reconfiguration paths for faults $(1,2)$, $(2,2)$, and $(2,1)$ in Fig. 1 all simultaneously. Thus it provides higher yield/reliability compared to the first type. We discuss the dynamic node covering method in the next section.

In order to maximally utilize the spare CLBs, rectilinear reconfiguration paths from faults to spares need to be optimally determined (i.e., if there exist such paths for all faults, they need to be found). We present network-flow based reconfiguration algorithms for both node-disjoint and edge-disjoint FPGA designs that determine such paths in Sec. 3. In previous work, network-flow based reconfiguration algorithms have been proposed for VLSI/WSI arrays in [12]. Since our dynamic node covering method is meant to be used online, reconfiguration speed is important. In Sec. 4, we present an effective technique for speeding up our reconfiguration algorithms that exploits the regular array structure of the flow graph and that provides as much as 20 times speedup. In Sec. 5, we analyze this speedup technique and verify the analysis empirically. Sec. 6 presents reconfigurability results for node- and edge-disjoint and single- and double-spare FPGA designs. Finally, we conclude in Sec. 7.

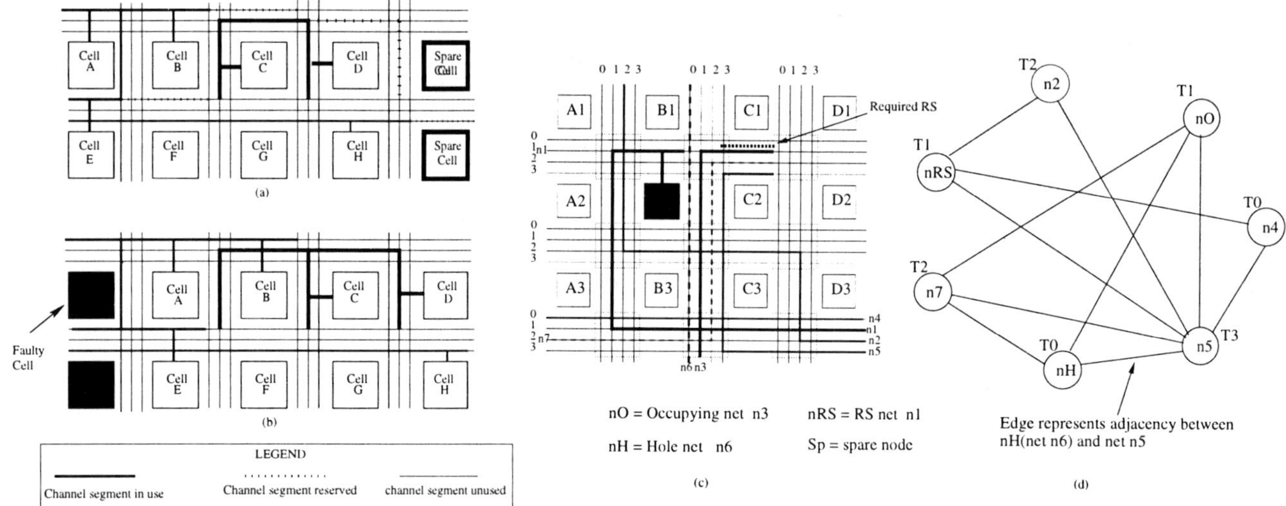

Figure 2: Fault tolerance using the static node covering method in a 1S-C FPGA: (a) Cover segments associated with nets in the FPGA. (b) Reconfiguration around faulty cells A and E using cover segments and (static) straight reconfiguration paths to the right. Reconfiguration using the dynamic node covering method: (c) Presence of occupying net (O-net) n3 prevents a straightforward insertion of a reserved segment in the RS channel. Therefore the O-net must be moved to another track, possibly bumping other nets, to make room for the reserved segment. (d) Overlap graph used to determine transition tree for FPGA circuit in [c].

2 Background: Dynamic Node Covering

The dynamic FT method [13] was developed to reduce the track overhead incurred in implementing the static method. It is similar to the static method except that reconfiguration paths for tolerating faults are not predetermined, instead they depend upon the particular set of faults to be reconfigured around.[1] The fact that reconfiguration paths in the dynamic method depend upon the fault set means that the assignment of cover cells to dependent cells is not static. This also means that RS insertions are required only along the actual reconfiguration paths used, in contrast to requiring RSs at all branch points for nets along the whole FPGA. By not statically reserving wire segments, having flexibility for reconfiguration paths, and requiring RS insertions only along such paths, a better utilization of the unused wiring segments and tracks is obtained. This leads to a much lower track overhead and better fault tolerance for the dynamic FT method compared to the static one.

The dynamic nature of the method requires the actual position of the fault to be known to identify the RSs required. Since the routing for the FPGA has already been completed, this brings into question the availability of the wire segment where an RS has to be inserted. This is discussed next.

2.1 Reserved Segments and Occupying and Hole Nets

For any required RS, if the required wire segment where the RS is to be inserted is vacant, i.e., no net has been routed through it, the RS insertion is done by including this segment in the net that is connected to the dependent cell, so that its connectivity can be taken over by the cover cell. If the required wire segment is occupied by another net, i.e., some other net has already been routed through that wire segment, then the RS insertion cannot be made directly because the required segment is not available. As shown in Fig. 2(c), the net requiring the RS extension is termed the *RS net* and the net occupying the required wire segment is termed the *occupying net* (O-net). The existence of O-nets for the required RSs gives rise to a requirement that there should be at least as many vacant segments as required RSs in the channel segment where these RSs have to be inserted. When there is a vacant segment on a section of the channel requiring the RS (the *RS channel*) on a certain track T_i, any net that passes through the channels adjacent to the RS-channel but does not pass through the RS-channel on the same track T_i is referred to as a *hole net*.

The problem can now be stated as follows. The RS net and O-net are on the same track. The RS net has to be extended by one segment (*RS-insertion*). This requires the O-net to move out of its current track. Let a *transition* be defined as the movement of net n_i on a track T_j to another track T_k. This transition may result in the net n_i bumping into one or more nets on track T_k. These nets will have to move out of their current track T_k, giving rise to a transition for each of them. This gives rise to a transition sequence which will finally terminate in "spare" nodes, which are vacant segments of appropriate lengths to which a bumped net can move in without bumping any other net. When such a vacant segment is part of on occupied track then no spare track overhead is incurred, whereas when it is part of a spare track then

[1] Note that for edge-disjoint reconfiguration paths that skip nodes (i.e., in which covering can take place between non-adjacent cells), RSs of segment length > 1 are required. Specifically, if u covers v and is at a distance of t from it, then RSs of length up to t are required for u to connect to nets originally connected to v.

an overhead of an extra track is incurred. Clearly, the set of transitions takes on a tree structure, termed a *transition tree*, with the spares forming the leaf nodes. The RS insertion is successful if a transition tree rooted at the corresponding O-net can be found whose leaves are spare nodes, such a transition tree is termed a *converging transition tree*. We next briefly discuss a model that can be used for efficiently determining a converging transition tree.

2.2 The Overlap Graph

The *overlap graph* (OG) is a graph representation of the circuit routing on the FPGA. This graph is an undirected graph with the circuit nets represented by the nodes of the graph. In the overlap graph $OG(V, E)$, the set of nets $N = \{n_1, n_2, \ldots, n_m\}$ in the circuit routing is represented by a set of nodes/vertices $V = \{n_1, n_2, \ldots, n_m\}$. We use $n_i^{T_j}$ to denote a net n_i on track T_j. There exists an edge between n_i and n_j in the OG iff nets n_i and n_j share a *channel*[2] in the FPGA. Figs. 2(c) and (d) show nets n_2 and n_{RS} having an edge between them because they are routed through a common channel on the left of the faulty cell. Also, the net $n_6^{T_0}$ is routed through the adjacent channel in the area of the faulty cell but not in the channel where the RS is required. The wire segment on track T_0 in the RS channel is vacant. So n_6 is termed the hole net.

The overlap graph can be used as an effective model in the evaluation of the required transition tree. Since $OG(V, E)$ represents the circuit routing on the FPGA, the movement of nets involved in a transition tree can be seen as a tree in the graph. Obviously, a converging transition tree should end with the final transitions of nets into tracks where they do not bump into any other nets, i.e., they end in spare segments, which correspond to the spare (leaf) nodes in the transition tree.

For a given circuit routing and a specific cell fault, it is possible to identify the RS net, the O-net, and the H-net in the OG. The O-net has to be moved out of its current track to accommodate the RS. Since the transition $n_i^{T_j \rightarrow T_k}$ of net n_i from track T_j to another track T_k may result in the net bumping into one or more of its children on that track, we associate a heuristic cost with each net transition. The heuristic attempts to measure the cost of bumpings—bumping into a large net is more expensive than bumping into a small net or a number of small nets with total length (in terms of number of track segments) the same as or smaller than the length of the large net. The heuristic is used as a guide in creating the transition tree by choosing those net transitions that are less costly. This reduces the branching factor of the tree path and hence the amount of perturbation of nets, thus making it more likely for the transitions to converge with a minimal overhead of spare tracks. Three different transition cost heuristics have been evaluated in [13]. For the best heuristic, the track overhead for tolerating one fault per row (the same fault pattern as in the static method), and for a total of four faults, for a number of benchmark circuits, is only 16% and 4.5%, respectively. This establishes the superiority of the dynamic FT approach over the static one.

To tolerate arbitrary fault patterns, however, straight reconfiguration paths will no longer be sufficient. Reconfiguration paths with possibly multiple bends will be needed and they may also intersect each other at nodes (edge-disjoint paths). Intersection of two paths at a node has the effect of one of the paths "skipping" the intersecting node. Optimal or near-optimal techniques for finding such reconfiguration paths in a faulty FPGA are desirable for maximal fault tolerance. Once these paths are determined, reconfiguration will be achieved by inserting RSs as required along these paths using the techniques of [13] for determining converging transition trees. In the rest of this paper, we develop fast optimal algorithms for determining reconfiguration paths in a faulty FPGA.

As mentioned earlier, there are two types of reconfiguration paths, *node-disjoint* and *edge-disjoint*. In the next section, we present network-flow based algorithms to determine reconfiguration paths of these two types.

3 Reconfiguration Algorithm

First, define a *FPGA flow graph* for a FT FPGA as follows.

Definition 1 *A* FPGA flow graph *for a faulty FT FPGA has a vertex corresponding to each primary cell in the FPGA and has two unidirectional, unit-capacity edges directed in opposite directions between vertex pairs which have corresponding cell pairs that are either east-west or north-south neighbors in the FPGA. Vertices in the flow graph corresponding to faulty primary cells in the FPGA are sources. The flow graph has an additional vertex which is a sink (representing nonfaulty spares in the FPGA) which has edges incident on it from vertices corresponding to neighbors of nonfaulty spare cells in the FPGA. Vertices that are neither sources nor sink have unbounded capacities for an edge-disjoint FPGA design and unit capacities for a node-disjoint FPGA design.*

Assuming the 7×5 array of primary cells inside rectangle ABCD in Fig. 3(a) represents an FPGA and that it is a 2S-RC design (i.e., it is surrounded by spares on all sides), the corresponding FPGA flow graph would be as in Fig. 3(b). Note that there is no edge in Fig. 3(b) corresponding to the faulty spare on the right in row 9 of Fig. 3(a). We are now ready to demonstrate the equivalence between the FPGA reconfiguration and maximal flow problems.

Theorem 1 *The problem of determining a maximal set of reconfiguration paths to reconfigure faults in the node- and*

[2] A channel is the set of all track segments between two adjacent switchboxes of the FPGA.

edge-disjoint FT FPGA designs is equivalent to the problem of determining a maximal flow in the corresponding FPGA flow graph.

Proof: It is clear from the definition of FPGA flow graph (Def. 1) that a flow in the flow graph corresponds to a rectilinear reconfiguration path from a fault to a spare in the actual FPGA hardware. The fact that all edges in the FPGA flow graph have unit capacities implies that reconfiguration paths must be edge disjoint. Vertices that are neither sources nor sink have unbounded capacities in the flow graph for an edge-disjoint FPGA design to allow edge-disjoint reconfiguration paths that may not be node disjoint, i.e., that may be intersecting. However, these vertices have unit capacities for a node-disjoint FPGA design to allow only node-disjoint reconfiguration paths. Thus by solving the maxflow problem for this flow graph, a set of reconfiguration paths to tolerate the maximum number of faults possible can be found. □

Figs. 3(a) and (b) show the correspondence between reconfiguration paths in the FPGA and flows in the FPGA flow graph.

Theorem 2 *A maximal set of reconfiguration paths to tolerate as many faults as possible in the node- and edge-disjoint FT FPGA designs can be found by applying the lift-to-front preflow-push algorithm of [2] to the corresponding FPGA flow graph.*

Proof: This follows from Theorem 1 and the fact that the lift-to-front preflow-push algorithm finds a maximal flow in the flow graph to which it is applied [2]. □

In our simulations, we used the $O(|V|^3)$ lift-to-front preflow-push algorithm of [2], which runs in $O(N^3)$ time since there are $\Theta(N)$ vertices in the flow graph. Since the flow graph under consideration is planar, we can use a more efficient, although not as simple to code, maxflow algorithm meant especially for planar graphs given in [7] that runs in $O(N^{1.5}\log N)$ time.

Reconfiguration paths obtained using the above approach may either be supportable with the unused or spare tracks and track segments or extra tracks may be needed, which cause a track overhead. Clearly, it would be desirable to judiciously utilize the spare tracks and track segments and to minimize the track overhead. This is accomplished by associating with each edge from a vertex u to a vertex v in the flow graph discussed above a cost that estimates the track-overhead cost of inserting RSs in order for v to cover u. This cost can be determined as follows. Let $RS(v,u)$ be the set of RSs that need to be inserted for v to cover u, and let $O(v,u)$ be the set of corresponding occupying nets. Then the cost of arc (u,v) in the flow graph will be the sum of the minimum or best transition costs of the nets in $O(v,u)$, and is given by

$$\sum_{n_i \in O(v,u)} \min\{cost(n_i^{T_j \to T_k}) | T_k \neq T_j\}$$

where $cost()$ is a heuristic cost function. Then a set of reconfiguration paths that results in the maximum possible number of faults being reconfigured and at the same time also incurs minimum track overhead can be found by solving the mincost flow problem on this modified flow graph [1].

4 Speeding Up Reconfiguration

In this section, we present an effective technique to significantly speed up the reconfiguration algorithm. Fast reconfiguration is needed especially in long-life mission critical systems possibly operating in hazardous and/or unmaintained environments (e.g., spacecrafts, satellites, remote-sensing stations) where multiple faults can accumulate over the life of the mission. The speedup technique discussed applies to both node- and edge-disjoint FPGA designs, the only difference being that vertices that are neither sources nor sinks in the flow graph have unit capacities in the former case and unbounded capacities in the latter case.

4.1 The Technique for Double-Spare Designs

For simplicity of exposition, we first consider the reconfiguration algorithm for the double-spare case in which there are spares on all four sides of the FPGA. Figure 3(a) shows a 14×8 array of primary cells with a 10-fault pattern including a faulty spare in the rightmost column in row 9; assume for the moment that it is a double-spare design, although the figure actually depicts a single-spare design with a spare column on the right and a spare row at the bottom. Define the *circumscribing rectangle* corresponding to a fault pattern as the set of primary cells in the rectangle circumscribing all primary-cell faults and all primary cells adjacent to spare faults. This is rectangle (A,B,C,D) in Fig. 3(a).

The reconfiguration problem in the double-spare case is essentially equivalent to finding reconfiguration paths for all faults to unique boundary cells of the circumscribing rectangle, since from there the paths can be extended straight outward from the rectangle to spares in the same row (for boundary cells on the left and right sides) or column (for boundary cells on the top and bottom sides). For example, for the fault $(9,4)$ in Figure 3(a), we first find a path to the boundary cell $(11,4)$, and from there extend it straight outward to the spare in the bottom row and the same column. Although not shown in Figure 3(a), paths formed till boundary cells on the left and top sides of the circumscribing rectangle are extended outward to the spares on the left and top sides of the array, respectively. Thus, the reconfiguration problem in the double-spare case is equivalent to solving the maxflow problem in the subgraph of the original graph discussed in Sec. 3 consisting of vertices and edges confined to the circumscribing rectangle and in which boundary-cell

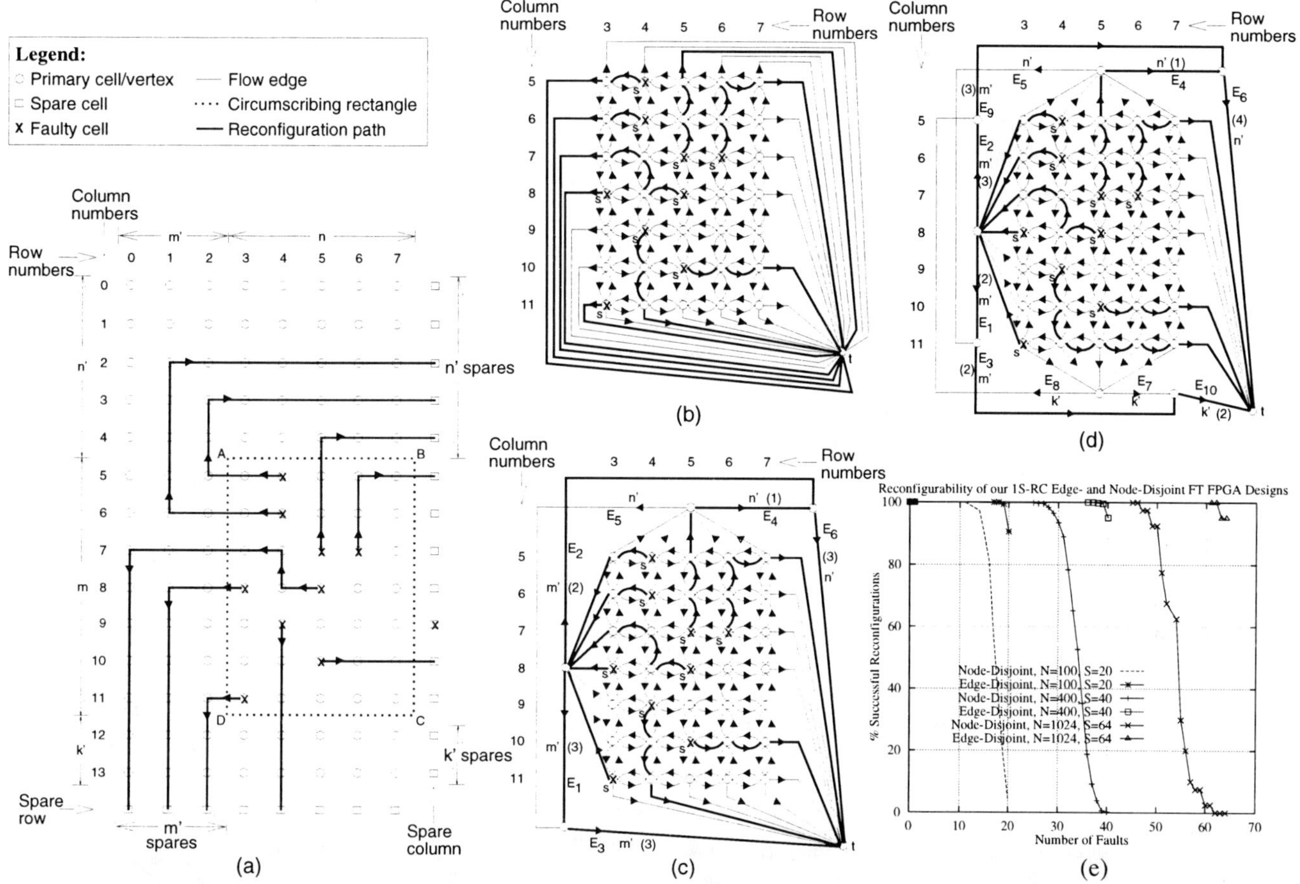

Figure 3: (a) An example fault reconfiguration showing the basis of the fast reconfiguration algorithm with the circumscribing rectangle identified with dotted lines. (b) The flow graph for the fast reconfiguration algorithm in the double-spare row-column case. (c) The flow graph for the fast reconfiguration algorithm in the single-spare row-column case. (d) The flow graph in the single-spare column case. (e) Reconfigurability of edge- and node-disjoint FT FPGA designs for arrays of 100, 400, and 1024 cells for the single-spare row-column case.

vertices are connected to the sink. The maxflow graph for the above fault pattern is shown in Figure 3(b). Note that, as before, a faulty spare (e.g., the spare fault in row 9) means that there is no corresponding edge in the maxflow graph. By reducing the number of vertices in the equivalent maxflow problem, we can speed up the reconfiguration algorithm. We will analyze the expected amount of speedup and give empirical speedup results in Sec. 5.

4.2 The Technique for Single-Spare Row-Column Designs

Next, consider the case of 1S-RC FPGA designs. The additional constraint here is that there are no spares on the left and top sides of the array, and hence paths formed till boundary cells on these sides of the circumscribing rectangle will need to bend to access spares on the right and bottom sides of the array. This is depicted in Figure 3(a) for the example fault pattern considered above. In general, let the circumscribing rectangle be of dimensions $m \times n$ and let it located a distance of m' from the left and n' from the top boundary of the array; $m = 7, n = 5, m' = 3$ and $n' = 5$ in Fig. 3(a). From our observation above, flow graphs for the double- and single-spare cases, depicted in Figs. 3(b) and (c), respectively, should be the same, except that the latter should incorporate the additional constraint on routing reconfiguration paths from the left and top boundary points of the circumscribing rectangle to spares on the right and bottom. How this additional constraint is incorporated in Fig. 3(c) by edges $E_1 - E_3$, all of capacity m', and edges $E_4 - E_6$, all of capacity n', is explained next.

Of all reconfiguration paths exiting the left side of the circumscribing rectangle, a maximum of m' paths may go to the bottom spares (since there are only m' cell columns to the left of the circumscribing rectangle to route these paths)—this restriction is modeled by edge E_1, and a maximum of m' paths may bend and access the spares on the right—this is modeled by edge E_2. Similarly, of the paths exiting the top side, a maximum of n' paths each may access spares on the right and bottom sides of the array—these restrictions are modeled by edges E_4 and E_5, respectively. Furthermore, since there are only m' bottom spares to the left of the circumscribing rectangle, no more than m' paths exiting the left and top sides can access these spares—this is modeled by edge E_3. Edge E_6 models a similar restriction for spares on the right. The numbers in parenthesis next to the above flow edges in Fig. 3(c) represent the actual flow amount in them for the example fault pattern considered in Fig. 3(a). Thus solving maxflow on the above graph is equivalent to solving the reconfiguration algorithm in the 1S-RC case.

4.3 The Technique for Single-Spare Row/Column Designs

Finally, consider the case of single-spare row or column FPGA designs (see Fig. 3(d)). Here we show how our technique is applied for 1S-C FPGA (one in which there is a spare column on the right); application for 1S-R FPGA is similar. Assume that the circumscribing rectangle of Fig. 3(a) is located a distance of k' from the bottom boundary of the array. Reconfiguration paths exiting the rectangle on the top, left, and bottom sides must bend and access the n' and k' spares on the right to the top and bottom, respectively, of the array. By arguments similar to that made for Fig. 3(c), it is clear why the pairs of edges (E_1, E_2), (E_4, E_5), and (E_7, E_8) in Fig. 3(d) should have capacities m', n', and k', respectively. Of the reconfiguration paths exiting the bottom and left sides of the rectangle, only a maximum of m' can access the top spares—this is modeled by edge E_9; and of these and the reconfiguration paths exiting the top side of the rectangle, only a maximum of n' can access the top n' spares—this is modeled by edge E_6. By symmetry, it is easy to see how edges E_3 and E_{10} model the remaining flow constraints. It should be noted in Fig. 3(d) that since only two spares can be accessed at the bottom of the array (because $k' = 2$), the reconfiguration path for fault $(8, 5)$ in Fig. 3(a) has been diverted upwards and to the right in Fig. 3(d), and that for fault $(9, 4)$ has been diverted to spare $s^r_{11,*}$.

5 Speedup Analysis

We now estimate the expected speedup from using the above technique over the original algorithm of Sec. 3 for a $\sqrt{N} \times \sqrt{N}$ array assuming that faults are distributed randomly across the array. Recall that the time complexity of the reconfiguration algorithm is determined by the number of vertices in the circumscribing rectangle of the fault pattern. In the following, we determine, for a given fault size, the probabilities for circumscribing rectangles of different sizes. Consider an $i \times j$ rectangular subset of the array spanning rows i' through $i' + i - 1$ and columns j' through $j' + j - 1$. Given a fixed-size random fault pattern F, the probability of the event $E_0 \equiv E[i' : i'+i-1, j' : j'+j-1]$ of F lying within this rectangle is

$$p_{i,j} = P(E_0) = \frac{\binom{i \cdot j}{|F|}}{\binom{N}{|F|}} = \frac{(i \cdot j)!\,(N - |F|)!}{N!\,(i \cdot j - |F|)!},$$

$$\text{for } i > 0,\ j > 0,\ |F| \leq i \cdot j, \text{ and}$$
$$= 0, \text{ otherwise.} \quad (1)$$

Note that we do not use i' and j' to index the probability $p_{i,j}$ since it is independent of the location of the circumscribing rectangle. Let $E_1 \equiv E[i' : i' + i - 2, j' : j' + j - 1]$, $E_2 \equiv E[i'+1 : i'+i-1, j' : j'+j-1]$, $E_3 \equiv E[i' : i'+i-1, j' : j' + j - 2]$, and $E_4 \equiv E[i' : i' + i - 1, j' + 1 : j' + j - 1]$. Then, the probability that the fault pattern is circumscribed by the above rectangle, i.e., the probability that all $|F|$ faults are confined to the above rectangle and at least one fault lies on each boundary of the rectangle, is

$$q_{i,j} = P(E_0) - P(E_1 \cup E_2 \cup E_3 \cup E_4). \quad (2)$$

The second probability on the right hand side of Eq. 2 is given by the inclusion-exclusion formula [14]

$$P(E_1 \cup E_2 \cup E_3 \cup E_4) = S_1 - S_2 + S_3 - S_4, \quad (3)$$

where S_k is the sum of the probabilities of any k events among the E_i's, $1 \leq i \leq 4$, occuring simultaneously. For example,

$$S_2 = P(E_1 \cap E_2) + P(E_1 \cap E_3) + P(E_1 \cap E_4) + P(E_2 \cap E_3) + P(E_2 \cap E_4) + P(E_3 \cap E_4). \quad (4)$$

Note that the probabilities of intersecting events can be computed from Eq. 1. For example,

$$\begin{aligned} P(E_1 \cap E_2) &= P(E[i' : i' + i - 2, j' : j' + j - 1] \cap E[i' + 1 : i' + i - 1, j' : j' + j - 1]) \\ &= P(E[i' + 1 : i' + i - 2, j' : j' + j - 1]) \\ &= p_{i-2,j}. \end{aligned} \quad (5)$$

Thus we can compute $q_{i,j}$ in Eq. 2 using Eqs. 1 and 3.

Let the function $\Gamma(|V|)$ denote the average complexity of the maxflow reconfiguration algorithm on a $|V|$-vertex flow graph. Then, since there are $(\sqrt{N} - i + 1) \cdot (\sqrt{N} - j + 1)$ different possible locations for a $i \times j$ circumscribing rectangle in a $\sqrt{N} \times \sqrt{N}$ array, the average complexity of the fast reconfiguration algorithm for a given fault size $|F|$ is

$$T(N, |F|) = \sum_{i,j=1}^{\sqrt{N}} (\sqrt{N} - i + 1) \cdot (\sqrt{N} - j + 1) \cdot q_{i,j} \cdot \Gamma(i \cdot j), \quad (6)$$

and the speedup obtained is

$$S(N, |F|) = \frac{\Gamma(N)}{T(N, |F|)}. \quad (7)$$

We collected speedup results, averaged over ten runs, for the $O(N^3)$ reconfiguration algorithm of Sec. 3 for edge-disjoint FPGA designs. Table 1 depicts empirical speedups obtained for a 1024-cell node-disjoint FPGA array for five different fault sizes, viz., $|F| = 2, 4, 8, 16, 32$. It also gives corresponding analytical speedups obtained from Eq. 7 assuming the average complexity of the reconfiguration algorithm is $\Gamma(N) = \Theta(N^{1.8})$. Assuming this average complexity gives us the best fit for the analytical speedup with the empirical one for $|F| = 2$ among $\Theta(N^3), \ldots, \Theta(N^{1.9})$, $\Theta(N^{1.8})$, $\Theta(N^{1.7})$, etc. As can be seen, the empirical and analytical speedups are in good agreement over the entire range of $|F|$ values. Note that by using the fast reconfiguration algorithm, we are able to solve the reconfiguration problem in a fraction of the time taken by the regular algorithm. Clearly, as is evident from Table 1 also, speedups will be higher for smaller than larger fault sizes, since the circumscribing rectangles will be smaller in the former compared to the latter case. For the same reason, it is clear that, for a given fault size, speedups will be higher for larger arrays than smaller ones. Moreover, since defects on an FPGA are likely to be localized to small regions, faults are more likely to be clustered than uniformly distributed across the array, so that the circumscribing rectangles will be smaller. Hence, speedups obtained will be more than that predicted by the above analysis.

Fault Size	Empirical Speedup	Analytical Speedup
2	23.05	22.43
4	3.34	4.55
8	2.13	2.07
16	1.25	1.38
32	1.10	1.13

Table 1: Empirical and analytical speedups obtained for a 1024-cell edge-disjoint FT FPGA array for five different fault sizes assuming in the analysis that the average complexity of the reconfiguration algorithm is $\Theta(N^{1.8})$.

6 Reconfigurability of Edge- and Node-Disjoint FT FPGA Designs

Here we present reconfigurability results for the edge- and node-disjoint FPGA designs obtained by using the maxflow-based reconfiguration algorithm of Sec. 3 and Monte Carlo simulations averaged over 300-1000 samples. In Fig. 3(e) we plot the percentage of successful reconfigurations for various fault sizes for the single-spare row-column and double-spare (not shown) row-column cases, respectively, of the above designs. We denote the number of primary cells by N and the number of spares by S. Note that the reconfigurability of the edge-disjoint design is 100% for all fault sizes except those of size $S-2$ or greater—of course it is possible to tolerate only faults of sizes S or less. Even for these large-sized faults, the reconfigurability is 90% or better and in most cases close to 100%. Furthermore, this is much better than the reconfigurability of the node-disjoint design for large fault sizes. These results also demonstrate that the spare-cell utilization in the edge-disjoint design is close-to-optimal.

7 Conclusions

We presented dynamic node covering based FT FPGA designs for increasing yield and for use in mission-critical systems. Two types of designs were considered: one supporting rectilinear node-disjoint and the other supporting rectilinear edge-disjoint reconfiguration paths. By having reconfiguration paths depend upon actual faults and inserting RSs only along actual reconfiguration paths, the dynamic method incurs much less overhead for the same reliability compared to the static method. To facilitate fast on-line reconfiguration, a speedup technique that speeds up reconfiguration time by as much as 20 times, depending upon the fault set, was presented. The amount of speedup obtainable on average using the technique was analyzed and verified empirically. Finally, we presented reconfigurability results for both the node- and edge-disjoint FT FPGA designs. These show that the reliability achievable via the dynamic node covering approach is indeed high and very close to the best possible with a given number of spares. Future work will explore minimization of track overhead for several real FPGA circuits by incorporating transition costs in the flow graph and solving the resulting mincost flow problem.

References

[1] R.K. Ahuja, et al., *Network Flows*, Prentice Hall, 1993.

[2] T.H. Cormen, et al., *Intro. to Algorithms*, McGraw Hill, 1990.

[3] F. Hanchek and S. Dutt, "Node-covering based defect and fault tolerance methods for increased yield in FPGAs," *Proc. Int. Conf. VLSI Design*, pp. 225–229, Jan., 1996.

[4] F. Hanchek and S. Dutt, "Methodologies for tolerating logic and interconnect faults in FPGAs," *IEEE Trans. Comp.*, special Issue on Dependable Computing, Jan. 1998, pp. 15-33.

[5] N. Hastie and R. Cliff, "The implementation of hardware subroutines on FPGAs," *Proc. CICC*, pp. 31.4.1–31.4.4, 1990.

[6] F. Hatori, *et al.*, "Introducing redundancy in FPGAs," *Proc. IEEE CICC*, pp. 7.1.1–7.1.4, 1993.

[7] S. Khuller and J. Naor, "Flow in planar graphs with vertex capacities," Technical report UMIACS-TR-91-102, CS-TR-2715, University of Maryland, College Park, MD, June 1991.

[8] V. Kumar, et al., "An approach for yield enhancement of program. gate arrays," *Proc. ICCAD*, pp. 226–229, Nov. 1989.

[9] J. McDonald, et al., "A fine grained, highly fault tolerant system based on WSI and FPGA technology," *FPGAs*, W. Moore and W. Luk (eds.), Abingdon EE & CS Books, Abingdon, England, pp. 114–126, 1991.

[10] J. Narasimhan, et al., "Yield enhancement of program. ASIC arrays by reconfiguration of circuit placements," *IEEE T-CAD of ICs and Syst.*, Vol. 13, No. 8, pp. 976–986, Aug. 1994.

[11] K. Roy and S. Nag, "On routability for FPGAs under faulty conditions," *IEEE TC*, Vol. 44, pp. 1296–1305, Nov. 1995.

[12] V.P. Roychowdhury, et al., "Efficient algorithms for reconfiguration in VLSI/WSI arrays," *IEEE Trans. Comp.*, Vol.39, No.4, pp.480-489, Apr. 1990.

[13] V. Shanmugavel, "Low overhead fault reconfiguration techniques for FPGAs," *M.S. Thesis*, Dept. of EECS, Univ. of Illinois at Chicago, IL, 1998.

[14] A. Tucker, *Applied Combinatorics*, John Wiley & Sons, New York, pp. 307, 1984.

Two-Step Algorithms for Maximal Diagnosis of Wiring Interconnects

Wenyi Feng

FPGA Software Core Group
Lucent Technologies
1247 S Cedar Crest Blvd
Allentown PA 18103

Fred J. Meyer and Fabrizio Lombardi

Electrical & Computer Engineering
Northeastern University
360 Huntington Ave
Boston MA 02115

Abstract

We give two algorithms for maximal diagnosis of wiring networks without repair under a general fault model. Maximal diagnosis [7] consists of identifying all diagnosable faults under the assumptions that each net can have multiple drivers and receivers and can be affected by any number of short and open faults. This process is equivalent to verifying all connections between inputs and outputs. Matrices represent the connections in fault-free and faulty networks.

All algorithms discussed are adaptive and have their tests divided into two phases. Our first algorithm exploits a unique condition for verifying the connections; our second algorithm maps the connection verification problem to a bipartite graph. All algorithms use an independent test set [2] for the first test phase.

Simulation results show that the proposed algorithms outperform previous algorithms for maximal diagnosis, in terms of the number of tests. The total time complexity for computing the test sequences and analyzing the output response is polynomial.

1 Introduction

Diagnosing the interconnects on a printed circuit board is an important procedure in the boundary scan architecture standard [1]. In this standard, an architecture is defined so that each primary I/O pin of each chip is associated with a boundary scan cell to facilitate in-place testing of complex digital systems. Each chip has a boundary scan register, which is comprised of the boundary scan cells. Testing the board consists of exploiting the scan chain generated by cascading the boundary scan registers of the individual chips [1]. Board testing consists of testing the individual chips and the wiring between them. Boards may have thousands of nets in the interconnect, so the problem of wiring diagnosis is substantial.

Several papers have dealt with the problem of constructing test sets for diagnosing a wiring network [2, 4, 5, 6, 7, 8, 10, 11, 12]. A common fault model considers stuck-at faults, as well as bridging (short) faults and open faults (usually modeled as stuck-at). Some works assume that a net cannot be simultaneously affected by shorts and opens, and thus test for these separately.

A general framework for detection and location of interconnect faults was given in [5]. The property of diagonal independence was proposed as a sufficient condition for one-step diagnosis without repair. Reference [7] has considered diagnosis under this general fault model—i.e., the simultaneous existence of open and short faults on a net. A walking–1 sequence is necessary and sufficient for one-step maximal diagnosis. Also, two adaptive algorithms were given for *maximal diagnosis,* which requires identifying all *diagnosable* faults with arbitrary short and open faults and no repair. This is equivalent to verifying all connections in the wiring network (determining, for each receiver, which drivers drive it). Adaptiveness was used to (possibly) reduce the number of test vectors compared to the worst case complete walking–1 sequence.

To model the faults for maximal diagnosis, we use a connection matrix, which describes, without ambiguity, the effect of any type and number of faults in the network. Not all matrices are possible. A *valid connection matrix* is one that can result from any combination of short and open faults; it is independent of the original fault-free connection matrix. Herein, we characterize the properties of a valid connection matrix. Maximal diagnosis consists of successfully determining which valid connection matrix an interconnect has.

2 Preliminaries

We let the fault-free interconnect consist of $Netnum$ nets, where each net may have zero or more drivers and zero

0-7695-0213-X/99 $10.00 © 1999 IEEE

or more receivers. We denote the i–th driver (j–th receiver) as D_i (R_j). There are M drivers, $i = 1, \ldots, M$ and there are N receivers, $j = 1, \ldots, N$. We often refer to a driver as an *input* and a receiver as an *output*.

We assume that only open faults (broken wires) and bridging faults (shorted wires) occur. There can be any number of these. We model shorts by OR-ing together the signals that are driving the short (wired-OR model). We assume that a floating output will be observed as a logical 0. (If a floating output is a 1, then one additional test (all 0 inputs) might be necessary.)

- *Parallel Test Vector* (PTV): a vector applied to all inputs in parallel.
- *Sequential Test Vector* (STV): the vector experienced by a single input, over a period of time, due to a sequence of PTVs.
- *Test Set* (or Test Sequence), S: the set of all STVs represented as a table. Each column of S is a PTV and each row of S is an STV.
- *Sequential Response Vector* (SRV): the response of an output to a test sequence.
- *Syndrome:* the SRV of a faulty output.
- *OR-cover:* a vector, V_i, OR-covers another vector, V_j, if, for every bit position in V_j with a value of 1, the corresponding bit in V_i is also 1. For example, vector (1101) OR-covers vector (1001). The OR-cover (or simply cover) is used in the wired-OR fault model.
- *Independent Test Set:* a test set, S is an independent test set if no STV_i covers any other $STV_j, j \neq i$.

2.1 Review

In one-step diagnosis, the test results are analyzed only after the entire test set has been applied to the interconnect under test [8, 9, 11]. In adaptive diagnosis, part of the tests are applied, the results analyzed, and then further tests are applied [3, 7, 10]. We will only consider adaptive two-step diagnosis. Based on the response to the first test sequence, a second test sequence is applied. The response to both test sequences is then analyzed to arrive at the diagnosis.

In [7], two (adaptive) two-step diagnostic algorithms were proposed for maximal diagnosis, referred to as A_1 and A_2. The total testing time will depend on the length of the two test sequences, as well as the amount of time necessary to construct the second test sequence (and the final diagnostic computation).

A_1 applies a maximal independent test set, S_M, for the first step. By analyzing the output response, the inputs are divided into two groups: for a net i, if $STV_i = SRV_i$ and SRV_i is unique, then i is put in Group 0; else, net i is put in Group 1. The second step applies a walking–1 sequence for the nets in Group 1 and all–0 vectors for all nets in Group 0. The total number of PTVs using A_1 is $p + F$. p tests are needed for the independent test set; p is the smallest integer satisfying $C^p_{\lfloor \frac{p}{2} \rfloor} \geq M$. ($C^a_b$ is the number of combinations, a choose b.) F tests are needed for the second step, and F is the number of nets in Group 1. Algorithm A_2 [7] also uses an independent test set in step 1. Algorithm A_2 does not achieve maximal diagnosis so we consider it no further.

3 Connection Matrix Analysis

There may be any number of faults in the interconnect, but they are all limited to shorts and opens. As a result, a receiver either floats or is driven by one or more of the drivers; no other functionality is possible despite the faults. To diagnose the network, therefore, it is sufficient to determine, for each receiver, which of the drivers are driving it, if any. Examining further, we see that the correct (intended) operation of the network is irrelevant to diagnosis. For any network, open faults could exist that disconnect all drivers and all receivers from whatever intervening fabric exists. Whereupon, short faults could exist to establish any desired driver-receiver connections.

To characterize maximal diagnosis, we require that we correctly determine the driver-receiver connections that exist. A *connection matrix,* C, is a boolean matrix. C has dimensions $M \times N$, where each of the M rows corresponds to a driver, and each of the N columns corresponds to a receiver. Each element, C_{ij}, of C is 1 if the connection between D_i and R_j is present; otherwise, $C_{ij} = 0$.

Lemma 1 *In an interconnect without buffers, and any number of short or open faults, the connection matrix, C, has no 2×2 submatrix with precisely 3 entries set to 1.*

For the case of configurable interconnect, where we would be testing whether the interconnect was successfully configured, Lemma 1 will apply if the configuration is accomplished with symmetrical devices, such as pass transistors. We say that a C matrix satisfying Lemma 1 is a *valid connection matrix.* We assume that the interconnect is bufferless, so only valid connection matrices are possible. Reference [7] also made this assumption, although it was left unstated.

The number of ways to distribute n distinct elements into *precisely* m non-distinct groups (no group being empty) is given by $S(n, m)$, which is the Stirling number of the second kind.

$$S(n,m) = \begin{cases} 1 & m = 1 \\ \sum_{i=1}^{n-(m-1)} C^{n-1}_{i-1} S(n-i, m-1) & m > 1 \end{cases}$$

Theorem 1 *The number of* valid *connection matrices of a wiring network with M inputs and N outputs is* $\sum_{k=0}^{\min\{M,N\}} k! S(N+1, k+1) S(M+1, k+1)$.

Figure 1 shows the number of valid connection matrices for different small values of M and N. (The number from Theorem 1 is symmetrical in M and N.) We also plot the total number of 0–1 matrices, including invalid ones, for comparison. The plot is on a binary logarithmic scale. For example, there are 2^{36} possible binary 6×6 matrices, because there are $6 \cdot 6 = 36$ elements of such a matrix. However, there are only $\approx 2^{20.5}$ valid 6×6 connection matrices.

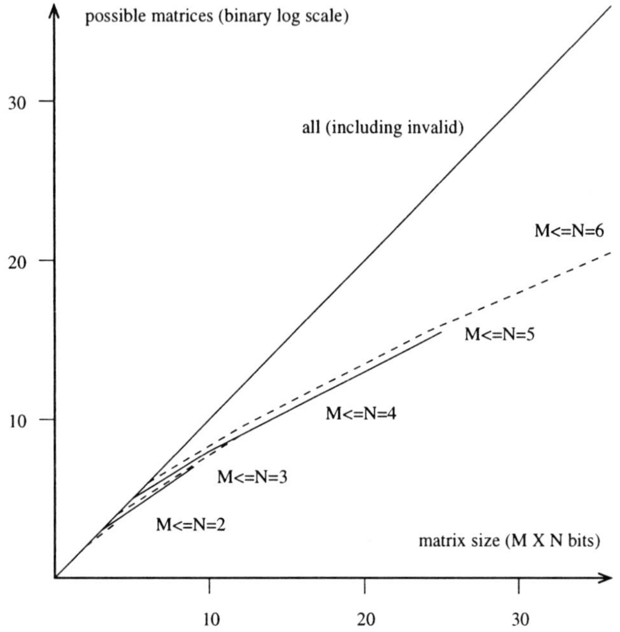

Figure 1. Number of valid connection matrices.

4 Two-Step Diagnosis Algorithms

Reference [7] gives two adaptive algorithms, A_1 and A_2. Since A_2 is not correct, we are only interested in new algorithms compared to A_1. We will give two new algorithms that we denote as A_3 and A_4.

Like [7], we use an independent test set [2] for the first test sequence. We then analyze the response to construct the second test sequence. Reference [7] speaks in terms of nets, rather than drivers and receivers, and thus makes assumptions about multi-driver nets having already been tested to ensure they are capable of being driven by only one driver at a time. In our model, we do not require this. In fact, we allow multiple simultaneous drivers to be defined as the correct (fault-free) behavior. Algorithm A_1 [7] is easily modified to do this as well by performing its computation with respect to drivers rather than nets.

4.1 Two-Step Algorithm A_3

We use an independent test set [2] for the initial test sequence. A property of this sequence is that, if any two or more STVs are wired together (OR-ed), the resulting SRV cannot equal any of the STVs. So, if we observe any SRV_j equal to any STV_i, we know that the receiver R_j is being driven by the driver D_i and by no other driver—i.e., we know the column vector corresponding to R_j in the connection matrix, C. From Lemma 1, we also know that column vectors are either equal or nonoverlapping in their ones. As a result, we also can determine the row vector in C corresponding to driver D_i: it will have 1 entires in all locations, C_{ik}, where the k–th column vector corresponds to STV_i; it will have 0 entries everywhere else.

From these observations, we can improve Algorithm A_1 to get Algorithm A_3, given in Figure 2.

1. Apply an independent test set [2]. Collect the output response.
2. For all $i = 1$ to M, for all $j = 1$ to N, if $STV_i = SRV_j$, then set $C_{ij} = 1$, else set $C_{ij} = 0$. Declare the rows (drivers) of C that are all zeros as being in Group 1; declare the nonzero rows as being in Group 0.
3. Apply a walking–1 test sequence to the drivers in Group 1 while holding all other drivers to 0. Collect the output response.
4. Declare matrix C' as the output response of the walking–1 test sequence (column vectors correspond to SRVs). Update C by bitwise OR-ing it with the result of the walking–1 test sequence, $C = C + C'$.

Figure 2. Algorithm A_3.

Theorem 2 *Algorithm A_3 achieves maximal diagnosis.*

If A_3 is applied to the interconnect given in Figure 3, in Step 2 all inputs go into Group 1, so in Step 3 a walking–1 sequence (8 PTVs) is applied to all the nets and all faults are diagnosed. Indeed, in this problematic case, our Algorithm A_3 actually produces a second test sequence identical to Algorithm A_1 (Algorithm A_2 of [7] fails in this case).

4.2 Two-Step Algorithm A_4

Algorithm A_4, given in Figure 4 can place more drivers in Group 0 than Algorithm A_3 can.

Consider Step 2. Figure 5 shows an example bipartite graph that could result from an independent test set. The masks are initialized to all zeros and are discussed later. The edges shown as dashed lines are the only edges where an SRV equals an STV. Algorithm A_1 [7] looks for such

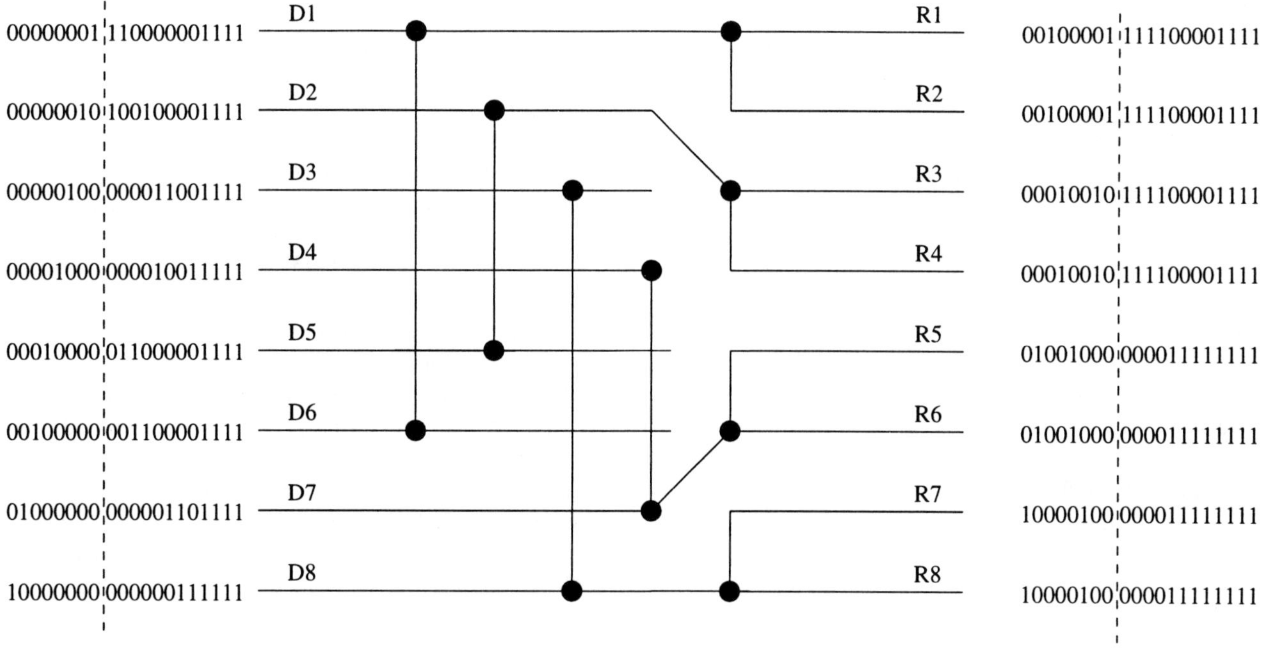

Phase 2 Phase 1

Figure 3. Example of Algorithm A_3.

1. Apply an independent test set [2]. Collect the output response.
2. Initialize connection matrix C to all zeros. Construct a bipartite graph: the drivers/receivers form the nodes in the two partitions; an edge between D_i and R_j exists if SRV_j OR-covers STV_i. Scan the bipartite graph for instances of required support (basically, D_i is required to support R_j if D_i has a bit set (1) that no other neighbor of R_j has set). A more detailed explanation is given in the text. For each instance of required support: record the necessary support in C, then remove all edges from the supporting driver in the graph. At the end, any drivers that still have edges are declared to be in Group 1; the other drivers are in Group 0.
3. Apply a walking–1 test sequence to the drivers in Group 1 while holding all other drivers to 0. Collect the output response.
4. Declare matrix C' as the output response of the walking–1 test sequence (column vectors correspond to SRVs). Update C by bitwise OR-ing it with the result of the walking–1 test sequence, $C = C + C'$.

Figure 4. Algorithm A_4.

edges, but requires that the receiver's SRV not equal any other SRV. But here, $SRV_1 = SRV_3 = SRV_5 = SRV_6 = SRV_7$. So Algorithm A_1 does not place driver D_7 in Group 0. As a result, A_1's second test sequence is a walking–1 across all 7 drivers. Contrast this with Algorithm A_3, which records the connections in the matrix C. It knows that D_7 drives R_1, R_3, R_5, R_6, and R_7. (It also knows that D_7 does not drive R_4.) So, Algorithm A_3 places D_7 in Group 0, and its second test sequence is a walking–1 across 6 drivers.

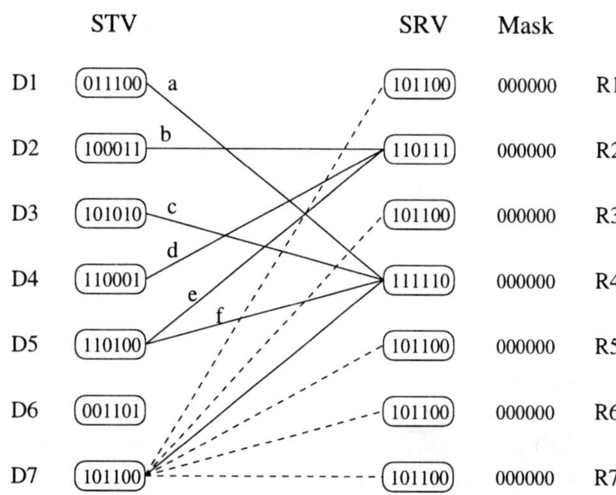

Figure 5. Original bipartite graph.

Step 2 of Algorithm A_4 works from the original bipartite graph and successively removes as many edges as it can. When it cannot remove any more edges, it places all the edgeless drivers in Group 0. Since D_7 is the sole neighbor of R_7, it has a "unique bit" not provided by any other driver that is a neighbor of R_7 in the bipartite graph. A unique bit is the condition the algorithm is looking for, so it will always find these cases and place drivers like D_7 in Group 0. So, A_4 is catching all the cases that A_3 catches. Moreover, we see that Algorithm A_4 will do better than A_3, because driver D_6 has no edges.

Consider one of the other receivers, R_2. Its support comes from edges b, d, and e. Looking for unique bits of support, we see that the fourth bit from the left is only present in STV_5 (edge e). Following Step 2 of Algorithm A_4: we record the support in C, setting $C_{5,2} = 1$, then we remove the edges of D_5—e and f. The result is shown in Figure 6, where we have also processed R_7 and thus removed the edges from D_7.

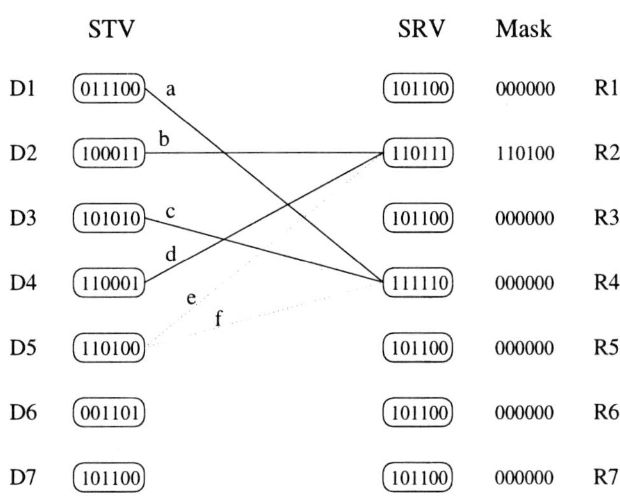

Figure 6. Bipartite graph in middle of Step 2.

The mask field is for recording what support has already been accounted for. Since we determined that D_5 is wired to R_2, we updated R_2's mask by OR-ing it with STV_5. We also removed D_5's edge f with R_4 from the bipartite graph. But in that case, we know that D_5 is not wired to R_4 (bufferless interconnect), so R_4's mask has not been changed.

Now that we have a non-zero mask, we can see how to use it. We continue to process R_2. When considering whether R_2 gets any unique support we examine its remaining edges (from D_2 and D_4). First, D_4. We mask STV_4 (bitwise AND with the complement of R_2's mask) to get: $STV_4 \wedge \overline{Mask_2} = (110001) \wedge \overline{110100} = (000001)$, call it $Sup(D_4)$. The mask makes sure we are ignoring bit positions where support is already coming from a removed edge (in our case, from driver D_5). We compare this with the support possible from all other neighbors of R_2. We take the union (OR) of all other neighbors (there is only D_2) to get (100011). We mask this to get $(100011) \wedge \overline{110100} = (000011)$, call it $Sup(\overline{D_4})$. (Equally as well, we could omit masking (100011).) We see that D_4 does not provide a unique bit of support (specifically, $Sup(D_4) \vee Sup(\overline{D_4}) = Sup(\overline{D_4})$). We now try D_2. We mask STV_2 to get (000011) and we mask the union of R_2's other neighbors to get (000001). We see that D_2 provides a unique bit of support, so we know it must be wired to R_2. We update C, setting $C_{2,2} = 1$, then remove all edges from D_2. The mask for R_2 is updated by OR-ing it with STV_2.

When we process R_4, we see that both D_1 and D_3 provide unique bits of support for SRV_4. At this point, the only edge remaining in the graph is from D_4 to R_2. Algorithm A_4 is unable to remove this edge—indeed, we cannot know whether D_4 and R_2 are connected, and must test for this. Algorithm A_4 places D_4 in Group 1 and all other drivers in Group 0. In Step 3 of Algorithm A_4, the walking–1 test sequence consists of a single PTV with D_4 set to 1.

For space, we omit the implementation details for Step 2. These include various steps, such as first partitioning the receivers into cohorts that have identical SRVs.

Theorem 3 *Algorithm A_4 achieves maximal diagnosis.*

5 Comparison of Two-Step Algorithms

We compare two aspects of the two-step algorithms: (1) how many tests they generate and (2) their computational time complexity. Given the same independent test set used for each algorithm as its first test sequence, the total number of PTVs depends only on the second test sequence.

Theorem 4 *The total number of PTVs for Algorithms A_1, A_3, and A_4 is always greatest for A_1 and least for A_4.*

To gauge the improvement, we conducted experiments with random interconnects. We held the number of receivers equal to the number of drivers, varied the number of drivers up to 500, and randomly generated valid connection matrices to represent the interconnect. For the first test sequence, we always applied a maximal independent test set (minimal number of PTVs for an independent test set). The difference in the total number of PTVs, therefore, lies in the number of walking–1 PTVs each algorithm generates for its second test sequence. Figure 7 plots the size of the second test sequence for Algorithms A_1, A_3, and A_4.

Let there be M drivers, N receivers, and P PTVs in the first test sequence (independent test set). In the worst case, the total test sequence must include as a subsequence a walking–1 across all M drivers, which is $O(M^2)$. It must also collect and process the N SRVs for these M tests, which is $O(NM)$. So the I/O for the algorithms is $O(M(N + M))$.

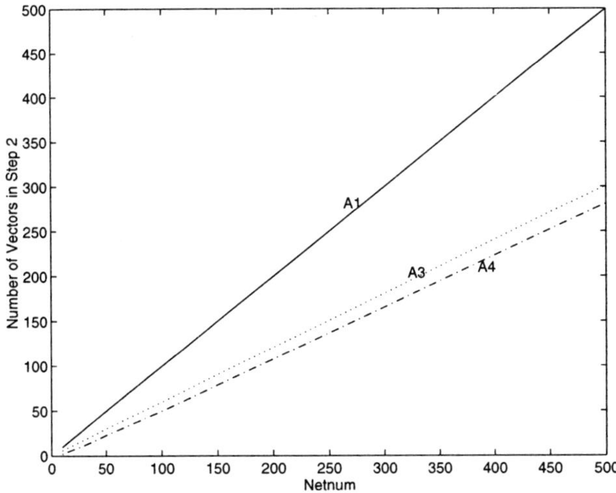

Figure 7. Average test size for Algorithms A_1, A_3, and A_4.

Theorem 5 *The computational time complexities of the two-step adaptive diagnosis algorithms are:* A_1, $O(M(N+M))$*;* A_3, $O(M(N+M))$*; and* A_4, $O(M(N+M+\min\{2^P, N\}P\log M))$.

P is $\Omega(\log M)$. For good results, in practice, we never need to let P exceed $\Theta(\log M)$. With $P \in \Theta(\log M)$, the time complexity of Algorithm A_4 is $O(M(N+M+\min\{M,N\}\log^2 M))$ or, equivalently, $O(M(N^2+M^2+NM\log^2 M)/(N+M))$.

6 Simulation Results

The first test sequence is an independent test set, consisting of STVs none of which OR-cover each other [2]. We define an independent test set by two parameters, (P, k), where P is the number of PTVs (the length of each STV) and k is the number of ones in each STV. So, a (P, k) independent test set can have as many as C_k^P STVs. Also, since we must have M STVs, one for each driver, we need to be large enough so that $C_{\lfloor P/2 \rfloor}^P \geq M$.

For a large system, say a PCB with $M = 10,000$ nets, the minimal possible P is 16 ($k = 8$), which would equate to about 170,000 scan shifts in the first test sequence. We will see below that using larger P will be helpful. For large M, the worst case computational complexity of computing the second test sequence is larger than the scan count. For $M = 10,000$, this is over a million instructions on a 64–bit machine in the worst case. The algorithm's complexity tends to approach the worst case only when there are nets with many drivers.

We conducted experiments to see how the choice of P and k affect the test set. For the first experiment, we set $M = N = 50$ and generated random wiring networks. For the independent test set, we set $P = 12$ and varied k. We picked the 50 actual STVs at random from the pool of C_k^P possible STVs. Figure 8 plots the number of tests needed for the second test sequence, using Algorithm A_4. It steadily decreases as we reduce k.

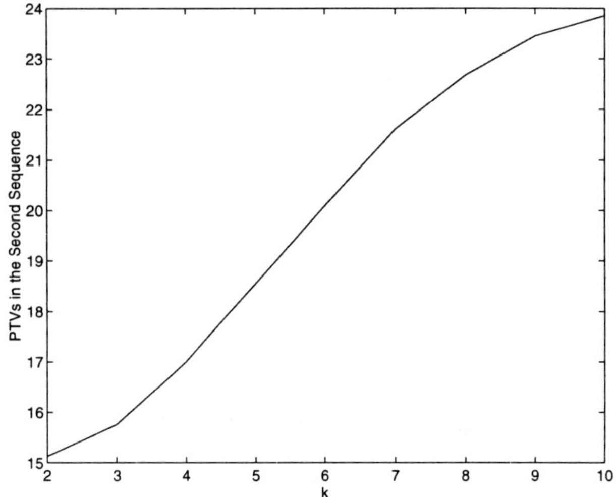

Figure 8. Non-maximal independent test set varying k ($M = N = 50$).

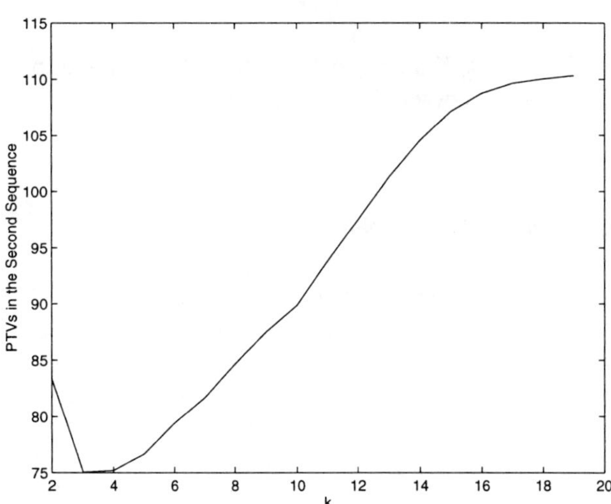

Figure 9. Non-maximal independent test set varying k ($M = N = 200$).

Smaller k is superior in general, because it provides more opportunity for unique bits of support. However, choosing the smallest possible k does not always result in the shortest test sequence. Figure 9 is a similar experiment. Here we set $M = N = 200$, fixed P at 21, and varied k. The length of the first test sequence is always 21. The average length of the second test sequence is minimized when $k = 3$. Despite this anomaly, minimizing k is a solid rule of thumb.

These experiments set P higher than necessary so we could vary k, but is this advantageous? We conducted an experiment where we varied P, while choosing k as small as possible (such that $C_k^P \geq M$). We again generated random wiring networks (valid connection matrices). Figures 10 and 11 plot the results. The first test sequence has P PTVs. Increasing P pays dividends by reducing the length of the second test sequence. However, the optimum for P is near the minimum for P.

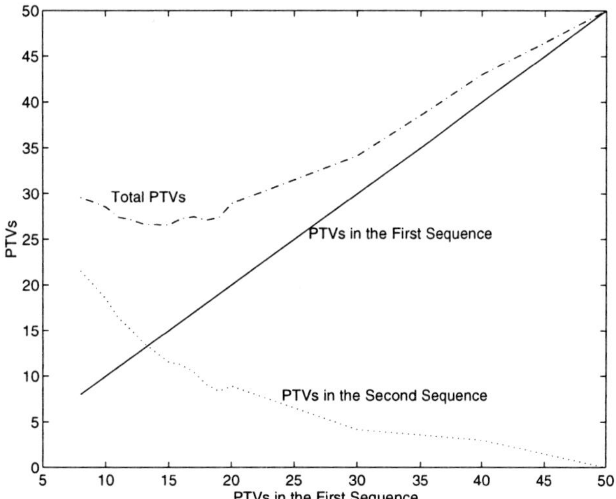

Figure 10. Trading off the length of the two test sequences ($N = M = 50$).

6.1 Single-Driver Nets

We want to consider cases with a bounded number of faults. Previously, we allowed arbitrary networks, because multiple faults could transform any fault-free network into any valid network. Now we restrict our attention to those fault-free networks where each receiver is driven by at most one driver. In the extreme case, each driver will also drive only one receiver, and we would have a bus. Additional receivers help to diagnose faults, so a bus is the worst case here, and we indeed use a bus in these experiments.

We set $M = N = 500$ and declared the fault-free network to be a bus (connection matrix is an identity matrix). We introduce a variable, f, which is the number of faulty receivers. For each value f and for each simulation run, we threw random faults at the wiring network. We stopped when we reached f faulty receivers. Each fault was either a short or an open. The relative frequency of shorts and opens can vary in systems, so we did one experiment where shorts

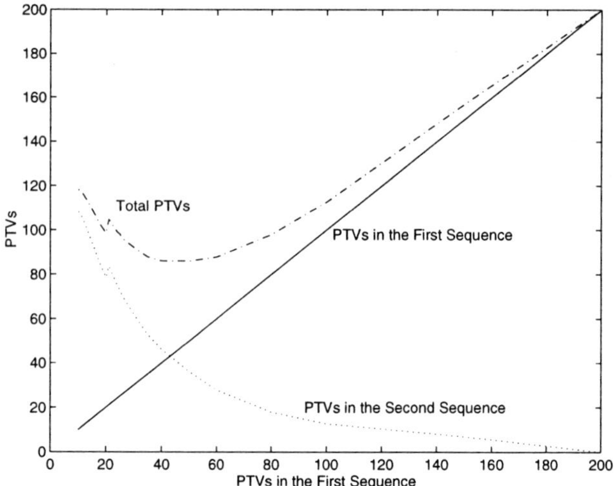

Figure 11. Trading off the length of the two test sequences ($N = M = 200$).

predominate and another where opens predominate. Each short bridged two random wires on the bus. Each open fault was either open at a driver or at a receiver. (If a bus line were involved in more than one short, in addition to an open, then there would be additional possible locations. Since we are dealing with a relatively small number of random faults, we ignore this distinction.)

We recorded the number of PTVs needed for the second test sequence and averaged them over the simulation runs. Figure 12 plots the results.

With Algorithm A_3, the independent test set will find that $M - f$ of the receivers are correct. A_3 will construct a walking–1 test sequence spanning the drivers corresponding to the f faulty receivers. This is confirmed in Figure 12. We varied the number of faulty nets in Figure 12 from 5 to 100.

Algorithm A_4 potentially can do better. It might identify some disconnected drivers or unique bits of support. In this experiment, we again varied (P, k). For each P, we set k to be minimal. Increasing P did decrease the length of the second test sequence. However, it was not easy to overcome the penalty due to having more PTVs in the first test sequence. Using Algorithm A_4 with a $(16, 3)$ independent test set did not become as good as $(13, 4)$ until f was over 20. Likewise, a $(33, 2)$ independent test set did not become superior to the $(16, 3)$ one until f was over 80.

7 Conclusions

We proposed two-step algorithms for maximal diagnosis of wiring networks under a general fault model. Maximal diagnosis consists of identifying all diagnosable faults under the assumption that each net can have multiple drivers and receivers, and any number of short and open faults. The maximal diagnosis requirement is equivalent to identifying whether a wiring connection exists between each driver and each receiver. So we described these networks with a connection matrix.

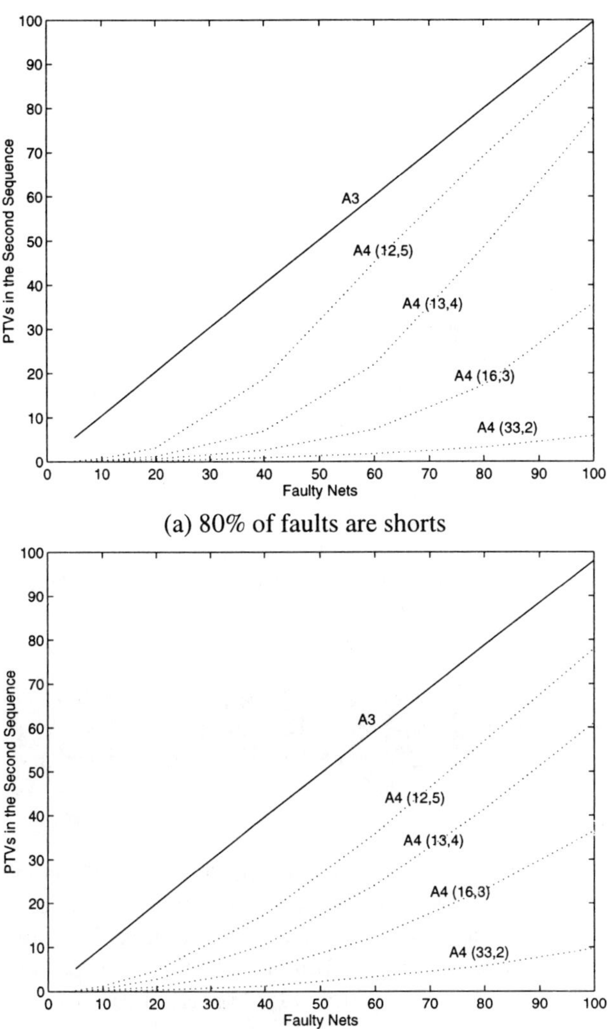

(a) 80% of faults are shorts

(b) 80% of faults are opens

Figure 12. Bus network with bounded multiple faults ($N = M = 500$).

Our first algorithm, A_3, leads to smaller test sequences than Algorithm A_1 in [7], while having the same time complexity. Algorithm A_2 in [7] does not achieve maximal diagnosis. Our second algorithm, A_4, uses a bipartite graph to represent the possible connections after the first test sequence. Its computational time complexity is only slightly greater—typically no more than a factor of $\log^2 M$, where M is the number of drivers.

All these algorithms use an independent test set [2] for the first test sequence. Algorithms A_1 and A_3 do not depend on the particular independent test set used, so it is most efficacious to use the smallest such test set possible. We showed, however, that Algorithm A_4's results can improve by using a larger independent test set.

References

[1] J. C. Chan, "Boundary walking test: An accelerated scan method for greater system reliability," *IEEE Trans. Rel.*, vol. 41, no. 4, 1992, pp. 496–503.

[2] W. T. Cheng, J. L. Lewandowski, and E. Wu, "Diagnosis for Wiring Interconnects," *IEEE Int. Test Conf.*, pp. 565–571, 1990.

[3] C. Feng, W. K. Huang, and F. Lombardi, "A New Diagnosis Approach for Short Faults in Interconnects," *IEEE Fault-Tol. Comp. Symp.*, Pasadena CA, pp. 331–339, June 1995.

[4] A. Hassan, J. Rajski, and V. K. Agrawal, "Testing and Diagnosis of Interconnects Using Boundary-Scan," *IEEE Int. Test Conf.*, pp. 126–137, 1985.

[5] N. Jarwala and C. W. Yau, "A New Framework for Analyzing Test Generation and Diagnosis Algorithms for Board Interconnects," *IEEE Int. Test Conf.*, pp. 71–77, 1989.

[6] W. H. Kautz, "Testing for faults in wiring networks," *IEEE Trans. Comput.*, vol. 23, no. 4, 1974, pp. 358–363.

[7] J. C. Lien and M. A. Breuer, "Maximal Diagnosis for Wiring Networks," *IEEE Int. Test Conf.*, pp. 96–105, 1991.

[8] T. Liu, X.-T. Chen, F. Lombardi, and J. Salinas, "Layout-Driven Detection of Bridge Faults in Interconnects," *IEEE Symp. on DFT of VLSI Sys.*, pp. 105–113, 1996.

[9] J. Salinas, Y.-N. Shen, and F. Lombardi, "A sweeping line approach to interconnect testing," *IEEE Trans. Comput.*, vol. 45, no. 8, Aug. 1996, pp. 917–929.

[10] W. Shi and K. Fuchs, "Optimal interconnect diagnosis of wiring networks," *IEEE Trans. VLSI Sys.*, vol. 3, no. 2, June 1995, pp. 430–436.

[11] P. T. Wagner, "Interconnect Testing with Boundary Scan," *IEEE Int. Test Conf.*, pp. 52–57, 1987.

[12] C. W. Yau and N. Jarwala, "A Unified Theory for Designing Optimal Test Generation and Diagnosis Algorithms for Board Interconnects," *IEEE Int. Test Conf.*, pp. 71–77, 1989.

Fault Identification Algorithmic: A New Formal Approach

Béchir AYEB*
University of Sherbrooke
RiFa Lab / DMI
Sherbrooke (PQ)
CANADA J1K 2R1
ayeb@dmi.usherb.ca

Abstract

Much research has been devoted to system-level diagnosis. Two issues have been addressed. The first of these is diagnosability, The second is the design of fault identification algorithms. This paper focuses on the second of these concerns. This paper investigates the process of fault identification itself, introduces a new formal approach, and proposes a fault identification algorithm which runs in $O(n^2\sqrt{\tau}/\sqrt{\log n})$, $\tau < \frac{n}{2}$.

1 Prologue

Consider a system **S** of n units (e.g., subsystems, modules, chips, processors), where each unit is assigned a particular subset of the remaining units to test. The complete collection of tests is called the **connection assignment** and can be represented by a directed graph $G\langle V, E\rangle$ where V is a finite set of vertices, each vertex representing a unit of **S**, and E is a set of directed edges, each representing a test between a pair of units.

An **outcome**, denoted by a_{ij}, is associated with each edge (v_i, v_j) in E, where $a_{ij} = 1$ (resp. $a_{ij} = 0$) if v_i evaluates (i.e., tests) v_j as faulty (resp. fault-free). The set of outcomes associated with the edges of the corresponding graph of **S** is called a **syndrome**.

Of course, when the tester is fault-free the outcome is deterministic. That is, if v_i is fault-free then $a_{ji} = 0$ provided that v_j is fault-free. If v_i is faulty then $a_{ji} = 1$ provided that v_j is fault-free. When the tester is faulty, things are a bit complicated and we should eventually take assumptions. Under the **PMC model** [21] (also called the symmetric model), no assumptions are made.[1] The outcome provided by a faulty tester may be either 0 or 1.

A syndrome is said to be **consistent** with F, a subset of units, if it may be obtained when F is the set of all faulty units. A system **S** is called **τ-diagnosable** if, given a syndrome, all the (permanent) faulty units in **S** can be identified provided that the number of faulty units does not exceed τ.

Two related issues are worth addressing here. The first concerns the necessary and sufficient conditions for a system **S** to be τ-diagnosable. Considering the PMC model, it has been provided in [15].[2]

Lemma 1 (HAKIMI & AMIN [15]) *A system* **S** *is* τ*-diagnosable iff:* $n \geq 2\tau + 1$, $\Gamma(v) \geq \tau, \forall v \in V$, *and* $|\Gamma(V')| > p, \forall V' \subset V$ *such that* $|V'| = n - 2\tau + p$ *and* $0 \leq p \leq \tau - 1$.
□□□

Similar results have been obtained in [1], [13], and [23]. Let us now turn to the second issue which concerns the design of fault identification algorithms for τ-diagnosable systems. Under the PMC model, we have the following results: (1) The KAMEDA ET AL algorithm runs in $O(\tau|E|)$ [17]; (2) The DAHBURA & MASSON algorithm runs in $O(n^{2.5})$ [13]; (3) The SULLIVAN algorithm runs in $O(\tau^3 + |E|)$ [24].

This paper is concerned with the second issue, that is, fault identification algorithms. We first shed some light on the process of fault identification and yields a simple algorithm to identify all faulty units. The proposed algorithm runs in $O(n^2\sqrt{\tau}/\sqrt{\log n}), \tau < \frac{n}{2}$.

* This work is supported by Federal Grant OGP0121468; NSERC.

[1] In [7], a new model is proposed. It assumes that $a_{ij} = 1$ whenever both units u_i and v_j are faulty. This model is known as the **BGM model**; it is also called the asymmetric model.

[2] As usual, we have: $\Gamma(v_i) = \{v_j/(v_i, v_j) \in E\}$ and $\Gamma^{-1}(v_i) = \{v_j/(v_j, v_i) \in E\}$. If V_1 and V_2 are two given sets then (1) $|V_1|$ denotes the cardinality of set V_1; (2) $V_1\backslash V_2$ denotes set difference; (3) $\Gamma(V_1) = (\bigcup_{v\in V_1} \Gamma(v))\backslash V_1$; (4) $\Gamma^{-1}(V_1) = (\bigcup_{v\in V_1} \Gamma^{-1}(v))\backslash V_1$.

0-7695-0213-X/99 $10.00 © 1999 IEEE

This bound is not however tight, but it depends on solving other related problems. Hence, subsequent improvements are possible but they do not alter the basic results given in this paper.

The rest of this paper is organized as follows. Section 2 provides problem formulation and an illustrative example. It also presents D, a fault identification algorithm with the complexity mentioned above. Finally, Section 3 summarizes this paper and presents concluding remarks.

2 Our Framework

Due to space limitation, the paper has been drastically shortened. Results are stated without proof and several steps have been simplified. The complete version, including details and proofs, is available in [3], a 20-page research report.

2.1 Formulation

A **System S** under diagnosis is a pair $\langle \mathcal{U}, \tau \rangle$ where $\mathcal{U}$ is a finite set of constants $\{u_1, \cdots, u_n\}$ representing the units of **S**, and τ is an integer denoting the diagnosability of **S**.

To formalize[3] the notion of a syndrome corresponding to a given system **S**, we introduce the following distinguished predicate [6]. The unary predicate $\text{UU}(x), x \in \mathcal{U}$ is interpreted as meaning the unit x is **unreliable**– i.e., faulty. Using the UU(.) predicate, we formalize the outcomes composing the syndrome of the system under diagnosis as follows. Let u_i and u_j be two units of $\mathcal{U}$. If $a_{ij} = 0$ then we write $\neg\text{UU}(u_i) \Rightarrow \neg\text{UU}(u_j)$ Conversely, if $a_{ij} = 1$ then we write $\neg\text{UU}(u_i) \Rightarrow \text{UU}(u_j)$. Observe that $a_{ij} = a_{ji} = 1$ yields the same formula.

Clearly, a syndrome, hereafter denoted by Σ, consists of a set of formulas which have the following forms: (1) $\neg\text{UU}(u_i) \Rightarrow \neg\text{UU}(u_j)$ which is equivalent to the clause $(\text{UU}(u_i) \vee \neg\text{UU}(u_j))$, or (2) $\neg\text{UU}(u_i) \Rightarrow \text{UU}(u_j)$, which could rewritten as $(\text{UU}(u_i) \vee \text{UU}(u_j))$.

As in [6], we suppose that we have a conventional deduction system, denoted here as $\models_{sld}$, with two inference rules. Let Φ and Ψ be two literals, then the first rule is the standard Modus Ponens: if Φ holds and $\Phi \Rightarrow \Psi$ holds, then Ψ holds– e.g., if $\text{UU}(x)$ holds and $\text{UU}(x) \Rightarrow \text{UU}(y)$ holds then $\text{UU}(y)$ holds. The second is the resolution rule adapted to $\models_{sld}$: if $\Phi \Rightarrow \Psi$ holds and $\neg\Phi \Rightarrow \neg\Pi$ holds, then $\Pi \Rightarrow \Psi$ holds. For the sake of completeness, we add the following axiom $[\forall x \in \mathcal{U}, \text{UU}(x) \oplus \neg\text{UU}(x)]$ to our deduction system $\models_{sld}$. This axiom states that any unit must be *exclusively* unreliable (i.e., faulty) or not unreliable (i.e., fault-free).

Observe that the only predicate which could occur in all formulas handled by $\models_{sld}$, our deduction system, is $\text{UU}(x)$, where $x \in \mathcal{U}$, the given set of units. Therefore, all conjunctions and clauses in this paper are necessarily built using $\text{UU}(x)$ predicate, where $x \in \mathcal{U}$. If Φ is a formula, then $U(\Phi)$ denotes the set of units occurring in Φ. Since units in $U(\Phi)$ could occur in positive or negative literals, then $U^+(\Phi)$ denotes all units occurring in positive literals, whereas $U^-(\Phi)$ denotes those occurring in negative literals. Let $\Psi = \text{UU}(u) \wedge \text{UU}(v) \wedge \neg\text{UU}(p) \wedge \neg\text{UU}(q) \wedge \neg\text{UU}(r)$ be a formula; then $U(\Psi) = \{u, v, p, q, r\}$, $U^+(\Psi) = \{u, v\}$, and $U^-(\Psi) = \{p, q, r\}$.

Now, we can define a diagnosis as follows.

Definition 1 *Let* $\mathbf{S}\langle \mathcal{U}, \tau \rangle$ *be a system under diagnosis. Then a* **Diagnosis** *for* **S** *w.r.t syndrome* Σ *is a conjunction* Δ *such that: (1)* $|U^+(\Delta)|$ *is minimal w.r.t set cardinality; (2)* $\Delta \models_{sld} \Sigma$*; and (3)* $\{\Delta \cup \Sigma\}$ *is consistent.* □□□

The following properties are simple consequences of the above definition and make a first connection with the definition of a diagnosis used in the system-level literature.

Property 1 *Let* $\mathbf{S}\langle \mathcal{U}, \tau \rangle$ *be a system under diagnosis. If* Δ *is a diagnosis for* **S** *w.r.t syndrome* Σ*, then the following statements hold: (1)* $\forall x \in \{\mathcal{U} \backslash U^+(\Delta)\}, \forall y \in U^-(\Delta), (\neg\text{UU}(x) \Rightarrow \neg\text{UU}(y)) \notin \Sigma$. *(2)* $\forall x, y \in \mathcal{U}, (\neg\text{UU}(x) \Rightarrow \text{UU}(y)) \in \Sigma \Rightarrow x \in U^+(\Delta) \vee y \in U^+(\Delta)$. *(3) If* $\mathbf{S}\langle \mathcal{U}, \tau \rangle$ *is* τ*-diagnosable then* Δ *is necessarily unique and* $|U^+(\Delta)| \leq \tau$. □□□

Property 2 *Let* $\mathbf{S}\langle \mathcal{U}, \tau \rangle$ *be a system under diagnosis. Consider* Σ*, a syndrome of* **S***, and let* Δ_1 *and* Δ_2 *be two conjunctions such that: (1)* $|U^+(\Delta_1)| \leq \tau$, $|U^+(\Delta_2)| \leq \tau$*, (2)* $U^+(\Delta_1) \neq U^+(\Delta_2)$, $U^+(\Delta_1) \cap U^+(\Delta_2) \neq \emptyset$*, (3)* Δ_1 *is a diagnosis for* **S** *w.r.t* Σ*, and (4)* Δ_2 *is a diagnosis for* **S** *w.r.t* Σ*. Then* $\mathbf{S}\langle \mathcal{U}, \tau \rangle$ *is* **not** τ*-diagnosable.* □□□

Consider Φ, a set of formulas, and Π, a conjunction. Π is called an implicant of Φ provided that $\Pi \models \Phi$. Let Π be an implicant of Φ; then Π is called a **prime implicant** provided that if Π' is an implicant of F and $\Pi' \models \Pi$ then $\Pi = \Pi'$. In what follows, we focus

[3]The following notation is used through this paper: Capital Greek letters (e.g., Π, Δ, Σ) denote formulas. End-of-alphabet lower-case letters x, y, z denote variables, while other lower-case letters (e..g., $u, v, u_i, v_j, a, b, c, \ldots$) denote constants. Calligraphic characters (e.g., $\mathcal{U}, \mathcal{U}_v$) denote sets. Integers are denoted by lower-case Greek letters–e.g., τ, ρ, μ. The Symbol $\wedge$ (resp. $\vee$, resp. $\neg$, resp. $\oplus$, resp. $\Rightarrow$) denotes *and* (resp. *or*, resp. *not*, resp. *exclusive*, resp. *implies*). Finally, $\backslash$ operator denotes set difference, while $|\mathcal{E}|$ denotes the cardinality of the set $\mathcal{E}$.

only on prime implicants; we will write **p-implicants** to denote prime implicants. As in [6], the following property is immediate.

Property 3 *Let* $\mathbf{S}\langle\mathcal{U},\tau\rangle$ *be a system under diagnosis and* Σ *its syndrome. If* Δ *is a p-implicant of* Σ *such that* $U+(\Delta)$ *is minimal w.r.t set cardinality, then* Δ *is a diagnosis of* $\mathbf{S}\langle\mathcal{U},\tau\rangle$. □□□

2.2 An Illustrative Example

For the sake of illustration, let us borrow the following example from DAHBURA & MASSON [13]. Let $\mathbf{S_{dm}}\langle\mathcal{U}_{dm},\tau_{dm}\rangle$ be the system under diagnosis, where $\mathcal{U}_{dm}=\{a,b,c,d,e,f,g,h,i\}$ and $\tau_{dm}=4$. Fig. 2.1 depicts $\mathbf{S_{dm}}$ together with Σ_{dm}, its corresponding syndrome.

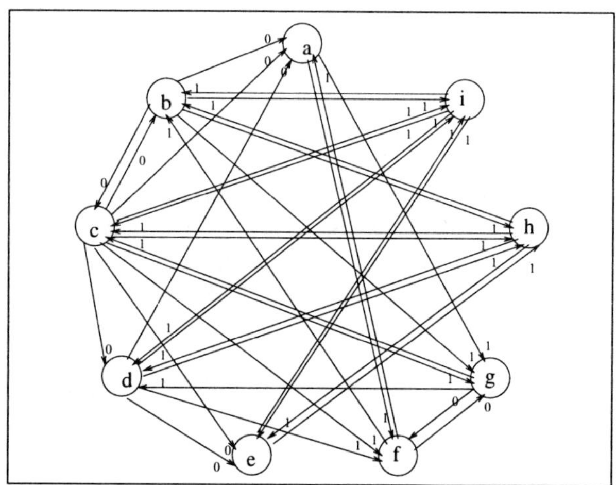

Fig. 2.1: Illustrative Example– $\mathbf{S_{dm}}\langle\mathcal{U}_{dm},\tau_{dm}\rangle$.

$$\Sigma_{dm}\left\{\begin{array}{l}(\mathrm{UU}(b)\vee\neg\mathrm{UU}(a)),(\mathrm{UU}(c)\vee\neg\mathrm{UU}(a)),\\(\mathrm{UU}(d)\vee\neg\mathrm{UU}(a)),(\mathrm{UU}(c)\vee\neg\mathrm{UU}(b)),\\(\mathrm{UU}(b)\vee\neg\mathrm{UU}(c)),(\mathrm{UU}(c)\vee\neg\mathrm{UU}(d)),\\(\mathrm{UU}(c)\vee\neg\mathrm{UU}(e)),(\mathrm{UU}(d)\vee\neg\mathrm{UU}(e)),\\(\mathrm{UU}(f)\vee\neg\mathrm{UU}(g)),(\mathrm{UU}(g)\vee\neg\mathrm{UU}(f)),\\(\mathrm{UU}(i)\vee\mathrm{UU}(b)),(\mathrm{UU}(c)\vee\mathrm{UU}(i)),\\(\mathrm{UU}(d)\vee\mathrm{UU}(i)),(\mathrm{UU}(i)\vee\mathrm{UU}(e)),\\(\mathrm{UU}(h)\vee\mathrm{UU}(b)),(\mathrm{UU}(c)\vee\mathrm{UU}(h)),\\(\mathrm{UU}(d)\vee\mathrm{UU}(h)),(\mathrm{UU}(e)\vee\mathrm{UU}(h)),\\(\mathrm{UU}(a)\vee\mathrm{UU}(g)),(\mathrm{UU}(b)\vee\mathrm{UU}(g)),\\(\mathrm{UU}(c)\vee\mathrm{UU}(g)),(\mathrm{UU}(g)\vee\mathrm{UU}(d)),\\(\mathrm{UU}(f)\vee\mathrm{UU}(a)),(\mathrm{UU}(f)\vee\mathrm{UU}(b)),\\(\mathrm{UU}(c)\vee\mathrm{UU}(f)),(\mathrm{UU}(d)\vee\mathrm{UU}(f))\end{array}\right\}$$

Considering the syndrome Σ_{dm}, $\mathbf{S_{dm}}\langle\mathcal{U}_{dm},\tau_{dm}\rangle$ admits the following diagnosis:

$\Delta_{dm}=\neg\mathrm{UU}(a)\wedge\neg\mathrm{UU}(b)\wedge\neg\mathrm{UU}(c)\wedge\neg\mathrm{UU}(d)\wedge\neg\mathrm{UU}(e)\wedge\mathrm{UU}(f)\wedge\mathrm{UU}(g)\wedge\mathrm{UU}(h)\wedge\mathrm{UU}(i)$

2.3 Theoretical Issues

Lemma 2 *Let* $\mathbf{S}\langle\mathcal{U},\tau\rangle$ *be a system under diagnosis and* Σ *its syndrome. Then we have the following:* $\forall x,y,z\in\mathcal{U},\Sigma\models_{sld}(\neg\mathrm{UU}(x)\Rightarrow\neg\mathrm{UU}(y))\wedge\Sigma\models_{sld}(\neg\mathrm{UU}(y)\Rightarrow\mathrm{UU}(z))\Rightarrow\Sigma\models_{sld}(\neg\mathrm{UU}(x)\Rightarrow\mathrm{UU}(z))$. □□□

While the importance of Lemma 2 will be shown in §2.4, the following lemmas are ready to offer us an immediate result, the status of a given unit.

Lemma 3 *Let* $\mathbf{S}\langle\mathcal{U},\tau\rangle$ *be a system under diagnosis and* Σ *its syndrome. Then we have:* $\forall x,y\in\mathcal{U},\mathrm{UU}(x)\wedge[\Sigma\models_{sld}(\neg\mathrm{UU}(y)\Rightarrow\neg\mathrm{UU}(x))]\Rightarrow\Sigma\models_{sld}\mathrm{UU}(y)$. □□□

Lemma 4 *Let* $\mathbf{S}\langle\mathcal{U},\tau\rangle$ *be a system under diagnosis and* Σ *its syndrome. Then we have:* $\forall x,y\in\mathcal{U},\Sigma\models_{sld}(\neg\mathrm{UU}(x)\Rightarrow\neg\mathrm{UU}(y))\wedge\Sigma\models_{sld}(\neg\mathrm{UU}(y)\Rightarrow\mathrm{UU}(x))\Rightarrow\Sigma\models_{sld}\mathrm{UU}(x)$. □□□

Assuming that $\mathbf{S}\langle\mathcal{U},\tau\rangle$, the system under diagnosis, is diagnosable, we introduce the following definition.

Definition 2 *Let* $\mathbf{S}\langle\mathcal{U},\tau\rangle$ *be a system under diagnosis, then the* **Actual Diagnosis** *for* **S** *w.r.t* Σ, *its syndrome, is a conjunction, denoted by* $\underline{\mathbf{\Delta}}$, *such that (1)* $U(\underline{\mathbf{\Delta}})=\mathcal{U}$, *i.e., the state (reliable or not) of each unit is specified in* $\underline{\mathbf{\Delta}}$, *and (2)* $\underline{\mathbf{\Delta}}\models_{sld}\Sigma$, *i.e.,* $\underline{\mathbf{\Delta}}$ *holds in the intended interpretation.* □□□

Considering $\underline{\mathbf{\Delta}}$, the following lemma is immediate.

Lemma 5 *Let* $\mathbf{S}\langle\mathcal{U},\tau\rangle$ *be a system under diagnosis and* Σ *its syndrome. If* Δ *is a diagnosis for* $\mathbf{S}\langle\mathcal{U},\tau\rangle$ *w.r.t* Σ, *then* $\underline{\mathbf{\Delta}}\models_{sld}\Delta$. □□□

The following proposition is straightforward but it serves our purpose.

Proposition 1 *Let* Φ *be a set of formulas and* $\Pi_1,\cdots,\Pi_m$ *the set of its p-implicants. If* Φ *is consistent and complete, then there exists among* $\Pi_1,\cdots,\Pi_m$ *at least one p-implicant which necessarily holds.* □□□

Lemma 6 *Let* $\mathbf{S}\langle\mathcal{U},\tau\rangle$ *be a system under diagnosis and* Σ *its syndrome. Suppose that* $\Delta_1,\cdots,\Delta_m$ *are the p-implicants of* Σ. *Then among them, there exists at least one p-implicant* Δ_k *such that:* $\underline{\mathbf{\Delta}}\models_{sld}\Delta_k$. □□□

Considering Lemma 6 together with Definition 1, we obtain:

Corollary 1 *Let* $\mathbf{S}\langle\mathcal{U},\tau\rangle$ *be a system under diagnosis and* Σ *its syndrome. If* Δ *is a diagnosis for* $\mathbf{S}\langle\mathcal{U},\tau\rangle$ *w.r.t* Σ, *then* Δ *is a p-implicant of* Σ. □□□

Lemma 7 *Let* $\mathbf{S}\langle\mathcal{U},\tau\rangle$ *be a system under diagnosis and* Σ *its syndrome. Suppose that* $\Delta_1,\cdots,\Delta_m$ *are the p-implicants of* Σ. *Assuming that* $\mathbf{S}$ *is* τ*-diagnosable, then there exists one and only one p-implicant* Δ *among* $\Delta_1,\cdots,\Delta_m$ *such that:* $|U^+(\Delta)| \leq \tau$. □□□

Let GENERATE(Σ) be a procedure to compute the set of p-implicants for Σ, a given set of clauses. Suppose that SELECT primitive picks up the p-implicant which is minimal w.r.t set cardinality. Then by using Lemma 7, we obtain a first diagnosis algorithm, A, shown in Fig. 2.2.

```
A(S⟨U,τ⟩,Σ)
|  PIs ← GENERATE(Σ)
|  Δ ← SELECT(PIs)
|  Return(Δ)
L
```

Fig. 2.2: A– Abstract Algorithm

Clearly, A is an abstract algorithm and several versions could be derived. It is also inefficient as we will investigate efficiency in the next subsection. In this vein, the following corollaries characterize (un)reliable units.

Corollary 2 *Let* $\mathbf{S}\langle\mathcal{U},\tau\rangle$ *be a system under diagnosis and* Σ *its syndrome. Consider* $u \in \mathcal{U}$ *and suppose that* $\neg\text{UU}(u)$ *holds, then for any p-implicant* Δ *of* Σ, *we have:* $u \in U^+(\Delta) \Rightarrow |U^+(\Delta)| > \tau$. □□□

Corollary 3 *Let* $\mathbf{S}\langle\mathcal{U},\tau\rangle$ *be a system under diagnosis and* Σ *its syndrome. Consider* $u \in \mathcal{U}$ *and suppose that for any* Δ, *a p-implicant of* Σ, *we have* $u \notin U^+(\Delta)$; *then* $\neg\text{UU}(u)$ *holds.* □□□

As a matter of fact, a diagnosis could be built recursively, as shown by the following lemma.

Lemma 8 *Let* $\mathbf{S}\langle\mathcal{U},\tau\rangle$ *be a system under diagnosis and* Σ *its syndrome. Considering* $v \in \mathcal{U}$ *and supposing that* $\text{UU}(v)$ *holds, let us build* $\mathbf{S}'\langle\mathcal{U}',\tau'\rangle$, *a new system under diagnosis, and* Σ', *its syndrome, such that* $\mathcal{U}' = \mathcal{U}\backslash\{v\}$, $\tau' = \tau - 1$, *and* Σ' *consists of all formulas of* Σ *except those which include* v. *Then all previous lemmas and corollaries hold for* $\mathbf{S}'\langle\mathcal{U}',\tau'\rangle$. □□□

2.4 Implementation Issues

As one could expect, previous results and namely A Algorithm, is rather useless. This cannot afford us practical ways to diagnose unreliable units. Ultimately, computing the p-implicants of a given syndrome is rather expensive– indeed the process could be exponential [6]. We must therefore seek efficient ways to build diagnoses. Intuitively, we want to take advantage of the nature of our formulas.

Let us focus on Σ, a given syndrome. Let us denote by Σ^* the conjunctions of all clauses which can be deduced from Σ. Formally, we have: $\Sigma \models_{sld} \Sigma^*$.

Observe that since $\mathcal{U}$ is finite, the set of all formulas which can be deduced from Σ under $\models_{sld}$ is necessarily finite. Moreover, $\models_{sld}$ is sound and valid by definition. Finally, Σ is assumed to be consistent and complete, Σ^* is also consistent and complete. From the operational viewpoint, Σ^* includes all clauses in Σ and possibly new (deduced) clauses which are founded on Lemma 2. In our example, Σ^* coincides with Σ, namely because DAHBURA & MASSON have arranged the syndrome such that the set of clauses remains minimal and the status of units cannot be stated easily.

Let us now focus on the nature of the clauses included in Σ^*. Any clause in Σ^* could be either (1) $(\text{UU}(x) \vee \text{UU}(y))$, or (2) $(\text{UU}(x) \vee \neg\text{UU}(y))$, where $x, y \in \mathcal{U}$. Let us then split Σ^* into two subsets Σ^+ (resp. Σ^-) including all clauses of the first (resp. second) form.

A close examination of our deduction system shows that clauses in Σ^- are from clauses in Σ. On the other hand, clauses in Σ^+ are generated from a combination of clauses in Σ^+ and Σ^-, using the resolution rule. From an informational standpoint, clauses in Σ^- convey little information. A clause such as $(\text{UU}(u) \vee \neg\text{UU}(v))$ states that if u is reliable then v is also reliable. On the other hand, a clause in Σ^+ (e.g., $(\text{UU}(u) \vee \text{UU}(v))$) states that at least u or v is unreliable.

Considering the above remarks, let us focus on Σ^+ and call all clauses in Σ^+ **conflicts**. Intuitively, a conflict clause $(\text{UU}(u) \vee \text{UU}(v))$ tells us that there is conflict between units u and v and one of them is necessarily unreliable. In fact, the computation of a diagnosis for a system under diagnosis $\mathbf{S}\langle\mathcal{U},\tau\rangle$ w.r.t Σ, its syndrome, turns out in resolving all conflicts in Σ^+. From a theoretical standpoint, computing a diagnosis w.r.t Σ^+ instead of Σ^* does not convey the same information. In particular, such a diagnosis does not specify the state of reliable units. Indeed, for any prime implicant Δ of Σ^+, we have $U^-(\Delta) = \{\}$. Hence, a unit which is not stated explicitly to be unreliable is assumed to be reliable. In fact, such an assumption was already made in our initial Definition 1 but not in Definition 2. On the other hand, diagnosis computation w.r.t Σ^+ is computationally attractive.

Consider Σ^+ a given set of conflicts, and let $x \in \mathcal{U}$ be a given unit. Let us then denote by Σ_x^+ the set of conflicts in which x occurs. Similarly, let $\mathcal{U}_x$ be the subset of units occurring in Σ_x^+. Note that $x \in \mathcal{U}_x$.

Finally, let us denote by $\overline{\Sigma_x^+}$ the subset of remaining conflicts which do not include units occurring in $\mathcal{U}_x$. Then we have:

Lemma 9 *Let* $\mathbf{S}\langle\mathcal{U},\tau\rangle$ *be a system under diagnosis and* Σ^+ *the set of its conflicts. Consider* $u \in \mathcal{U}$ *and suppose that* $|\Sigma_u^+| = \rho$; *then* $\text{UU}(u)$ *holds iff:* $|\Delta| > \tau - \rho$, *where* Δ *denotes the p-implicant of* $\overline{\Sigma_u^+}$ *such that* $|U(\Delta)|$ *is minimal w.r.t set cardinality.* □□□

Considering Lemma 9, we can now design another algorithm to build a diagnosis. The C algorithm is shown in Fig. 2.3.

```
C(𝒰, τ, Σ*)
  Begin
  Δ ← ∅
   For x ∈ 𝒰
    Let ρ = |Σx+|
    PIs ← GENERATE(Σx+ (overlined))
    Δ ← SELECT(PIs)
    If |Δ| > τ − ρ
     Then Let UU(x) in Δ
     Else Let ¬UU(x) in Δ
    Fi
   Od
  RETURN(Δ)
  End
```

Fig. 2.3: C– Concrete Algorithm

Back to our example, let us take unit a, we have: $\Sigma_a^+ = \{(\text{UU}(a) \vee \text{UU}(f)), (\text{UU}(a) \vee \text{UU}(g))\}$, $\rho = 2$, $\overline{\Sigma_a^+} = \{(\text{UU}(i) \vee \text{UU}(b)), (\text{UU}(c) \vee \text{UU}(i)), (\text{UU}(d) \vee \text{UU}(i)), (\text{UU}(i) \vee \text{UU}(e)), (\text{UU}(h) \vee \text{UU}(b)), (\text{UU}(c) \vee \text{UU}(h)), (\text{UU}(d) \vee \text{UU}(h)), (\text{UU}(e) \vee \text{UU}(h)),\}$, while $\Delta = (\text{UU}(i) \wedge \text{UU}(h))$ stands for a minimal p-implicant. Since $|\Delta| = 2$, it follows that $\neg\text{UU}(a)$ is in $\boldsymbol{\underline{\Delta}}$. Hence, unit a is then reliable. On the other hand, consider unit f, we obtain: $\Sigma_f^+ = \{(\text{UU}(f) \vee \text{UU}(a)), (\text{UU}(f) \vee \text{UU}(b)), (\text{UU}(f) \vee \text{UU}(c)), (\text{UU}(f) \vee \text{UU}(d))\}$, $\rho = 4$, $\overline{\Sigma_f^+} = \{(\text{UU}(i) \vee \text{UU}(e)), (\text{UU}(e) \vee \text{UU}(h)),\}$, and $\Delta = \text{UU}(e)$. This time, we have $|\Delta| = 1$ and $\text{UU}(f)$ is in $\boldsymbol{\underline{\Delta}}$. Unit f is then unreliable.

Yet, C algorithm is still not efficient because it uses p-implicants. However, let us first observe that computing a p-implicant which is minimal w.r.t set cardinality coincides with computing a minimal vertex cover in a bipartite graph [19, 9]. Most importantly, we are not interested in computing the p-implicant which is minimal w.r.t set cardinality, but rather in knowing its size. Therefore, using Konig's result [19], we know that the size of a maximal matching of a bipartite graph is also the size of a minimal vertexes cover. These remarks yield a diagnosis algorithm, called D, depicted in Fig. 2.4. From an abstract view, D algorithm works in similar way than C algorithm. The main difference is that D algorithm represents formulas in Σ^* as a graph to handle size of maximal matching rather than size of p-implicants. However, the mapping is not straightforward and raises several subtleties. These are explained later, when commenting the stages of the algorithm.

For now, let us turn our attention to the computation of Σ^*. For this end, Proposition 1 together with the definition of an order on units play a central role. As noted in §2.4 (paragraph 3), Σ^* coincides with Σ in our example. However, this is not always the case. Intuitively, the order aims at driving the inference process, particularly when using Lemma 2, and obtaining Σ^* in $O(n^2 \log n)$. Consider two clauses $(\neg\text{UU}(u) \vee \text{UU}(v)), (\text{UU}(u) \vee \text{UU}(w))$, we have to define the following order $u \prec v \prec w$. A such an order, where u precedes the other ubits, starts the inference process with clauses including unit u to generate new clauses (i.e., $(\text{UU}(v) \vee \text{UU}(w))$ which will be added to Σ^*. Details are in [3].

Now, we are ready to comment D algorithm. It requires four parameters: (1) $\mathcal{U}$, the set of units; (2) τ, the maximum number of faulty units; (3) EMM_{Σ^+}, the maximal matching of the corresponding graph; (4) μ, the size of EMM_{Σ^+}. To provide the third parameter, we proceed as follows.

Start by generating Σ^*, then build $BG_{\Sigma^+}\langle V^r, V^g, E\rangle$, a bipartite graph for Σ^+. If x is a unit occurring in Σ^+, then let us color it twice, once red, denoted by x^r, and then green, denoted by x^g. The set of vertices (units) V^r (resp. V^g) includes all red (resp. green) units. Put the red vertices on the left side and the green ones on the right side of BG_{Σ^+}. If $(\text{UU}(u) \vee \text{UU}(v))$ is a conflict in Σ^+ then build two edges (u^r, v^g) and (v^r, u^g) and put them in E. From a computational viewpoint, BG_{Σ^+} doubles both the number of units and the number of conflicts in Σ^+. For convenience, let us introduce the following conventions. If $x \in \mathcal{U}$ is a unit, then x^r (resp. x^g) denotes the red (resp. green) vertex in V^r (resp. V^g). When the color does not matter, we write x^*. Finally, if x^* denotes a colored vertex in V^r or V^g, then x stands for the "original" unit in $\mathcal{U}$.

Finally, compute a maximal matching of $BG_{\Sigma^+}\langle V^r, V^g, E\rangle$ to obtain EMM_{Σ^+}. Using the procedure of [2], this could be done in $O(n'^{1.5}\sqrt{m/\log n'})$, where n' (resp. m) is the size of the set of vertices (resp. edges) in BG_{Σ^+}. We have $n' \leq 2n$, where $n = |\mathcal{U}|$. Assuming[4] that

[4] In fact, if x^* has more than τ edges, then $\text{UU}(x)$ trivially holds.

the number of edges for each vertex does not exceed τ, then $m \leq n'\tau$. Summing up, the complexity of this stage is in $O(n^2\sqrt{\tau}/\sqrt{\log n})$. Set μ to the size of EMM_{Σ^+}.

Let us denote by EMM_{Σ^+} (resp. VMM_{Σ^+}) the subset of edges (resp. vertices) included in a maximal matching of $BG_{\Sigma^+}\langle V^r, V^g, E\rangle$, the corresponding bipartite graph of Σ^+. As mentioned above, the set of edges of BG_{Σ^+}, doubles the number of conflicts in Σ^+. Ultimately, it doubles the size of the maximal matching [3]. Now, we are ready to comment each stage.

```
D(U, τ, EMM_Σ+, μ)
| % Stage 1.0:  Initialization
|   U⁻ = {}
|   U⁺ = {}
| % Stage 2.0:  Diagnosis
|   For x ∈ U
|   |  Stage 2.1:  Initialization
|   |  A ← ADJ{x^r}
|   |  ρ ← |A|
|   |  ν ← 0
|   |  Stage 2.2:  Updating EMM_Σ+ w.r.t x^r
|   |  If (x^r, y^g) ∈ EMM_Σ+
|   |  |  Then
|   |  |  |  ν ← ν + 1
|   |  |  |  A ← A\y^g
|   |  |  L
|   |  L
|   |  Stage 2.3:  Updating EMM_Σ+ w.r.t ADJ{x^r}
|   |  For y ∈ A
|   |  |  If (z^r, y^g) ∈ EMM_Σ+
|   |  |  |  Then
|   |  |  |  |  If ∃y'^g ∈ ADJ{z^r} ∧ (z^r, y'^g) ∉ EMM_Σ+
|   |  |  |  |  |  Then ν ← 2τ
|   |  |  |  |  |  Else  ν ← ν + 1
|   |  |  |  |  L
|   |  |  |  L
|   |  |  L
|   |  L
|   |  % Stage 2.4:  Decision w.r.t Lemma 9
|   |  If μ − ν > 2τ − ρ
|   |  |  Then U⁺ ← U⁺ ∪ {x}
|   |  |  Else  U⁻ ← U⁻ ∪ {x}
|   |  L
|   L
| % Stage 3.0:  Termination
|   Δ_D = (⋀_{x∈U⁺} UU(x) ∧ ⋀_{x∈U⁻} ¬UU(x))
END.
```

Fig. 2.4: D Algorithm.

Stage 1.0 simply initializes two sets U^+ and U^-, the sets of unreliable and reliable units respectively. Similarly, **Stage 3.0** collects units in U^+ and U^- to build the final diagnosis Δ.

Stage 2.0 uses Lemma 9 to determine the status of each unit $x \in U$. Stage 2.1 is merely initialization, where A denotes the set of vertices adjacent to x^r, ρ denotes the size of A, and ν, set to 0, will serve as a counter. The primitive $\text{ADJ}\{x^*\}$ returns the subset of units which are adjacent to x^* in BG_{Σ^+}. A conventional preprocessing with an appropriate data structure ensures that $\text{ADJ}\{x^*\}$ can be done in $O(1)$.

Stage 2.2 and Stage 2.3 aims at computing the size of a minimal p-implicant of $\overline{\Sigma}^+_x$. Referring to BG_{Σ^+}, this amounts to computing the size of a maximal matching of BG_{Σ^+}, when removing vertex x^r as well as all vertices adjacent to x^r. Instead of computing a new maximal matching, Stage 2.2 and Stage 2.3 actually update the size of EMM_{Σ^+}.

Assume that $\text{ADJ}\{x^r\} = \{y_1^g, \cdots, y_k^g\}$. If there is an edge $(x^r, y_j^g) \in EMM_{\Sigma^+}$, then the size of EMM_{Σ^+} must be decremented by one. That is the task of Stage 2.2, where ν counts the number of edges deleted from EMM_{Σ^+}. Again, a simple data structure ensures that such a test can be done in $O(1)$.

Consider $A = \text{ADJ}\{x^r\}\backslash y_j^g$. Stage 2.3 must proceed as follows. Whenever EMM_{Σ^+} includes (z^r, y_i^g) such that $y_i^g \in A$, then the initial size of EMM_{Σ^+} has to be decremented by one, except in the following particular case: there is an edge $(z^r, y'^g) \in E$ such that $y'^g \notin VMM_{\Sigma^+}$.

Fortunately, such a particular case occurs only when x^r, the unit being considered, is unreliable. Indeed, suppose that x^r is reliable (i.e., $\neg\text{UU}(x)$ holds); then by definition $\forall y \in A, \text{UU}(y)$. Since $(z^r, y_i^g) \in EMM_{\Sigma^+}$, it follows that $\neg\text{UU}(z^r)$. Hence, we have $\forall y' \in \text{ADJ}\{z'^r\}, \text{UU}(y')$. Moreover, we have $\forall y' \in \text{ADJ}\{z'^r\}$, $\exists (z'^r, y') \in EMM_{\Sigma^+}$. Summing up, the particular case occurs only when x is an unreliable unit. Formally, we have the following property.

Property 4 *Let x be a unit in $\mathcal{U}$ and suppose that $\text{ADJ}\{x^r\} = \{y_1^g, \cdots, y_k^g\}$ the subset of units adjacent to x^r in BG_{Σ^+}. If EMM_{Σ^+} is a maximal matching of BG_{Σ^+}, then we have: $\forall z \in \mathcal{U}, \forall y^g \in \text{ADJ}\{x^r\}, z^r \neq x^r \wedge (z^r, y^g) \in EMM_{\Sigma^+} \wedge$
$\exists y'^g \in \text{ADJ}\{z^r\} \wedge (z^r, y'^g) \notin EMM_{\Sigma^+} \Rightarrow \text{UU}(x)$.* □□□

As in Stage 2.2, variable ν in Stage 2.3 counts the number of edges deleted from EMM_{Σ^+}. Note that ν is set to a high value (e.g., 2τ) when the particular case described above is encountered. Testing for such a case could be done in $O(1)$, provided a simple preprocessing which indicates for each unit x^r whether $\text{ADJ}\{x^r\} \subseteq VMM_{\Sigma^+}$.

Stage 2.4 uses Lemma 9 to determine the status of each unit. Finally, note that Stage 2.0 is in $O(n)$, while preprocessing (e.g., building $\text{ADJ}\{x\}$ could be done in $O(n^2)$). Summing up, we obtain the following lemmas.

Lemma 10 (Correctness) *Let $\mathbf{S}\langle\mathcal{U}, \tau\rangle$ be a system under diagnosis and Σ its syndrome. If $\boldsymbol{\Delta}$ denotes* *the actual diagnosis of* $\mathbf{S}\langle\mathcal{U},\tau\rangle$ *w.r.t* Σ *and* Δ_D *is the diagnosis generated by algorithm* D*, then* $\underline{\mathbf{\Delta}} = \Delta_D$. □□□

Lemma 11 (Complexity) *The complexity of the* D *algorithm is in* $O(n^2\sqrt{\tau}/\sqrt{log\ n})$*, which corresponds to the complexity computing a maximal matching for a bipartite graph.* □□□

Note that the D algorithm is basic in the sense that it does not test certain particular cases, where it could be stated straightforwardly that a unit is reliable or unreliable. However, these particular cases, discussed in [3], do not change the overall complexity, which depends on the complexity of computing a maximal matching for a bipartite graph.

3 Epilogue

3.1 Related Work

Using the proposed framework, it is straightforward to capture the essence[5] of both KAMEDA ET AL [17] and SULLIVAN [24] algorithms– see [3] for details. This paper is in fact rooted in DAHBURA & MASSON's proposal [13]. Therefore, several similarities could be drawn between the two proposals. Our proposal differs from the work of DAHBURA & MASSON on at least three levels. On the conceptual level, it seems that the ultimate goals of the work are different. The goal of DAHBURA & MASSON is specifically to obtain an efficient and elegant diagnosis algorithm. On the other hand, our primary aim is to investigate the diagnosis computation process. Consequently, the proposed D algorithm appears as an incidental result. Unlike DAHBURA & MASSON's work, ours requires no diagnosability criteria thanks to our use of p-implicants. On the decision level, the status of each unit is determined according to different criteria. In particular, the D algorithm is based on Lemma 9 and uses the Konig's Theorem [19], while the DAHBURA & MASSON algorithm uses Hall's Theorem [16] and is based on an elegant labeling procedure. Finally, on the level of implementation, both algorithms take advantage of maximal matching. The DAHBURA & MASSON algorithm requires the computation of a maximal matching in a general graph, whereas the D algorithm uses a bipartite graph. Hopefully, computation of a maximal matching is much easier for a bipartite graph. Its theoretical complexity, which is now in $O(n^2\sqrt{\tau}/\sqrt{log\ n})$, may be reduced still further. Obviously, there is no simple way to adapt the DAHBURA & MASSON algorithm in [13] to handle bipartite graphs without altering the essence of the algorithm.[6]

Yet, we do not believe that the D algorithm is in practice more efficient than that of DAHBURA & MASSON. The new bound, which is in $O(n^2\sqrt{\tau}/\sqrt{log\ n})$ compared to $O(n^{2.5})$, is rather theoretical. As a matter of fact, experimentation shows that backtracking algorithms (e.g., the SULLIVAN algorithm which is in $O(\tau^3 + |E|)$) are the most efficient [12]. In fact, the ultimate goal of this paper is not take part in a competition, but rather to shed some light on the process of diagnosis.

3.2 Concluding Remarks

The ultimate objective of this paper is to present an investigation[7] of diagnosis computation process in τ-diagnosable systems. Such an investigation yields a simple diagnosis algorithm whose (theoretical) complexity is attractive– $O(n^2\sqrt{\tau}/\sqrt{log\ n})$ compared to $O(n^{2.5})$ the best known complexity. This work could be extended in several directions. The first direction consists in studying non-PMC models [7, 22], intermittent faults [25, 8]. In the same vein, distributed diagnosis is another area, where investigation is worthwhile. The preliminary results [4, 5] are quite encouraging but much work remains to be done.

There are several challenges which remains to be tackled. It is unclear whether simple criteria can be found to determine straightforwardly the status of a unit. That is, given a unit x, is it possible to say whether x is reliable or not simply by exploring a *constant* number of other units? In [18], a thorough investigation is provided and a deep case-by-case analysis remains to be done.

Acknowledgments

I appreciated the encouragements of Dr. Tony Dahbura, the co-author of [13]. His elegant algorithm (with Prof. G. Masson) has triggered this work aiming at the analysis of the essence of an efficient computation of diagnoses by using the concept of maximal matching. I would also like to thank my colleague Prof. D. Ziou, who spent a (very) long time, while I am presenting multiple versions of this work.

[5]Actually, we showed that it is possible to provide a counter-example for KAMEDA ET AL [17] algorithm in [3].

[6]A recent correpondence with Dr. A. Dahbura has drawn our attention to [11] which is built on a bipartite graph. A deep analysis of [11] is ongoing. We believe however that this work goes beyond using bipartite graphs. It rather proposes a new approach shedding deep insights on the diagnosis process itself.

[7]See research report [3] for a thorough investigation.

References

[1] F. J. Allan, T. Kameda, and S. Toida. An Approach to the Diagnosability Analysis of a System. *IEEE, Transactions on Computers*, 25:1040–1042, October 1975.

[2] H. Alt, N. Blum, K. Mehlhorn, and M. Paul. Computing a Maximum Cardinality Matching in a Bipartite Graph in Time $O(n^{1.5}\sqrt{m/log\, n})$. *Information Processing Letters*, (37):237–240, February 1991.

[3] B. Ayeb. Fault Identification in System-Level Diagnosis: An $O(n^2\sqrt{\tau}/\sqrt{logn})$ Algorithm. Research Report, 20 pages # DMI-218, Université de Sherbrooke, 1998.

[4] B. Ayeb. Reliability: Circumventing vs Identifying Faults (Bridging the Gap). In *Proceedings of 2nd IMACS International Conference on Computational Engineering in Systems Applications*, pages (3)129–133, Hammamet (TN), April 1–4 1998.

[5] B. Ayeb and A. Farhat. The Byzantine Problem: Masking and Demasking Faults. *Research Report # 219, Submitted*, 1998.

[6] B. Ayeb, P. Marquis, and M. Rusinowitch. Preferring Diagnoses By Abduction. *IEEE Transactions on Systems, Man and Cybernetics*, 23:792–808, May 1993.

[7] F. Barsi, F. Grandoni, and P. Maestrini. A Theory of Diagnosability of Digital Systems. *IEEE, Transactions on Computers*, C-25(6):585–593, 1976.

[8] D. M. Blough, G. F. Sullvian, and G. M. Masson. Intermittent Fault Diagnosis in Multiprocessor Systems. *IEEE, Transactions on Computers*, 41(11):1430–1441, November 1992.

[9] J. A. Bondy and U. S. R. Murthy. *Graph Theory and Applications.* Elsevier North-Holland, New York, 1976.

[10] D. Coppersmith and S. Winograd. Matrix Multiplication via Arithmetic Progressions. *IEEE, Transactions on Computers*, 9(3):251–280, 1990.

[11] A. Dahbura and G. Masson. A Practical Variation of the $O(n^{2.5})$ Fault Diagnosis Algorithm. In *Proceedings of FTCS*, pages 428–433, 1984.

[12] A. T. Dahbura, J. J. Laferrera, and L. L. King. A Performance Study of System-Level Fault Diagnosis Algorithms. In *Proceedings of 4th. Phoenix Conf. on Computers and Communication*, pages 469–473, Scott Sdak, AR (USA), 1985.

[13] A. T. Dahbura and G. M. Masson. An $O(n^{2.5})$ Fault Identification Algorithm for Diagnosable Systems. *IEEE, Transactions on Computers*, 33:486–492, June 1984.

[14] A. Goralcikova and V. Koubek. A Reduct and Closure Algorithms for Graphs. In Springer Heidelberg, editor, *Proceedings Conf. on Mathematical Foundations of Computer Science, LNCS 74*, pages 301–107, 1979.

[15] S. L. Hakimi and A. T. Amin. Characterization of Connection Assignement of Diagnosable Systems. *IEEE, Transactions on Computers*, pages 86–88, January 1974.

[16] P. Hall. On Representatives of Subsets. *J. London Math. Soc.*, 10:26–30, 1935.

[17] T. Kameda, S. Toida, and F. J. Allan. A Diagnosing Algorithm for Networks. *Information and Control*, 29:141–148, 1975.

[18] M. A. Kennedy and G. G. L Meyer. The PMC System Level Fault Model: Cardinality Properties of the Implied Faulty Sets. *IEEE, Transactions on Computers*, 38(3):478–480, March 1989.

[19] D. Konig. Graphes and Matrices (Hungarian). *Mat. Fiz. Lapok*, 38:116–119, 1931.

[20] K. Mehlhorn. *Data Structures and Efficient Algorithms.* Springer Verlag, New York, 1984.

[21] F. P. Preparata, G. Metze, and R. T. Chien. On the Connection Assignement Problem of Diagnosable Systems. *IEEE, Transactions on Electronic Computers*, EC-16(6):848–854, December 1967.

[22] A. Sengupta and A. T. Dahbura. On Self-Diagnosable Multiprocessor Systems: Diagnosis by the Comparison Approach. *IEEE, Transactions on Computers*, 41(11):1386–1396, November 1992.

[23] A. K. Somani, V. K. Agarwal, and D. Avis. A Generalized Theory for System Level Diagnosis. *IEEE, Transactions on Computers*, C-36(5):538–546, May 1987.

[24] G. F. Sullivan. An $O(t^3 + |E|)$ Fault Identification Algorithm for Diagnosable Systems. *IEEE, Transactions on Computers*, 37(4):388–397, April 1988.

[25] C. L. Yang and G. M. Masson. A Fault Identification Algorithm for t_i-Diagnosable Systems. *IEEE, Transactions on Computers*, C-35(6):503–510, June 1986.

Session 6B

Fast Abstracts I

Session 7A

CORBA and Group Communication

Chair: Richard Buskens
Bell Laboratories, USA

A Fault Tolerance Framework for CORBA

L. E. Moser, P. M. Melliar-Smith and P. Narasimhan *
Department of Electrical and Computer Engineering
University of California, Santa Barbara 93106
moser@ece.ucsb.edu, pmms@ece.ucsb.edu, priya@alpha.ece.ucsb.edu

Abstract

We describe a Fault Tolerance Framework for CORBA that provides fault tolerance management and core services, implemented above the ORB for ease of use and customization, and fault tolerance mechanisms, implemented beneath the ORB for transparency and efficiency. Strong replica consistency is facilitated by a multicast engine that provides reliable totally ordered delivery of multicast messages to the replicas of an object. Transparency to the application allows application programmers to focus on their applications rather than on fault tolerance, and transparency to the ORB allows existing commercial CORBA ORBs to be used without modification. The Fault Tolerance Framework adheres to CORBA's objective of interoperability by ensuring that different implementations of the specifications of the framework can interoperate and that non-fault-tolerant objects can interwork with fault-tolerant objects.

1 Introduction

The Object Management Group (OMG) has developed the Common Object Request Broker Architecture (CORBA) [11] as a standard for distributed object computing. The CORBA standard is based on a client/server, object-oriented style of computing. The application programmer defines an interface for each application class in the OMG's Interface Definition Language (IDL), a declarative language that is independent of the particular programming language in which the classes are implemented. The Object Request Broker (ORB) of CORBA locates the server object on behalf of a client object and packages the client's method invocations, and the server's responses, into messages, defined by the General Internet Inter-ORB Protocol (GIOP) and by the Internet Inter-ORB Protocol (IIOP), the mapping of GIOP onto TCP/IP.

*This research has been supported by the Defense Advanced Research Projects Agency in conjunction with the Office of Naval Research and the Air Force Research Laboratory, Rome, under Contracts N00174-95-K-0083 and F3602-97-1-0248, respectively.

Although CORBA provides portability, location transparency, and interoperability of applications across heterogeneous platforms (architectures, operating systems, and languages), it lacks support for fault tolerance. Recently, the OMG has recognized the need for fault tolerance through its Request for Proposals (RFP) [12] for a fault tolerance standard for CORBA. In this paper, we describe the key components of the Fault Tolerance Framework [8] that we have proposed to the OMG in response to that RFP.

Fault tolerance for CORBA could be provided entirely through CORBA service objects, located above the ORB, with application-level interfaces written in IDL. While it is necessary to expose some interfaces of the framework, particularly those for management, to the application for ease of use and customization, it is less desirable to expose the more difficult aspects of fault tolerance, such as replica consistency and fault recovery, through application-level interfaces. Moreover, implementation of fault tolerance above a CORBA ORB is not necessarily the most efficient approach due to the overhead of the ORB in the communication paths.

On the other hand, fault tolerance for CORBA could be provided through mechanisms within or underneath a CORBA ORB, but that makes it difficult for the application to interface to, and manage, the operation of the framework. Moreover, such an approach exploits complex ORB or operating system facilities that are difficult for the application programmer to understand and customize. However, a framework implemented within or underneath the ORB has the advantage of transparency due to its minimal visibility at the application level. Additionally, a framework based on this approach avoids the ORB overheads and therefore should be more efficient.

The Fault Tolerance Framework that we have developed achieves the benefits of both approaches in a novel manner, through the combination of mechanisms implemented underneath the ORB for transparency and efficiency, and services implemented above the ORB for application-level control and ease of use.

0-7695-0213-X/99 $10.00 © 1999 IEEE

2 Architectural Overview

Figure 1 shows the Fault Tolerance Framework, which provides interfaces for the following services and mechanisms:

- **Fault Tolerance Management Services** that allow application designers to describe the static fault tolerance properties of their applications. The replication and fault tolerance of the application objects are automatic and transparent to such users, who run their unmodified applications on the unmodified commercial ORBs of their choice.
- **Fault Tolerance Core Services** that allow the application program to exercise dynamic control over replication and recovery from faults, for example, by requiring an application object to be replicated on specific processors. These services operate at the level of application objects, without exposing how object replication and recovery are implemented.
- **Fault Tolerance Mechanisms** that allow the application program or the Fault Tolerance Core Services to exercise precise control over the creation and location of individual object replicas, and direct control over recovery. The interfaces to the mechanisms are critical for interoperability within a fault-tolerant system.

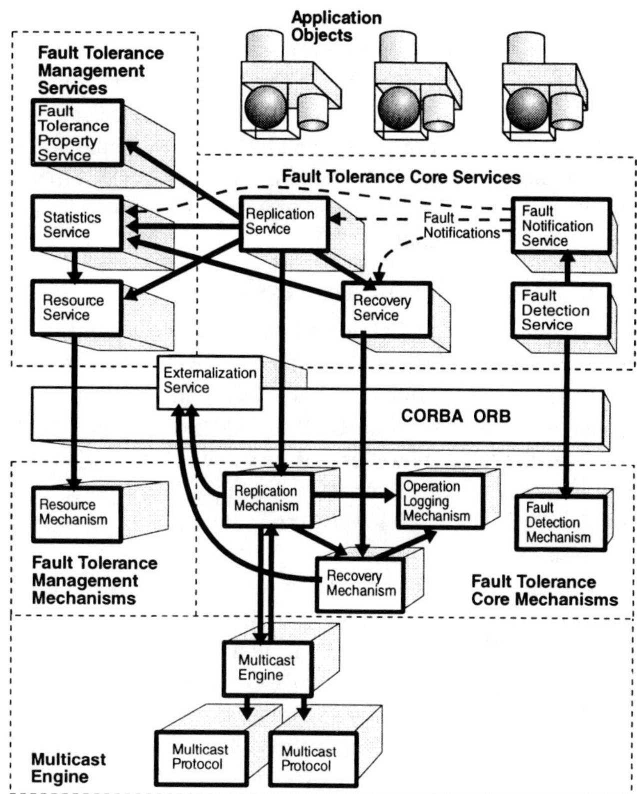

Figure 1: The structure of the Fault Tolerance Framework.

The Fault Tolerance Management and Core Services are implemented as CORBA objects above the ORB. The Fault Tolerance Mechanisms are implemented as pseudoobjects (native code) beneath or within the ORB. Several components of the Fault Tolerance Framework have both service and mechanism counterparts, *e.g.*, the Replication Service and the Replication Mechanism. The intent is not duplication of effort or code but, rather, the separation of a component into service-level and mechanism-level modules that together provide the required functionality. The service-level module provides a user-accessible and customizable interface, while the mechanism-level module provides an efficient implementation of the infrastructure required by the service-level counterpart.

The Fault Tolerance Framework employs a Multicast Engine that provides reliable totally ordered delivery of multicast messages in a model of virtual synchrony to maintain strong replica consistency. Space constraints preclude a description of the Multicast Engine.

2.1 Replication Domains

A *replication domain* is a set of replicated objects under the control of a single implementation of the Fault Tolerance Core Services. Multiple implementations of the Fault Tolerance Core Services can coexist, and can even share the same processors and use the same Fault Tolerance Core Mechanisms. For example, in a wide-area application, there can be Fault Tolerance Core Services at each physical site that handle objects replicated within the local area, and Fault Tolerance Core Services that handle objects replicated across several sites within the wide area. Each replication domain has a unique replication domain identifier, provided by the application designer, who records this in the Fault Tolerance Property Service.

2.2 Object Replication

The Fault Tolerance Framework supports the individual object as the basic unit of replication. The *replicas of an object*, also referred to as *object replicas* or more simply *replicas*, implement the same IDL interface and have the same implementation source code. The behavior of each object must be deterministic.

An *object group*, also referred to as a *replicated object*, is the set of replicas of an object. It has no physical manifestation and is not located on any specific processor (because that processor might fail). The application does not access the object replicas directly (because a replica might fail). The replicated object continues to exist, even though processors or individual object replicas fail. Each object group has an object group identifier, which is unique within a replication domain.

Cold, warm and hot passive replication, and active replication with and without majority voting, are supported. The appropriate choice of replication policy is made for each object individually, concentrating fault tolerance where it is needed, without incurring unnecessary costs where less stringent fault tolerance or slower recovery is acceptable. Resistance to arbitrary faults requires active replication with majority voting and a more robust multicast protocol [10]; we focus our discussion here on protection against crash (fail-silent) faults.

2.3 Object Group Addressing

The Fault Tolerance Framework, uses two different kinds of Interoperable Object References (IORs), object IORs and object group IORs. An object IOR is an ordinary IOR, generated and used by an ORB, to address an object that it hosts; the ORB, however, has no knowledge of whether the object is a replica. An object group IOR is generated by the Replication Service and is used by the application to address a replicated object.

An object group IOR is like an ordinary IOR except that it contains the replication domain identifier and the object group identifier, rather than the identifier of a physical processor and a port number. Some ORBs send messages to verify that the host actually exists and that the object exists on that processor. The Replication Mechanism intercepts such messages and performs the required checks against the mappings established by the Replication Service.

An object group IOR appears to the ORB to be a reference to an object on some other processor, even if one of the replicas of the object group is actually on the same processor. This triggers the ORB to communicate with the object by using IIOP, which can be intercepted, rather than by using local invocations.

2.4 Strong Replica Consistency

The Fault Tolerance Framework employs several mechanisms to maintain strong replica consistency. In particular, it employs a Multicast Engine that provides reliable totally ordered delivery of multicast messages. The invocations of methods on the replicas, and the corresponding responses, are contained in multicast messages. Because the messages are delivered in the same total order at each object replica, the methods are executed by each replica in the same order. This consistent ordering of messages is the basic mechanism for ensuring that the states of the replicas remain consistent.

In addition, to maintain strong replica consistency, the Fault Tolerance Framework detects and suppresses duplicate invocations (responses) that are generated by two or more replicas of an object. It also provides transfer of state between replicas, ensuring that all of the replicas agree on which method executions precede the state transfer and which follow it. Moreover, it guarantees consistent scheduling of concurrent threads of execution by enforcing a single thread of control inside each object and disallowing direct access by one object to the data of another object.

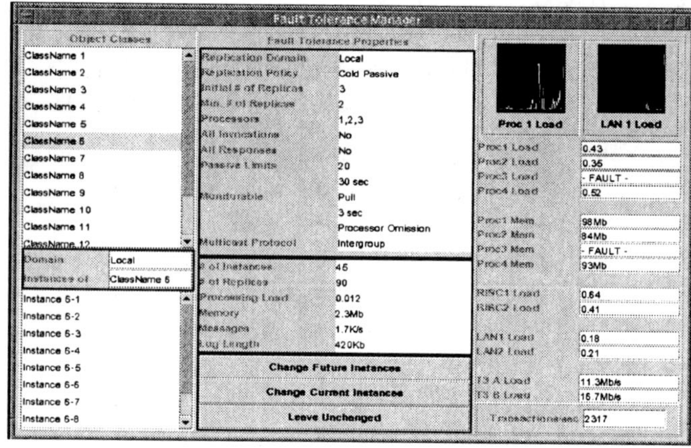

Figure 2: A prototype GUI for the Fault Tolerance Property Service. Selection of application classes and instances are shown in the left panel, editing of fault tolerance properties in the center panel, and display of faults and utilization of resources in the right panel.

2.5 Replication of Fault Tolerance Services

The Fault Tolerance Services are implemented as standard CORBA objects that are actively replicated and thus protected against faults. It may not be obvious that such a service object can control its own replication and protect itself against faults. The technique is, however, well-understood and was first used in the SIFT aircraft flight control computer [16].

If one or more, but not all, of the replicas fail, the Fault Tolerance Services can invoke the methods that recover, or create, replicas of their own objects. As long as at least one replica is operational, the Fault Tolerance Services can operate normally, protecting themselves and the system against faults.

3 Management Services/Mechanisms

3.1 Fault Tolerance Property Service

System management for the Fault Tolerance Framework is the selection, or creation, of policies that alter the behavior of the system, primarily fault tolerance behavior. Most of the properties are set at design/deployment time, and some of them can be modified later.

A graphical user interface (GUI) for the Fault Tolerance Property Service, shown in Figure 2, allows the application designer or system administrator to define static fault tolerance properties for an application class within a replication domain.

3.2 Resource Service and Mechanism

The Resource Service exploits the Resource Mechanism located on each processor to determine the available resources, *e.g.*, processing and memory resources. The Resource Service provides a list of the available resources to the Replication Service, when the Replication Service

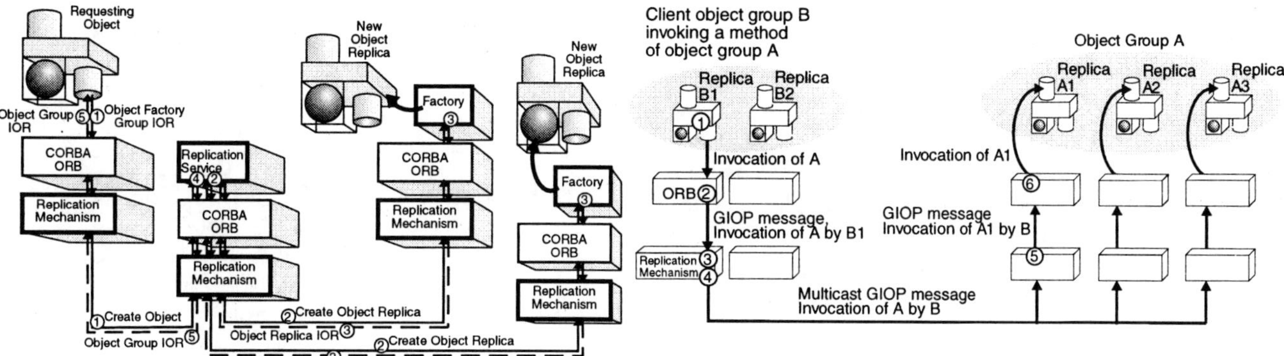

When the application invokes a factory to create a new object:

1. The Replication Mechanism intercepts the invocation and routes it to the Replication Service.
2. The Replication Service decides where to create the object replicas and then invokes the factories on those processors to create the object replicas.
3. The factories return object replica IORs for the replicas to the Replication Service.
4. The Replication Service creates a unique object group IOR and establishes a mapping between the object group and the object replicas. It communicates this mapping to the Replication Mechanism.
5. The Replication Service returns the object group IOR to the application that requested the creation of the object.

Figure 3: The creation of a new (replicated) object.

When an object group B invokes a method of object group A:

1. An object replica $B1$ uses the IOR of object group A to dispatch the invocation.
2. The ORB notes that the IOR of the invoked object group A appears to refer to an object on some other processor and constructs a GIOP message, whose destination is object group A and whose source is the individual replica $B1$.
3. The Replication Mechanism, using the mapping tables provided to it by the Replication Service, replaces the invoking replica $B1$ in the source field by object group B.
4. The Replication Mechanism then encapsulates the GIOP message in a multicast message and multicasts it to the processors hosting the replicas of object group A.
5. At each of those processors, the Replication Mechanism replaces the invoked object group A in the destination field of the message by the individual replica $A1$, $A2$ or $A3$ on that processor, and passes the GIOP message to the ORB.
6. The ORB invokes the individual replica $A1$, $A2$ or $A3$ on its respective processor.

Figure 4: The invocation of an object group.

invokes it. The Resource Mechanism exploits native operating system mechanisms to determine current resource utilizations.

The Resource Service allows the application designer to define a *fault containment region* as a property of a resource. Two resources having the same fault containment region may experience correlated faults, for example, processors in a shared memory multiprocessor. The Replication Service will not assign replicas of the same object to resources within the same fault containment region.

3.3 Statistics Service

A minimal Statistics Service receives event notifications from the other components of the Fault Tolerance Framework and records statistics relevant to fault tolerance, including creation of objects and replicas, occurrence of faults, time to recover from faults and availability and utilization of resources. The application designers may extend or replace this minimal service with custom software, so that it collects information of direct interest to them.

4 Core Services/Mechanisms

4.1 Replication Service/Mechanism

The Replication Service operates in conjunction with the Replication Mechanism to create and delete object replicas within a single replication domain. The Replication Service obtains its instructions from the application designer via the Fault Tolerance Property Service regarding which application objects to replicate and how to replicate them. It obtains information about the available resources (*e.g.*, processing and memory resources) and their current utilization from the Resource Service. The Replication Service subscribes to the Fault Notification Service to be notified of faults.

The Replication Service interface, provided to the application, allows the creation (deletion) of object groups, and also the creation (deletion) of individual object replicas on specific processors. This interface returns object group IORs, rather than object IORs for the individual replicas. The Replication Mechanism interface, accessible only to the Replication Service, allows access to the object IORs of the replicas. Figure 3 shows the role of the Replication Service and Mechanism when the application creates an object.

To create an object replica, the Replication Service uses the Recovery Service to make the replica *operational*, which entails making the replica's state consistent with that of the other replicas. For a passively replicated object, the Replication Service informs the Recovery Service of the replica that is chosen as the primary replica, and the order in which the other replicas should be used for the selection of subsequent primary replicas in the event of faults.

Figure 4 shows the role of the Replication Service and Mechanism when an object group is invoked. To ensure that the states of the replicas do not become inconsistent because the same invocation is executed multiple times, the Replication Mechanism detects and suppresses duplicate invocations (responses), as shown in Figure 5. Those duplicates that are not detected and suppressed at the source are detected and suppressed at the destinations.

The Replication Service, through the fault reports it receives from the Fault Notification Service, can remove a faulty replica from an object group, or can create a new replica, to maintain the desired fault tolerance requirements. Removal of a replica from an object group by the Replication Service causes the Replication Mechanism to terminate that replica. Immediate removal of a faulty replica is not essential. If the faulty replica continues to generate invocations (responses), the Replication Mechanism will detect and suppress duplicate invocations (responses).

4.2 Recovery Service/Mechanism

The Recovery Service, in conjunction with the Recovery Mechanism, provides fault recovery for passive replication, and activates new objects for both passive and active replication. The Recovery Service subscribes to the Fault Notification Service. If the Recovery Service receives a report that a nonprimary replica has failed during an operation, then no recovery action needs to be taken, because the primary replica continues to perform the operation.

For a cold passively replicated object, when the primary replica fails, the new primary replica does not yet exist. Thus, the Recovery Service must first invoke the Replication Service to create the new primary replica on the appropriate processor. Following this, the Recovery Service instructs the Recovery Mechanism to obtain, from the Operation Logging Mechanism, the most recent state transfer message and the set of invocation and response messages that follow that state transfer message. The Recovery Mechanism then applies the state transfer message to the new primary replica, followed by the set of invocation and response messages, as above. The steps are shown in Figure 6.

For a warm passively replicated object, the state transfer message has already been applied by the backup replica. Thus, the Recovery Manager needs to retrieve only the recent invocation and response messages from the log and apply them to the new primary replica.

Multiple invocations on other objects, and even responses, can be generated by the original and the new primary replicas. The Replication Mechanism detects and suppresses such duplicates.

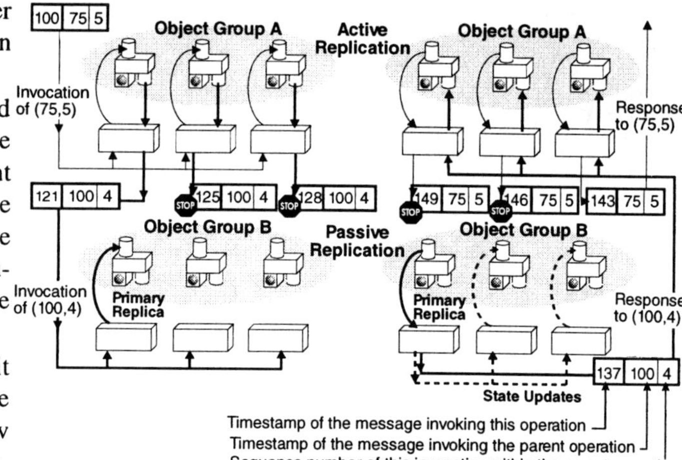

Object group A contains three active replicas and object group B contains three passive replicas.

- Some client object (not shown in the figure) invokes a method with invocation identifier $(100,(75,5))$ on object group A. Each of the replicas in A executes the method, which results in the invocation of other methods, including the one with invocation identifier $(121,(100,4))$ on object group B.
- The timestamp of the "parent" invocation that resulted in the subsequent invocations is 100. If the method invocation on object group B is the fourth in the sequence of invocations triggered by the execution of the parent invocation then, at each replica in A, the operation identifier for the invocation of B is $(100,4)$.
- The Replication Mechanism for one of the replicas in object group A multicasts a message containing the invocation identifier $(121,(100,4))$. When the Replication Mechanism at another replica in object group A receives this message, it suppresses its own replica's invocation also with operation identifier $(100,4)$.
- The primary replica in object group B then executes the method, after which the Replication Mechanism transfers the state of the primary replica to the nonprimary replicas in object group B and multicasts the response to object group A using the response identifier $(137,(100,4))$. Note that the invocation identifier $(121,(100,4))$ and the corresponding response identifier $(137,(100,4))$ refer to the same operation and thus have the same operation identifier $(100,4)$.
- At the end of the operation, the Replication Mechanism at one of the replicas in object group A multicasts the response using the response identifier $(143,(75,5))$. When the Replication Mechanism at another replica in object group A receives this message, it suppresses its own replica's response for $(75,5)$.

Figure 5: Detection and suppression of duplicate invocations (responses).

4.3 Fault Detection Service/Mechanism

The Fault Detection Service monitors objects (typically replicas of an object), verifying that they continue to operate, and generates fault reports, using the Fault Detection Mechanism. The Fault Detection Service depends on user-defined timeouts to generate suspicions that objects are faulty, though other mechanisms may be used. An object that is slow in producing a response, or that has a faulty communication link, may be suspected by the fault detector, even though the object itself has not actually failed.

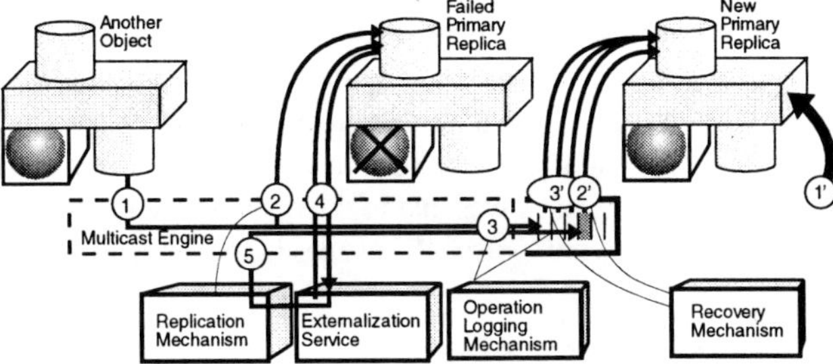

If a cold passively replicated object is invoked and the primary replica does not fail:

1. The Replication Mechanism dispatches the GIOP message containing the invocation of the passively replicated object using the Multicast Engine, which encapsulates the GIOP message in a multicast message and multicasts it.
2. The Recovery Mechanism applies the received message to the primary replica.
3. The Operation Logging Mechanism logs, but does not apply, the message at the other (nonprimary) replicas.
4. The Externalization Service allows the Replication Mechanism to obtain the state of the primary replica.
5. The Replication Mechanism dispatches the GIOP message containing the state of the primary replica to the other (nonprimary) replicas using the Multicast Engine.

If the primary replica fails:

1.′ The Replication Mechanism loads the new primary replica into its processor if it is not already loaded.

2.′ The Recovery Mechanism determines a new primary replica, extracts the most recent state transfer message from the log and then applies it to the new primary replica.

3.′ The Recovery Mechanism extracts subsequent invocation messages from the log and applies them to the new primary replica.

Figure 6: The role of the various services and mechanisms in cold passive replication.

The Fault Detection Service supports both pull monitoring and push monitoring. In the push monitoring model, an object reports periodically to the Fault Detection Service to confirm that it is alive. In the pull monitoring model, the Fault Detection Service periodically invokes a method on an object, which must respond confirming that it is still alive. Objects that fail to report or fail to respond are reported as faulty by the Fault Detection Service.

The Fault Detection Service detects only object faults; other components in the system detect other types of faults. For example, the Multicast Engine detects processor faults and network faults, the Resource Service detects resource overload faults, and the Replication Service detects inadequate replication faults. Some types of faults might be detected by the application objects themselves.

4.4 Fault Notification Service

The Fault Notification Service receives fault reports from the fault detectors and, in turn, generates fault notifications to other objects. Both application objects that need fault notifications, and service objects including the Replication, Recovery and Statistics Services, subscribe to the Fault Notification Service.

The Fault Notification Service might generate multiple fault notifications for a fault report that it receives. For example, a fault report for a processor results in a fault notification for each of the object replicas hosted by that processor. Similarly, a fault report for an object group triggers fault notifications for each of its object replicas. If a fault is reported for the last replica of an object group, a notification is generated for the object group as a whole. An application needs to register selectively for fault notifications to avoid receiving a large number of simultaneous correlated notifications.

4.5 Operation Logging Mechanism

The Operation Logging Mechanism maintains, for each object replica, a log of messages, which contains a record of invocations and responses, as well as state transfer messages, for that object. To achieve reasonable efficiency (in terms of storage and time for logging), the Operation Logging Mechanism is implemented as pseudoobjects beneath the ORB, which are present on each processor. Conceptually, a separate log is maintained for each object replica; physically, the implementation may share storage and retrieval facilities across many logs.

State transfer is performed by the *getstate* and *setstate* methods, which must be coded by the application programmer as part of the application object. Alternatively, if the ORB provides an Externalization, Objects by Value or Persistent State Service, those can be exploited to perform state transfer.

5 Prototype Implementation

We have implemented the Fault Tolerance Mechanisms of the Fault Tolerance Framework in our prototype Eternal system [7, 9], using unmodified commercial ORBs, including Inprise's VisiBroker, Iona's Orbix, Xerox PARC's ILU, Object-Oriented Concept's ORBacus and Washington University's real-time TAO ORB. The implementation is designed for Solaris 2.6 but can also operate on Linux. A port to WindowsNT is in progress. The Fault Tolerance Management and Core Services have been specified and their implementation is underway. The underlying mechanisms are the difficult part of the Fault Tolerance Framework to implement; the services are essential for the practical deployment of the Framework but their implementation is relatively straightforward.

The current implementation exploits library interpositioning, which is less dependent on operating system specific mechanisms and has lower overheads than our initial implementation, which was based on intercepting the */proc* interface of the Solaris operating system. Either approach (library interpositioning or using */proc*) allows the mechanisms of the Fault Tolerance Framework to be used with diverse commercial ORBs, with no modification of either the ORB or the application. The only stipulation is that the vendor's implementation of CORBA must support IIOP, as mandated by the CORBA standard.

The mechanisms that the Fault Tolerance Framework employs to ensure replica consistency are implemented beneath the ORB and, thus, are transparent to the application and to the ORB. The overheads are in the range of 7-15% for remote invocations with triplicated clients and triplicated servers. These low overheads include the cost of interception and replication, as well as that of multicasting GIOP messages using the Totem multicast group communication system [6].

For example, using Sun UltraSPARC2 167 and 200 MHz workstations and 100 Mbit/s Ethernet, a remote invocation and response with an unreplicated client and an unreplicated server running over VisiBroker, without the mechanisms of the Fault Tolerance Framework, requires 0.330 ms. In this case, the client and server communicate using IIOP messages transmitted over TCP/IP.

Using the mechanisms of the Fault Tolerance Framework, for the same platform and application, with three-way actively replicated client and server objects running over VisiBroker, a remote invocation and response required 0.369 ms, which represents an overhead of 12% over the unreplicated case. These measurements involved an actively replicated client object repeatedly invoking an actively replicated server object using deferred synchronous communication without message packing. The Operation Logging Mechanism did not contribute to the measured overheads because it was not required for state transfer.

With three-way passively replicated clients and servers, a remote invocation and response required 0.374 ms, which represents an overhead of 15% over the unreplicated case. These measurements involved a passively replicated client object, with the primary client replica repeatedly invoking the passively replicated server object. In the absence of a standard CORBA service that provides externalization, the state transfers for both client and server objects were hand-coded.

Little difference in the time for invocations and responses was observed between cold (no state transfers), warm (state transfer every fourth invocation) and hot (state transfer every invocation) passive replication, because the state transfers largely overlap the invocations and responses. Cold passive replication, of course, imposes a lower processing load on the processors hosting the nonprimary replicas. With cold passive replication, for the nonprimary replicas, the Replication and Operation Logging Mechanisms accounted for 1.2% of the CPU load, while the ORB and the nonprimary replicas imposed no load on the CPU at all. With hot passive replication, for the nonprimary replicas, the Replication and Operation Logging Mechanisms accounted for 5% of the CPU load, with the ORB and the nonprimary replicas exhibiting similar CPU usage, entirely for state transfers. The main overhead in both cases was due to the operating system and networking software, with CPU usages in the range of 20%.

6 Related Work

Several systems have been developed that augment CORBA application objects with fault tolerance. These systems vary in the level of fault tolerance provided to the application, in the transparency provided to the application and the ORB, and in the performance overheads incurred.

The Electra toolkit implemented on top of Horus provides support for fault tolerance by replicating CORBA objects, as does Orbix+Isis on top of Isis [1, 5]. Both Electra and Orbix+Isis integrate the replication and group communication mechanisms into the ORB and require modification of the ORB. Unlike the Fault Tolerance Framework, Electra and Orbix+Isis are non-hierarchical object systems and support only active replication.

The Maestro toolkit [15] includes an IIOP-conformant ORB with an open architecture that supports multiple execution styles and request processing policies. The replicated updates execution style can be used to add reliability and high availability properties to client/server CORBA applications in settings where it is not feasible to make modifications at the client side.

The AQuA framework [2] employs the Ensemble/Maestro [14, 15] toolkits, the Quality Objects (QuO) runtime, and the Proteus dependability property manager. Based on the requirements communicated by the QuO runtime and the faults that occur, Proteus determines the type of faults to tolerate, the replication policy, the degree of replication, the type of voting to use and the location of the replicas, and dynamically modifies the configuration to meet those requirements. The AQuA gateway translates CORBA object invocations into messages that are transmitted via Ensemble, and detects and filters duplicate invocations (responses). The AQuA framework is more similar to the Fault Tolerance Framework than the other systems described here.

The Object Group Service (OGS) [3] provides fault tolerance for CORBA applications through a set of services implemented on top of the ORB. OGS is itself composed of several CORBA services including a group service, a consensus service, a monitoring service and a messaging service, each of which can be used as a stand-alone CORBA service. The service approach, adopted by OGS, exposes the replication of objects to the application program, but allows the application programmer to modify the class library and customize the services more easily.

The Distributed Object-Oriented Reliable Service (DOORS) [13] adds support for fault tolerance to CORBA by providing replica management, fault detection, and fault recovery as service objects above the ORB. Unlike the above systems and the Fault Tolerance Framework, DOORS focuses on passive replication and is not based on group communication and virtual synchrony. The DoorMan management interface monitors DOORS and the underlying system to fine-tune the functioning of DOORS and to take corrective action by migrating objects, if their hosts are suspected of being faulty.

Using a quite different approach from that of the Fault Tolerance Framework, Killijian *et al* [4] have defined a metaobject protocol for implementing fault-tolerant applications based on the use of inheritance and reflection. Their approach allows control by the user at the metalevel, but is heavily language dependent.

7 Conclusion

The Fault Tolerance Framework, described here, is novel in its use of a combination of services and mechanisms to provide fault tolerance for CORBA. The mechanisms are optimally implemented beneath the ORB for transparency and efficiency, and the services are implemented above the ORB for ease of use and customization by the application.

Strong replica consistency is ensured for CORBA applications by means of a reliable totally ordered message delivery service, detection of duplicate invocations and duplicate responses, transfer of state between replicas of an object ensuring that the replicas of an object agree on which method executions precede the state transfer and which follow it, and consistent scheduling of concurrent threads of execution.

The Fault Tolerance Framework can be used transparently or controlled directly by the application program, depending on the degree of control that the application requires. Transparency to the application allows the benefits of fault tolerance to become available to a much wider range of applications and users, with less effort on the part of the application programmer. Transparency to the ORB allows fault tolerance to be provided using unmodifed commercial implementations of CORBA.

References

[1] K. P. Birman and R. van Renesse, *Reliable Distributed Computing with the Isis Toolkit*, IEEE Computer Society Press, Los Alamitos, CA, 1994.

[2] M. Cukier, J. Ren, C. Sabnis, W. H. Sanders, D. E. Bakken, M. E. Berman, D. A. Karr and R. E. Schantz, "AQuA: An adaptive architecture that provides dependable distributed objects," *Proceedings of the IEEE 17th Symposium on Reliable Distributed Systems*, West Lafayette, IN (October 1998), pp. 245-253.

[3] P. Felber, R. Guerraoui and A. Schiper, "The implementation of a CORBA Object Group Service," *Theory and Practice of Object Systems*, vol. 4, no. 2 (1998), pp. 93-105.

[4] M. O. Killijian, J. C. Fabre, J. C. Ruiz-Garcia and S. Chiba, "A metaobject protocol for fault-tolerant CORBA applications," *Proceedings of the IEEE 17th Symposium on Reliable Distributed Systems*, West Lafayette, IN (October 1998), pp. 127-134.

[5] S. Landis and S. Maffeis, "Building reliable distributed systems with CORBA," *Theory and Practice of Object Systems*, vol. 3, no. 1, (April 1997), pp. 31-43.

[6] L. E. Moser, P. M. Melliar-Smith, D. A. Agarwal, R. K. Budhia and C. A. Lingley-Papadopoulos, "Totem: A fault-tolerant multicast group communication system," *Communications of the ACM*, vol. 39, no. 4 (April 1996), pp. 54-63.

[7] L. E. Moser, P. M. Melliar-Smith and P. Narasimhan, "Consistent object replication in the Eternal system," *Theory and Practice of Object Systems*, vol. 4, no. 2 (1998), pp. 81-92.

[8] L. E. Moser, P. M. Melliar-Smith and P. Narasimhan, *Fault tolerance for CORBA*, Technical Report 98-27, Department of Electrical and Computer Engineering, University of California, Santa Barbara, OMG Technical Document orbos/98-10-08, October 1998.

[9] P. Narasimhan, L. E. Moser and P. M. Melliar-Smith, "Replica consistency of CORBA objects in partitionable distributed systems," *Distributed Systems Engineering*, vol. 4, no. 3 (September 1997), pp. 139-150.

[10] P. Narasimhan, K. P. Kihlstrom, L. E. Moser and P. M. Melliar-Smith, "Providing support for survivable CORBA applications with the Immune system," *Proceedings of the IEEE 19th International Conference on Distributed Computing Systems* (May/June 1999), Austin, TX.

[11] Object Management Group, *The Common Object Request Broker: Architecture and Specification*, Revision 2.2, OMG Technical Document formal/98-07-01, February 1998.

[12] Object Management Group, *Fault-Tolerant CORBA Using Entity Redundancy: Request for Proposals*, OMG Technical Document orbos/98-04-01, April 1998.

[13] J. Schonwalder, S. Garg, Y. Huang, A. P. A. van Moorsel and S. Yajnik, "A management interface for distributed fault tolerance CORBA services," *Proceedings of the IEEE Third International Workshop on Systems Management*, Newport, RI (April 1998), pp. 98-107.

[14] R. van Renesse, K. Birman, M. Hayden, A. Vaysburd and D. Karr, "Building adaptive systems using Ensemble," *Software - Practice and Experience*, vol. 28, no. 9 (July 1998), pp. 963-979.

[15] A. Vaysburd and K. Birman, "The Maestro approach to building reliable interoperable distributed applications with multiple execution styles," *Theory and Practice of Object Systems*, vol. 4, no. 2 (1998), pp. 73-80.

[16] J. Wensley, P. M. Melliar-Smith, *et al*, "SIFT: Design and analysis of a fault-tolerant computer for aircraft control," *Proceedings of the IEEE*, vol. 66, no. 10 (October 1978), 1240-1255.

The Performance of Database Replication with Group Multicast *

JoAnne Holliday Divyakant Agrawal Amr El Abbadi
Department of Computer Science, University of California, Santa Barbara, CA 93106, USA
{joanne46,agrawal,amr}@cs.ucsb.edu

Abstract

Replication with update-anywhere capability while maintaining global synchronization and isolation has long been thought impractical. Protocols have been proposed for distributed replicated databases that take advantage of atomic broadcast systems to simplify message passing and conflict resolution in hopes of making replication efficient. This paper presents performance measurements on a simulation of a replicated database using those protocols. The results show that with the proper group broadcast mechanism, replication with update-anywhere capability is indeed practical.

1 Introduction

Gray et al., in "The Dangers of Replication and a Solution" [6], state that database replication with write-anywhere capability, full serializability, and isolation is impractical because the number of deadlocks will rise as the third power of the number of nodes in the network. Also, since writing to all replicas is part of the transaction, the number of database operations (the transaction size) grows with the degree of replication and the probability of aborts and deadlocks grows as the fifth power of the transaction size. This has lead to a great deal of research into primary-copy models that restrict where updates can occur and schemes which relax consistency, atomicity and isolation requirements. In order to reduce the cost of writes, the database community has moved from the traditional read-one, write-all update protocols with Two Phase Locking (2PL) or Global TimeStamp, to variations which use quorum-based protocols and lazy update propagation.

Another part of the distributed systems community interested in fault-tolerance, has developed systems which provide group communication primitives to support distributed applications. Systems such as ISIS [4], Amoeba [9], and Totem [2], provide reliable message broadcast with delivery guarantees, atomicity and ordering properties. The expectation is that these systems will solve the replication problem. An application would issue a single command to the group communication system to send messages to all participating sites, thus updating all replicas at once. This would indeed reduce update costs, however, these sample applications consider transactions consisting of a single object update. Real transactions require reliability, atomicity, and ordering on a group of operations, not just a single operation. This mismatch is starting to receive some attention [13], and efforts for reconciliation have just begun [10, 1].

Two main benefits are expected from group broadcast. The application design will be simpler and the performance of the replicated system will be better. Update protocols have been proposed for distributed replicated databases that take advantage of broadcast communications [1]. We found that the design of the database and update protocols was not noticeably simpler. In fact, the replicated system must still have a concurrency control protocol, and dealing with deadlock is not straightforward. The design process also showed us that the broadcast systems had many features we did not need which we thought would hurt performance. We were therefore skeptical about the performance improvements.

In this paper we explore the benefits of atomic broadcasts for the management of replicated databases. The update protocols use the atomic broadcast primitives to simplify message passing and conflict resolution in hopes of making replication efficient. For concreteness we investigate a particularly important application of replication, namely a highly available server in an Internet environment. A heavily loaded database server, with requests continuously being generated from the Internet, may be implemented as a replicated database on a small number of servers on a local area network. In order to determine whether broadcast based protocols can provide good performance for replicated databases, we built a detailed simulation of a distributed replicated database. We then conducted a series of experiments to determine the tradeoffs among the different protocols and to explore advantages of replication in a broadcast based system. The results show that, with the proper group broadcast mechanism, replication with update-anywhere capability is indeed viable.

Section 2 defines our system model and Section 3 discusses the specific replicated data update protocols used. Section 4 describes our simulation program. In Section 5 we present the results of our experiments. The paper concludes with a discussion in Section 6.

2 System and communication model

In this paper we investigate the design of a highly available database server in an Internet environment. If the server is implemented as a single database, it may easily become congested and be a bottleneck. We therefore consider repli-

*This work was partially supported by NSF grant CCR97-12108.

0-7695-0213-X/99 $10.00 © 1999 IEEE

cating several copies of the database (or perhaps only the hot-spot pages) on multiple sites connected by a local area network. We refer to them as *server copies*. Each server copy could be connected directly to the Internet or there could be a controller which accepts the Internet requests and forwards them to one of the server copies. The former approach would avoid the potential bottleneck of the controller. The latter approach could ensure a balanced load among the replicas. In this paper, we allow both system configurations.

A replicated database is a collection of data items that are replicated at multiple sites [3]. We assume that the database is fully replicated and users interact with the database by invoking *transactions* at any one of the server copies. A transaction is a sequence of read and write operations on the data items that is executed atomically. We assume that all read operations are executed before all write operations. Since strict two-phase locking is widely used to enforce serializability, we assume that concurrency control is locally enforced by strict two phase locking at all server sites. However, this is not sufficient to ensure correctness as a transaction can be initiated at any one of the database copies and an update protocol is needed to ensure *one-copy serializability*. Thus, our goal is to find update protocols to keep all copies consistent while achieving superior performance.

We assume that the server copies are fail-stop and the communication subsystem connecting them provides primitives to broadcast messages to a group of sites. These group multicast services ensure reliable totally ordered message broadcasting. In order to achieve the ordered delivery of messages, messages that are received at a site are delayed and not delivered to the application until they can be delivered in the proper order. In addition to ordering and reliability, group multicast systems keep track of group membership and report site failures. In this paper we consider atomic broadcast with the following properties [7]: If a correct (non-failed) site broadcasts a message m, the primitive ensures that the message will be delivered to all operational sites. Furthermore, if a site delivers a message m, then all operational sites deliver m. This is the "all-or-nothing" property. A message is delivered at most once, and only if it was actually broadcast. If sites p and q deliver broadcast messages m and m', then m and m' are delivered in the same order at all sites.

Several atomic broadcast systems have been proposed. We now discuss one of those systems: Totem. Totem [2] was developed at UCSB and provides totally ordered multicasts to process groups with low, predictable latency. It uses a token circulating on a logical ring. A site can broadcast messages only when it has the token, giving the messages a total order. Performance remains good at heavy loads because the need to wait for the token is offset by the lack of contention on the Ethernet. Totem offers *agreed* delivery and *safe* delivery. Both options are totally ordered; however, safe delivery waits until all sites have received the message before any site can deliver the message to its application. Our protocols require only agreed delivery, however, the larger delay of safe delivery was used in our model to give realistic results under less-than-ideal conditions. Performance measurements were made using Sun SparcStations on a 100 Mbit Ethernet with no special hardware [5].

3 Atomic broadcast based update protocols

We now briefly describe a set of replicated data update protocols which use atomic broadcast primitives as their means for communication with the other replicas and ensure *one-copy serializability* [1]. The idea underlying each of these protocols is that since the communication subsystem supports totally ordered atomic broadcasts, operations can be processed one at a time at every site in the same order. These protocols tolerate failures because the broadcast mechanism masks all such failures.

3.1 Protocol A1: broadcast all

This is the simplest protocol for managing replicated data and is presented primarily as a benchmark to compare with the other protocols. This protocol requires that a transaction initiated at a server site broadcasts all its operations (read or write) to all other sites using the atomic broadcast. Since lock requests can be delayed, transactions may deadlock. Since every site performs the same operations in the same order, deadlock resolution can be localized to each site. It is important for the correctness of this protocol (and the next one) that every site detects and resolves the deadlock the same way. If deterministic deadlock detection techniques are used at every site to resolve the deadlock, we are guaranteed that the same transactions will be selected for deadlock resolution.

3.2 Protocol A2: broadcast writes

An obvious drawback with the previous protocol is that read operations are performed globally (i.e., broadcasting read lock requests to all database sites), which is an overkill. In the database context, it is generally expected that read operations are significantly more frequent than write operations. Hence, localizing the execution of read operations is desirable and should result in significant performance improvements.

In this protocol, we execute read operations locally and broadcast only write operations. A read operation is executed locally after obtaining a read lock, and a write operation is broadcast to all copies of the database. When the lock manager at site S receives a write request from T_i, it checks if the lock can be granted. If granting is successful, the operation is executed. If the lock cannot be granted, it is because the requested data page, x, is either locked by readers or a writer. If x is locked by a writer, the write operation is blocked at S and any potential deadlock is resolved using the appropriate deadlock resolution mechanism. Since write operations are performed globally, a cycle involving write operations will be detected at every site in the system and resolved consistently. If on the other hand, the lock is held by some readers, for every transaction T_j that holds a read lock on x, the lock manager checks whether T_j has already broadcast a commit. (Note that T_j was initiated at S.) If so, the lock manager blocks the write request until it receives T_j's commit. If S has not sent T_j's commit, T_j is aborted and T_i is granted the write lock. If T_j is not read-only, T_j's abort is broadcast to release all locks held by T_j at other sites. There can never be a deadlock cycle involving read operations. Finally, T_i terminates by broadcasting a commit operation. Since the atomic broadcast has the "all-or-nothing" property, there is no need to employ an atomic commitment protocol.

3.3 Protocol A3: delayed broadcast writes

This protocol attempts to completely localize transaction execution. This is achieved by deferring update operations until commit time, when a single message with all updates is sent to all other sites. A transaction, T_i, executes a read operation locally while a write operation is deferred until T_i is ready to commit. To terminate, T_i broadcasts its deferred writes to all sites. On receiving the writes, the lock manager on site S grants all write locks to T_i atomically, and then the writes are executed at S. After all the writes of T_i are executed locally, T_i broadcasts its commit operation to all sites. T_i terminates after the delivery and execution of its commit locally.

This protocol is also based on reading one copy and writing all copies of replicated objects. It has the added benefit that deadlocks are not possible. This is because all the write locks for a transaction are obtained in a single atomic step at the local lock manager. Conflicts with read locks are dealt with by aborting read operations and the transactions they belong to. There is thus no need to check for deadlocks.

3.4 Protocol A4: single broadcast transactions

Since all write operations are known to all sites and they will be eventually executed, the question arises if the extra broadcast of the commit operation is superfluous. To use a single broadcast, this protocol maintains a version number with each page in the database. A transaction T_i executes a read operation locally and a write operation is deferred until T_i is ready to commit. When the site that initiated T_i is ready to commit T_i, if T_i is a read-only transaction, the decision to commit is done locally and no message is broadcast. Otherwise the site broadcasts the set of reads with their version numbers and the set of writes. On receiving the set of reads and writes of T_i, the lock manager at a site S first checks if the version of the items read by T_i are obsolete (that is if any of the versions on S are greater than the versions read by T_i). If so, T_i is aborted. Otherwise, S proceeds with the attempt to atomically grant all the write locks. If a write lock cannot be granted due to a conflict with a read operation, the reading transaction is aborted and T_i receives the lock. Once all write locks are obtained, S executes the write operations and increments the version numbers of each data-item. T_i terminates at S as soon as it atomically obtains the write locks and successfully executes its write operations.

3.5 To broadcast or not to broadcast?

The above protocols use atomic broadcasting to manage replicated databases. Atomic broadcast tools can be quite expensive in terms of message passing overhead as compared to point-to-point communication. Due to the order guarantees, multiple rounds of message passing may be needed by the broadcast system. However, the replicated data protocols A2, A3, and A4 exploit these total order guarantees to attain several advantages.

If point-to-point communication primitives are used, operations at remote sites must be acknowledged before transaction execution can proceed. When atomic broadcasts with delivery guarantees are used, acknowledgements for operation requests are redundant. Since the state in which an operation is executed is identical at all sites, the response to all operations is the same. Elimination of explicit acknowledgements at the application level reduces the communication cost of executing transactions. One of the main problems encountered when two-phase locking is used in a distributed environment is the need for distributed deadlock detection. In these protocols, global deadlock is impossible. Note also that atomic broadcast eliminates the possibility of deadlock on a single object, since concurrent and competing requests for the same page will be delivered to and processed by every database site in the same order. Even local multiple-object deadlocks cannot occur in the protocols A3 and A4. Finally, a two-phase commit protocol to ensure atomic commitment is not needed since all sites will uniformly make the same decisions.

The main question this paper addresses is whether these advantages outweigh the overhead involved in implementing atomic broadcast. We address this question by designing a detailed simulation to study the performance of replication using broadcasts.

4 The simulation model

We used a detailed simulation model of a replicated database for our experiments. Previous studies [11] have shown that neglecting to model resources can greatly affect the conclusions. Therefore, in our model the transactions and site databases must contend for the CPU, data disk, log disk,

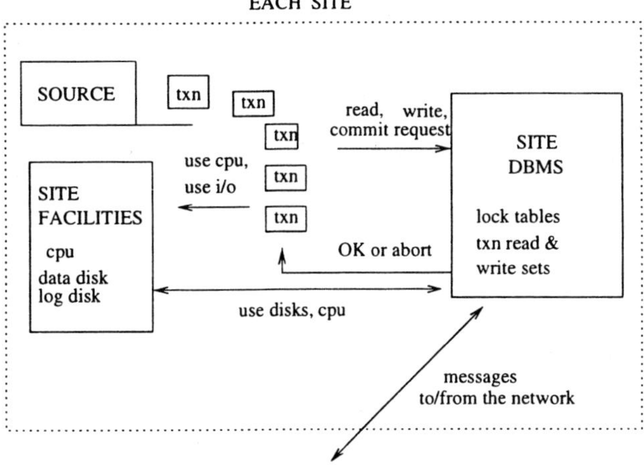

Figure 1: Model Structure of a Single Site

and network services. The structure of the model [10, 11] for each site is shown in Figure 1.

Each site in the database model has a *Source* which generates transactions. This corresponds to the transactional requests arriving from the Internet. The transaction interarrival time determines the load on the system. As the interarrival time is made shorter, the load increases (there is no multiprogramming level to limit the number of active transactions vying for data pages and resources). This is the "open" queuing model, and is appropriate for a system accepting requests from users on the Internet.

Transactions are modeled as sequences of read and write operations, where all the reads are done before the writes. The write set is a subset of the read set, so there are no "blind writes". A transaction makes a read or write request to the site DBMS. After the operation is done, the transaction "thinks" for a while before presenting the next operation. This think time could represent the time needed to transmit the results to the user, analyze the results and send the next operation.

The *Site DBMS* has a collection of 1000 data pages which are replicated at each site. These 1000 data pages could be a subset of a larger database that is replicated for high throughput. By making the number of pages small, we will be able to study data contention issues more easily. A page is assumed to be 2K and is the locking granularity as well as the data disk block granularity. The DBMS uses Strict Two-Phase Locking to ensure local serializability. The DBMS maintains the lock tables and a table of active transactions with the locks they currently hold. The site DBMS uses the network when the update protocol calls for the broadcast or receipt of a message. Each site DBMS has a deadlock detection routine for use with protocols that are susceptible to local deadlocks, i.e., A1 and A2. A Wait-For-Graph is maintained and is checked for cycles each time an edge is added. The deadlocked transaction with the highest transaction ID is chosen as the victim. Victims are aborted and restarted after a delay.

Parameter	*Meaning*	Value
InterTm	Transaction interarrival time	varies
NumSites	Number of sites	varies
NumDisks	Number of data disks per site	1
MinDiskTm	Smallest data disk access time	4 ms
MaxDiskTm	Max data disk access time	14 ms
CPUInitDisk	CPU time to access disk	0.4 ms
LogDiskTm	Time for forced write of log	10 ms
LogPageSz	Number of log records/page	100
HitRate	Probability of cache hit	0.8
LockTime	CPU time needed to handle lock requests	0.006

Table 1: System Parameters

Parameter	*Meaning*	Value
ReadSetMin	Smallest read set size	6
ReadSetMax	Maximum read set size	10
ROPercent	Percentage of r-o transactions	75%
WriteSetMin	Smallest write set size	1
WriteSetMax	Maximum write set size	4
CPUPageTm	CPU time per a data page	1.0 ms
IntThinkTm	Time between sucessive operation requests	10 ms

Table 2: Transaction Parameters

The Site DBMS lock manager was carefully designed so that we could guarantee that each site grants locks to operations in the order in which they are broadcast to it. Thus, the operations will appear to be performed in the same order at all sites. Traditionally, there are no constraints on the lock manager as to the order in which it services operations from its input queue. When two-phase locking is used, operations arrive at the lock manager for consideration. If the lock is granted, the lock manager forwards the associated I/O (read/write) request to the data-manager. As soon as the operation is forwarded, the lock manager considers the next operation in its input queue. If the lock manager is multi-threaded, the order in which locks are granted may not be the same as the order in which requests are delivered by the broadcast service. Since the proposed protocols rely on the broadcast delivery order of operation, the lock manager has to be single-threaded. Also, when several lock requests are pending for a page, the choice of which request is considered next after the release of a lock on that page must be the same at all lock managers. This guarantees that all lock managers grant locks in the same order at every site and hence ensure the same synchronization decision at every site.

The system parameters of the model are given in Table 1 along with their values. The parameters governing the generation and behavior of transactions are given in Table 2. Transaction *response time* measured in milliseconds is the most important measurement. If an individual transaction had to be aborted, the restart delay, as well as the first partial and second total execution time (assuming only one restart was necessary), is included in the response time. Thus, the true cost of aborts is reported in the response time measurements. System *throughput*, measured in transactions committed per second, is also important in comparing results with different numbers of sites in the distributed system.

The Totem multicast system is modeled with four parameters. Each broadcast and receive operation uses a certain amount of the CPU, *CPUMsgSend* and *CPUMsgRcv*, set to 0.7ms and 0.5ms respectively. Before a message is distributed to the other sites by the network, it is delayed by *SendDelay* (0.48ms times the number of sites), which models waiting for the token in Totem. The message also uses the network with *NetFacUse* (0.2ms times the message size). The simulation model achieves total order delivery by having a *network* module with a single input queue for messages to be broadcast. The order in which messages are put into the queue determines their eventual delivery order. The *network* module removes a message from its input queue and distributes it to all site input queues before considering the next message.

5 Experimental results

In this section, we present the results of a variety of experiments that were conducted. The overall goals of the experiments were to evaluate the relative performance of the various replication protocols that use atomic broadcast as a means of communication and to ascertain the advantages of replication as a means for improving overall system performance.

All measurements in these experiments were made by running the simulation until a 95% confidence interval was achieved for each data point. This was typically 15,000 to 30,000 transactions. The confidence intervals were typically one to two milliseconds wide.

5.1 Response time analysis

The first experiment measured response time in milliseconds as a function of transaction interarrival time, in milliseconds for all four protocols. An interarrival time of 50 means that every 50 milliseconds a new transaction starts at each site. One purpose of the experiment was to verify our intuitive assessment of how the protocols would perform. We modeled systems of three server copy sites on a LAN using Totem and the results are shown in Figure 2.

As expected, A1, which broadcasts all operations, had a much greater response time than the other protocols under all loading conditions. Protocol A1 is not included in subsequent experiments. Protocol A4, which requires a single broadcast per update transaction, performed best. We were, however, surprised that there was not a greater separation

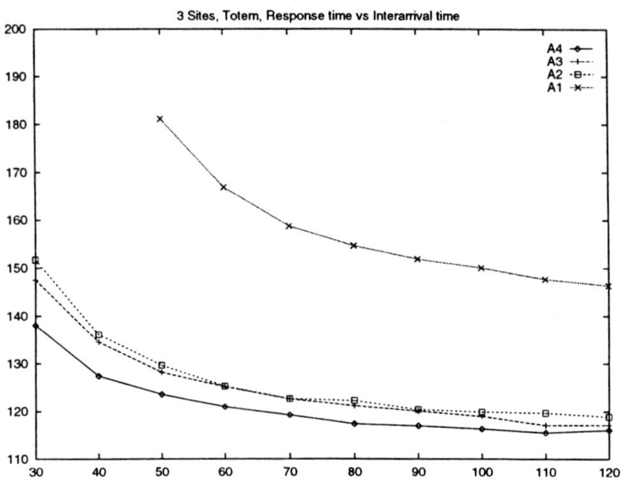

Figure 2: Response vs Interarrival time for 3 sites

between A2, which requires a broadcast per write and A3 which only requires two broadcasts per update transaction. The main reason seems to be due to the increased resource contention. In fact, both A3 and A4 pay a penalty in terms of wait time for the disk and CPU that A2 does not have. We considered the mean queue length for the data disk for A2, A3, and A4 at an interarrival time of 70 milliseconds on a three site system. For A2 the mean disk queue length was 0.292. For A3 and A4, it was 0.310 and 0.308 respectively. Recall that protocols A3 and A4 do all write operations at once, rather than one at a time with a *think time* in between as is done in A2. Thus, although all three protocols are making statistically the same requests, the distribution of the timing of those requests makes a difference. Apparently, the natural interleaving of resource use with other processing that A2 does (and that occurs in any multi-programming environment) is an advantage in spite of having to use the network to broadcast every write request. In our simulation, the data manager handles requests in the order they arrive, and does not reorder them for convenience or optimization. There is therefore a tradeoff between the benefit achieved by the data manager being able to rearrange operations and the benefit achieved by imposing a system-wide total order on the operations.

Another important observation is the substantially better response time of A4 when compared to both A3 and A2. This is primarily due to the fact that transactions using protocol A4 never have to wait for a page lock. Blocking readers are aborted and writers must have completed their writes and committed before the current transaction is considered. For A2 and A3 at an interarrival rate of 70 ms, the abort ratios (the ratio of transaction aborts to transaction commits) are similar and the blocking ratios (the ratio of the number of times a transaction was forced to wait for a lock to the number of transaction commits) were 0.008 and 0.004,

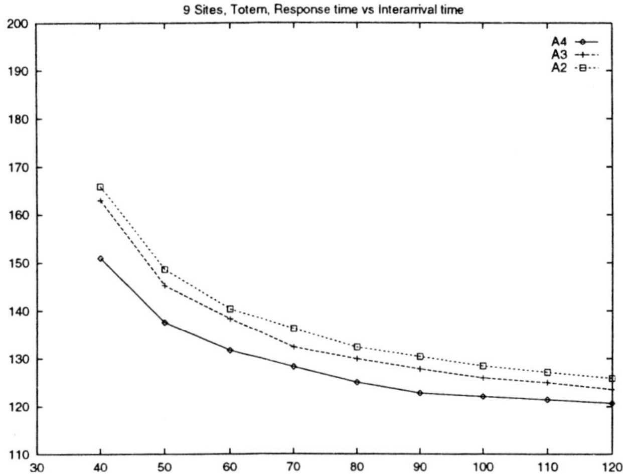

Figure 3: Response time vs Interarrival time for 9 site System

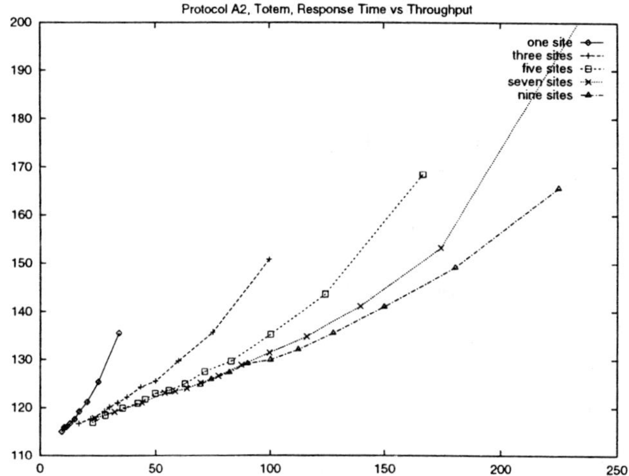

Figure 4: Response time vs Throughput, Protocol A2

respectively. For A4 under the same conditions, the abort ratio was slightly higher, but the blocking ratio was zero.

We increased the number of server copy sites from three to nine and studied the relative performance of A2, A3, and A4. The response times (Figure 3) increased for all three protocols in similar proportions. The smallness of the increase was unexpected given that the system has tripled in size. We therefore studied the system with increased network delays. The response time for A3 at an interarrival time of 110ms on a three site system is 117.08 milliseconds and on a nine site system it is 124.92ms. We tripled the network costs for nine site system, and got a response time of 134.79ms. We conclude from this set of experiments that, given the relatively low network communication costs, the replicated data management protocols perform quite well.

These experiments were repeated using the Amoeba system [9] as the broadcast mechanism. The results, which are reported in [8], were substantially the same.

5.2 Varying degree of replication

In this experiment we investigate the benefits of replication on throughput. To compare the performance of a single protocol on systems with a varying number of sites, response time is shown as a function of throughput in Figure 4. This is because the transaction load on a nine-site system is three times as much as that on a three-site system for the same transaction interarrival time. Throughput is the number of transaction committed by the system per second. The measurements for a one-site system were made by setting the number of sites to one and the message broadcast cost to zero. In this way, the measurements represent the use of a centralized database using ordinary Two-Phase-Locking with no replication.

The results in Figure 4 show the advantages of replication for just the A2 protocol. A2 is a simple extension to protocols already in use, so these results are especially gratifying. Our first observation is that in a non-replicated system, the maximum throughput that could be reached before the effect of queuing for resources and the multiplicative effect of aborts overloaded the system was 34 transactions per second. If higher throughput is desired, it seems that replication must be used. As the number of server copies increases, the system can handle larger throughput. For example, neither one- nor three-copy systems could handle a throughput of 150 transactions per second. However, a five-site system handled it with an average response time of 162ms, a seven-site system had response time 145ms, and a nine-site system, 140ms. Note that a nine-site system can handle a throughput of 225 transactions per second with a fairly reasonable response time of 165 ms.

The results for A3 and A4 were not much different from A2, and are not shown. Using protocol A4, a nine-site system can handle 150 transactions per second with a response time of 130 ms, whereas with protocol A2 a nine-site system handling 150 transactions per second had a response time of 141 ms.

5.3 Reduced resource contention

One of the challenges for replication is its ability to scale up well as system performance improves. One may question whether, with reduced resource contention (faster network, faster disk), would the protocols be able to handle the increased data contention resulting from increased load. We must demonstrate that the data contention caused by replication and our protocols will scale up reasonably with increased load. In the previous experiments, resource contention, particularly contention for the data disk, seemed to be the most important factor limiting throughput. How would our protocols perform with the best resources available today? Totem was evaluated on a 100 Mbit Ethernet [5]. One gigabit Ethernets are available today, so in this exper-

Parameter	New Value
MinDiskTm	2 ms
MaxDiskTm	4 ms
CPUInitDisk	0.1 ms
LogDiskTm	3 ms
HitRate	0.95
NetFacUse	0.02*MsgSize
SendDelay	0.2*NumSites

Table 3: Parameter Changes

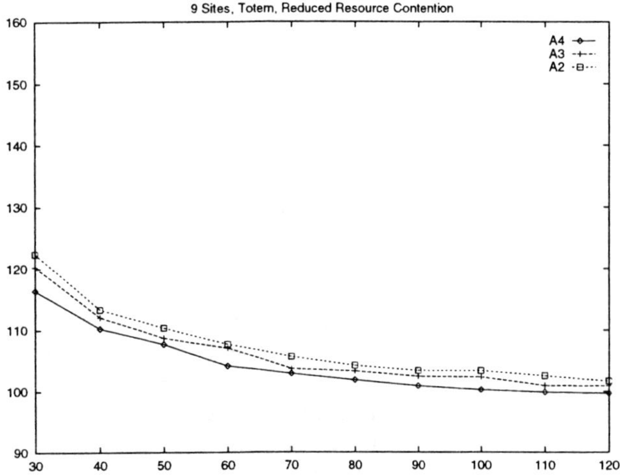

Figure 5: Reduced Resource Contention, 9 sites

iment we decrease the network usage parameter. Also, the Totem *Agreed Delivery* will be modeled instead of the more expensive *Safe Delivery*. Ruemmler and Wilkes [12] point out that disk drives such as the HP97560 with data caching can complete about 50 percent of requests in 3 milliseconds or less. In a replicated database, it may not be necessary to keep a copy on disk at all sites. Therefore the hit rate was increased and the disk access time shortened from 4 – 14 to 2 – 4 ms in this reduced resource contention model.

Table 3 summarizes the parameters changes. The results are shown in Figure 5. The scale on the Y-axis has been changed since the response times are much shorter. It is interesting that the difference in performance between the protocols becomes negligible and all of the protocols perform better. In our previous example of a nine site system, protocol A4 had a response time of 125 ms at an interarrival time of 80ms. Now, with reduced resource contention, protocol A4 has a response time of 102 ms at the same transaction interarrival time. Similar results were observed for a three site system, Since network costs are negligible and the disk is faster so the queuing effects are less important, the overhead for all protocols becomes comparable.

5.4 No read-only transactions

Our final experiment explores the case where the system is under heavy update load. Note that in all previous experi-

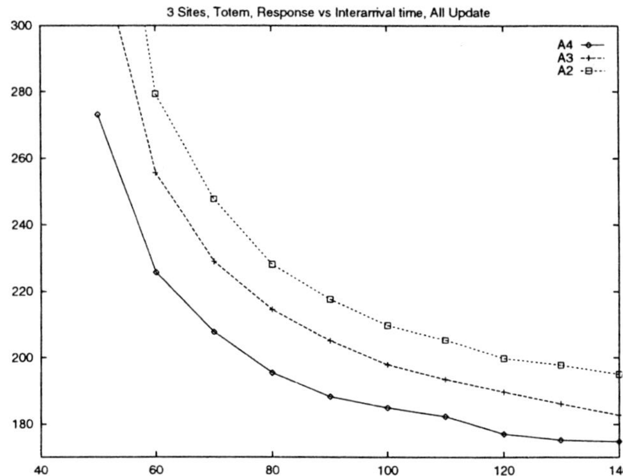

Figure 6: No RO, Response vs Interarrival time, 3 sites

ments, most of the transactions (75%) were read-only and only 26% of the update transaction's operations were write operations. This is a reasonable setting for most commercial databases. However, we wanted to study the performance of the replicated protocols under stress. We therefore eliminated all read-only transactions and required all transactions to have on average 5 to 6 write operations out of a total of 10 to 12 operations. In Figure 6 we plot the resulting response time for a three site system. Obviously the average response time per transaction is more than in the read-only dominated system. In a three site system, protocol A4 had a response time of 117 ms at an interarrival time of 80ms. Now, with all transactions updating, protocol A4 has a response time of 195 ms at the same transaction interarrival time.

Although the relative performance of the protocols is still as expected, we notice a more significant difference in the absolute performance of the three protocols, due to the increased write rate. The distinction between A2 and A3 is now substantial since more communication overhead is incurred by A2. A4 performs quite well considering the load on the system.

6 Discussion

We were quite pleased with the simulation results. The increase in throughput capacity as the number of sites increased caused us to ask, "Why were the response times so good?" Familiar models of replication predict that data contention and message cost will multiply, causing response times to soar out of control as the number of sites and the load on the system increases.

With a group multicast system to handle messaging, sending a message to all other sites is a single, relatively fast operation. The time required does depend on the number of sites, N; however, the factor is small (240 microseconds) and the dependency is N rather than N^2. Our protocols may not perform well with 100 or 1,000 sites (the multicast systems have much different characteristics at those sizes), but replications up to nine sites appear to give a definite throughput advantage. In our protocols, there can be no global deadlocks. Local deadlocks are possible in A1 and A2, but they are extremely rare since a transaction that wants to write to a data page that is read-locked by another simply aborts the reader rather than waiting.

Broadcast-based replication does not add to the probability of aborts as it does in the point-to-point model. In that model, a transaction must avoid abortion at each site in order to survive and commit and each site carries a small but non-zero probability of abortion. In our model, if a transaction survives at one site and is able to commit at that site, it must survive and be able to commit at every other site. Also, a transaction running at a site does not have to wait until its commit request is acknowledged and approved by all other sites. It is enough for the transaction to know that the commit message is assured a place in the total order of message delivery, and the transaction can commit locally. This has a positive effect on the response time.

We can also compare our model to the primary or master copy model. In the primary copy model, each data page or data object has a *primary* site and all other copies of the data are secondary. Read operations can be done on any copy, but a write can be performed only by obtaining a lock on the primary copy (the update is then propagated to the secondary copies). The restriction to the primary copy serializes write requests at a single site, thus overcoming the confusion of replication. The primary-copy model has been shown in numerous studies to have acceptable performance. The primary-copy system gives the improved performance because there is a single entity dictating the serialization order and the secondary copies are just copies. Our replicated system also has a single entity dictating the serialization order, except that this entity is not the primary copy but rather the group multicast service which imposes a total order on the operations. Thus, we might see performance similar to the primary-copy model.

In conclusion, in spite of common attacks on the practical benefits of replication, we believe that broadcast support holds the promise of actually delivering these benefits. Broadcast-based replication should be revisited, now that the performance of broadcast systems has improved. The protocols we presented show that replication may be the sole avenue for achieving high throughput. Two of these protocols are especially worthy of note. The broadcast writes protocol (A2) provides good overall response time, while requiring only minor modifications to standard transaction execution models. The single broadcast protocol (A4), on the other hand, eliminates operation blocking and thus provides excellent response time performance. Finally, we observe that all the experiments considered less than 10 sites. This is due to restrictions on the broadcast system Totem. We are currently exploring a wide area network version of these protocols that would allow increased scalability both in terms of number of sites and the extent of the network.

References

[1] D. Agrawal, G. Alonso, A. El Abbadi, I. Stanoi, "Exploiting Atomic Broadcast in Replicated Databases," *EuroPar'97, Proc. 3rd International EuroPar Conf*, Passau, Germany, August 1997.

[2] Y. Amir, L.E. Moser, P.M. Melliar-Smith, D.A. Agarwal, P. Ciarfella, "The Totem Single-Ring Ordering and Membership Protocol," *ACM Transactions on Computer Systems* 13(4), Nov. 1995, p311-342.

[3] P.A. Bernstein, V. Hadzilacos, N. Goodman, *Concurrency Control and Recovery in Database Systems*. Addison Wesley, Reading MA., 1987.

[4] K.P. Birman, R. Van Renesse, *Reliable Distributed Computing with the ISIS Toolkit*. IEEE Computer Society Press, Los Alamitos, CA, 1994.

[5] R.K. Budhia. *Performance Engineering of Group Communication Protocols*. Ph.D. Dissertation. ECE Department, Univ. of California at Santa Barbara, August 1997

[6] J. Gray, P. Helland, P. O'Neil, and D. Shasha. The Dangers of Replication and a Solution. In *Proc. ACM SIGMOD 1996 Int'l Conf. Management of Data*, Montreal, Quebec, pages 173-182, 1996.

[7] V. Hadzilacos, S. Toueg. "Fault-tolerant Broadcast and Related Problems". S. Mullender, editor, *Distributed Systems*, p.97-147. Addison-Wesley, 1993.

[8] J. Holliday, D. Agrawal, A. El Abbadi, "The Performance of Database Replication with Group Multicast" Technical Report TRCS99-11, Computer Science Department, Univ. of California, Santa Barbara, 1999.

[9] M.F. Kaashoek, A.S. Tanenbaum, S.F. Hummel, H.E. Bal, "An Efficient Reliable Broadcast Protocol", Operating Systems Review, Vol. 23, pp.5-19, Oct. 1989.

[10] B. Kemme, G. Alonso, "A Suite of Database Replication Protocols based on Group Communication," *18th International Conf. on Distributed Computing Systems* (ICDCS 98), Amsterdam, The Netherlands, May 1998.

[11] R. Agrawal, M. Carey, M. Livny, "Concurrency Control Performance Modeling: Alternatives and Implications" and M. Carey, M. Livny, "Conflict Detection Tradeoffs for Replicated Data". In V. Kumar, editor, *Performance of Concurrency Control Mechanisms in Centralized Database Systems*, Prentice Hall, 1996.

[12] C. Ruemmler, J. Wilkes, "An Introduction to Disk Drive Modeling," *IEEE Computer* 27(3) p17-29, March 1994.

[13] A. Schiper, M. Raynal. "From Group Communication to Transactions in Distributed Systems," *Communications of the ACM*, 39(4) p.84-87, April 1996.

Design, Implementation and Performance Evaluation of a CORBA Group Communication Service

Shivakant Mishra, Lan Fei, and Guming Xing
Department of Computer Science
University of Wyoming, P.O. Box 3682
Laramie, WY 82071-3682, USA.

Abstract

This paper describes the design, implementation, and performance evaluation of a CORBA group communication service. It also evaluates the effect of CORBA in implementing a group communication service. The main conclusion is that CORBA can be used to implement group communication services and therby achieve interoperability in a heterogeneous computing environment. However, there is a substantial performance cost. As a result, current CORBA technology is not suitable for implementing high performance group communication services.

1. Introduction

Group communication services have been successfully used to construct highly available, dependable, and real-time applications [15, 3, 2, 12, 1]. However, these services have mostly been implemented on a homogeneous, distributed computing environment, i.e. a computing environment in which all computing components are of similar architecture and run the same system software. This has been a major limitation. With increasing diversity in hardware and software technology, most modern computing environment are heterogeneous in nature.

In this paper, we address this problem of operating group communication services in a heterogeneous, distributed computing environment. We describe the implementation and performance of a group communication service, called the timewheel group communication service [10, 11], using the Common Object Request Broker Architecture (CORBA) [16]. While mechanisms for persistence, transactions, event channels, etc. have been designed for CORBA, there is no support for object replication. Group communication services are an important mechanism for supporting object replication. So, a secondary goal of this paper is to provide object replication support for CORBA by implementing a CORBA group communication service.

Other efforts in this direction include [7, 9, 6, 5, 14]. The approach adopted in [7] and [9] consists of modifying and extending the ORB with group communication mechanism. This approach is termed as *integration* approach in [6]. The approach adopted in [6] consists of providing group communication as a service on top of ORB. This approach is termed as *service* approach. A qualitative comparison of these two approaches in [6] indicates that a service approach is preferable, because it follows the basic philosophy behind CORBA: the ORB should provide minimal functionalities to allow interoperability between heterogeneous objects. The integration approach violates this basic philosophy. In addition, the integration approach results in a loss of portability and interoperability, because it forces application implementations to be ORB dependent (depending on the group communication service integrated in the ORB), and servers and clients need to use the same ORB implementation.

For these reasons, we decided to use the service approach for implementing the timewheel group communication service using CORBA. It is clear from the description in [6] that a group communication service can be implemented as a service on top of ORB. However, how practical is it to provide group communication on top of an ORB? What is the performance overhead of such an implementation? In this paper, we provide answers to these questions by comparing the CORBA implementation of the timewheel group communication service with another implementation of the same service that does not use CORBA (and hence does not provide interoperability properties). We also discuss in detail the sources of performance overhead due to CORBA for implementing a group communication service.

0-7695-0213-X/99 $10.00

We have implemented the timewheel group communication service in two ways. The first implementation uses the UDP socket interface, and runs on a network of SGI (indy) workstations running IRIX 6.2. This implementation is described in detail in [10] and [11]. In this paper, we will refer to this implementation as the socket implementation. The second implementation uses the IONA Orbix 2.3, and runs on a network of SGI (Indys) workstations running IRIX 6.2, Sun Sparcstations running Solaris, PCs running Windows 95, and PCs running Windows NT 4.0. In this paper, we will refer to this implementation as the CORBA implementation. We provide a performance comparison between the performance measured from the first implementation on a network of SGI workstations and the performance measured from the second implementation which runs only on the SGI workstations.

2. Background

2.1. CORBA

Common Object Request Broker Architecture (CORBA) defines a framework for developing object-oriented, distributed applications. It supports the construction and integration of object-oriented software components in a heterogeneous, distributed computing environment. Two major components of CORBA are Interface Definition Language (IDL) and Object Request Broker (ORB). IDL is used for specifying the interfaces of CORBA objects. It enables CORBA-compliant applications to be language independent. The interface definition specifies which member functions are available to a client without making any assumptions about the implementation of the object. To invoke member functions on a CORBA object, a client needs only the object's IDL definition. CORBA objects use the ORB as an intermediary to facilitate network communication. A CORBA ORB delivers requests to objects and returns any response to clients making the requests. The key feature of ORB is the transparency of its facilitation of client/server communication. When a client invokes a members function on a CORBA object via the IDL interface, the ORB intercepts the function call and redirects the function call across the network to the target object. The ORB then collects the results and returns them to the client.

2.2. Timewheel Group Communication

The timewheel group communication service [10, 11] consists of a clock synchronization protocol, a group membership protocol, and an atomic broadcast protocol. It is designed for a timed asynchronous distributed system model [4], and supports nine group communication semantics simultaneously: three kinds of ordering semantics—*unordered*, *total ordered*, and *time ordered*, three kinds of atomicity semantics—*weak*, *strong*, and *strict*, and one termination semantic. Users can dynamically choose these semantics when broadcasting an update, i.e. a user may broadcast one update with one pair of order and atomicity semantics, and another update with another pair. In particular, this service provides an ordering of update deliveries that preserve causality arising due to "hidden" communication channels [8]. This service provides good overall performance in the absence as well as presence of communication or processor failures.

2.3. CORBA vs Socket Implementation

Group communication services have typically been implemented using UDP or TCP sockets. While a socket implementation of a group communication service provides excellent performance, its employment in a heterogeneous, distributed computing environment is very difficult and requires excessive amount of work. This is because sockets are specific to operating systems. In BSD Unix systems, sockets are are a part of the operating system kernel, while in MS-DOS, Windows, MacOS, and OS/2, sockets are in the form of user libraries. In addition, a socket-based implementation of a group communication service supports only a single-language applications.

We have addressed this limitation by implementing the timewheel group communication service using CORBA. There are several reasons for choosing CORBA. The first and the most important reason is that CORBA is an extremely popular middleware for constructing distributed applications in a heterogeneous distributed computing environment. The second reason is that CORBA is platform independent. CORBA ORB is a standardized infrastructure mechanism for networking that is same on all operating system platforms. This implies that a single implementation of a group communication service using CORBA will run on all operating systems. This is in contrast to different versions of sockets on different operating system platforms.

The third reason is that CORBA is language independent. Every application object connects to the CORBA ORB and communicates with other objects by the standardized interface defined by the CORBA IDL that supports multiple language mapping. This implies that applications may be written in different languages and still use a group communication service implemented using CORBA. Finally, the standardized ORB and IDL interfaces make a significant reduction in complexity. With sockets in a system with N nodes, the number of interfaces is N×N, while with CORBA ORB, only N interfaces are required. Integration of an additional node requires developing N+1 new interfaces in socket implementation, while only one new interface in CORBA implementation.

3. Design and Implementation

Figure 1 shows the relationship between application clients, application servers, and a group communication service. An application with high availability, dependability, and/or real-time responsiveness requirements is constructed by implementing application servers on multiple machines. These application servers replicate the application state and use a group communication service to coordinate their activities in the presence of concurrent event occurrences, asynchrony, and processor or communication failures. Application clients that need application services interact with one of the application servers. A detailed description of the design and implementation of timewheel group communication service using UDP sockets is given in [10] and [11]. Here, we focus on how CORBA has been used to facilitate various communication requirements of this service.

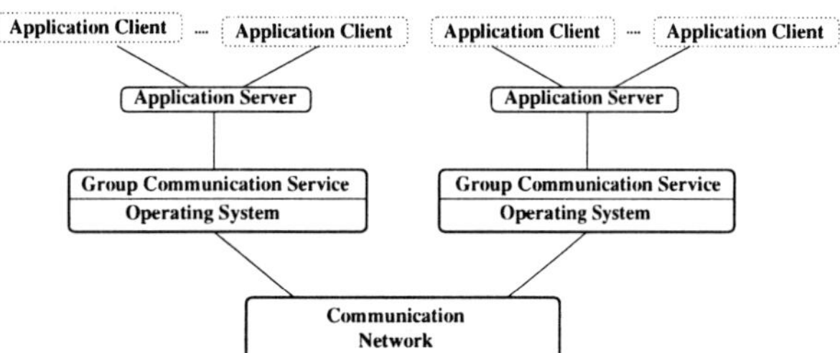

Figure 1. Relationship between application clients, servers, and group communication service.

3.1. CORBA Interfaces

We use two important properties of CORBA: standardized ORB and remote invocation. In addition, we also use interface inheritance and object factories in our implementation. In accordance with the relationship between application clients, application servers, and a group communication service (see Figure 1), each group member provides two sets of IDL interfaces: *members_interface* and *application_interface*. The members_interface specifies interactions between different group members, and the application_interface specifies interactions between an application server and a group member. Together, these two interfaces allow different application servers and different group members to run on machines that have different architectures and run different operating systems. In addition, these interfaces allow the implementation of application servers and group members in different programming languages.

Group members running on different hosts communicate with one another via the ORB by using the members_interface. This interface allows different group members to run on machines of different architectures and use different programming languages for their implementation. Figure 2 shows the usefulness of this interface. The ORB makes remote invocation in CORBA as simple as a local function call. In our design, message transfer between different group members has been facilitated by passing messages as parameters of the remote invocation.

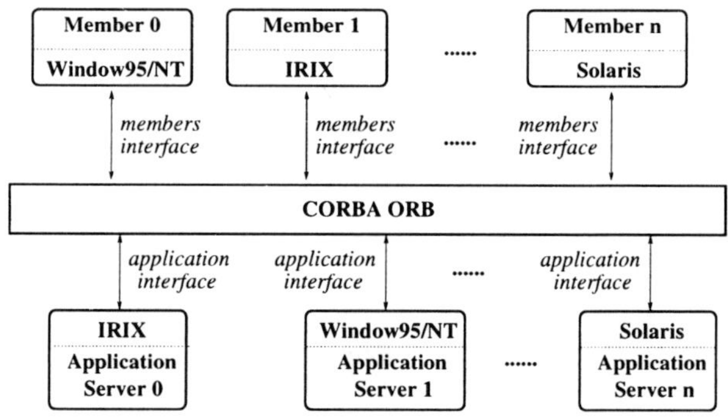

Figure 2. Heterogeneity via the members and application interfaces.

An application server invokes various group communication service operations by using the application_interface. This allows application servers and group members to run on different machines of different architectures. In addition, this interface also enables an application server and a group member to be implemented in different programming languages. Figure 2 shows the usefulness of this interface.

3.2. Member Implementation

Each group member is implemented as a set of two processes: *protocol process* and communication process. The protocol process is responsible for implementing all the timewheel group communication functionalities. In particular, it processes messages sent by other members, services application server requests, implements atomicity, order, and termination semantics, maintains a consistent group membership, and so on.

The communication process is responsible for receiving messages from other group members. As soon as a message is received by the communication process, it passes that message to the protocol process. Figure 3 shows this design of a group member. The application_interface is implemented in the protocol process and the members_interface is implemented in the communication process. A protocol process sends a message to another group member by directly invoking an appropriate interface function specified in the communication process of the other member. As soon as a message is received by a communication process, it passes this message to the local protocol process. This communication between protocol process and application process can be accomplished by using any interprocess communication primitive provided by the operating system. For example, a pipe or socket-based communication may be used.

There are three important reasons for implementing a group member as a set of two processes. First, it provides a clean separation between the implementation of the group communication service functionalities and the communication mechanisms used. Second, this design simplifies extending a group communication service implementation to become CORBA compliant, and hence, provide the heterogeneity properties. Finally, this design facilitates a sequential (event-based) implementation of a group communication service, which is a preferred method of implementation of a group communication service [13].

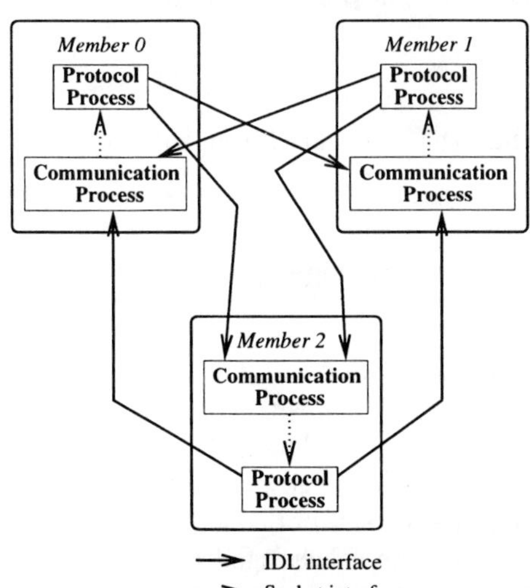

Figure 3. Implementation of a group member.

4. Performance Evaluation

There are four performance indices we have measured: *throughput*, average broadcast *delivery time*, average broadcast *stability time*, and average number of messages exchanged per atomic broadcast. Throughput of a group communication service is defined as the number of updates delivered per second at each member for a given update arrival rate. The broadcast delivery time is defined as the duration between the moment an update is entrusted to a group member and the moment the update is delivered by every group member. The broadcast stability time is the duration between the moment a member receives an update to be broadcast and the moment all members learn that the update is *stable*, i.e. it has been received by all group members. Finally, the number of messages per atomic broadcast includes all messages sent by different group members to complete the broadcast of an update. Since, the timewheel group communication service provides several different semantics, we provide a performance comparison for several different group communication semantics.

4.1. Throughput

We measured the throughput for a group size of three, in which all group members broadcast updates at a uniform rate. Figures 4 and 6 show the throughput measured for two sets of group communication semantics. Throughput for the other sets of group communication semantics are similar. The number of updates delivered per second is approximately equal to the total number of update broadcasts per second for up to about 50 update broadcasts per seconds. After that the number of updates delivered per second becomes smaller than the number of updates broadcast per second. The maximum number of updates delivered per second varies between 125 and 150 for different group communication semantics. This maximum occurs at around 350 update broadcasts per second.

For a comparison, we have included the throughput measured from the socket implementation of the timewheel group communication service in Figures 5 and 7. The throughput measured from the CORBA implementation is significantly lower (about 10-15 times lower) than that measured from the socket implementation.

4.2. Delivery Time

The average delivery time measured for a group of size 3 is reported in Table 1 for various group commu-

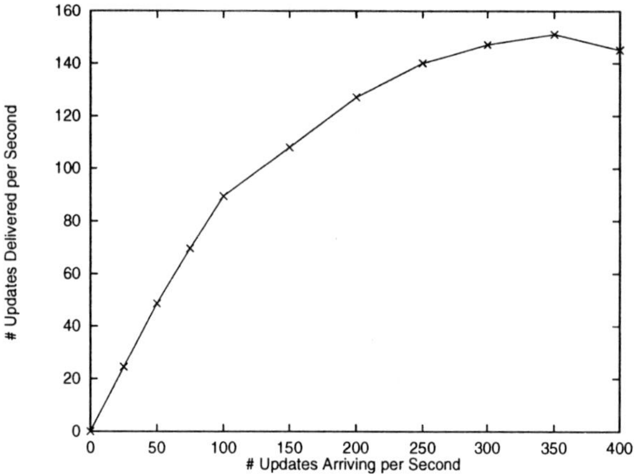

Figure 4. Throughput (weak atomicity, no order) CORBA implementation.

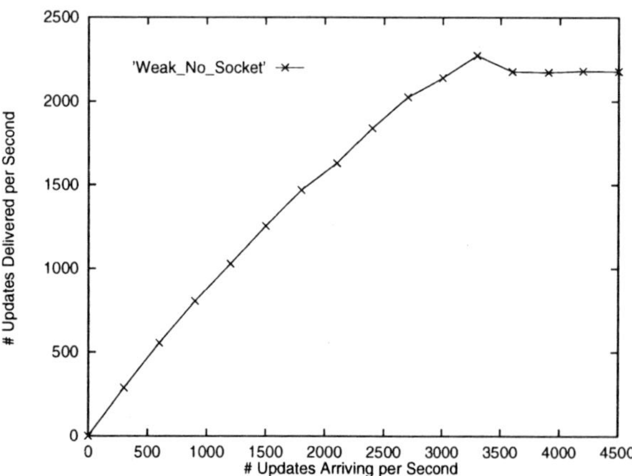

Figure 5. Throughput (weak atomicity, no order) socket implementation.

nication semantics. For a comparison, we have also included the corresponding delivery times measured from the socket implementation. The delivery times measured from the CORBA implementation is significantly higher (about 8-10 times higher) than that measured from the socket implementation.

4.3. Stability Time

The average stability time measured for a group of size 3 is reported in Table 2 for various group communication semantics. For a comparison, we have also included the corresponding stability times measured from the socket implementation. Once again we notice that the stability times measured from the CORBA implementation is significantly higher (about 8-10 times higher) than that measured from the socket implementation.

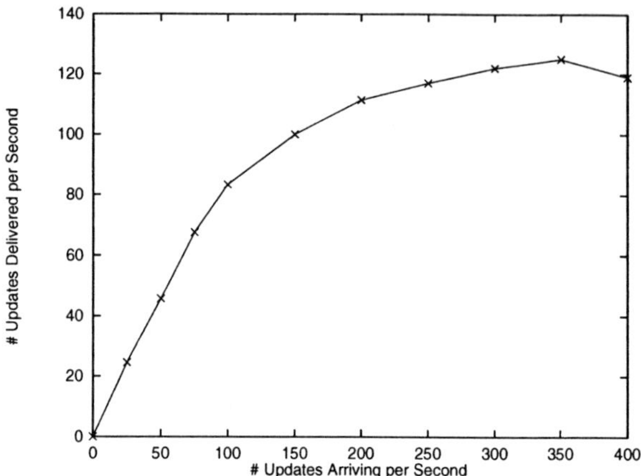

Figure 6. Throughput (strong atomicity, time order) CORBA implementation.

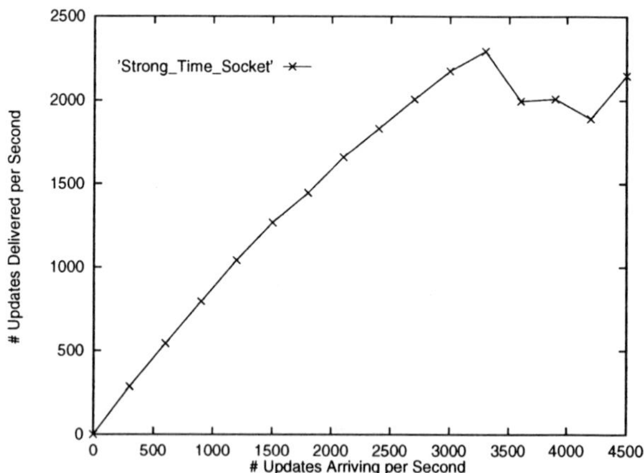

Figure 7. Throughput (strong atomicity, time order) socket implementation.

4.4. Number of Messages

The average number of messages exchanged per atomic broadcast is shown in Table 3. Again, for a comparison, we have included the corresponding number of messages exchanged per update broadcast measured from the socket implementation. The average number of messages exchanged per update broadcast in the CORBA implementation of the timewheel group communication service is about twice the number of messages exchanged per update broadcast in the socket implementation.

Semantics		Interarrival Time			
		2.0	5.0	8.0	10.0
Wk Atm & Ttl Ord	Socket	2.58	1.9	1.49	1.5
	CORBA	22.7	17.7	12.1	11.5
Strn Atm & Tm Ord	Socket	2.6	2.0	1.5	1.5
	CORBA	23.4	17.8	12.9	12.6
Strc Atm & No Ord	Socket	2.6	2.1	1.5	1.55
	CORBA	24.0.8	17.3	12.7	12.0
Strc Atm & Ttl Ord	Socket	2.62	2.13	1.52	1.6
	CORBA	24.7	17.7	12.4	11.8

Table 1. Delivery time (msec)

Semantics		Interarrival Time			
		2.0	5.0	8.0	10.0
Wk Atm & No Ord	Socket	5.5	4.0	3.99	4.18
	CORBA	52.8	39.9	33.5	32.0
Wk Atm & Ttl Ord	Socket	5.5	4.9	4.2	4.22
	CORBA	50.6	40.5	35.3	32.1
Strn Atm & Tm Ord	Socket	5.51	4.9	4.22	4.22
	CORBA	52.6	40.2	33.6	33.1
Strc Atm & No Ord	Socket	5.5	4.9	4.2	4.21
	CORBA	53.1	39.5	34.3	33.0

Table 2. Stability time (msec)

4.5. Performance Analysis

The only difference between the CORBA implementation and the socket implementation of the timewheel group communication service is the method used for interprocess communication. CORBA implementation uses the CORBA remote object invocation via OrbixORB, while the socket implementation uses UDP sockets. So, in order to understand the reasons for extra performance overhead in the CORBA implementation, we measured the average one-way communication delay between two SGI workstations for UDP sockets and OrbixORB.

For a message size of 100 bytes (approximate size of the timewheel proposal and decision messages), the average one-way communication delay was measured to be about 0.6 milliseconds for UDP sockets and 2.5 milliseconds for OrbixORB. This indicates that the communication delay in UDP is nearly four times smaller than that in OrbixORB. As we increased the message size, this difference decreased. However, since messages in the timewheel group communication service are of smaller sizes (around 100 bytes), the one-way communication delay difference between the two implementations is expected to be about four times.

Implementation Technique	Interarrival Time			
	2.0	5.0	8.0	10.0
Socket	2.0	2.9	4.0	5.0
CORBA	4.3	5.5	8.1	10.5

Table 3. Number of messages per broadcast

It seems improbable that this difference of four times in one-way communication delay can result in a difference of 10-15 times in the performance of the group communication service. To understand this, we measured the average processing times of proposal and decision messages in the two implementations. The processing time of a message is defined as the time span between the moment a member sends that message and the moment that message has been processed by all members.

The reason for concentrating on the the processing times of proposal and decision messages is that these two messages determine the minimum duration of each processing cycle in the timewheel group communication service. A key to improving the performance of the timewheel group communication service is to reduce the processing times of these two messages. In addition, a measurement of the processing times of these two messages gives an indication of the processing times of other messages. The average processing times of the proposal and decision messages are shown in Tables 4 and 5 for the two implementations of the timewheel group communication service.

Semantics	Socket	CORBA
Tm Ord & Strc Atm	0.95	7.6
Strn Atm & Ttl Ord	0.9	6.48
Wk Atm & No Ord	0.9	4.8
Strc Atm & No Ord	0.95	6.39

Table 4. Proposal processing times (msec)

The processing times of a proposal message in the CORBA implementation of the timewheel group communication service is about 5-8 times higher than the corresponding processing times in the socket implementation. Similarly, the processing times of a decision

Semantics	Socket	CORBA
Tm Ord & Strc Atm	1.1	12.4
Strn Atm & Ttl Ord	1.07	9.67
Wk Atm & No Ord	1.04	7.45
Str Atm & No Ord	1.1	10.6

Table 5. Decision processing times (msec)

message in the CORBA implementation of the timewheel group communication service is about 7-10 times higher than the corresponding processing times in the socket implementation. The difference in the one-way communication delay between the two implementations is one factor that contributes to this difference in message processing times. In addition, the difference in the one-way communication delay results in some queued up proposal/decision messages to be dropped from the buffers (flow control mechanism). These dropped messages are then retransmitted, resulting in an additional increase in the average message processing times in the CORBA implementation. Thus, a relatively small difference in one-way communication delay results in a significant difference in the performance of the group communication service.

The extra performance overhead in all four performance indices in the CORBA implementation can be explained by the difference in one-way communication delay and the difference in the processing times of the proposal and decision messages. The increase in message processing times results in a decrease in the throughput of the CORBA implementation of the timewheel group communication service. Increase in the average delivery and stability times is a result of increased one-way communication delay and increased message processing times in the CORBA implementation. Finally, increase in the number of messages per update broadcast is a result of increased message retransmissions, which in turn results from increased one-way communication delay and increased message processing times in the CORBA implementation.

5. Discussion

The key question we have addressed in this paper is how practical a CORBA implementation of a group communication service is. We expected that there will be some performance degradation by using CORBA instead of UDP sockets. However, the extent of performance degradation that we observed was a surprise to us. Our measurements show that there is a significant performance overhead due to CORBA. The throughput is lowered by 10-15 times, delivery and stability times are increased by 8-10 times, and number of messages exchanged per update broadcast increased by about 2 times.

There are three important reasons for this significant performance degradation. First, the one-way communication delay in the CORBA ORB (OrbixORB) is about four times the one-way communication delay in UDP sockets for smaller sized messages. The reason for this is that a remote object method invocation in CORBA has to go through several layers of abstractions to get serviced by the server object. A remote object invocation has to go through the client stub code to the ORB, which then forwards it to the remote server, where it must go through the server skeleton code to be finally processed by the server object. Each level of abstraction in this path adds some time delay.

Second, the timewheel group communication service relies heavily on a large amount of interprocess communication to achieve an update broadcast or to form a new group. This means that the relatively inefficient CORBA communication methods are repeatedly invoked. This compounds the performance degradation due to dropping of messages followed by their retransmissions.

Finally, the Orbix IDL that we used did not have a full mapping to C++ data types. For instance, this IDL does not support the *long long* data type, which has been used at several places in the implementation of the timewheel group communication service to represent time variables. For example, ordering mechanisms, a timely rotation of the decider role, use of timers in the timewheel group membership protocol, time representation in the clock synchronization protocol, and all the time measurements in our performance measurement depend on a correct representation of the time variables. Because Orbix IDL does not support *long long* data type, we had to explicitly perform some extra data type conversions in our implementation. This added to the performance overhead of the CORBA implementation of the timewheel group communication service.

While the results presented here are based on an implementation of the timewheel group communication service, they can be generalized for any group communication service. This is because the three reasons for performance degradation mentioned above are present in any group communication service. The message sizes in a group communication service are generally small, and so, the one-way communication delay will be significantly higher in a CORBA implementation than in a UDP socket-based implementation of a group communication service. Group communication services in general rely on large amount of interprocess communication, and so, the difference in one-way communication delay will result in additional performance degradation in a CORBA implementation due to dropping of messages and their corresponding retransmissions. Finally, group communication services use time variables for various purposes, such as to detect the failure of a group member. So, there will be a need for data type conversion in a CORBA implementation that will incur additional performance overhead.

The main conclusion we can draw from this work is that while current CORBA technology can be used to provide heterogeneity properties to group communication services, it is not suitable for implementing *high performance* group communication services. However, it should be noted that the substantial performance overhead due to CORBA to implement a group communication service does not mean that a CORBA implementation of a group communication service is useless. The performance provided by a CORBA implementation of a group communication service is still good enough to satisfy the requirements of a large number of applications that have high availability and high dependability requirements, but do not have high performance requirements.

Operation in a heterogeneous, distributed computing environment is an important requirement for constructing modern applications. CORBA provides a simple and easy-to-use method for implementing group communication services for a heterogeneous, distributed computing environment. At present, there are no other simple alternatives that may be used for implementing group communication services in a heterogeneous, distributed computing environment. The current CORBA technology is suitable for implementing heterogeneous group communication services as long as we are willing to accept its substantial performance overhead. We have identified some important reasons for the poor performance of a CORBA implementation of a group communication service. With additional work in the CORBA technology, it is expected that these performance cost will go down in future.

References

[1] Y. Amir, L. Moser, P. Melliar-Smith, D. Agarwal, and P. Ciarfella. The totem single-ring ordering and membership protocol. *ACM Transactions on Computing Systems*, 13(4):311–342, 1995.

[2] K. Birman, A. Schiper, and P. Stephenson. Lightweight causal and atomic group multicast. *ACM Transactions on Computer Systems*, 9(3):272–314, Aug 1991.

[3] F. Cristian. Understanding fault-tolerant distributed systems. *Communications of ACM*, 34(2):56–78, Feb 1991.

[4] F. Cristian and C. Fetzer. The timed asynchronous system model. Technical Report CSE97-519, Dept of Computer Science and Engineering, University of California, San Diego, La Jolla, CA, 1997.

[5] M. Cukier, J. Ren, C. Sabnis, W. Sanders, D. Bakken, M. Berman, D. Karr, and R. Schantz. Aqua: An adaptive architecture that provides dependable distributed objects. In *Proceedings of the 17th Symposium on Reliable Distributed Systems*, West Lafayette, IN, Oct 1998.

[6] P. A. Felber, B. Garbinato, and R. Guerraoui. The design of a corba group communication service. In *Proceedings of the 15th Symposium on Reliable Distributed Systems*, Niagara-on-the-Lake, Canada, Oct 1997.

[7] IONA and Isis. *An Introduction to Orbix+Isis*. IONA Technologies Ltd. and Isis Distributed Systems, Inc., 1994.

[8] L. Lamport. Time, clocks, and the ordering of events in a distributed system. *Communications of the ACM*, 21(7):558–565, Jul 1978.

[9] S. Maffeis. Adding group communication and fault tolerance to corba. In *Proceedings of the 1995 USENIX Conference on Object Oriented Technologies*, Monterey, CA, Jun 1995.

[10] S. Mishra, C. Fetzer, and F. Cristian. The timewheel asynchronous atomic broadcast protocol. In *Proceedings of the 1997 International Conference on Parallel and Distributed Processing Techniques and Applications*, pages 1239–1248, Las Vegas, NV, Jun 1997.

[11] S. Mishra, C. Fetzer, and F. Cristian. The timewheel group membership protocol. In *Proceedings of the Workshop on Fault Tolerant Parallel and Distributed Systems*, Orlando, FL, Apr 1998.

[12] S. Mishra, L. Peterson, and R. Schlichting. Consul: A communication substrate for fault-tolerant distributed programs. *Distributed Systems Engineering*, 1(2):87–103, Dec 1993.

[13] S. Mishra and R. Yang. Thread-based vs event-based implementation of a group communication service. In *Proceedings of the 12th International Parallel Processing Symposium & 9th Symposium on Parallel and Distributed Processing*, Orlando, FL, Apr 1998.

[14] L. E. Moser, P. M. Melliar-Smith, and P. Narasimhn. Consistent object replication in the eternal system. *Theory and Practice of Object Systems*, 4(2), 1998.

[15] F. Schneider. Implementing fault-tolerant services using the state machine approach: A tutorial. *ACM Computing Surveys*, 22(4):299–319, Dec 1990.

[16] J. Siegel. *CORBA Fundamentals and Programming*. John Wiley & Sons, Inc., 1996.

An Execution Service for a Partitionable Low Bandwidth Network

Takako M. Hickey and Robbert van Renesse*

Abstract

As the amount of scientific data grows to the point where the Internet bandwidth no longer supports its transfer, it becomes necessary to make powerful computational services available near data repositories. Such services allow remote researchers to start long-running parallel computations on the data. Current execution services do not provide remote users with adequate management facilities for this style of computing.

This paper describes the PEX system. It has an architecture based on partitionable group communication. We describe how PEX maintains replicated state in the face of processor failures and network partitions, and how it allows remote clients to manipulate this state. We present some performance numbers, and close with discussing related work.

1 Introduction

Dozens of particle accelerators around the world individually collect terabytes of data each year from experiments [9]. Satellites send terabytes worth of observation to earth each day [8]. Much of this data is stored near where it was generated or received. The state-of-the-art in networking is not such that the data can be made available anywhere, and in any case copyright laws may prevent shipping the data. Due to the large amounts of data, replication is not usually possible, and caches cannot be made large enough to provide significant hit ratios.

Thus it makes sense to set up computation services close to where the data is stored. Typically, computation on this type of data (observations) can be easily parallelized, resulting in significant speed-up. The individual computations require little or no interaction, and a cluster of computers on a conventional network is inexpensive and well-suited for this type of processing.

The typical `rsh`-style of remote computation, common in Unix processing, does not provide convenient access to the remote resources. The problem is that some scientific computations require hundreds of processes [9, 8]. Creation of the processes is relatively simple, but keeping track of hundreds is difficult.

As on individual computers, there is a need for a processing service that organizes related processes into sessions. A user should be able to add processes to a session, list running (or recently terminated) processes, and be able to terminate a session with a single command. In addition, it might be useful for a session to be shared among several users. These users would be cooperating on the same scientific computation, but would not necessarily be co-located.

Sessions must be able to tolerate failures. A single session may exist for days or weeks. If a process crash eradicates the session, or if a network failure renders the session inaccessible, hundreds of processes may run unmanaged and would most likely be inaccessible, consuming resources but not performing useful work.

An execution service provides more than just process placement or load balancing. It should:

- support long-running, parallel computation;
- support process placement based on application-defined placement functions (such as data location);
- be tolerant of processor failures and network partitions;
- support heterogeneity of CPU types and operating systems;
- support cooperation between multiple, remote users.

This paper describes the *PEX service*. The contributions of this work are:

- a study of issues related to partitionable operation of distributed services, and remote execution services in particular;
- a demonstration of the use of group communication protocols in such services;
- a software architecture and implementation of a remote execution service, as well as experimental results.

The rest of the paper is organized as follows. Section 2 presents the architecture. In Section 3, we present the client interface. Section 4 describes a reliable RPC mechanism that is used to implement this interface. In Section 5, we

*The work reported was supported in part by ARPA/ONR grant N00014-96-J-1014, ARPA/RADC grant F30602-96-1-0317, NASA/ARPA grant NAG-2-893, and AFOSR grant F49620-94-1-0198.

0-7695-0213-X/99 $10.00 © 1999 IEEE

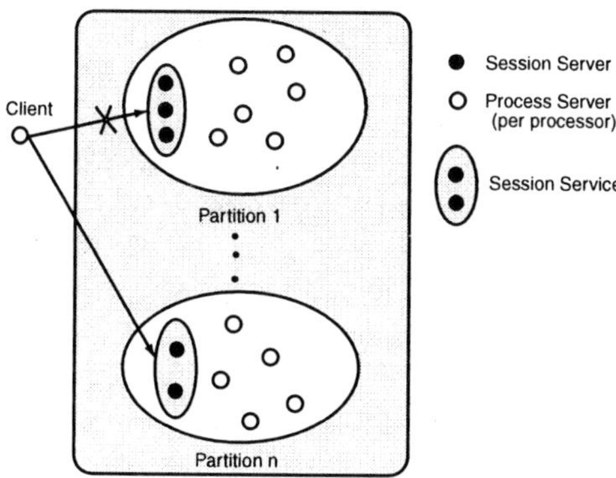

Figure 1. PEX architecture

describe how PEX deals with processor failures and network partitions. Section 6 reports on the performance of the initial implementation. Section 7 compares PEX to other work, and Section 8 gives conclusions.

2 The PEX Architecture

PEX makes use of a *partitionable group membership service* [2]. The service provides consistent information to the processes about the partition that they are in, and supports ordered communication within each partition.

Figure 1 shows the PEX architecture. An *institute* is a collection of processors connected by a small collection of local area networks, such as those used in academic departments or medium-sized companies. Each institute organizes its processors in a *processor group.* Each processor runs a *process server*, which handles execution and termination of processes running on that processor. A small number of processors (typically, two or three) each run a *session server.* Session servers together provide the *session service*, which provides an access point for users (within or outside the institute) that want to use processors in the processor group. We will use the term *client* to describe users of the session service.

The partitionable membership service manages both the processor group, which is large, and a group of session servers, which is small. The session service group needs to be small, because it maintains replicated information that would be hard to scale to the entire processor group.

The session service maintains three types of replicated objects: the processor database, sessions, and records for outstanding user requests. The *processor database* maintains information about the processors in the local processor group. For each processor, it maintains attributes such as CPU type and speed, operating system, amount of physical memory, local data sets, accessibility, and load. Based on this information, and information provided along with each process creation request (such as which data set it needs to access), the service can do informed process placement.

Sessions are sets of processes currently running or recently terminated. Having sessions simplifies management of related processes and facilitates cooperation between clients. With PEX arbitrating user requests to the shared session, multiple clients can safely manage an application concurrently. All processes in a session have to run in the same processor group. Sessions and the processor database are replicated to improve availability and load sharing.

Client request records describe on-going and recently completed client requests. They are replicated to avoid the loss of a request or reply when a session server fails, and also to filter duplicate requests submitted to more than one session server.

Before creating a session, a client has to decide on the institute where the session should run. Currently, we assume that the client knows which institute stores the data set that the computation needs; eventually, we hope to use a fault-tolerant directory service for storing and retrieving this information.

3 Management Interface

This section describes the RPC interface that clients use to manipulate sessions. The major types of requests are listed in Table 1.

Before requesting that the session service start processes, a client must create a session using `SessionCreate`. The session service returns a unique session identifier. Once a session is created, clients can add processes to it using `ProcessCreate`. Arguments to a `ProcessCreate` request are a session identifier, processor specifications, process properties, a set of commands (one for each architecture), plus a *recovery instruction.* The reply to `ProcessCreate` includes process identifiers for each of the started processes and a list of commands that failed to start. PEX ensures that, at the time of creation, each process identifier refers to a unique object across all partitions. This is accomplished by adopting the already unique RPC identifier attached to the requests (see Section 4).

The processor specifications argument is a disjunctive list of conjunctive criteria used to select processors (e.g., [OS type = SunOS & load $<$ 1.0] $\vee$ [OS type = WinNT & data sets include EOS]). The session service selects a set of processors by testing each conjunctive criteria against the processor database. The process properties argument specifies characteristics of processes to be started. Some processors may restrict types of processes that they run (e.g., only those belonging to a particular user).

Each entry in the command set is a list of processor characteristics followed by a normal shell-style command. This allows execution of different versions of the same command

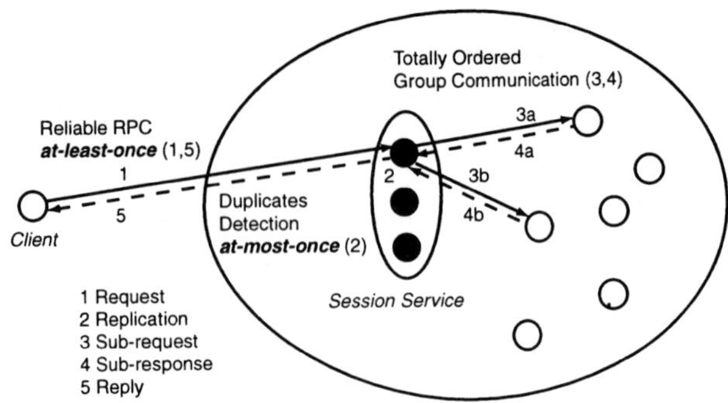

Figure 2. Exactly-once execution

based on processor architecture or operating system. The recovery instruction argument specifies the action that the session service should take in certain situations (such as whether to restart a process after a processor failure).

Clients can wait for processes using `SessionWait` or `ProcessWait`. `SessionWait` returns a reply when the last process in a session completes. `ProcessWait` waits for a particular process to complete. Using `SessionKill` or `ProcessKill`, processes can be terminated explicitly. The state of on-going sessions and processes can be examined using `SessionGetState` and `ProcessGetState`. Clients should destroy a session once it is no longer necessary using `SessionDestroy`.

4 Handling Client Requests

Carrying out a client request exactly-once is desirable not only because it avoids wasting resources, but because it simplifies maintaining consistency and coordinating multiple clients sharing the same session. However, achieving exactly-once execution is complicated when replicated objects are involved, since retransmissions of RPC requests may be dispatched to different servers. Servers must coordinate in order to filter out duplicated requests.

This section describes client-to-service and intra-service mechanisms that together ensure exactly-once execution per partition per view of client requests. The first subsection describes a reliable RPC mechanism that clients use to ensure at-least-once delivery of requests to the session service. The second subsection describes the mechanisms that the session service uses to ensure at-most-once execution of received client requests. Together they provide the desired behavior (see Figure 2).

4.1 At-Least-Once Semantics

Clients access their sessions by sending requests to session servers and receiving responses. RPC requests and responses are sent over TCP/IP connections. Before the first request, a client must select one of the session servers. For this, the client maintains a *confidence value* between 0 and 1 for each session server. When initiating an RPC to the service for the first time, the client picks the server that has the highest confidence value. A confidence value of 0 implies that the server is certainly down, while 1 implies that it is certainly up. Initially, the value is set to 0.5, and 0.1 is added to it every minute until it reaches 1. When a connection breaks, the confidence value of the corresponding server is halved, and a new server is chosen.

Connections to session servers are cached until they break or until the connection table in the operating system fills. In case of such communication problems, the client keeps choosing new servers and retransmitting the RPC request until it receives a corresponding response to the RPC request. That is, the client never gives up, so at-least-once semantics are achieved.

For each new RPC request, the client creates a new RPC identifier that consists of the client address and a sequence number that is incremented for each new RPC request. Retransmissions of the same RPC request, typically sent to different servers, carry the same RPC identifier.

Clients may obtain server addresses using the *White Pages service* (WP). This service maps ASCII service names (such as "Session Service") to a list of TCP/IP addresses for servers that implement the named service. Each server periodically sends a `Refresh` request to the WP service (currently, once a minute). The WP service lists those servers that have refreshed in this way during the last ten minutes. Each institute runs its own WP service. The RPC mechanism automatically contacts the WP service at the institute of choice (in this case, where the client wants to create the session). The WP service is replicated in way similar to the session service described in the next section.

4.2 At-Most-Once Semantics

This section describes mechanisms that the session service uses to detect duplicate requests to ensure at-most-once execution of each client request. Combined with the at-least-once delivery provided by our RPC facility, exactly-once execution of each client request is achieved.

As mentioned previously, session servers and process servers that serve the same processor group use group membership and totally ordered communication protocols. These protocols ensure that all servers agree on the delivery order of messages and on group membership changes relative to the message ordering. Agreement simplifies the task of consistency maintenance of replicated objects.

A client request is delivered initially to one of the servers. We call this server the *request manager*. Requests that can modify server state must be handled by all servers in the same order and at most once. A simple way of achieving this is by having the request manager multicast the request to the session service group. Each server executes the

Request	Arguments	Response
SessionCreate		session-id
ProcessCreate	session-id, processor specs, process properties, command list, recovery instruction	process-id list, failed commands
SessionWait	session-id	status
ProcessWait	session-id, process-id	status, small output
SessionKill	session-id	status
ProcessKill	session-id, process-id	status
SessionGetState	session-id	session state
ProcessGetState	session-id, process_id	process state
SessionDestroy	session-id	status

Table 1. Session management interface

request. If a request arrives at two different servers at approximately the same time, then they are both multicast, but the second to be delivered can be filtered automatically. In general, this approach to replication is costly because each server has to execute the request. More importantly, if request processing is non-deterministic, this approach does not work because the state of the servers would diverge.

These problems can be cured by adopting a primary-backup approach, where one of the servers, called the *primary*, carries out the request. The primary then multicasts a *state update* message to the other servers. The state update message describes how the backups should modify their state to replicate the primary. The main disadvantage of this approach is that a failure of the primary means that a fail-over delay is incurred (due to the length of failure detection and the subsequent agreement protocol).

To get the best of both approaches, PEX uses a hybrid protocol. Upon receiving a client request, the request manager carries out the non-deterministic part of computation but without actually changing state. The request manager then forwards the request, along with the result of the non-deterministic computation, to all servers, including itself. Since the session service group uses totally ordered communication, all servers receive these forwarded requests in the same order and will stay synchronized with each other.

When a session server receives a forwarded request, the server checks whether it has a *client-request record* with the same RPC identifier. If not, the request is new and the server creates a client request record for it. Next, the session server carries out the deterministic portion of processing, which may include generating, but not sending, *sub-requests* to one or more process servers. After the processing completes, only the request manager forwards sub-requests, if any, to the selected process servers. Process servers that receive a sub-request do processing and reply to all session servers when that processing is done. When all sub-requests have completed, each session server deterministically generates a reply and stores it in the server's client-request record. The request manager also sends the reply to the client. This way the correct state of the process is known by the session service, even if the request manager fails.

If a session server receives a client request for which it already has a client-request record, then it checks to see if the current request manager has failed (that is, removed from the process group). If it has, then the recipient of the retransmitted request becomes the new request manager. The new request manager checks the current state of the request. If the processing is completed, then it sends back the reply to the client. If it is still being processed, then it resends any sub-requests for which no replies were received, since it is possible that the sub-requests were lost. (To avoid duplicate processing of sub-requests, these messages contain a unique identifier as well.) After that, the protocol can be completed as normally.

5 Restoring Consistency

This section describes how the session service deals with server failures and network partitions. Instead of replicating entire processes themselves, only some of the objects implemented by these processes are replicated. Much of this section is devoted to discussing which objects are replicated, and how consistency of these objects is ensured.

Crashes and partitions are announced by the group membership service in the form of *view-changes*. In asynchronous distributed systems, it is impossible to distinguish the case of a processor being failed from the case of slow processor. The group membership protocol "solves" this problem by erroneously (but consistently) marking a slow processor as having failed. This is practical, because computation on other processors can then continue unimpeded.

A problem created by this solution is that a processor that joins a group might not be a newly started member with no state, but an old member that has partitioned away sometime ago and continued processing. In this case, it is possible for replicas of a single object to have divergent states at view-changes. To our knowledge, all existing group communication systems, if they support partitioned operations at all, adopt the primary partition state at view-changes. While algorithmically simple, this approach is unsatisfying when dealing with long running computations; by throwing away the state of a minority partition it is possible to lose the results calculated in a computation that has run a long time, simply because the primary partition did not know about it.

In general, constructing a consistent state out of divergent versions is application dependent. We designed PEX with a small set of replicated objects having states for which construction of consistent states is relatively easy: the process servers do not maintain replicated objects at all, and session servers maintain only three types of replicated objects: processor database, sessions (which contain process objects), and client-request records. We present state-merge algorithms for each of these.

5.1 Reconstruction of the Processor Database

PEX keeps the processor database consistent by reconstructing it from scratch when there is a view-change, rather than by trying to reconcile divergent versions of the database. Reconstruction is possible because the session service only uses the entries of accessible processors. The entries of inaccessible processors may differ at the different servers, but this does not matter.

The state of an accessible processor is known by the process server that is running on the processor. After a view-change, each process server multicasts its state to all session servers so that they can independently recreate the processor database. Ultimately, this scheme may not scale, since this means that potentially hundreds of processors broadcast a message on the network at the same time. Although we have not found these broadcasts to be a problem, we in the future may adopt a more sophisticated algorithm similar to those used in the other replicated objects described below.

5.2 Merging Session Object Replicas

A session is described by a *session object*, which in turn consists of a set of *process objects*. After a partition there may be multiple concurrent versions of the same session object, and ditto for a process object. Merging two versions of a session object involves making sure that every replica of a resultant session object contains the same set of process objects and that each process object refers to a single (live) process. PEX accomplishes this in two phases. In the first phase, the following subsets of the process objects are built:

- live set: processes that are up and running
- dead set: processes that have terminated
- kill set: (duplicate) processes that need to be killed
- restart set: (failed) processes that need to be restarted

Note that processes in the dead set are terminated only in this partition. They may still be running and be accessible in other partitions.

```
if Svr1 = Svr2 & alive(Svr1) then
    add(live, P1)
else if alive(Svr1) & dead(Svr2) then
    add(live, P1)
else if dead(Svr1) & alive(Svr2) then
    add(live, P2)
else if dead(Svr1) & dead(Svr2) then
    if to_restart(P1) then
        add(restart, P1)
    else
        add(dead, P1)
else if rank(Svr1) < rank(Svr2) then
    add(live, P1)
    add(kill, P2)
else
    add(live, P2)
    add(kill, P1)
```

Figure 3. Merging process object

In the second phase, the processes in the kill set are terminated and the processes in the restart set are restarted. (For efficiency, PEX actually reconciles the client-request records in between the two phases, since this merge may make additional changes to the sets.) We will now discuss these phases in more detail.

Group membership services allow the election of one member as *coordinator* of a partition. When partitions merge, the coordinators of the (old) partitions broadcast the state of the sessions in their respective partitions. Each session server merges these states pairwise. This ensures that the set of process objects in each session object is the same across all replicas provided that the merge operation used is deterministic and commutative.

The algorithm for merging two versions, P1 and P2, of the same process object is shown in Figure 3. If the two versions refer to the same process, only one is added to the set; if only one of the processes is accessible, the live one is used; if both are dead, it is placed into kill or restart set depending on the client's recovery instruction; otherwise (both are live processes) the rank of process server managing conflicting processes is used to pick a process to keep alive deterministically.

Merging two session objects takes the union of all process objects known by either session, while checking uniqueness of each process object. The union might include old processes that clients tried to remove, but this approach requires less space than maintaining the histories of session operations in each partition, which would be required to do a better job. Furthermore, clients can always get the state of sessions after merging and kill those processes that are not needed.

The same process identifier can refer to different processes. This happens when a client is partitioned from the original process and starts a new one. After the session objects merge, and only if both process servers are available, the one with the lowest rank is chosen and the other is terminated. If both process servers are unavailable, the process is restarted, possibly creating a third version of it.

After ensuring that each session replica contains the same process objects, the session service makes sure that there is exactly one physical process running for each process object with running state by killing processes in the kill set and restarting processes in the restart set.

The process server restarts a process by executing the same command used to start the process originally. It is up to the application to save its state if necessary. Restarting a process is similar to creation of a new process in that it involves nondeterministically picking a processor. However, rather than replicating the processor selection (which takes extra rounds of messages), one session server is put in charge of selecting a process server and sending a request to it. The process server in turn sends its reply back to all session servers. This way, the fact that the restarted process exists will be recorded, even if the session server that sent the request to the process server failed.

5.3 Merging Client-Request Record Replicas

As in merging session objects, merging client-request records proceeds in two phases. A request record contains sub-request records, each representing a message that has been sent to a different process server. Since request processing involves a non-deterministic selection of processors, processing the same client request again may not necessarily result in the same set of sub-requests. Rather than dealing with individual sub-requests, PEX simply adopts one of the request record versions at random in its entirety.

For requests that call for operations on all processes in a session (e.g., `SessionWait`), this approach might overlook some of these processes. This happens if processes not known by the partition where the requests were issued were later merged in. This is not a problem, since the same scenario can happen in a failure-free case, when a client adds a process while an old session-wide request is still being processed.

The first phase of merging request records is similar to that of session objects. It consists of the coordinator of each partition broadcasting the state of each replicated object on a view-change, and having each session server independently merge received states pairwise. Similar to process objects, the up/down status of the request manager is used to decide which version of the request record to keep, breaking ties using the ranks of the request managers.

As a result of processes terminating and restarting, some of the requests being served may not make sense (e.g., waiting for a dead process) or may become automatically done (e.g., killing an already dead process). The second phase of merging request records makes sure that requests represented are either being served or, if they are done, a reply is sent back to the client. [4] describes this algorithm in more detail.

6 Performance

PEX was written in Ocaml [6] over the Ensemble group communication system [3]. We used two applications for performance measurements: `dsh` and `omake`. `dsh` is a simple shell-like application that reads in a list of commands to execute along with pre-defined composable machine selection criteria (e.g., [7] describes criteria that work well even when processor load information is old). These are submitted to the execution service using the API of Section 3. `omake` is a parallel make program.

We ran our tests on Intel Pentium PCs running LINUX and on Sun SparcStations running either SunOS4 or Solaris. The processors were of mixed speeds, and connected by a collection of 10 and 100 Mbit/sec Ethernets.

6.1 Basic Operations

PEX is primarily intended for running long sessions. However, in order to measure the overhead of creating sessions and processes, we used sessions that only ran one short command (namely, Unix `uptime`). We measured the time between having `dsh` send a request and receive a response for the `SessionCreate`, `ProcessCreate`, and `SessionDestroy` operations. We ran our tests with session servers on three Pentium processors and process servers on SparcStations. Processor selection was random.

Table 2 shows the results for varying numbers of process servers. It takes longer to start many processes rather than a few, but even the longest time is negligible if processes are expected to run for hours, days, or even weeks.

We also measured the time it took to run `uptime` using `sh` and `rsh` on Sparc20 stations. For these measurements, we ran the command 100 times and took the average. These times are not strictly comparable to the `dsh` numbers presented, since we used the Unix `time` facility for measuring the overhead rather than `gettimeofday` system calls that we used inside our own programs. Despite this potential shortcoming of our measurements, it is instructive to note that run time using `dsh` is comparable to the best-case of starting the command locally. The reason that `dsh` is not faster is that it uses `sh` for parsing commands.

`rsh` is almost an order of magnitude slower than `dsh`. Doing this comparison is not entirely fair, since `rsh` and `dsh` have different goals. Among other overheads in `rsh`, a new `rsh` daemon is started for every invocation, and the output of the process created has to be captured and returned

Command	#Servers	Total (msec)	SessCreate	ProcCreate	SessDestroy
`uptime`	1	140			
`sh`	1	210			
`rsh`	1	1700			
`dsh`	1	208	10	51	3
`dsh`	2	293	9	56	2
`dsh`	4	326	9	66	2
`dsh`	8	462	9	126	2
`dsh`	16	506	9	119	2
`dsh`	32	817	8	201	2

Table 2. Performance of basic operations

to the user. With `dsh`, no daemons are started, and all processes run under a guest account.

6.2 Merging Divergent Versions

One of the concerns with replicated objects is the time overhead involved in maintaining consistency. PEX merges versions of replicated objects on view-changes. This section demonstrates that time overhead of merging replicated objects is negligible compared to the time it takes to install a view-change by the group membership service.

We did two experiments. In the first experiment, we measured the time it takes to reconstruct the processor database, while varying the number of process servers in the group. In the second experiment, we measured the time to merge session objects and request records, while varying the number of sessions. Each session contained a single process running Unix `sleep`. In both experiments, we ran the session servers on Pentium processors running LINUX and the process servers on SparcStations running SunOS.

PEX merges objects at view-change installations. Causing view-changes to happen for our experiments requires adding or killing a session or process server. This happens automatically in the first experiment. For the second experiment, we induced view-changes by periodically starting and crashing session servers.

Figure 4 shows the time it takes to reconstruct the processor database as a function of the number of process servers. The time to reconstruct the processor database is negligible compared to the view-change overhead. (The experiment was run only once for each number of process servers, and therefore outliers are visible.)

Figure 5 shows the time it takes to merge *all* replicated objects as a function of the number of sessions. This time includes reconstructing the processor database, but the overhead is approximately constant, since the number of process servers is now fixed. The merge overhead is approximately linear in the number of sessions and negligible compared to the overhead of view-changes.

Our experiment results raises a question: is it worth using a group membership service, since it is the source of most overhead in PEX? We believe the answer is yes. The

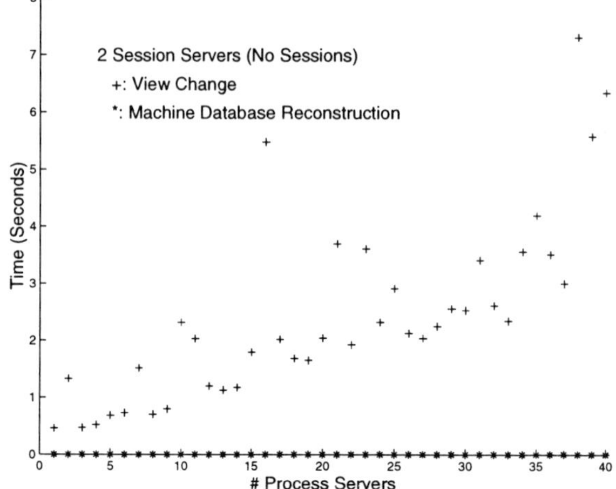

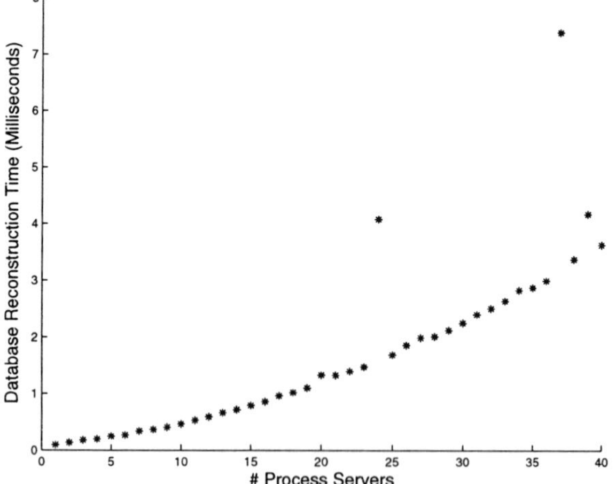

Figure 4. Processor database reconstruction

membership service provides automatic location and incorporation of new session and process servers, detection of their inaccessibility, so client requests do not stall, and ordered communication that facilitates replication. Were we to build such facilities within PEX, then we would have had to write significantly more code, and we would probably

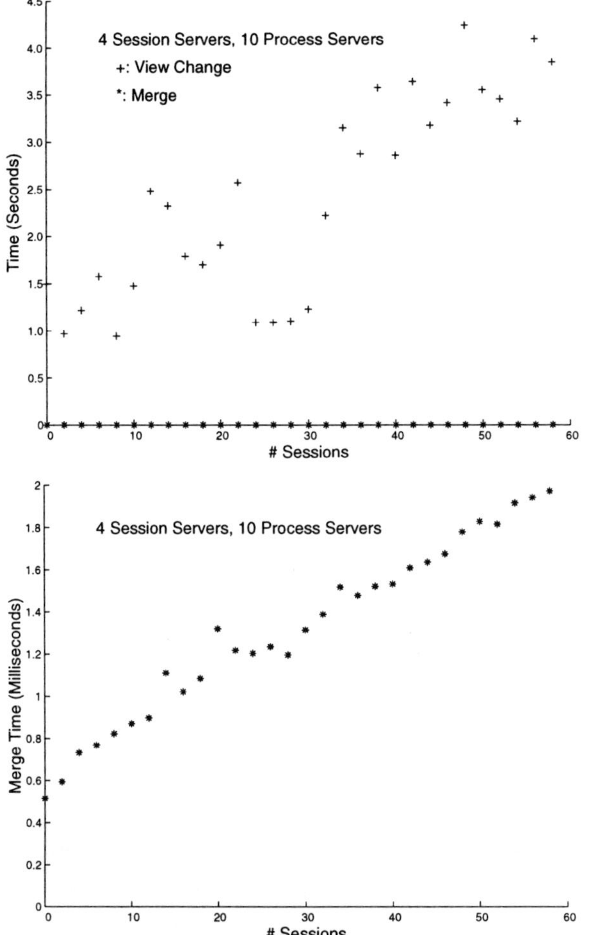

Figure 5. Merging divergent objects

not see much in the way of performance improvements at the end of that exercise.

7 Related Work

The PEX project is concerned with two sets of issues: load sharing in a distributed system, and partitionable operation. For an extensive overview of related work concerning these issues, see the full paper [4, 5]. Due to space limitations, we only mention the Relacs and Locus systems here.

Relacs [1] is a partitionable group communication system, much like Ensemble, and they suggest a number of partitionable applications. To our knowledge PEX is the only application actually implemented that handles non-trivial merging of replicated objects.

The LOCUS file system [10] developed a simple conflict detection mechanism based on *version vectors*. multiple writer conflicts, but not read-write conflicts. The LOCUS designers reasoned that this shortcoming is acceptable for most file systems, where files are independent of each other. LOCUS also developed a conflict resolution algorithm for directories. For other files, manual intervention is usually necessary. LOCUS includes a transparent execution environment for homogeneous processors.

8 Conclusion

PEX is an execution service for a partitionable low bandwidth network. PEX maintains highly available and long-running sessions of processes on behalf of users anywhere on the Internet. Besides the service itself, the contributions of our work include techniques for maintaining replicated objects that can partition and re-merge, and a demonstration of the use of the group membership paradigm.

Acknowledgments

The initial idea for building a remote execution service grew out of discussions with Mark Hayden. We thank Gary Adams, Ken Birman, Jason Hickey, Fred Schneider, and anonymous referees for comments on drafts of this paper.

References

[1] Ozalp Babaoglu, Renzo Davoli, Alberto Montresor, and Roberto Segala. System support for partition-aware network applications. In *Proceedings of the 18th International Conference on Distributed Computing Systems*, Amsterdam, The Netherlands, October 1998. IEEE Computer Society.

[2] Kenneth P. Birman. *Building Secure and Reliable Network Applications*. Manning, 1996.

[3] Mark Hayden. *The Ensemble System*. PhD thesis, Cornell University, January 1998.

[4] Takako M. Hickey. *Availability and Consistency in a Paritionable Low Bandwidth Network*. PhD thesis, Cornell University, August 1998.

[5] Takako. M. Hickey and Robbert Van Renesse. An execution service for a partitionable low bandwidth network. *http://www.cs.cornell.edu/home/rvr/papers/pex.ps*, 1999.

[6] Xavier Leroy. *The Objective Caml system release 1.07*. INRIA, Paris, France, March 1998.

[7] Michael Mitzenmacher. How useful is old information? In *Proceedings of the Sixteenth Annual ACM Symposium on Principles of Distributed Computing*, Santa Barbara, CA, USA, August 1997. ACM SIGACT-SIGOPS.

[8] NASA. Earth Observation System. http://eos.nasa.gov.

[9] Aleta Ricciardi, Michael Ogg, and Eric Rothfus. The Nile system architecture: Fault-tolerant, wide-area access to computing and data resources. In *Proceedings of Computing in High Energy Physics*, Rio de Janeiro, September 1995.

[10] Bruce Walker, Gerald Popek, Robert English, Charles Kline, and Greg Thiel. The LOCUS distributed operating system. In *Proceedings of the Ninth ACM Symposium on Operating Systems Principles*, pages 49–70, Bretton Woods, New Hampshire, October 1983. ACM SIGOPS.

Session 7B

Coding and On-Line Testing

Chair: Hideo Fujiwara
Nara Institute of Science and Technology, Japan

Automatic Design of Optimal Concurrent Fault Detector for Linear Analog Systems

Emmanuel SIMEU, Arno W. PETERS, Iyad RAYANE
TIMA-Laboratory,
46 Av. Félix Viallet F-38031 Grenoble, France
Emmanuel.Simeu@imag.fr

Abstract

This paper presents a generalized strategy for optimal design of on-line integrated fault detector for linear analog systems. The method consists in processing the available node voltage signals to provide a residual signal that carries information about the faults. Contrary to previously proposed techniques dealing only with the particular case of state variable systems, the use of extra circuitry with the objective of concurrent fault detection is extended here without limitation to a larger class of linear analog systems for which the state variables do not necessary need to be available as measurable voltages. This requires the use of an extended state space model for any linear analog system. For this purpose, an algorithm providing the extended state space model from a netlist description is developed and implemented.

1. Introduction

A novel fault detection methodology based on the use of analytical rather than physical redundancy has emerged and is increasingly discussed. For this purpose, the inherent redundancies contained in the static and dynamic relationships among the system input and measured signals are exploited. In other words, a mathematical model of the system or a part of it is used. In this paper, the problem of concurrent model-based fault detection is discussed for linear analog systems. Generally, the basic principle of concurrent testing techniques consists in exploiting the mathematical knowledge available on the monitored system to generate a fault indicating signal (called residual). The residuals express the difference between the signals coming from the actual system and the information provided by the system nominal model in the normal operation. When the mathematical model is an accurate representation of the nominal system behavior, the residuals generated characterize the system operating mode : close to zero in normal operation, different from zero if there is a mismatch. The goal is to detect the faults of interest and their causes early enough so that a failing of the overall system can be avoided. Residuals are generated on-line by means of dedicated additional hardware into the system data flow graph. The idea of designing additional hardware for error detection and fault tolerance was applied to FFT networks by Jou and Abraham in [1]. Chatterjee used the checksum codes developed in the above work in [2] for concurrent error detection in linear analog and switched-capacitor state variable systems. In contrast to the previous works using algorithm-based fault tolerance ([3], [4]) the error detection process is directly hard-wired into the system using additional detection circuitry. The method proposed in [2] is applicable only to state variable systems. Such systems consist of a serial interconnection of integrators and summers (realized with op-amps). The availability for physical connection of all the state variables facilitates redundancy generation and the design of concurrent error detection schemes. In the approach proposed in this paper, the use of extra circuitry with the objective of on-line fault detection is extended to a larger class of linear analog systems, with detection dedicated circuitry often comparable to those used in the previous works, for only state variable systems. The scheme that is proposed here involves the elimination of unknown state variables by aggregation using linear combinations of input, output and available node signals. Test dedicated hardware is optimized by a reduction of the number of integration (or derivations) required for residual generation. To minimize the overhead for implementation, information contained on any circuit node available for measurement should be usable as input of the detector scheme. This required a mathematical model of the circuit providing not only the classical behavioral relationships between the circuit input and its functional output, but also an appropriated modeling of the signal on any internal node.

In this paper, a symbolic method to derive an appropriated state space model, from any linear analog circuit netlist

0-7695-0213-X/99 $10.00

description is described. The algorithm presented in section 2 is implemented to transform the netlist description (Spice netlist for example) of linear analog circuit, into an extended space state model usable for residual generation. A dead-beat observers method described in section 3 uses the previous extended state model to generate the equations describing the optimal fault detector circuitry, for a large class of linear analog circuit.

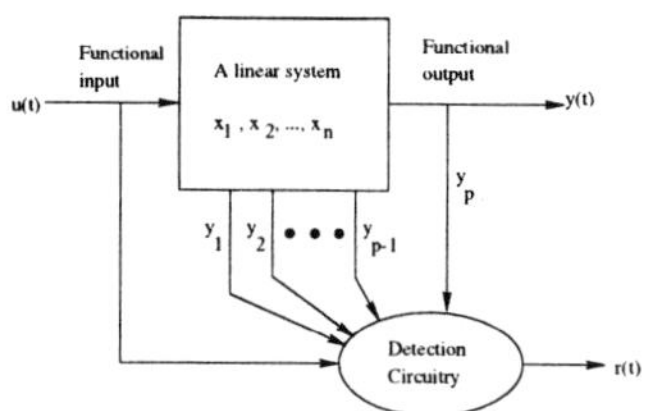

Figure 1. Residual generation scheme.

2. From netlist to extended state space model

The first step of any model based fault detection method is the determination of an appropriate mathematical behavioral model of the system under test. The mathematical knowledge available on this model is then exploited to generate a residual that will be used as fault indicating signal. Taking into account the system nominal model, the residual is obtained by the processing of available signals provided by sensors and actuators. Electronic circuits are driven by voltage sources and current sources. Hence, there are no actuators to the circuit other than these sources. Also, there are no additional sensors necessary to measure voltages.

2.1. Modeling requirements for concurrent testing

The few publications that focus on on-line error detection for electronic circuits deal with fully available systems [2]. For this type of circuit, all state variables are voltages and can be easily tapped from the circuit under test. When the system state variables are not directly connectable, on line fault detection can be perform using the classical input/output behavioral model, that is generally used for functional output simulation. Unfortunately, the use of such a simulation model for concurrent testing of analog circuit would be too costly in term of additional circuitry. Measuring currents is problematic because the corresponding signals have to be read with minimal disturbance to the primary function of the circuit under test. It is assumed in this paper that only circuit node voltages are available for measurement. The corresponding node voltage are assumed to be read through voltage followers without disturbance of initial functionality of the circuit under test. Figure 1 shows that the residual is build from the functional outputs and the internal node voltages of the circuit. Contrary to the models generally used for functional output simulation, the extended model required for fault detection must also give :
• an estimation of the signal on any internal node;
• a model for unknown inputs or noise effects ;
• a model for fault effects.
In the extended model, the circuit unknown inputs modeling the noise sources are clearly differentiated to the faulty behavior. The required extended model for the circuit may have the following state equations form :

$$\dot{\mathbf{x}} = \mathbf{A}\,\mathbf{x(t)} + \mathbf{B}\,\mathbf{u(t)} + \mathbf{E}\,\mathbf{d(t)} + \mathbf{K}\,\mathbf{f}; \quad (1)$$
$$\mathbf{y(t)} = \mathbf{C}\,\mathbf{x(t)} + \mathbf{D}\,\mathbf{u(t)} + \mathbf{F}\,\mathbf{d(t)} + \mathbf{G}\,\mathbf{f}. \quad (2)$$

In these equations, $\mathbf{x(t)}$ is the state vector of size $\mathbf{n}$, $\mathbf{u(t)}$ is the input vector, $\mathbf{y(t)}$ is the output vector of size $\mathbf{p}$. Each output component $\mathbf{y_i(t)}$ represents the voltage signal on node number $\mathbf{i}$. $\mathbf{d(t)}$ is a vector modeling the effects of unknown inputs and disturbances when vector $\mathbf{f}$ models the fault effects. $\mathbf{A}$, $\mathbf{B}$, $\mathbf{C}$, $\mathbf{D}$, $\mathbf{E}$, $\mathbf{F}$, $\mathbf{G}$ and $\mathbf{K}$ are matrixes with time invariant components and appropriate dimensions. A similar model has been used in the topic of automatic control for fault detection and identification [5]. The problem that has to be solved is : how to derive such extended state space model from the classical analog circuit description tools.

2.2. Netlist description of analog circuits

The choice of a model to represent a dynamical system depends on the situation and the type of analysis required. Among the modeling techniques available for analog circuit representation : Circuit diagrams; Block diagrams; Bond graphs, netlist description. The netlist representation is not really usual for analog systems. It is generally used as an intermediary stage between the previous representation techniques and the mathematical behavioral models, usable for system simulation. Figure 2 shows the schematic and the corresponding netlist for a fourth order low pass filter.

2.3. Causal variable/equation dependency matrix

Any linear element in a SPICE circuit description defines a topologic equations. The connections of different elements in a circuit give possible additions of Kirchoff node equations. For simplicity and without loss of generality, the noise caused by the effects of resistors heating is the only unknown inputs taken into account in the system modeling. Their influence can be modeled as a small voltage source E_R in series with the resistor. This voltage source is an unknown input because it cannot be measured or controlled. This modeling can easily be extended to any other

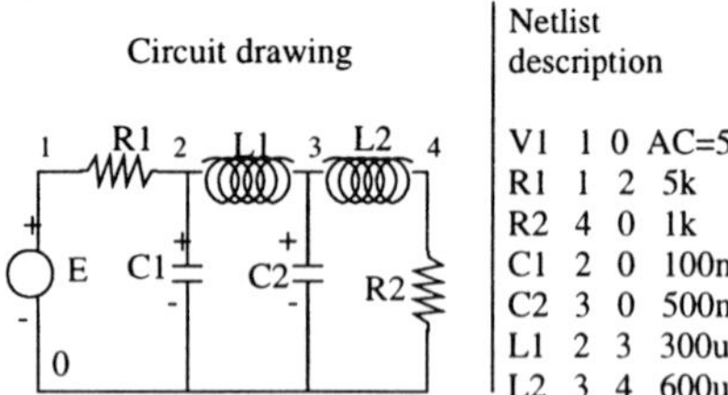

Figure 2. Circuit schematic and netlist for a fourth order low pass filter.

type of noise disturbing the system nominal behavior. A state equation is an equation containing one or more signal derivatives sx_i and the corresponding state variable is the signal x_i. Variables that are indexed are: derived state variables $sx_1, \ldots, sx_n$, current variables i_{XX} and node variables $u_0, \ldots, u_j$. Equations are subdivided: state equations, node equations and topology equations. For the fourth order low pass filter (Figure 2) the following variables are identified:

- derived state variables: sx_0, sx_1, sx_2 and sx_3
- current variables: $i_{R_1}, i_{R_2}, i_{C_1}, i_{C_2}, i_{L_1}$ and i_{L_2}
- voltage potential variables: u_0, u_1, u_2, u_3 and u_4;
- input variables: V_1;
- unknown input variables: E_{R_1} and E_{R_2}.

With the method outlined in this section, the following equations are obtained:

- State equations

$$-sx_0 \cdot C_1 + i_{C_1} = 0;$$
$$-sx_1 \cdot C_2 + i_{C_2} = 0;$$
$$-sx_2 \cdot L_1 + (u_2 - u_3) = 0;$$
$$-sx_3 \cdot L_2 + (u_3 - u_4) = 0.$$

- Topology equations

$$-V_1 + (u_1 - u_0) = 0;$$
$$-i_{R_1} \cdot R_1 + (u_1 - u_2 - E_{R_1}) = 0;$$
$$-i_{R_2} \cdot R_2 + (u_4 - u_0 - E_{R_2}) = 0;$$
$$-x_0 + (u_2 - u_0) = 0;$$
$$-x_1 + (u_3 - u_0) = 0;$$
$$-x_2 + i_{L_1} = 0;$$
$$-x_3 + i_{L_2} = 0;$$
$$u_0 = 0.$$

- Kirchoff node equations

$$-i_{R_1} + i_{C_1} + i_{L_1} = 0;$$
$$+i_{R_2} - i_{L_2} = 0;$$
$$+i_{C_2} - i_{L_1} + i_{L_2} = 0.$$

A matrix that holds the variable/equation dependencies can be constructed. The rows of the matrix correspond to successive equations and the columns of the matrix index a variable. The matrix is filled with zeros and ones. A one (black point) in position (r, c) indicates equation r contains the variable c. A zero indicates that the equation does not contain this variable. Figure 3 (before causality, on the left side of the figure) shows how this translates into a variable/equation dependency matrix. Each row represents an equation in the order given above. Each column represents a variable also in the order given above. In this step, it's a

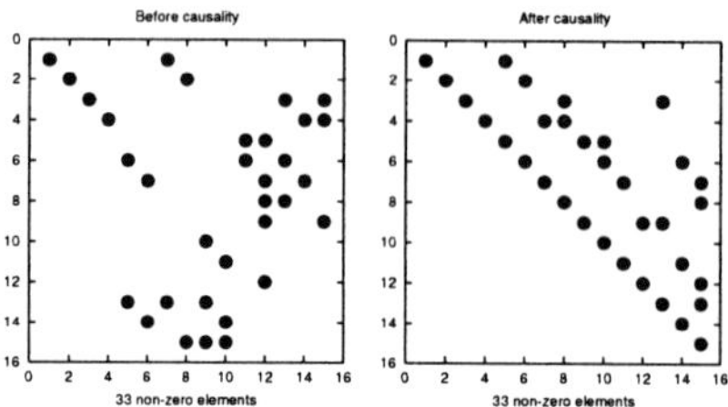

Figure 3. V/E dependency matrix for fourth order low pass filter.

question of arranging equations and variables in such a way that they can be successively and easily solved. Causality is assigned to initial non-causal equations stored in the adjacency matrix. The degree of dependency is calculated for each of the following depending variables: derived state variables (sx_X); current variables: (i_{R_X}, i_{C_X}, i_{L_X}) and node voltage potential variables: (u_X).

The degree of dependency $nd(\sigma)$ assigned to each depending variable σ is equal to the number of equations that contain the variable σ. As the input signal, state variables x_X are considered as explicit variables. The calculation of the dependency degree of such explicit variable is not useful in this section. In the example of the low pass filter, the initial dependency degree for each variable is

- $sx_0, sx_1, sx_2, sx_3 \Longrightarrow 1$
- $i_{R_2}, i_{C_1}, i_{C_2}, u_1, u_4 \Longrightarrow 2$
- $i_{L_1}, i_{L_2}, i_{R_1}, u_2, u_3 \Longrightarrow 3$
- $u_0 \Longrightarrow 5$.

The algorithm of Figure 4 is run in order to assign a causal order to equations. Each step of the algorithm of Figure 4 solves a variable σ_k and an equation Eq_k. The weighting of unsolved variables must be adjusted by decreasing the degree of dependency of unsolved variables that are used in equation Eq_k. Finding multiple dependency equations means the existence of loops that have to be solved later on. In this case, the remaining variables are reordered on weighted dependency. Lowest dependency degree come first; highest dependency degree last. If the number of equations/variables is n, it can be proved that the algorithm presented here can assign causality in worst-case time complexity of

$$O\Big(\sum_{k=1}^{n} k \log k\Big) \leq O\left(n^2 \log n\right).$$

Figure 3 (after causality, on the right) shows the causal variable/equation dependency matrix (CDM) for the fourth order low pass filter. The columns of the figure on the right hold the variables: $sx_0, sx_1, sx_2, sx_3, i_{C_1}, i_{C_2}, u_4, u_3, i_{R_1}, i_{L_1}, i_{R_2}, u_1, u_2, i_{L_2}, u_0$. The rows show the equations:

$$\begin{aligned}
-sx_0 \cdot C_1 + i_{C_1} &= 0;\\
-sx_1 \cdot C_2 + i_{C_2} &= 0;\\
-sx_2 \cdot L_1 + (u_2 - u_3) &= 0;\\
-sx_3 \cdot L_2 + (u_3 - u_4) &= 0;\\
-i_{R_1} + i_{C_1} + i_{L_1} &= 0;\\
+i_{C_2} - i_{L_1} + i_{L_2} &= 0;\\
-i_{R_2} \cdot R_2 + (u_4 - u_0 - E_{R_2}) &= 0;\\
-x_1 + (u_3 - u_0) &= 0;\\
-i_{R_1} \cdot R_1 + (u_1 - u_2 - E_{R_1}) &= 0;\\
-x_2 + i_{L_1} &= 0;\\
+i_{R_2} - i_{L_2} &= 0;\\
-V_1 + (u_1 - u_0) &= 0;\\
-x_0 + (u_2 - u_0) &= 0;\\
-x_3 + i_{L_2} &= 0;\\
u_0 &= 0.
\end{aligned}$$

Similar results were obtained for other types of circuits.

2.4. Deriving the nominal model

Using the causal variable/equation dependency matrix, the system can be solved by a simple back-substitution of variables starting at the last equation and working up to the first. The back-substitution gives a number of state equations of signal variables depending only on the explicit variables (inputs signal or state variables) and the component parameters. Any equation with a single dependency has the following form :
$\gamma z + \delta_1 x_1 + \delta_2 x_2 + ... + \delta_n x_n + \eta u$
where z is the corresponding depending variable, $x_1, x_2, ..., x_n$, are the state variables and u is the input signal. This equation can be written in the following explicative form, expressing the depending variable as function of the input signal and state variables :
$z = \Gamma_1.x_1 + \Gamma_2.x_2 + ... + \Gamma_n.x_n + \Upsilon.u$
Isolating the variables selected by the causality assignment process yields the following equations in the case of the

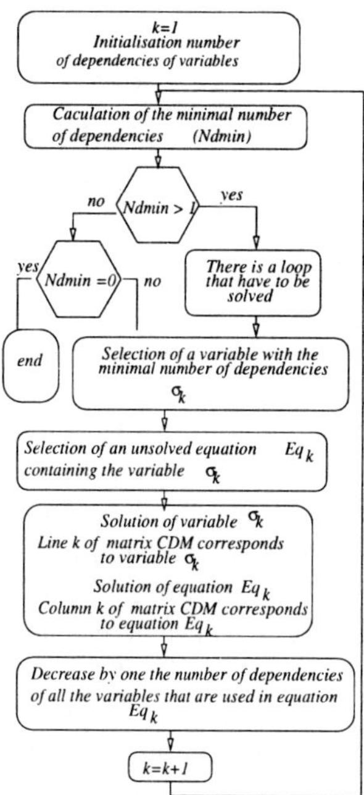

Figure 4. Causal dependency matrix algorithm.

low pass filter:

$$\begin{aligned}
sx_0 &= i_{C_1}/C_1;\\
sx_1 &= i_{C_2}/C_2;\\
sx_2 &= (u_2 - u_3)/L_1;\\
sx_3 &= 1/L_2 \cdot u_3 - u_4/L_2;\\
i_{C_1} &= i_{R_1} - i_{L_1};\\
i_{C_2} &= i_{L_1} - i_{L_2};\\
u_4 &= R_2 \cdot i_{R_2} + (u_0 + E_{R_2});\\
u_3 &= u_0 + x_1;\\
i_{R_1} &= -1/R_1 \cdot u_2 + (u_1 - E_{R_1})/R_1;\\
i_{L_1} &= x_2;\\
i_{R_2} &= i_{L_2};\\
u_1 &= u_0 + V_1;\\
u_2 &= u_0 + x_0;\\
i_{L_2} &= x_3;\\
u_0 &= 0.
\end{aligned}$$

Now, these equations have to be put into matrix form with the state variables split off from the element parameters. The equations expressing the state variable derivatives (sx_i) function of input signal and state variables constitute the state dynamic equation. The equations giving the node voltage signals (u_j) function of input signal and state variables form the system output equation. The nominal model has the following expressions.

$$\dot{\mathbf{x}} = \begin{pmatrix} \frac{-1}{R_1C_1} & 0 & \frac{-1}{C_1} & 0 \\ 0 & 0 & \frac{1}{C_2} & \frac{-1}{C_2} \\ \frac{1}{L_1} & \frac{-1}{L_1} & 0 & 0 \\ 0 & \frac{1}{L_2} & 0 & \frac{-R_2}{L_2} \end{pmatrix} \mathbf{x} + \begin{pmatrix} \frac{1}{R_1C_1} \\ 0 \\ 0 \\ 0 \end{pmatrix} V_1$$

$$\begin{pmatrix} y_1 \\ y_2 \\ y_3 \end{pmatrix} = \begin{pmatrix} u_2 \\ u_4 \\ u_3 \end{pmatrix} = \begin{pmatrix} 1 & 0 & 0 & 0 \\ 0 & 0 & 0 & R_2 \\ 0 & 1 & 0 & 0 \end{pmatrix} \mathbf{x} + \begin{pmatrix} 0 \\ 0 \\ 0 \end{pmatrix} V_1$$

2.5. Unknown input and fault model

Noise generated by the elements should *not* be considered as a fault; their effect is temporary and does not affect the functionality of the circuit. For simplicity and without loss of generality, it is assumed here that only resistors (and conductors) generate noise. Their influence is modeled as a small voltage source E_R in series with the resistor. This voltage source is an unknown input to the system because it cannot be measured or controlled. This modeling can easily be extended to any other type of noise disturbing the system nominal behavior. The machinery described in subsections 2.3–2.4 derives the matrixes for the unknown inputs. For the fourth order low pass filter, the unknown input model is:

$$E = \begin{pmatrix} \frac{1}{R_1C_1} & \frac{1}{R_1C_1} \\ 0 & 0 \\ 0 & 0 \\ 0 & 0 \end{pmatrix} \qquad F = \begin{pmatrix} 0 & 0 \\ 0 & 0 \\ 0 & 0 \end{pmatrix}$$

Noise affects the state variables because $\mathbf{E}$ is non-zero. But noise does not directly influence the outputs as $\mathbf{F}$ is zero.

Fault models describe how fault processes interact with the function of the hardware. A linear approximation around the nominal model is used to extract a fault model. Matrices $\mathbf{A}$ and $\mathbf{B}$ can be concatenated as they are affected by the same element faults.

$$\begin{pmatrix} \mathbf{A} + \Delta\mathbf{A}\mathbf{f} & \mathbf{B} + \Delta\mathbf{B}\mathbf{f} \end{pmatrix} \tag{3}$$

The nominal symbolic matrix for each element is substituted by a linear approximation. Any faulty element X in the circuit is replaced by a power series as follows:

$$X \mapsto X \cdot \left(1 + \frac{dX}{X} + O\left(\frac{dX}{X}^2\right)\right).$$

This substitution is made for each element in the symbolic matrix. Then the fault matrix can be extracted without difficulty. The power series $O(\cdot)$ nullified and the fault matrix can then be subtracted from the nominal matrix to obtain the difference matrix. This gives the linear approximation for the difference variables for each element.

3. The detection circuit design

The extended state space model derived in the previous section for linear analog circuits is used in this section to design an optimal error detection circuit. The detection circuitry is built using the dead-beat observer principle. The observer is combined so that its output is zero under nominal conditions and non-zero in faulty conditions.

3.1. Optimal dead-beat observer

It is assumed that the circuit model can be described with Equations (1) and (2). In general, state vector $\mathbf{x}$ is not directly measurable from the circuit under test. The error detection circuitry must use only available measurable signals : input vector $\mathbf{u}$, and output vector $\mathbf{y}$. The unknown state parameters of vector $\mathbf{x}$ have to be eliminated from Equations (1) and (2). This goal is achieved by expressing the successive derivatives of the output vector $\mathbf{y}$ explicitly in terms of $\mathbf{x}$, $\mathbf{u}$, $\mathbf{d}$ and $\mathbf{f}$. For simplicity and without loss of generality, only single input is considered. The k successive first derivatives of the output vector are given by the following equations :

$$\begin{aligned} \mathbf{y}^{(0)}(t) &= \mathbf{C}\mathbf{x}^{(0)}(t) + \mathbf{D}\mathbf{u}^{(0)}; \\ \mathbf{y}^{(1)}(t) &= \mathbf{C}\mathbf{A}\mathbf{x}^{(0)}(t) + \mathbf{C}\mathbf{B}\mathbf{u}^{(0)}(t) + \mathbf{D}\mathbf{u}^{(1)}(t); \\ &\vdots \\ \mathbf{y}^{(k)}(t) &= \mathbf{C}\mathbf{A}^k\mathbf{x}^{(0)}(t) + \mathbf{C}\mathbf{A}^{k-1}\mathbf{B}\mathbf{u}^{(0)}(t) + \cdots + \\ &\quad + \mathbf{C}\mathbf{A}\mathbf{B}\mathbf{u}^{(k-2)}(t) + \mathbf{C}\mathbf{B}\mathbf{u}^{(k-1)}(t) + \mathbf{D}\mathbf{u}^{(k)}(t). \end{aligned}$$

To obtain the equations for $\mathbf{d}$, substitute in the above equations $\mathbf{E}$ for $\mathbf{B}$ and $\mathbf{F}$ for $\mathbf{D}$; likewise for $\mathbf{f}$, substitute $\mathbf{K}$ for $\mathbf{B}$ and $\mathbf{G}$ for $\mathbf{D}$.

These equations can be grouped in the following matrix form :

$$Y^{[k]} = \mathbf{Ob}_k\mathbf{x}(t) + \mathbf{H}_u^{[k]}U^{[k]} + \mathbf{H}_d^{[k]}D^{[k]} + \mathbf{H}_f^{[k]}F^{[k]} \tag{4}$$

where

$$Y^{[k]} = \begin{pmatrix} \mathbf{y}^{(0)}(t) \\ \mathbf{y}^{(1)}(t) \\ \vdots \\ \mathbf{y}^{(k)}(t) \end{pmatrix}; \; U^{[k]} = \begin{pmatrix} \mathbf{u}^{(0)}(t) \\ \mathbf{u}^{(1)}(t) \\ \vdots \\ \mathbf{u}^{(k)}(t) \end{pmatrix};$$

$$D^{[k]} = \begin{pmatrix} \mathbf{d}^{(0)}(t) \\ \mathbf{d}^{(1)}(t) \\ \vdots \\ \mathbf{d}^{(k)}(t) \end{pmatrix}; \; F^{[k]} = \begin{pmatrix} \mathbf{f}^{(0)}(t) \\ \mathbf{f}^{(1)}(t) \\ \vdots \\ \mathbf{f}^{(k)}(t) \end{pmatrix} \; \mathbf{Ob}_k = \begin{pmatrix} \mathbf{C} \\ \mathbf{CA} \\ \vdots \\ \mathbf{CA}^k \end{pmatrix}. \tag{5}$$

and

$$\mathbf{H}_u^{[k]} = \begin{pmatrix} \mathbf{D} & \mathbf{0} & \dots & \mathbf{0} & \mathbf{0} \\ \mathbf{CB} & \mathbf{D} & \ddots & \mathbf{0} & \mathbf{0} \\ \mathbf{CAB} & \mathbf{CB} & \ddots & \mathbf{0} & \mathbf{0} \\ \vdots & \vdots & \ddots & \ddots & \vdots \\ \mathbf{CA}^{k-1}\mathbf{B} & \mathbf{CA}^{k-2}\mathbf{B} & \dots & \mathbf{CB} & \mathbf{D} \end{pmatrix}; \quad (6)$$

The matrix $\mathbf{H}_d^{[k]}$ (respectively $\mathbf{H}_f^{[k]}$) is obtained from the expression of matrix $\mathbf{H}_u^{[k]}$ by substituting $\mathbf{B}$ by $\mathbf{E}$ (respectively by $\mathbf{K}$) and $\mathbf{D}$ by $\mathbf{F}$ (respectively by $\mathbf{G}$). The integer k is number of output derivatives required for residual generation. k will also be the order of the residual, i.e. the number of integration needed in the residual generation scheme. Generally, in the case of electronic circuits, more than one integration is rarely necessary. If n is the order of the system, then $\mathbf{Ob}_k\ |_{k=n-1}$ is the observability matrix of the system. In the nominal conditions ($d(t) = f(t) = 0$) Equation (4) has the following simpler form :

$$Y^{[k]} = \mathbf{Ob}_k\mathbf{x}(t) + \mathbf{H}_u^{[k]}U^{[k]} \quad (7)$$

In Equation (7), it is clear that the signal vectors $Y^{[k]}$ (node signal vector) and $U^{[k]}$ (input vector) are assumed to be measurable, when the state vector $x(t)$ is not necessarily available for connection. The basic idea of the residual generation method presented in this paper consists of eliminating the unknown variable in Equation (7). This elimination may be performed by combination of equations or by projection. The projection technique consists of determining the subspace P_s of all the vectors $\mathbf{v}$ defined by Equation (8).

$$P_s = \{\mathbf{v}|\mathbf{v}^{\mathrm{T}}\mathbf{Ob_k} = 0\} \quad (8)$$

Every vector $\mathbf{v}_j$ of the subspace P_s can be used to generate a scalar residual $r_j(t)$ that can be used for a parity chek. Equation (9) will just do that.

$$r_j(t) = \mathbf{v}_j^{\mathrm{T}}\left(Y^{[k]} - \mathbf{H}_u^{[k]}U^{[k]}\right) \quad (9)$$

Using Equations (4) and (8), the expression of the residual r_j become

$$\begin{aligned} r_j(t) &= \mathbf{v}_j^{\mathrm{T}}\left(\mathbf{Ob_k x(t)} + \mathbf{H}_d^{[k]}D^{[k]} + \mathbf{H}_f^{[k]}F^{[k]}\right) \\ &= \mathbf{v}_j^{\mathrm{T}}\left(\mathbf{H}_d^{[k]}D^{[k]} + \mathbf{H}_f^{[k]}F^{[k]}\right) \end{aligned}$$

From this explicative form, it is clear that the residual r_j is a function of $\mathbf{d}$ and $\mathbf{f}$ but not function of input $\mathbf{u}$. Hence r_j can be used for the purpose of fault detection. When there is no fault ($\mathbf{f} = 0$), then r_j is only influenced by unknown inputs, $\mathbf{d}$. When however a fault occurs ($\mathbf{f} \neq 0$) r_j is influenced by both $\mathbf{f}$ and $\mathbf{d}$ and its value increases. Thus, a fault can be detected by checking the increment of r_j caused by $\mathbf{f}$. For the low pass filter of Figure (2), an application of the relations defined in Equation 5 (for $k = 1$) gives

$$Y^{[1]T} = \begin{pmatrix} y_1 & y_2 & y_3 & \dot{y}_1 & \dot{y}_2 & \dot{y}_3 \end{pmatrix}, U^{[1]T} = \begin{pmatrix} u & \dot{u} \end{pmatrix}$$

$$\mathbf{Ob}_1 = \begin{pmatrix} 1 & 0 & 0 & 0 \\ 0 & 0 & 0 & R_2 \\ 0 & 1 & 0 & 0 \\ \frac{-1}{R_1C_1} & 0 & \frac{-1}{C_1} & 0 \\ 0 & \frac{R_2}{L_2} & 0 & \frac{-R_2^2}{L_2} \\ 0 & 0 & \frac{1}{C_2} & \frac{-1}{C_2} \end{pmatrix}, \mathbf{H}_u^{[1]} = \begin{pmatrix} 0 & 0 \\ 0 & 0 \\ 0 & 0 \\ \frac{1}{R_1C_1} & 0 \\ 0 & 0 \\ 0 & 0 \end{pmatrix} \quad (10)$$

Since $\mathbf{Ob}_1$ is not a full line-rank matrix, the subspace P_s orthogonal to $\mathbf{Ob}_1$ and defined by Equation 8 is not *zero*. It is easy to verify that the vectors $\mathbf{v}_1$ and $\mathbf{v}_2$ defined by Equation (11) belong to P_s

$$\begin{aligned} \mathbf{v}_1^{\mathrm{T}} &= \begin{pmatrix} R_2 & R_1 & 0 & R_1R_2C_1 & 0 & R_1R_2C_2 \end{pmatrix}; \\ \mathbf{v}_2^{\mathrm{T}} &= \begin{pmatrix} 0 & 0 & R_2 & C_1R_2^2 & -L_2 & C_2R_2^2 \end{pmatrix}. \end{aligned} \quad (11)$$

According to Equation (9), the vectors $\mathbf{v}_1$ and $\mathbf{v}_2$ can be used to provide two independent residuals $r_1(t)$ and $r_2(t)$ defined respectively by the following equations.

$$\begin{aligned} r_1(t) &= R_2y_1 + R_2y_2 + R_{-1}R_2C_1\dot{y}_1 + R_{-1}R_2C_2\dot{y}_3 - \frac{u}{R_1C_1} \\ r_2(t) &= R_2y_3 + R_2^2C_1\dot{y}_1 - L_2\dot{y}_2 + R_2^2C_2\dot{y}_3 \end{aligned} \quad (12)$$

More generally, to any linear combination of form $\mathbf{v}_j = \delta_1\mathbf{v}_1 + \delta_1\mathbf{v}_2$ corresponds a scalar residual defined by Equation (9). Equation (13) gives the general expression of such a scalar residual.

$$r_j(t) = \alpha_0y_1 + \beta_0y_2 + \gamma_0y_3 + \alpha_1\dot{y}_1 + \beta_1\dot{y}_2 + \gamma_1\dot{y}_3 + \lambda_0u \quad (13)$$

Where the design parameters α_0, β_0, γ_0, α_1, β_1, γ_1 and λ_0 are function of vector $\mathbf{v}_j$.

Ideally, the resulting detector should react strongly under the presence of a fault but should not react to unknown inputs to the system, like noise. The following equations put these words into mathematical rigor.

$$\mathbf{v}_j^{\mathrm{T}}\mathbf{H}_f^{[k]} \neq 0; \quad (14)$$

$$\mathbf{v}_j^{\mathrm{T}}\mathbf{H}_d^{[k]} = 0. \quad (15)$$

Finding a vector $\mathbf{v}_j^{\mathrm{T}}$ that satisfies Equations (8)–(15) creates a residue that is unaffected by unknown inputs but is affected by a fault. These equations may not yield a solution. An optimal approximation can be used. It is useful to define a performance measurement that shows in a way how much the detector is sensitive to faults and insensitive to unknown inputs. The following performance index satisfies these constraints:

$$P = \frac{\|\mathbf{v}_j^T \mathbf{H}_d^{[k]}\|}{\|\mathbf{v}_j^T \mathbf{H}_f^{[k]}\|} \tag{16}$$

where $\|\cdot\|$ is the 2-norm; the largest singular value of the matrix. Minimizing P will yield the desired residual.

3.2. Residual implementation

Normally, the implementation of the residual r_j using Equation (9) requires the differentiation of the output and input signals. This operation is prone to error. Integrating the Equation (13) once (k times in the general case) replaces differentiation by integration. The drawback of this trick is a potentially unstable pole at $s = 0$. The stabilization is obtained by using a negative feedback factor $P = -p_0$ of the residual output into the detection circuit. To provide a stable residual signal, pure integrator has to be replaced by a one a order filter. The division of the Laplace transform of relations (13) by $(s + p_0)$ gives the expression of filtered residual r_{fj}, usable for on line fault detection.

$$r_{fj}(s) = \frac{\alpha_0 y_1(s) + \beta_0 y_2(s) + \gamma_0 y_3(s) + \lambda_0 u(s)}{s + p_0} + \frac{+s\alpha_1 y_1(s) + s\beta_1 y_2(s) + s\gamma_1 y_3(s)}{s + p_0} \tag{17}$$

The use of a one order transfer function provides a mean to control the sensitivity of the residual signal to tolerances in component values. As in [2], the residual filter also allows an adjustment of the response of the test circuitry to sharp transients. The general scheme of the residual block diagram an the corresponding detection circuit schematic are given on Figures 5 and 6 respectively. The size of the detection circuitry is only function of the number k of output derivatives required in the residual generation process. This number depends on the quality of information available on node voltages and not on the size of the circuit under test.

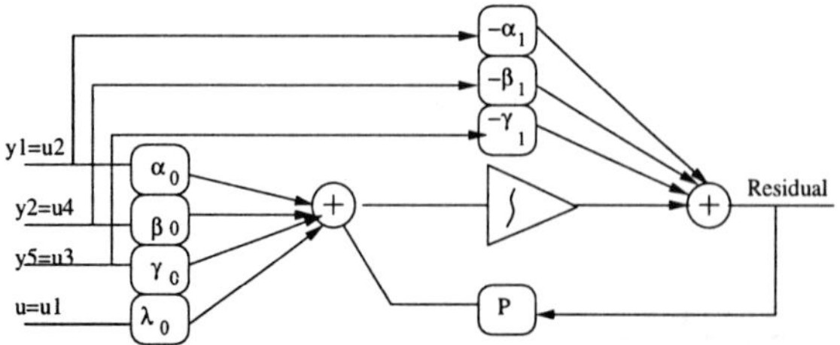

Figure 5. Block diagram of the error detection circuit.

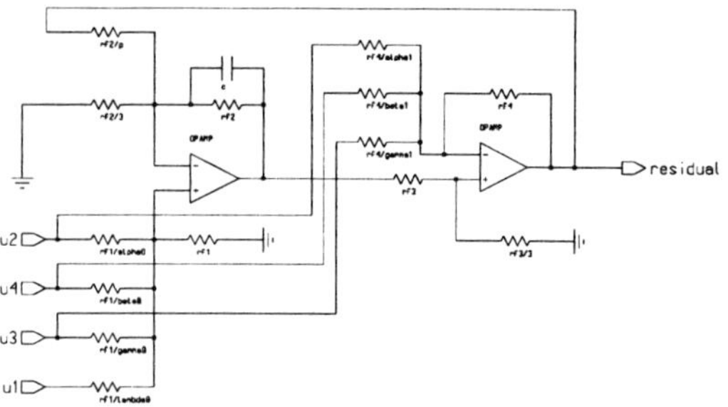

Figure 6. Schematic of one order detection circuit.

4. Simulation results

The method described in the previous sections has been applied to different type of analog circuits including biquadratic filter, high pass filter, Pierce oscillator, and to the low pass filter example of Figure 2. For simplicity, the results presented in this section correspond to the low pass filter circuit of Figure 2 only. The results obtained for the other circuits where very similar and are not presented here.

In all simulations, the following component values were used : $R_1 = 5\,\text{k}\Omega$, $R_2 = 1\,\text{k}\Omega$, $C_1 = 1\,\mu\text{F}$, $C_2 = 5\,\mu\text{F}$, $L_1 = 30\,\text{mH}$ and $L_2 = 60\,\text{mH}$.

It was first verified that any of the generated residual was very close to zero in the fault free condition. The single fault simulation was applied on the circuit model. Positive and negative parametric faults were simulated on each element separately, when the other elements were held at their nominal value. The overall shapes of the residual were generally very close for symmetric negative and positive offsets (the figures show only the residuals for positive offsets). The threshold value is defined by a previous simulation that take into account components tolerances. The results represented on Figures 7 and 8 are obtained on two independent residuals for $+/-50\%$ parametric faults. The results are summarized in the Tables 1 and 2 that hold the maximum gain values associated with each residual for each faulty element. For the first residual, we can see from For the first residual, the threshold can be fixed at 0.035. Then figure 7 and table 1 show that faults on R_1 and R_2 will be detected up to about 5000 rad/sec. Faults on C_2 will only be detected in the frequency range 500–5000 rad/sec. Faults on the other elements will not be detected.

The second residual can use a threshold of 0.08. Faults on R_2 will be detected up to 2000 rad/sec; faults on R_1 can be detected up to 5000 rad/sec and faults on C_2 show up in the range 200–5000 rad/sec.

Every residual covers a different spectrum of possible faults. To obtain better results, it may be possible to combine different residuals with different spectrum and fault

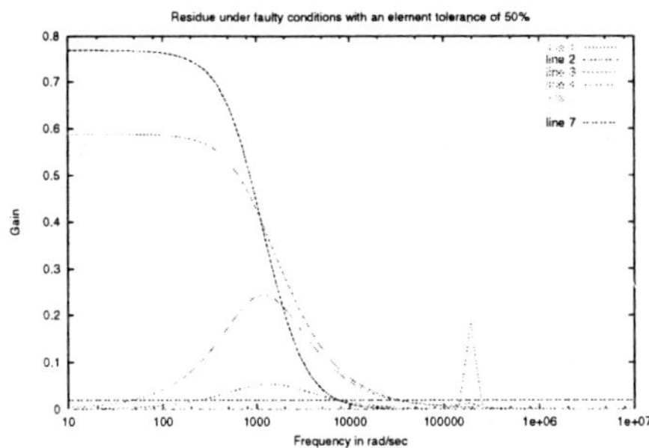

Figure 7. First residue under faulty conditions.

Table 1. Maximum response for first residual.

element offset	+50%	−50%
R_1	0.588	1.428
R_2	0.769	0.909
C_1	0.0548	0.162
C_2	0.244	0.322
L_1	0	0
L_2	0	0

coverage. But we are still looking for a formal method. The choice for a residual or possibly a combination of residuals can depend on

- the allotted space for the error detection circuitry;
- the desired fault coverage;
- the operational frequency range;
- the criticality of faults covered (in terms of effects gravity and occurrence probability).

In the end, the designer has to choose between maximum fault coverage and minimum space.

5 Conclusion

The first part of this paper deals with the generation of an extended symbolic model for linear analog circuits from its netlist description. This extended model required for efficient on-line fault detection comprises state space matrices for the nominal model, an unknown noise input model and a fault model. The noise sources are modeled by the unknown inputs. Fault models are generated from a sensitivity analysis of the symbolic state space model. From the previous extended model of the circuit, an optimal concurrent error detection circuitry is derived in the second part of this paper. The detector optimality request here corresponds to maximal sensitivity to faults and minimal sensitivity to unknown inputs.

Contrary to previously proposed methods on concurrent fault detection of linear analog circuits, the methodology presented in this paper is usable for any linear analog circuit, state variable or non. Further development should focus on the extension to non-linear problems. As a first step, non-linearity can be captured in the unknown input vectors. Techniques on how this can be accomplished for electronic networks have yet to be developed.

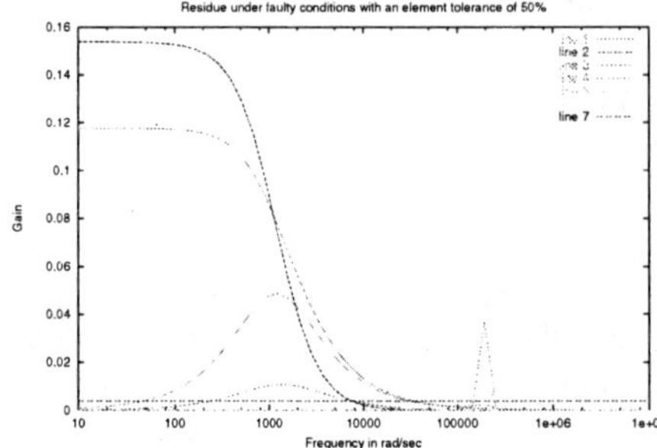

Figure 8. Second residue under faulty conditions.

Table 2. Maximum response for second residual.

element offset	+50%	−50%
R_1	0.118	0.286
R_2	0.154	0.182
C_1	0.0110	0.0324
C_2	0.0488	0.0645
L_1	0	0
L_2	0	0

References

[1] Jou, J.Y. and J.A. Abraham, *Fault tolerant FFT networks*, IEEE Transactions on Computers, 37, May 1988, pp 548–561.

[2] Chatterjee, A., *Concurrent Error Detection and Fault Tolerance in Linear Analog Integrated Circuits Using Continuous Checksums*, IEEE Transactions on VLSI Systems, vol 1 (1993), no 2, pp 138–150.

[3] Nair, V.S.S. and J.A. Abraham, *Real-Number Code for Fault Tolerance Matrix Operations on Processor Array*, IEEE Transactions on Computers, vol 39 (1990), no 4, pp 426–435.

[4] Reddy, L.N. and P. Banerjee, *Algorithm-Based Fault Detection for Signal Processing Applications*, IEEE Transactions on Computers, vol 39 (1990), no 10, pp 1304–1308.

[5] Frank, P.M., *Fault diagnosis in dynamical systems using analytical and knowledge based redundancy—A survey and some new results*, Automatica, vol 26 (1990), no 3, pp 459–474.

Some transmission time analysis for the parallel asynchronous communication scheme*

Luca G. Tallini
Dipartimento Di. Tec.,
Politecnico di Milano,
Via Bonardi, 3, 20133 Milano, ITALY.
E-mail: luca.tallini@polimi.it

Bella Bose
Department of Computer Science,
Oregon State University,
Corvallis, OR, 97331, USA.
E-mail: bose@cs.orst.edu

Abstract

In asynchronous buses, the sender encodes a data word with a code word from an unordered code and transmits it on the parallel bus lines. In this paper, some transmission time analysis for the above parallel asynchronous communication scheme are presented. It is proved that the average transmission time for a code word is a strictly increasing function of the weight, w, of the code word and it approaches the worst transmission time possible when w goes to infinity. This implies that the low weight codes result in a faster implementation of the above communication scheme. This paper also analyzes the transmission time performance of the recently introduced proximity detecting codes; further, some efficient low constant weight code designs are described.

Keywords: Asynchronous communication, delay-insensitive codes, unordered codes, constant weight codes, proximity detecting codes, low weight codes.

1. Introduction

Unordered codes [9], [5], [3], [4], [1] are used to achieve parallel asynchronous communication in asynchronous busses in which the transmission time on each individual bus line may vary from line to line due to different shapes, lengths and physical states of the bus lines. In asynchronous busses, the common scheme to communicate is the one in which the sender encodes a data word with a code word from an unordered code and transmits it on the parallel bus lines. The i-th component of the code word is transmitted on the i-th line of the bus, in such a way that an electrical transition of the line represents a 1 and an absence of transition represents a 0. Researchers in [9], [4], have modeled this communication scheme as a situation in which the sender communicates with the receiver using n parallel tracks (the bus lines) by rolling marbles (that correspond to an electrical transition of the lines) in the tracks. If the i-th component of the code word is a 1 then the sender rolls a marble in the i-th track of the bus. Because of the different topologies and physical states of the tracks, the amount of time a marble takes to travel from the source to the destination is unknown and may differ from track to track or even from roll to roll. But it is non-negative and finite; namely, marbles eventually do arrive after they have been rolled onto a track. Since there is no clock telling the receiver when the code word has been received completely (namely, when all the 1/marbles of the code word have reached the destination), the only way the receiver has to realize the complete reception of the code word is to make a membership test of the current word in the unordered code at the receiver end of the bus. For example, if the unordered code employed in the communication scheme is a constant weight w code of length n [6], [7], the receiver can figure out the complete reception of the code word by checking, at the receiver end of the bus, that the current word has w 1's. Once complete reception is detected, the receiver sends an acknowledgment signal to the sender indicating that it is ready to receive the next code word.

This paper presents some transmission time analysis for the above parallel asynchronous communication scheme. The transmission time of a word is equal to the elapsed time between the time when all the marbles of the word are first placed on the bus lines and the time when the receiver detects the complete reception of the word. In the usual implementation of the scheme, the receiver detects the complete reception of the word when the last marble of the word is received. Obviously, the transmission time of a word of weight w depends on the transmission time of the w 1/marbles constituting the word. For $j = 1, 2, \ldots, w$ let X_j be the elapsed time for the j-th marble of the word. The X_j's can be modeled as non-negative random variables over the real numbers. Under the most natural assumption of that these X_j's are continuous, independent and all uniformly distributed over the interval $[t_{min}, t_{max}]$, we have shown that the average transmission time of a word of weight w is

$$\overline{T}(w) = t_{min} + \frac{w}{w+1}(t_{max} - t_{min}). \tag{1}$$

Further, if we assume that the X_j's are continuous, independent and all exponentially distributed over the interval $[t_{min}, +\infty)$ with parameter λ, then the average transmission time of a word of weight w is

$$\overline{T}(w) = t_{min} + \frac{H_w}{\lambda}, \tag{2}$$

where $H_w = 1+1/2+1/3+\ldots+1/w$ is the w-th harmonic number. Note that in both distributions the following properties hold. **P1)** $\overline{T}(w+1) > \overline{T}(w)$; namely, the average transmission time of a word is a strictly increasing function of the weight of the word, and **P2)** if $p(x)$ is the cumulative distribution function (cdf) of the X_j's, then $\lim_{w\to+\infty} \overline{T}(w) = \sup\{x \in \mathbb{R} : p(x) \in [0,1)\}$; namely, as w goes to infinity, $\overline{T}(w)$ goes to the supremum (the least upper bound) of the inverse image of the interval $[0, 1)$ with respect to the function $p(x)$, $p^{-1}([0,1))$. In the first probability

*This work was supported by the National Science Foundation under Grant MIP-9705738.

distribution the supremum is t_{max} and in the second it is $+\infty$. Note that $p^{-1}([0,1))$ contains the set of values where the cdf $p(x)$ increases, so that, as w goes to infinity, the average transmission time becomes as worst as it can possibly be. We have also proved that the properties **P1** and **P2** hold under very general hypothesis on X_j's. In particular, we show that such properties hold independently from the cdf of the non-negative, independent and equally distributed random variables X_j's, provided that the X_j's are not almost always equal to a common constant. Because of space limitation, this result is not proved in this paper. However, this result implies that low weight codes results in a faster implementation of the parallel asynchronous communication scheme.

In section 3, we present a transmission time analysis for the proximity detecting codes recently introduced by Vaidya and Perisetty in [8]. Their very interesting idea is to use certain t-proximity detecting (t-PD) codes to allow the receiver to send the acknowledgment signal to the sender when all but t of the transmitted 1/marbles of a code word have been received. Examples of t-PD codes are constant weight codes, for all t [8]. In general, we have proved that, if the X_j's are continuous non-negative, independent and equally distributed, then the average transmission time for a code word of a t-PD code is equal to

$$\overline{T}_{t-PD}(w) = (w-t)\binom{w}{t}\int_0^1 p^{-1}(y)y^{w-t-1}(1-y)^t\,dy; \quad (3)$$

with $p^{-1}(y)$ being the inverse of the cumulative distribution function, $p(x)$, of the X_j's. In particular, we show that if the X_j's are independent and all uniformly distributed over the interval $[t_{min}, t_{max}]$, then the transmission time for a code word of a t-PD code is

$$\overline{T}_{t-PD}(w) = t_{min} + \frac{w-t}{w+1}(t_{max} - t_{min}). \quad (4)$$

In this case, a t-PD code with average weight per code word w' is faster to implement than a 0-PD code (or unordered code) with average weight per code word w iff $w'-w < t(w+1)$. If the X_j's are independent and all exponentially distributed over the interval $[t_{min}, +\infty)$ with parameter λ, then

$$\overline{T}_{t-PD}(w) = t_{min} + \frac{H_w - H_t}{\lambda}. \quad (5)$$

Also in this case, a t-PD code with average weight per code word w' is faster to implement than a 0-PD code with average weight per code word w if $w' - w < H_t w$. Note that the assumptions $w' - w < t(w+1)$ and $w' - w < H_t w$ are very reasonable and are satisfied by all the codes presented in [8].

In Section 4, some simple low constant weight code (i.e., constant weight codes whose weight is low) designs are given. In Section 5 some conclusions are drawn and some comparisons are given.

2. The transmission time analysis

Before proceeding with our analysis we need to recall some concepts and notations from probability theory and these can be found, for example, in [2].

Let $(\Omega, \mathcal{A}, P)$ be a probability space, where Ω is the event space, $\mathcal{A} \subseteq \mathcal{P}(\Omega)$ ($\stackrel{\text{def}}{=}$ the power set of Ω) is a σ-field (or σ-algebra) of sets and $P : \mathcal{A} \longrightarrow \mathbb{R}^+$ is a probability measure over Ω. A real valued random variable, X, is nothing but a measurable function from Ω to $\mathbb{R}$; that is, $X : \Omega \longrightarrow \mathbb{R}$ and the inverse images of the open intervals of $\mathbb{R}$ are elements of the σ-field $\mathcal{A}$. In this way, it is possible to define the mean value of X as the real number

$$E[X] \stackrel{\text{def}}{=} \int_\Omega X(\psi)\,P(d\psi),$$

where the above integral is the Lebesgue integral of X over Ω. It is very well known, from probability theory, that random variables are suited to describe uncertain quantities and that their mean values are certain quantities which "best" represent them. The probabilistic behavior of any random variable, X, is characterized by its cumulative distribution function (cdf), $p_X : \mathbb{R} \longrightarrow [0,1] \subseteq \mathbb{R}$, which is defined as

$$p_X(x) \stackrel{\text{def}}{=} P(\{\psi \in \Omega : X(\psi) \leq x\}).$$

This function is monotone non-decreasing, right-continuous, and satisfies $p_X(-\infty) \stackrel{\text{def}}{=} \lim_{x\to-\infty} p(x) = 0$ and $p_X(+\infty) \stackrel{\text{def}}{=} \lim_{x\to+\infty} p(x) = 1$. When the function $p_X(x)$ takes on at most a finite number of possible values, the random variable X is said to be simple. In this case, $p_X(x)$ is a step function. If p_1, p_2, ..., p_m are the step sizes at x_1, x_2, ..., x_m respectively, where $x_1 < x_2 < \ldots < x_m$, then $p_X(x) = \sum_{i:x_i \leq x} p_i$ and

$$E[X] = \sum_{i=1}^{m} x_i p_i = x_1 p(x_1) + \sum_{i=2}^{m} x_i(p(x_i) - p(x_{i-1})). \quad (6)$$

When the function $p_X(x)$ is an absolutely continuous function, the random variable X is said to be (absolutely) continuous. In this case, there exists almost everywhere the derivate, $p'_X(x)$, of $p_X(x)$ which is called probability density function (pdf) of X. Such pdf satisfies $p'(x) \geq 0$, for all $x \in \mathbb{R}$. Further, $p_X(x) = \int_{-\infty}^{x} p'_X(y)\,dy$ and

$$E[X] = \int_{-\infty}^{+\infty} x p'_X(x)\,dx. \quad (7)$$

To begin our analysis, let $(\Omega, \mathcal{A}, P)$ be a probability space, $\mathcal{X} = \{X_i : i \in \mathcal{I}\}$, $\mathcal{I}$ index set such that $|\mathcal{I}| \geq |\mathbb{N}|$, be a set of non-negative random variables over Ω and, for all $w \in \mathbb{N}$, let X_1, X_2, ..., X_w be w random variables taken from $\mathcal{X}$. In our problem, $X_j : \Omega \longrightarrow \mathbb{R}^+$, $j \in [1, w]$, represents the elapsed time of the j-th marble (i.e., the elapsed time between the time it is put on its track and the time it is received) and $\mathcal{X}$ represents a "basket" of random variables from where X_j's are picked. Also, consider the random variable $Y_w : \Omega \longrightarrow \mathbb{R}^+$, defined as

$$Y_w(\psi) \stackrel{\text{def}}{=} \max_{j\in[1,w]} X_j(\psi), \qquad \text{for all } \psi \in \Omega.$$

Note that Y_w is the elapsed time of the word (i.e., the elapsed time between the time all marbles of the word are first placed on the tracks and the time the last marble is received). In other words, Y_w is a random variable which represents the transmission time of the word of weight w, when the usual asynchronous communication scheme is used. Based on $\mathcal{X}$, the problem is then to find the mean value of Y_w; or at least, some information concerning it. First note that, independently from the set $\mathcal{X}$, the sequence $\{E[Y_w]\}_{w\in\mathbb{N}}$ is monotone non-decreasing. In fact, $Y_w(\psi) = \max_{j\in[1,w]} X_j(\psi) = \max\{Y_{w-1}(\psi), X_w(\psi)\} \geq Y_{w-1}(\psi)$, for all $\psi \in \Omega$; hence

$$E[Y_w] = \int_\Omega Y_w(\psi)\,P(d\psi) \geq \int_\Omega Y_{w-1}(\psi)\,P(d\psi) = E[Y_{w-1}].$$

Is it possible to say more ? For example, under which hypothesis on $\mathcal{X}$ (the weakest) the above inequality is strict ? What is the value of $\lim_{w\longrightarrow+\infty} E[Y_w]$? Since the sequence $\{E[Y_w]\}_{w\in\mathbb{N}}$ is monotone non-decreasing, this limit is an upper bound on $E[Y_w]$.

For the time being, assume that $\mathcal{X}$ is a set of **independent and equally distributed** random variables, and let us compute $E[Y_w]$ for some known distributions. First, note that the above assumptions are very reasonable because, a priori, the lines of the bus are designed to be equal and the signals are independent, meaning that a signal in one line will not interfere with the signal in another line. Now, if $\mathcal{X}$ is a set of independent random variables and the X_j's are taken from $\mathcal{X}$, then

$$p_{Y_w}(x) = P(\{\psi\in\Omega : Y_w(\psi) \le x\}) =$$

$$P(\{\psi\in\Omega : \max_{j\in[1,w]} X_j(\psi) \le x\}) =$$

$$P(\{\psi\in\Omega : X_1(\psi) \le x \text{ and } \ldots \text{ and } X_w(\psi) \le x\}) =$$

$$P\left(\bigcap_{j=1}^{w}\{\psi\in\Omega : X_j(\psi) \le x\}\right) =$$

$$\prod_{j=1}^{w} P(\{\psi\in\Omega : X_j(\psi) \le x\}) = \prod_{j=1}^{w} p_{X_j}(x).$$

If $\mathcal{X}$ is also a set of equally distributed random variables with common cdf, $p(x)$, then $p(x) = p_{X_1}(x) = p_{X_2}(x) = \ldots = p_{X_w}(x)$ and

$$p_{Y_w}(x) = p^w(x). \tag{8}$$

As a first example, assume that $\mathcal{X}$ is a set of **continuous random variables uniformly distributed** over the interval $[a,b]$ of the real numbers, $a < b$. In this case

$$p(x) = \begin{cases} 0 & \text{if } x\in(-\infty,a), \\ (x-a)/(b-a) & \text{if } x\in[a,b], \\ 1 & \text{if } x\in(b,+\infty), \end{cases} \tag{9}$$

so that, from (7) and (8),

$$E[Y_w] = \int_{-\infty}^{+\infty} x p'_{Y_w}(x)\,dx = \int_{-\infty}^{+\infty} xwp^{w-1}(x)p'(x)\,dx =$$

$$\int_a^b xw\left(\frac{x-a}{b-a}\right)^{w-1}\frac{1}{b-a}\,dx = a + \frac{w}{w+1}(b-a);$$

which is exactly the relation (1). Note that $E[Y_w]$ satisfies the following two properties. **P1**) the sequence $\{E[Y_w]\}_{w\in\mathbb{N}}$ is strictly increasing with w and **P2**) $\lim_{w\to+\infty} E[Y_w] = b$; namely, as w approaches infinity, the average transmission time approaches the worst case transmission time possible.

Now, as a second example, assume that $\mathcal{X}$ is a set of **continuous random variables exponentially distributed** over the real interval $[a,+\infty)$ with parameter $\lambda\in\mathbb{R}^+$. In this case

$$p(x) = \begin{cases} 0 & \text{if } x\in(-\infty,a), \\ 1-e^{-\lambda(x-a)} & \text{if } x\in[a,+\infty), \end{cases} \tag{10}$$

so that, from (7) and (8),

$$E[Y_w] = \int_{-\infty}^{+\infty} x p'_{Y_w}(x)\,dx = \int_{-\infty}^{+\infty} xwp^{w-1}(x)p'(x)\,dx =$$

$$\int_0^1 p^{-1}(y)wy^{w-1}\,dy,$$

with $x = p^{-1}(y) = a - \log_e(1-y)/\lambda$. Hence,

$$E[Y_w] = \int_0^1 way^{w-1}\,dy - \int_0^1 w\frac{1}{\lambda}y^{w-1}\log_e(1-y)\,dy.$$

Now,

$$\int_0^1 way^{w-1}\,dy = a,$$

whereas, integrating by parts,

$$\int y^{w-1}\log_e(1-y)\,dy = \int \log_e(1-y)\,d\frac{y^w}{w} =$$

$$\frac{y^w}{w}\log_e(1-y) + \frac{1}{w}\left[\int\frac{1}{1-y}\,dy - \int\frac{(1-y^w)}{1-y}\,dy\right].$$

Since

$$\int\frac{1}{1-y}\,dy = -\log_e(1-y),$$

$$\int\frac{(1-y^w)}{1-y}\,dy = \int\sum_{j=0}^{w-1} y^j\,dy = \sum_{j=0}^{w-1}\int y^j\,dy = \sum_{j=1}^{w}\frac{y^j}{j}$$

and $\lim_{y\to1}(1-y^w)\log_e(1-y) = 0$ it follows that,

$$\int_0^1 w\frac{1}{\lambda}y^{w-1}\log_e(1-y)\,dy = -\frac{1}{\lambda}\sum_{j=1}^{w}\frac{1}{j}.$$

All this imply that

$$E[Y_w] = a + \frac{1}{\lambda}\sum_{j=1}^{w}\frac{1}{j} = a + \frac{H_w}{\lambda},$$

where $H_w \stackrel{\text{def}}{=} 1 + 1/2 + 1/3 + \ldots + 1/w$ is the w-th harmonic number. The above relation is exactly (2). In this case also, $E[Y_w]$ satisfies the properties **P1** and **P2** mentioned above. **P1**) the sequence $\{E[Y_w]\}_{w\in\mathbb{N}}$ is strictly increasing with w and **P2**) as w approaches infinity, the average transmission time approaches the worst case; i.e., $\lim_{w\to+\infty} E[Y_w] = +\infty$.

As a last example, assume that $\mathcal{X}$ is a set of **simple random variables** taking, with probability different from zero, the values $t_1, t_2, \ldots, t_m$, where $t_1 < t_2 < \ldots < t_m$ and $m \ge 2$. In this case, Y_w is also a simple random variable taking, with probability different from zero, $t_1, t_2, \ldots, t_m$ and, using (6) and (8), it follows (note that $p_{Y_w}(t_m) = 1$),

$$E[Y_w] = t_1 p_{Y_w}(t_1) + \sum_{i=2}^{m} t_i(p_{Y_w}(t_i) - p_{Y_w}(t_{i-1})) =$$

$$t_m - \sum_{i=1}^{m-1}(t_{i+1}-t_i)p_{Y_w}(t_i) = t_m - \sum_{i=1}^{m-1}(t_{i+1}-t_i)p^w(t_i).$$

Again in this case, **P1**) the sequence $\{E[Y_w]\}_{w\in\mathbb{N}}$ is strictly increasing with w and **P2**) as w goes to infinity, the average transmission time approaches the worst case transmission time possible. This is because $\lim_{w\to+\infty} E[Y_w] = t_m$.

We have proved that the properties **P1**) and **P2**) hold in general for any cumulative distribution function, $p(x)$. Because of the space limitation, the proof is not given.

3. The analysis for proximity detecting codes

In [8], Vaidya and Perisetty proposed proximity detecting (PD) codes to improve the performance of an asynchronous channel. If certain assumptions can be made on relative delays on the wires of the bus, a t-PD code can be used to allow the receiver to send the acknowledgment signal to the sender when all but t non-zero transmitted bits have been received. In this case, the receiver detects the complete reception of a word when all but t marbles of it have arrived at the destination. Examples of t-PD codes are constant weight codes, for all t. In the case of t-proximity detection, the transmission time of a word is represented by the random variable $Y_w^{(t)} : \Omega \longrightarrow \mathbb{R}^+$, defined as

$$Y_w^{(t)}(\psi) \stackrel{\text{def}}{=} (w-t)\text{-th smallest (or (t+1)-th biggest) element in the set } \{X_1(\psi), X_2(\psi), \ldots, X_w(\psi)\},$$

with $X_j \in \mathcal{X}$, $j \in [1, w]$. Note that $Y_w^{(0)}$ is the biggest element in the set $\{X_1(\psi), X_2(\psi), \ldots, X_w(\psi)\}$ and is equal to the random variable of the previous section, $Y_w^{(1)}$ is the second biggest element in the set $\{X_1(\psi), X_2(\psi), \ldots, X_w(\psi)\}$, and so on. As in the case $t = 0$, for any fixed t, the sequence $\{E[Y_w^{(t)}]\}_{w \in \mathbb{N}}$ is monotone non-decreasing because $Y_w^{(t)}(\psi) \geq Y_{w-1}^{(t)}(\psi)$, for all $\psi \in \Omega$. In general, theorems, which are similar to those given in Section 2 for $Y_w^{(0)}$, can be stated and proved for $Y_w^{(t)}$, $t > 0$.

For simplicity, assume that $\mathcal{X}$ is a set of **independent and equally distributed** random variables having common cdf $p(x)$. In this case the cdf of $Y_w^{(t)}$ is

$$p_{Y_w^{(t)}}(x) = P(\{\psi \in \Omega : Y_w^{(t)}(\psi) \leq x\}) =$$

$$P(\{\psi \in \Omega : (w-t) \text{ or more of the } X_j\text{'s are} \leq x\}) =$$

$$P(\bigcup_{h=0}^{t} \{\psi \in \Omega : \text{exactly } (w-t+h) \text{ of the } X_j\text{'s are} \leq x\}) =$$

$$\sum_{h=0}^{t} P(\{\psi \in \Omega : \text{exactly } (w-t+h) \text{ of the } X_j\text{'s are} \leq x\}) =$$

$$\sum_{h=0}^{t} \binom{w}{w-t+h} p^{w-t+h}(x)(1-p(x))^{t-h}$$

and so,

$$p_{Y_w^{(t)}}(x) = \sum_{h=0}^{t} \binom{w}{h} p^{w-h}(x)(1-p(x))^h. \quad (11)$$

If we assume that the random variables of $\mathcal{X}$ are also **continuous** with pdf $p'(x)$, then the pdf of $Y_w^{(t)}$ can be obtained using the following important identity of functions. If, for all $n, m \in \mathbb{N}$, $I_{n,m}(z) \stackrel{\text{def}}{=} \int z^n(1-z)^m \, dz$ then

$$I_{n,m}(z) = \sum_{i=0}^{m} \frac{1}{n+1} \frac{\binom{m}{i}}{\binom{n+1+i}{n+1}} z^{n+1+i}(1-z)^{m-i}. \quad (12)$$

This identity can be proved integrating by parts and solving a recurrence relation. Now, from (12) with $n = w - t - 1$, $m = t$ and $z = p(x)$, and (11), it follows

$$I_{w-t-1,t}(p(x)) = \int p^{w-t-1}(x)(1-p(x))^t p'(x) \, dx =$$

$$\frac{1}{(w-t)\binom{w}{t}} \sum_{h=0}^{t} \binom{w}{h} p^{w-h}(x)(1-p(x))^h = \frac{p_{Y_w^{(t)}}(x)}{(w-t)\binom{w}{t}}.$$

This implies that the pdf of $Y_w^{(t)}$ is

$$p'_{Y_w^{(t)}}(x) = (w-t)\binom{w}{t} p^{w-t-1}(x)(1-p(x))^t p'(x)$$

and

$$E[Y_w^{(t)}] = \int_{-\infty}^{+\infty} x p'_{Y_w^{(t)}}(x) \, dx =$$

$$(w-t)\binom{w}{t} \int_{-\infty}^{+\infty} x p^{w-t-1}(x)(1-p(x))^t p'(x) \, dx =$$

$$(w-t)\binom{w}{t} \int_0^1 p^{-1}(y) y^{w-t-1}(1-y)^t \, dy, \quad (13)$$

with $p^{-1}(y)$ being the inverse of the function $p(x)$. This last relations give (3).

For example, assume that $\mathcal{X}$ is a set of **continuous random variables uniformly distributed** over the interval $[a, b]$ of the real numbers. In this case, from (9), $y = p(x) = (x-a)/(b-a) \iff x = p^{-1}(y) = (b-a)y + a$. Hence, from (13),

$$E[Y_w^{(t)}] = (w-t)\binom{w}{t} \int_0^1 [(b-a)y + a] y^{w-t-1}(1-y)^t \, dy.$$

But, from (12),

$$\int_0^1 y^{w-t-1}(1-y)^t \, dy = \frac{1}{(w-t)\binom{w}{t}} \quad (14)$$

and

$$\int_0^1 y^{w-t}(1-y)^t \, dy = \frac{1}{(w+1)\binom{w}{t}},$$

so, $E[Y_w^{(t)}] = a + (w-t)/(w+1)(b-a)$; which is exactly (4).

Now, assume that $\mathcal{X}$ is a set of **continuous random variables exponentially distributed** over the interval $[a, +\infty)$ with parameter λ. In this case, from (10), $y = p(x) = 1 - e^{-\lambda(x-a)} \iff x = p^{-1}(y) = a - \log_e(1-y)/\lambda$. Hence, from (13), $E[Y_w^{(t)}] =$

$$(w-t)\binom{w}{t} \int_0^1 \left(a - \frac{\log_e(1-y)}{\lambda}\right) y^{w-t-1}(1-y)^t \, dy.$$

It can be proved that

$$\int_0^1 \log_e(1-y) y^{w-t-1}(1-y)^t \, dy = -\frac{(H_w - H_t)}{(t+1)\binom{w}{t+1}}.$$

The above relation and (14) give $E[Y_w^{(t)}] = a + (H_w - H_t)/\lambda$; which is exactly (5).

4. Some simple low constant weight code designs

This section presents some low constant weight codes which are very efficient in terms of speed if used to realize an asynchronous communication system. Their speed performance will be quantified in Section 5. Such codes are also efficient in terms of complexity; i.e., it is easy to convert a data word to a code word and vice versa. In fact, the encoding and decoding can be accomplished in parallel with fast and small combinational circuits. Further, the codes are efficient in terms of redundancy; i.e., the number, r, of extra check bits required to encode k data bits is relatively small. Let $\mathcal{S}_w^k$ indicate the set of all words of length k and weight w. With DC(n, k, w) we indicate a binary block code of length n, constant weight w and k information bits [6].

4.1. Design of a DC$(n = 4, k = 2, w = 1)$ code

Here, we give a very simple method to encode $k = 2$ data bits into a constant weight code of length $n = 4$ and weight $w = 1$. The design is defined in the following table representing the truth table of the encoding function $\mathcal{E} : \mathbb{Z}_2^2 \longrightarrow \mathcal{S}_1^4$ for the code.

x_1x_2	$\overset{\mathcal{E}}{\longleftrightarrow}$	$y_1y_2y_3y_4$
00		0001
01		0010
10		0100
11		1000

The encoding function $\mathcal{E}$ can be realized as

$$\mathcal{E}(x_1x_2) = (x_1 \cdot x_2, x_1 \cdot \overline{x_2}, \overline{x_1} \cdot x_2, \overline{x_1} \cdot \overline{x_2}).$$

Whereas, the decoding function $\mathcal{E}^{-1}$ can be realized as

$$\mathcal{E}^{-1}(y_1y_2y_3y_4) = (y_1 \vee y_2, y_1 \vee y_3).$$

Note that, concatenating this code with itself it is possible to obtain very simple DC$(n = 2k, k, w = 0.5k)$ codes which require the same number of redundant bits as the usual dual-rail code, but the number of 1's in each code word is only half that of a dual-rail code word.

4.2. Design of a DC$(n = 7, k = 4, w = 2)$ code

Here, we give a simple method to encode $k = 4$ data bits into a constant weight code of length $n = 7$ and weight $w = 2$. The design is defined in the following table representing the truth table of the encoding function $\mathcal{E} : \mathbb{Z}_2^4 \longrightarrow \mathcal{S}_2^7$ for the code.

x_1x_2	x_3x_4	$\overset{\mathcal{E}}{\longleftrightarrow}$	$y_1y_2y_3$	$y_4y_5y_6y_7$
00	00		000	0101
00	01		000	0011
00	10		000	1100
00	11		000	1010
01	00		001	0001
01	01		001	0010
01	10		001	0100
01	11		001	1000
10	00		010	0001
10	01		010	0010
10	10		010	0100
10	11		010	1000
11	00		100	0001
11	01		100	0010
11	10		100	0100
11	11		100	1000

The encoding function $\mathcal{E}$ can be realized as

$$\mathcal{E}(x_1x_2x_3x_4) = (x_1 \cdot x_2, x_1 \cdot \overline{x_2}, \overline{x_1} \cdot x_2, x_3 \cdot x_4 \vee \overline{x_1} \cdot \overline{x_2} \cdot x_3,$$
$$x_3 \cdot \overline{x_4} \vee \overline{x_1} \cdot \overline{x_2} \cdot \overline{x_4}, \overline{x_3} \cdot x_4 \vee \overline{x_1} \cdot \overline{x_2} \cdot x_4, \overline{x_3} \cdot \overline{x_4} \vee \overline{x_1} \cdot \overline{x_2} \cdot \overline{x_3}).$$

Whereas, $\mathcal{E}^{-1}(y_1y_2y_3y_4y_5y_6y_7) =$

$$(y_1 \vee y_2, y_1 \vee y_3, y_4 \vee \overline{y_6} \cdot \overline{y_7}, y_6 \vee \overline{y_5} \cdot \overline{y_7}).$$

Note that, concatenating this code with itself it is possible to obtain DC$(n = 1.75k, k, w = 0.5k)$ codes which have the same features as the codes given in the previous subsection but are less redundant.

4.3. Design of a DC$(n = 13, k = 8, w = 3)$ code

Here, we give a method to encode $k = 8$ data bits into a constant weight code of length $n = 13$ and weight $w = 3$. Note that any constant weight 3 coding method requires at least 5 extra check bits to encode 8 bit data. This is because there are $2^8 = 256$ data words of length 8 and $\binom{12}{3} = 220 < 256$. Further, using 5 check bits, 8 is the maximum length of information word that can be made constant weight 3. In fact, $2^8 = 256 \leq \binom{13}{3} = 286$ and $\binom{14}{3} = 364 < 2^9 = 512$. In this respect, as the previous codes, this code is optimal from the redundancy point of view. The code design is also simple because the whole coding system (encoder plus decoder) for this code can be implemented using less than 1070 transistors with a depth of less than 30 transistors.

The code is described following the encoding scheme introduced in [6]. Consider the following 11 "balancing functions"

$$f_i \overset{\text{def}}{=} \langle \Gamma_i \rangle : \mathcal{D}_i \longrightarrow \mathcal{C}_i, \quad i \in [1, 11]$$

defined as follows.

$$\begin{aligned}
f_1 &\overset{\text{def}}{=} \langle\{00000, 00001, 00011\}\rangle : \mathcal{D}_1 \longrightarrow \mathcal{S}_1^8 \cup \mathcal{S}_2^8 \cup \mathcal{S}_3^8, \\
f_2 &\overset{\text{def}}{=} \langle\{00010, 00110\}\rangle : \mathcal{D}_2 \longrightarrow \mathcal{S}_1^8 \cup \mathcal{S}_2^8, \\
f_3 &\overset{\text{def}}{=} \langle\{01100\}\rangle : \mathcal{D}_3 \longrightarrow \mathcal{S}_1^8, \\
f_4 &\overset{\text{def}}{=} \langle\{11000\}\rangle : \mathcal{D}_4 \longrightarrow \mathcal{S}_1^8, \\
f_5 &\overset{\text{def}}{=} \langle\{10001\}\rangle : \mathcal{D}_5 \longrightarrow \mathcal{S}_1^8, \\
f_6 &\overset{\text{def}}{=} \langle\{00101\}\rangle : \mathcal{D}_6 \longrightarrow \mathcal{S}_1^8, \\
f_7 &\overset{\text{def}}{=} \langle\{00100\}\rangle : \mathcal{D}_7 \longrightarrow \mathcal{S}_2^8, \\
f_8 &\overset{\text{def}}{=} \langle\{01000\}\rangle : \mathcal{D}_8 \longrightarrow \mathcal{S}_2^8, \\
f_9 &\overset{\text{def}}{=} \langle\{10000\}\rangle : \mathcal{D}_9 \longrightarrow \mathcal{S}_2^8, \\
f_{10} &\overset{\text{def}}{=} \langle\{01010\}\rangle : \mathcal{D}_{10} \longrightarrow \mathcal{S}_1^8, \\
f_{11} &\overset{\text{def}}{=} \langle\{10100\}\rangle : \mathcal{D}_{11} \longrightarrow \mathcal{S}_1^8,
\end{aligned} \tag{15}$$

where,

$$\begin{aligned}
\mathcal{D}_1 &\overset{\text{def}}{=} \mathcal{S}_1^8 \cup \mathcal{S}_2^8 \cup \mathcal{S}_3^8, \\
\mathcal{D}_2 &\overset{\text{def}}{=} \mathcal{S}_6^8 \cup \mathcal{S}_7^8, \\
\mathcal{D}_3 &\overset{\text{def}}{=} 000(\mathcal{S}_0^5 \cup \mathcal{S}_4^5 \cup \mathcal{S}_5^5), \\
\mathcal{D}_4 &\overset{\text{def}}{=} 001(1\mathcal{S}_2^4 \cup 0\mathcal{S}_4^4), \\
\mathcal{D}_5 &\overset{\text{def}}{=} 010(1\mathcal{S}_2^4 \cup 0\mathcal{S}_4^4), \\
\mathcal{D}_6 &\overset{\text{def}}{=} 100(1\mathcal{S}_2^4 \cup 0\mathcal{S}_4^4), \\
\mathcal{D}_7 &\overset{\text{def}}{=} 011(\mathcal{S}_2^5 \cup \mathcal{S}_3^5) \cup 001(0\mathcal{S}_3^4 \cup 1\mathcal{S}_3^4), \\
\mathcal{D}_8 &\overset{\text{def}}{=} 110(\mathcal{S}_2^5 \cup \mathcal{S}_3^5) \cup 010(0\mathcal{S}_3^4 \cup 1\mathcal{S}_3^4), \\
\mathcal{D}_9 &\overset{\text{def}}{=} 101(\mathcal{S}_2^5 \cup \mathcal{S}_3^5) \cup 100(0\mathcal{S}_3^4 \cup 1\mathcal{S}_3^4), \\
\mathcal{D}_{10} &\overset{\text{def}}{=} 111(1\mathcal{S}_0^4 \cup 0\mathcal{S}_2^4 \cup 1\mathcal{S}_4^4), \\
\mathcal{D}_{11} &\overset{\text{def}}{=} 111(0\mathcal{S}_1^4 \cup 1\mathcal{S}_1^4).
\end{aligned}$$

The function f_1 is the identity function, the function f_2 is the complement function and the remaining functions will be defined further down. The functions $f_i : \mathcal{D}_i \longrightarrow \mathcal{C}_i$'s are one-to-one and $\{\mathcal{D}_i\}_{i \in [1,11]}$ is a partition of the set of data words $\mathbb{Z}_2^8$ so that, in the encoding process, a data word $X \in \mathcal{D}_{ib}$ is encoded as $\mathcal{E}(X) = f_{ib}(X)C$, with $C \in \Gamma_{ib}$ chosen such that $w(\mathcal{E}(X)) = w(f_{ib}(X)) + w(C) = 3$. Note that there always exist such a C. The index ib is called the balancing index (of X). Since the Γ_i's are pairwise disjoint, the check symbol C "encodes" which balancing function (i.e., balancing index) has been used during the encoding process so that decoding of $\mathcal{E}(X) = YC$, with $Y \in \mathbb{Z}_2^8$ and $C \in \Gamma_{ib} \subseteq \mathbb{Z}_2^5$, is a matter of computing $X = \mathcal{E}^{-1}(YC) = f_{ib}^{-1}(Y)$. The whole coding scheme can be implemented in parallel as explained in [6]. Now, the functions f_i's are very simple together with their inverses. In fact, the function f_1 and f_2 are straightforward, and the remaining functions can be efficiently computed in parallel implementing the following Boolean expressions. The function f_3 is defined in the following truth table

x_1x_2	x_3x_4	x_5x_6	x_7x_8	$\overset{f_3}{\longleftrightarrow}$	$y_1y_2y_3y_4$	$y_5y_6y_7y_8$
00	01	01	11		1000	0000
00	01	10	11		0100	0000
00	01	11	01		0010	0000
00	01	11	10		0001	0000
00	01	11	11		0000	1000
00	00	11	11		0000	0100
00	00	00	00		0000	0010

and can be efficiently computed in parallel implementing the Boolean expressions $f_3(x_1x_2x_3x_4x_5x_6x_7x_8) =$

$$(x_4\cdot\overline{x_5}, x_4\cdot\overline{x_6}, x_4\cdot\overline{x_7}, x_4\cdot\overline{x_8}, x_4\cdot x_5\cdot x_7\cdot x_8, \overline{x_4}\cdot x_5, \overline{x_4}\cdot\overline{x_5}, 0).$$

Whereas, the function f_3^{-1} can be computed with the Boolean expressions $f_3^{-1}(y_1y_2y_3y_4y_5y_6y_7y_8) =$

$$(0, 0, 0, \overline{y_6}\cdot\overline{y_7}, \overline{y_1}\cdot\overline{y_7}, \overline{y_2}\cdot\overline{y_7}, \overline{y_3}\cdot\overline{y_7}, \overline{y_4}\cdot\overline{y_7}).$$

The function f_4 is defined in the following truth table

x_1x_2	x_3x_4	x_5x_6	x_7x_8	$\overset{f_4}{\longleftrightarrow}$	$y_1y_2y_3y_4$	$y_5y_6y_7y_8$
00	10	11	11		1000	0000
00	11	11	00		0100	0000
00	11	10	10		0010	0000
00	11	10	01		0001	0000
00	11	00	11		0000	1000
00	11	01	01		0000	0100
00	11	01	10		0000	0010

and can be efficiently computed in parallel implementing the Boolean expressions $f_4(x_1x_2x_3x_4x_5x_6x_7x_8) =$

$$(\overline{x_4}, \overline{x_7}\cdot\overline{x_8}, \overline{x_6}\cdot\overline{x_8}, \overline{x_6}\cdot\overline{x_7}, \overline{x_5}\cdot\overline{x_6}, \overline{x_5}\cdot\overline{x_7}, \overline{x_5}\cdot\overline{x_8}, 0).$$

Whereas, the function f_4^{-1} can be computed with the Boolean expressions $f_4^{-1}(y_1y_2y_3y_4y_5y_6y_7y_8) =$

$$(0, 0, 1, \overline{y_1}, \overline{y_5}\cdot\overline{y_6}\cdot\overline{y_7}, \overline{y_3}\cdot\overline{y_4}\cdot\overline{y_5}, \overline{y_2}\cdot\overline{y_4}\cdot\overline{y_6}, \overline{y_2}\cdot\overline{y_3}\cdot\overline{y_7}).$$

The function f_5 and f_6 are defined and computed by first applying a cyclic shift of $x_1x_2x_3$ one and two times to the left respectively, and then applying the function f_4. Their inverses can be simply obtained by undoing this process. The function f_7 is defined in the following truth table

x_1x_2	x_3x_4	x_5x_6	x_7x_8	$\overset{f_7}{\longleftrightarrow}$	$y_1y_2y_3y_4$	$y_5y_6y_7y_8$
01	11	10	00		1000	1000
01	11	01	00		1000	0100
01	11	00	10		1000	0010
01	11	00	01		1000	0001
01	10	01	11		0100	1000
01	10	10	11		0100	0100
01	10	11	01		0100	0010
01	10	11	10		0100	0001
00	11	01	11		0010	1000
00	11	10	11		0010	0100
00	11	11	01		0010	0010
00	11	11	10		0010	0001
00	10	01	11		0001	1000
00	10	10	11		0001	0100
00	10	11	01		0001	0010
00	10	11	10		0001	0001
01	11	00	11		1100	0000
01	11	11	00		0011	0000
01	10	00	11		0000	1100
01	10	11	00		0000	0011
01	11	01	01		1010	0000
01	11	10	10		0101	0000
01	10	01	01		0000	1010
01	10	10	10		0000	0101
01	11	01	10		1001	0000
01	11	10	01		0110	0000
01	10	01	10		0000	1001
01	10	10	01		0000	0110

and can be efficiently computed in parallel implementing the Boolean expressions

$$\begin{aligned}
y_1 &= x_2\cdot x_4\cdot\overline{x_5} \vee \overline{x_6}\cdot\overline{x_7}\cdot\overline{x_8},\\
y_2 &= x_2\cdot x_4\cdot x_5\cdot x_7 \vee x_2\cdot x_4\cdot x_5\cdot x_8 \vee x_2\cdot x_4\cdot x_7\cdot x_8 \vee\\
&\quad x_2\cdot x_5\cdot x_6\cdot x_7 \vee x_2\cdot x_5\cdot x_6\cdot x_8 \vee x_2\cdot x_5\cdot x_7\cdot x_8 \vee\\
&\quad x_2\cdot x_6\cdot x_7\cdot x_8,\\
y_3 &= x_4\cdot x_5\cdot x_6 \vee x_4\cdot x_5\cdot x_8 \vee x_4\cdot x_6\cdot x_8,\\
y_4 &= \overline{x_2}\cdot\overline{x_4} \vee x_2\cdot x_4\cdot x_5\cdot x_6 \vee x_2\cdot x_4\cdot x_5\cdot x_7 \vee x_2\cdot x_4\cdot x_6\cdot x_7,\\
y_5 &= x_2\cdot\overline{x_4}\cdot\overline{x_5} \vee x_6\cdot x_7\cdot x_8 \vee \overline{x_6}\cdot\overline{x_7}\cdot\overline{x_8},\\
y_6 &= x_2\cdot\overline{x_4}\cdot\overline{x_6} \vee x_5\cdot x_7\cdot x_8 \vee \overline{x_5}\cdot\overline{x_7}\cdot\overline{x_8},\\
y_7 &= x_2\cdot\overline{x_4}\cdot\overline{x_7} \vee x_5\cdot x_6\cdot x_8 \vee \overline{x_5}\cdot\overline{x_6}\cdot\overline{x_8},\\
y_8 &= x_2\cdot\overline{x_4}\cdot\overline{x_8} \vee x_5\cdot x_6\cdot x_7 \vee \overline{x_5}\cdot\overline{x_6}\cdot\overline{x_7}.
\end{aligned}$$

The function f_7^{-1} can be computed as

$$\begin{aligned}
x_1 &= 0,\\
x_2 &= y_1 \vee y_2 \vee y_3\cdot y_4 \vee \overline{y_3}\cdot\overline{y_4},\\
x_3 &= 1,\\
x_4 &= y_1 \vee y_3 \vee y_2\cdot y_4,\\
x_5 &= y_1\cdot y_5 \vee \overline{y_1}\cdot\overline{y_5},\\
x_6 &= \overline{y_1}\cdot\overline{y_2}\cdot\overline{y_6} \vee \overline{y_1}\cdot\overline{y_3}\cdot\overline{y_4}\cdot\overline{y_6} \vee y_1\cdot\overline{y_2}\cdot\overline{y_5}\cdot\overline{y_7}\cdot\overline{y_8},\\
x_7 &= \overline{y_1}\cdot\overline{y_3}\cdot\overline{y_7} \vee \overline{y_1}\cdot\overline{y_2}\cdot\overline{y_4}\cdot\overline{y_7} \vee y_1\cdot\overline{y_3}\cdot\overline{y_5}\cdot\overline{y_6}\cdot\overline{y_8},\\
x_8 &= \overline{y_1}\cdot\overline{y_4}\cdot\overline{y_8} \vee \overline{y_1}\cdot\overline{y_2}\cdot\overline{y_3}\cdot\overline{y_4} \vee y_1\cdot\overline{y_4}\cdot\overline{y_5}\cdot\overline{y_6}\cdot\overline{y_7}.
\end{aligned}$$

Also in this case, the function f_8 and f_9 can be computed by first applying a cyclic shift of $x_1x_2x_3$ one and two times to the left respectively, and then applying the function f_7. Their inverses can be simply obtained by undoing this process. The function f_{10} is defined in the following truth table

x_1x_2	x_3x_4	x_5x_6	x_7x_8	$\overset{f_{10}}{\longleftrightarrow}$	$y_1y_2y_3y_4$	$y_5y_6y_7y_8$
11	11	11	11		1000	0000
11	10	11	00		0100	0000
11	10	10	10		0010	0000
11	10	10	01		0001	0000
11	10	00	11		0000	1000
11	10	01	01		0000	0100
11	10	01	10		0000	0010
11	11	00	00		0000	0001

and can be efficiently computed in parallel implementing the Boolean expressions $f_{10}(x_1x_2x_3x_4x_5x_6x_7x_8) =$

$$(x_4 \cdot x_5, \overline{x_4} \cdot x_5 \cdot x_6, \overline{x_4} \cdot x_5 \cdot x_7, \overline{x_4} \cdot x_5 \cdot x_8,$$

$$\overline{x_4} \cdot x_7 \cdot x_8, \overline{x_4} \cdot x_6 \cdot x_8, \overline{x_4} \cdot x_6 \cdot x_7, x_4 \cdot \overline{x_5}).$$

Whereas, the function f_{10}^{-1} can be computed with the Boolean expressions $f_{10}^{-1}(y_1y_2y_3y_4y_5y_6y_7y_8) =$

$$(1, 1, 1, y_1 \vee y_8, y_1 \vee y_2 \vee y_3 \vee y_4,$$

$$y_1 \vee y_2 \vee y_6 \vee y_7, y_1 \vee y_3 \vee y_5 \vee y_7, y_1 \vee y_4 \vee y_5 \vee y_6).$$

Finally, the function f_{11} is defined in the following truth table

x_1x_2	x_3x_4	x_5x_6	x_7x_8	$\overset{f_{11}}{\longleftrightarrow}$	$y_1y_2y_3y_4$	$y_5y_6y_7y_8$
11	11	10	00		1000	0000
11	11	01	00		0100	0000
11	11	00	10		0010	0000
11	11	00	01		0001	0000
11	10	10	00		0000	1000
11	10	01	00		0000	0100
11	10	00	10		0000	0010
11	10	00	01		0000	0001

and can be efficiently computed in parallel implementing the Boolean expressions $f_{11}(x_1x_2x_3x_4x_5x_6x_7x_8) =$

$$(x_4 \cdot x_5, x_4 \cdot x_6, x_4 \cdot x_7, x_4 \cdot x_8, \overline{x_4} \cdot x_5, \overline{x_4} \cdot x_6, \overline{x_4} \cdot x_7, \overline{x_4} \cdot x_8).$$

Whereas, the function f_{11}^{-1} can be computed with the Boolean expressions $f_{11}^{-1}(y_1y_2y_3y_4y_5y_6y_7y_8) =$

$$(1, 1, 1, y_1 \vee y_2 \vee y_3 \vee y_4, y_1 \vee y_5, y_2 \vee y_6, y_3 \vee y_7, y_4 \vee y_8).$$

Now we turn our attention to the computation of the balancing index ib and the check symbol C. For $X \in \mathbb{Z}_2^l$, $l \in \mathbb{N}$, let $m_i(X) = 0$ if $w(X) < i$ and $m_i(X) = 1$ if $w(X) \geq i$. The bit $m_i(X)$ is the i-th component of the vector $m(X) = 1^{w(X)}0^{l-w(X)}$. For simplicity and clarity of exposition, assume that ib is represented in unary by a binary vector of length 11 and weight 1 whose i-th component is 1 iff $ib = i$. For example, $ib = 00100000000$ stands for $ib = 3$. In the encoding process,

$$ib = i_1i_2i_3i_4i_5i_6i_7i_8i_9i_{10}i_{11}$$

can be computed from $X = X_LX_R$, with $X_L, X_R \in \mathbb{Z}_2^4$, as

$$\begin{aligned}
i_1 &= m_1(X) \cdot \overline{m_4(X)}, \\
i_2 &= m_6(X) \cdot \overline{m_8(X)}, \\
i_3 &= \overline{m_1(X_L)} \cdot \overline{m_1(X_R)} \vee \overline{m_1(X_L)} \cdot m_4(X_R) \vee \\
&\quad \overline{x_1} \cdot \overline{x_2} \cdot \overline{x_3} \cdot x_4 \cdot m_3(X_R), \\
i_4 &= \overline{x_1} \cdot \overline{x_2} \cdot x_3 \cdot \left(x_4 \cdot m_2(X_R) \cdot \overline{m_3(X_R)} \vee \overline{x_4} \cdot m_4(X_R)\right), \\
i_5 &= \overline{x_1} \cdot x_2 \cdot \overline{x_3} \cdot \left(x_4 \cdot m_2(X_R) \cdot \overline{m_3(X_R)} \vee \overline{x_4} \cdot m_4(X_R)\right), \\
i_6 &= x_1 \cdot \overline{x_2} \cdot \overline{x_3} \cdot \left(x_4 \cdot m_2(X_R) \cdot \overline{m_3(X_R)} \vee \overline{x_4} \cdot m_4(X_R)\right), \\
i_7 &= \overline{x_1} \cdot x_2 \cdot x_3 \cdot \left(x_4 \cdot m_1(X_R) \cdot \overline{m_3(X_R)} \vee \overline{x_4} \cdot m_2(X_R) \cdot \right. \\
&\quad \left. \overline{m_4(X_R)}\right) \vee \overline{x_1} \cdot \overline{x_2} \cdot x_3 \cdot m_3(X_R) \cdot \overline{m_4(X_R)}, \\
i_8 &= x_1 \cdot x_2 \cdot \overline{x_3} \cdot \left(x_4 \cdot m_1(X_R) \cdot \overline{m_3(X_R)} \vee \overline{x_4} \cdot m_2(X_R) \cdot \right. \\
&\quad \left. \overline{m_4(X_R)}\right) \vee \overline{x_1} \cdot x_2 \cdot \overline{x_3} \cdot m_3(X_R) \cdot \overline{m_4(X_R)}, \\
i_9 &= x_1 \cdot \overline{x_2} \cdot x_3 \cdot \left(x_4 \cdot m_1(X_R) \cdot \overline{m_3(X_R)} \vee \overline{x_4} \cdot m_2(X_R) \cdot \right. \\
&\quad \left. \overline{m_4(X_R)}\right) \vee x_1 \cdot \overline{x_2} \cdot \overline{x_3} \cdot m_3(X_R) \cdot \overline{m_4(X_R)}, \\
i_{10} &= m_4(X_L) \cdot \overline{m_1(X_R)} \vee x_1 \cdot x_2 \cdot x_3 \cdot \overline{x_4} \cdot m_2(X_R) \cdot \\
&\quad \overline{m_3(X_R)} \vee m_4(X_L) \cdot m_4(X_R), \\
i_{11} &= x_1 \cdot x_2 \cdot x_3 \cdot m_1(X_R) \cdot \overline{m_2(X_R)}.
\end{aligned}$$

Note that $X \in \mathcal{D}_j$ iff $i_j = 1$ and $i_h = 0$ for $h \neq j$. According to the definition (15) of the balancing functions, the check symbol $C = c_1c_2c_3c_4c_5$ can be computed from X as

$$\begin{aligned}
c_1 &= i_4 \vee i_5 \vee i_9 \vee i_{11}, \\
c_2 &= i_3 \vee i_4 \vee i_8 \vee i_{10}, \\
c_3 &= m_7(X) \cdot \overline{m_8(X)} \vee i_3 \vee i_6 \vee i_7 \vee i_{11}, \\
c_4 &= m_1(X) \cdot \overline{m_2(X)} \vee m_6(X) \cdot \overline{m_7(X)} \vee \\
&\quad m_7(X) \cdot \overline{m_8(X)} \vee i_{10}, \\
c_5 &= m_1(X) \cdot \overline{m_2(X)} \vee m_2(X) \cdot \overline{m_3(X)} \vee i_5 \vee i_6.
\end{aligned}$$

During the decoding process, the balancing index ib can be computed from C as

$$i_1 = \overline{c_1} \cdot \overline{c_3} \cdot c_5 \vee \overline{c_1} \cdot \overline{c_2} \cdot \overline{c_3} \cdot \overline{c_4} \cdot \overline{c_5},$$

$$\begin{aligned}
i_2 &= \overline{c_2} \cdot c_4 \cdot \overline{c_5}, & i_7 &= \overline{c_1} \cdot \overline{c_2} \cdot c_3 \cdot \overline{c_4} \cdot \overline{c_5}, \\
i_3 &= c_2 \cdot c_3, & i_8 &= \overline{c_1} \cdot c_2 \cdot \overline{c_3} \cdot \overline{c_4}, \\
i_4 &= c_1 \cdot c_2, & i_9 &= c_1 \cdot \overline{c_2} \cdot \overline{c_3} \cdot \overline{c_5}, \\
i_5 &= c_1 \cdot c_5, & i_{10} &= c_2 \cdot c_4, \\
i_6 &= c_3 \cdot c_5, & i_{11} &= c_1 \cdot c_3.
\end{aligned}$$

Note that $C \in \Gamma_j$ iff $ib = j$.

Concatenating this code with itself it is possible to obtain efficient DC($n = 1.625k, k, w = 0.375k$) codes.

5. Concluding remarks

The results proven in Section 2 and Section 3 imply that, for fixed $t \geq 0$, the t-PD codes whose code words contain a low number of 1's result in a faster implementation of the asynchronous communication scheme. In particular, low constant weight codes, such as the codes proposed in Section 4, are very well suited for this application.

For example, assume that $\mathcal{X}$ is a set of continuous random variables uniformly distributed over the interval $[t_{min}, t_{max}]$ of the time domain. In this case, if t_{ack} is the transmission time of the acknowledgment signal and

$$\Delta t \stackrel{\text{def}}{=} t_{max} - t_{min},$$

then, on average, the system cycle time, $\overline{P}_{t-PD}(w)$, using the t-proximity detection scheme is given by,

$$\overline{P}_{t-PD}(w) = t_{ack} + \overline{T}_{t-PD}(w) = t_{ack} + t_{min} + \frac{w-t}{w+1}\Delta t.$$

Now we distinguish the two cases which follow.

If $t_{ack} + t_{min} > \Delta t$ then, as soon as the first 1/marble of the transmitted word reaches the end of the bus, the receiver can send the acknowledgment signal to the sender so that it sends the next word. In other words, if the code employed is a constant weight w code, it is possible to communicate using the $(w-1)$-proximity

Table 1. Minimum speed-up comparisons.

	0-PD	1-PD	2-PD	3-PD	4-PD	5-PD	6-PD	7-PD	8-PD
DC($w=1$)	25.9%	88.8%	-	-	-	-	-	-	-
DC($w=2$)	13.3%	41.7%	88.8%	-	-	-	-	-	-
DC($w=3$)	7.9%	25.9%	51.1%	88.8%	-	-	-	-	-
DC($w=4$)	4.9%	18.1%	34.9%	57.4%	88.8%	-	-	-	-
DC($w=5$)	3.0%	13.3%	25.9%	41.7%	61.9%	88.8%	-	-	-
DC($w=6$)	1.7%	10.2%	20.2%	32.2%	46.9%	65.3%	88.8%	-	-
DC($w=7$)	0.7%	7.9%	16.2%	25.9%	37.4%	51.1%	67.9%	88.8%	-
DC($w=8$)	0.0%	6.3%	13.3%	21.4%	30.8%	41.7%	54.5%	70.0%	88.8%
BC($w=5.36$)	2.5%	-	-	-	-	-	-	-	-
1-VP($w=7.29$)	0.5%	7.4%	-	-	-	-	-	-	-
2-VP($w=7.73$)	0.2%	6.7%	14.1%	-	-	-	-	-	-

detection scheme. Note that, in this case, the intersymbol interference problem described in [4] does not occur. With $(w-1)$-proximity detection, the average system cycle time is

$$\overline{P}_{(w-1)-PD}(w) = t_{ack} + t_{min} + \frac{1}{w+1}\Delta t,$$

which is a strictly decreasing function of the weight of the transmitted word. Hence, in this case the use of high weight codes (codes whose code words contain a large number of 1's) results in a faster implementation of the communication scheme. Note that the high weight codes can be obtained by simply complementing low weight codes (such as the codes given in Section 4).

If instead, $t_{ack}+t_{min} \leq \Delta t$ then, to be safe from the intersymbol interference problem mentioned above, t-proximity detection is possible only for $t \in [0, w-2]$ which depends on the particular case (i.e., on the particular relative delays of the wires). We can still analyze the worst case behavior. Since the system cycle time increases with $t_{ack}+t_{min}$, the worst case occurs when

$$t_{ack} + t_{min} = \Delta t, \tag{16}$$

so that,

$$\overline{P}_{t-PD}(w) = \Delta t + \frac{w-t}{w+1}\Delta t = \frac{2w-t+1}{w+1}\Delta t.$$

For example, let's compare the performance of the usual dual-rail code, used as 0-PD code, with the performance of the DC($n = 13, k = 8, w = 3$) code proposed in Subsection 4.3, used as 1-PD code. For the dual-rail code:

$$\overline{P}_{0-PD}^{dual-rail} = \overline{P}_{0-PD}(w=8) = \frac{17}{9}\Delta t = 1.889 \cdot \Delta t.$$

For the proposed code:

$$\overline{P}_{1-PD}^{proposed} = \overline{P}_{1-PD}(w=3) = \frac{6}{4}\Delta t = 1.500 \cdot \Delta t.$$

This means that using the second communication scheme instead of the first, one gets at least the following speed-up:

$$\text{minimum speed-up} = \left(\frac{\overline{P}_{0-PD}^{dual-rail}}{\overline{P}_{1-PD}^{proposed}} - 1\right) \cdot 100 =$$

$$\left(\frac{1.889}{1.500} - 1\right) \cdot 100 = 25.9\%.$$

But in many cases, such as for off-chip data transfer, hypothesis (16) is optimistic and Δt may be much greater than $t_{ack} + t_{min}$. In such cases, the speed-up is much more than the one just given. Table 1 shows other comparisons with respect to the dual-rail code with $k = 8$ information bits used as a 0-PD code. In the Table, the codes DC(w) are constant weight w codes. The code BC($w = 5.36$) is a Berger like code designed to minimize the average weight per code word. The codes 1-VP($w = 7.29$) and 2-VP($w = 7.73$) are systematic t-PD codes, $t = 1, 2$ respectively, given in [8].

Finally, note that analogous conclusion can be drawn for distributions which are different from the uniform distribution.

References

[1] V. Akella, N. H. Vaidya and G. R. Redinbo, "Limitations of VLSI implementation of delay-insensitive codes", *Proceedings FTCS-26*, IEEE Computer Society Press, Los Alamitos, California, pp. 208–217, 1996.

[2] P. Billingsley, *Probability and Measure*, Jhon Wiley & Sons, New York, 1979.

[3] M. Blaum, *Codes for Detecting and Correcting Unidirectional Errors*, IEEE Computer Society Press, Los Alamitos, California, 1993.

[4] M. Blaum and J. Bruck, "Delay-insensitive pipelined communication on parallel busses", *IEEE Transactions on Computers*, vol. 44, pp. 660–668, May 1995.

[5] B. Bose, "On unordered codes", *IEEE Transactions on Computers*, vol. 40, pp. 125–131, Feb. 1991.

[6] L. G. Tallini and B. Bose, "Design of efficient balanced and constant weight codes for VLSI systems", *IEEE Transaction on Computers*, vol. 47, pp. 556–572, May 1998.

[7] L. G. Tallini and B. Bose, "Balanced codes with parallel encoding and decoding", to appear on *IEEE Transaction on Computers*,

[8] N. H. Vaidya and S. Perisetty, "Systematic proximity-detecting codes", *IEEE Transactions on Information Theory*, vol. 43, pp. 1852–1863, Nov. 1997.

[9] T. Verhoeff, "Delay-insensitive codes – an overview", *Distributed Computing*, vol. 3, pp. 1–8, 1988.

Fault Tolerance, Channel Coding and Arithmetic Source Coding Combined

G. Robert Redinbo and Ranjit Manomohan
Department of Electrical and Computer Engineering
University of California
Davis, CA 95616-5294

Abstract

A complete source and channel coding system is protected from both channel errors and errors emanating from internal hardware failures by introducing redundancy in the source encoding and decoding procedures as well as infrequently inserting parity symbols generated by a burst-detecting convolutional code. The combined protected system can detect errors in any significant subsystems whether from transmission errors or hardware faults. The arithmetic source coding procedures are augmented with a few checking operations which detect failure effects at each iteration of the algorithm. The normal input symbol sequence has a parity symbol inserted sparsely; every n^{th} symbol is determined by a high-rate burst-detecting convolutional code. These parity values provide end to end error detection for channel and hardware-based errors. The favorable probability of detection performance is evaluated, and the low overhead costs as measured by increased compression length of the modified source coding procedure are determined.

Introduction

Data that are produced by a source and conveyed to a user can be transformed in many ways to increase the efficiency and reliability of the communications process. The classic work of Shannon on Information Theory [1,2] shows how it is possible to first encode the source so as to minimize the average length of the compressed symbols, and secondly, how to incorporate error-correcting codes so that arbitrarily low probability of error can be achieved over the transmission channel. Lossless source coding transforms the data representation without losing any information.

There has been increased interest in combining the source and channel coding functions to increase efficiencies, e.g., see references of [3]. Nevertheless, no fundamental principles of information theory are violated by examining alternative methods of achieving source and channel coding. This paper addresses the protection of data that are source encoded using arithmetic coding methodologies. In a departure from previous approaches, the system is designed to withstand not only transmission errors, but errors resulting from internal hardware failures in all parts of the implementation including protecting the encoders and decoders.

The following section describes pertinent fundamental operations of arithmetic coding. Then protection methods for detecting errors arising from any part of the system are developed. Special checks internal to the computations of the arithmetic coding are defined and external protection is introduced by sparsely inserting parity symbols determined by a burst-detecting convolutional code. The next section shows the effectiveness of these methods by displaying the dramatic improvement in detecting errors of any kind. The overhead cost measured by the degradation in compression length is evaluated. The final section describes extending these protection methods to practical systems such as those using adaptive procedures. Simulation results verify performance levels.

Transmission of Arithmetic Coding Compressed Data

An important and optimal source coding technique is arithmetic coding so named because it transforms input symbols using arithmetic subintervals of the unit interval. The output digits are grouped into variable length blocks to represent each input symbol. Arithmetic encoders with binary output groups will be considered only because of the prevalent use of binary logic.

The fundamental principles and operations of arithmetic coding will be explained for a zeroth-order source, meaning a source whose symbol alphabet is assigned a probability mass function [2]. The source alphabet containing A symbols will be denoted by S.

$$S = \{s_1, s_2, \ldots, s_A\} \qquad ; |S| = A \tag{1}$$

$$f_i = \Pr(s_i) \quad i = 1, 2, \ldots, A$$

The encoding algorithm partitions subintervals according to a distributed function $\{F_i\}$ associated with these probability values.

$$F_i = \sum_{j=1}^{i-1} f_j \qquad ; \; i = 2, 3, \ldots, A+1 \tag{2}$$

$$F_1 = 0 \qquad ; \; F_{A+1} = 1 \text{ (by probability properties)}$$

An arithmetic encoder accepts a sequence of source symbols, say $s_{i_1}, s_{i_2}, \ldots, s_{i_k}, \ldots$, and translates them into a sequence of binary bit groups, each group having a variable number of bits, $b_{i_1}, b_{i_2}, \ldots, b_{i_k}, \ldots$,

$$s_{i_r} \rightarrow b_{i_r} \qquad ; r = 1, 2, \ldots, k, \ldots \tag{3}$$

This basic encoding is depicted in Figure 1a. The bits that are transmitted represent the bits in a binary expansion of a dyadic fractional number which falls within an interval as developed inside the encoder.

This research was supported in part by Grant ONR N00014-95-1-1190.

0-7695-0213-X/99 $10.00 © 1999 IEEE

$\text{Bits}\{b_{i_1}, b_{i_2}, \ldots, b_{i_r}\} \rightarrow B_r$ Dyadic Fraction

Each input symbol in the input sequence is associated with a subinterval of the real line interval [0,1)-half open unit interval.

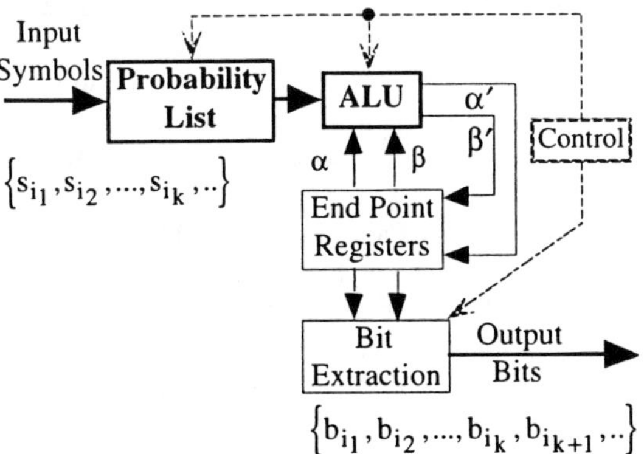

(a) Arithmetic Encoder

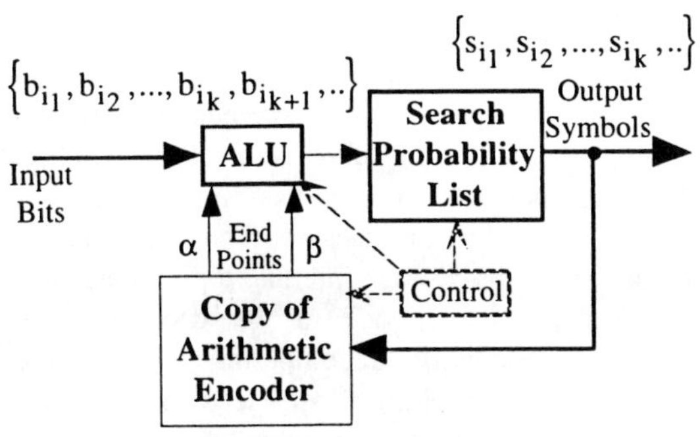

(b) Arithmetic Decoder

Figure 1. Basic Structures of Arithmetic Encoder and Decoder

Successive subintervals are formed by partitioning the subinterval related to the previous symbol. Say the kth input symbol, s_{i_k}, has been assigned a subinterval $[\alpha_k, \beta_k)$. The next subinterval is $[\alpha_{k+1}, \beta_{k+1})$ associated with $s_{i_{k+1}}$.

$$[\alpha_{k+1}, \beta_{k+1}) \subset [\alpha_k, \beta_k) \tag{4}$$

For maximum compression the new subinterval is selected from partitioning $[\alpha_k, \beta_k)$ as determined by the distribution function values for index i_{k+1} and $(i_{k+1}+1)$. The length of the base subinterval $[\alpha_k, \beta_k)$ is denoted by λ_k.

$$\lambda_k = \beta_k - \alpha_k \; ; \; \alpha_{k+1} = \lambda_k F_{i_{k+1}} + \alpha_k \; ; \; \beta_{k+1} = \lambda_k F_{(i_{k+1}+1)} + \alpha_k \tag{5}$$

The compressed output bits grouped in $b_{i_{k+1}}$ assigned to the new input symbol i_{k+1} are easily determined by examining any number in the new subinterval $[\alpha_{k+1}, \beta_{k+1})$. However, there are judicious choices for an interior point which are used in practical implementations [1,2,4]. Nevertheless, the number of bits in group $b_{i_{k+1}}$ is dictated by the exponent t_{k+1} satisfying the following inequalities involving the new subinterval's length λ_{k+1}.

$$\lambda_{k+1} = \beta_{k+1} - \alpha_{k+1} \quad ; \left|\text{Bits}\{b_{i_{k+1}}\}\right| = t_{k+1} \quad ; \frac{1}{2^{t_{k+1}}} \le \lambda_{k+1} < \frac{1}{2^{(t_{k+1}-1)}} \tag{6}$$

Generally, only two items need to be maintained during the encoding of a sequence of input symbols. Either the two interval endpoints α_k and β_k or one endpoint and the interval's length, e.g., α_k and λ_k, are sufficient to define the interval representing the source coding of input symbol s_{i_k} [5].

Practical implementations of arithmetic coding confront several issues, numerical precision and representation formats. Nevertheless, the theoretical requirements outlined above are all that are necessary to motivate and examine protection against hardware failures and channel error corruption. A method called rescaling [2,4] eliminates the growing precision requirements of ever smaller subintervals as newer input symbols are processed. The theory of arithmetic coding guarantees that all items in the algorithm can be scaled periodically without altering the encoded output bits. The impact of computer number representations leads to dual representatives of the same numerical value, possibly producing situations of underflow or overflow [2]. Such situations are resolved at later steps in the encoding sequence, but they can cause the need for large buffers and widely varying output rates

The arithmetic decoder, the data expansion operation, translates the compressed data bits back into their original symbols even though the corresponding bits are grouped by variable lengths. The decoder employs a copy of the encoder to remove the effects of previously decoded bits on the subinterval endpoints as they are computed, Figure 1b. The decoder's ALU computes a dyadic fraction that must fall between two probability distribution function values which represent the input alphabet. Theses consecutive values identify the proper decoded symbol's index. For current endpoint α_k and length λ_k, the dyadic fraction represented by the received bits to date, B_k, can be used to calculate a fraction pointing into the proper distribution function's interval.

$$\text{Compute}\left(\frac{B_k - \alpha_k}{\lambda_k}\right) \Rightarrow \{F_i\}\text{Interval} \Rightarrow \text{Symbol index } i_k \tag{7}$$

The output bits of the data compressor, the arithmetic encoder, are transmitted or recorded for use at another place or time. Clearly, even a single bit error can have a disastrous effect on the arithmetic code decoding process, and so channel error-correcting codes are generally employed. However any coding scheme, no matter how elaborate, can be overwhelmed. There have been several recent articles addressing combined source and channel coding to increase the efficiency and error-correcting capabilities [6-11]. On the other hand, hardware failures can occur in any of the subsystems in the arithmetic encoder or decoder. Very little research has been directed towards such problems with most of it focused on channel decoder fault tolerance [12-15].

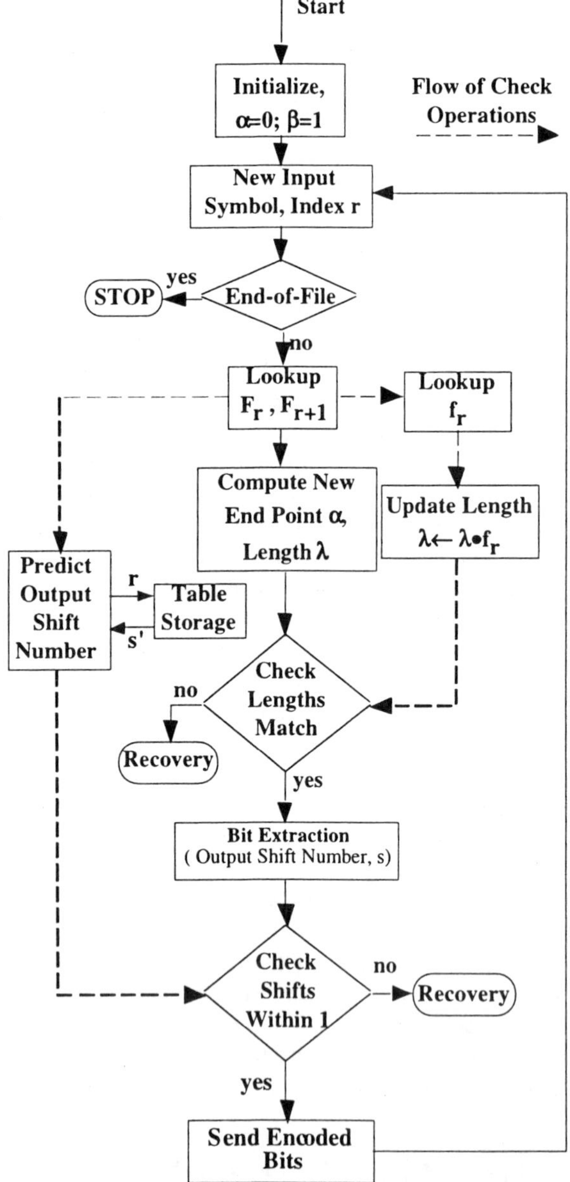

Figure 2. Internal Arithmetic Encoder Checks

Since hardware failures in the arithmetic encoder and decoder can impact virtually any operations, the resulting errors are generally modeled as affecting some numerical result. The most general error model supporting failures is to add real number errors to the correct result; this is a model that does not require errors to be actually additive at the hardware level. This is the high level model employed in algorithm-based fault tolerance (ABFT) designs for example [16, Section 3.12]. The error models vary by subsystem. The transmission channel and the outputs of the channel code encoder and decoder will have errors modeled at the bit level. Failures in the arithmetic encoder and decoder can be viewed as introducing numerical errors. It will be assumed that errors in the five subassemblies, data compressor, channel encoders, transmission channel, channel decoders and data expander are statistically independent

System Protection Methods, Internal and External

The feedback nature of the arithmetic encoding and decoding algorithms make it very difficult to detect errors due to internal failures, even temporary ones. The basic encoding and decoding operations, equations (5) and (7), clearly show how previously computed endpoints and interval lengths are used in subsequent steps. The central part of all the operations in these assemblies involve the computation of interval parameters. The first part of this section describes how the internal operations of the encoding steps, also repeated in the decoder, may be protected by efficiently recomputing some internal parameters, thusly, checking most steps in the encoder. This technique is simpler than just duplicating all encoding steps and comparing the two results at each iteration.

The fundamental steps in the encoding algorithm are shown in Figure 2, following the solid line of arrows. Two different simple calculations are also performed as denoted by flows designated by dashed lines. A comparable length value is computed by using the previous length value λ, as verified in the preceding stage, scaling by the stored probability mass value associated with the present input symbol. Simultaneously, the same interval length is computed as the difference of the upper and lower endpoints. These two versions are checked for a match to the precision of the stored probability value. Any single error in either the lookup process for the distribution function or probability values, or any computational error in the numerical operations is immediately detected. Here, as is common practice in fault tolerance methodologies, only one error is assumed in one part, with all remaining steps error-free.

The second internal check protects the selection of how many bits are placed in each output group at the conclusion of each encoding pass. The theory of arithmetic coding guarantees that, after possibly a delay, several bits in the representation of the affiliated interval's endpoints are identical, and thus may be sent. It can be shown also that the predicted number of this shift can be precomputed and stored, since they are related to the expansion of the probability mass function for each input symbol index. However, due to accumulated small fractions, this shift amount can differ only one shift if at all.

Both of the internal checks are very effective at detecting errors in numerical operations and memory accessing steps. The two checks are performed by bit comparators while the alternate length computation requires an additional multiplication. The predicted shift amount is stored in a memory table. Combined, the extra features are not equal to completely duplicating the encoder. The small amount of unprotected resources will be covered by external features described next.

In a classic source channel dichotomy, any failure in the data compressor's hardware produces errors that cannot be detected anywhere else in the overall system. Likewise, any failures that produce errors in the data expander are passed directly to the destination without detection. The underlying problem is that there is no error-detecting redundancy in either the encoder or decoder [6]. No published method addresses failures in the source and channel encoding and decoding hardware subsystems.

The channel coding error-correcting codes, either block or convolutional types, encode and decode bits by grouping them into blocks or subblocks regardless of their intrinsic meaning as outputs of a source encoder. That is fine from an information theory viewpoint, but troublesome when faults in the source encoding or decoding hardware are considered. A fault can cause errors in channel bits that span more than one code word or subblock in a convolutional code's case. Hardware based errors can cause bursts of errors which are passed though the channel error-detecting mechanisms without notice. Hence, redundancy should be introduced before or in the source coding process where the input symbols retain their fixed block structure.

One method of inserting sparse amounts of redundancy for fault tolerance and channel error control purposes in outlined in Figure 3a where a bank of parallel high-rate binary convolutional encoders are employed to regularly but infrequently produce a parity symbol that is then inserted among the normal input symbols. Each input symbol is viewed as being represented by k binary bits, and the resulting bit streams are encoded by k parallel binary encoders as detailed in Figure 3b.

The binary code selected is from the class of high-rate, burst-detecting and correcting codes called Berlekamp-Preparata-Massey (BPM) after their independent discoveries [17,18]. They can be designed for any parameter n yielding a rate (n-1)/n convolutional code with constraint parameter

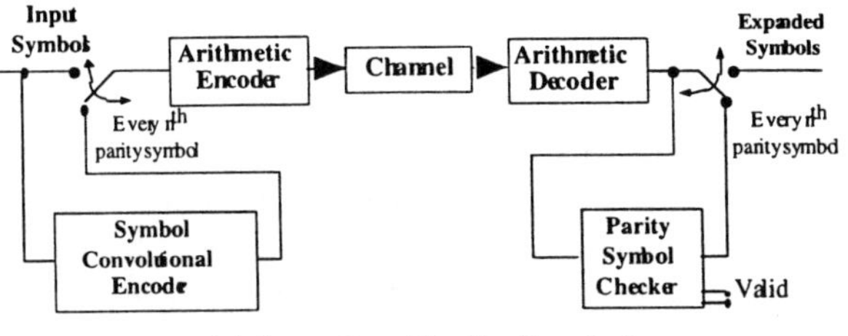

(a) Inserting Parity Symbols in Arithmetic Coded Stream

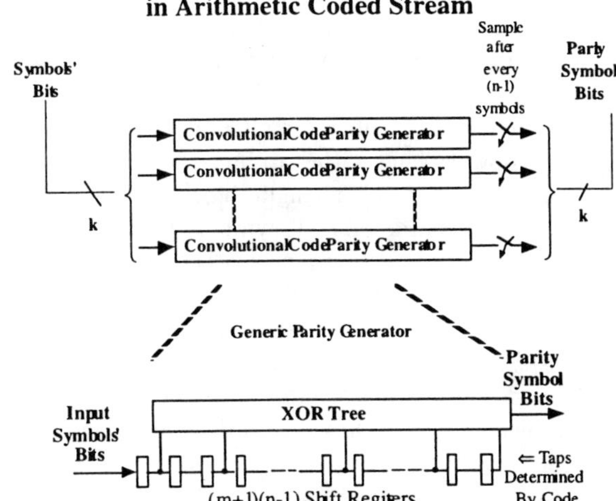

(b) Symbol Convolutional Encoder

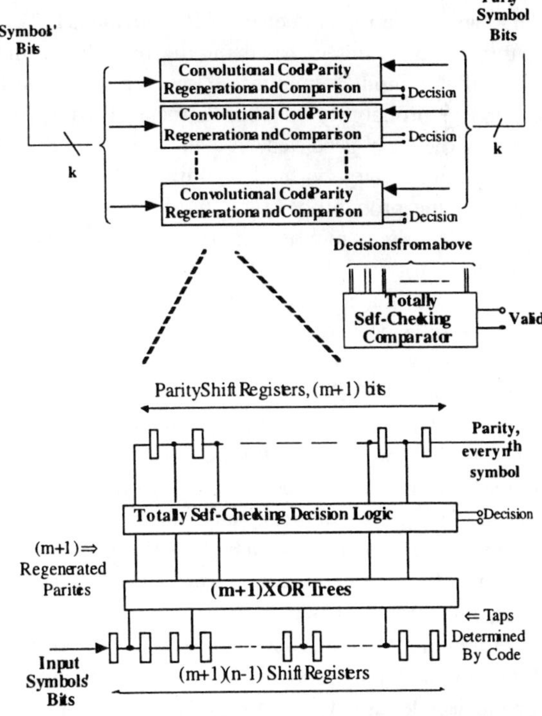

(c) Parity Symbol Checker

Figure 3. Externally Protecting Transmission and Arithmetic Coding Systems

$m = (2n - 1)$. These codes can detect the onset of bursts of errors provided there has been m blocks, n bits per block, without errors preceding the present burst.

The BPM class of burst-detecting convolutional codes generates a parity symbol of k bits after (n-1) symbols. This parity symbol is then inserted into the normal stream of symbols at the arithmetic encoder's output. Of course, this infrequent parity symbol does not convey any additional information from the source, and so the efficiency of the source coding is degraded slightly, as will be analyzed shortly. However, this form of redundancy permits detection capabilities for all errors introduced by subsystems downstream. The arithmetic decoder at the destination receives variable length blocks of bits from which it reconstructs the original symbols in the error-free case. Every n^{th} symbol now represents a parity symbol. The burst-detecting structure of the code is recreated at the destination by regenerating the parity symbol values from other decoded symbols and comparing each with the related symbol decoded directly. The error decisions are combined in a fault-tolerant manner providing a dual-rail logic signal "valid" (See Figure 3c).

As long as only one subsystem in the protected subsystem, Figure 3c, fails, this scheme will detect the beginning of erroneous behavior. The standard technique for addressing communication errors is to request a repeated transmission, known as automatic-repeat-request (ARQ) methods [17].

Arithmetic encoding is based on the probability mass function of the input symbols. However, what is the corresponding probability function associated with parity symbols as they are generated? It can be shown that the parity symbols are virtually uniformly distributed regardless of the probability function of the regular input symbols when the number of tap positions used to compute the parity values is relatively large. The inserted parity symbols are not compressed by the arithmetic encoding process but greatly increases the probability of detecting errors and failures.

Coverage and Efficiency

Simple analyses will access the effectiveness of the fault tolerance method proposed in Figure 3 which provides for detection of errors whether due to the transmission channel or a result of hardware failures in any subsystem. The main goal is to ensure no faulty data are passed from the system without signaling erroneous conditions; detecting methods are of paramount importance.

End to end protection relies ultimately on the detection facilities in the parity symbol checks following the arithmetic decoder as detailed in Figure 3c. This part of the overall protected system is designated as Region 4 in Figure 4b and contains several totally self-checking comparators and decision logic arrays that are self-protecting by design [19,20]. Note, as in most fault tolerance methodologies, dual-rail logic is used at the output. It is assumed that any failures are mutually exclusive either in a comparator or in the surrounding logic.

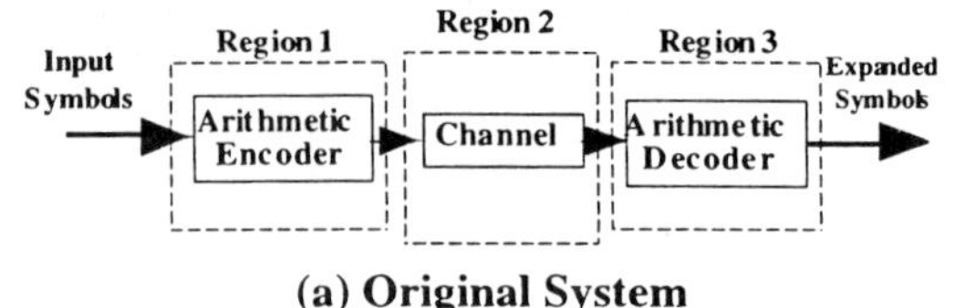

(a) Original System

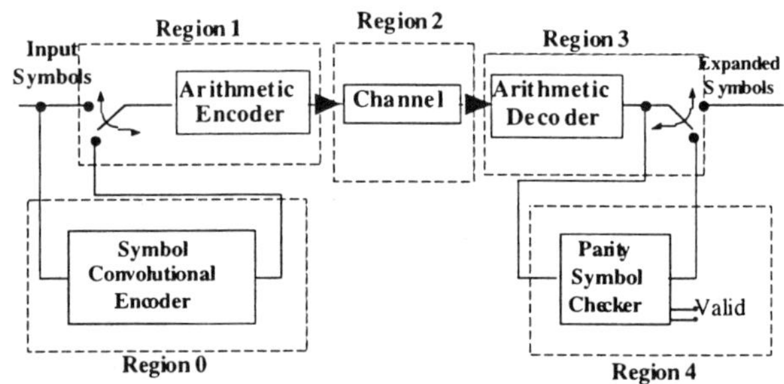

(b) Error Regions in Protected system

Figure 4. Subsystem Error Containment Regions in Original and Protected System

It is easy to see that errors resulting from any one other region's failure in Figure 4b will be detected by an error-free Region 4. However, it is possible in general that two regions producing errors will not lead to detectable errors by Region 4 resources. This is because errors can compensate one another. Nevertheless, even under these restrictions great improvement in protection are possible when compared with an unprotected system, Figure 4a.

A simple probability analysis involving bounding techniques will demonstrate protection coverage. The probability of undetected errors is a good measure of the protection level. A central question is: when adding additional resources for error detection, does the extra exposure to further errors lead to a net decrease in the probability of undetected errors?

Figure 4a shows the regions of a standard arithmetic source coding and transmission system that contain hardware or transmission facilities which can introduce errors. Assume each region has a probability of error which describes events leading to errors passing out of the region, i.e., $P_i = P$ (Errors out of Region i). It is easy to evaluate the probability of undetected errors in the unprotected system Figure 4a, $P_{UNPRTCD}(UDE)$, the complement of the event of no errors in all subsystems.

$$P_{UNPRCTD}(UDE) = 1 - \prod_{i=1}^{3} (1 - P_i) \quad (8)$$

On the other hand, the proposed protected system may may be lower bounded by considering the probability of at most one subsystem in error.

$$P_{PRCTD}(DE) \geq$$

$$Q(DE) = P(\text{one or fewer subsystems in error}) \quad (9a)$$

$$Q(DE) = \prod_{j=0}^{4}\left(1-P_j\right) + \sum_{i=0}^{4}\{P_i\}\prod_{\substack{j=0 \\ j\neq i}}^{4}\left(1-P_j\right) \quad (9b)$$

The probability of undetected errors, $P_{PRTCD}(UDE)$, is related to $P_{PRTCD}(DE)$, and may be overbounded using Q(DE)

$$P_{PRCTD}(UDE) \leq 1 - Q(DE) \quad (10)$$

A comparison plot between $P_{UNPRCTD}(UDE)$ and the upper bound for $P_{PRTCD}(UDE)$ is shown in Figure 5, where both axes employ logarithmic scales. For purposes of this plot, all subsystems are assumed to have equal probabilities of error, just to simplify the presentation. The curve in Figure 5 representing the protected system is an upper bound so the true probability of undetected errors lies below it, increasing the differences displayed. There are overhead costs associated with the great improvements in protection exhibited in Figure 5. The periodic insertion of parity symbols degrades the efficiency of the arithmetic source encoding process by increasing the average length of the output.

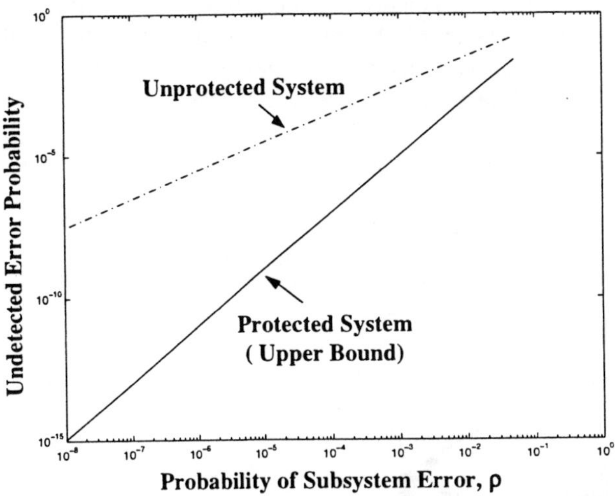

Figure 5. Probability of Undetected Error, Protected and Unprotected Systems, versus Probability of Subsystem Error

The optimum average length for an arithmetic coder operating on a stationary memoryless source is equal to the source entropy H(X) [1,2]. In a similar way, it is possible to develop the average length $\overline{T}$ for the protected system assuming a similar source. The parameter of the code n and the size of the symbol alphabet, 2^k, are quite evident in the final equation for $\overline{T}$

$$\overline{T} = \frac{(n-1)}{n}H(x) + \frac{k}{n} \quad (11)$$

The code rate (n-1)/n scales the basic source entropy H(x) which is the average length for the unprotected system Figure 4a. The extra additive factor k/n represents the number of bits in the basic input symbol divided by the code's subblock length n.

One measure of the overhead cost is the dimensionless ratio of $\overline{T}$ to the original average length H(x), subtracting 1 to get the fractional increase due to protection features. This may be rewritten by considering two independent parameters, the code rate R=(n-1)/n and the compression ratio factor ξ=H(X)/k . The factor ξ represents the amount of compression length H(x) divided by the maximum entropy of symbols over k-dimensional binary space.

$$\gamma = R - 1 + \frac{1}{n\xi} \qquad ;R = \frac{n-1}{n},\quad \xi = \frac{H(x)}{k} \quad (13)$$

Figure 6 shows the overhead factor γ for various sizes of code subblock n as a function of the compression factor ξ. For better compression factors (smaller values of ξ), the overhead cost γ increases because the parity symbols requiring maximum length infrequently begin to dominate the desirable effects of compression. Normal compression factors are above 0.3 so codes can be selected with overhead costs below 20%.

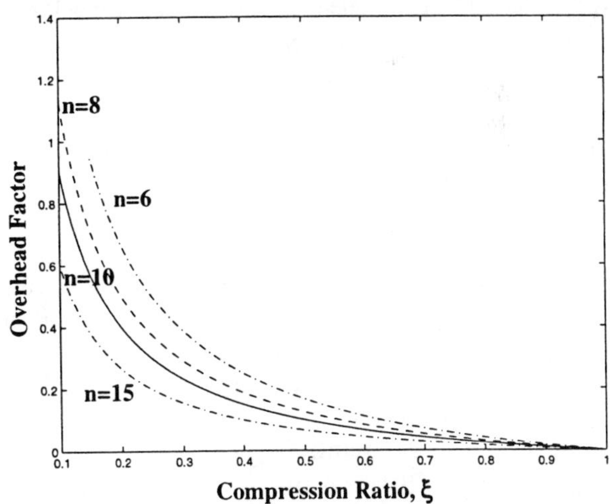

Figure 6. Overhead versus Compression Ratio Factor

Practical Considerations and Simulations

Arithmetic coding systems employed in practice do not use a static probabilistic model. Such a model is usually unavailable and creating it would require the algorithm to operate on two passes. Instead practical versions of arithmetic coding systems estimate the probability function based on the input symbol's observed history and is called adaptive encoding because the important probability characterization is adapted as the source symbols are observed [2, Chapter 8]. As long as the encoder and decoder follow the same estimation rules and there are no errors. The probability values are generally approximated by using a histogram; the probability of a symbol is its occurrence number divided by the total number of symbols in a long observation period.

The widely available implementation of arithmetic coding by Witten et. al.[23] was used for simulations. Both static and adaptive versions of the arithmetic coding implementations were modified by including the error checking procedures proposed earlier with parity symbols generated by a parallel bank of 8 rate 9/10 convolutional encoders. Most of the simulations employed the adaptive method because the static systems are truly a subset of the adaptive one. A brief description of the changes required in the implementation code from [23] is described below through some pseudo-code snippets.

The adaptive version of the algorithm adjusts the model after every symbol is encoded which means that there may be a change in the predicted number of bits shifted for every symbol. The predicted number of bits output while encoding each symbol is estimated by the following expression:

|Total number of symbols| - |Frequency of current symbol|

where |x| denotes the number of bits required to represent x. Since both of the terms in the expression above can change when the model is updated, both variables must be tracked. This is achieved by the pseudo-code fragment given below:

```
/* In procedure update_model */
if (frequency_of_current_symbol>
(2^|frequency_of_current_symbol|))
then inc |frequency_of_current_symbol|;
if (total_number_of_symbols >
(2^|total_number_of_symbols|))
then inc |total_number_of_symbols|;
```

Similar steps have to be taken when the table of the probabilities of the symbols overflows its numerical storage space and its values are resized to fit in the given bounds. The pseudo-code fragment that implements these operations are shown below:

```
if(total_number_of_symbols >
Maximum_allowed) then begin
Halve_the_frequency_of_each_symbol_in_the_
table();
dec |frequency_of_each_symbol|;
end;
```

The adaptive model also employs a table of the frequencies of the parity symbol. This table is maintained and updated in a similar fashion as the normal frequency count table.

The encoder must check after each symbol is processed to ensure that the right number of shifts have been made. Also, computations are verified by requiring the interval length be recomputed and checked with current interval length.

```
/* In procedure encode_symbol */
if( high - low != recomputed_interval)
        ERROR_IN_COMPUTATION();
if( Number_of_Bits_Output !=
|Total number of symbols| - |Frequency of
current symbol|±1 )
        ERROR_IN_COMPUTATION();
```

Parity generation by the convolution encoder banks is straightforward, and the parity symbols are handled by the arithmetic encoder using the parity symbol distribution, which quickly approaches a uniform one, leading to no compression of the checking symbols.

The results of the simulation closely model the theoretical expectations. Of primary interest are the overhead of the parity symbols and their probability distribution.

The overhead factor is observed for varying levels of compression and is shown in Figure 7. The theoretical or expected curve from equation(11) for a rate 9/10 convolutional code employing byte symbols is also shown. This curve shows the best possible results that can be obtained. In adaptive arithmetic coding, the entropy H(x) can be thought of as varying continuously and each data point in the scatter plot models running the experiment on the various instantaneous static probability distributions. An observation of the ratio of parity symbols to the information symbols throughout the experiment results in a scatter plot as shown in Figure 7. The scatter plot is very close to the curve where the overhead is around 15 - 20% for moderate compression ratios. Arithmetic coding in most practical cases gives a compression of 1.5 to 2 times and this overhead is acceptable for the protection of both the source and the channel coding system.

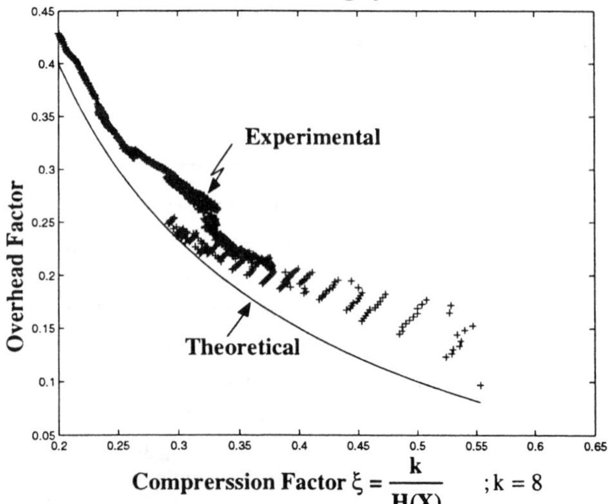

Comprerssion Factor $\xi = \frac{k}{H(X)}$;k = 8

Figure 7. Experimental Overhead Costs

Conclusions

A complete system protected from both hardware failures and channel errors has been described. The combination of a few assertions in the source encoder combined with the infrequent insertion of parity symbols is shown to achieve good protection at very low overhead. The application of this system is seen in transmission systems using ARQ techniques where not only the channel but also the digital electronics are prone to errors. Most data compression systems incorporate arithmetic coding as the last stage and this work is proposed for use in the final stage of a compression system like the JPEG.

References

[1] T. M. Cover and J. A. Thomas, *Elements of Information Theory*. New York, NY: John Wiley & Sons, Inc., 1991.

[2] D. Hankerson, G.A. Harris and P. D. Johnson, Jr., *Introduction to Information Theory and Data Compression.* Boca Raton, FL: CRC Press, 1998.

[3] N. Demir and K. Sayood, "Joint Source/Channel Coding for Variable Length Codes," Proceedings Data Compression Conference (DCC'98), Snow Bird, Utah, pp. 139-148, 1998.

[4] G. G. Langdon, Jr., "An Introduction to Arithmetic Coding," *IBM Journal of Research and Development*, vol. 28, pp. 135-149, March 1984.

[5] C. B. Jones, "An Efficient Coding System for Long Source Sequences," *IEEE Transactions on Information Theory*, vol. IT-27, pp. 280-291, May 1981.

[6] C. Boyd, J. G. Cleary, S. A. Irvine, I. Rinsma-Melchert and I. H. Witten, "Integrating Error Detection into Arithmetic Coding," *IEEE Transactions on Communications*, vol. 45, pp. 1-3, January 1997.

[7] I. Kozintsev, J. Chou and K. Ramchandran, "Image Transmission using Arithmetic Coding based Continuous Error Detection," Proceedings Data Compression Conference (DCC'98), Snow Bird, Utah, pp. 339-348, 1998.

[8] I. Kozintsev, J. Chou and K. Ramchandran, "The Role of Arithmetic Coding based Continuous Error Detection in Digital Transmission Systems," Proceedings IEEE International Symposium on Information Theory, Cambridge, MA, pg. 290, 1998.

[9] G. F. Elmasry and Y. Bar-Ness, "An Automatic Repeat Request Scheme for Error Detection and Correction of Compressed Data," Proceedings of the 1996 Conference on Information Science and Systems, Vol. 1, Princeton, NJ, pp. 561-566, 1996.

[10] G. F. Elmasry, " An Automatice Repeat Request Scheme for Joint Lossless-Source and Channel Codes," Proceedings Thirty-Fourth Annual Allerton Conference on Communication, Control and Computing, Urbana-Champaign, Il, pp. 102-111, 1996.

[11] G. F. Elmasry, "Arithmetic Coding Algorithm with Embedded Channel Coding," *Electronics Letters*, vol. 33, No. 20, pp. 1687-1688, 1997.

[12] G. R. Redinbo, " Fault-Tolerant Decoders for Cyclic Error-Correcting Codes," *IEEE Transactions on Computers*, Vol. C-36, No. 1, pp. 47-63, 1987.

[13] I. M. Boyarinov, "Self-Checking and Self-Correcting Decoder Circuits for Deleting Single Error Bytes," *Automatic Control and Computer Sciences (Russian Translation)*, vol. 25, pp. 75-79, 1991.

[14] I. M. Boyarinov, "Self-Checking Decoding Algortihm for Reed-Solomon Codes," pp. 63-68 in *Errro Control, Cryptology, and Speech Compression.* A. Chmora and S. B. Wicker (Editors) Workshop on Information Protection, Moscow Russia, Berlin:Springer-Verlag, 1993.

[15] G. R. Redinbo, L. M. Napolitano and D. D. Andaleon, "Multibit Correcting Data Interface for Fault-Tolerant Systems," *IEEE Transactions on Computers*, Vol. 42, No. 4, pp. 433-446, 1993.

[16] D. K. Pradhan, *Fault-Tolerant Computer System Design.* Upper Saddle River, New Jersey: Printice-Hall, 1996.

[17] S. Lin and D. J. Costello, Jr., *Error Control Coding: Fundamentals and Applications.* Englewood Cliffs, NJ: Prentice Hall, 1983

[18] W. W. Peterson and E. J. Weldon, Jr., *Error-Correcting Codes, Second Edition.* Cambridge, MA: The MIT Press, 1972.

[19] B. W. Johnson, *Design and Analysis of Fault-Tolerant Digital Systems.* Reading, MA: Addison-Weslet Publishing Company, 1989.

[20] J. Wakerly, *Error Detecting Codes, Self-Checking Circuits and Applications*, New York, NY: North-Holland, 1978.

[21] A. Papoulis, *Probability, Random Variables, and Stochastic Processes (Second Edition).* New York: McGraw-Hill Book Company, 1984.

[22] D. F. Elliot and K. R. Rao, *Fast Transforms Algorithms, Analyses, Applications.* New York: Academic Press, Chapter 8, 1982.

[23] I.H.Witten, R.M. Neal, and J.G.Cleary, "Arithmetic coding for data compression", *Communications of the ACM*, vol. 30, pp. 520-540, 1987.

On the Necessity of On-line-BIST in Safety-Critical Applications – A Case-Study

Andreas Steininger
TU Vienna, Inst. für Technische Informatik
Treitlstr. 3/182/2, A-1040 Vienna, Austria
Andreas.Steininger@tuwien.ac.at

Christoph Scherrer
TU Vienna, Inst. für Meß- und Schaltungstechnik
Gusshausstr. 25/354, A-1040 Vienna, Austria
Christoph.Scherrer@tuwien.ac.at

Abstract

This paper analyzes the effect of dormant faults on the mean time to failure (MTTF) of highly reliable systems. The analysis is performed by means of Markov models that allow quantifying the effect of dormant faults and other vital reliability parameters. It turns out that the presence of dormant faults can drastically reduce the MTTF of a system, particularly if the operating system allows a sporadic ("event-driven") change from a regular mode of operation to another mode. Virtually every practical system involves such a change, at least in case of emergency.

It is demonstrated that on-line built-in self-test (BIST) is an effective means to overcome the deteriorating effect of dormant faults and re-establish a high MTTF. A very moderate test period may already be sufficient. The analysis is performed for the example of a fail-silent communication system for safety-critical real-time applications.

1. Introduction

In the past decades the market for safety-related distributed computing systems has been dominated by low and medium-volume applications such as avionics control systems. A recent trend in the automotive industry to replace vital mechanical components by electronic systems dramatically changes this situation. Computing systems like ABS, the engine controller and steer-by-wire take charge of safety-critical tasks that directly control the movement of the vehicle (SAE class C [1]). This emerging market segment is much more competitive and cost-sensitive than the traditional ones.

Driven by this motivation new system architectures are sought that can provide a comparable level of reliability without incurring the high cost incident to the massive redundancy used in the traditional solutions. Fail-silent architectures have come forth as a promising solution in this respect (e.g. [2,3]). These architectures are based on the assumptions of single faults and fail-silent nodes. While the role of the error detection coverage for the fail-silence property is widely recognized, the implications of the single-fault assumption are often underestimated.

This paper employs Markov models to identify the parameters crucial to the reliability of a fail-silent system. We concentrate on the effects of dormant faults. These are known to be particularly hazardous, as they tend to accumulate across the components of redundant systems, hence violating the single-fault assumption.

Built-in-self-test (BIST) has been widely accepted by the fault-tolerant computing community as a means to ensure system integrity. Until recently BIST has been mainly utilized for quality management after the manufacturing process or prior to the start of safety critical missions. If applied during the mission BIST has the potential to prevent fault accumulation. The inclusion of on-line BIST into our model allows us to quantify its contribution to system reliability. To illustrate the respective conclusions we apply our considerations to a (hypothetical) steer-by-wire system based on the Time-Triggered Architecture (TTA).

In section 2 we give a short introduction to the properties of TTA. The assumptions and terminology our models are based on will be discussed in sections 3 and 4. A preliminary assessment of the required system coverage is carried out in section 5. Section 6 refines the Markov model to account for the effects of dormant faults and on-line BIST. Section 7 concludes the paper.

2. Description of the target system

2.1. Application

In a steer-by-wire system [4] there is one computing node located at each steered wheel to collect and preprocess the local sensor inputs and to control the steering actuator of the wheel. Further computing nodes are responsible for calculating and coordinating the individual angles of the wheels,

0-7695-0213-X/99 $10.00 © 1999 IEEE

considering the inputs from the steering wheel sensors, the feedback from the wheel sensors and diverse environmental conditions. The communication between these subsystems plays a vital role in the system architecture. As steering is a highly safety-relevant task, the demands on dependability and fault-tolerance are very high. In particular the failure of any single system component must not lead to a failure of the whole system. Moreover, the high dynamics of the steering process puts stringent requirements on the real-time capabilities of the communication system.

In a highly competitive market like the automotive all these requirements must still be met in a cost-effective way. Cabling cost makes the use of a serial (two-wire) broadcast bus instead of a point-to-point network imperative.

2.2. Time-Triggered Architecture

The Time-Triggered Architecture (TTA) [2] fulfills all the above requirements and is therefore considered by many leading automotive companies for their next-generation communication systems. One central property of TTA is the existence of a fault-tolerant global time-base. In contrast to event-driven systems this global time base controls all activities in the system. This guarantees highly predictable system behavior even in peak-load situations. In particular the access to the communication network is performed according to a static TDMA schedule.

Figure 1 shows the system architecture: A set of distributed Fault-Tolerant Units (FTUs) exchanges messages over a serial communication channel. Each FTU is composed of two identical Smallest Replaceable Units (SRUs) that operate in active redundancy. To avoid a single point of failure the communication channel is also dual-redundant and protected from "babbling idiots" by a Bus Guardian [13].

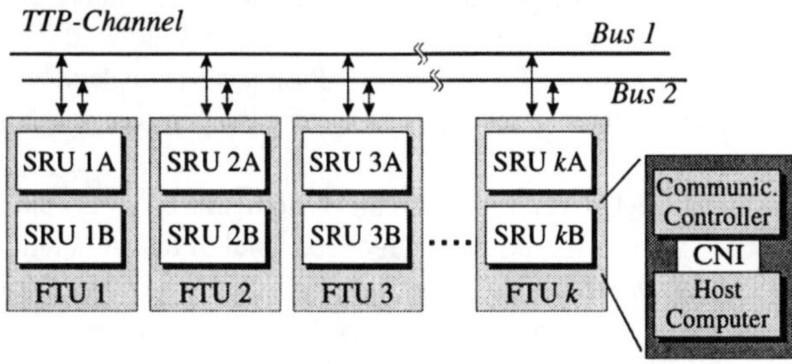

Figure 1: Example System Architecture of TTA

The SRU is divided into two subsystems: The *host* performs the application-specific tasks and maintains the sensor/actuator-interface, while the *communication controller* is responsible for message exchange, global time base and other protocol related tasks. Both subsystems represent error containment regions. They communicate via the Communication Network Interface (CNI). The CNI makes one subsystem appear like an abstract source and sink of data for the other one, and no temporal information can cross it. In this way it acts as a temporal firewall between the two subsystems.

The simple structure of the CNI allows fitting the host to the needs of the application, while the communication controller always remains the same. Therefore it is economically attractive to integrate the communication controller into a VLSI chip. A prototype of this TTA controller chip has already been put into operation.

3. Implied assumptions

3.1. Scope of consideration

This paper concentrates on the reliability aspects of the communication controller which is a generic building block of every distributed fault-tolerant system based on TTA. The understanding of the reliability of the communication system is essential for the system designer to determine the overall reliability of a specific system like the steer-by-wire system of our example. The strict decoupling provided by the CNI justifies the assumption that the operation of the host computer and the sensor/actuator components has no influence on the reliability of the communication.

3.2. Fail-silence assumption

A computing node is called fail-silent, if it produces either correct outputs at specified instances of time or no outputs at all. Two domains of fail-silence violations can be identified: Failure to deliver the required service at the specified instant of time and/or providing wrong data to the other participants of the communication. In the specific case of our communication controller fail-silence violations in the time domain are extremely critical. An SRU that transmits messages at arbitrary points in time corrupts other messages and thus prevents any communication on the busses, hence the implementation of the Bus Guardian. Fail-silence violations in the value domain are quite easily covered by a transmission CRC and optionally by an additional end-to-end CRC provided by the hosts.

The *fail-silence coverage* is the proportion of faults that are detected and properly handled before they lead to a fail-silence violation. Obviously the fail-silence coverage of an SRU is largely determined by its error detecting capabilities.

A system-architecture based on fail-silent SRUs is very economic, since it requires a lower degree of replication than a system in which the SRUs can fail uncontrolled. Fail-silence is also a prerequisite for installing a broadcast bus, which yields a considerable reduction of cabling cost as compared with other network topologies.

3.3. Single-fault assumption

Based on the fail-silence property of the SRUs the duplicated system structure of TTA allows tolerating any single failure of a component without the loss of service. In this context a "component" is either an SRU or a single bus. This *single-fault assumption* is a most usual design paradigm of fault-tolerant systems. It is invalidated in the following cases:

- If a single event affects more than one component at one point in time, we encounter *correlated faults.* Design faults and single points of failure fall in this category. As the prevention of correlated faults is a design issue these will not be considered here any further.
- If the system has not completely recovered from one component failure before the next one occurs, we encounter *near coincident faults* [7]. Varying environmental conditions in a vehicle, for instance, may result in bursts of faults. To minimize the impact of near coincident faults on system reliability the down-time of each SRU must be kept as short as possible.
- If faults may reside in the system without being activated and removed, there is the risk of *fault accumulation* across different components. On-line testing effectively aids in eliminating such dormant faults.

4. Terminology

4.1. Dormant faults

A fault may reside in an SRU for an indefinite period, the fault dormancy period, without having any effect on the service provided by the SRU. Since the moment of fault activation is determined by system activity, dormant faults often reside in parts of the system that are rarely exercised.

In a fault-tolerant system not all resources are allocated for the execution of regular tasks. In general the design includes dedicated logic and memory to take action in case of exceptional conditions. A well recognized problem [12] is to ensure that these system resources work properly when needed, since they often represent the last means to prevent a disaster.

In the worst case dormant faults can accumulate in both SRUs. This, in turn, leads to an instantaneous failure of the system when it switches to modes of operation that utilize the corrupted system resources. One way to overcome this problem is to periodically run an online-test to uncover dormant faults and to orderly repair the impaired SRU as long as redundancy is available.

4.2. Error detection versus on-line self-test

Testing involves exercising the unit with a set of predefined inputs and comparing the outputs of the circuit with a known-good reference. If this type of test is performed autonomously within the controller it is called a built-in self-test (BIST), if it is furthermore performed while system operation is ongoing, the test is called an on-line BIST. The major strength of on-line BIST is that a dormant fault can be detected before it becomes activated by normal system activity.

Error detection involves concurrently comparing the operation of the component or a set of components to a set of rules. Such rules typically consist of knowledge of control flow paths, execution time limits, codes, comparisons among redundant components, or various forms of reasonableness checks applied to input and output values. Error detection does not involve exercising the system but relies on the system operation to excite the components and cause fault activation. The major drawback of error detection is its inability to detect dormant faults in areas of the unit that are not exercised.

In general, error detection is responsible for enforcing the fail-silence assumption, while on-line BIST is capable of detecting dormant faults and thus enforces the single-fault assumption.

5. Basic system level reliability model of TTA

The *mean time to failure (MTTF)* of a system is the expected time a system will operate before the first failure occurs [5]. In the following we will use this parameter to quantify the quality of our target system with respect to reliability.

Markov models are widely applied to analyze the reliability properties of a system and to determine the MTTF. They provide a means to establish a correspondence between failure of the system and failure of a system component. The Markov model commonly used for the reliability analysis of systems composed of fail-silent computing nodes is described in [6]. We can directly apply this model to our TTA system:

An FTU composed of two identical fail-silent SRUs operating in active redundancy can assume three different states that have the following impact on the system service:

(α) Both SRU are working, the system is operative and fault-tolerant

(β) One SRU has shut down, the system still provides the required service, but with a reduced level of fault-tolerance.

(ω) The system has failed because both SRUs have shut down (spare exhaustion) or at least one SRU has violated the fail-silence assumption.

Figure 2 shows the corresponding Markov graph. As usual, constant failure rates of the SRUs are assumed to keep the model time-invariant. It is further assumed that an automatic repair action can re-establish SRU operation, provided that the preceding SRU shutdown has been orderly. An orderly shutdown implies that the SRU error has been properly detected and handled, which occurs with a probability c, the *fail-silent coverage* [7]. An automatic SRU repair is assumed to occur with a constant *repair rate* ρ (the inverse of the mean time to repair *MTTR*). Note that the failure rate λ refers to the SRU rather than the system in this discussion.

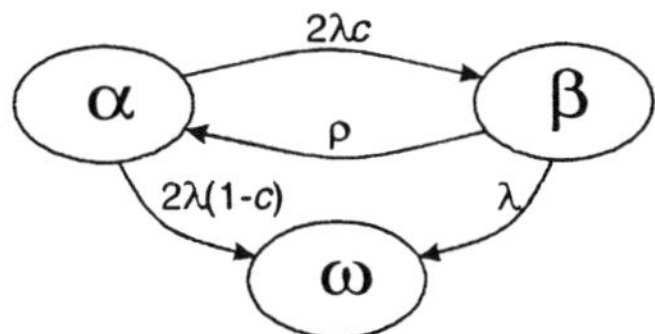

Figure 2: Markov model for a system composed of two redundant fail-silent nodes

The solution of this model for the mean time to failure of our system is [8]

$$MTTF_{sys} = \frac{1}{2\lambda} \cdot \frac{1 + \frac{\lambda}{\rho}(1+2c)}{\frac{\lambda}{\rho} + (1-c)} \qquad (1)$$

under the assumption that operation is started in state α, i.e. the system is initially fault free.

5.1. Known system parameters

SRU failure rate: The communication system comprises the TTA chip and a few external components like an EPROM and bus drivers. A failure rate estimation according to MIL217E [9] leads to an overall SRU failure rate of approximately $25 \cdot 10^{-6}$ per hour or a MTTF of 40000 hours (4.5 years). This estimation appears quite conservative, but comparably substantiated alternatives are not available. As motivated in section 3.1 we assume that host failures do not influence the dependability of the system communication established by TTA.

Required MTTF for the system: The usual requirement in civil avionics is "less than 10^{-9} catastrophic failure conditions per hour of operation" [10], which equals a $MTTF_{sys}$ of 10^9 hours. No comparable standardized values for automotive applications can be found in the literature, however, it is widely agreed that a safety-critical application like steer-by-wire should also achieve an MTTF of 10^9 hours. Two arguments make this requirement quite reasonable:

(a) Although car accidents are much less catastrophic than airplane crashes, the huge population of cars makes accidents much more likely. A failure rate of 10^{-9} per hour implies a 9.5% risk that in a sample of 1 million cars at least one will encounter a failure of the steer-by-wire system within 100 hours of operation.

(b) The steer-by-wire system is only one of many safety-critical electronic control systems in a car and the failure of any of them may lead to an accident.

Since the communication system plays a central role for the overall system dependability we directly apply the MTTF requirement to it.

Repair rate: For our example system we estimate that error detection and automatic (on-line) repair can be performed within an interval of 100ms (SRU restart). In case of a permanent fault we assume that measures on higher level are taken (degraded service, mechanical backup, garage stop) to prevent spare exhaustion. The proposed Markov model in general and the repair rate in particular do not include such measures.

5.2. Impact of the fail-silence coverage

The denominator of equation (1) suggests that a tradeoff between coverage and repair rate can be made. To assess the contribution of the fail-silence coverage alone let us assume perfect repair rate $\rho \to \infty$, which means $\rho >> \lambda$ in practice:

$$\lim_{\rho \to \infty} MTTF_{sys} = \frac{1}{2\lambda(1-c)} \qquad (2)$$

The term (1-*c*) in the denominator on the right side of equation (2) leads to an extreme sensitivity of $MTTF_{sys}$ to changes in *c*, particularly in the area of interest near *c*=100%.

To attain the desired system failure rate of 10^{-9} per hour, a non-coverage (1-*c*) below 0.002% is required. This is a very ambitious goal [11]. Note that the inclusion of further redundant SRUs into an FTU is an improper means here: The transition rate of $2 \cdot \lambda(1-c)$ from state α to state ω shown Figure 2 reflects the fact that a fail-silence violation in any one of the two SRUs leads to a system failure. By combining *n* SRUs into an FTU we even increase this transition rate to $n \cdot \lambda(1-c)$.

5.3. Impact of the repair rate

The effect of the repair rate on $MTTF_{sys}$ can be studied by assuming perfect coverage in equation (1):

$$\lim_{c \to 100\%} MTTF_{sys} = \frac{1}{2\lambda} \cdot \left(\frac{\rho}{\lambda} + 3 \right) \qquad (3)$$

For the practically relevant area of $\rho / \lambda >> 3$ we find a linear influence of ρ on $MTTF_{sys}$. Given the SRU failure rate λ and the desired $MTTF_{sys}$ we can further calculate a minimum requirement of 1.25 per hour for the repair rate. According to equation (1) a fail-silence coverage of 99.998% is required to achieve the desired $MTTF_{sys}$ of 10^9 with the assumed repair rate of 10 per second.

The most important conclusion from the above considerations is that the fail-silence coverage is much more critical to system reliability than the repair rate. This fact is well understood and widely recognized. The effect of fault accumulation, however, is much less often accounted for in reliability concepts. In the following we will use our target system as an example to present a systematic and quantitative analysis of the effect of dormant faults.

6. Extended reliability model

The third order Markov model presented so far does not account for dormant faults and testing. In the following we will develop a sixth order model that also incorporates dormant faults, system mode switching to activate these faults as well as testing. This model shall help us identify the most important parameters of system reliability and provide insight into their interrelation. Based on this understanding we can finally discuss potential contributions of on-line testing.

Table 1 gives an overview of the system states distinguished in the model. A failure occurs when either SRU violates the fail-silence assumption due to an uncovered fault in either mode of operation or when both SRUs have shut down.

Table 1: States considered in the extended system model

SRU A	SRU B	State
no fault	*no fault*	α
Down	*no fault*	β
no fault	*dormant fault*	β'
Dormant fault	*dormant fault*	β''
Down	*dormant fault*	ω'
failure		ω

Figure 3 shows the Markov graph of the sixth order model. The following notation is applied: λ denotes the overall failure rate of the communication controller, whereas δ refers to the failure rate portion of the sporadically used system resources and is given as a percentage of λ. The coverage and non-coverage is denoted by c and $(1-c)$, respectively. The switch rate σ quantifies the rate at which exceptional events cause the system to activate the sporadically utilized system resources. Since the operation of both SRUs is driven by the global time we assume that the switching takes place at the same instant in time for both SRUs. The test rate τ denotes the product of testing coverage and the rate at which the SRUs are tested. At this point it is interesting to observe that a non-optimal test coverage can be compensated for by a higher test rate (to some degree). As opposed to switching we assume that testing is performed asynchronously on both SRUs. This approach avoids spare exhaustion in case that both SRUs are affected by dormant faults (state β"). Finally, ρ denotes the repair rate. In Table 2 the transitions between the system states are discussed.

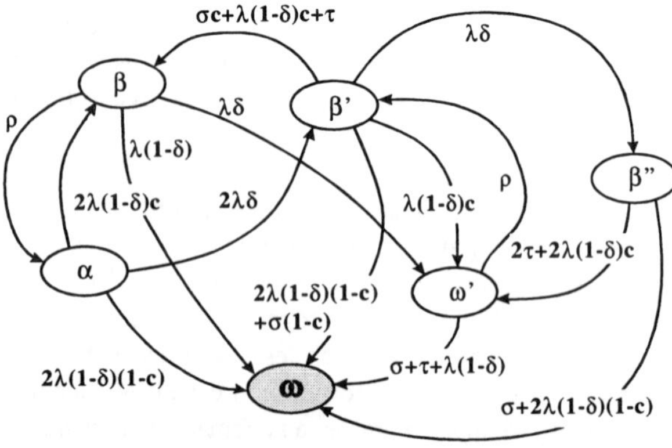

Figure 3: Sixth order Markov model including dormant faults

The sixth order model has been solved using the generic solution given in [8]. Due to the high number of terms a simple algebraic presentation directly showing the influence of single parameters could not be derived. In the following we will discuss selected graphical presentations instead.

6.1. Impact of dormant faults on the MTTF

In the first step we want to find out how the inclusion of dormant faults into our model impacts $MTTF_{sys}$. For this purpose we apply the values for c and ρ that we have obtained from the third order model to the sixth order model now. As we did not consider any on-line testing yet, we set the test rate τ to 0 and vary the proportion δ of dormant faults and the switch rate σ, while studying $MTTF_{sys}$. Figure 4 shows the result.

We observe a significant drop of $MTTF_{sys}$ down to 10^5 in the worst case. In fact, there are only three cases for which the desired MTTF level can actually be achieved.

(1) No dormant faults ($\delta = 0$): This trivial case essentially represents the view of the third order model.

(2) Very high switch rates ($\sigma > 10^3$ per hour): All system resources are frequently exercised, therefore dormant faults become activated very soon and the danger of fault accumulation is minimized. This situation appears quite ideal, however, it is contradictory to our initial assumption according to which part of the system resources are dedicated to handle unforeseen events. As a remarkable consequence a high rate of unforeseen events apparently improves $MTTF_{sys}$.

(3) Extremely low switch rates ($\sigma < 10^{-8}$ per hour): Even if dormant faults will very likely reside in the system in this case, they become activated extremely infrequently, hence their impact on $MTTF_{sys}$ is low. Note that the switch period is of the same magnitude as $MTTF_{sys}$ – a condition impossible to meet in a practical system.

In general the estimation of the switch rate may become very difficult. The periodic nature of the Time-Triggered Architecture used in our example provides detailed knowledge of the resource utilization, however, error handling paths are activated irregularly in TTA, as well. As a consequence we can not guarantee our switch rate to be sufficiently high for case (2) to apply. Obviously the results gained from the third order model are too optimistic and we have to find a way to defeat the effect of dormant faults in our application. We have

Table 2: Transitions in the sixth order Markov model

Transition	Rate	Meaning
$\alpha \rightarrow \beta$	$2\lambda(1-\delta)c$	*Either SRU* is affected by a fault and shuts down while the other continues to operate fault-free
$\alpha \rightarrow \beta'$	$2\lambda\delta$	*Either SRU* is affected by a dormant fault but continues to provide its service.
$\alpha \rightarrow \omega$	$2\lambda(1-\delta)(1-c)$	*Either SRU* is affected by a non-covered non-dormant fault and violates the fail-silent assumption
$\beta \rightarrow \omega$	$\lambda(1-\delta)$	The *still working* SRU is affected by a non-dormant fault, either leading to spare exhaustion (if covered) or to a fail-silent violation (if not covered)
$\beta \rightarrow \omega'$	$\lambda\delta$	The *still working* SRU is affected by a dormant fault.
$\beta \rightarrow \alpha$	ρ	The SRU being down is repaired.
$\beta' \rightarrow \omega$	$2\lambda(1-\delta)(1-c)$ $+\sigma(1-c)$	(1) *Either SRU* is affected by a non-covered non-dormant fault violating the fail-silent assumption. (2) The system switches and the dormant fault now being activated is not covered.
$\beta' \rightarrow \omega'$	$\lambda(1-\delta)c$	The *fault-free SRU* is also affected by a covered non-dormant fault, leading to a shut-down of this SRU.
$\beta' \rightarrow \beta''$	$\lambda\delta$	The *fault-free SRU* is affected by a dormant fault.
$\beta' \rightarrow \beta$	σc $+\lambda(1-\delta)c$ $+\tau$	(1) The system switches and the dormant fault now being activated is covered. (2) The *SRU affected by the dormant fault* is additionally affected by a non-dormant fault that is covered. (3) The dormant fault is detected by testing.
$\omega' \rightarrow \beta'$	ρ	The *SRU being down* is repaired.
$\omega' \rightarrow \omega$	σ $+\tau$ $+\lambda(1-\delta)c$	(1) The system switches thus activating the dormant fault. This leads either to a spare exhaustion or a fail silence violation. (2) Testing uncovers the dormant fault and shuts down the *only SRU that remained working.* (3) The *SRU affected by a dormant fault* is affected by a non-dormant fault.
$\beta'' \rightarrow \omega$	σ $+2\lambda(1-\delta)(1-c)$	(1) The system switches, which activates both dormant faults. (2) *Either SRU* is affected by a non-covered non-dormant fault, leading to a fail-silent violation.
$\beta'' \rightarrow \omega'$	2τ $+2\lambda(1-\delta)c$	(1) *Either SRU* is tested and shut down. (2) *Either SRU* is affected by a non-dormant fault that is covered.

already seen that the provision of further redundant SRUs is not only an expensive solution, but even deteriorates the MTTF, as it increases the risk of fail-silence violations. Therefore our options are (a) an increase of the coverage or (b) elimination of the dormant faults by on-line BIST.

6.2. Improvements by coverage increase

In section 5.2 we noticed the high sensitivity of $MTTF_{sys}$ to changes in c. This suggests to increase the coverage to compensate for the negative effect of dormant faults. To get a feeling for limitations of this approach, let us first assume perfect coverage. This leads to a graph similar to that in Figure 4, this time, however, with an increased MTTF level. Figure 5 shows the intersections of this graph with horizontal planes for $MTTF_{sys}$ = 10^8, 10^9 and 10^{10}. The shaded area indicates combinations of σ and δ that yield insufficient $MTTF_{sys}$.

As expected we can quite easily handle all proportions of dormant faults, if switch rates are very high or extremely low. Like before, however, $MTTF_{sys}$ shows a distinct minimum at a switch rate near $\sigma = 4.4 \cdot 10^{-4}$. Note that even with 100% coverage we can attain the desired $MTTF_{sys}$ of 10^9 only if the proportion of dormant faults is below 1.1%. For non-perfect coverage this proportion becomes even smaller.

Increasing coverage to accommodate a proportion below 1% of dormant faults does not appear very promising when the minimum coverage requirements are already at a level of 99.998%. We will therefore investigate the capabilities of on-line BIST in the following.

6.3. Improvements by On-line BIST

As already outlined in section 4.2 on-line BIST has the potential to detect dormant faults. With a properly selected test rate we should be able to detect and remove dormant faults before they accumulate. Let us assume the proportion of dormant faults is δ = 15%. From the above discussion we know that no more than δ = 1.1% can be handled without testing, even with perfect coverage. So the expectations on testing implied by this assumption are quite high.

Figure 6 illustrates the situation for non-zero test rates. It shows the coverage required to attain the desired $MTTF_{sys}$ of 10^9 over switch rate σ and test rate τ. The solid line shows the

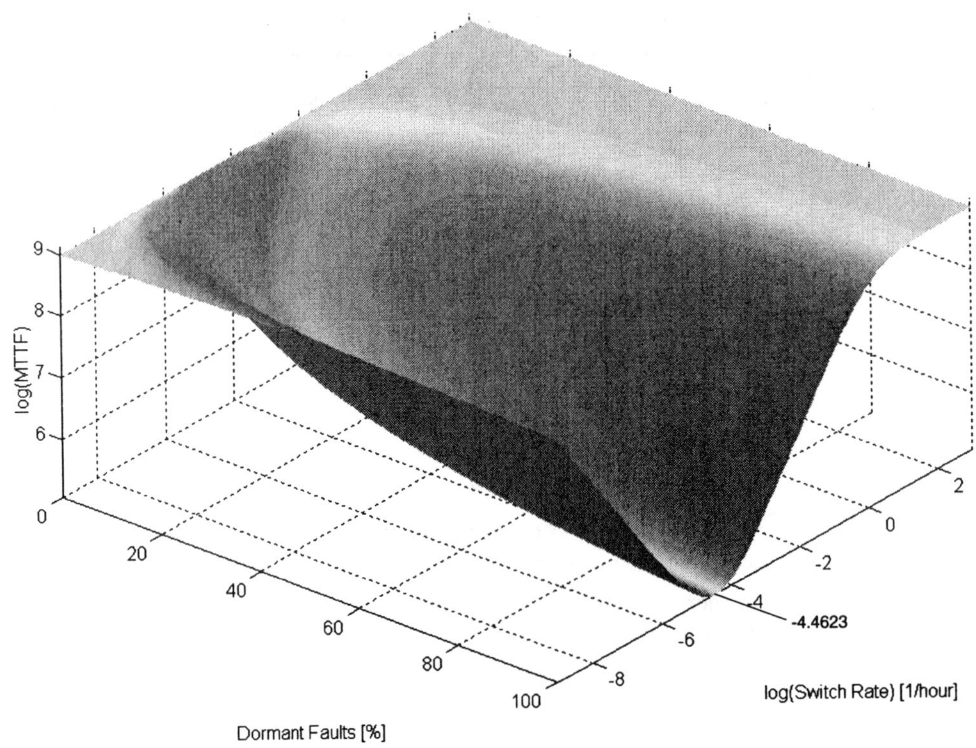

Figure 4: Impact of dormant faults on the mean time to failure of the system

intersection of this graph with the horizontal plane for c = 99.998%.

The result is quite impressive: As long as we keep the test rate above the moderate level of 0.4 per hour, we can sustain the desired MTTF with the coverage of 99.998%. With a test rate higher than the switch rate we can even relax the coverage requirements to 99,9976%. This latter effect can be explained

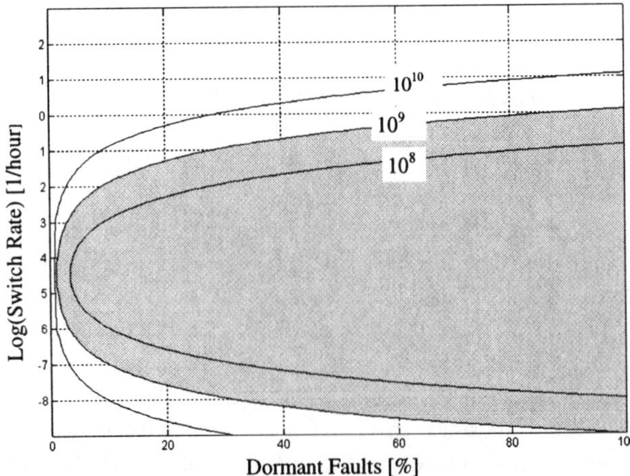

Figure 5: Valid combinations of switch rate and proportion of dormant faults for perfect coverage

as follows: If on-line BIST allows us to detect and remove all dormant faults before they become activated, only the remaining proportion of non-dormant faults becomes effective. This yields the same result as using a reduced SRU failure rate (85% in our example) in the simplified model. The coverage gain, however is not too significant. By far more important is the fact that on-line BIST allows us to guarantee that the desired MTTF can be sustained for any arbitrary switch rate. The required test rate of about 0.4 per hour corresponds to a test period of 2.5 hours. As the mission time of our steer-by-wire system exceeds this period, we can not rely on the start-up tests that must be performed anyway to ensure that mission starts in state α. We rather have to employ a dedicated on-line BIST additionally.

7. Conclusion

We have studied the impact of dormant faults on the MTTF of high reliability communication systems. It turned out that neglecting the influence of dormant faults leads to a severe overestimation of the MTTF of several orders of magnitude in the worst case. The elaboration of a Markov model clearly revealed that on-line testing of sporadically utilized system resources is indispensable to provide the required MTTF of 10^9 hours in the presence of dormant

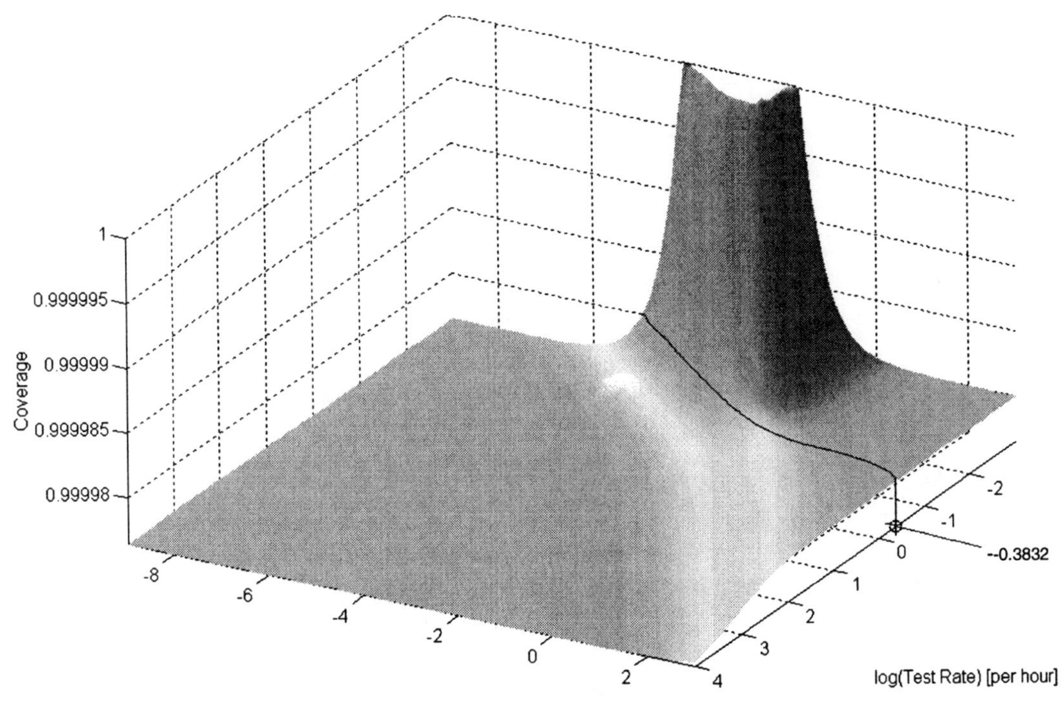

Figure 6: Coverage requirements over switch rate and test rate

faults. Interestingly, even a moderate test rate is sufficient to compensate for the deteriorating effect of dormant faults on the MTTF. The model further showed that the high requirements on the error detection coverage can not significantly be relaxed by on-line BIST.

To illustrate the conclusions from our model we have applied our considerations to a steer-by-wire system based on the Time-Triggered Architecture. We have tried to give quantitative results, but are well aware of the fact that much more effort is needed to attain trustworthy results for a 10^9 system. Among the critical issues are the validation of the coverage including confidence intervals and the variance of the MTTF. In this sense the results are hypothetical, but parameter variations have shown that the qualitative message still holds.

Future work will concentrate on the examination of how to integrate on-line BIST and start-up BIST into the TTA controller chip and merge them with factory BIST most economically.

8. References

[1] Class C Application Requirement Considerations. *SAE Recommended Practice J2056/1*, Society of Automotive Engineers, 6/1993.

[2] H. Kopetz, and G. Grünsteidl, "TTP- A Protocol for Fault-Tolerant Real-Time Systems", *IEEE Computer*, January 1994, pp. 14-23.

[3] D. Powell, P. Verissimo, G. Bonn, F. Waeselynck, and D. Seaton, "The Delta-4 Approach to Dependability in Open Distributed Computing Systems", *Proc. FTCS-18,* IEEE CS press, June 1988, pp. 246-251.

[4] G. Heiner, and T. Thurner, "Time Triggered Architecture for Safety-Related Distributed Real-Time Systems in Transportation Systems", *Proc. FTCS-28*, IEEE CS press, June 1998, pp. 402-407.

[5] B.W. Johnson, *Design and Analysis of Fault Tolerant Systems*, Addison-Wesley, Reading, MA, 1989.

[6] T. Arnold, "The Concept of Coverage and Its Effect on the Reliability Model of a Repairable System",. *IEEE Transactions on Computers*, vol. C-22, no. 3, March 1973, pp. 251-254.

[7] J. McGough, M. Smotherman, and K. Trivedi, "The Conservativeness of Reliability Estimates Based on Instantaneous Coverage", *IEEE Transactions on Computers*, vol. C-34, no. 7, July 1985, pp. 602-609.

[8] D. Siewiorek, and S. Swarz, *Reliable Computer Systems: Design and Evaluation*, 2nd edition, Digital Press, Bedford, MA 1992.

[9] Reliability Prediction of Electronic Equipment, *Military Handbook MIL-HDBK-217E*, United States Department of Defense.

[10] B. Littlewood, and L. Strigini, "Validation of Ultra-High Dependability for Software-based Systems", in B. Randell, J. Laprie, H. Kopetz, B. Littlewood (eds.) *Predictably Dependable Computing Systems*, ESPRIT Basic Research Series, Springer 1995, pp. 473-493

[11] D. Powell, E. Martins, J. Arlat, and Y. Crouzet, "Estimators for Fault Tolerance Coverage Estimation", *Proc. FTCS-23,* IEEE CS press, June 1993, pp. 228-237.

[12] M. Nicolaidis, S. Noraz, and B. Courtois, "A Generalized Theory of Fail-Safe Systems", *Proc. FTCS-19*, IEEE CS press, June 1989, pp. 398-406.

[13] Ch. Temple, "Avoiding the Babbling-Idiot Failure in a Time-Triggered Communication System", *Proc. FTCS-28*, IEEE CS press, June 1998, pp. 218-227.

Session 7C

Fast Abstracts II

Session 8A

Software Demonstrations and Practical Experience Reports

Chair: Jeff Zhou
AlliedSignal Inc., USA

Winckp: a Transparent Checkpointing and Rollback Recovery Tool for Windows NT Applications

P. Emerald Chung
Woei-Jyh Lee

Bell Laboratories
Lucent Technologies
emerald@lucent.com
woeijhylee@lucent.com

Yennun Huang

AT&T Labs
yen@research.att.com

Deron Liang
Chung-Yih Wang

Institute of Information
Academia Sinica
drliang@sinica.edu.tw
cywang@sinica.edu.tw

Abstract

The goal of Winckp is to transparently checkpoint and recover applications on Windows NT. The definition of transparency is no modifications to applications at all, period. There is no need to get source code, or object code. It does not involve compilation, linking or generation of a different executable. We employ window message logging/replaying to recreate states that are otherwise difficult to recover by checkpointing alone. In the paper, we describe the design and implementation of Winckp, and present the challenges and limitations. The software is available for download from http://www.bell-labs.com/projects/swift.

1 Introduction

Windows NT has become a popular computing platform for building new applications due to the proliferation of software tools and components and the potential lower hardware cost. The telecommunication industry has also started to build fault-tolerant and highly available systems on NT.

We have been working on the NT-SwiFT project to understand the fault-tolerance and high availability requirements of applications running on NT. NT-SwiFT currently contains a set of components which add fault-tolerant capabilities to applications on Windows NT and Winckp is one of them.

Winckp supports five major functions.

- Checkpoint: store the state of an application process in persistent storage.
- Rollback: roll back the state to the last checkpoint in the same process.
- Recover: restore the last checkpoint in a new process.
- Logging: store window messages such as keystrokes, mouse movements and mouse clicks in persistent storage.
- Replay: replay logged window messages.

Additional features include (1) support of file rollback; (2) support of multiple threads; (3) console display recovery; (4) partial replay of window messages; (5) configurable replay speed.

2 User Interface

2.1 Graphical User Interface

The Winckp GUI is shown in Fig. 1. The user clicks the "Run App" button to start an application, and clicks the "Snapshot" button at any time to checkpoint the application; the user clicks the "Recover" button to *roll back* the application to the last checkpoint. If the application process has died, the user can click the "Run App" button again to start the last application and click the "Recover" button to *recover* the last checkpointed state in the new process.

An application process state consists of data, stack, heap, thread context, and some kernel objects. If the recovery of an application requires a rollback of files, the user must check the "Include files" box before running the application.

Winckp can also be used to log and replay mouse and keyboard events of an application. The feature is turned on by clicking the "Start recording" button. The event log is truncated every time the "Snapshop" button is clicked. If the "Playback" button is clicked, Winckp replays all mouse and keyboard events starting from the last snapshot.

The Winckp GUI is suitable for Window-based applications that are constantly waiting for a mouse or keyboard event to change its state, such as games. Winckp can save the state between moves and rollback can be used as a generic undo operation.

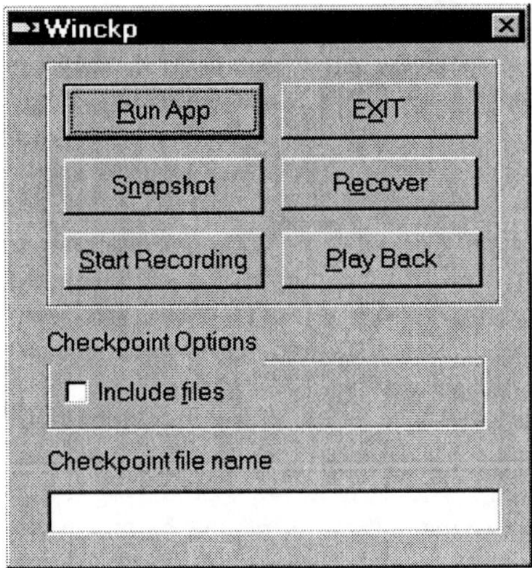

Figure 1 The Winckp GUI

2.2 Command Line Interface

Winckp is also useful for long-running scientific programs which usually require periodic checkpointing. We design a command line interface, ckprun, for this purpose. The usage of ckprun is shown in Table 1.

```
Usage:
CKPRUN [/F ckpf] [/I t] [/X] app.exe

[/F ckpf] specifies checkpoint file
name
[/I t] specifies the time between
checkpoints.
[/X ] No checkpoint and recovery of
files.
[/R ] Recover execution from
checkpoint
```

Table 1 Ckprun command line interface

2.3 Library Interface

The Winckp GUI and ckprun are two separate executables. The basic functions for checkpointing and recover are implemented in a library, *libwinckp.dll* and the functions for logging and replaying window messages are in *libwinrec.dll*. This architecture allows people to embed checkpointing or logging in their applications by linking with either of these two DLLs.

3 Implementation

3.1 Checkpoint and Rollback

Winckp is implemented from scratch to use only Win32 APIs. Winckp leverages a set of Win32 functions that allow a process to alter another process. Microsoft created many of these functions for use by debuggers [Richter97-18]. Winckp starts the application by calling `CreateProcess()`. To take a snapshot, Winckp suspends all threads and stores state information into files. During a rollback operation, all threads are also suspended. The state information is restored from files. Winckp resets all thread contexts then resumes all threads.

If the application process has died, Winckp starts a new process, suspends its main thread, restores all state information, and then resumes all threads.

Winckp injects a checkpointing thread into the target application. This thread is in charge of saving system-call-related info in stable storage and replaying the system calls during rollback or recovery.

3.2 Threads

Winckp and the target applications are running as two separate processes. NT allows a process to obtain and set the thread context for threads in a different process. Winckp obtain and restore the thread context using `GetThreadContext()` and `SetThreadContext()`. Winckp also recreates and terminates threads if the number of threads at the time of the last snapshot is different from the number at the recovery time.

3.3 Memory

Winckp saves an application's memory including data, heap and stack. The memory image is obtained and restored using `ReadProcessMemory()` and `WriteProcessMemory()`. Winckp determines the address and the amount of memory to save as follows. An NT process has about 2GB of private address space, ranging from 0x00010000 to 0x7FFEFFFF [Richter97-3], but not every region in this space needs to be saved. The `VitualQueryEx()` system call allows us to examine the space region by region. It is necessary to save a memory region only if its write access is enabled and if its physical storage is committed [Richter97-5]. Winckp also stores the MEMORY_BASIC_INFORMATION structure along with each memory region. During a rollback operation, all threads are suspended. Winckp calls `WriteProcessMemory()` to restore the memory content.

3.4 Files

To checkpoint and recover files, Winckp uses a system call interception mechanism to intercept file-related system calls, such as `CreateFile()`, `WriteFile()`, etc. Winckp records each handle value and the parameters used to create the handle. In recovery, Winckp recreates all the handles by replaying the calls with the recorded parameters. An issue is that the values of the recovered handles may be different from their checkpointed values. Winckp creates a mapping of old handle values to the new handle values. The system call interception routines replace the old handle values with the new values before making the real call.

To make sure file content is consistent, Winckp generates idempotent undo logs for all file updates. The undo logs are played at the recovery time.

3.5 Window objects

Winckp intercepts a subset of functions in USER32.dll and GDI32.dll, such as `CreateWindow()` and `CreateDC()`. The recovery of window handles and other GDI objects has been a very difficult task due to the dependency among these objects and the fact that they are not isolated from other processes or kernel.

To recover a window handle, Winckp first starts a new process and let the new process create all related windows. Afterwards, Winckp creates a mapping between the old window handle value and the new window handle value. We replace the old value by new value in the checkpoint file before restoring it back to memory. It works for a small set of applications, such as winmine.exe and solitaire.exe. However, a more generic mechanism is necessary and it depends on an in-depth understanding of NT windows management.

3.6 Window messages

Winckp records events coming from the mouse and keyboard. The Win32 subsystem provides a hook that allows a user application to monitor system events such as keyboard strokes, window messages, debugging information, etc., and to react to these events through a user-defined callback procedure. User applications may specify those system events of interest and install the corresponding callback procedures via the Win32 API.

Winckp captures these events by calling `SetWindowsHookEx()` with flag WH_JOURNALRECORD. Keyboard events and mouse events are copied from the Win32 system's message queue to our callback procedure. These events are kept in a log file. To replay, we insert these events one by one in their timestamp order back to the Win32 system message queue by installing the WH_JOURNALPLAYBACK callback procedure. The Win32 system temporarily disables the inputs from keyboard and mouse when the WH_JOURNALPLAYBACK callback procedure is installed. It executes only the events fed from the callback procedure until our event log is over or the WH_JOURNALPLAYBACK callback procedure is uninstalled.

4 Limitations

Winckp currently has the following limitations:

(1) System calls: If a snapshot takes place in the middle of a system call, Winckp does not store any kernel state. It may become a problem during recovery.

(2) Thread ID and thread handle value: Current Winckp rolls back the number of threads to the number in the last snapshot state. A dead thread is recreated. The recreated thread usually has a different thread handle and thread ID. Applications depend on thread handle and thread ID may not work.

(3) Synchronization objects: All kernel objects used for synchronization are not recovered if they no longer exist, such as events and mutexes.

(4) Interprocess communication: The current implementation does not support recovery of interprocess communications, such as COM calls or socket calls.

(5) Playback nondeterminism: Since playback involves the whole display area, it involves all windows in other processes. There is no guarantee from Winckp that the state of all windows at the beginning of playback is the same as the beginning of recording. In addition, changing the playback speed may also affect the outcome. For instance, the Windows may interpret two single clicks as a double click or vice versa.

5 Related work

5.1 Windows Checkpointing Software

A similar checkpointing facility was developed at Intel [Srouji98]. The main differences are (1) it requires a different build process to replace an application's startup function with their checkpoint DLL startup code; (2) it utilizes the QueueUserAPC() mechanism on NT to replay all system calls at recovery by application threads, while our system calls are replayed by the injected thread; (3) it does not roll back any persistent storage; (4) it does not handle GUI programs; (5) it does not log or replay window messages.

There is a checkpointing facility on the Brazos parallel programming environment [Abdel-Shafi 99]. To support thread migration, Brazos currently implements a subset of Winckp functions including saving the thread context, stack and memory.

5.2 UNIX Checkpointing Software

On UNIX, transparent checkpointing is now very well studied. The discussions can be found in [Litzkow 97][Plank 95][Wang 95].

6 Summary

Windows NT is very complex and it is open to all sorts of hardware/driver configurations. As a result, it has been perceived as less reliable than UNIX and there is a rapidly increasing need for application-level fault-tolerance on Windows NT.

In this paper, we described our experience in implementing checkpointing on Windows NT. In general, NT supports more mechanisms needed to enable the implementation of checkpointing. However, the recovery of NT kernel objects or GUI objects is not yet well understood. There remain a lot of challenges.

7 Acknowledgement

The authors would like to thank Binh Vo for his help in the development of Winckp, Yi-Min Wang for his discussions on the UNIX libckp implementation, and Chandra Kintala for his support of the work.

8 Reference:

[Abdel-Shafi 99] H. Abdel-Shafi et al, "Efficient User-Level Thread Migration and Checkpointing on Windows NT Clusters", to appear in the 3rd USENIX Windows NT Symposium, 1999.

[Huang98] Y. Huang, P. Chung, C. Kintala, C. Wang and D. Liang, "Software Implemented Fault Tolerance on Windows NT", 2nd USENIX Windows NT Symposium, pp. 47-55, Seattle, Washington, August, 1998.

[Litzkow 97] M. Litzkow et al, "Checkpoint and Migration of UNIX Processes in the Condor Distributed Processing System," Univ. of Wisconsin-Madison, CS TR #1346, April 1997.

[Richter97-3] J. Richter, "Processes", Chapter 3, in *Advanced Windows,* Ed. 3, pp.33-72, Microsoft Press, 1997.

[Richter97-5] J. Richter, "Win32 Memory Architecture", Chapter 5, in *Advanced Windows.*

[Richter97-18] J. Richter, "Breaking Through Process Boundary Wall", Chapter 18, in *Advanced Windows.*

[Plank 95] J. Plank, M. Beck and G. Kingsley, "Libckpt: Transparent Checkpointing Under UNIX", 1995 Usenix Conference.

[Srouju 98] J. Srouji et al., "A Transparent Checkpoint Facility on NT," *Proceedings of the 2nd USENIX NT Symposium,* Seattle, Washington, pp. 77-85, 1998.

[Wang95] Y. Wang and Y. Huang and K. Vo and P. Chung and C. Kintala, "Checkpoint and its applications", *Proceedings of the 25th IEEE Fault Tolerant Computing Symposium,* Pasadena, California, pp. 22-31, 1995.

A User-level Checkpointing Library for POSIX Threads Programs*

William R. Dieter James E. Lumpp, Jr.
Department of Electrical Engineering
University of Kentucky
Lexington, KY 40506, USA
{dieter,jel}@dcs.uky.edu

Abstract

Several user-level checkpointing libraries that checkpoint Unix processes have been developed. However, they do not support multithreaded programs. This paper describes a user-level checkpointing library to checkpoint multithreaded programs that use the POSIX threads library provided by Solaris 2. Experiments with programs from the SPLASH-2 benchmark suite showed a 3% to 10% increase in execution time with checkpointing enabled, plus an additional overhead for saving the program's state. The checkpointing library described here is available at http://www.dcs.uky.edu/~chkpt/.

1. Introduction

A multithreaded program's state can be divided into private state and shared state. A thread's *private state* includes its program counter, stack pointer, and registers. Its *shared state* includes everything common to all threads in the process, such as the address space and open file state. A multithreaded checkpointing library must save and recover the program's shared state and each thread's private state.

User-level thread libraries are implemented outside the kernel using timers to preempt a thread when its time slice is over. User-level threads cannot take advantage of a symmetric multiprocessor (SMP) because the kernel is not aware of the threads. Implementing a checkpointing library for a user-level threads package is a straightforward extension of a single-threaded checkpointing library because a user-level multithreaded process is no different from a single-threaded process from the operating system's point of view.

With *kernel-level threads*, the kernel schedules threads and keeps track of their state. Not only must the checkpointing library save and restore the address space of the process to recover the thread state, but it must also call the kernel to restart threads during recovery.

Section 2 describes the checkpointing library. Section 3 discusses the performance of programs using the library. Section 4 discusses related work. More details on the library's implementation and capabilities can be found in [3].

2. Implementation

Modifying the kernel to support checkpointing would tie the checkpointing library to the operating system and require the user to install a modified operating system kernel. Many users are not willing or not able to install a custom kernel, particularly if they are using a remote machine owned by someone else. Our checkpointing library is implemented at the user level to improve portability. While complete portability is the goal, parts of the checkpointing library, as described later, must be platform dependent.

2.1. Limitations

The checkpointing library supports programs that access regular files sequentially and use signals, but at least one signal must be available to the checkpointing library (`SIGUSR1` by default). The library does not support programs that randomly access files or communicate with other processes. In addition, the checkpointing library does not support POSIX semaphores, thread-specific data functions, or thread cancellation functions. The reasons for these limitations and their implications can be found in [3]. However, these limitations are no more restrictive than those imposed by single-threaded checkpointing libraries, and some of them can be removed, with additional run-time overhead.

2.2. Synchronization

The checkpointing library sends Unix signals to all the threads to synchronize them at a checkpoint. Each thread must run the signal handler, save its private state, and wait

*This research was supported by the National Science Foundation under Grant CDA-9502645 and the Advanced Research Projects Agency under Grant DAAH04-96-1-0327.

0-7695-0213-X/99 $10.00 © 1999 IEEE

for all the other threads, but a thread may not be able to run the signal handler. For example:

1. Thread 1 locks mutex M
2. Thread 1 blocks on a condition, unlocking mutex M
3. Thread 2 locks mutex M
4. Both threads receive the checkpointing signal
5. Thread 2 runs the signal handler and waits for thread 1

When a thread unblocks from a condition variable it locks the mutex it unlocked when it blocked. Thread 1 cannot unblock from the condition variable to run the signal handler because to unblock it must relock mutex M, which thread 2 has locked. If thread 2 unlocks mutex M when it enters the signal handler, thread 1 can run the signal handler when it receives the signal. However, thread 2 must relock mutex M before any thread tries to access data protected by mutex M.

The checkpointing library handles this by tracking thread calls while the program runs so it can unlock and relock mutexes during a checkpoint to preserve the program's correctness. The checkpointing library intercepts thread library calls to track how many threads exist, their identifiers, which threads are blocked on condition variables, and which mutexes they have locked in the *thread table*. The checkpointing library also intercepts file open and close calls to track the file name associated with each file descriptor. So the open file state can be restored from a checkpoint.

2.3. Saving a checkpoint

The *checkpoint thread*'s sole purpose is to initiate checkpoints. It blocks until it is time to do so. During checkpointing the *main thread* (the thread created when the process starts) and the *child threads* (all the other threads) handle the checkpoint signal (SIGUSR1) signal differently. Checkpoints proceed as follows:

1) Set the `prevent_locks` **flag.** The checkpoint thread sets the `prevent_locks` flag to prevent any thread from locking a mutex. Without the flag, a thread that receives the SIGUSR1 later than other threads may lock a mutex that a thread in the checkpointing signal handler has unlocked.

2) Send SIGUSR1 **to all threads.** The checkpointing thread then sends a SIGUSR1 signal to every thread, including itself. When a thread receives a SIGUSR1, it runs the SIGUSR1 handler unless it is blocked on a condition variable and another thread has locked the mutex associated with the condition variable (see section 2.2).

3) Unlock mutexes. Each thread unlocks every mutex it has locked and sets a flag indicating the mutex has been unlocked. Unlocking mutexes allows threads that blocked because a mutex was locked to enter the signal handler.[1]

4) Wait for the child threads. The main thread waits for all the child threads to signal they are ready.

5) Save the private thread state. Each child thread writes its private state to its entry in the thread table.

6) Signal the main thread. Each child thread indicates that it has saved its private state.

7) Wait for the main thread. The child threads block until the main thread signals them.

8) Save the file state. The main thread records the current file pointer offset in each open file.

9) Clear the `prevent_locks` **flag.** The main thread clears the `prevent_locks` flag.

10) Save the process state. The main thread saves the thread table, the process's memory mappings, and the process's address space to a checkpoint file.

11) Signal child threads. The main thread wakes up the child threads.

12) Relock mutexes. Each thread relocks the mutexes it unlocked in step 3 in two phases as follows:

12a) Lock held mutexes (locking phase 1). Each thread locks all the mutexes it had locked when the checkpoint started. Each thread waits until every thread has finished phase 1 before continuing with phase 2.

12b) Lock condition wait mutexes (locking phase 2). Each thread attempts to lock the any mutexes it was blocked waiting to lock when the checkpoint started along with mutexes it released before the checkpoint to wait on a condition variable. In phase 2, a thread may try to lock a mutex that another thread has already locked. In that case it blocks while locking the mutex in the signal handler, but this is the desired result because it was blocked on a condition variable or trying to lock a mutex when the thread got the signal. At this point the program continues as if the checkpoint had not happened.

Thread synchronization functions may not be safe to call in a signal handler depending on how they are implemented [1, section 6.6]. However, threads must synchronize during a checkpoint and must unlock mutexes to allow all threads to run. We assume locking a mutex in a signal handler is safe as long the mutex has not already been locked by the same thread, and unlocking a mutex in a signal handler is safe as long at it was locked by the same thread.

2.4. Restoring from a saved checkpoint

When a program recovers from a checkpoint, it starts with a single thread. During initialization, the checkpoint library restores the program as follows:

[1] Some threads may continue executing while others enter the checkpoint signal handler because Unix does not guarantee when signals will be delivered. Threads that have not received a SIGUSR1 are prevented from locking a mutex unlocked by a process in the signal handler because of the `prevent_locks` flag. The checkpointing thread uses thread synchronization to guarantee every thread will see the `prevent_locks` flag set before locking the mutex in the intercepted mutex lock call.

1) Restart threads. The main thread opens the checkpoint file, reads the saved thread table, and restarts a new thread for each thread in the original program. We assume the thread library can assign thread identifiers during recovery in the same order in which it assigned them when the program first ran. While true for Solaris 2.6, this assumption may not be true for other thread libraries [3].

2) Restore thread stack pointers. Next, the main thread waits while the child threads restore their own stack pointers.

3) Wait for the main thread. The child threads wait for the main thread to finish restoring the program's state.

4) Restore main thread stack. Once the child threads have blocked, the main thread restores its own stack pointer.

5) Remap the process's address space The main thread maps each segment from the checkpoint file into the program's address space except the main thread stack. The checkpointing library then reads the main thread's stack.

6) Restore main thread stack pointer The main thread restores its stack pointer and jumps to the code it was executing when it saved the checkpoint.

7) Restore the file state The main thread opens all the files that were open during the checkpoint and moves the file pointer to its position at the time of the checkpoint.

To finish restoring, the program runs steps 11 and 12 of the checkpointing algorithm described in section 2.3.

3. Performance Results

The two main sources of checkpointing overhead are saving the checkpoint to disk and the intercepting thread and file I/O calls. We ran several multithreaded programs with and without the checkpointing library to measure the checkpointing overhead. We ran the tests on a single processor, 125 MHz Sparc-20 with 64 MB of RAM running Solaris 2. Checkpoints were saved to an NFS mounted disk exported from an identical Sparc-20 over 100 Mbps Ethernet.

Most of the overhead comes from tracking mutex lock and unlock thread library calls. We calculated the average amount of time to lock and unlock a mutex by timing a loop that locked and unlocked a mutex one million times and dividing the time by one million. Without the checkpointing library linked, each lock and unlock pair took approximately 0.33 μs compared to 5.5 μs with the checkpointing library.

Figure 1 shows the performance of the checkpointing library with two application programs, Barnes and Radiosity, from the SPLASH-2 benchmark suite [15]. Barnes simulates a group of particles interacting in three dimensions. Radiosity renders a three dimensional scene. The "Checkpointing Disabled" curve shows the application's execution time without any checkpointing overhead. As the number of threads increases, execution time of the program increases gradually because of thread synchronization. The "Checkpointing Enabled, No Checkpoints" curve shows the application's execution time with the checkpointing library enabled, but without saving any checkpoints. The "Checkpointing Enabled, One Checkpoint" curve shows the program's execution time when the checkpointing library saves one checkpoint during the program's execution.

Barnes with checkpointing enabled took 3% longer on average than with checkpointing disabled even though no checkpoints are saved. On average checkpointing added 10% to the execution time of Radiosity in the same case. The extra overhead with Radiosity is expected because it spends a higher percentage of time in synchronization [15].

The amount of time required to save the checkpoint is large percentage of execution time for these relatively short-running programs. The user can reduce the percentage of execution time spent saving checkpoints by increasing the checkpoint interval.

4. Related work

Checkpointing libraries such as Libckpt, Condor, and libckp run on several versions of Unix, but are not designed for multithreaded programs [10, 12, 14].

Plank and Li describe several algorithms for reducing latency when saving checkpoints on multiprocessor machines[11]. Their algorithms could be used to improve the efficiency of our checkpointing library.

Many researchers have worked on checkpointing for distributed systems [2, 4, 5, 7, 8, 9, 13]. Distributed checkpointing algorithms are primarily concerned with forming consistent global checkpoints state either by coordinating all of the processors or by building a consistent checkpoint from independent checkpoints. Our checkpointing library uses the thread library's memory consistency guarantees ensure checkpoints are consistent.

5. Conclusion

Our user-level checkpointing library can checkpoint multithreaded programs that use kernel-level threads. It added about 5 μs to a mutex lock and unlock pair. For two programs from the SPLASH-2 benchmark suite checkpointing added 3% and 10% to execution time. Programs with similar synchronization patterns will incur similar overhead. Saving process state to disk incurs a substantial amount of overhead, and we are considering optimizations to reduce the overhead of writing a checkpoint to disk.

Currently we are working on reducing the overhead of intercepting thread library calls, integrating the checkpointing library into the Unify distributed shared memory li-

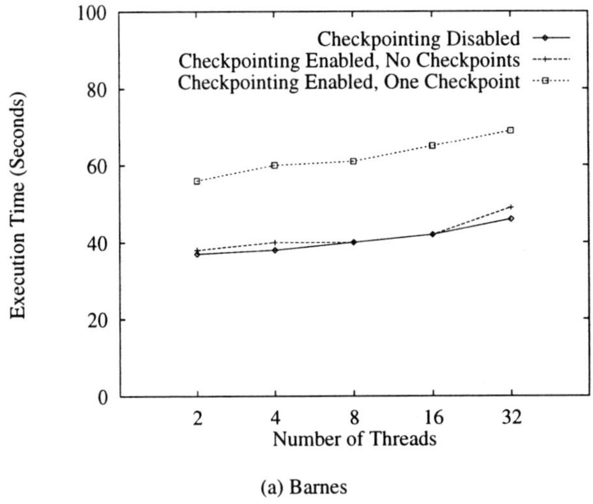

(a) Barnes

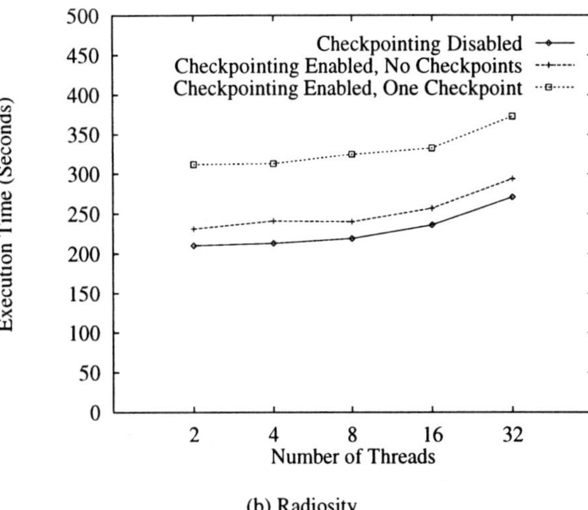

(b) Radiosity

Figure 1. These graphs show how the execution time of two SPLASH-2 benchmark programs are affected by increasing the number of threads. The execution time does not decrease with more threads because the program was run on a single processor machine.

brary [6], porting the checkpointing library to other operating systems, and adding features found in other checkpointing libraries.

References

[1] D. R. Butenhof. *Programming with POSIX Threads*. Addison-Wesley, 1997.

[2] K. M. Chandy and L. Lamport. Distributed snapshots: Determining global states of distributed sytems. *ACM Trans. Comput. Syst.*, 3(1):63–75, Feb. 1985.

[3] W. R. Dieter and J. E. Lumpp. User-level checkpointing of posix threads. Technical Report CEG-99-004, University of Kentucky, Department of Electrical Engineering, Lexington, KY 40506–0046, http://www.dcs.uky.edu/~chkpt, 1999.

[4] E. N. Elnozahy, D. B. Johnson, and W. Zwaenepoel. The performance of consistent checkpointing. In *Proceedings of the Symposium on Reliable Distributed Systems*, pages 39–47, Oct. 1992.

[5] E. N. Elnozahy and W. Zwaenepoel. On the use and implementation of message logging. In *Proceedings of the International Symposium on Fault-Tolerant Computing*, pages 298–307, June 1994.

[6] J. Griffioen, R. Yavatkar, and R. Finkel. Unify: A scalable approach to multicomputer design. *IEEE Computer Society Bulletin of the Technical Committee on Operating Systems and Application Environments*, 7(2), 1995.

[7] R. Koo and S. Toueg. Checkpointing and rollback-recovery for distributed systems. *IEEE Trans. Softw. Eng.*, SE-13(1):23–31, May 1987.

[8] P.-J. Leu and B. Bhargava. Concurrent robust checkpointing and recovery in distributed systems. In *Proceedings of the International Conference on Data Engineering*, pages 154–163, Feb. 1988.

[9] D. Manivannan, R. H. B. Netzer, and M. Singhal. Finding consistent global checkpoints in a distributed computation. *IEEE Transactions on Parallel and Distributed Systems*, July 1997.

[10] J. S. Plank, M. Beck, G. Kingsley, and K. Li. Libckpt: Transparent checkpointing under Unix. In *USENIX Winter 1995 Technical Conference*, Jan. 1995.

[11] J. S. Plank and K. Li. Low-latency, concurrent checkpointing for parallel programs. *IEEE Transactions on Parallel and Distributed Systems*, 5(8):874–879, Aug. 1994.

[12] T. Tannenbaum and M. Litzkow. Checkpointing and migration of unix processes in the condor distributed processing system. *Dr. Dobbs Journal*, Feb. 1995.

[13] Y.-M. Wang, P.-Y. Chung, I.-J. Lin, and W. K. Fuchs. Checkpoint space reclamation for uncoordinated checkpointing in message-passing systems. *IEEE Transactions on Parallel and Distributed Systems*, 6(5):546–554, May 1995.

[14] Y.-M. Wang, Y. Huang, K.-P. Vo, P.-Y. Chung, and C. Kintala. Checkpointing and its applications. In *Proceedings of the International Symposium on Fault-Tolerant Computing*, pages 22–31, June 1995.

[15] S. C. Woo, M. Ohara, E. Torrie, J. P. Singh, and A. Gupta. The splash-2 programs: Characterization and methodological considerations. In *Proceedings of the International Symposium on Computer Architecture*, pages 24–36, June 1995.

The DSPNexpress 2.000 Performance and Dependability Modeling Environment

Christoph Lindemann, Andreas Reuys, and Axel Thümmler
University of Dortmund
Department of Computer Science
44221 Dortmund, Germany
{cl, reuys, thummler}@cs.uni-dortmund.de
http://www4.cs.uni-dortmund.de/~Lindemann/

Abstract

This paper describes the latest version of the software package DSPNexpress, a tool for modeling with deterministic and stochastic Petri nets (DSPNs). Novel innovative features of DSPNexpress 2.000 constitute an efficient numerical method for transient analysis of DSPNs with and without concurrent deterministic transitions. In particular, DSPNexpress 2.000 can perform transient analysis of DSPNs without concurrent deterministic transitions in three orders of magnitude less computational effort than the previously known method. Furthermore, DSPNexpress 2.000 contains an effective numerical method for steady-state analysis of DSPNs with concurrent deterministic transitions.

1. Innovative Features of DSPNexpress

To effectively employ model-based evaluation of computer and communication systems, software environments are needed that simplify model specification, modification, as well as automate quantitative analysis. Due to the complexity of practical modeling applications requiring sophisticated solution methods, the development of effective software tool support for stochastic Petri nets is an active research area. Software packages for stochastic Petri nets include GreatSPN [4], QPN-tool [2], SPNP [6], SURF-2 [3], and UltraSAN [12].

This paper describes the latest version of one such software package, the DSPNexpress 2.000 modeling environment. The previous version of DSPNexpress, DSPNexpress1.5 is known for its highly efficient numerical method for steady state analysis of deterministic and stochastic Petri nets (DSPNs, [1]) without concurrent deterministic transitions [8], [9]. This numerical method analyzes complex DSPNs with four orders of magnitude less computational effort that the previously known method implemented in the version 1.4 of the package GreatSPN. Novel innovative features of the DSPNexpress 2.000 include:

(1) Efficient numerical method for transient analysis of DSPNs without concurrent deterministic transitions based on an iterative numerical solution of one-dimensional Volterra integral equations [10]. As shown in Section 4, this method can perform numerical transient analysis of complex DSPNs in some minutes CPU on a modern workstation.

(2) An implementation of an effective numerical method for transient and steady-state analysis of DSPNs with two deterministic transitions concurrently enabled. These tasks require numerical solution of two-dimensional Volterra equations by an iterative scheme and direct quadrature, respectively. On a modern workstation, transient analysis of quite complex DSPNs (i.e., with 10 thousand tangible markings with moderate stiffness in the parameter settings) requires about 40 minutes of CPU time [11], steady-state analysis less than 10 minutes of CPU time.

(3) Orthogonal software architecture especially tailored to numerical analysis of the stochastic process underlying a discrete-event stochastic system with exponential and deterministic events (i.e., a Markov regenerative process [5] or a generalized semi-Markov process [10]) based on interprocess communication with UNIX sockets rather than writing intermediate results in files.

(4) Plug-and-play interface such that numerical solvers can easily be utilized to quantitative evaluation of arbitrary discrete-event stochastic systems with exponential and deterministic events specified in other modeling formalisms than just DSPNs (e.g., hardware systems represented as finite state machines).

In previous work, transient analysis of DSPNs was always based on the restriction that deterministic transitions are not concurrently enabled. Choi, Kulkarni, and Trivedi observed that the marking process underlying a DSPN with this restriction is a Markov regenerative stochastic process [5]. They introduced a numerical method for transient analysis of such DSPNs based on numerical inversion of Laplace-Stieltjes transforms. More recently, German et al. developed a numerical method for transient analysis of DSPNs based on the approach of supplementary variables [7]. While these methods are certainly of theoretical interest, they are both not suitable for application in practical dependability modeling projects.

The remainder of this paper is organized as follows. Section 2 describes the software architecture of DSPNexpress 2.000. The graphical interface of the package is briefly recalled in Section 3. To illustrate the applicability of DSPNexpress 2.000 for practical dependability modeling projects, we present performance curves of the newly implemented transient solver in Section 4. Finally, concluding remarks are given.

2. The Software Architecture of the Numerical Solvers

The core of the package DSPNexpress constitutes the solution engine for discrete-event stochastic systems with exponential and deterministic events. The software architecture of this solution engine and its software modules are shown in Figure 1. The solution engine is drawn as the big white rectangular box. The six software modules are drawn as rectangles. These software modules are invoked from the solution engine as UNIX processes. Interprocess communication with sockets drawn as broken ellipses is employed for passing intermediate results from one module to the next.

Steady state analysis of DSPNs without concurrent deterministic transitions relies on analysis of an embedded Markov chain (EMC) underlying such DSPNs [1]. To efficiently derive the probability matrix of this EMC, the concept of a subordinated Markov chain (SMC) was introduced. Recall that a SMC associated with a state

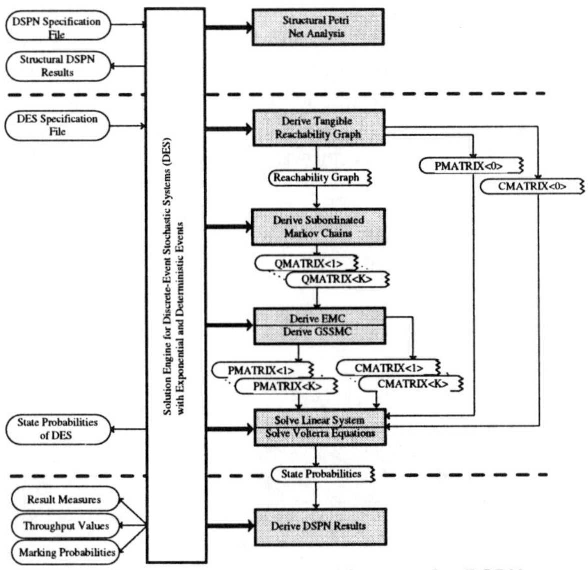

Figure 1. The solver architecture for DSPNs

s_i is a CTMC whose states are given by the transitive closure of all states reachable from s_i via the occurrence of exponential events [9]. After generating the reachability graph comprising of tangible markings (states) of the DSPN, for each state the generator matrix of its SMC is derived. These tasks are performed in the modules *Derive Tangible Reachability Graph* and *Derive Subordinated Markov Chains*, respectively. Entries of this probability matrix are computed by transient analysis of the SMCs. Subsequently, a linear system corresponding to the stationary equations of the EMC is solved. These task are performed in the submodules *Derive EMC* and *Solve Linear System*.

Transient analysis of DSPNs is based on the analysis of a general state space Markov chain (GSSMC) embedded at equidistant time points nD (n = 0,1,2,...) of the continuous-time marking process. The Chapman Kolmogorov equations of the GSSMC constitute a system of Volterra integral equations [11]. Steady state analysis of DSPNs with concurrent deterministic transitions relies on the same approach [10]. The transition kernel of the GSSMC specifies one-step jump probabilities from a given state at instant of time nD to all reachable new states at instant of time (n+1)D. Key drivers for the computational efficiency of the GSSMC approach constitute the separability and piece-wise continuity of the transition kernel [11]. Furthermore, the elements of the transition kernel can effectively be determined by an extension of the concept of subordinated Markov chains. Numerical computation of kernel elements relies also on transient analysis of these CTMCs. This task is performed in submodule *Derive GSSMC.* Subsequently, for transient analysis a number of iterations corresponding to the mission time are performed on the system of Volterra equations [11] whereas for steady state analysis a linear system is solved for each mesh point [9], [10]. This task is performed in the submodule *Solve Volterra Equations.*

We would like to point out that only the front end and the back end of the solution engine is tailored to DSPNs. That is instead of a DSPN specification file provided by the graphical interface of DSPNexpress, a specification file of an arbitrary discrete-event stochastic system with exponential and deterministic events (e.g., finite state machines) could be quantitatively evaluated by the solution engine of DSPNexpress using an appropriate filter.

3. The Graphical User Interface

Of course, the package DSPNexpress also provides a user-friendly graphical interface running under X11. To illustrate the features of this graphical interface, consider the snapshot shown in Figure 2. The first line displays the name of the package *DSPNexpress* and the actual version *2.000,* the affiliation of the authors, *University of Dortmund, Computer Systems and Performance*

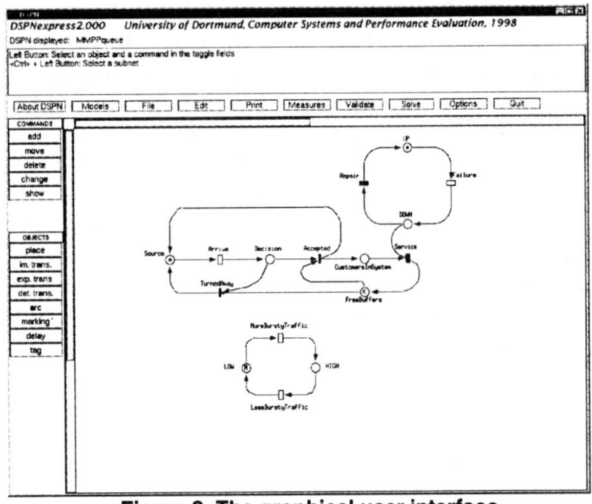
Figure 2. The graphical user interface

Evaluation Group, and the year of release *1998.* A DSPN of a single-server, finite-capacity queue with failure and repair is displayed. The model is named *MMPPqueue* because customers arrive according to a Markov modulated Poisson process. Recall that in DSPNs three types of transitions exist: immediate transitions drawn as thin bars fire without delay, exponential transitions drawn as empty bars fire after an exponentially distributed delay whereas deterministic transitions drawn as black bars fire after a constant delay.

At any time, DSPNexpress provides on-line helpmessages displayed in the third line of the interface. The command line and the object line are located on the left side of the interface. The buttons are located in a vertical line between the on-line help line and the working area. The working area constitutes the remaining big rectangle which contains the graphical representation of the DSPN *MMPPqueue.* This DSPN is displayed with the options *tags on.* Thus, each place and each transition of this DSPN is labeled (e.g., *Source*, *Arrive*, *Decision, Service*, etc.). A detailed description of the features of the graphical interface is given in [9].

4. Application Example

To illustrate the applicability of the transient solver of DSPNexpress 2.000 for practical dependability modeling projects, we consider a DSPN for an MMPP/D/1/K queue with breakdown and repair. The DSPN is shown in the working area of the graphical interface in Figure 2. The K tokens residing in place *FreeBuffers* in the initial marking represent the finite number of buffers of the single-server queueing system. The number tokens residing the place *LOW* control the mean firing time of the exponential transition *Arrive.* That is, the Markov modulated Poisson arrival stream is represented by defining the firing delay of the exponential transition *Arrive* dependent on the number of tokens in the place *LOW.* The number of tangible markings of this DSPN is given by

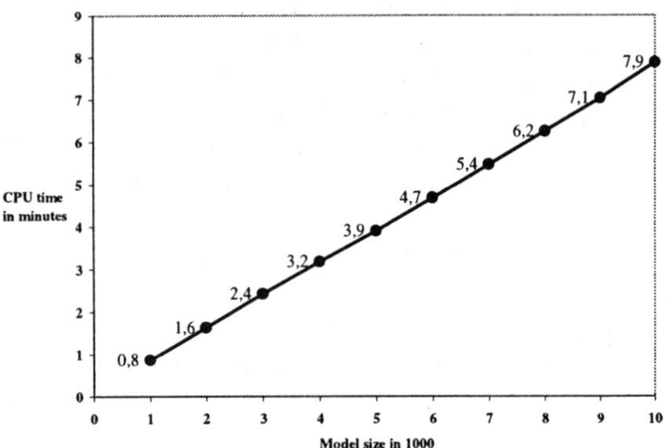

Figure 3. CPU time versus model size

$2 \cdot (K+1) \cdot (N+1)$. The constant service requirement is assumed as D = 1.0. We assume that after a failure the partly completed service is lost and is restarted after repair. In all experiments, model parameters of the Markov modulated arrival process are set such that the effective arrival rate λ_{eff} = 0.9. At time t = 0, zero customers reside in the queue and the system is *UP.* Failures of the system are assumed to be exponentially distributed. Repair times are assumed to be constant The experiments have been performed on a Sun Sparc Enterprise station with 1 GByte main memory running the operating system SunOS5.6. For the performance tests the CPU time has been measured by the UNIX system call *clock.* Figure 3 plots the CPU time required for computing the transient solution at instant of time t = 100 for increasing model size. We observe a linear growth of CPU time. This is due to the exploitation of the separability of the transition kernel of the GSSMC resulting in an almost linear growth of the nonzero kernel elements to be considered in the iterative scheme [11]. Figure 4 plots the memory requirements for storing the nonzero elements of the transition kernel versus model size and, thus, provides further evidence along this line. In these experiments, the number of discretization steps employed in the numerical quadrature is M = 10. A DSPN of an MMPP/D/1/K queue with failure and repair was already considered in [7] and a computational effort of 100 hours of CPU was reported. Figures 3 and 4 show

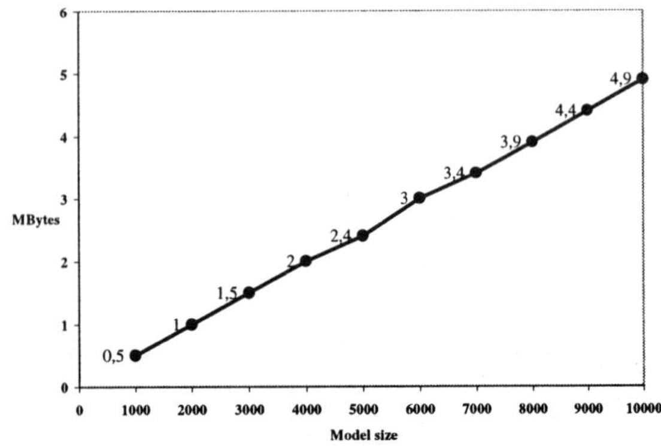

Figure 4. Memory requirements versus size

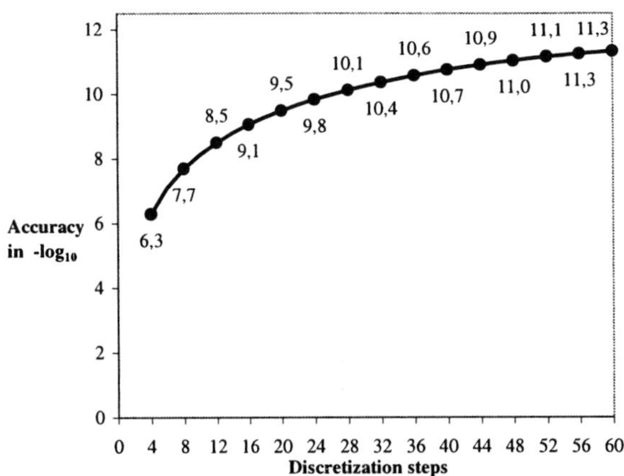

Figure 5. Numerical accuracy

that the software package DSPNexpress performs numerical transient analysis of such DSPNs three orders of magnitude faster than the previously known numerical method based on the approach of supplementary variables [7]. Since the DSPN does not contain concurrently enabled deterministic transitions, the stationary of time-averaged state probabilities of its marking process can be computed by an embedded Markov chain as already implemented in the previous version of the software package DSPNexpress [8]. Note that by setting the mission time sufficiently long, the transient solver can also be employed for computing stationary or time-averaged distributions. We use this fact for estimating the numerical accuracy achieved by the newly implemented transient solver for a given numerical quadrature of the Volterra integral equations. Figure 5 plots the accuracy of the stationary distribution of the DSPN achieved by the transient solver versus the number of discretization points employed in the iterative scheme. We observe that for already 10 discretization points a numerical accuracy of less that 10^{-7} is obtained

5. Conclusions

This paper provided an overview of DSPNexpress 2.000, the new version of a widely distributed software package for modeling with deterministic and stochastic Petri nets. While the previous version of DSPNexpress was known for its highly efficient numerical solver for stationary analysis of DSPNs without concurrent deterministic transitions [8], DSPNexpress 2.000 also provides a method for transient analysis of DSPNs [11]. Furthermore, both the stationary analysis and the transient analysis is no longer restricted to the case that deterministic transitions cannot be concurrently enabled [10].

To illustrate the applicability of the newly implemented transient solver of DSPNexpress for practical dependability projects, we presented curves for an MMPP/D/1/K queue with failure and repair plotting the CPU time and memory requirements versus model size and mission time, respectively. For this DSPN, the transient solver of DSPNexpress implementation based on the GSSMC approach [9], [11] requires a couple of minutes of CPU time on a modern workstation whereas as reported in [7] the previously known method requires more than 100 hours of CPU time.

6. References

[1] M. Ajmone Marsan and G. Chiola, On Petri Nets with Deterministic and Exponentially Distributed Firing Times", in: *G. Rozenberg (Ed.) Advances in Petri Nets 1987, Lecture Notes in Computer Science 266*, 132-145, Springer 1987.

[2] F. Bause, P. Buchholz, and P. Kemper, QPN-tool for the Specification and Analysis of Hierarchically Combined Queueing Petri Nets, in: H. Beilner, F. Bause (Eds.) *Quantitative Evaluation of Computing and Communication Systems,* Lecture Notes in Computer Science, Vol. 977, pp. 224-238, Springer 1995.

[3] C. Beounes et al., SURF-2: A Program for Dependability Evaluation of Complex Hardware and Software Systems, *Proc. 23rd Int. Symp. on Fault-Tolerant Computing, Toulouse France,* 668-673, 1993.

[4] G. Chiola, G. Franceschinis, R. Gaeta, and M. Ribaudo, GreatSPN 1.7: Graphical Editor and Analyzer for Timed and Stochastic Petri Nets, *Performance Evaluation,* **24**, 47-68, 1995.

[5] H. Choi, V.G. Kulkarni, and K.S. Trivedi, Transient Analysis of Deterministic and Stochastic Petri Nets, in: *M. Ajmone Marsan (Ed.) Application and Theory of Petri Nets 1993, Lecture Notes in Computer Science 691*, 166-185, Springer 1993.

[6] G. Ciardo, J. Muppala, and K.S. Trivedi, SPNP: Stochastic Petri Net Package, *Proc. 3rd Int. Workshop on Petri Nets and Performance Models Kyoto Japan,* 142-151, 1989.

[7] A. Heindl and R. German, A Fourth Order Algorithm with Automatic Step Size Control for the Transient Analysis of DSPNs, *Proc. 7th Int. Workshop on Petri Nets and Performance Models, Saint Malo, France,* 60-69, 1996.

[8] Ch. Lindemann, DSPNexpress: A Software Package for the Efficient Solution of Deterministic and Stochastic Petri Nets, *Performance Evaluation,* **22**, 3-21, 1995.

[9] Ch. Lindemann, *Performance Modelling with Deterministic and Stochastic Petri Nets*, John Wiley & Sons 1998.

[10] Ch. Lindemann and G.S. Shedler, Numerical Analysis of Deterministic and Stochastic Petri Nets with Concurrent Deterministic Transitions, *Performance Evaluation, Special Issue Proc. of PERFORMANCE '96*, **27&28**, 565-582, 1996.

[11] Ch. Lindemann and A. Thümmler, Transient Analysis of Deterministic and Stochastic Petri Nets with Concurrent Deterministic Transitions, (submitted for publication).

[12] W.H. Sanders, W.D. Obal, M.A. Qureshi, and F.K. Widjanarko, The UltraSAN Modeling Environment, *Performance Evaluation,* **24**, 89-115, 1995.

The Galileo Fault Tree Analysis Tool

Kevin J. Sullivan
University of Virginia
Dept. of Computer Science

sullivan@cs.virginia.edu

Joanne Bechta Dugan
University of Virginia
Dept. of Electrical Engineering

jbd@virginia.edu

David Coppit
University of Virginia
Dept. of Computer Science

coppit@cs.virginia.edu

Abstract

We present Galileo, a dynamic fault tree modeling and analysis tool that combines the innovative DIF-Tree analysis methodology with a rich user interface built using package-oriented programming. DIFTree integrates binary decision diagram and Markov methods under the common notation of dynamic fault trees, allowing the user to exploit the benefits of both techniques while avoiding the need to learn additional notations and methodologies. Package-oriented programming (POP) is a software architectural style in which large-scale software packages are used as components, exploiting their rich functionality and familiarity to users. Galileo can be obtained for free under license for evaluation, and can be downloaded from the World-Wide Web.

1. Introduction to Galileo

Software and reliability engineering researchers at the University of Virginia in are collaborating on the Galileo project, an experiment in the use of *package-oriented programming (POP)* to deliver innovative engineering analysis techniques supported by functionally rich, industrially viable software tools. *POP* is the use of standard, off-the-shelf software packages as components [5][6][7] It supports the *DIFTree* technique for efficient modular analysis of dynamic fault trees [1].

Galileo is a research prototype software tool for dynamic fault tree analysis that runs on personal computers running Microsoft's *Windows 95*, *98* or *NT* operating systems. Galileo hosts *DIFtree* in a richly functional easy-to-use tool, the vast bulk of the user-level function of which is provided by a tightly integrated framework comprising Microsoft's *Word* and *Internet Explorer* programs and Visio Corporation's *Visio Technical* drawing program. The user interface is based on the familiar Microsoft Windows "MFC" user interface style. The tool enables engineers to edit and display fault trees in textual and graphical form through widely used, commercially-supported, volume-priced components that are easy to use in engineering practice. Our POP software development approach has allowed the construction of a tool that has the potential to be far richer, easier to use and more easily changed than would otherwise possible at a comparable level of development cost and code complexity. Some of the important features of Galileo are as follows:

- supports the *DIFTree* modular dynamic fault tree analysis approach
- allows the user to edit a fault tree in either a textual or graphical representation, and provides an automatic rendering between the two views
- exploits the user interfaces and other features of off-the-shelf packages, e.g., zoom, find-and-replace, print preview, cut-and-paste, etc.
- provides on-line documentation through an embedded internet browser and World-Wide Web pages

0-7695-0213-X/99 $10.00 © 1999 IEEE

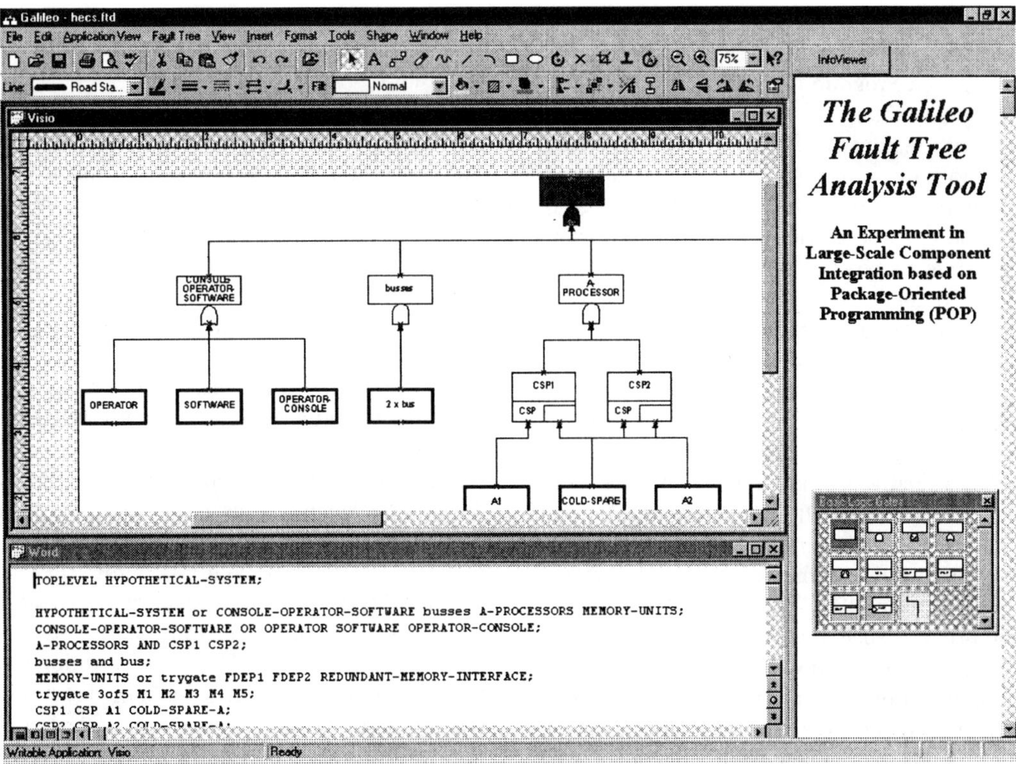

Figure 1. A screenshot of Galileo

Figure 1 shows a screenshot of the current version of Galileo. The upper left window shows the graphical view, hosted by Visio. The lower left window shows the same fault tree in textual format, as hosted by Word. The right side shows the on-line help, hosted by Internet Explorer. Because the graphical view provided by Visio is currently selected for viewing, Galileo presents to the user the Visio menus and toolbars combined with the Galileo menus. When either of the other views is selected, the menus and toolbars are updated to reflect the interfaces of those components.

2. The *DIFTree* Analysis Approach

DIFtree (Dynamic Innovative Fault Tree)[1] is a modeling methodology and analysis algorithm providing a unique approach for reliability analysis of complex computer-based systems. *DIFtre*e combines static and dynamic fault tree analysis techniques using a modular approach. It is unique in several aspects.

First, the decomposition of dynamic fault trees into modules uses an efficient algorithm to identify independent sub-trees. These sub-models can be solved separately using the most appropriate underlying methods, allowing exacts solution to be obtained efficiently.

Second, the sub-models are classified as either static or dynamic, depending on the temporal relationships between the input events. Static gates express failure criteria in terms of combinations of events. Dynamic gates express the failure criteria in terms of combinations and order of occurrence for input events. A static sub-tree is one containing no dynamic gates. Static sub-trees are solved using combinatorial methods based on binary decision diagrams (BDDs). Dynamic sub-trees are solved with Markov methods. DIFtree combines the sub-tree results into an exact solution for the given tree.

Third, modeling imperfect fault coverage is critical to correct evaluation of computer-based systems, so we include this capability in both the static and dynamic solution techniques.

Fourth, the solution of static fault trees using methods based on BDDs, and including imperfect coverage in this solution, is unique to our approach[4]. The BDD approach to static fault tree analysis is an innovation that has significant potential for the analysis of large models.

Fifth, the dynamic fault tree model allows the analysis of systems with complex redundancy management in a relatively simple manner. Factors that often complicate analysis include cold, warm and hot spares, spares which are shared among several different components, and functional dependencies. These are handled by the DIFtree dynamic gates.

3. Package-Oriented Programming

Package-Oriented Programming (POP) is a research project investigating the reuse and integration of standard, large-scale components. By large-scale we mean components whose implementations are on the order of a million or more lines of code. We are interested in large-scale reuse because without it, it appears that it will be impossible to build sophisticated engineering modeling tools quickly and inexpensively. Conformance of components to a standard integration architecture is meant to ensure that components can be integrated without undue cost or effort.

In the particular domain of tools, we see the following structure. Core analysis algorithms can often be implemented in a relatively small amount of code (perhaps thousands or tens of thousands of lines). The problem is building usability-engineered, interoperable, easy-to-learn, and well-documented tool "superstructures" that run on commodity Windows-based computers and that provide such features as rich graphical interfaces, cut-and-paste drawings, constraint-based layout, and the many other amenities typical in shrink-wrapped software. It is the code for this superstructure that we believe tends to dominate development costs in tools that are built largely from scratch.

Our work suggests that an approach based on the integration of just a few massive, commercially available, volume-priced components provides an effective attack on the tool superstructure development problem. In order to explore and evaluate POP, we are developing Galileo. Galileo hosts the DIFtree codes in a usability superstructure based on the tight integration of multiple shrink-wrapped packages. Galileo uses Microsoft Word 97 to present a textual view of a fault tree and Visio Technical 5.0 to present a graphical view. Galileo keeps multiple views consistent in a compiler-like manner that the user invokes by menu selection. The underlying analysis code is invoked in the same way. The application windows are composed into a single tool window using Microsoft's Active Document architecture. This mechanism manages the integration of package and Galileo menu items. Galileo also uses Microsoft's Internet Explorer for on-line help and to support user interaction with each other and with the Galileo developers (e.g., for purposes of bug reporting, troubleshooting and for requesting enhancements).

Evidence suggests that Galileo is close to being an industrially viable tool. We performed a case study on the use of Galileo at the Lockheed Martin Corporation. An engineer there concluded that Galileo has tremendous potential to aid reliability engineers in that corporation (as reported in an internal study of the tool). Galileo has been acquired by over 150 enterprises in 32 countries, although it is not easy for us to know how large the active installed base is. Galileo is distinguished in several ways with respect to component integration.

First, Galileo is based on tight integration of multiple, widely used, shrink-wrapped commercial-off-the-shelf packages. It is not built on a single package; instead it integrates packages as co-equal components.

Second, it uses these packages to present multiple views of an engineering model (i.e., fault tree). Microsoft Word presents the tree being edited in a textual form based on the *Galileo fault tree language.* Visio presents the tree as a structured technical drawing using Galileo shapes and behaviors programmed within Visio. A potentially significant advantage of this approach is that it reduces user learning costs by presenting sophisticated modeling and analysis codes through packages that users already understand how to use. Third, Galileo keeps views consistent in a manner based on an analogy with a compiler. In Galileo, you edit a fault tree in either textual or graphical form, and, when you are ready, you ask Galileo to "compile" it into the other form. Unlike a traditional compiler, though, Galileo translates in both directions. Fourth, Galileo achieves tight integration of component packages within a single, overall Galileo tool window.

There are several areas in which Galileo falls short today. One of the most pressing is in graphical editing. We have not yet programmed sufficiently rich graphical layout or editing capabilities. The tool draws fault trees automatically from textual representations, but only on a single drawing page no matter how large the tree. Similarly, editing the graphical representation requires low-level manipulation of Visio gate and connector shapes. We are now adding support to overcome these deficiencies. In particular, we plan to add higher level graphical editing functions (e.g., add a gate) that do not require low-level drawing operations (e.g., drop a connector then connect it to the required gates). We are also planning for enhancements in the underlying analysis codes to be discussed in future publications.

4. An example

As an example of the capability of the Galileo fault tree analysis package, we present an analysis of the ASID-MAS system (see Figure 2), originally analyzed using HARP in [3]. There are two interesting reasons to revisit this particular fault tree. First, at the time when this system was analyzed using HARP, the dynamic fault tree did not include the hot spare gate. Galileo includes the hot spare gate, which can easily model pooled spares and which simplifies the fault tree model considerably. The underlying Markov model did not change, but it could be described more succinctly. Second, Galileo modularized the fault tree

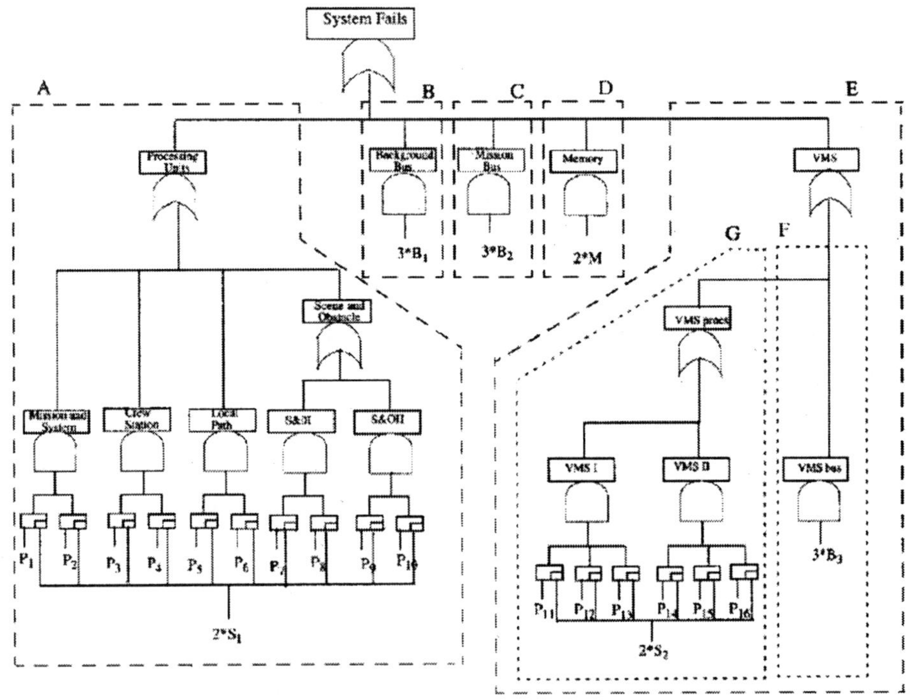

Figure 2. The ASID-MAS Fault Tree

into seven independent subtrees: 4 static and 3 dynamic. Without modularization, the entire tree needed to be converted into a single Markov chain for analysis. The resulting Markov chain was too big for exact analysis; [3] reports unreliability bounds based on a truncated Markov chain. With modularization, the resulting Markov chains for the dynamic subtrees could be generated and solved completely. The largest Markov chain contains more than 28000 states and 87000 transitions.

5. How to Obtain Galileo for Evaluation

Galileo is available on the World-Wide Web, free of charge, under license for evaluation purposes (URL: http://www.cs.virginia.edu/~ftree/). Galileo runs on Microsoft Windows 95, 98, and NT. It requires either or both of Microsoft Word 95 or 97 and Visio Corporation's Visio Technical 5.0. If *Internet Explorer* is available, Galileo will use it. If it is not available, it is not possible to browse the user documentation from within the tool. A 166 MHz "Pentium-class" computer is recommended, with at least 32 MB of main memory, and 50 MB of disk space. Installation involves the unzipping of the archive, and the execution of a standard setup program.

References

[1] J. Dugan, K. Venkataraman, and R. Gulati, "DIFtree: A software package for the analysis of dynamic fault tree models," *Proc. 1997 Reliability and Maintainability Symposium*, January 1997.

[2] R. Gulati and J. Dugan, "A modular approach for analyzing static and dynamic fault trees," in *Proc. Reliability and Maintainability Symposium,* January 1997.

[3] J. Dugan, S.J. Bavuso and M.A. Boyd, "Dynamic fault tree models for fault tolerant computer systems," *IEEE Transactions on Reliability*, Volume 41, Number 3, pages 363-377, September 1992.

[4] S.A. Doyle and J. Dugan, "Dependability assessment using binary decision diagrams," In *Proc. IEEE International Symposium on Fault-Tolerant Computing*, FTCS-25, June 1995.

[5] K.J. Sullivan, J. Cockrell, S. Zhang, and D. Coppit, "Package-oriented programming of engineering tools," In *Proc. 19th International Conference on Software Engineering*, pages 616-617, Boston, Massachusetts, 17-23 May 1997, IEEE.

[6] K.J. Sullivan and J.C. Knight, "Building Programs from Massive Components," *Proc. 21st Annual Software Engineering Workshop*, Greenbelt, MD, Dec. 4—5, 1996.

[7] K.J. Sullivan and J.C. Knight, "Experience Assessing an Architectural Approach to Large-Scale, Systematic Reuse," *Proc. 18th International Conference on Software Engineering, Berlin, March 1996, pp. 220—229.*

Session 8B

Special Seminar: Intrusion Detection

Moderator:
Roy Maxion, Carnegie Mellon University, USA

Speakers:
Marc Dacier, IBM Research, Switzerland
Sami Saydjari, DARPA Information Technology Office, USA

Special Seminar: Intrusion Detection

Organizer: Roy A. Maxion, Carnegie Mellon University

Marc Dacier

Global Security Analysis Laboratory
IBM Research
Saumerstrasse 4
CH-8803 Ruschlikon, Switzerland
Internet: dac@zurich.ibm.com

Sami Saydjari

Information Technology Office
Defense Advanced Research Projects Agency
3701 North Fairfax Drive
Arlington, Virginia 22203 USA
Internet: ssaydjari@darpa.mil

In the early days of computing, when system components included relays and vacuum tubes, failures would occur as often as once every million cycles. In those days, hardware was considered to be the primary locus of undependability. Later, following many innovative, fault-tolerance solutions for hardware problems, software became the dominant contributor to undependability. As fault tolerance expanded its scope to cover software issues, other assaults on dependability began to appear, one of which remains largely unaddressed: errors at the user-interface. In the last several years, however, a new, more sinister menace to dependability has emerged, disrupting computer operations worldwide: intrusions by unauthorized users. A recent example is the infamous Melissa virus, which caused large-scale denials of service. This latest addition to the arsenal of threats against dependability is called the intentionally malicious fault.

FTCS has historically been concerned about dependability and the threats against it. As new kinds of faults have appeared over the years, the international fault-tolerance community has risen to the challenge of preventing, removing, tolerating and forecasting them, all in the interest of making systems more reliable, or survivable. To address the concerns raised by the newest class of faults, malicious ones, the FTCS-29 Program Committee invited two of the world's most informed speakers on the topic to present the technical, strategic and tactical issues of developing and deploying intrusion-detection systems.

Marc Dacier's topic is: *intrusion detection vs. detection of errors caused by intentionally malicious faults.* Although research on intrusion detection has been carried out for more than two decades, it has recently received increased attention due to the success of the Internet. A recent survey conducted by the IBM Global Security Laboratory indicates that more than 20 intrusion-detection products are now available on the market, whereas two years ago there were only three. Despite this growth of product offerings, intrusion-detection solutions are still in their infancy. Not only is there a lack of understanding of what an intrusion really is, but also how it should be handled. Moreover, from a technical point of view, many critical issues remain unsolved.

In this talk, Marc presents what has been done in the intrusion domain in the past, and highlights new research directions that need to be addressed. He will highlight the relationship between intrusion detection and fault tolerance, drawing on the body of knowledge that has been developed within the traditional dependability community, and noting the opportunities for these two communities to work together to solve this important problem.

Sami Saydjari's topic is: *the detection of novel, previously unseen attacks.* Although intrusion detection is a field still in its infancy, two broad approaches have evolved: pattern-based detection and anomaly-based detection. Pattern-based detection, sometimes called misuse-based detection, relies on matching known patterns of attacks already suffered. Anomaly-based detection, on the other hand, relies on detecting behaviors that are abnormal with respect to some normal standard. An example is that of a masquerader trying to hide behind someone else's login; unless the masquerader is clever indeed, his activities will stand out as anomalous against a victim's profile of normal behavior. Anomaly-based detection techniques appear to hold the best hope of detecting new variants of attacks.

Sami emphasizes that although there exist some low-level sensors that can detect known attacks, the research community must move quickly in learning how to detect novel attacks at much higher detection rates (state of the art is around 80%) while keeping the false positive rates very low (0.1% or better). Detecting novel attacks will require better anomaly detection algorithms. Achieving a 99.9% detection rate will require gaining a firm understanding of the "sweet spots" of various detection algorithms, as well as an understanding of how to fuse the results of the best of the best. There is also a need to better represent knowledge of attack patterns in a canonical form, to be able to share that knowledge across multiple detection tools, and to be able to judge tools on the basis of how effectively they use knowledge, as opposed to which tool can include the largest corpus of precompiled (pattern-based) knowledge into its on-line database.

The session concludes with an open discussion of how research communities can work together to reduce undependability caused by intentionally malicious faults.

0-7695-0213-X/99 $10.00 © 1999 IEEE

Session 8C

Posters and Round Table

Chair: Nirmal Saxena
Stanford University, USA

Session 9A

Checkpointing II

Chair: Neeraj Suri
Boston University, USA

An Analysis of Communication Induced Checkpointing

Lorenzo Alvisi *‡ Elmootazbellah Elnozahy† Sriram Rao*‡ Syed Amir Husain‡ Asanka De Mel‡

‡ Department of Computer Sciences, U. T. Austin

†IBM Austin Research Lab, Austin, Texas, USA.

Abstract

Communication induced checkpointing (CIC) allows processes in a distributed computation to take independent checkpoints and to avoid the domino effect. This paper presents an analysis of CIC protocols based on a prototype implementation and validated simulations. Our result inidcate that there is sufficient evidence to suspect that much of the conventional wisdom about these protocols is questionable.

1 Introduction

There are three styles for implementing application-transparent rollback-recovery in message-passing systems, namely coordinated checkpointing, message logging, and communication-induced checkpointing (CIC) [5]. Both coordinated checkpointing and message logging have received considerable analysis in the literature [6, 12, 14, 15], but little is known about the behavior of CIC protocols. This paper presents an experimental analysis of these protocols through a prototype implementation and reveals several of their theoretical and pragmatic characteristics.

CIC protocols are believed to have several advantages over other styles of rollback-recovery. For instance, they allow processes considerable autonomy in deciding when to take checkpoints. A process can thus take a checkpoint at times when saving the state would incur a small overhead [10, 13]. CIC protocols also are believed to scale up well with a larger number of processes since they do not require the processes to participate in a global checkpoint. But there is a price to pay for these advantages. First, the protocol-specific information piggybacked on application messages occasionally "induces" processes to take forced checkpoints before they can process the messages. Second, processes have to pay the overhead of piggybacking information on top of application messages, and they also need to keep several checkpoints on stable storage. These advantages and disadvantages are clearly qualitative and potentially arguable. A purpose of our work is to shed some light on these issues using quantitative metrics drawn from a real system.

To this end, we have implemented three CIC protocols—the original one by Briatico et al [2], and two recent protocols [1, 7] based on the Z-path theory [11]— and we have examined their performance using two metrics, namely the average number of forced checkpoints a protocol causes and its running time. The first metric is important because forced checkpoints negate the autonomy advantage of CIC protocols. Also, they contribute substantially to the performance and resource overheads. A good CIC protocol therefore tries to limit these forced checkpoints to the extent possible. The experiments use four compute-intensive programs from the NPB 2.3 benchmark suite [3], which is a representative of a class of applications that have traditionally been the primary users of checkpointing protocols. We then use the implementation in part to validate a simulation model that we built to study further the scalability of the protocols and their behaviors under different communication patterns.

Our results reveal several important properties of CIC protocols and highlight several implementation and theoretical issues that were not addressed in the literature. We hope that our work will be a first step in investigating an area that thus far has been only subject to theoretical research.

*This author supported in part by the National Science Foundation (CAREER award CCR-9734185, Research Infrastructure Award CDA-9734185, and DARPA/SPAWAR grant N66001-98-8911).

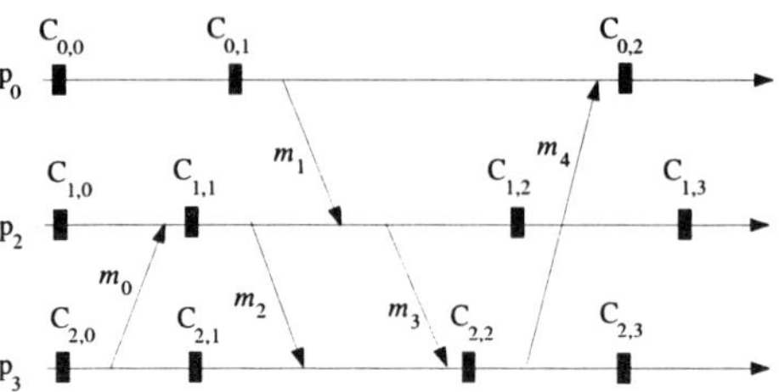

Figure 1 : A distributed computation. $C_{i,j}$ denotes the jth checkpoint of process p_i.

2 Background

This section reviews the three protocols used in the experiments, along with some necessary definitions. The description is inevitably terse and covers only the features necessary to follow the experimental work described later.

2.1 Definitions

Local checkpoints: A process may take a local checkpoint any time during the execution. The local checkpoints of different processes are not coordinated to form a global consistent checkpoint [4].

Forced checkpoints: To guard against the domino effect, a CIC protocol piggybacks protocol-specific information to application messages that processes exchange. Each process examines the information and occasionally is forced to take a checkpoint according to the protocol.

Useless checkpoints: A useless checkpoint of a process is one that will never be part of a global consistent state [18]. In Figure 1, checkpoint $C_{2,2}$ is an example of a useless checkpoint. Useless checkpoints are not desirable because they do not contribute to the recovery of the system from failures, but they consume resources and cause performance overhead.

0-7695-0213-X/99 $10.00

Checkpoint intervals: A checkpoint interval is the sequence of events between two consecutive checkpoints in the execution of a process.

2.2 Z-paths and Z-cycles

Z-paths: A Z-path (zigzag path) is a special sequence of messages that connects two checkpoints. Let $\rightarrow$ denote Lamport's happen-before relation [9]. Given two local checkpoints $C_{i,m}$ and $C_{j,n}$, a Z-path exists between $C_{i,m}$ and $C_{j,n}$ if and only if one of the following two conditions holds:

1. $m < n$ and $i = j$; or
2. There exists a sequence of messages $[m_0, m_1, , m_z]$, $z \geq 0$, such that:
   (a) $C_{i,m} \rightarrow send_i(m_0)$;
   (b) $\forall l < z$, either $deliver_k(m_l)$ and $send_k(m_{l+1})$ are in the same checkpoint interval, or $deliver_k(m_l) \rightarrow send_k(m_{l+1})$; and
   (c) $deliver_j(m_z) \rightarrow C_{j,n}$ where $send_i$ and $deliver_i$ are communication events executed by process p_i. In Figure 1, $[m_1, m_2]$ and $[m_1, m_3]$ are examples of Z-paths.

Z-cycles: A Z-cycle is a Z-path that begins and ends with the same checkpoint. In Figure 1, the Z-path $[m_4, m_1, m_3]$ is a Z-cycle that involves checkpoint $C_{2,2}$.

2.3 Z-cycles and CIC

CIC protocols do not take useless checkpoints. These protocols recognize that the creation of useless checkpoints depends on the occurrence of specific patterns in which processes communicate and take checkpoints [8]. Informally, these protocols recognize potentially dangerous patterns and break them before they occur. This intuition has been formalized in an elegant theory based on the notion Z-cycles. A key result in this theory is that a local checkpoint is useless if it is involved in a Z-cycle [8, 11]. Hence, to avoid useless checkpoints it suffices that no Z-path ever becomes a Z-cycle. Enforcing the no-Z-cycle ($\mathcal{NZC}$) condition may require that a process save additional forced checkpoints in addition to its local checkpoints. There are two approaches to avoiding Z-cycles. The first approach uses a function that associates a timestamp with each checkpoint. The protocol guarantees, through forced checkpoints if necessary, that (*i*) if there are two checkpoints $C_{i,m}$ and $C_{j,n}$ such that $C_{i,m} \rightarrow C_{j,n}$, then $ts(C_{j,n}) \geq ts(C_{i,m})$, where $ts(C)$ is the timestamp associated with checkpoint C; and (*ii*) consecutive local checkpoints of a process have increasing timestamps. The second approach relies instead on preventing the formation of specific checkpoint and communication patterns that may lead to the creation of a Z-cycle. Protocols that follow this approach do not adopt a specific function for associating timestamps with checkpoints. However, for these protocols there always exists an equivalent time-stamping function that would cause the same forced checkpoints [8].

2.4 Briatico, Ciuffoletti and Simoncini (BCS)

In BCS, each process p_i maintains a logical clock lc_i that functions as p_i's checkpoint timestamp. The timestamp is an integer variable with initial value 0 and is incremented according to the following function:

1. lc_i increases by 1 whenever p_i takes a local checkpoint.
2. p_i piggybacks on every message m it sends a copy of the current value of lc_i. We denote the piggybacked value as $m.lc$.
3. Whenever p_i receives a message m, it compares lc_i with $m.lc$. If $m.lc > lc_i$, then p_i sets lc_i to the value of $m.lc$ and takes a forced checkpoint before processing the message.

The set of checkpoints having the same timestamps in different processes is guaranteed to be a consistent state. Therefore, this protocol guarantees that there is always a recovery line corresponding to the lowest timestamp in the system, and the domino effect is prevented.

2.5 Hélary, Mostefaoui, Netzer and Raynal (HMNR)

The HMNR protocol uses the observation that if checkpoints' timestamps always increase along a Z-path (as opposed as simply non-decreasing, as required by rule (*i*) above), then no Z-cycle can ever form. It is thus possible to design functions that take advantage of this observation. Hélary et al start with the following simple scheme which would require each process to maintain a logical clock, as in BCS, and to apply the following rules:

1. lc_i increases by 1 whenever p_i takes a local or forced checkpoint.
2. Whenever p_i sends a message m, it piggybacks on m a copy of lc_i, and we denote this value by $m.lc$ as before.
3. Whenever p_i receives a message m, it compares lc_i with $m.lc$. If $m.lc > lc_i$, then p_i sets lc_i to the value of $m.lc$.

Then, they refine the protocol using more sophisticated observations and requiring that processes append more information. Figure 2, adapted from [7], shows how this simple timestamp function can be used to decide when to take a checkpoint. Let $ts(m)$ denote the timestamp piggybacked on message m. When process p_1 receives message m_0, if $ts(m_0) \leq ts(m_1)$ then certainly $ts(C_{0,0}) \leq ts(C_{2,1})$ and there is no need for a forced checkpoint. If $ts(m_0) > ts(m_1)$, however, delivering m_1 may create the possibility of generating a Z-path along which the timestamps do not increase. A straightforward way to avoid this risk is to force p_1 to take a checkpoint before delivering m_0, thereby breaking the Z-path. It may be possible, however, for p_1 to avoid taking a forced checkpoint by using a more sophisticated timestamp function. For instance, a function that piggybacks on application messages information about the logical clocks of all processes may give process p_1 more information to decide if a forced checkpoint is really necessary. In Figure 2 (b), if p_1 knows that the value of p_2's local clock is at least x when it is about to deliver m_0, then even if $ts(m_0) > ts(m_1)$, p_1 does not need to take a forced checkpoint if $ts(C_{0,0}) \leq ts(m_1) \leq x < ts(C_{2,1})$. HNMR uses this observation and more sophisticated ones to reduce the number of forced checkpoints while still ensuring that the timestamps always increase along a Z-path. In [7], Hélary et al present several CIC algorithms. For our experiments, we have used the most sophisticated one, which reduces as much as possible the number of forced checkpoints.

2.6 Baldoni, Quaglia and Ciciani (BQC)

The BQC protocol does not prevent forced checkpoints by using an explicit function to timestamp checkpoints [1]. Rather, this protocol enforces $\mathcal{NZC}$ by preventing the formation of patterns of checkpoints and communication that may result in the creation of

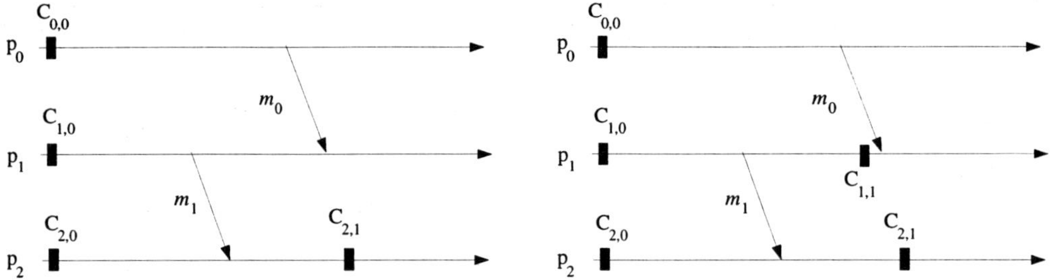

Figure 2 : To checkpoint or not to checkpoint?

a Z-cycle. In particular, BQC prevents the creation of suspected Z-cycles. Figure 3 shows the structure of a suspected Z-cycle. In this example, process p_i would take a checkpoint before delivering message m_2, in order to avoid a potential Z-cycle that includes m_0 and m_1 and involves checkpoint $C_{0,1}$. Note that a suspected Z-cycle is not necessarily a Z-cycle. For instance, there is no Z-cycle in Figure 3 unless there is an actual Z-path starting with m_0 and ending with m_1 between $C_{i,0}$ and $C_{0,1}$. This information may or may not be available to process p_i when it receives m_2. If the information is not available, the protocol opts for safety and takes a forced checkpoint before delivering m_2. If the information is available, however, the protocol refrains from taking a forced checkpoint. The actual protocol propagates n^2 values on each application message to help processes detect suspected Z-cycles and suppress them using forced checkpoints [1]. The reference also contains a formal characterization of the notion of suspected Z-cycle and a proof that a protocol that prevents suspected Z-cycle also satisfies $\mathcal{NZC}$ [1].

3 Implementation Issues

An implementation of CIC must deal with several pragmatic issues that are typically left out of protocol specifications. We describe how we resolved these issues in our implementation.

3.1 Autonomy in Local Checkpoints

A stated advantage of CIC protocols is that they prevent the domino effect while allowing processes considerable autonomy in deciding when to take local checkpoints. An efficient implementation of CIC must therefore adopt a checkpointing policy that exploits this autonomy and translates it into a benefit. In general, this requires a good understanding of the application and of the execution environment. For example, detailed knowledge of the application may allow processes to take checkpoints when the size of the live variables is small [10, 13].

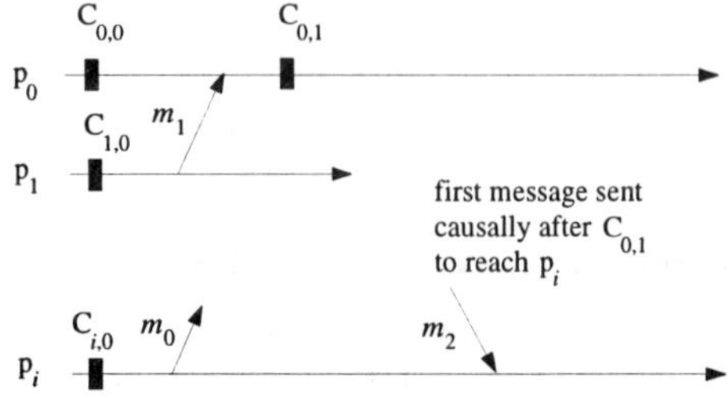

Figure 3 : A suspect Z-cycle involving checkpoint $C_{0,1}$.

In our study, we have chosen a set of compute-intensive, long-running applications that have traditionally been the main beneficiary of checkpointing protocols. We have found that either the complexity of the application program precludes investing the effort in defining a reasonable checkpoint placement policy, or that the application structure does not reveal points within the execution where taking a checkpoint is more advantageous than others. Therefore, we have resolved to use a probabilistic distribution to emulate what an autonomous application would do in deciding on where to place the local checkpoints. In addition, we have also used the traditional policy of taking checkpoints at regular intervals. The results were similar; indeed, one of the first conclusions that we reached in our implementation is that even with a deep understanding of the applications' structure, no policy for taking local checkpoints can reasonably be adopted without considering the effect of the forced checkpoints that occur because of communication events. For example, a pre-run analysis may decide on the execution points during which it is most "convenient" to schedule local checkpoints within a particular process. But if this policy ignores the forced checkpoints, then it is possible to schedule a local checkpoint immediately after a forced checkpoint. In this case, taking the local checkpoint will result in additional work and overhead, with no substantial reduction of the amount of work at risk. A more reasonable decision may then be to postpone taking the local checkpoint. In any case, the autonomy of deciding when to take checkpoints seems to be limited by the occurrence of forced checkpoints due to interactions with other processes.

3.2 Non-blocking Checkpointing in CIC

The benefits of non-blocking checkpointing in reducing the performance overhead of checkpointing protocols have been clearly established [6, 14]. Non-blocking checkpointing allows the application to resume computation as soon as possible and to schedule the actual writing of the checkpoint concurrently with the application execution. The result is that saving the checkpoint to stable storage does not become a bottleneck that impedes application progress. However, using non-blocking checkpointing in CIC introduces potential inconsistencies with the specification of the protocols. To understand why, consider the situation where a process p_i takes a non-blocking checkpoint (local or forced) and then sends a message m to another process p_j; assume furthermore that the CIC protocol being used requires p_j to take a forced checkpoint before delivering m. Recall that all CIC protocols maintain the invariant that no Z-cycles may form and no useless checkpoint is ever taken: hence, the forced checkpoint of p_j should never be useless and no Z-cycles can include it. However, suppose that p_i fails after sending m, but before p_i's checkpoint has been entirely written to stable storage. The failure of p_i makes the checkpoint taken by p_j useless, thereby violating the protocol invariant. The problem is not just cosmetic, because several such communication events may occur while several non-blocking checkpoints are being written to stable storage according to an implementation of non-blocking checkpointing. Therefore, it may be possible for many checkpoints on stable storage to be rendered useless because a failure of some process in the system occurred before one or more of its checkpoints were saved on stable storage. Indeed, in situations like this, Z-cycles do form and useless checkpoints are taken. There are two solutions to this problem. The first one blocks any outgoing messages from a process until all its non-blocking checkpoints have been written to stable storage. The messages are buffered and released only when a process receives notification from the checkpointing agent that the checkpoint has been saved. There is a penalty to pay for this modification, but it is preferable to disallowing non-blocking checkpointing altogether. It is interesting to note here that this solution shows how a pragmatic consideration may require a modification in the protocol itself to maintain its invariant. The second solution that we considered is to simply allow these temporary Z-cycles to form, and hope that the checkpoints will be written before a failure actually occurs. In a sense, this is an optimistic implementation of CIC, which may allow Z-cycles to form temporarily while some checkpoints are being written to stable storage. If the optimistic assumption holds, then the invariant of the protocol is preserved and no useless checkpoints are ever taken. However, if the assumption is violated because of a failure, then some of the checkpoints that would have otherwise be part of the recovery line will have to be discarded. The benefit of this optimistic alternative is that the overhead is small and does not require any modification to the protocol as specified. After an interesting debate among the authors, it was resolved to use the second solution for its simplicity and because failures are supposedly rare. It is important however for future implementers to understand the subtle issues involved with the pragmatic choices described here and how they may affect the protocol implementation.

4 Experiments and Analysis

The testbed for this study consists of four 300-MHz Pentium-II based workstations connected by a 100MB/s Ethernet. Each workstation has two processors, 512MB of RAM, and a 4GB disk used to implement stable storage. The machines ran Solaris 2.6, and used Suns f77 and C compilers. The testbed is part of the Egida tool [16], which includes support for incremental checkpointing and implements non-blocking checkpointing by forking off a child process that writes the checkpoint to stable storage. The applications under study consist of four MPI [17] programs from the NPB 2.3 benchmark suite [3]. These programs represent common computational loads in fluid dynamics applications and typify the kind of applications that have traditionally benefited from checkpointing; their characteristics are given in Table 1.The performance metrics we report are the number of forced checkpoints that a protocol causes and the performance overhead. We use a combination of experiments on the prototype implementation, and then we use the prototype itself to validate a simulator that we built to study CIC protocol further, under different communication patterns and environments.

4.1 The Measured Performance of CIC Protocols

The first set of experiments consists of running each of the four applications under the three protocols and for two local checkpoint placement policies. The first policy triggers local checkpoints according to an exponential distribution with a mean checkpoint interval (μ) set to 360 seconds, while the second policy uses the same probabilistic distribution but with the mean checkpoint interval set to 480 seconds. Table 2 shows the results of the experiments. It reports the execution time of the entire application, in addition to the per-process average number of local and forced checkpoints. For convenience, the average per-process total number of checkpoints is also reported. The table also reports the per-process average checkpoint size (either local or forced).

Analysis The results reveal a few issues. In BCS and HMNR, the number of forced checkpoints is essentially the same. In contrast, the BQC protocol is showing a comparatively larger number of forced checkpoints when compared to the other two.. The reason for this can be ascribed to the communication pattern of the applications under study. These applications use a common iterative structure to solve a computationally intensive problem in which processes exchange partial results and resume. This leads to a communication pattern that mimics a periodic broadcast. Under this pattern, the BQC protocol seems to be too "eager" in preventing Z-cycles compared to BCS and HMNR. Furthermore, two additional effects seem to occur:

1. Many suspected Z-cycles end up causing forced checkpoints without actually being a menace.
2. It is often the case that more than one process "volunteer" in parallel to break the same suspected Z-cycle by forcing checkpoints.

Consider Figure 4. In this example, we see process p_2 take a forced checkpoint because of message m_3, not knowing that process p_1 has already broken the suspected Z-cycle (part (2) of the figure). Similarly, process p_0 takes a forced checkpoint because of message m_2, not knowing that process p_1 has already broken the Z-cycle using checkpoint $C_{1,1}$. This behavior continues for a while under the communication pattern used by our applications. This suggests that there is a disadvantage to using CIC protocols that suspect Z-cycles or that are eager to prevent a Z-cycle from forming before it is actually clear that one is indeed forming. In contrast, protocols that use time-stamping functions adopt a lazy approach: they prevent the formation of Z-cycles only at the last possible moment, and therefore work better. Additionally, the results show that the alleged benefit of process autonomy in placing local checkpoints does not materialize in practice. Under the best circumstances, a process takes twice as many forced checkpoints as local ones. The curious notion of process autonomy in distributed systems where all processes become inter-dependent seems to be on shaky ground. The results also point out to another serious problem with CIC protocols in general, namely the unpredictability of the checkpointing rate. In all experiments, the protocols ended up taking more checkpoints than could be anticipated based on the local distribution of checkpoint placement. For BCS and HMNR, the number of forced checkpoints was generally twice the number of local ones. For BQC, the ratio was worse. The ratio in itself is a function of the application, the number of processes, and the checkpoint placement. The fact that it is unpredictable makes the protocols cumbersome to use in practice, because it is difficult to plan ahead of time the actual stable storage requirements and the mean checkpointing interval. Contrast this with consistent checkpointing protocols where the number of checkpoints and required stable storage can be estimated with great certainty beforehand [6]. The table also points to another negative aspect of using CIC protocols. The performance overhead when considering the running time was relatively bad, reaching between 5 % to

Application	NPB Specific Info.	Messages/sec.	Message Size (Avg.) (KB)	Exec. Time (sec.)
bt	Class A	6	50.5	1530
cg	Class B	14	60.7	1516
lu	Class A	54	3.7	975
sp	Class A	17	43.4	1222

Table 1: Characteristics of the benchmarks used in the experiments.

Application	Protocols	μ	Number of Checkpoints Local	Forced	Total	Ckpt Size (MB)	Exec.Time (sec.)
bt	BCS	360	6	13	19	69.5	1777
		480	4	9	13	70.9	1715
	HMNR	360	5	11	16	70.5	1709
		480	4	9	13	71.0	1683
	BQC	360	6	54	60	41.5	1875
		480	4	39	43	41.0	1819
cg	BCS	360	5	11	16	17.6	1683
		480	4	9	13	18.9	1655
	HMNR	360	5	11	16	17.7	1655
		480	3	10	13	19.1	1643
	BQC	360	5	24	29	8.5	1689
		480	3	16	19	13.5	1665
lu	BCS	360	4	9	13	10.7	1051
		480	2	4	6	11.0	1033
	HMNR	360	4	9	13	10.8	1035
		480	2	4	6	11.0	1015
	BQC	360	4	33	37	6.6	1050
		480	2	14	16	6.0	1036
sp	BCS	360	5	11	16	20.8	1339
		480	3	7	10	21.2	1290
	HMNR	360	5	11	16	20.7	1320
		480	3	7	10	21.1	1300
	BQC	360	5	37	42	11.8	1362
		480	3	31	34	12.2	1329

Table 2: Performance of three CIC protocols for two checkpoint intervals and four applications.

20 % of the execution time. This behavior is actually common in systems where checkpoints are not coordinated and processes communicate frequently [6]. In these situations, when a process takes a local checkpoint independent of the others it inevitably slows down because of the state saving and memory copying that occur during the checkpoint. This in turn delays the production of the expected partial result that the process will send to others in the next communication round. Consequently, the slowdown affects other processes even if they are not taking checkpoints in the meantime. The resulting slowdowns stagger quickly and have a cumulative effect because many of these independent checkpoints occur at different times [6]. Finally, we would like to note that incremental checkpointing seems to mitigate some of the effects of having to take so many checkpoints (forced or local). The results show that the average per-process checkpoint size goes down as the frequency of checkpointing increases, just as one would expect. In summary, lazy protocols that use time-stamping to break Z-cycles perform better than eager protocols that take forced checkpoints as soon as they suspect a Z-cycle. The unpredictability of the actual number of checkpoints to be taken (forced and local) makes these protocols cumbersome to use in practice because no reasonable planning of resources and checkpointing frequency can be made without understanding the application and its communication patterns. Also, it seems that any hope of a benefit for allowing processes to take independent checkpoints is thwarted by the fact that a process ends up taking at least twice as many forced checkpoints than local ones. And finally, CIC protocols share some of the negative performance properties of independent checkpointing when used in computations where the processes are tightly coupled and communicate frequently.

4.2 Scalability and Effects of Communication Patterns

To assess the effect of increasing the number of processes on the protocol performance, we constructed a simulator to measure the number of forced checkpoints for each of the three protocols. We first validated the simulator using the measured number of forced checkpoints for 4 processes, and we then used it to estimate the number of forced checkpoints for different numbers of processors and different communication patterns. Figure 5 shows the results for the three protocols as the number of processes in the computation varies. Two different sets of measurements are reported. The first set is for a random distribution of messages with a relatively low load, where each process sends an average of 10 messages between each two consecutive local checkpoints. That is, in this simulation processes do not communicate much and communicate

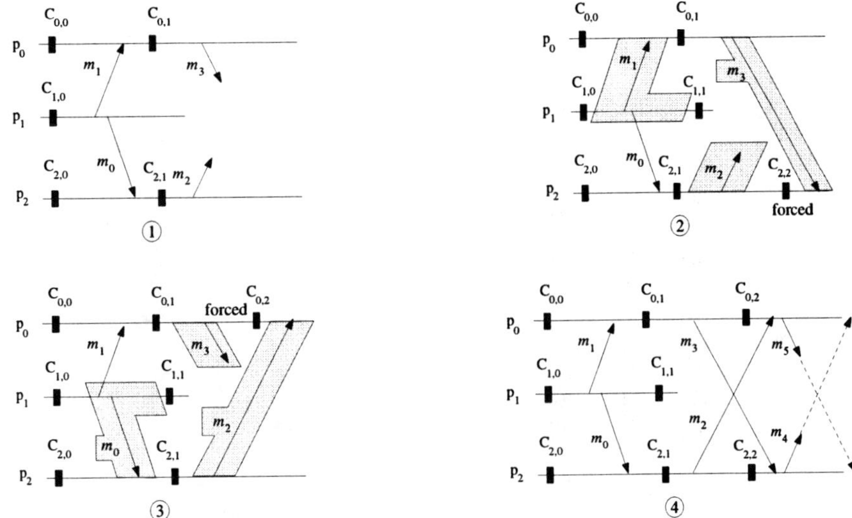

Figure 4 : Anomalies in detecting suspect Z-cycles.

with different processes equally at random and at random intervals. During this simulation, 119 local checkpoints were taken on average. The second set of measurements shows the same results but with a different communication pattern in which each process talks to two designated neighbors at uniform intervals. A process sends about 500 messages between each two consecutive local checkpoints. This communication pattern is representative of those that occur in distributed over-relaxation algorithms.

Analysis The results show that, in general, the communication pattern strongly affects the behavior of CIC protocols. This is expected. But the results also show that CIC protocols do not scale well. In both cases, there is an almost linear increase in the number of forced checkpoints per process as the number of processes increase. For this set of applications, at least, the conventional wisdom that these protocols scale better because they do not resort to global coordination is not true. The results also show that CIC protocols seem to favor random patterns of communications with low loads.

4.3 An Adaptive Local Checkpointing Policy

The results of the experiments so far suggest that a flurry of forced checkpoints occur throughout the system as a result of one process taking a local checkpoint. It is plausible that if forced checkpoints are not taken into account, a local checkpointing policy may take a local checkpoint shortly after a forced checkpoint has been taken. Such a local checkpoint advances the recovery point of the process by a very short amount compared to the previous forced checkpoint. Furthermore, this local checkpoint is likely to trigger more forced checkpoints in other processes, escalating the phenomenon even further. It may be argued that the resulting overhead can be limited by using incremental checkpointing, and that therefore the local checkpoint does not have to save a lot of state on stable storage if a forced checkpoint has been taken recently. But we contend that taking a checkpoint, however small, always has an overhead associated with it, if only to compute the state that must be saved and to arrange for the copy-on-write to implement non-blocking checkpointing. However it may be, this overhead cannot be ignored. Therefore, there is very little to gain by taking this local checkpoint, while there is a potential for larger overhead. To fix this problem, we experimented with an adaptive local checkpointing policy that refrains from taking a scheduled local checkpoint if a forced checkpoint has occurred during the last T seconds, where T is a parameter. Figure 6 shows the resulting number of local and forced checkpoints for the four applications and the three protocols under study. We report three measurements, one with the adaptive policy disabled (T = 0) and two for different values of T (60 and 90 seconds). For each T, the table shows the number of local and forced checkpoints under each of the three protocols. The measurements for different applications are reported separately.

Analysis The results show that taking forced checkpointing into account reduces the number of local checkpoints, which in turn reduces the number of forced checkpoints. The results are more pronounced for the BQC protocol. These results show two things:

1. A successful local checkpoint placement policy must contain a dynamic element that accounts for the occurrence of forced checkpoints. The simple policy "let us checkpoint every x seconds" does not work well.
2. A successful local checkpoint placement policy must adapt to the application communication patterns as they change during execution. This would reduce the frequency of checkpoints when the communication load is heavy and the frequency of forced checkpoints is high, and vice versa.

Our recommendations once more outline the unpredictability that faces a user of CIC protocols in practice, though they outline plausible solutions. It is perhaps possible to come up with better placement policies than the one we outlined here, but this is out of the paper's scope.

5 Conclusions

We have conducted several experiments to analyze the behavior and characteristics of communication-induced checkpointing for a class of compute intensive distributed applications. Our results show that:

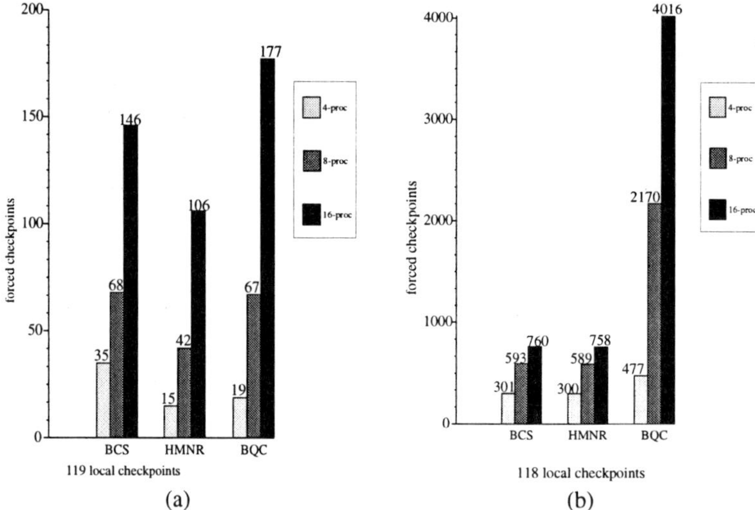

Figure 5 : The effect of adaptive local checkpointing: Number of local and forced checkpoints for the three protocols under values of T for the four applications under study.

1. CIC protocols that use an eager approach to preventing Z-cycles by taking forced checkpoints whenever they suspect the formation of a Z-cycle are bound to perform worse than lazy protocols that use a time-stamping function to prevent a Z-cycle at the last possible second.

2. CIC protocols do not scale well with a larger number of processes. We have found that the number of forced checkpoints increases almost linearly with the number of processes.

3. A process takes at least twice as many forced checkpoints as local ones. Therefore, the touted benefit of autonomy of CIC protocols in allowing the processes to take independent checkpoints does not seem to materialize in practice.

4. There is a considerable unpredictability in the way CIC protocols behave in practice. The amount of stable storage required, performance overhead, and number of forced checkpoints depend greatly on the number of processes, the application, and the communication pattern. This unpredictability makes the use of CIC protocols in practice more cumbersome than other alternatives.

5. A successful placement policy of local checkpoints must be dynamic, must account for forced checkpoints, and must adapt to changes in the application behavior.

6. CIC protocols seem to perform best when the communication load is low and the pattern is random. Regular, heavy load communication patterns seem to fare worse.

We would like to stress that the results are only valid for the application set that we have studied—we lay no claim that these results generalize to all applications. Nevertheless, we believe that there is sufficient evidence to suspect that much of the conventional wisdom about these protocols is questionable and that more experimental work to investigate these protocols further.

References

[1] R. Baldoni, F. Quaglia, and B. Ciciani. A VP-Accordant Checkpointing Protocol Preventing Useless Checkpoints. In *Proceedings of the IEEE Symposium on Reliable Distributed Systems*, pages 61–67, 1998.

[2] D. Briatico, A. Ciuffoletti, and L. Simoncini. A Distributed Domino-Effect Free Recovery Algorithm. In *Proceedings of the IEEE International Symposium on Reliability Distributed Software and Database*, pages 207–215, December 1984.

[3] NASA Ames Research Center. NAS Parallel Benchmarks. http://science.nas.nasa.gov/Software/NPB/, 1997.

[4] K. M. Chandy and L. Lamport. Distributed snapshots: determining global states of distributed systems. *ACM Transactions on Computer Systems*, 3(1):63–75, February 1985.

[5] E. N. Elnozahy, D. B. Johnson, and Y. M. Wang. A Survey of Rollback-Recovery Protocols in Message-Passing Systems. Technical Report CMU-CS-96-181, Carnegie Mellon University, 1996.

[6] E. N. Elnozahy, D. B. Johnson, and W. Zwaenepoel. The Performance of Consistent Checkpointing. In *Proceedings of the Eleventh Symposium on Reliable Distributed Systems*, pages 39–47, October 1992.

[7] J. M. Hélary, A. Mostefaoui, R. H. B. Netzer, and M. Raynal. Preventing Useless Checkpoints in Distributed Computations. In *Proceedings of IEEE International Symposium on Reliable Distributed Systems*, pages 183–190, 1997.

[8] J. M. Hélary, A. Mostefaoui, and M. Raynal. Virtual precedence in asynchronous systems: concepts and applications. In *Proceedings of the 11th Workshop on Distributed Algorithms*. LNCS press, 1997.

[9] L. Lamport. Time, Clocks, and the Ordering of Events in a Distributed System. *Communications of the ACM*, 21(7):558–565, July 1978.

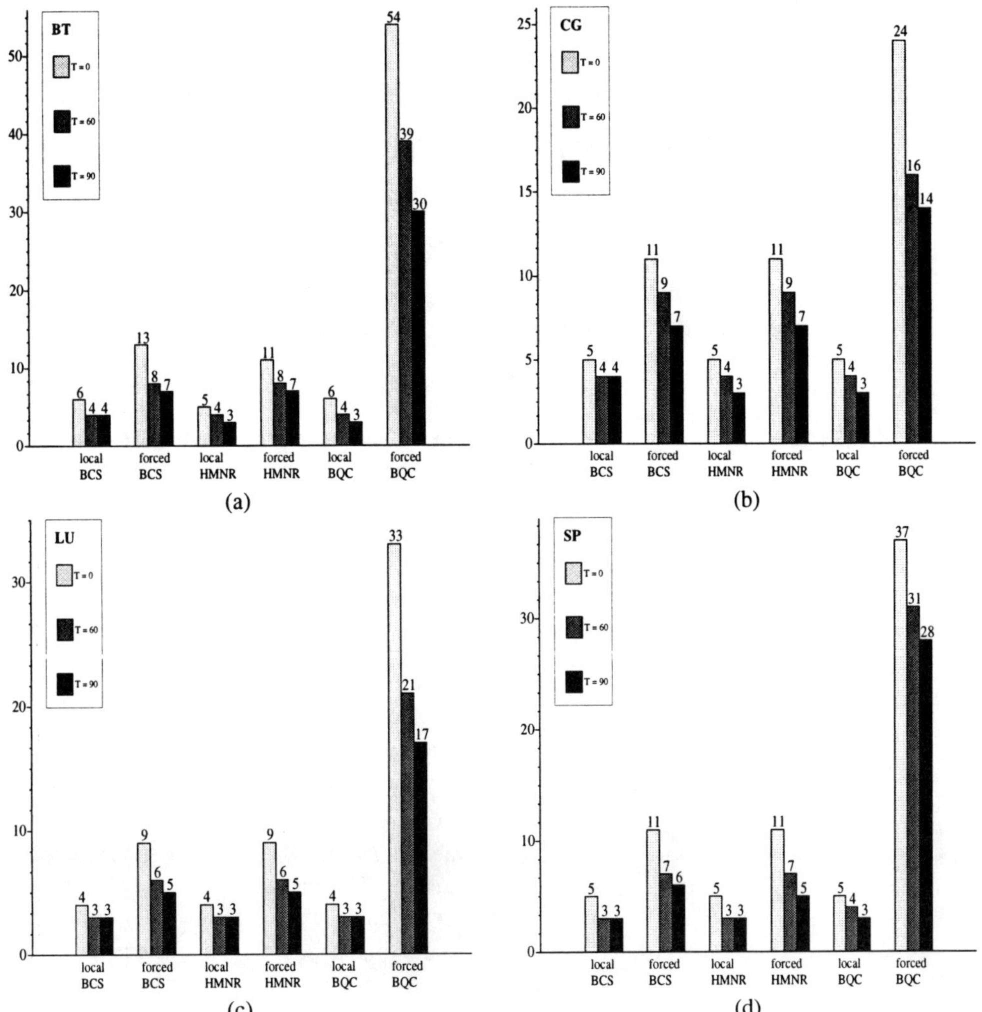

Figure 6 : The effect of adaptive local checkpointing: Number of local and forced checkpoints for the three protocols under values of T for the four applications under study.

[10] C. C. Li and W. K. Fuchs. CATCH: Compiler-assisted techniques for checkpointing. In *Proceedings of the 20th International Symposium on Fault-Tolerant Computing*, pages 74–81, 1990.

[11] R. Netzer and J. Xu. Necessary and Sufficient Conditions for Consistent Global Snapshots. Technical Report 93-32, Department of Computer Sciences, Brown University, July 1993.

[12] N. Neves and W. K. Fuchs. RENEW: A Tool for Fast and Efficient Implementation of Checkpoint Protocols. In *Proceedings of the 28th IEEE Fault-Tolerant Computing Symposium (FTCS)*, Munich, Germany, June 1998.

[13] J. S. Plank, M. Beck, and G. Kingsley. Compiler-assisted memory exclusion for fast checkpointing. *IEEE Technical Committee on Operating Systems Newsletter, Special Issue on Fault Tolerance*, pages 62—67, December 1995.

[14] J. S. Plank, M. Beck, G. Kingsley, and K. Li. Libckpt:Transparent checkpointing under Unix. In *Proceedings of the USENIX Technical Conference*, pages 213–224, January 1995.

[15] J. S. Plank and K. Li. Faster checkpointing with $N+1$ parity. In *Proceedings of the Twenty Fourth International Symposium on Fault-tolerant Computing (FTCS-24)*, pages 288—297, June 1994.

[16] S. Rao, L. Alvisi, and H. M. Vin. Egida: An Extensible Toolkit for Low-overhead Fault-tolerance. In *Proceedings of the IEEE Fault-Tolerant Computing Symposium (FTCS-29)*, Madison, WI, June 1999.

[17] M. Snir, S. Otto, S. Huss-Lederman, D. Walker, and J. Dongarra. *MPI: The Complete Reference*. Scientific and Engineering Computation Series. The MIT Press, Cambridge, MA, 1996.

[18] Y. M. Wang and W. K. Fuchs. Optimisitic message logging for independent checkpointing in message-passing systems. In *Proceedings of the 11th Symposium on Reliable Distributed Systems*, pages 147–154, October 1992.

The Average Availability of Parallel Checkpointing Systems and Its Importance in Selecting Runtime Parameters

James S. Plank Michael G. Thomason
Department of Computer Science, University of Tennessee
[plank,thomason]@cs.utk.edu

Abstract

Performance prediction of checkpointing systems in the presence of failures is a well-studied research area. While the literature abounds with performance models of checkpointing systems, none address the issue of selecting runtime parameters other than the optimal checkpointing interval. In particular, the issue of processor allocation is typically ignored. In this paper, we briefly present a performance model for long-running parallel computations that execute with checkpointing enabled. We then discuss how it is relevant to today's parallel computing environments and software, and present case studies of using the model to select runtime parameters.

1 Introduction

Performance prediction of checkpointing systems is a well-studied area. Most work in this area revolves around selecting an *optimal checkpoint interval*. This is the frequency of checkpointing that minimizes the expected execution of an application in the presence of failures. For uniprocessor systems, selection of such an interval is for the most part a solved problem [19, 26]. There has been important research in parallel systems [12, 25, 28], but the results are less unified.

To date, most checkpointing systems for long-running distributed memory computations (e.g. [4, 5, 13, 22, 24]) are based on *coordinated checkpointing* [8]. At each checkpoint, the global state of all the processors is defined and stored to a highly available stable storage. If any processor fails, then a replacement processor is selected to take the place of the failed processor, and then all processors restore the saved state of the computation from the checkpoint.

When a user must execute a long-running application on a distributed memory computing system, he or she is typically faced with an important decision: How many processors should the application use? Most programs for such environments require the user to choose such a value before the computation begins, and once underway, the value may not change. On a system with no checkpointing, the application typically employs as many as are available for the most parallelism and the shortest running time. However, when a system is enabled with checkpointing, then the answer is less clear. If all processors are used for the application and one fails, then the application may not continue until that processor is repaired and the whole system may recover. If fewer processors are used for the application, then the application may take longer to complete in the absence of failures, but if a processor fails, then there may be a *spare* processor standing by to be an immediate replacement. The application will spend less time down due to failures. Consequently, selecting the number of processors on which to run the application is an important decision.

In this paper, we model the performance of coordinated checkpointing systems where the number of processors dedicated to the application (termed a for "active") and the checkpoint interval (termed I) are selected by the user before running the program. We use the model to determine the *average availability* of the program in the presence of failures, and we show how average availability can be used to select values of a and I that minimize the expected running time of the program. We then give examples of parameter selection using parallel benchmarks and failure data from a variety of parallel workstation environments.

The significance of this work is that it addresses an important runtime parameter selection problem that has not been addressed heretofore.

2 The System Model

We are running a parallel application on a distributed memory system with N total processors. Processors are interchangeable. The application uses exactly $a \leq N$ processors, a being chosen by the user. Processors may fail and be repaired. We term a processor as *functional* when it can be used to execute the application. Otherwise it is *failed and*

0-7695-0213-X/99 $10.00 © 1999 IEEE

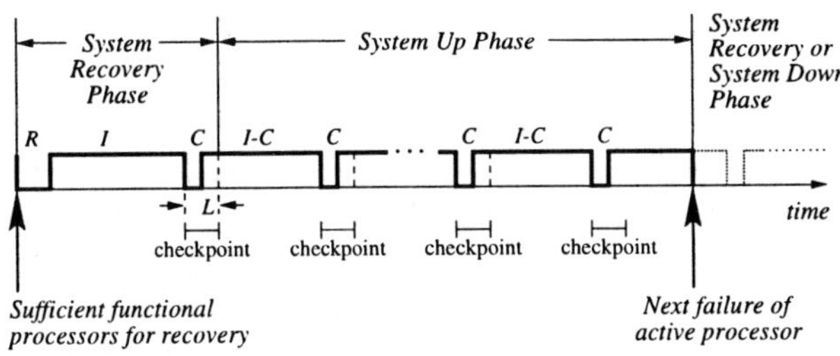

Figure 1. The sequence of time between the recovery of an application from a failure, and the failure of an active processor.

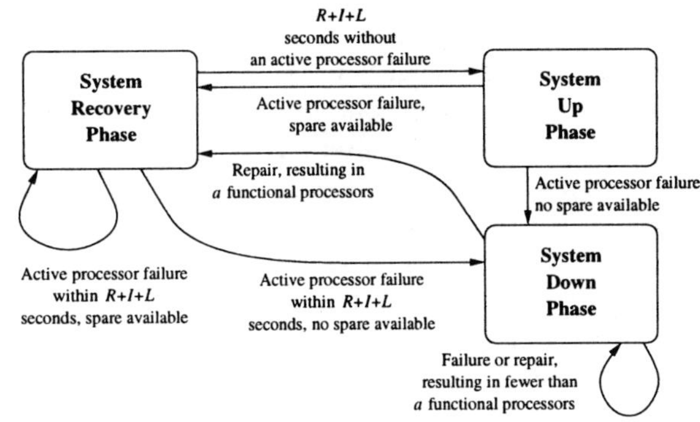

Figure 2. Phase transition diagram.

under repair. We assume that interoccurrence times of failures for each processor are independent and identically distributed (*iid*) as exponential random variables with the same failure rate $\lambda > 0$. Likewise, repairs are *iid* as exponential random variables with repair rate θ. Occurrences of failures or repairs at exactly the same instant have probability 0 for the exponential probability laws.

When the user initiates the application, it may start running as soon as there are a functional processors. If, after I seconds, none of the a processors has failed, a checkpoint is initiated. This checkpoint takes L seconds to complete, and once completed it may be used for recovery. L is termed the "checkpoint latency." The checkpoint adds C seconds of overhead to the running time of the program. C is termed the "checkpoint overhead." Many checkpointing systems use optimizations such as "copy-on-write" so that $C \ll L$, which improves performance significantly [26]. While there are no failures among the a processors, checkpoints are initiated every I seconds. I must be greater than or equal to L so that the system is never attempting to store multiple checkpoints simultaneously.

When an active processor fails, the application is halted and a replacement is sought. If there are no replacements, then the application must stand idle until there are again a functional processors. When there are a functional processors, the application is restarted from the most recently completed checkpoint. This takes R seconds (termed the "recovery time"), and when recovery is finished, execution begins at the same point as when the checkpoint was initiated. I seconds after recovery is complete, checkpointing begins anew. This process continues until the program completes. To illustrate the system model, see Figure 1, which depicts a segment of time between the recovery of an application and the failure of an active processor.

While the application is running, the S=N-a processors not being employed by the application are termed "spares." Their failure and subsequent repair does not affect the running of the application while the active processors are functional. It is only when an active fails that the status of the spares is important (i.e. that the number of non-failed active and spare processors numbers at least a, so that recovery may begin immediately).

To help in the explanation of the performance model, we partition the execution of a checkpointing system into three phases. They are depicted in Figure 1.

System Recovery Phase: This phase is initiated by recovery from a checkpoint. It ends either upon the successful completion of the first checkpoint following recovery (i.e. if no active processor fails in $R + I + L$ seconds), or when an active processor fails within $R + I + L$ seconds of the phase's inception.

System Up Phase: This phase is initiated by the completion of the first checkpoint after recovery. It ends when an active processor fails.

System Down Phase: This phase occurs whenever there are fewer than a functional processors. The application cannot execute during this phase. It ends as soon as a processors are functional again.

The phase transition diagram for this system is depicted in Figure 2. In this diagram, the only failures that cause transitions are failures to active processors. The failure and subsequent repair of spare processors is only important when an active processor fails. The status of the spares then determines whether the next phase is a System Recovery or System Down phase.

3 Calculating Availability

In the following sections, we introduce a discrete-parameter, finite-state Markov chain [10, 16] $\mathcal{M}$ to study the *availability* of the distributed memory checkpointing system described above. *Availability* is defined to be the fraction of time that the system spends performing *useful work*, where useful work is time spent performing computation on the application that will never be redone due to a failure. In other words, this is the time spent executing the application before a checkpoint completes. If time is spent executing the application, but an active processor fails before the next checkpoint completes, then that part of the application must be re-executed, and is therefore not useful. Likewise, recovery time, checkpoint overhead, and time spent in the System Down Phase also do not contribute to useful work.

Suppose that the running time of an application with checkpointing is $U + D$ seconds. This is the sum of time spent performing useful work (U) and time spent not performing useful work (D). The availability of the system during that time is: $A = U/(U + D)$.

Given the parameters N, a, C, L, R, I, λ and θ, we use $\mathcal{M}$ to determine the average availability A of the parallel system. A is an asymptotic value for the availability of a program whose running time approaches infinity. A can be used to approximate the availability of executing a program with a long running time, or of many executions of a program with a shorter running time.

The determination of availability is useful in the following way. The user of a parallel checkpointing system is confronted with an important question: What values of a and I minimize the expected running time of the application? Using large values of a can lower the running time of the program due to more parallelism. However, it also exposes the program to a greater risk of not being able to run due to too few functional processors. Similarly, increasing I improves the performance of the program when there are no failures, since checkpointing overhead is minimized. However, it also exposes the program to a greater recomputing penalty following a failure. Thus, we look for an optimal combination of a and I to minimize the expected running time of a program in the presence of failures and repairs.

Suppose the user can estimate the failure-free running time RT_a of his or her program when employing a active processors and no checkpointing. Moreover, suppose the user can estimate C_a, L_a and R_a. Additionally, suppose that λ and θ are known. Then the user can select any value of a and I, and compute the average availability $A_{a,I}$ of the system. The value $RT_a/A_{a,I}$ is then an estimate of the program's expected running time in the presence of failures. Thus, the user's question may be answered by choosing values of a and I that minimize $RT_a/A_{a,I}$.

In Section 6, we show nine examples of this kind of parameter selection.

4 Realism of the Model

This calculation is only useful if the underlying model has basis in reality. The model of the checkpointing system with parameters C, L, R and I mirrors most coordinated checkpointing systems that store their checkpoints to a centralized storage. Examples of these are the public-domain checkpointers MIST [4], CoCheck [22, 24], and Fail-Safe PVM [13], as well as several unnamed checkpointers that have been employed for research projects [9, 17].

A priori selection of I and a is a requirement all all the above systems. Moreover, parallel programs such as the NAS Parallel benchmarks [1], and all programs based on the MPI standard [15] have been written so that the user selects a fixed number of processors a on which to execute.

The modeling of failures and repairs as *iid* exponential random variables has less grounding in reality. Although such random variables have been used in many research papers on the performance of uniprocessor and multiprocessor checkpointing systems (see [19, 26] for citations), the studies that observe processor failures have shown that the time-to-failure and time-to-repair intervals are extremely unlikely to belong to an exponential distribution [19].

Nonetheless, there are three reasons why performance evaluations based on exponential random variables have utility. First, when failures and repairs are rare, independent events, their counts may be approximated by Poisson processes [2]. Poisson counts are equivalent to exponential interoccurrence times [10], meaning that if failures and repairs are rare (with respect to I, C, R, L, etc), their TTF distributions may be approximated by an exponential. Second, if the true failure distribution has an increasing failure rate (like the workstation failure data in [14]) rather than the constant failure rate of the exponential distribution, then the results of this paper provide a conservative (i.e. lower bound) approximation of the availability. Third, simulation results on real failure data [19] have shown in the uniprocessor case that the determination of the optimal value of I using an exponential failure rate gives a good first-order approximation of the optimal value of I determined by the simulation.

Thus, in the absence of any other information besides a mean time to failure and a mean time to recovery for processors, the availability calculation in this paper can be a reasonable indicator for selecting optimal values of a and I.

5 The Markov Chain $\mathcal{M}$

In this following sections, we define a discrete-parameter, finite-state Markov chain [10, 16] $\mathcal{M}$ to study the availability of parallel checkpointing systems. A more detailed description of $\mathcal{M}$ (with examples) is in [21].

Given values of N and a (and $S = N - a$), $\mathcal{M}$ consists of $N + S + 2$ states, partitioned into three groups based on the three phases defined above. States are entered and exited when any of the events depicted in Figure 2 occur.

System Recovery States: There are $S + 1$ System Recovery States, labeled $[R : s]$ for $0 \leq s \leq S$. Each state $[R : s]$ is entered following a failure which leaves a functional processors to perform the application and s spares.

State $[R : 0]$ may also be entered from the System Down State $[D : a-1]$ when a processors become functional. Once a System Recovery State is entered, it is not exited until either $R+I+L$ seconds have passed with no active processor failure, or an active processor fails before $R+I+L$ seconds have passed. The number of functional spares during this time is immaterial. It is only at the instant that the state is exited that the number of functional spares is important. Note that if $N > a$, there are no transitions into state $[R : S]$, and it may be omitted. If N equals a, then there is one System Recovery State: $[R : 0]$.

System Up States: There are $S+1$ System Up States, labeled $[U : s]$ for $0 \leq s \leq S$. Each state $[U : s]$ is entered from a System Recovery State when $R+I+L$ seconds have passed with no active processor failures. The value of s depends on the number of functional spare processors at the time the state is entered. System Up States are exited when an active processor fails. At that time, the total number of functional processors p determines the next state. If $p \geq a$, then System Recovery State $[R : p-a]$ is entered. If $p = a-1$ (no functional spares at the time of failure), then System Down State $[D : a-1]$ is entered.

System Down States: There are a System Down States, labeled $[D : p]$ for $0 \leq p < a$. State $[D : p]$ is entered whenever a failure or repair leaves the system with exactly p functional processors. No computation may be performed in a System Down State, since there are not enough processors. System Down States are exited whenever there is a processor failure or repair. If the resulting total number of functional processors p' is less than a, then the transition is to $[D : p']$. Otherwise, $p' = a$, and the transition is to $[R : 0]$.

5.1 Birth-Death Markov Chain $\mathcal{S}^{s,\tau}$

In order to define the transition probabilities out of the System Recovery and System Up states, we need to have some notion of the number of functional spares at the time of the transition. For this determination, we employ a second Markov chain $\mathcal{S}^{s,\tau}$.

The solution of Markov chain $\mathcal{S}^{s,\tau}$ yields a $(s+1) \times (s+1)$ matrix $Q^{s,\tau}$ of probabilities. Suppose that there are s processors, and at a certain time, exactly i of them are functional. Entry $q_{i,j}^{s,\tau}$ of $Q^{s,\tau}$ is the probability that exactly j of those s processors are functional τ seconds later. Obviously $\sum_{j=0}^{s} q_{i,j}^{s,\tau} = 1$ for each i. We use $Q^{s,\tau}$ to define the transition probabilities from the System Recovery and System Up states.

For brevity, we do not give an exact description of $\mathcal{S}^{s,\tau}$. Such a description, complete with examples, may be found in [21]. In general Markov chain theory, $\mathcal{S}^{s,\tau}$ is a *continuous-parameter, finite-state, birth-death Markov chain* [7, 16], and $Q^{s,\tau}$ is easy to calculate with standard matrix operations.

We use three values of τ in the calculations below:

τ_1: the mean time to the first failure (*MTTF*) among a active processors with *iid* exponential failures: $\tau_1 = \frac{1}{a\lambda}$.

τ_2: the length of time during which there must be no failure in order to leave the System Recovery Phase successfully: $\tau_2 = R+I+L$.

τ_3: the conditional *MTTF*, given a failure within the first $R+I+L$ seconds in the System Recovery Phase:

$$\tau_3 = \frac{1}{a\lambda} - (\tau_2)\frac{e^{-a\lambda(\tau_2)}}{1-e^{-a\lambda(\tau_2)}} = \tau_1 - \tau_2\frac{e^{-a\lambda\tau_2}}{1-e^{-a\lambda\tau_2}}.$$

5.2 Transition Probabilities

In this section, we define the transition probabilities between states of $\mathcal{M}$. The sum of all probabilities emanating from a state must equal one.

System Recovery States: Transitions out of a System Recovery State $[R : i]$ are based on the time $\tau_2 = R+I+L$. The probability of the event "no active processor failure during interval τ_2" is $e^{-a\lambda\tau_2}$. Thus, the probability of a transition to a System Up State is $e^{-a\lambda\tau_2}$. The specific System Up State depends on the number of functional spares at the end of the interval. This probability is given by Q^{S,τ_2}. In particular, the probability of a transition from $[R : i]$ to $[U : j]$ is $(e^{-a\lambda\tau_2})(q_{i,j}^{S,\tau_2})$.

The probability of an active processor failure during the interval τ_2 is $1-e^{-a\lambda\tau_2}$. Such a failure causes a transition either to a System Recovery State or to System Down State $[D : a-1]$. Again, the exact state depends on the number of spares at the time of the failure. We calculate the transition probabilities with Q^{S,τ_3}, based on the the conditional *MTTF* given a failure in the interval τ_2. The probability of a transition to state $[R : j]$ is $(1-e^{-a\lambda\tau_2})(q_{i,j+1}^{S,\tau_3})$. The probability of a transition to state $[D : a-1]$ is $(1-e^{-a\lambda\tau_2})(q_{i,0}^{S,\tau_3})$.

System Up States: Transitions out of a System Up State $[U : i]$ are based on τ_1, the *MTTF* of the first processor in a set of a processors[1]. This failure causes a transition either to $[D : a-1]$ (when there are no spares at the time of failure), or to $[R : j]$ (when there are $j+1$ spares). The transition probabilities are defined by Q^{S,τ_1}. The probability of a transition to state $[D : a-1]$ is $(q_{i,0}^{S,\tau_1})$. The probability of a transition to state $[R : j]$ is $(q_{i,j+1}^{S,\tau_1})$.

System Down States: Transitions out of a System Down State occur whenever there is a failure or repair. In state $[D :$

[1]Note that the "memoryless" property of *iid* exponentials means that the *MTTF* is independent of how long the processors have already been functional. Therefore, even though at the beginning of state $[U : i]$, the processors have already been functional for $R+I+L$ seconds, their *MTTF* remains τ_1.

$p]$, there are $p < a$ functional processors that are subject to failure rate λ, and $N-p$ failed processors that are subject to repair rate θ. Their cumulative distribution function is $F(t) = 1 - e^{-(p\lambda+(N-p)\theta)t}$. A property of this form of the exponential *cdf* is that whenever an event does occur, the probability that it is a repair is $(N-p)\theta/(p\lambda + (N-p)\theta)$ and that it is a failure is $p\lambda/(p\lambda+(N-p)\theta)$ [7]. These two ratios are independent of the time the event occurs. Thus, the transition probability to state $[D : p+1]$ (or to state $[R : 0]$ if $p = a-1$) is $(N-p)\theta/(p\lambda+(N-p)\theta)$, and the transition probability to state $[D : p-1]$ is $p\lambda/(p\lambda+(N-p)\theta)$.

5.3 Transition Weightings

We label each transition $\mathcal{T}$ with two weightings, $U_\mathcal{T}$ and $D_\mathcal{T}$. $U_\mathcal{T}$ is the average amount of useful work performed in the state which the transition is leaving, and $D_\mathcal{T}$ is the average amount of non-useful work. Our description is based on the states which the transitions are leaving:

System Recovery States: A transition $\mathcal{T}_{R\to R}$ from state $[R : i]$ to $[R : j]$ indicates that a failure has occurred before the first checkpoint completes. Therefore, $U_{\mathcal{T}_{R\to R}} = 0$, and $D_{\mathcal{T}_{R\to R}} = \tau_3$. The transitions from $[R : i]$ to $[D : a-1]$ have the same weightings. A transition $\mathcal{T}_{R\to U}$ from state $[R : i]$ to $[U : j]$ indicates that no failure has occurred in the first $R+I+L$ seconds. Therefore $U_{\mathcal{T}_{R\to U}} = I$, and $D_{\mathcal{T}_{R\to U}} = R + L$.

System Up States: Let $\mathcal{T}_U$ be any transition from a System Up State. The values of $U_{\mathcal{T}_U}$ and $D_{\mathcal{T}_U}$ are computed with reference to the checkpoint interval I. The probability of the event "no active processor failure in an interval I" is $e^{-a\lambda I}$ and the probability of its complement is $1-e^{-a\lambda I}$. These two events are the outcomes of a Bernoulli trial [10] for which the mean number of trials until a failure is $M = \frac{e^{-a\lambda I}}{1-e^{-a\lambda I}}$. In other words, M is the mean number of intervals I completed until the first active processor failure occurs.

Therefore, $U_{\mathcal{T}_U} = M(I-C)$. The amount of non-useful work is $D_{\mathcal{T}_U} = MC + (\tau_1 - IM)$. This includes MC for the overhead of all the successful checkpoints plus the mean duration of the last, unsuccessful interval.

System Down States: Let $\mathcal{T}_{[D:p]}$ be any transition from System Down State $[D : p]$. Obviously, $U_{\mathcal{T}_{[D:p]}} = 0$. $D_{\mathcal{T}_{[D:p]}}$ is the mean time of occupancy in state $[D : p]$: $1/(p\lambda + (N-p)\theta)$.

5.4 Calculating $A_{a,I}$

The transition probabilities of $\mathcal{M}$ may be represented in a square matrix **P**. Each state of $\mathcal{M}$ is given a row of **P** such that P_{ij} is the probability of the transition from state i to state j. Similarly, the weightings may be represented in the matrices **U** and **D**. We use the long-run properties of $\mathcal{M}$ to compute A. $\mathcal{M}$ is a recurrent chain with well-defined, asymptotic properties [11, 16]. In particular, the long-run, unconditional probability of occupancy of state i in terms of number of transitions is entry π_i in the unique solution of the matrix equation $\Pi = \Pi\mathbf{P}$ where $\sum_i \pi_i = 1, \pi_i > 0$.

Once Π is obtained, the availablility $A_{a,I}$ may be calculated as the ratio of the mean useful time per transition to the mean total time per transition:

$$A_{a,I} = \frac{\sum_{i,j} U_{ij}\pi_i P_{ij}}{\sum_{i,j}(U_{ij} + D_{ij})\pi_i P_{ij}}.$$

$A_{a,I}$ may then be used to obtain optimal values of a and I as detailed in Section 3. Greater detail on this process, complete with example calculations, is available in [21]. We have encapsulated the process in the form of Matlab scripts, which are available on the web at **http://www.cs.utk.edu/~plank/plank/avail/**.

6 Case Studies

In the following sections, we detail nine case studies of parameter selection in checkpointing systems. We selected three long-running parallel applications from the NASA Ames NAS Parallel Benchmarks [1]. These are the BT (block tridiagonal solver), LU (linear equation solver), and EP (random number generator) applications.

Name	r	z
BT	(Matrix Size)^3	(Matrix Size)^2
LU	(Matrix Size)^3	(Matrix Size)^2
EP	$\frac{\text{\# random numbers}}{2^{26}}$	1 (constant)

Table 1. Basic application data

For the purposes of parameter selection, RT_a, C_a, L_a, and R_a must be functions of a. Amdahl's law has been shown to characterize the NAS Benchmarks very well according to number of processors a and a performance metric r based on the input size [23]. Thus, we calculate RT_a using a slightly enhanced statement of Amdahl's law:

$$RT_a = \frac{b_1 r}{a} + \frac{b_2}{a} + b_3 r + b_4.$$

We assume that C_a, L_a, and R_a are proportional to the total global checkpoint size CS_a, and that the global checkpoint is composed of global data partitioned among all the processors (such as the matrix in BT and LU), and replicated/private data for each processor. Thus, CS_a is a function of a and a size metric z:

$$CS_a = c_1 za + c_2 a + c_3 z + c_4.$$

The first two terms are for the replicated/private data and the second two are for the shared data. The BT, LU and EP applications have clear definitions of r, and z which are included in Table 1.

For each application, we used timing and checkpoint size data from a performance study of the NAS benchmarks on a network of Sparc Ultra workstations [3]. From these, we used Matlab's regression tools to calculate the coefficients b_i and c_i. These are listed in Table 2.

Coef.	BT	LU	EP
b_1	1.551e-02	9.400e-03	1.059e+02
b_2	-3.788e+01	-3.441e+01	1.980e+02
b_3	3.643e-04	1.560e-04	5.767e+00
b_4	-6.425e-01	-6.989e+00	-4.122e+01
c_1	1.875e-04	5.650e-04	0
c_2	1.952e+00	4.594e-01	1.700e+00
c_3	8.345e-02	1.882e-02	0
c_4	-2.790e+01	-1.838e+01	0

Table 2. The coefficients b_i and c_i.

We constructed three processing environments for our case studies. All three are based on published checkpointing and failure/repair data. We assume that all are composed of 32 processors and exhibit the same processing capacity as the Ultra Sparc network in [3]. However, they differ in failure rate, repair rate and checkpointing performance. The environments are detailed in Table 3 and below.

HIGH is a high-performance environment characterized by low failure rates and excellent checkpointing performance. The failure and repair rates come from the **PRINCETON** data set in [19], where failures are infrequent, and the checkpointing performance data comes from CLIP [5], a checkpointer for the Intel Paragon, which has an extremely fast file system. In **HIGH**, C, L and R are equal because CLIP cannot implement the copy-on-write optimization.

MEDIUM is a medium-performance workstation network such as the Ultra Sparc network from [3]. We use workstation failure data from a study on workstation failures on the Internet [14], and checkpointing performance data from a PVM checkpointer on a similar workstation network [17].

Environment	λ	θ	$\frac{C_a}{CS_a}$	$\frac{L_a, R_a}{CS_a}$
HIGH	$\frac{1}{32.7 \text{ days}}$	$\frac{1}{1.30 \text{ days}}$	$\frac{1 \text{ sec}}{24.8 \text{ MB}}$	$\frac{1 \text{ sec}}{24.8 \text{ MB}}$
MIDDLE	$\frac{1}{13.0 \text{ days}}$	$\frac{1}{2.02 \text{ days}}$	$\frac{1 \text{ sec}}{2.04 \text{ MB}}$	$\frac{1 \text{ sec}}{0.120 \text{ MB}}$
LOW	$\frac{1}{70 \text{ min}}$	$\frac{1}{75 \text{ min}}$	$\frac{1 \text{ sec}}{1.00 \text{ MB}}$	$\frac{1 \text{ sec}}{0.200 \text{ MB}}$

Table 3. Failure, repair and checkpointing data for the three processing environments.

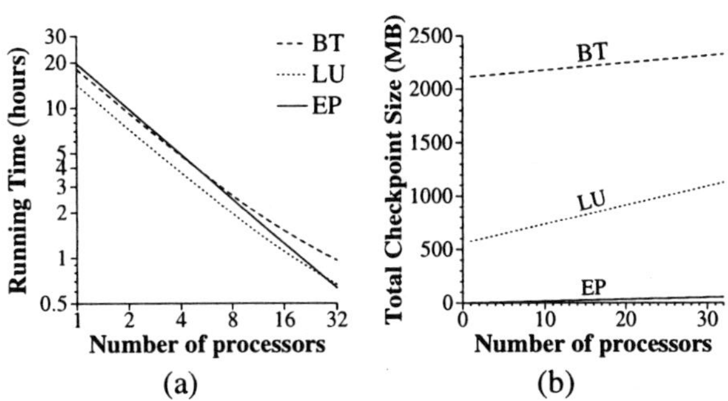

Figure 3. (a): Running time (RT_a) of the applications as a function of the number of processors. (b): Checkpoint size (CS_a) as a function of the number of processors.

Finally, **LOW** is based on an idle-workstation environment such as the one supported by CosMiC [6], where workstations are available for computations only when they are not in use by their owners. Failure and repair data was obtained by the authors of [6], and the checkpointing performance data was gleaned from performance results of CosMiC's transparent checkpointer **libckp** [27]. It is assumed that the copy-on-write optimization yields an 80% improvement in checkpoint overhead [18]. The failure rate of **LOW** is extremely high, which is typical of these environments.

For each application, we selected a problem size that causes the computation to run between 14 and 20 hours on a single workstation with no checkpointing or failures. These are matrix sizes of 160 and 175 for BT and LU respectively, and 2^{35} random numbers for EP. We then calculate values of RT_a for $1 \leq a \leq 32$. These are plotted in Figure 3(a) (using a log-log plot, meaning perfect speedup is a straight line). As displayed by this graph, EP shows the best scalability as a increases. BT and LU scale in a roughly equal manner. In these instances, BT takes a little longer than LU. We assume that the programming substrate recognizes processor failures (as does PVM).

The total checkpoint size CS_a for each application and value of a is calculated using the data in Table 2, and then plotted in Figure 3(b). BT has very large checkpoints (over 2 GB). The checkpoints in LU are smaller, but grow faster with a. EP's checkpoints are very small (1.7 MB per processor).

7 Experiment

For each value of a from 1 to 32, we determine the value I_{opt} of I that minimizes $A_{a,I}$. This is done using Matlab, with a straightforward parameter sweep and iterative refinement of values for I_{opt}, making sure that $I_{opt} \geq L_a$. We

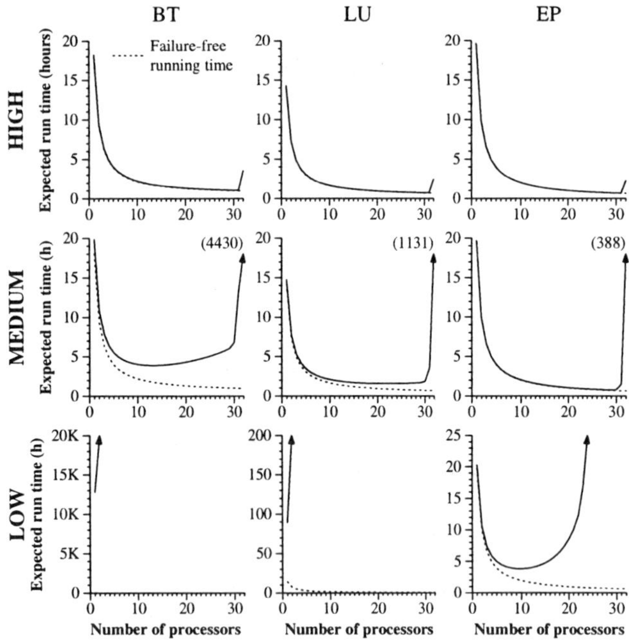

Figure 4. Optimal expected running times of all case studies in the presence of failures as a function of a.

then calculate $RT_a/A_{a,I_{opt}}$, which is the optimal expected running time of the application in the presence of failures. These are plotted using the solid lines in Figure 4. Arrows indicate when these values go beyond the extent of the Y-axes. In the **MEDIUM** cases, the values for $a = 32$ are noted. Dotted lines plot RT_a to compare $RT_a/A_{a,I_{opt}}$ to the failure-free running times. The optimal values of a and I are shown in Table 4.

The first thing to note about Figure 4 and Table 4 is that the optimal value of a varies widely over all cases. In the **HIGH** processing environment, the optimal a in all cases is 31, meaning that it is best to always have a spare processor available in case of failure. If no spare is available, then the application spends a significant amount of idle time waiting for failed processors to be repaired.

In the **MEDIUM** processing environment, the optimal a ranges from 13 to 29. The optimal a is smaller than in **HIGH** because of more frequent failures and much larger latencies, overheads, and recovery times. Of the applications, EP has the highest value of a_{opt} and the best running times. This is mainly because of its smaller checkpoints.

In the **LOW** processing environment, BT and LU have poor expected running times. The optimal values of a are one, and the expected running times are 12791 hours (533 days) and 89 hours (3.7 days) respectively. The reason for these large running times is that $R + L$ is 5.9 hours for BT and 1.6 hours for LU. Both of these are larger than the single processor *MTTF* of 1.2 hours. Thus, even when I equals L, most of time of these applications is spent executing code that will not be checkpointed. The EP application has much smaller checkpoints (its largest $R + L$ value is 0.15 hours), and therefore spends more time performing useful work. It achieves an acceptable optimal running time of 3.85 hours with $a_{opt} = 10$.

As shown by the dotted lines in Figure 4 and the rightmost column of Table 4, checkpointing and failures add very little overhead in the **HIGH** processing environment. In the **MEDIUM** environment, the smaller checkpoints of EP lead to good performance in the presence of failures, while LU and BT perform less well. In the **LOW** environment, BT is basically unrunnable. Given the nature of the environment and the size of the application, LU's performance is barely passable, and EP's is decent. It is worth noting that although checkpointing and process migration environments have been built for idle workstation environments [4, 6, 22], this is the first piece of work that attempts to characterize the performance of large parallel applications on such environments.

8 Related Work

As stated above, there has been much work on checkpointing performance prediction in the presence of failures for uniprocessor and multi-processor (again, see [19, 26] for citations). However, this is the first paper that considers the use of spare processors to take the place of failed active processors. Of note is the work of Wong and Franklin [28], which assumes that the program may reconfigure itself during execution to use a variable number of processors. However, as stated in Section 4, the majority of parallel programs and checkpointing environments do not allow reconfiguration (e.g. [1, 4, 9, 13, 17, 20, 22, 24]).

9 Conclusion

We have presented a method for estimating the average running time of a long-running parallel program, enabled with coordinated checkpointing, in the presence of failures and repairs. This method allows a user to perform an optimal selection of the checkpointing interval and number of active processors. We have shown case studies of three applications from the NAS parallel benchmarks executing on three different but realistic parallel processing environments. Our results show that the optimal number of active processors can vary widely, and that the selection of the number of active processors can have a significant effect on the average running time. We expect this method to be useful for those executing long-running programs on parallel processing environments that are prone to failure.

Application	Processing Environment	a_{opt}	I_{opt} (hours)	$A_{a_{opt},I_{opt}}$	$RT_{a_{opt}}$ (hours)	$RT_{a_{opt}}/A_{a_{opt},I_{opt}}$ (hours)	Overhead of failures and checkpointing
BT	**HIGH**	31	1.16	0.947	0.98	1.04	6.1%
BT	**MEDIUM**	13	5.07	0.458	1.77	3.87	119%
BT	**LOW**	1	2.94	0.00141	18.1	12791	70756%
LU	**HIGH**	31	0.80	0.961	0.68	0.71	4.4%
LU	**MEDIUM**	22	2.19	0.557	0.87	1.56	80%
LU	**LOW**	1	0.80	0.159	14.2	89.4	529%
EP	**HIGH**	31	0.17	0.986	0.65	0.66	1.5%
EP	**MEDIUM**	29	0.33	0.923	0.70	0.75	7.1%
EP	**LOW**	10	0.033	0.515	1.98	3.85	94%

Table 4. Optimal a and I for all tests.

There are three directions in which to extend this work. First, we can attempt to illuminate the method with stochastic simulation based on *iid* exponential failure and repair intervals. This can both validate the model, as in [12], and point to interesting areas of research. Second, we can explore the impact of the assumption of *iid* exponential failures and repairs, by performing simulation based on real failure data, as in [19]. Third, we can attempt to study a wider variety of checkpointing systems, such as two-level [25] and diskless checkpointing systems [20].

10 Acknowledgements

This material is based upon work supported by the National Science Foundation under grants CDA-9529459 and CCR-9703390. The authors thank Emerald Chung, Darrell Long and Richard Golding, for providing failure and repair data, Kim Buckner and Erich Strohmaier for help in obtaining performance data, and Henri Casanova for discussions of the model.

References

[1] D. Bailey *et al.* The NAS parallel benchmarks 2.0. Tech. Rep. NAS-95-20, NASA Ames Research Center, Dec. 1995.

[2] A. D. Barbour, L. Holst, and S. Janson. *Poisson Approximation.* Clarendon Press (Oxford University), Oxford, UK, 1992.

[3] K. Buckner. Timings and memory usage for the NAS parallel benchmarks on a network of Ultra workstations. Tech. Rep. CS-98-408, Univ. of Tenn., 1998.

[4] J. Casas *et al.* MIST: PVM with transparent migration and checkpointing. In *3rd Annual PVM Users' Group Meeting*, Pittsburgh, PA, May 1995.

[5] Y. Chen *et al.* CLIP: A checkpointing tool for message-passing parallel programs. In *SC97: High Perf. Networking and Comp.*, Nov. 1997.

[6] P. E. Chung *et al*, Checkpointing in CosMiC: a user-level process migration environment. In *Pac. Rim Int. Symp. on Fault-Tol. Systems*, Dec. 1997.

[7] D. R. Cox and H. D. Miller. *The Theory of Stochastic Processes.* Chapman and Hall Ltd., London, UK, 1972.

[8] E. N. Elnozahy, D. B. Johnson, and Y. M. Wang. A survey of rollback-recovery protocols in message-passing systems. *ACM Computing Surveys*, to appear.

[9] E. N. Elnozahy, D. B. Johnson, and W. Zwaenepoel. The performance of consistent checkpointing. In *11th Symp. on Rel. Dist. Sys.*, pp. 39–47, Oct. 1992.

[10] W. Feller. *An Introduction to Probability Theory and Its Applications (Third Edition).* John Wiley & Sons, Inc., NY, 1968.

[11] J. G. Kemeny and J. L. Snell. *Finite Markov Chains.* Van Nostrand, Princeton, NJ, 1960. Republished by Springer-Verlag, NY, 1976.

[12] G. P. Kavanaugh and W. H. Sanders. Perf. analysis of two time-based coordinated checkpointing protocols. In *Pac. Rim Int. Symp. on Fault-Tol. Sys.*, 1997.

[13] J. León, *et al.* Fail-safe PVM: A portable package for distributed programming with transparent recovery. Tech. Rep. CS-93-124, Carn. Mel. Univ., 1993.

[14] D. Long, A. Muir, and R. Golding. A longitudinal survey of internet host reliability. In *14th Symp. on Rel. Dist. Sys.*, pp. 2–9, Sep. 1995.

[15] Message Passing Interface Forum. MPI: A message-passing interface standard. *International Journal of Supercomputer Applications*, 8(3/4), 1994.

[16] E. Parzen. *Stochastic Processes.* Holden-Day, San Francisco, CA, 1962.

[17] J. S. Plank. Improving the performance of coordinated checkpointers on networks of workstations using RAID techniques. In *15th Symposium on Reliable Distributed Systems*, pp. 76–85, October 1996.

[18] J. S. Plank, M. Beck, G. Kingsley, and K. Li. **Libckpt**: Transparent checkpointing under Unix. In *Usenix Winter Tech. Conf.*, pp. 213–223, Jan. 1995.

[19] J. S. Plank and W. R. Elwasif. Experimental assessment of workstation failures and their impact on checkpointing systems. In *28th Int. Symp. on Fault-Tol. Comp.*, pp. 48–57, June 1998.

[20] J. S. Plank, K. Li, and M. A. Puening. Diskless checkpointing. *IEEE Transactions on Parallel and Distributed Systems*, 9(10):972–986, October 1998.

[21] J. S. Plank and M. G. Thomason. The average availability of multiprocessor checkpointing systems. Tec. Rep. CS-98-403, Univ. of Tenn., Nov. 1998.

[22] J. Pruyne and M. Livny. Managing checkpoints for parallel programs. In *Workshop on Job Scheduling Strategies for Parallel Processing (IPPS '96)*, 1996.

[23] H. D. Simon and E. Strohmaier. Amdahl's law and the statistical content of the NAS Parallel Benchmarks. *Supercomputer*, 11(4):75–88, 1995.

[24] G. Stellner. CoCheck: Checkpointing and process migration for MPI. In *10th International Parallel Processing Symposium*, pp. 526–531. Apr. 1996.

[25] N. H. Vaidya. A case for two-level distributed recovery schemes. In *ACM SIGMETRICS Conf. on Meas. and Modeling of Computer Sys.*, May 1995.

[26] N. H. Vaidya. Impact of checkpoint latency on overhead ratio of a checkpointing scheme. *IEEE Transactions on Computers*, 46(8):942–947, August 1997.

[27] Y-M. Wang *et al.* Checkpointing and its applications. In *25th Int. Symp. on Fault-Tol. Comp.*, pp. 22–31, June 1995.

[28] K. F. Wong and M. Franklin. Checkpointing in distributed systems. *Journal of Parallel & Distributed Systems*, 35(1):67–75, May 1996.

Session 9B

Testing

Chair: Kozo Kinoshita
Osaka University, Japan

Reducing Test Application Time for Full Scan Embedded Cores *

Ilker Hamzaoglu and Janak H. Patel
Center for Reliable & High-Performance Computing
University of Illinois, Urbana, IL 61801

Abstract

We propose a new design for testability technique, Parallel Serial Full Scan (PSFS), for reducing the test application time for full scan embedded cores. Test application time reduction is achieved by dividing the scan chain into multiple partitions and shifting in the same vector to each scan chain through a single scan in input. The experimental results for the ISCAS89 circuits showed that PSFS technique significantly reduces both the test application time and the amount of test data for full scan embedded cores.

1 Introduction

Chips with multiple embedded cores, called *system-on-chip*, are becoming more prevalent in the industry, since the core-based design approach considerably reduces the design time through design reuse. However, testing embedded cores is a challenging problem, because of the limited access to the core peripheries, i.e. inputs and outputs [3, 6, 17, 18]. There are three major peripheral access techniques; *parallel direct access*, *functional access* and *serial boundary scan access* [18].

Parallel access technique provides direct access to core peripheries by either using dedicated chip I/O pins or by sharing the chip I/O pins by multiplexing and demultiplexing them with other signals. Functional access technique provides access to core peripheries by justifying the test patterns and propagating the fault effects using the user defined logic surrounding the core. Serial access technique provides indirect but full access to core peripheries by using a boundary scan chain around the core. Although the serial access technique increases the test application time for the cores due to serial access to the core peripheries, it is currently the most realistic approach for providing peripheral access to the embedded cores [18].

The full scan technique is a widely adopted DFT technique in the industry for reducing the complexity of test generation for sequential circuits to a combinational circuit test generation problem by making all the memory elements in the circuit both controllable and observable through a scan chain. However, since controlling (observing) the flip-flops are done by serially shifting in (out) the values to (from) the memory elements, full scan technique increases the test application time. Several techniques are proposed to reduce the test application time for full scan circuits, e.g. parallel direct access [9], hybrid test generation scheme [10, 15, 16], multiple scan chains [12, 15] and ordering flip-flops in a single scan chain [13]. However, these techniques are not effective for the full scan circuits used as embedded cores which we refer to as *full scan embedded cores*. The general structure of a full scan embedded core is shown in Figure 1.

Since hybrid test generation (HTG) technique uses sequential test generation, it generates large test sets. Since some of these vectors do not require shifting in the values to the memory elements and the input values are directly applied to the primary inputs, it reduces the test application time for standalone full scan circuits. However, if serial access technique is used for test access, then the test application time can be quite large because the primary input values in each vector should be serially shifted into the boundary scan. In addition, since it generates a large test set, HTG scheme makes it more difficult to use the functional access technique by increasing the number of vectors that have to be justified at the core inputs. Finally, since HTG technique requires sequential test generation, it may not be applicable to large cores.

Multiple scan chains (MSC) technique requires separate input/output pins for each scan chain. This requirement makes it more difficult to use the parallel access technique by increasing the number of core pins and the routing overhead. The same requirement makes it more difficult to use the functional access technique too by increasing the number of values that should be justified at the core inputs. On the other hand, if the serial access technique is used for test access, the MSC technique does not reduce the test application time. Because the input values that will be shifted into each scan chain first should be seri-

*This research was supported in part by the Semiconductor Research Corporation under contract SRC 97-DJ-482 and in part by DARPA under contract DABT63-95-C-0069.

0-7695-0213-X/99 $10.00 © 1999 IEEE

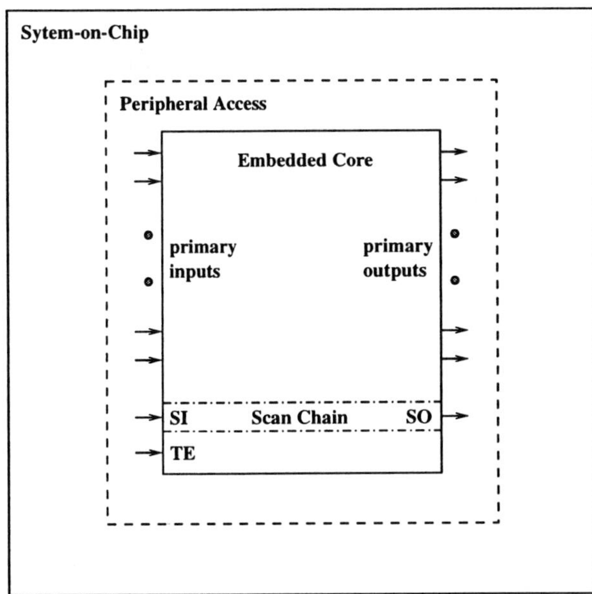

Figure 1: Full Scan Embedded Core

ally shifted into the boundary scan and then shifted into the scan chains in parallel. Similarly, the test responses in the scan chains first should be shifted out to the boundary scan in parallel and then serially shifted out from the boundary scan. Therefore, the test application time becomes the same as the test application time for full scan cores using a single scan chain.

Parallel direct access to all the memory elements are impractical for embedded cores, since even the direct access to the core inputs and outputs are limited. Even though single scan chain reconfiguration technique reduces the test application time to some degree, it is possible to reduce the test application time further.

In this paper, we propose a new DFT technique, *Parallel Serial Full Scan (PSFS)*, for reducing the test application time for the full scan embedded cores. Since the PSFS technique does not use any additional test access pins other than the ones used in the full scan technique and it does not require large number of test vectors, it is applicable to the full scan cores using any of the three peripheral access techniques; serial, parallel or functional access.

The PSFS techniques reduces the test application time by dividing the scan chain into multiple partitions and shifting in the same vector to each scan chain through a single scan in input. The outputs of the scan chains are observed through a multiple input signature analyzer (MISR). In order to test the faults that cannot be detected by this organization and the faults aliased by the MISR, PSFS technique also preserves the single scan chain structure using extra multiplexers and a simple control structure. Since the performance of the PSFS technique is dependent on the scan chain configuration, i.e. the number of the scan chains used and the assignment of the memory elements to the scan chains, we propose a heuristic technique for computing an optimal scan chain configuration that produces a minimal test application time.

In addition to reducing the test application time, PSFS technique has another important advantage for testing full scan cores. Since for each test vector, in addition to the primary input values, only the input values for the longest scan chain should be stored in the tester, PSFS technique reduces the tester storage requirements and the amount of test data that should be transfered from the tester to the core and from the core back to the tester. This is especially important for large system-on-chips with multiple cores [7].

We enhanced ATOM, our advanced ATPG system for combinational circuits [4], to generate test vectors under the single stuck at fault model for the embedded cores incorporating the PSFS technique. The experimental results showed that for the ISCAS89 circuits the PSFS technique reduces the total test application time by 82%, and it reduces the total test data by 67%.

In addition to significantly reducing the test application time and the amount of test data, the PSFS technique is also very effective in terms of the other performance metrics. In particular, it only uses combinational test generation, thus it is applicable to large cores. It doesn't degrade the performance of the core in normal mode more than the full scan technique. It doesn't require any additional test access pins other than the scan in, scan out and test enable pins used by the full scan technique. It only incurs a small amount of hardware overhead, and it provides 100% combinational fault coverage.

In this paper, we applied the PSFS technique only to the flip-flops of a full scan core, and we assumed that the inputs and the outputs of the core will be accessed by any one of the peripheral access techniques. However, if the serial boundary scan access technique is used for test access to the core, then it is possible to apply the PSFS technique to both the flip-flops of the core and the boundary scan flip-flops for the inputs and the outputs of the core by considering all of these flip-flops as a single scan chain and by dividing this scan chain into multiple partitions and shifting in the same vector to each scan chain through a single scan in input and observing the outputs of the scan chains through a MISR. This way the test application time can be reduced further.

A similar technique to PSFS is proposed in [11] for testing multiple independent circuits simultaneously by using a single input to support the scan chains in all

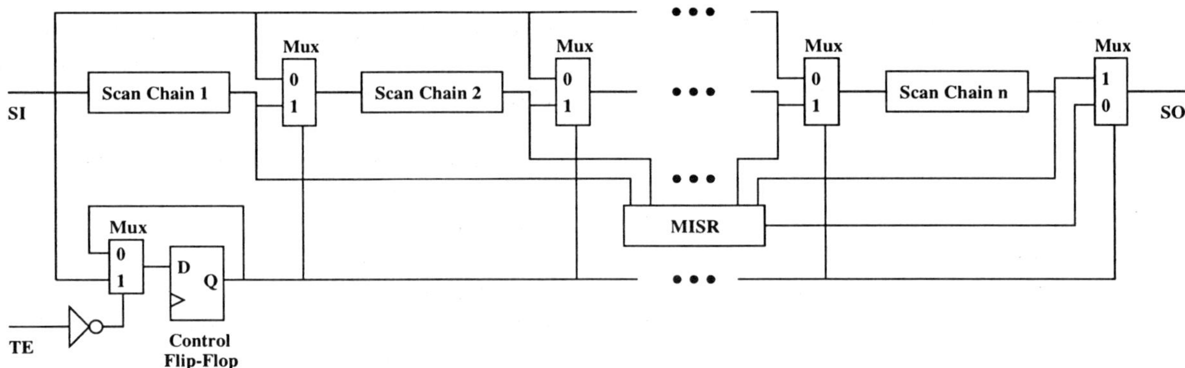

Figure 2: Parallel Serial Full Scan (PSFS) Technique

the circuits. The number of scan chains is equal to the number of circuits, and the memory elements of each circuit is assigned to its scan chain. The only design parameter is the order of the memory elements in each scan chain. Since the circuits are independent, all the detectable faults in each circuit are still detectable under this organization. PSFS technique, on the other hand, is proposed for testing a single full scan embedded core. The number of scan chains, the distribution of the memory elements to the scan chains, and the order of the memory elements in each scan chain are all design parameters for the PSFS technique. In addition, since PSFS technique is applied to a single full scan core, some of the detectable faults in the core may not be detectable when the same logic values are shifted into the multiple scan chains in the core.

The rest of the paper is organized as follows. Section 2 presents the PSFS technique. The algorithm for finding an optimal scan chain configuration is described in Section 3. Section 4 describes the test generation algorithm used to generate a minimal test set for a given scan chain configuration. The experimental results are given in Section 5. Finally, Section 6 presents the conclusions.

2 Parallel Serial Full Scan Technique

We propose a new DFT technique, *Parallel Serial Full Scan (PSFS)*, for reducing the test application time for full scan embedded cores. The full scan embedded cores incorporating the PSFS technique are called *PSFS cores*. The organization of the flip-flops of a PSFS core is shown in Figure 2. The PSFS technique reduces the test application time for the embedded cores without using any additional test access pins other than the ones used in the full scan technique, i.e. scan in (SI), scan out (SO), and test enable (TE).

As in the full scan cores, the TE input controls the operation of the PSFS cores. When the TE is 0, the core operates in the normal mode. The operation of the PSFS cores in the normal mode is same as the full scan cores. When the TE is 1, the core operates in the test mode. The operation of the PSFS cores in the test mode is controlled by the control flip-flop (CFF). When the CFF is 1, the PSFS core operates in the *serial test mode*. The operation of the PSFS core in the serial test mode is same as the operation of the full scan cores in the test mode, i.e. the new values are shifted into each flip-flop serially through SI input, and the previous values of all the flip-flops are shifted out serially through SO output. When the CFF is 0, the PSFS core operates in the *parallel test mode*. In the parallel test mode, shifting in the input values into the flip-flops and shifting out the test response from the flip-flops are done in parallel.

We will now explain the operation of the PSFS cores in the test mode in more detail. PSFS technique divides the single scan chain in a full scan core into multiple partitions. The input of the first scan chain is driven by the SI input. The input of the other scan chains is driven either by the output of the previous scan chain or by the SI input. The selection is done by a 2-to-1 multiplexer (MUX) which is controlled by the CFF. When the CFF is 0, each scan chain is driven by the SI input, thus the same logic values are shifted into each scan chain in parallel. When the CFF is 1, each scan chain is driven by the previous scan chain, thus the flip-flops behave as a single serial scan chain.

The output of each scan chain is connected both to the MUX driving the next scan chain and to a multiple input signature analyzer (MISR). The PSFS technique uses the MISR to compress the test response of the embedded core that is stored in its flip-flops. Since the output of each scan chain is connected to a different data input of the MISR, the size of the MISR used in a PSFS core is equal to the number of scan chains used in the core. In this work, we used two different type 2 (internal-XOR) MISRs, a 6-bit and a 16-bit MISR with the primitive characteristic polynomials $P(x) =$

x^6+x+1 and $P(x) = x^{16}+x^9+x^7+x^4+1$ respectively.

The *SO* output of the PSFS core is driven either by the output of the last scan chain or by the output of the MISR. The selection is done by a 2-to-1 MUX which is controlled by the CFF. When the CFF is 0, the output of the MISR is shifted out through the *SO* output. When the CFF is 1, *SO* output is driven by the output of the last scan chain, thus the flip-flops behave as a single serial scan chain.

In summary, when the CFF is 0, the same logic values are shifted into each scan chain in parallel through the *SI* input, the outputs of the scan chains are compressed using a MISR, and the output of the MISR is observed through the *SO* output. On the other hand, when the CFF is 1, the flip-flops behave as a single serial scan chain, i.e. the new values are shifted into each flip-flop serially through *SI* input, and the previous values of all the flip-flops are shifted out serially through *SO* output.

The parallel test mode is used to reduce the test application time. However, since the same logic values are shifted into each scan chain, some of the testable faults may not be detected under the parallel test mode. Moreover, the use of a MISR for response compaction may cause some of the faults to be aliased. The serial test mode is used to test these faults, thus providing 100% combinational fault coverage. The test vectors applied under the serial test mode are called *serial vectors*, and the test vectors applied under the parallel test mode are called *parallel vectors*.

3 Scan Chain Configuration

The effectiveness of the PSFS technique for reducing the test application time is dependent on the scan chain configuration, i.e. the number of the scan chains used and the assignment of the flip-flops to the scan chains. Therefore, we propose a heuristic technique for computing an optimal scan chain configuration that provides a minimal test application time.

3.1 Number of Scan Chains

As the number of scan chains increases, the amount of parallelism also increases and the parallel vector length decreases, thus decreasing the test application time. However, using a large number of scan chains increases the number of faults that cannot be tested using the parallel test mode, thus increasing the number of serial vectors, which starts increasing the test application time. As the number of scan chains increases, the hardware overhead of the PSFS technique also increases, i.e. large number of MUXes, a large MISR and extra routing are needed.

Since, for a given core, it is computationally prohibitive to compute the optimum number of scan chains, in this work we selected the number of scan chains by trying to avoid using a small or a large number of scan chains relative to the number of flip-flops used in the core. Based on this criterion, in our experiments, we used 6 scan chains for the cores with less than 200 flip-flops, and 16 scan chains for the cores with less than 2000 flip-flops.

3.2 Mapping Flip-Flops to Scan Chains

Finding the optimum scan chain configuration that will produce the minimum number of test cycles is an NP-hard problem. Because it requires solving the problem of generating a minimum size stuck at test set for a given combinational circuit which is proven to be NP-hard [8]. Even for the special case of evenly distributing the flip-flops to the scan chains, the number of different scan chain configurations with possibly different test application times is

$$\prod_{N_{SC}=1}^{MaxN_{SC}} \frac{F!}{\left(\frac{F}{N_{SC}}\right) * N_{SC}!}$$

where F is the total number of flip-flops, N_{SC} is the number of scan chains used, and $MaxN_{SC}$ is the maximum number of scan chains that can be used. Thus, it is computationally prohibitive to search the entire scan chain configuration space for finding the optimum scan chain configuration. Therefore, we propose a heuristic mapping technique for finding an optimal scan chain configuration. The heuristic assumes that the number of scan chains in the circuit (N_{SC}) is given and it tries to map the flip-flops to these scan chains such that a minimal test application time is achieved.

Two inputs of a circuit are said to be *compatible* if they can be shorted together without introducing any redundant stuck at fault in the circuit, otherwise these two inputs are called *incompatible* [2]. In the parallel testing mode, the corresponding flip-flops in each scan chain is assigned the same logic value. This restriction may prevent the detection of some of the combinationally testable faults thus increasing the test application time by increasing the number of serial vectors necessary to achieve 100% fault coverage. However, if all of these flip-flops are compatible with each other, then this restriction cannot introduce any artificial redundancies. Therefore, our heuristic mapping technique tries to assign pairwise compatible flip-flops to the same position in each scan chain.

Since the exact techniques for checking the compatibility of two flip-flops are computationally expensive, they may not be applicable to large circuits. Therefore, we used the heuristic technique described in [2] for deciding whether two flip-flops are compatible or not.

	x_1	x_2	x_3	x_4
t_1	X	1	0	1
t_2	1	0	1	1
t_3	0	0	0	0
t_4	1	1	X	0
t_5	X	0	X	X

Figure 3: Partially Specified Test Set Matrix

The heuristic technique first generates a complete partially specified test set for the full scan circuit without using any test set compaction algorithm. The resulting test set can be represented as a two dimensional matrix where each row is a test vector and each column is the values that will be assigned to a single flip-flop of the circuit. Two columns, in this matrix, are compatible if for every row their corresponding logic values are same or at least one of them is a don't care (X). An example test set matrix is shown in Figure 3 in which only the columns x_1 and x_3 are pairwise compatible. If two columns in a given test set matrix are compatible, then the corresponding two flip-flops are compatible. However, if two columns are incompatible, it is not possible to conclude that the corresponding flip-flops are incompatible. Because it is possible that in a different test set the columns corresponding to these two flip-flops may be compatible. Therefore, this heuristic technique may fail to prove the compatibility of two compatible flip-flops.

A *compatibility class* is a set of flip-flops that are pairwise compatible. Assigning pairwise compatible flip-flops to the same position in each scan chain requires finding the compatibility classes of size at most N_{SC}. We used a common greedy heuristic for solving this problem. The heuristic technique considers each flip-flop one at a time. The first flip-flop is assigned to the first compatibility class. If the next flip-flop is compatible with the first one, it is also assigned to the same compatibility class, otherwise it is assigned to a new compatibility class. If the next flip-flop is compatible with all the flip-flops in an existing compatibility class which has less than N_{SC} flip-flops, then it is added to that class, otherwise it is assigned to a new compatibility class and so on.

Once the compatibility classes are computed, our heuristic mapping technique uses this information for mapping the flip-flops to the scan chains. It first sorts the compatibility classes in the descending order of their cardinality. Starting from the first position in each scan chain, it assigns the flip-flops in each compatibility class of size N_{SC} to the same position in each scan chain, i.e. the flip-flops in the first compatibility class of size N_{SC} is assigned to the first position in each scan chain and so on. Then, it assigns the flip-flops in each compatibility class of size $S > \frac{2}{3} * N_{SC}$ to the same position in the first S scan chains and fills in the same position in the remaining scan chains using the flip-flops in the compatibility classes of size $S \leq \frac{2}{3} * N_{SC}$. Finally, it assigns the flip-flops in each of the remaining compatibility classes of size $S \leq \frac{2}{3} * N_{SC}$ to the same position in the first S scan chains leaving the same position in the remaining scan chains empty.

The second step of the heuristic mapping technique may cause some of the faults to be untestable in the parallel test mode, since some of the flip-flops that are assigned to the same position in each scan chain may be incompatible. This increases the number of serial vectors necessary to achieve 100 % fault coverage, thus increasing the test application time. However, this assignment reduces the size of the longest scan chain, thus reducing the test application time. The number of artificial redundancies introduced and the amount of reduction achieved in the longest scan chain size depends on the number of incompatible flip-flops assigned to the same position in each scan chain. If this number is large, then this may increase the test application time more than it helps to decrease it. Therefore, in order to reduce the size of the longest scan chain without causing a large number of artificial redundancies, the heuristic technique assigns at most $\frac{1}{3} * N_{SC}$ incompatible flip-flops to the same position in each scan chain.

In order to assess the effectiveness of the heuristic optimal mapping technique, we also measured the performance of the PSFS technique using a different mapping technique, called default mapping, which does not try to find an optimal scan chain configuration that produces a minimal test application time. The default mapping technique distributes the flip-flops evenly to each scan chain using the flip-flop order given in the circuit description, i.e. the flip-flops 1 to n are assigned to scan chain 1, the flip-flops $n+1$ to $2n$ are assigned to scan chain 2, and so on, where $n = (number\ of\ flip-flops)\ /\ (number\ of\ scan\ chains)$.

Example: Consider a full scan embedded core with 27 flip-flops. Suppose that 6 scan chains are used in the circuit. As shown in Figure 4, the default mapping technique assigns the flip-flops evenly to each scan chain using the flip-flop order given in the circuit description, i.e. 1 to 27. Suppose that the heuristic for computing compatibility classes computed 7 compatibility classes for the core flip-flops as shown in Figure 4. The optimal mapping technique assigns the flip-flops to the scan chains using this compatibility in-

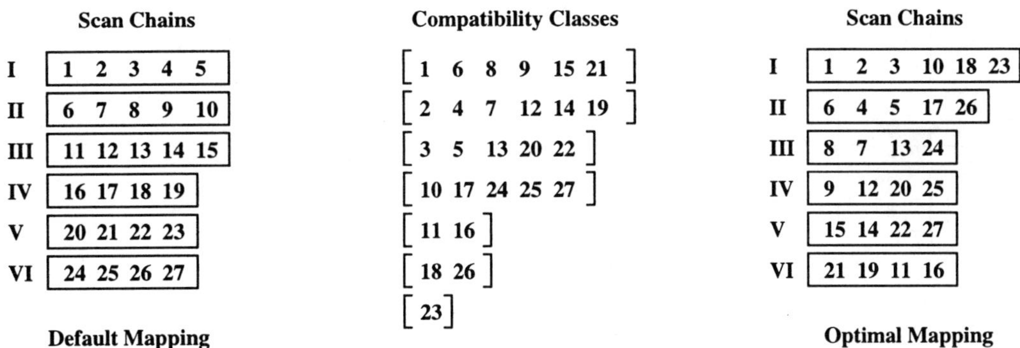

Figure 4: Scan Chain Configuration Example

formation as explained in this section. The resulting scan chain configuration is shown in Figure 4.

4 Test Generation

The problem of generating the minimum size test set for a given scan chain configuration is NP-hard, because it requires solving the problem of generating a minimum size stuck at test set for a given combinational circuit which is proven to be NP-hard [8]. In this work, therefore, we used the heuristic test set compaction algorithms dynamic compaction and redundant vector elimination [5] for generating compact test sets.

Test generation process for a given scan chain configuration proceeds as follows. First, a minimal test set that detects all the faults that are detectable under the parallel test mode is generated. During the test generation process for the parallel test mode, the test generation constraints imposed by the scan chain configuration, i.e. the flip-flops assigned to the same position in each scan chain should be assigned the same logic value in each test vector, are taken into account. Next, the MISR is fault simulated for the vectors in this test set and the faults aliased by the MISR are identified. Finally, using the serial test mode a minimal test set that detects the aliased faults and the faults that are undetectable using the parallel test mode is generated. The final test set is the union of the test set with the parallel test vectors and the one with the serial test vectors.

5 Experimental Results

In order to generate test vectors for the PSFS cores under the single stuck at fault model, we enhanced ATOM, our advanced ATPG system for combinational circuits [4], and we implemented a sequential circuit fault simulator, based on PROOFS algorithm [14], for simulating a MISR and incorporated it into ATOM. ATOM and the new extensions are implemented in C++. The test application time for the small ISCAS89 circuits is already very small, because the number of flip-flops and the size of the minimal test set are quite small for these circuits [5]. Therefore, we tested ATOM on the large ISCAS89 circuits [1]. We assumed that these circuits are used as full scan embedded cores. The performance results are obtained on a 200 MHz Pentium Pro PC with 128MB RAM running Linux 2.0.0 using GNU CC version 2.8.0. In all the experiments, a backtrack limit of 6 is used in ATOM, and all the test sets generated by ATOM have 100% fault coverage.

The experimental results for the full scan embedded cores are presented in Table 1. The last four columns in this table present the number of test vectors in the minimal test set, the number of cycles necessary to test the core, the amount of test data in number of bits that should be stored in the tester for testing the core, and the test generation time in seconds respectively. The test application time for a full scan core is computed as $F + (1 + F) * V$, where F is the number of flip-flops and V is the number of test vectors.

The experimental results for the PSFS cores using the default and the optimal scan chain configuration techniques are presented in Tables 2 and 3 respectively. The columns in these tables present the core name, the number of scan chains used, the number of flip-flops in the longest scan chain, the number of parallel test vectors, the number of faults that cannot be detected under the parallel test mode, the number of faults aliased by the MISR, the number of serial test vectors used for testing both the aliased faults and the faults that cannot be detected under the parallel test mode, the number of cycles necessary to test the core, the amount of test data in number of bits that should be stored in the tester for testing the core, and the test generation time in seconds respectively. The experimental results for the PSFS cores presented in these tables are obtained by assuming that the parallel access technique is used for test access to the core inputs and outputs. Therefore, the

Core	Inputs	Outputs	Flip-Flops	Test Vectors	Test Cycles	Test Data (bits)	Time(s)
s5378	35	49	179	111	**20159**	**49062**	11.5
s9234	36	39	211	159	**33919**	**79023**	57.4
s13207	62	152	638	236	**151442**	**351640**	68.9
s15850	77	150	534	126	**67944**	**163170**	156.3
s35932	35	320	1728	16	**29392**	**60976**	117.3
s38417	28	106	1636	99	**163699**	**337194**	148.0
s38584	38	304	1426	136	**195498**	**434384**	215.5

Table 1: Performance Results for Full Scan Embedded Cores

Core	Scan Chains	Longest Scan Chain	Parallel Test Vectors	Undetectable Faults	Aliased Faults	Serial Test Vectors	Test Cycles	Test Data (bits)	Time(s)
s5378	6	30	132	65	0	28	**9349**	**31384**	18.1
s9234	6	36	181	932	1	57	**19036**	**54936**	156.6
s13207	16	40	136	1174	6	137	**93815**	**244114**	119.2
s15850	16	34	152	472	0	26	**19816**	**78510**	205.4
s35932	16	108	31	0	0	0	**5233**	**17701**	231.2
s38417	16	103	303	116	0	34	**88927**	**218824**	720.5
s38584	16	90	190	891	0	49	**88747**	**255686**	472.7

Table 2: Performance Results for PSFS Cores Using Default Scan Chain Configuration

Core	Scan Chains	Longest Scan Chain	Parallel Test Vectors	Undetectable Faults	Aliased Faults	Serial Test Vectors	Test Cycles	Test Data (bits)	Time(s)
s5378	6	33	186	0	1	1	**6724**	**28342**	22.4
s9234	6	44	214	0	0	0	**9893**	**34882**	109.6
s13207	16	42	277	0	0	0	**12609**	**82546**	124.6
s15850	16	40	235	6	1	3	**11832**	**76030**	314.2
s35932	16	108	16	0	0	0	**3598**	**9136**	238.9
s38417	16	140	264	2	16	6	**48840**	**129732**	593.5
s38584	16	90	236	0	8	2	**25864**	**129580**	526.6

Table 3: Performance Results for PSFS Cores Using Optimal Scan Chain Configuration

test application time for a PSFS core is computed as $1+F_{LSC}+(1+F_{LSC})*V_P+S+1+F+(1+F)*V_S$, where F is the number of flip-flops in the circuit, F_{LSC} is number of flip-flops in the longest scan chain, S is the number of scan chains, V_P is the number of parallel test vectors and V_S is the number of serial test vectors.

The test generation time for the PSFS cores using the heuristic optimal mapping method presented in Table 3 does not include the test generation time for generating the partially specified test sets. It includes the time to compute the optimal mapping given a partially specified test set and the test generation time using this scan chain configuration.

The comparisons of the test application time and the amount of test data for the full scan cores and the PSFS cores are presented in Table 4.

The results show that the PSFS technique is quite effective in reducing the test application time and the test storage requirements for the ISCAS89 circuits even if the default mapping method is used. The test generation time for the default scan chain configuration is also quite small. Though this may not be the case for every full scan embedded core, if the default mapping method provides a satisfactory test application time reduction, this avoids the design time for using the heuristic optimal mapping technique. These results also show that for some embedded cores the layout information can be used to configure the scan chains to reduce the routing overhead of the PSFS technique without sacrificing the advantage of reduced test application time.

The results also show that the PSFS technique using the heuristic optimal mapping method significantly reduces the test application time and the test storage requirements for full scan cores. For the ISCAS89 circuits, the total test application time is reduced by 82%, and the total test data is reduced by 67%. The results show that the heuristic optimal mapping technique is more effective than the default mapping technique. The design time for computing the optimal scan chain

Core	Test Application Time					Test Data				
	Full Scan	PSFS with Default Scan Chain		PSFS with Optimal Scan Chain		Full Scan	PSFS with Default Scan Chain		PSFS with Optimal Scan Chain	
	Test Cycles	Test Cycles	Percent Reduction	Test Cycles	Percent Reduction	Test Data (bits)	Test Data (bits)	Percent Reduction	Test Data (bits)	Percent Reduction
s5378	20159	9349	54 %	6724	67%	49062	31384	36%	28342	42%
s9234	33919	19036	44%	9893	71%	79023	54936	31%	34882	56%
s13207	151442	93815	38%	12609	92%	351640	244114	31%	82546	77%
s15850	67944	19816	71%	11832	83%	163170	78510	52%	76030	53%
s35932	29392	5233	82%	3598	88%	60976	17701	71%	9136	85%
s38417	163699	88927	46%	48840	70%	337194	218824	35%	129732	62%
s38584	195498	88747	55%	25864	87%	434384	255686	41%	129580	70%

Table 4: Comparison of Performance Results

configuration and the test generation time for this configuration is also very small.

The effectiveness of the PSFS technique for a core depends on the existence of the compatible flip-flops in that core. Even though the PSFS technique is very effective for the ISCAS89 circuits, if the flip-flops of a full scan core is highly incompatible, then it may not be very effective for reducing the test application time for that full scan core.

The results also showed that for some of the circuits parallel vectors alone achieved 100% fault coverage and the MISR did not cause any aliasing. Since no serial vectors are needed for these circuits, there is no need to preserve the single serial scan structure using the extra multiplexers and the control structure. Therefore, the PSFS technique incurs a much smaller hardware overhead for these circuits.

6 Conclusions

We proposed a new DFT technique, Parallel Serial Full Scan (PSFS), for reducing the test application time for full scan embedded cores without using any additional test access pins other than the ones used for the full scan technique. The experimental results for the ISCAS89 circuits showed that this technique significantly reduces both the test application time and the amount of test data for full scan embedded cores.

References

[1] F. Brglez, D. Bryan, and K. Kozminski, "Combinational Profiles of Sequential Benchmark Circuits", in *Proc. of the Int. Symp. on Circuits and Systems*, pp. 1929-1934, May 1989.

[2] C. Chen and S. K. Gupta, "A Methodology to Design Efficient BIST Test Pattern Generators", in *Proc. of the Int. Test Conf.*, pp. 814-823, October 1995.

[3] I. Ghosh, N. K. Jha, and S. Dey, "A Low Overhead Design for Testability and Test Generation Technique for Core-based Systems", in *Proc. of the Int. Test Conf.*, pp. 50-59, October 1997.

[4] I. Hamzaoglu and J. H. Patel, "Deterministic Test Pattern Generation Techniques", in *Proc. of the VLSI Test Symp.*, pp. 446-452, April 1998.

[5] I. Hamzaoglu and J. H. Patel, "Test Set Compaction Algorithms for Combinational Circuits", in *Proc. of the Int. Conf. on Computer-Aided Design*, pp. 283-289, November 1998.

[6] V. Immaneni and S. Raman, "Direct Access Test Scheme - Design for Block and Core Cells for Embedded ASICS", in *Proc. of the Int. Test Conf.*, pp. 488-492, October 1990.

[7] A. Jas and N. A. Touba, "Test Vector Decompression via Cyclical Scan Chains and Its Application to Testing Core-Based Designs", in *Proc. of the Int. Test Conf.*, pp. 458-464, October 1998.

[8] B. Krishnamurthy and S. B. Akers, "On the Complexity of Estimating the Size of a Test Set", *IEEE Trans. on Computers*, pp. 750-753, August 1984.

[9] S. Lee and K. G. Shin, "Design for Test Using Partial Parallel Scan", *IEEE Trans. on Computer-Aided Design*, pp. 203-211, February 1990.

[10] S. Y. Lee and K. K. Saluja, "An Algorithm to Reduce Test Application Time in Full Scan Designs", in *Proc. of the Int. Conf. on Computer-Aided Design*, pp. 17-20, November 1992.

[11] K. Lee, J. Chen, and C. Huang, "Using a Single Input to Support Multiple Scan Chains", in *Proc. of the Int. Conf. on Computer-Aided Design*, pp. 74-78, November 1998.

[12] S. Narayanan, R. Gupta, and M. Breuer, "Optimal Configuring of Multiple Scan Chains", *IEEE Trans. on Computer-Aided Design*, pp. 1121-1131, September 1993.

[13] S. Narayanan and M. Breuer, "Reconfiguration Techniques for a Single Scan Chain", *IEEE Trans. on Computer-Aided Design*, pp. 750-765, June 1995.

[14] T. M. Niermann, W. Cheng, and J. H. Patel, "PROOFS: A fast, memory-efficient sequential circuit fault simulator", *IEEE Trans. on Computer-Aided Design*, pp. 198-207, February 1992.

[15] D. K. Pradhan and J. Saxena, "A Design for Testability Scheme to Reduce Test Application Time in Full Scan", in *Proc. of the VLSI Test Symp.*, pp. 55-60, April 1992.

[16] E. M. Rudnick and J. H. Patel, "A Genetic Approach to Test Application Time Reduction for Full Scan and Partial Scan Circuits", in *Proc. of Int. Conf. on VLSI Design*, pp. 288-293, January 1995.

[17] N. A. Touba and B. Pouya, "Testing Embedded Cores Using Partial Isolation Rings", in *Proc. of the VLSI Test Symp.*, pp. 10-16, April 1997.

[18] Y. Zorian, "Test Requirements for Embedded Core-based Systems and IEEE P1500", in *Proc. of the Int. Test Conf.*, pp. 191-199, October 1997.

Synthesis of Circuits Derived from Decision Diagrams – Combining Small Delay and Testability –

Harry Hengster *

Bernd Becker

Institute of Computer Science, Albert-Ludwigs-University, Freiburg i.Br., Germany
email: <hengster,becker>@informatik.uni-freiburg.de

Abstract

We present a synthesis for testability approach to obtain EXOR-based circuits with inherently small delay. The starting point of our approach is a functional specification given in form of a so-called Kronecker Functional Decision Diagram *(KFDD). The KFDD is transformed into a circuit by using a composition method based on* Boolean Matrix Multiplication. *Efficient algorithms working on the KFDD are applied during synthesis to avoid the creation of* constant *lines. Thereby full stuck-at fault testability is guaranteed by construction.*

Moreover, tests for all faults can be derived efficiently from the graph of the KFDD. Thus, it is not necessary to apply automatic test pattern generation *(ATPG) to compute test sets for the synthesized circuits or to check for redundancies. Area and delay of the circuits can be further improved by merging of* equivalent *gates. Altogether, our approach makes it possible to combine high speed with full testability for circuits derived from KFDDs.*

Finally, the efficiency of the proposed methods is demonstrated by experiments.

1. Introduction

Decision Diagrams (DDs) are a graph based data structure which was originally developed for the representation and manipulation of Boolean functions. In the meantime DDs as a data structure are widely used for various applications in verification, synthesis and testing (see e.g. [10, 11, 6, 15]). But the structure of the underlying graph, which results from a recursive decomposition of the functions to be represented, can also be used to derive circuit realizations for these functions.

Recently, such DD-based synthesis approaches have received more and more attention. Common to all these approaches is the idea, that structural properties of the DD and efficient DD manipulation algorithms can be successfully used to determine and optimize properties of the circuits themselves. Before concentrating on our synthesis approach we give a short review on several other examples demonstrating the validity of the concept:

The property of *Binary DDs* (BDDs) [9] that exactly one path is sensitized by a given input combination proves advantageous for the design of circuits with low power consumption [19]. For synthesis approaches mapping on *Pass Transistor Logic* (PTL) BDDs seem to be a good starting point. First promising results on how to transform a BDD to a PTL-circuit are reported e.g. in [27, 12, 16].

Using BDDs becomes also more and more popular in the area of (multiplexer-based) *Field Programmable Gate Arrays* (FPGAs). Here, the structure of BDDs simplifies the mapping process to the FPGAs [20].

Substitution of each node of a BDD by a subcircuit realizing the corresponding decomposition leads to multiplexer-based circuits (see e.g. [2, 4, 3]). Mapping more general (and thus more compact) forms of DDs to circuits is one possibility to introduce *EXOR* gates in the synthesis process, in addition to *AND* and *OR* used in standard logic synthesis tools [22, 5, 23, 25, 26, 28]. In general, *EXOR*-based synthesis has gained renewed interest, mainly due to new technologies which make this realization more practical, e.g. FPGA technologies have made it possible to utilize universal logic blocks which do not distinguish between the types of logic used [8, 21]. This calls for more integration of *EXOR*s into mainstream synthesis.

The synthesis approach proposed in this paper is based on *Kronecker Functional DDs* (KFDDs) [14], which are a generalization of BDDs. Whereas only one *AND/OR* based decomposition type is used in BDDs two additional *AND/EXOR* based decomposition types are used in KFDDs. Circuits derived from KFDDs by the above mentioned direct substitution process have nice testability properties on the one hand, but their delay is proportional to the number of primary inputs on the other hand [5]. The delay can be reduced by a method proposed in [18, 17]. Dependencies among the nodes of a DD are analyzed and a circuit is created, which combines these dependencies by *Boolean Matrix Multiplication* (BMM). This approach inherently produces circuits with small delay. Thus, it is more appropriate for modern VLSI systems, which are mostly designed to operate at high clock frequency. Additionally, it was shown in [18] for the restricted case of BDDs that the circuits are fully testable with respect to stuck-at faults and path-delay faults as long as *2-rail* logic is used, which causes additional area overhead and requires doubling the number of primary inputs and primary outputs. In [17] the

*This work was supported by DFG grant Be 1176/8-3.

0-7695-0213-X/99 $10.00 © 1999 IEEE

construction idea from [18] was generalized to KFDDs. For the circuits derived from KFDDs 2-rail logic no longer guarantees full testability.

In this paper we develop a synthesis for testability method that, in contrast to other advanced *EXOR*-based synthesis approaches [23, 25, 26, 28], combines small delay with full testability: starting from KFDDs as in [17] circuits with small delay are constructed and at the same time full stuck-at fault testability is guaranteed by construction. This is done without using 2-rail logic and thus avoids additional area consumption. On the contrary, full testability relies on the fundamental property that irredundancy is guaranteed for the considered circuits, as long as *constant* lines are avoided. (A constant line computes the same value for every assignment at the primary inputs.) A method is developed to avoid the construction of these lines during the synthesis process by an efficient algorithm based on the graph of the KFDD. Moreover, tests for all faults can also be derived efficiently from the graph of the KFDD. Thus, it is not necessary to apply *automatic test pattern generation* (ATPG) to compute test sets for the synthesized circuits or to check for redundancies. Area and delay of the synthesized circuits can be improved by merging of *equivalent* gates. (The outputs of equivalent gates evaluate to the same values for each assignment at the primary inputs.) Altogether, our approach makes it possible to combine high speed with full testability for circuits derived from KFDDs.

The paper is structured as follows: We start with preliminaries and review the concept of KFDDs in the next section. The synthesis for testability approach as well as the methods to avoid redundancies and to derive test sets are given in Section 3. The efficiency of the proposed methods is shown by experimental results in Section 4.

2. Preliminaries

In this paper we consider circuits consisting of *primary inputs (PI)*, *primary outputs (PO)*, *inverters (NOT)*, and *AND*, *OR*, and *EXOR* gates. In some technologies, like *Field Programmable Gate Arrays* (FPGAs) [8, 21], all basic gates are realized by the same structure and there is no extra cost for *EXOR* gates compared to other gates like *AND* and *OR*. Therefore, the *EXOR* gate will be considered as a basic gate type in this paper.

We briefly review the essential definitions of *Decision Diagrams* (DDs). For more details see [9, 14].

A DD is a graph based representation of Boolean functions over the variable set $X_n = \{x_1, x_2, \ldots, x_n\}$. A non-terminal node v of a DD is labeled with a variable from X_n and has exactly two outgoing edges $\mathrm{LOW}(v)$ and $\mathrm{HIGH}(v)$ leading to nodes $low(v)$ and $high(v)$, respectively. A terminal node v is labeled with 0 or 1 and has no successors. The set of nodes is divided into $n+1$ disjoint *levels*, denoted by $level_1, level_2, \ldots, level_n, level_{n+1}$. All non-terminal nodes labeled x_i belong to $level_i$ and the terminal nodes constitute $level_{n+1}$. The number of nodes in one level $w_i = |level_i|$ is called the *width* of $level_i$.

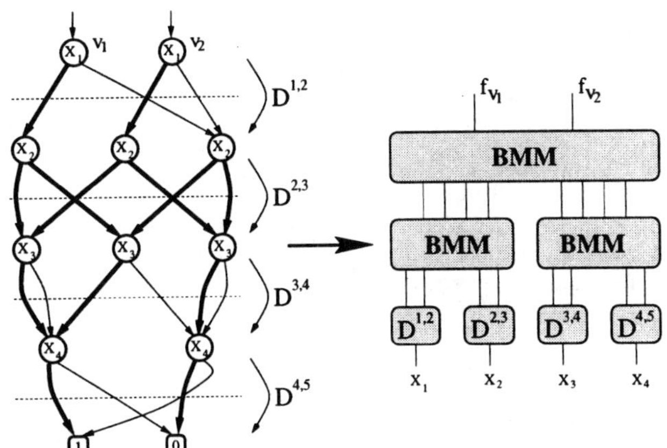

Figure 1. The concept of BMM transformation

To relate DDs to Boolean functions different *decomposition types* can be used. In a *Kronecker Functional Decision Diagram* (KFDD) *Shannon* (S), *positive Davio* (pD), or *negative Davio* (nD) decomposition can be chosen for all nodes in one level. The decomposition types for each level are given by a *Decomposition Type List* (DTL) $d := (d_1, d_2, \ldots, d_n)$, where $d_i \in \{S, pD, nD\}$.

Formally, KFDDs and their relation to Boolean functions can be defined as follows:

Definition 1 *A KFDD over X_n is given by a DD graph together with a fixed DTL $d := (d_1, \ldots, d_n)$. If v is a node at level i with label x then the function $f_v : \mathbf{B}^n \mapsto \mathbf{B}$ represented by node v is defined as:*

$$f_v = \begin{cases} \text{constant function } x & : \; i = n+1 \\ \overline{x} f_{low(v)} + x f_{high(v)} & : \; i \leq n \;\wedge\; d_i = S \\ f_{low(v)} \oplus x f_{high(v)} & : \; i \leq n \;\wedge\; d_i = pD \\ f_{low(v)} \oplus \overline{x} f_{high(v)} & : \; i \leq n \;\wedge\; d_i = nD \end{cases}$$

where $f_{low(v)}$ ($f_{high(v)}$) represents the function of node $low(v)$ ($high(v)$) and $\oplus$ denotes the EXOR operation.

In this paper we restrict to *ordered* [9] KFDDs without *complemented edges* [7]. Moreover, we consider *quasi-reduced* and *complete* KFDDs [17], i.e. isomorphic subgraphs are identified and each edge starting at a node in level l leads to a node in level $l+1$.

Example 1 *In Figure 1 a graphical representation of a quasi-reduced and complete KFDD is given. Labels are given inside the nodes. For a non-terminal node v the left (right) outgoing edge leads to $low(v)$ ($high(v)$). The KFDD in Figure 1 represents functions $f_{v_1} = x_1\overline{x}_3 \oplus x_1x_2x_3 \oplus \overline{x}_2x_3\overline{x}_4 \oplus \overline{x}_1x_2\overline{x}_3$ and $f_{v_2} = x_1\overline{x}_3 \oplus x_3\overline{x}_4 \oplus x_2x_3x_4$.*

3. The synthesis for testability approach

In the presented synthesis for testability approach a circuit description is derived from the graph of a KFDD representing the functions to be realized. We point out where care has to be taken to avoid redundant faults and develop an efficient method to incrementally derive tests for the faults

SynthesisForTestability (function $f \in B^{n,m}$)
// compute quasi-reduced and complete KFDD G for f
// without complemented edges;
$C = \emptyset$; // set of subcircuits to be combined by BMM
$T = \emptyset$; // test set
for ($l = 1, 2, ..., n$) {
    create subcircuit $C^{l,l+1}$ with an output line for each
    non-constant dependency in $D^{l,l+1}$ and derive tests $T^{l,l+1}$
    for faults at the *PI* x_l from G;
    $C = C \cup C^{l,l+1}$; $T = T \cup T^{l,l+1}$;
}
while ($|C| > 1$) {
    select $C^{k,s}$ and $C^{s,l}$; $C = C \setminus (C^{k,s} \cup C^{s,l})$;
    create BMM-circuit $C^{k,l}$ without constant lines and derive
    test set $T^{k,l}$ for faults at all newly created lines from G;
    $C = C \cup C^{k,l}$; $T = T \cup T^{k,l}$;
}
determine tests T^{out} for faults at the *POs*; $T = T \cup T^{out}$;
return (irredundant realization of function f, complete test set T);

Figure 2. Outline of the algorithm

at each newly created line. Since circuits without any redundant faults are produced there is no need for ATPG or resynthesis of the circuits to remove redundant faults. Thus, we do not only synthesize fully testable high speed circuits but we also generate test patterns for the circuits efficiently.

In the following we shortly describe the overall approach to derive a circuit description from a KFDD. Then, we discuss in detail testability aspects of the derived circuits. It is shown that the synthesis approach given in [17] can be modified to obtain fully testable circuits and complete test sets by efficient algorithms working on the graph of the KFDD.

A preview of the algorithm is given in Figure 2 to put the methods described in the following into perspective with respect to the overall synthesis for testability approach. The individual instructions will clarify in the remainder of this section.

3.1. The synthesis approach

The proposed synthesis approach is based on the fact that the function represented by a node v of a KFDD evaluates to 1 for assignment a iff an odd number of paths from v to the terminal node for function 1 are *active* for a [14]. Informally, a path from node v to v' is active for a given assignment, if the evaluation of the function represented by node v depends on the value of the subfunction rooted at v' for the given assignment.

Definition 2 *Let v be a node at level i of a KFDD with DTL d and let $a = (a_1, a_2, \ldots, a_n)$ be an assignment of Boolean values to the variables $x_1, x_2, \ldots, x_n$.*

- *Edge* LOW(v) *is active for a iff $(a_i = 0 \wedge d_i = S)$ or $d_i \in \{pD, nD\}$.*
- *Edge* HIGH(v) *is active for a iff $(a_i = 1 \wedge d_i \in \{S, pD\})$ or $(a_i = 0 \wedge d_i = nD)$.*
- *Path $\pi = \langle e_1, e_2, \ldots, e_p \rangle$ is active for a iff all edges e_i $(i = 1, 2, \ldots, p)$ are active for a.*

$d_{i,j}^{l,l+1}$	(diagram)	(diagram)	(diagram)	(diagram)
Shannon	$\overline{x}_l$	x_l	0	1
pos. Davio	1	x_l	0	$\overline{x}_l$
neg. Davio	1	$\overline{x}_l$	0	x_l

Figure 3. Dependencies in successive levels

Example 2 *In the quasi-reduced KFDD in Figure 1 the paths drawn with bold lines are active for the assignment $a = (0, 1, 1, 0)$. Thus, there are two active paths from node v_1 to the terminal node representing function 1 and one active path from node v_2, i.e. $f_{v_1}(a) = 0$ and $f_{v_2}(a) = 1$.*

3.1.1. BMM transformation

All assignments, for which an odd number of paths from node v_x^k to node v_y^l is active, are represented by the *dependency* $d_{x,y}^{k,l}$ of v_x^k upon v_y^l. Figure 3 shows how the dependency for any pair of nodes in successive levels and for any decomposition type of a KFDD is determined. The dependency matrix $D^{l,l+1}$ from level l to $l+1$ is formed by the dependencies $d_{i,j}^{l,l+1}$ for each pair of nodes $v_i^l \in level_l$ and $v_j^{l+1} \in level_{l+1}$. Note, that in each row of a dependency matrix $D^{l,l+1}$ at least all but two entries are 0 because every node has only two outgoing edges.

The next step is to define an operation $\circ$ to compose $D^{k,s}$ and $D^{s,l}$ to $D^{k,l}$. Then, it is possible to obtain the dependency matrix $D^{1,n+1}$ by iterative application of the operator $\circ$. This dependency matrix includes a representation of the functions represented by the KFDD.

The dependency matrix $D^{k,l} = D^{k,s} \circ D^{s,l}$ is defined by equation (1) for each pair of nodes $v_x^k \in level_k$ and $v_y^l \in level_l$. This equation defines the condition that node v_y^l is reached from node v_x^k by an odd number of paths (cf. Figure 4):

$$\begin{aligned} d_{x,y}^{k,l} &= d_{x,1}^{k,s} \cdot d_{1,y}^{s,l} \oplus d_{x,2}^{k,s} \cdot d_{2,y}^{s,l} \oplus \cdots \oplus d_{x,w_s}^{k,s} \cdot d_{w_s,y}^{s,l} \quad (1) \\ &= \bigoplus_{i=1}^{w_s} d_{x,i}^{k,s} \cdot d_{i,y}^{s,l} \end{aligned}$$

Since equation (1) corresponds to BMM, if the `exclusive-or` operation is substituted by the `or` operation, $\circ$ is called the BMM-operation.

Evaluating $d_{x,y}^{k,l}$ by equation (1) can result in a complex representation of a constant value. In this case a redundant line would be realized in the corresponding circuit realization. In Section 3.2 we present an efficient method based on the graph of the KFDD to detect constant dependencies. We will show that this method is sufficient to avoid any redundancies in the synthesized circuits.

3.1.2. Circuit realization

As already mentioned many entries of the dependency matrices have the constant value 0 and some may have the

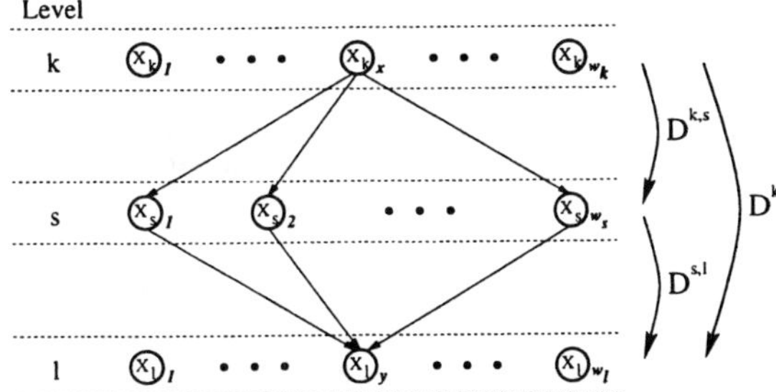

Figure 4. Composition by BMM

value 1. This causes constant values at the inputs of several gates. In the circuit realization all gates with constant inputs are recursively simplified.

The elements of the dependency matrices of successive levels $D^{l,l+1}$ are x_l, $\overline{x}_l$, 0, and 1. A subcircuit to realize such a dependency matrix consists only of the *PI* for x_l, lines, and inverters.

Equation (1) directly leads to 2-level *AND/EXOR* circuits, called *BMM-circuits*, which realize the BMM-operation. Since the BMM-operation $\circ$ is associative it is possible to combine the subcircuits as a balanced tree as shown in Figure 1. Thus, the functions represented by the KFDD can be realized by circuits with small delay.

During construction of a new subcircuit all tests for the faults in these new subcircuit can be derived from the graph of the KFDD. An efficient method is presented in the following section.

3.2. Completeness of the synthesis for testability approach

We consider *single stuck-at faults*. For a disquisition on stuck-at fault testability refer to [1].

In general, it is desirable to synthesize fully testable circuits, i.e. circuits which have no redundant faults. But, most synthesis tools do not guarantee that the resulting circuits are fully testable. The synthesis approach presented in Section 3.1 also results in circuits, which may have redundant faults. But we show that for these circuits redundant faults occur only at lines computing constant values. We present a method to avoid constant lines during the synthesis and we show that the resulting circuits have no redundant faults.

In Section 3.2.1 we show how to identify *all* lines, which would have a constant value in the circuit realization, by efficient algorithms on the graph of the KFDD during the synthesis procedure. Thus, it is possible to derive circuits without constant lines.

Furthermore, we show in Section 3.2.2 that in the synthesized circuits without constant lines no further redundant faults exist. Moreover, we present efficient methods to derive tests for the faults from the graph of the KFDD. Thus, we do not only synthesize fully testable high speed circuits but we also generate test patterns for the circuits efficiently.

In the following we frequently use an important property on active paths between two nodes in a KFDD:

Lemma 1 *Let $\mathcal{P}^{k,l}_{x,y} \neq \emptyset$ be the set of all paths from node v^k_x to v^l_y. An assignment $a = (a_k, a_{k+1}, \ldots, a_{l-1})$, for which exactly one path in $\mathcal{P}^{k,l}_{x,y}$ is active, can be computed in time $O(|V|)$, where $|V|$ is the number of nodes in the KFDD.*

Proof: The lemma can be proven formally by induction. We show how to choose the assignment and consider the complexity of the computation.

If there is at least one path $\langle \text{LOW}(v^k_x), e_{k+1}, \ldots, e_{l-1}\rangle$ in $\mathcal{P}^{k,l}_{x,y}$ then according to Definition 2 the value of a_k can be chosen such that $\text{LOW}(v^k_x)$ is active and $\text{HIGH}(v^k_x)$ is not active. Otherwise, all paths in $\mathcal{P}^{k,l}_{x,y}$ start with edge $\text{HIGH}(v^k_x)$. In this case, a_k is chosen such that $\text{HIGH}(v^k_x)$ is active. In both cases only one edge on the paths of $\mathcal{P}^{k,l}_{x,y}$ to a successor of node v^k_x is active. Then, the remaining values $a_{k+1}, a_{k+2}, \ldots, a_{l-1}$ of the assignment can be determined recursively considering the paths from this successor to v^l_y.

The set of paths $\mathcal{P}^{k,l}_{x,y}$ can be represented by marking the nodes on these paths in the graph of the KFDD. This can be achieved by a single *depth first search* (DFS) based traversal starting from node v^k_x. During this traversal at most the nodes in levels $k, k+1, \ldots, l$ have to be visited. This results in $O(|V|)$. □

3.2.1. Constant lines

The "direct" combination of two subcircuits by BMM may lead to constant lines, i.e. some lines may compute the same value for every assignment at the primary inputs. These lines would result in redundant stuck-at faults [1].

In the synthesized circuits constant lines result from constant dependencies between nodes in the KFDD. It is easy to determine all constant 0 dependencies. But constant 1 dependencies can be represented in a very complex way making it hard to recognize a tautology.

For example, the dependency of node v^1_1 upon v^5_1 in the KFDD presented in Figure 5 evaluates to $d^{1,5}_{1,1} = \overline{x}_1\overline{x}_2 \oplus (\overline{x}_1 x_2 \oplus x_1\overline{x}_2) \oplus x_1 x_2 = 1$. In the circuit realization this would lead to a redundant sa-1 fault at the line representing $d^{1,5}_{1,1}$. The standard approach would be to remove this redundant fault in a post-processing step. But identifying redundant lines in circuits may be very time consuming. Additionally, removing a redundancy can introduce new redundancies in the circuit and the test set for the original circuit is not guaranteed to be valid for the modified circuit. We will introduce a method to avoid constant lines during the synthesis resulting in circuits without redundant faults.

In the KFDD a constant 1 dependency corresponds to the situation that many paths from node v^k_x to v^l_y exist and for each assignment an odd number of these paths is active. According to Definition 2 both outgoing edges of v^k_x can only be active for a given assignment iff this node is decomposed by Davio decomposition. Then the edge $\text{LOW}(v^k_x)$ is always active and the edge $\text{HIGH}(v^k_x)$ is active for the appropriate assignment for x_k. In the following a HIGH-edge starting at a node decomposed by Davio decomposition is called a *DH-edge*.

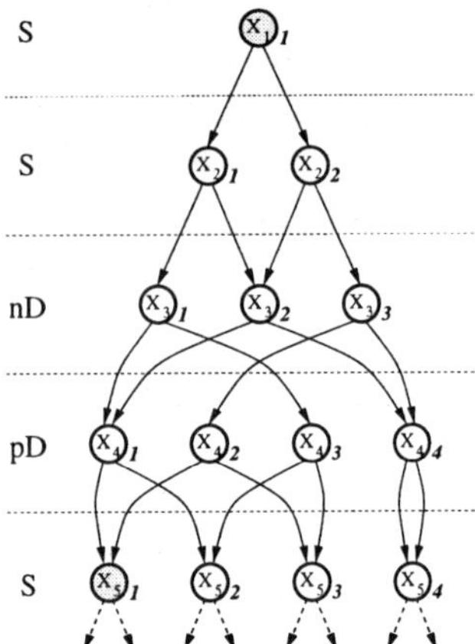

Figure 5. KFDD with $\overline{\text{DH}}$-dominator

A dominator relation between the nodes in the KFDD can be used to characterize constant 1 dependencies:

Definition 3 *Let $\mathcal{P}_x^{k,l}$ be the set of all paths from node v_x^k to any node in $level_l$. Then node $v_y^l \in level_l$ is a $\overline{\text{DH}}$-*dominator *of v_x^k iff the following holds:*

1. All paths in $\mathcal{P}_x^{k,l}$, which include no DH-edge, lead to v_y^l.
2. All paths in $\mathcal{P}_x^{k,l}$, which include at least one DH-edge, do not lead to v_y^l.

The following lemma shows that the $\overline{\text{DH}}$-dominator relation is the only situation, where an odd number of paths is active for each assignment. Thus, lines realizing constant value 1 in the synthesized circuits can be determined by checking for $\overline{\text{DH}}$-dominator relations in the KFDDs.

Lemma 2 *Node v_y^l is a $\overline{DH}$-dominator of v_x^k iff $d_{x,y}^{k,l} = 1$, i.e. $d_{x,y}^{k,l}$ is a constant 1 dependency.*

Proof: It is easy to see that exactly one path from node v_x^k to v_y^l is active for each assignment if v_y^l is a $\overline{\text{DH}}$-dominator of v_x^k. In the following, we show that at least one assignment exists, for which an even number of paths from v_x^k to v_y^l are active if v_y^l is not a $\overline{\text{DH}}$-dominator of v_x^k.

Depending on which condition of Definition 3 is violated, two cases have to be distinguished. Here we examine the case that at least one path in $\mathcal{P}_x^{k,l}$, which includes at least one DH-edge, leads to v_y^l.

Let $\text{DH}_{x,y}^{k,l}$ be the set of all paths from node v_x^k to v_y^l, which include at least one DH-edge. Analogously to Lemma 1 it can be shown that an assignment $a = (a_k, a_{k+1}, \ldots, a_{l-1})$ exists, for which exactly one path in $\text{DH}_{x,y}^{k,l}$ is active. Let π be this active path and let $\text{HIGH}(v_z^s)$ be an DH-edge on π. Now, consider assignment $\overline{a} = (a_1, a_2, \ldots, \overline{a}_s, \ldots, a_{l-1})$. We show that π is the only path which becomes inactive by switching from a to $\overline{a}$:

Since $\text{HIGH}(v_z^s)$ is a DH-edge all nodes in $level_s$ are decomposed by (positive or negative) Davio decomposition. Thus, all paths, which do not include an DH-edge starting at a node in $level_s$, are active for $\overline{a}$ iff they are active for a. All paths, which include an DH-edge starting at a node in $level_s$, cannot be active for $\overline{a}$ because the DH-edge is not active for $\overline{a}_s$. Since all these paths are in $\text{DH}_{x,y}^{k,l}$ only path π is active for a. Hence, an even number of paths are active for $\overline{a}$ if an odd number of paths are active for a and vice versa. □

A DFS based traversal can be used to check on the graph of a KFDD if a node v_x^k has a $\overline{\text{DH}}$-dominator at level l. The algorithm is based on the idea that node v_x^k cannot have a $\overline{\text{DH}}$-dominator at level l if at least one node v_z^s $(k < s \leq l)$ exists, for which the following holds: A path from v_x^k to v_z^s exists, which includes no DH-edge, and another path from v_x^k to v_z^s exists, which includes a DH-edge.

During a traversal the nodes in levels $k, k+1, \ldots, l$ have to be visited only once. Thus, we can conclude:

Lemma 3 *Each constant 1 dependency in a KFDD can be determined in time $O(|V|)$, where $|V|$ is the number of nodes in the KFDD.*

Altogether, we know that all constant dependencies can be determined efficiently. Applying the algorithm during the synthesis process allows to set the constant value in the corresponding dependency matrix and use this information during the remaining synthesis procedure. The gates already created to realize this line are recursively simplified.

Theorem 1 *It can be guaranteed in time $O(n \cdot w \cdot |V|)$ that a circuit realization derived from a KFDD has no constant lines, where $w = \max(w_1, w_2, \ldots, w_n)$ is the maximal width of any level in the KFDD.*

Proof: To combine all dependency matrices $D^{l,l+1}$ $(l = 1, 2, \ldots, n)$ only $n-1$ BMM-operations $D^{k,s} \circ D^{s,l}$ are necessary. Since the above method checks for a $\overline{\text{DH}}$-dominator of v_x^k at the entire level l and not only for one particular node, we have to apply the algorithm only w_k times for one BMM-operation. □

3.2.2. Full testability

Now, we show that the circuits without constant lines are fully testable, i.e. they have no redundant faults. Additionally, we present efficient methods to derive tests for all stuck-at faults. Thus, there is no need for ATPG.

We distinguish the following stuck-at 0 (sa-0) and stuck-at 1 (sa-1) faults in a circuit derived from a KFDD: Faults at the *PIs* and *POs* of the whole circuit; faults in the subcircuits realizing the BMM-operation; faults in the subcircuits realizing dependencies among nodes in successive levels.

We start with the analysis of testability for stuck-at faults at the *PIs* and *POs*. Note, that this lemma also holds for circuits generated by any other synthesis approach.

Lemma 4 *A test for any stuck-at fault at any PI or PO of a circuit realization can be derived from the KFDD in time $O(n)$.*

Proof: The sa-0 fault at a *PO* realizing function f can be tested with any assignment a resulting in $f(a) = 1$, i.e. any

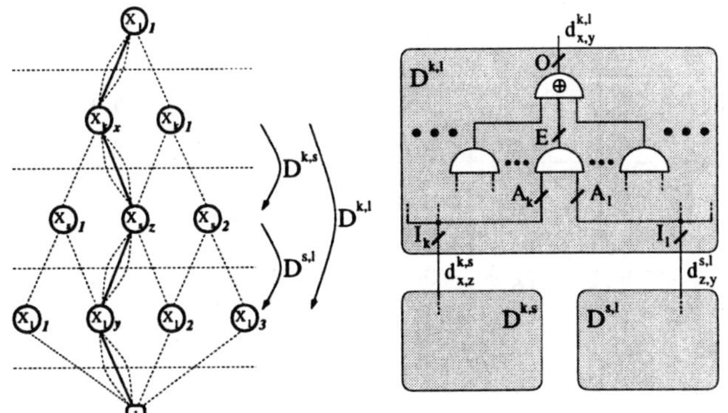

Figure 6. KFDD and BMM-circuit

satisfying assignment [14]. Similarly, the sa-1 fault can be tested with any non-satisfying assignment. These assignments can be derived from the graph of the reduced KFDD in time $O(n)$ [14].

Tests for the stuck-at faults at the *PIs* can also be derived from the graph of the KFDD in time $O(n)$. Details are omitted for shortness of the paper. □

Lemma 5 *A test for any stuck-at fault at any line in a BMM-circuit can be derived from the KFDD in time* $O(|V|)$.

Proof: We further subdivide the sa-0 and sa-1 faults in a BMM-circuit realizing $D^{k,l} = D^{k,s} \circ D^{s,l}$ according to the lines in this subcircuit (cf. the BMM-circuit in Figure 6): Inputs of the BMM-circuit for $D^{k,l}$ connected to the outputs of $D^{k,s}$ (*I_k-lines*) and inputs connected to the outputs of $D^{s,l}$ (*I_l-lines*). Inputs of the *AND* gates in $D^{k,l}$ connected to the outputs of $D^{k,s}$ (*A_k-lines*) and inputs connected to the outputs of $D^{s,l}$ (*A_l-lines*). Inputs of the *EXOR* gates (*E-lines*), which are equivalent to the outputs of the *AND* gates. Outputs of the BMM-circuit (*O-lines*), which are equivalent to the outputs of the *EXOR* gates.

To derive a test for a sa-0 fault at an I_k-line representing dependency $d^{k,s}_{x,z}$ we choose an assignment a, for which exactly one path π of the following form is active (cf. the KFDD in Figure 6): π starts in level 1, passes along nodes v^k_x, v^s_z, and any node in level l and ends at the terminal node representing the function 1. The circuit with the sa-0 fault corresponds to a circuit realization of a modified KFDD, in which the subpath of π from node v^k_x to level s is not active for assignment a, but all other paths are active for a if they are active in the original KFDD. Since π is the only path, which is active in the original KFDD and which is not active in the modified KFDD, an even number of paths are active in the original KFDD if an odd number of paths are active in the modified KFDD for a and vice versa. Hence, a is a test for the sa-0 fault. According to Lemma 1 the assignments to make each subpath of π active can be chosen in time $O(|V|)$.

A test for the sa-0 fault at a A_k-line representing dependency $d^{k,s}_{x,z}$ can be choosen analogously. In this case, the path π also has to pass along node v^l_y in level l.

Similarly, tests for the sa-0 faults at the I_l-line and A_l-line representing dependency $d^{s,l}_{z,y}$ and for the sa-1 faults at the I-lines and A-lines can be derived in time $O(|V|)$.

Faults at the E-lines are *dominated* [1] by faults at the A-lines and the same tests can be used. The O-lines are identical to I-lines of some other BMM-circuit or *POs*. □

Lemma 6 *A test for any stuck-at fault at any line in a subcircuit realizing dependencies among nodes in successive levels can be derived from the KFDD in time* $O(|V|)$.

It can easily be seen that all stuck-at faults in these subcircuits are equivalent to faults already considered in Lemma 4 and Lemma 5. Thus, tests can be derived by the methods already presented.

Theorem 2 *Tests for all stuck-at faults in a circuit realizing the dependencies of a KFDD can be derived from the KFDD in time* $O(|\mathcal{F}| \cdot |V|)$, *where* $|\mathcal{F}|$ *is the number of faults in the circuit.*

3.3. Merging equivalent gates

Dependencies between different pairs of nodes in level k and level l can be equivalent. In the circuits realizing the dependencies this would result in *equivalent gates*, i.e. gates of the same type with the same input lines. Since the outputs of equivalent gates always evaluate to the same values only one of the equivalent gates has to be realized and the output of this gate can be used for all lines originally connected to the output of any of the equivalent gates. Merging of equivalent gates can also be applied recursively.

Example 3 *In Figure 7 a KFDD and the corresponding circuit realization are given. Equivalent gates, which are not realized in the circuit, are shown by dotted lines. The lines connecting the outputs of the equivalent gates are drawn with bold lines. As it can already be seen from the structure of the KFDD the dependencies* $d^{1,3}_{1,2}$ *and* $d^{1,3}_{2,3}$ *are equivalent and the corresponding gates have to be realized only once.*

Merging of equivalent gates reduces the area and delay of the synthesized circuits. But after merging equivalent gates it cannot be guaranteed that the resulting circuits are still fully testable. This is because a stuck-at fault at the output of a merged gate corresponds to a *multiple stuck-at fault* [1] in the original circuit without merged gates whereas the test set derived by our approach is valid for single stuck-at fault only. Nevertheless, it turns out that after merging equivalent gates all faults are still detected by the test sets derived for the examined benchmark circuits.

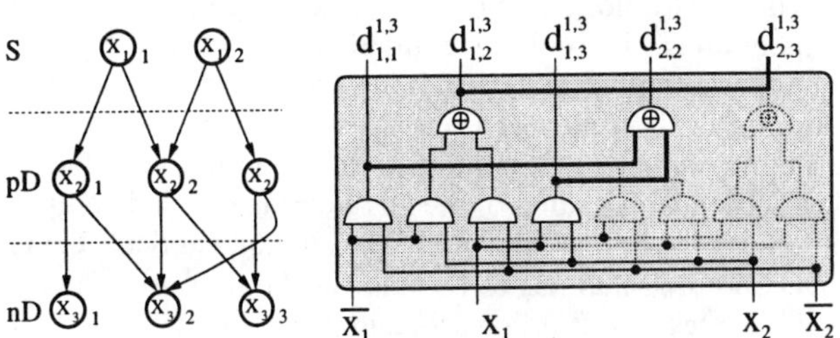

Figure 7. Merging equivalent gates

Circuit		KFDD		SFT				SFT + Merging			SIS		
name	$\#PI$	$\|G\|$	dom.	gates	delay	CPU	TPG	gates	delay	CPU	gates	delay	CPU
add6	12	48	14	117	15.2	1.4	<0.1	101	15.2	1.4	64	31.4	10.0
apex6	135	1673	1797	1068	33.2	38.8	13.6	970	31.8	37.8	775	38.8	14.4
gary	15	372	45	865	38.6	3.7	0.3	476	24.0	3.5	463	82.4	78.6
in7	26	174	100	236	17.2	2.3	0.1	191	15.6	2.3	113	21.0	2.4
rd53	5	22	6	41	10.8	0.4	<0.1	36	10.6	0.3	37	15.0	0.5
rd73	7	35	15	63	11.4	0.4	<0.1	48	10.6	0.4	61	30.0	2.4
s400	24	233	149	284	19.0	2.1	0.2	213	16.6	2.1	158	31.8	2.9
sao2	10	99	14	294	23.2	1.0	0.1	171	17.6	0.9	163	32.2	5.1
tial	14	517	45	2119	66.8	8.9	0.6	1029	30.2	8.2	229	37.8	761.9
vda	17	843	570	1663	57.8	13.8	1.8	689	28.6	12.9	509	25.2	96.5
vg2	25	159	61	367	21.4	6.5	0.1	342	22.2	6.5	102	16.6	1.8

Table 1. Results of the synthesis for testability approach and comparison

4. Experimental results

The proposed synthesis approach including the methods to avoid constant lines in the synthesized circuits and to derive tests for all stuck-at faults during the synthesis process has been implemented. Experimental results showing the efficiency of these methods are given in the following:

The first two columns of Table 1 show the name of the benchmark and the number of *PIs*, respectively.

Next, the number of nodes in the graph of the quasi-reduced KFDD are reported. The variable ordering and the DTL for the KFDD are computed similarly to the dynamic reordering methods proposed in [13]. Note, that the quality of the synthesized circuits can be further improved if more sophisticated algorithms are used to compute better variable orderings and DTLs. The next column shows the number of $\overline{\text{DH}}$-dominators in the graph of the KFDD identified during the synthesis process. This information has to be computed to guarantee that all synthesized circuits are fully testable.

The next four columns give the results obtained by our synthesis for testability approach without merging of equivalent gates, i.e. the obtained circuits are fully stuck-at fault testable. First, the size and delay of the synthesized circuits are given. We used only 2-input gates to take into account that gates with large fan-in need larger area to be realized and have longer delay than gates with small fan-in. The size of the circuits is measured as the number of 2-input gates. The delay is measured using the command *'print_delay -m unit-fanout'* of the synthesis tool SIS [24]. This takes into account the effect of large fan-out on the circuit delay.

The CPU-times on a SUN Sparc 20 are given in the next two columns. The column entitled "CPU" gives the CPU-time for the synthesis for testability process without computation of the complete test set. This time includes the construction of the KFDD, computation of the variable ordering and DTL, identification of the $\overline{\text{DH}}$-dominators, and computation of the circuit realization. The column entitled "TPG" gives the time that has to be paid for the derivation of the complete test set. It follows that up to one exception test set construction is almost for free. Since a test for each fault is generated by our approach we applied a (very simple) fault simulation based routine for compaction of the test set. The size of the obtained test sets is in the same range than test sets derived by other ATPG tools (at most three times larger than test sets derived by the command *'atpg'* of SIS).

To reduce the area overhead and to further improve the delay of the synthesized circuits we identified and merged equivalent gates during the synthesis process. The results for the circuits obtained with merging of gates are given in the next three columns. Although merging of gates does not guarantee to preserve testability, we obtain 100% fault coverage for all circuits with merged gates after simulation of the test sets computed by our approach.

The approaches presented in [26] and [28] also consider the *EXOR* gate during synthesis but no results on the delay are provided and different methods to report the size are used. Also no testability aspects are considered in [28]. Therefore, we used the synthesis tool SIS for comparison. SIS performs optimization based on *AND* and *OR* gates. The measurement of the size and the delay of the synthesized circuits is directly comparable to the circuits obtained by our method. The results for the benchmarks after optimization with SIS using script *'rugged'* are given in the last three columns of Table 1

The size of the circuits synthesized by our method is considerably smaller (40% on average) than the size obtained without merging of gates. However, it is still larger than for the SIS-circuits. Altogether 2674 gates are necessary for the circuits synthesized by SIS and our synthesis for testability approach requires 4266 gates. The delay is also improved by merging of equivalent gates. All circuits derived by our method have a delay of less than 32 ns and the average delay is 20.3 ns. On the contrary SIS derives a circuit realization with a delay of 82.4 ns for benchmark *gary* and the average delay for the SIS-circuits is 32.9 ns.

The CPU-time for the method with merging of gates is also slightly improved because less gates have to be stored in the data structure for the circuit description. The CPU-time for SIS is smaller than for our approach in two cases. But optimization by SIS needs tremendously long for circuit *tial.* Our synthesis method completes in less than 40 seconds for each benchmark. For circuit *apex6* the high CPU-time is mainly due to the variable ordering algorithm which needs relatively long time for circuits with large number of *PIs*. Altogether, our approach needs only 76.3 seconds to synthesize a fully testable circuit realization for all benchmarks, while SIS needs 976.5 seconds.

5. Conclusions

A method was presented to synthesize circuits from KFDDs combining small delay with full testability. Thereby, efficient algorithms on the graph of the KFDD were used to determine constant lines and to derive tests for all stuck-at faults in the circuit. Area and delay of the synthesized circuits was improved by merging of equivalent gates.

In its current form the approach presented in this paper relies on the fact that the whole circuit can be efficiently represented by a KFDD. To avoid a size explosion in such a monolithic KFDD approach and to make the approach applicable to larger circuits, for the future we plan to integrate a partitioning step: The circuit description first is transformed into a decomposed KFDD analogously to [12]. Then the basic synthesis approach presented in this paper can be applied to the decomposed KFDDs separately. In a recombination step the resulting subcircuits have to be merged to obtain a representation for the whole circuit.

References

[1] M. Abramovici, M. Breuer, and A. Friedman. *Digital Systems Testing and Testable Design*. Computer Science Press, 1990.

[2] P. Ashar, S. Devadas, and K. Keutzer. Gate-delay-fault testability properties of multiplexor-based networks. In *Int'l Test Conf.*, pages 887–896, 1991.

[3] P. Ashar, S. Devadas, and K. Keutzer. Path-delay-fault testability properties of multiplexor-based networks. *INTEGRATION, the VLSI Jour.*, 15(1):1–23, 1993.

[4] B. Becker. Synthesis for testability: Binary decision diagrams. In *STACS*, volume 577 of *LNCS*, pages 501–512. Springer Verlag, 1992.

[5] B. Becker and R. Drechsler. Synthesis for testability: Circuits derived from ordered Kronecker functional decision diagrams. In *European Design & Test Conf.*, page 592, 1995.

[6] B. Becker and R. Drechsler. Decision diagrams in synthesis - algorithms, applications and extensions -. In *VLSI Design Conf.*, pages 46–50, 1997.

[7] K. Brace, R. Rudell, and R. Bryant. Efficient implementation of a BDD package. In *Design Automation Conf.*, pages 40–45, 1990.

[8] S. Brown, R. Francis, J. Rose, and Z. Vranesic. *Field-Programmable Gate Arrays*. Kluwer Academic Publisher, 1992.

[9] R. Bryant. Graph - based algorithms for Boolean function manipulation. *IEEE Trans. on Comp.*, 35(8):677–691, 1986.

[10] R. Bryant. Symbolic Boolean manipulation with ordered binary decision diagrams. *ACM, Comp. Surveys*, 24:293–318, 1992.

[11] R. Bryant. Binary decision diagrams and beyond: Enabeling techniques for formal verification. In *Int'l Conf. on CAD*, pages 236–243, 1995.

[12] P. Buch, A. Narayan, A. Newton, and A. Sangiovanni-Vincentelli. Logic synthesis for large pass transistor circuits. In *Int'l Conf. on CAD*, pages 663–670, 1997.

[13] R. Drechsler and B. Becker. Dynamic minimization of OKFDDs. In *Int'l Conf. on Comp. Design*, pages 602–607, 1995.

[14] R. Drechsler and B. Becker. OKFDDs - algorithms, applications and extensions. In T. Sasao and M. Fujita, editors, *Representation of Discrete Functions*, pages 163–190. Kluwer Academic Publisher, 1996.

[15] R. Drechsler and B. Becker. Overview of decision diagrams. *IEE Proceedings*, 144:187–193, 1997.

[16] F. Ferrandi, A. Macii, E. Macii, M. Poncino, R. Scarsi, and F. Somenzi. Symbolic algorithms for layout-oriented synthesis of pass transistor logic circuits. In *Int'l Conf. on CAD*, 1998.

[17] H. Hengster, R. Drechsler, S. Eckrich, T. Pfeiffer, and B. Becker. AND/EXOR based synthesis of testable KFDD-circuits with small depth. In *Asian Test Symp.*, pages 148–154, 1996.

[18] N. Ishiura. Synthesis of multi-level logic circuits from binary decision diagrams. In *SASIMI*, pages 74–83, 1992.

[19] L. Lavagno, P. McGeer, A. Saldanha, and A. Sangiovanni-Vincentelli. Timed shannon circuits: A power-efficient design style and synthesis tool. In *Design Automation Conf.*, pages 254–260, 1995.

[20] V. Le, T. Besson, A. Abbara, D. Brasen, H. Bogushevitsh, G. Saucier, and M. Crastes. ASIC prototyping with area oriented mapping for ALTERA/FLEX devices. In *SASIMI*, pages 176–183, 1995.

[21] R. Murgai, R. Brayton, and A. Sangiovanni-Vincentelli. *Logic Synthesis for Field-Programmable Gate Arrays*. Kluwer Academic Publisher, 1995.

[22] A. Sarabi, P. Ho, K. Iravani, W. Daasch, and M. Perkowski. Minimal multi-level realization of switching functions based on Kronecker functional decision diagrams. In *Int'l Workshop on Logic Synth.*, pages P3a:1–6, 1993.

[23] T. Sasao, H. Hamachi, S. Wada, and M. Matsuura. Multilevel logic synthesis based on pseudo-Kronecker decision diagrams and local transformation. *IFIP WG 10.5 Workshop on Applications of the Reed-Muller Expansion in Circuit Design*, pages 152–160, 1995.

[24] E. Sentovich, K. Singh, L. Lavagno, C. Moon, R. Murgai, A. Saldanha, H. Savoj, P. Stephan, R. Brayton, and A. Sangiovanni-Vincentelli. SIS: A system for sequential circuit synthesis. Technical report, University of Berkeley, 1992.

[25] C. Tsai and M. Marek-Sadowska. Logic synthesis for testability. In *Great Lakes Symp. VLSI*, pages 118–121, 1996.

[26] C. Tsai and M. Marek-Sadowska. Multilevel logic synthesis for arithmetic functions. In *Design Automation Conf.*, pages 242–247, 1996.

[27] K. Yano, Y. Sasaki, K. Rikino, and K. Seki. Top-down pass-transistor logic design. *IEEE Jour. of Solid-State Circ.*, 31(6):792–803, June 1996.

[28] Y. Ye and K. Roy. Graph-based synthesis algorithms for AND/XOR networks. In *Design Automation Conf.*, pages 107–112, 1997.

Session 10A

Networking Issues II

Chair: Parmesh Ramanathan
University of Wisconsin at Madison, USA

Experimental Study of Internet Stability and Backbone Failures *

Craig Labovitz, Abha Ahuja, Farnam Jahanian
University of Michigan
Department of Electrical Engineering and Computer Science
1301 Beal Ave.
Ann Arbor, Michigan 48109-2122
{labovit, ahuja, farnam}@umich.edu

Abstract

In this paper, we describe an experimental study of Internet topological stability and the origins of failure in Internet protocol backbones. The stability of end-to-end Internet paths is dependent both on the underlying telecommunication switching system, as well as the higher level software and hardware components specific to the Internet's packet-switched forwarding and routing architecture. Although a number of earlier studies have examined failures in the public telecommunication system, little attention has been given to the characterization of Internet stability. We provide analysis of the stability of major paths between Internet Service Providers based on the experimental instrumentation of key portions of the Internet infrastructure. We describe unexpectedly high levels of path fluctuation and an aggregate low mean time between failures for individual Internet paths. We also provide a case study of the network failures observed in a large regional Internet backbone. We characterize the type, origin, frequency and duration of these failures.

1. Introduction

In a brief number of years, the Internet has evolved from a relatively obscure, experimental research and academic network to a commodity, mission-critical component of the public telecommunication infrastructure. Internet backbone failures that previously only impacted a handful of academic researchers and computer scientists, may now as easily generate millions of dollars of losses in e-commerce revenue and interrupt the daily routine of hundreds of thousands of end-users

*Supported by National Science Foundation Grant NCR-971017, and gifts from both Intel and Hewlett Packard.

The computer engineering literature contains a large body of work on both computer fault analysis, and the analysis of failures in the Public Switched Telephone Network (PSTN) [17, 1, 8]. Studies including [6, 18] have examined call blocking and call failure rates for both telephony and circuit switched data networks. Although a number of researchers have applied graph theoretic approaches to the study of faults in simulated, or theoretical networks [2], the topological stability and dynamics of deployed wide-area Internet Protocol (IP) backbones has gone virtually without formal study, with the exception of [9, 4, 3, 15].

In this paper, we describe an experimental study of Internet stability and the origins of failure in Internet protocol backbones. Unlike telephony networks, the stability of end-to-end Internet paths is dependent both on the underlying telecommunication switching system, as well as the higher level software and hardware components specific to the Internet's packet-switched forwarding, name resolution and routing architecture. Although a number of vendors provide mean-time to failure statistics for specific hardware components used in the construction of wide-area networks (e.g. power supplies, switches, etc.), estimations of the failure rates for IP backbones at a systemic level remain problematic.

The Internet exhibits a number of engineering and operational challenges distinct from those associated with telephony networks and applications. Most significantly, unlike switched telephony networks, the Internet is a conglomeration of thousands of heterogeneous dynamically packet switched IP backbones. Internet hosts segment application level streams into one or more independently routed IP datagrams. At the edge of every Internet backbone, routers forward these datagrams to the appropriate next-hop router in adjacent networks. Internet routers build next-hop routing tables based topological information exchanged in con-

0-7695-0213-X/99 $10.00

trol messages with other routers.

The most common inter-domain (exterior) routing protocol used between Internet providers is the Border Gateway Protocol (*BGP*) [5]. BGP route information includes a record of the inter-domain path the route has followed through different providers. We refer to this path record of as the route's *ASPath*.

Backbone service providers participating in the Internet core must maintain a complete map, or "*default-free*" routing table, of all globally visible network-layer addresses reachable throughout the Internet. At the boundary of each Internet Service Provider *(ISP)* backbone, peer border routers exchange reachability information to destination IP address blocks, or *prefixes*. A prefix may represent a single network, or a number of customer network addresses grouped into one larger, "supernet" advertisement. Providers commonly aggregate large numbers of customer networks into a single supernet announcement at their borders.

A number of studies, including [12, 15], have examined the stability of both Internet end-to-end paths and end-systems. We approach the analysis from a complimentary direction – by analyzing the internal routing information that gives rise to all end-to-end paths. Our study of the "default-free" routing information from the major Internet provides analysis of a supserset of all end-to-end Internet paths. For example, a single /8 route described in Section 3 may describe the availability of more than 16 million Internet end-systems. Our measurement infrastructure also allows the observation of higher frequency failures than described in [12, 15]. Overall, the significant findings of our work include:

- The Internet backbone infrastructure exhibit significantly less availability and a lower mean-time to failure than the Public Switched Telephone Network (PSTN).
- The majority of Internet backbone paths exhibit a mean-time to failure of 25 days or less, and a mean-time to repair of twenty minutes or less. Internet backbones are rerouted (either due to failure or policy changes) on the average of once every three days or less.
- Routing instability inside of an autonomous network does not exhibit the same daily and weekly cyclic trends as previously reported for routing between Inter provider backbones, suggesting that most inter-provider path failures stem from congestion collapse.
- A small fraction of network paths in the Internet contribute disproportionately to the number of long-term outages and backbone unavailability.

The remainder of this paper is organized as follows: Section 2 describes the infrastructure used in our characterization of backbone failures and the analysis of both inter and intra-domain path stability. Section 3 includes our analysis of the rate of failure and repair for both inter-domain Internet paths and intra-domain routes from a case study of a regional network. We also categorize the origins of failures during a one year study of this regional network. Finally, we compare the frequency and temporal properties of BGP and intra-domain routing data.

2. Methodology

Our analysis in this paper focuses on two categories of Internet failures: faults in the connections between service provider backbones, and failures occurring within provider backbones. Our data is based both on experimental measurements of deployed wide-area networks and data obtained from the operational records of a large regional Internet service provider. We use a number of tools developed by the MRT [14] and IPMA [7] projects for the collection, analysis and post-processing of our data.

We base our analysis of failures between service providers on data recorded by a central route collection probe, named RouteViews, located on the University of Michigan campus. We configured RouteViews to participate in remote BGP peering sessions with a number of cooperating regional and national backbone providers. Each of these backbone routers provided RouteViews with a continuous stream of BGP updates on the current state of the provider's default-free routing table between January 1997 and November 1998.

We base our analysis of intra-domain failures on a case study of a medium size regional network. The regional backbone interconnects educational and commercial customers in 132 cities via high speed serial lines and frame-relay links at speeds up to OC3 (155 MB). The network includes 33 backbone routers connected via multiple paths with links to several hundred customer routers. We use both recorded routing data and failure logs from this provider to categorize the type and frequency of different sources of failure.

We use a single provider case study due to the significant challenges of a more complete survey of internal failures across multiple providers. Factors limiting a more complete survey include the scale of the Internet, difficulties in the correlation of failure data amongst providers with different backbone infrastructure and fault monitoring practices, and the highly proprietary nature with which most provider's regard their failure data. As Paxson observed in [16], no single backbone, or snapshot of the Internet provides a valid representation of the heterogeneous and rapidly changing Internet. As a result, we do not claim our case study is representative of all providers. Instead, our focus in this paper is on comparing a source of intra-domain failure data with faults observed in the connectivity between providers.

For our intra-domain analysis, we first study the frequency and duration of failures using the operational monitoring logs from our case study provider. The monitoring system used by this provider includes a centralized network management station (CNMS) which periodically monitors all of router interfaces throughout the network using SNMP queries and the transmission/receipt of "ping" packets. We base our analysis on twelve months of CNMS logs from November 1997 to November 1998.

Our characterization of network failures used data culled from the trouble ticket tracking system managed by our case study provider's Network Operations Center (NOC). The NOC staff uses the trouble ticket information for tracking, troubleshooting and coordinating the resolution of detected network failures. During the course of normal operations, network operations staff manually create trouble tickets upon either the automated detection of a fault by the CNMS, or upon receipt of customer complaints.

3. Analysis

We divide our analysis in this section into three areas. We first examine the frequency and duration of failures observed in inter-provider backbone paths. Repeating the standard method of analysis used in computer systems, we examine the availability, mean-time to failure, and mean-time to repair for Internet routes. In the second subsection of our analysis, we explore the source, frequency and duration of internal backbone failures using the failure logs and routing data from our case-study provider. Finally, we discuss the relationship between the frequency of intra-domain failures and the behavior of inter-domain routing changes.

3.1. Analysis of Inter-domain Path Stability

In this section, we first turn our attention to failures observed in the inter-domain routing paths exchanged between core backbone providers. Specifically, we examine nine months of default-free BGP routing information recorded from three remote Internet Service Provider (*ISP*) backbone routers (ISP1, ISP2, ISP3). As noted in Section 2, the three providers represent a spectrum of different ISP sizes, network architecture and underlying transmission technology.

Our logs of routings updates from the three ISP routers provide BGP transition information about both the provider's own customer and transit routes, as well as routes received from other ISPs.

In our analysis, we examine the routing activity of each ISP independently. By this, we mean that if an ISP lacks a route to a given prefix destination, we consider that destination unreachable from that ISP even if other providers maintain a route to that destination. We define an inter-domain *fault* as the loss of an ISP's route to a previously reachable prefix.

In the taxonomy below, we distinguish between three classes of BGP routing table events observed from each provider:

Route Failure: A route is explicitly withdrawn and no alternative path to the prefix destination, or to a less specific aggregate network address, is available.

Route Repair: A previously failed route to a network prefix is announced as reachable. This also may include the addition of new customer routes, or the announcement of secondary, backup paths due to policy or network failures.

Route Fail-Over: A route is implicitly withdrawn and replaced by an alternative route with differing next-hop or ASPath attributes to the prefix destination. Route Fail-over represents the rerouting of traffic to a given prefix destination after a network failure. Recall from Section 1 that the ASPath represents the routing path of the prefix through different inter-connected autonomous systems.

Inter-domain Route Failures generally reflect faults in the connectivity between providers, or the internal loss of a provider's connectivity to multiple customer routers. Lacking internal knowledge of the policies and design of provider backbones, we cannot always distinguish between "legitimate" network failures, and certain classes of policy changes, consolidation amongst provider networks, or the migration of customers between providers.

We first look at the availability of inter-domain routes. We define the *availability* of a given default-free route from a provider as the period of time that a path to the network destination, or a less specific prefix, was present in the provider's routing table. We include less specific prefixes in our definition since as described in Section 1, provider's regularly aggregate multiple more

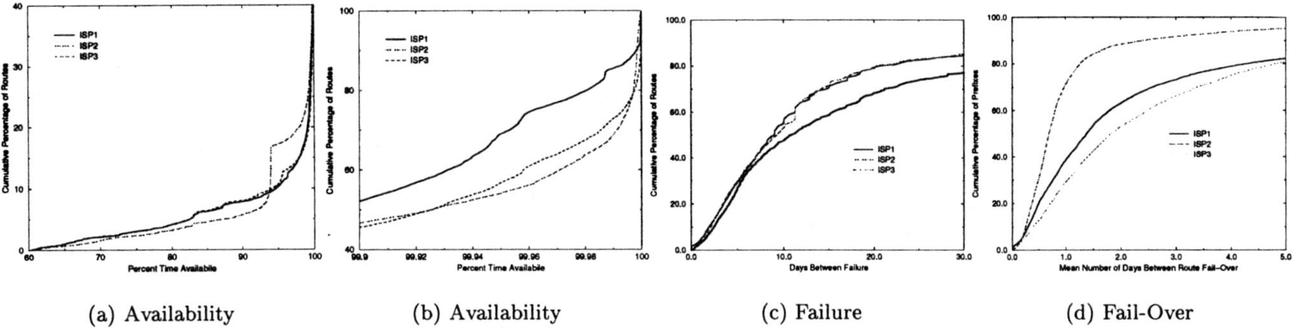

(a) Availability (b) Availability (c) Failure (d) Fail-Over

Figure 1. Cumulative distribution of the route availability of three service providers.

specific network addresses into a single supernet advertisement. We make several modifications to our data, described in [11], to more accurately reflect outages.

The graphs in Figure 1(a)(b) show the cumulative percentage of time default-free routes were available from each provider during our ten month study. The horizontal axis shows the percent time available; the vertical shows the cumulative percentage of routes with such availability. Both graphs in Figure 1(a)(b) represent the same data, but Figure 1(b) provides an expanded view of route availability above 99.9 percent.

A recent study study [8] found that the PSTN averaged an availability rate better than 99.999 percent during a one year period. From the graph in Figure 1(b), we see that the majority of Internet routes (65 percent) from all three providers exhibited an order of magnitude less availability. Only between 30 and 35 percent of routes from ISP3 and ISP2, and 25 percent of routes from ISP1 had availability higher that 99.99 percent of study period. Further, a significant 10 percent of the routes from all three providers exhibited under 95 percent availability. The availability of the three providers exhibit similar curves for most of Figure 1(a). The step in the curve for ISP3 at 95 percent availability represents a multi-hour loss of inter-provider connectivity due to an outage described in [11]. ISP1 exhibits significant less availability above 99.9 than ISP2 and ISP3 as evinced by the higher curve in Figure 1(b).

In addition to availability, we examine the rate of failure and fail-over in inter-domain paths. We define an inter-domain route *failure* as the loss of a previously available routing table path to a given network, or a less specific, prefix destination. A *fail-over* of a route represents a change in the inter-domain path (ASPath or NextHop) reachability of that route.

The two graphs in Figure 1 show the cumulative distribution of the mean number of days between route failures (c), and route fail-over (d) for routes from ISP1, ISP2 and ISP3. The horizontal axes represent the mean number of days between failures/fail-over; the vertical axes show the cumulative proportion of the ISP's routing table entries for all such events. Examining the graph in Figure 1(c), we see that the majority of routes (greater than 50 percent) from all three providers exhibit a mean-time to failure of fifteen days or more. By the end of thirty days, the majority (75 percent) of routes from all three providers had failed at least once. The distribution graphs for ISP1, ISP2 and ISP2 share a similar curve, with ISP1 exhibiting a slightly lower cumulative MTTF curve starting at ten days.

As noted earlier, most Internet providers maintain multiple, redundant connections to other providers. In the case of a single link or provider failure, routers will dynamically reroute around faults. Since not all Internet routes enjoy redundant connectivity, we focus our analysis on fail-over by modifying the vertical axis in Figure 1(d) to reflect a cumulative subset of interdomain routes – only those routes that exhibit multiple paths. Examining this graph, we see that majority of routes with redundant paths fail-over within two days. Further, only 20 percent of these routes from ISP1 and ISP3, and five percent from ISP2 do not fail over within five days. Both these mean-time to failure and fail-over results suggest a slightly higher incidence of failure in today's Internet than described in Paxson's 1994 study [15] which found 2/3's of Internet paths persisted for either days or weeks.

The graph in Figure 2(a) shows the cumulative distribution of the mean number of minutes between a route failure and repair. The horizontal axis shows the average time a route was unavailable; the vertical shows the cumulative percentage of all routes experiencing such an event. Since default-free routes announced by each ISP include routes transiting other providers, the mean-time to repair reflects both the time for fault resolution as well as the propagation delay of routing information through the Internet.

From Figure 2(a), we see that 40 percent of failures are repaired in under ten minutes. The majority (60 percent) are resolved within a half hour. After thirty minutes, the cumulative MTTR curves for all three providers demonstrates a heavy-tailed distribution, with slow asymptotic growth towards 100 percent. We can see the relationship between availability, MTTF and MTTR by examining the data for ISP1. The MTTF curve for ISP1 rose faster than ISP2 and ISP3 in Figure 1(c), but at a slower rate in the Figure 2(a) MTTR graph. The lower average mean-time to failure, but slower mean-time to repair contributes to ISP1's overall lower availability in Figure 1(a).

Overall, analysis of our MTTR data agrees with our qualitative findings in Section 3.2 that repairs not resolved within an hour usually represent more serious outages requiring significant engineering effort for problem diagnosis, or the replacement of faulty hardware. Our data also corroborates Paxson's findings [15] that most Internet outages are short-lived – lasting on the order seconds or minutes.

The above mean-time to repair data provides an indication of the average unavailability of a route, but it does not provide insight into the overall distribution of outage durations. In Figure 2(b) we show the cumulative distribution of outage durations for all three providers. The horizontal axis represents the duration of outages in hours on a logarithmic scale; the vertical axis represents the cumulative percentage of outages lasting the given duration or less. During the course of our study, we observed over six million outages. From Figure 2(b), we see that only 25 to 35 percent of outages from the three providers are repaired in under an hour. This data is in marked contrast to Figure 2(a) where the average repair time for a route failure is under a half hour. Analysis of the relationship between our failure duration data with the graph Figure 2(a) indicates that a small number of routes disproportionately contribute to overall unavailability. Or, more specifically, forty percent of routes exhibit multiple failures lasting between one hour and several days during our study. This result agrees with our findings in [9] that a small fraction routes are responsible for the majority of network instability.

3.2. Analysis of Intra-Domain Network Stability

In the last section, we examined the stability of inter-domain paths. We now focus on intra-domain failures using a case study of a regional provide described in Section 1. Intra-domain routing serves as the basis for much of the information exchanged in inter-domain routing and analysis of the faults associated with an intra-domain network also provides insight into failures in other areas of the Internet.

The graph in figure 2(c) shows the cumulative distribution of the mean-time to failure for two categories of router interfaces: backbone nodes and customer-sites. The horizontal axis represents the mean-time between interface failures; the vertical axis shows the cumulative percentage of interface failures at each mean-time. We define *backbone nodes* as router interfaces connected to other backbone routers via multiple physical paths. *Customer connections* represent router interfaces attached to the regional backbone via a single physical connection. As critical elements of the network infrastructure, backbone routers are closely monitored, and housed in telco-grade facilities with redundant power. In contrast, routers at customers nodes often are maintained under less ideal physical conditions and administration.

From Figure 2(c), we see that 40 percent of all interfaces experienced some failure within an average of 40 days, and five percent failed within a mean time of five days. Overall, the majority of interfaces (more than 50 percent) exhibit a mean-time to failure of forty days or more. This differs from our earlier analysis of BGP paths, which found the majority of inter-domain failures occur within 30 days. The curve of the better equipped and management backbone interfaces exhibits significantly lower MTTF than customer routers.

The step discontinuities in Figure 2(c) represent both the relationship between interfaces and an artifact of our data collection architecture. Specifically, interface failures tend to occur in groups due to power, maintenance and related outages simultaneously affecting all interfaces on a router. In addition, rare simultaneous failures of multiple redundant paths through the network may lead to a network partition and a disconnect between multiple router interfaces and the central data collection host.

The graph in Figure 2(d) shows the cumulative mean-time to repair for the two different categories of router interfaces described earlier. The horizontal axis shows the mean number of minutes to repair; the vertical shows the cumulative percentage of all interfaces averaging such repair duration. From the graph, we see that 80 percent of all failures are resolved in un-

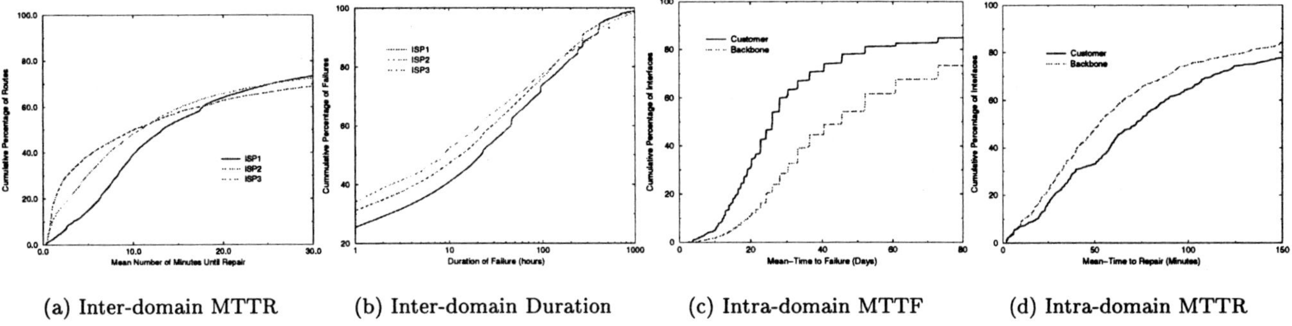

(a) Inter-domain MTTR (b) Inter-domain Duration (c) Intra-domain MTTF (d) Intra-domain MTTR

Figure 2. Mean time to repair and mean failure duration for inter and intra-domain routes.

der two hours. Further analysis of the data indicates that outages lasting longer than two hours usually represent long-term (several hours) outages which require significant engineering effort for problem diagnosis or the replacement of hardware or circuits.

3.3. Network Failures

In this section, we categorize the origins of the hardware, software and operational faults that gave rise to the intra and inter-domain failures described in the previous two subsections. As discussed in Section 2, we base our characterization of network failures on the operational trouble logs of a regional ISP.

Figure 3(a) shows a breakdown of all the outages recorded during our one-year case study (November 1997 to November 1998). As the diagnosis and categorization of outages remains an inexact science, several of the categories overlap and a few include some degree of ambiguity. The largest category at 16.2 percent, maintenance, refers to either a scheduled, or unscheduled emergency upgrade of software or hardware, or router configuration changes. A power outage (16 percent) includes either loss of power to a router, or a power failure in a PSTN facility which impacts one or more ISP circuits. Fiber or carrier failures (15.3 percent) usually result from a severed fiber optics link or a PSTN facility problem. Unreachable includes intermittent failures which mysteriously resolve themselves before an engineer investigates the outages. These unreachable outages usually result from PSTN maintenance or failures. A hardware problem (9 percent) includes a router, switch or power supply failure. Congestion refers to sluggishness, or poor connectivity between sites and usually represents link/router congestion on links, or router software configuration errors. A routing problem designation reflects errors with the configuration or interaction of routing protocols (OSPF, BGP, RIP). Most routing problems stem from human error and misconfiguration of equipment. Finally, the software problem category includes router software bugs.

From Figure 3, we see that majority of outages stem from maintenance, power outages and PSTN failures. Specifically, over 15 percent of all outages were due to sources outside of the provider's immediate control, including carrier and frame-relay failures. These percentages reiterate the observation in Section 1 that the reliability of IP backbones shares a significant dependence with the reliability of the underlying PSTN infrastructure. Approximately 16 percent of the outages were due to power outages. Power failures generally affect only customer routers which lack the same redundant power supplies as housed in backbone router facilities. Another 16 percent of the outages were planned maintenance outages. Overall, we note that most of these observed outages were not specifically related to regional IP backbone infrastructure (e.g. routers and software).

Further analysis of the data represented in Figure 3(a) shows the majority of outages were associated with individual customer sites rather than backbone nodes. This result is somewhat intuitive as backbone nodes tend to have backup power (UPS), more experienced engineers and controlled maintenance and upgrades.

Figure 3(b) shows number of interfaces, minutes down, and average number of interface failures for each backbone router monitored during our case study. From the table, we see that the overall uptime for all backbone routers averaged above 99.0 percent for the year. Further analysis of the raw data shows that these

Outage Category	Number of Occurrences	Percentage
Maintenance	272	16.2
Power Outage	270	16
Fiber Cut/Circuit/Carrier Problem	261	15.3
Unreachable	215	12.6
Hardware problem	154	9
Interface down	105	6.2
Routing Problems	104	6.1
Miscellaneous	86	5.9
Unknown/Undetermined/No problem	32	5.6
Congestion/Sluggish	65	4.6
Malicious Attack	26	1.5
Software problem	23	1.3

(a) Failure Categories

Router Name	# Interfaces	Percent Time Available	Average Number of Interface Failures	Average Minutes Down per Interface
bspop	14	99.74	17.79	1360.79
cmu	137	99.12	7.52	776.01
flint	16	99.88	7.94	625.5
flpop	20	99.9	4.45	506.7
grpop	49	99.67	11.8	1733.18
ironmt	9	99.82	18.33	955.11
jackson	19	99.82	9.26	926
lssu	3	99.69	68.33	1635.33
ltupop	36	99.81	10	1014.97
michnet1	17	99.96	3.76	210.65
michnet5	142	99.82	10.23	964.87
msu	49	99.87	8.55	686.8
mtu	15	99.71	15.93	1538.67
muskpop	43	99.7	12.77	1572.19
nmu	12	99.85	24.75	788.08
oakland	44	99.82	14.57	932.89
oakland3	8	99.9	10.88	520.38
saginaw	24	99.96	4.63	213.33
tcity	20	99.68	11.4	1697.45
umd	19	99.79	8.26	1098.74
wmu	60	99.88	7.55	617.58
wsu	36	99.84	10.69	824.75
wsu1	23	99.85	9.39	767.17

(b) Node Failures

Figure 3. Source and frequency of regional backbone failures.

averages are biased towards less availability by individual interfaces which exhibit a disproportionate number of failures. Specifically, the failure logs reveal a number of persistent circuit or hardware faults which repeatedly disrupt service on a given interface.

Since the trouble ticket system used in our study does not maintain outage duration statistics, we could not relate the duration of outages in Figure 3(b) with the source of outages in Figure 3(a). However, discussions with operations staff and empirical observations indicate that the duration of the most backbone outages tends be small – on the order of several minutes. Customer outages generally persist a bit longer – on the order of several hours. Specifically, most power outages and hardware failures tend to be resolved in four hours or less, and faults stemming from routing problems usually last under two hours. Carrier problems tend to be harder to estimate as the length of time down is independent of the regional provider.

3.4. Frequency

In this section, we examine frequency components of intra and inter-domain routing data. For this analysis, we define a routing update's *frequency* as the inverse of the inter-arrival time between routing updates; a high frequency corresponds to a short inter-arrival time. Other work has been able to capture the lower frequencies through both routing table snapshots [4] and end-to-end techniques [15]. Our measurement apparatus allowed a unique opportunity to examine the high frequency components of network failures.

Normally one would expect an exponential distribution for the inter-arrival time of routing updates, as they might reflect exogenous events, such as power outages, fiber cuts and other natural and human events. In our earlier analysis [9], we found a strong correlation between North American network usage and the level of inter-domain routing information at the major IXPs. Specifically, the graph of inter-domain route failures exhibited the same bell curve centered on 1pm EST as shown on most graphs of network traffic volume [11].

In this section, we repeat the analysis in [9] to identify frequency components in the inter-arrival internal routing updates exchanged within the backbone of our case study provider. We generated a correlogram, shown in [11], of both datasets generated by a traditional fast Fourier transform (FFT) of the autocorrelation function of the data. The graph of BGP data exhibits significant frequencies at seven days, and 24 hours. In marked contrast, the correlogram of intradomain routing information does not exhibit any significant frequency components. The absence of intradomain frequency components suggests much of BGP instability stems from a different class of failures than the hardware and software faults we described in the previous section. In particular, the lack frequency components supports the supposition in [9, 13] that significant levels BGP instability stem from congestion collapse.

As a mechanism for the detection of link-level or host failures, BGP uses the periodic TCP exchange of incremental routing updates and KeepAlives to test and maintain the peering session. If KeepAlives or routing updates are not received within a bounded time period (the router's Hold Timer), the peering session is severed, causing the withdrawal of all the peer's routes

– making them unreachable through the autonomous system and its downstream networks.

Because TCP end-stations adapt to network congestion by reducing the amount of available bandwidth, KeepAlive packets may be delayed during periods of peak network usage. Under these conditions, a KeepAlive may not be received before the remote BGP hold timer expires. This would cause peering sessions to fail at precisely those times when network load was greatest. The effect is most pronounced in internal BGP communication.

4. Conclusion

Our analysis confirms the widely held belief that the Internet exhibits significantly less availability and reliability than the telephony network. The detection of Internet failures is often far less problematic than identification of the failures' origins. Our characterization and analysis of backbone faults was hampered by the lack of standard fault reporting and measurement mechanisms across providers. A number of Internet engineering associations have called for the development of a uniform trouble ticket system schema and mechanisms for inter-provider sharing of the trouble ticket data. Based on our limited case-study of a regional provider, we found that most faults stemmed hardware and software not unique to the Internet's routing infrastructure.

In contrast to our analysis of the routing between providers, we did not find daily or weekly frequency components in our case-study of the internal routing of a regional provider. This absence supports our earlier findings [13] that Internet failures may stem from congestion collapse. Validation of this theory and correlation of faults amongst multiple providers remains an area for future research.

References

[1] R. Becker, L. Clark, D. Lambert, "Events Defined by Duration and Severity with an Application to Network Reliability", Technometrics, 1998.

[2] K. Calvert, M.B. Doar, E.W. Zegura, "Modeling Internet Topology," in *IEEE Communications Magazine*, June 1997.

[3] B. Chinoy, "Dynamics of Internet Routing Information," in *Proceedings of ACM SIGCOMM '93*, pp. 45-52, September 1993.

[4] R. Govindan and A. Reddy, "An Analysis of Inter-Domain Topology and Route Stability," in *Proceedings of the IEEE INFOCOM '97*, Kobe, Japan. April 1997.

[5] B. Halabi, "Internet Routing Architectures." New Riders Publishing, Indianapolis, 1997.

[6] Inverse Network Technology home page, http://www.inverse.net.

[7] Internet Performance Measurement and Analysis project (IPMA), http://www.merit.edu/ipma.

[8] R. Kuhn, "Sources of Failure in the Public Switched Telephone Network." IEEE Computer, Vol. 30, No. 4, April 1997.

[9] C. Labovitz, G.R. Malan, and F. Jahanian, "Internet Routing Instability," in *Proceedings of the ACM SIGCOMM '97*, Cannes, France, August, 1997.

[10] C. Labovitz, G.R. Malan, and F. Jahaniam, "Origins of Pathological Internet Routing Instability," in *Proceedings of the IEEE INFOCOM '98*, New York, March 1999.

[11] C. Labovitz, A. Ahuja, F. Jahanian, "Experimental Study of Internet Stability and Wide-Area Backbone Failures," University of Michigan CSE-TR-382-98, November 1998.

[12] D. Long, A. Muir, R. Golding, "A Longitudinal Survey of Internet Host Reliability," Hewlett Packard Technical Report, HPL-CCD-95-4, February, 1995.

[13] G.R. Malan, and F. Jahanian, "An Extensible Probe Architecture for Network Protocol Performance Measurement," in *Proceedings of the ACM SIGCOMM '98*, Vancouver, Canada, September 1998.

[14] Multi-Threaded Routing Toolkit, National Science Foundation Project (NCR-9318902).

[15] V. Paxson, "End-to-End Routing Behavior in the Internet," in *Proceedings of the ACM SIGCOMM '96*, Stanford, C.A., August 1996.

[16] V. Paxson, S. Floyd, "Why We Don't Know How to Simulate the Internet," in *Proceedings of the 1997 Winter Simulation Conference*," Atlanta, GA, 1997.

[17] D. Pradhan, "Fault Tolerant Computer System Design", Prentice Hall, New Jersey, 1996.

[18] Vital Signs, home page http://www.vitalsigns.com

A Columbus' Egg Idea for CAN Media Redundancy*

José Rufino
IST-UTL†
ruf@digitais.ist.utl.pt

Paulo Veríssimo
FC/UL‡
pjv@di.fc.ul.pt

Guilherme Arroz
IST-UTL
pcegsa@alfa.ist.utl.pt

Abstract

Network media redundancy is a clean and effective way of achieving high levels of reliability against temporary medium faults and availability in the presence of permanent faults. This is specially true of critical control applications such as those supported by the Controller Area Network (CAN). In our endeavor to provide CAN with media redundancy we ended-up devising a scheme which is extraordinarily simpler than previous approaches known for CAN or other LANs and field-buses.

1 Introduction

Continuity of service and determinism in message transmission delays are two fundamental requirements of fault-tolerant real-time applications. Though reliable real-time protocols can provide such guarantees in the presence of sporadic transient faults, they are helpless when faced with aggressive omission failure bursts or even permanent failure of the medium. There is no solution but using some form of space redundancy. Safety-critical applications would resort to full space-redundant network architectures, replicating media and attachment controllers, providing a broad coverage of faults and glitch-free communication [4, 6], at a high design and implementation cost. An alternative approach is simple media redundancy, such as it exists off-the-shelf in some standard LANs, or as developed in Delta-4 [11]. In these architectures, space redundancy is restricted to the physical - electrical signaling at the medium - level, which may lead to simpler and thus less expensive solutions. With the appropriate design techniques, the timeliness, reliability and accessibility guarantees achieved, satisfy a wide spectrum of fault-tolerant real-time applications, with exception of those with very stringent safety and timeliness requirements [16]. Cost-effectiveness and shorter design cycles are, among others, strong arguments in favor of using off-the-shelf LAN and field-bus technologies in the design of fault-tolerant distributed systems.

Field-buses are in essence a technology whose area of application requires continuity of service. They are widely used to convey information from and to the boundaries of the system: the sensors and the actuators. Systems intended for real-world interfacing are specially sensitive to the availability of the network infrastructure, that we address in this paper, in the context of the Controller Area Network (CAN) [5]. CAN is a low-cost field-bus that is getting more and more attractive for areas as diverse as shop-floor control, robotics, automotive or avionics. CAN is traditionally viewed as a robust field-bus. Together with protocol level extensive error checking capabilities, the use of differential two-wire communication medium and the use of physical level fault-tolerant mechanisms allows CAN to operate in the presence of one-wire failures in the network cabling [5]. However, these standard fault-tolerant mechanisms are helpless in the provision of CAN non-stop operation in harsher conditions, such as the simultaneous interruption of both wires in the network cabling.

The work presented here is part of a broader effort aiming at designing an embedded fault-tolerant distributed system around CAN. In previous works, regarding the definition of CAN fault-tolerant communication and time services [13, 12], we have assumed a system model where network components only temporarily refrain from providing service [17]. In this paper we substantiate that assumption by defining a CAN-based network infrastructure resilient to the permanent failure of physical layer components, such as medium partitions.

CAN-based redundant architectures using replicated buses have been identified as being too costly, when compared with alternative designs based on ring topologies [9]. An existing commercial redundant CAN solution implements a self-healing ring/bus architecture [9], but does not solve

---

* *Columbus' egg*: popular expression, with origin in a story about the navigator Christopher Columbus, that is widely used to refer an extremely simple solution to a difficult problem, hard to find, but that once known, looks trivial and even obvious. The navigator, in front of a meeting of lords, demonstrated how to make an egg stand on end... by cracking its shell in one of the poles!

† Instituto Superior Técnico - Universidade Técnica de Lisboa, Avenida Rovisco Pais, 1049-001 Lisboa, Portugal. Tel: +351-1-8418397/99 - Fax: +351-1-8417499. NavIST Group CAN WWW Page - http://pandora.ist.utl.pt/CAN.

‡ Faculdade de Ciências da Universidade de Lisboa, Campo Grande - Bloco C5, 1700 Lisboa, Portugal. Tel: +351-1-7500087 - Fax: +351-1-7500084. Navigators Home Page: http://www.navigators.di.fc.ul.pt.

0-7695-0213-X/99 $10.00 © 1999 IEEE

the problem of CAN continuity of service efficiently: ring reconfiguration takes time and meanwhile the network is partitioned.

In this paper, we do a systemic analysis of how bus redundancy mechanisms can be implemented in CAN. We started by studying the adaptation of techniques we had developed with success for LANs [15, 8]. Unexpectedly, we discovered that these techniques would become extremely complex to apply in the setting of CAN. Moreover, in this process we ended-up with a Columbus' egg idea: an extremely simple mechanism that makes bus-based redundancy easy to implement in CAN using off-the-shelf components.

The following discussion assumes the reader to be fairly familiar with CAN operation. In any case, we forward the reader to the relevant standard documents [5, 3], for details about the CAN protocol.

2 Related Work

The LAN-based media redundant architectures described in [15, 8] rely on the replication of the physical path – transmission medium and medium interfaces – used by the MAC[1] entities to communicate (channel). It is assumed: channel redundancy is used, through replicated media (physical and medium layers), but only one MAC layer; each transmission medium replica is routed differently, being reasonable to consider failures in different media as independent; all media are active, i.e. every bit issued from the MAC layer is transmitted simultaneously on all media.

In the implementation of LAN media redundancy [15, 8], one medium is selected at a time, for frame reception. A *frame-wise* strategy takes a decision at the start of each frame reception, based on the quality of the signals currently received from each medium. A complementary selection strategy, uses an indication on whether or not network errors occur during the reception of one frame, to choose the medium from which the next frame should be received. A *frame-wise* decision always supersedes an *error-based* selection, unless media switching is locked by fault treatment procedures, i.e measures to ensure the fault is passivated.

A similar approach can be found in the standard specification of some field-buses, such as WorldFIP [2] and PROFIBUS. An alternative dual-ring architecture is foreseen in PROFIBUS, when using fiber optics media [14]. In LONWORKS, a self-healing bus/ring architecture is specified [7]: each end of the bus terminates in an *intelligent switch* which is responsible for network reconfiguration in the event of an open-wiring fault in the network cabling. Since the switch is not replicated, it is a single-point of failure. The MIL-Std-1553 specifies a dual redundant bus option, but it also has a single-point of failure in a centralized bus controller: only one bus is active at a time with the bus controller initiating all message transfers.

[1] Medium Access Control.

3 CAN Physical Level Fault-Tolerance

In CAN, bus signaling takes one out of two possible representations: *recessive*, otherwise the state of an idle bus, occurs when all competing nodes send recessive bits; *dominant*, which always overwrites a recessive value. This behavior, together with the uniqueness of frame identifiers, is exploited for bus arbitration. A *carrier sense multi-access with deterministic collision resolution* policy is used: several nodes may jump on the bus at the same time, but while transmitting the frame identifier each node monitors the bus; for every bit, if the transmitted bit is recessive and a dominant value is monitored, the node gives up transmitting and starts to receive incoming data. Frames that have lost arbitration or have been destroyed by errors are automatically scheduled for retransmission.

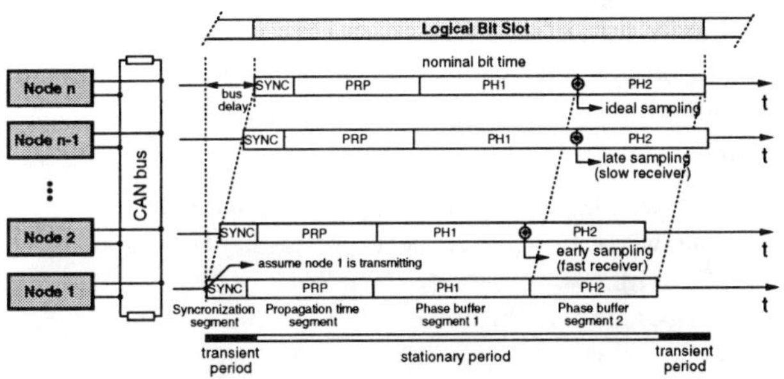

Figure 1. Sketch of CAN bus operation timing

Synchronization of receiver circuitry with the incoming bit stream is performed in CAN through a complex process that we summarize next. The nominal bit time is divided in four segments (Figure 1). The *propagation time segment* (PRP) accounts for physical level delays: the bus propagation time and the transmitter/receiver delays at the medium interface devices. The idea is to give enough time for signal stabilization along the bus before nodes perform sampling, which occurs at the end of the PH1 segment (Figure 1). Bus signal transitions are expected to lie within the *synchronization segment* (SYNC). Deviations from this ideal behavior produce phase errors which are compensated for by using one of the two *phase segments* as elastic buffers: the PH1 segment is lengthened in fast receivers, upon the detection of a phase error; slow receivers compensate phase errors by shortening PH2. Further details on bit synchronization can be found in [5].

With exception of the transient periods at bit boundaries, a single bit is present in the CAN bus line at a time. As a consequence, all nodes get the same bit – with regard the

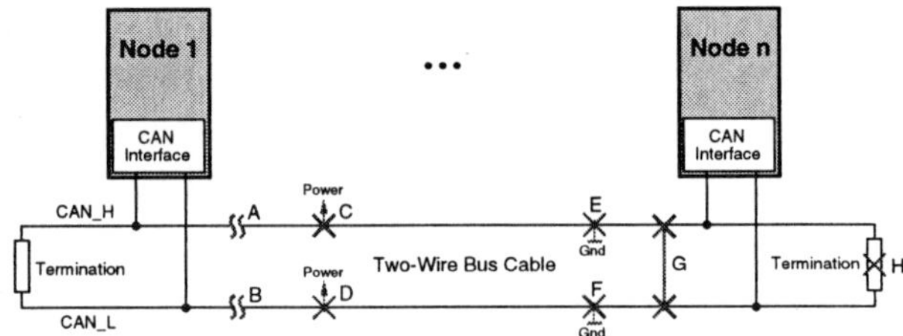

Figure 2. Resilience to medium failures in the ISO 11898 CAN standard

incoming stream – when sampling the bus[2]. Such kind of operation is known as *quasi-stationary*, and it will be of fundamental importance for the definition of CAN media redundancy strategies.

The CAN transmission medium is usually a two-wire differential line. The CAN physical layer specified in [5] allows resilience against some of the transmission medium failures illustrated in Figure 2, by switching from the normal two-wire differential operation to a single-wire mode. After mode switch-over bus operation is allowed to proceed, though with a reduced signal-to-noise ratio, in the presence of one of the following failures:

- one-wire interruption (A or B failures, in Figure 2);
- one-wire short-circuit either to power (C or D) or ground (E or F);
- two-wire short-circuit (G).

CAN medium interfaces that automatically switch to single-wire operation upon the detection of any of these failures and switch back to differential mode when recovered, are commercially available. Usually, such devices are intended for low-speed applications (up to 125 kbaud) with no more than 32 nodes [10]. One exception is the CAN interface described in [1].

The CAN bus line is usually terminated at both ends by its characteristic impedance [3]. Resilience to the failure of one termination (H failure, in Figure 2) can be achieved simply by taking into account the extra time needed for bus signal stabilization, when dimensioning the *propagation time segment* [5].

In any case, no standardized mechanisms exist to provide resilience to the simultaneous interruption of both bus line wires (A and B failures, in Figure 2). Upon such a failure, there may be subsets of the nodes which cannot communicate with each other. Because damaging of all wires in a bus line may result from single incidents with the network cabling, the probability of its occurrence is not negligible. The provision of resilience to CAN physical partitioning, through redundancy, is the objective of this paper.

[2] Although the sampled value may not be the same at all nodes, due to errors. Examples of causes for erroneous bit sampling are: electromagnetic interference, loss of synchronism or defective receiver circuits.

4 Redundancy Mechanisms for CAN

This section starts with a description of existing approaches to physical layer redundancy in CAN. Next, we analyze how LAN-based techniques could be adapted to CAN and finally present our Columbus' egg idea for CAN media redundancy.

Existing solutions

In [9] it is described a commercial solution (RED-CAN) that uses a self-healing ring/bus architecture to ensure resilience against open and short-circuits in the network physical wiring. Each RED-CAN node has its own reconfiguration switch. In case of failure, nodes perform a sequence of steps to find out the failure location and heal the physical network by isolating the failed segment. However, this reconfiguration process takes time and meanwhile the network is partitioned: communication blackouts can last as long as $100ms$. This is an extremely high figure when compared, for instance, with the worst-case time required by the standard CAN protocol to recover from severe network errors ($2.5ms@1Mbps$ - transmitter failure) [17].

Are redundant media bus architectures feasible ?

Our initial approach to the design of an infrastructure supporting CAN non-stop operation tries to exploit the techniques used in former works on LANs [15, 8], that proved quite effective. We maintain the assumptions stated in Section 2 for LAN-based approaches, but take into account the CAN own properties in the definition of media switching rules. For example, the *quasi-stationary* operation of CAN, guarantees the simultaneous reception at all redundant media interfaces of the same bit, in a given stream ordering.

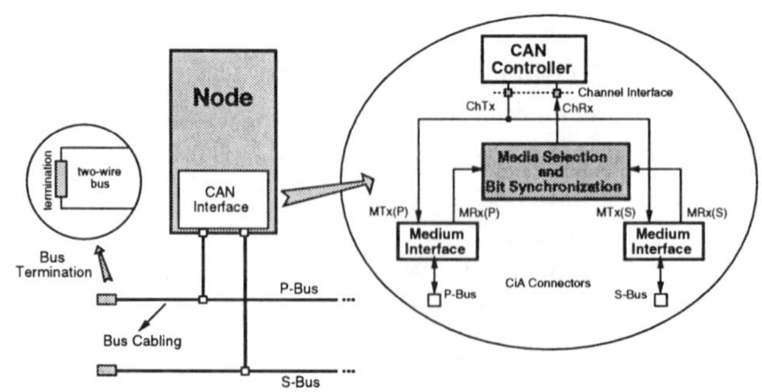

Figure 3. A complex approach to CAN media redundancy using off-the-shelf components

That property is exploited in the definition of a *frame-wise* strategy for CAN. The frame bit values are continuously compared and switching to a medium receiving a *dominant* value is required, whenever the current medium is receiving a *recessive* value at: the *start-of-frame* delimiter; within the frame arbitration field; at the *acknowledgment-slot*[3]. The reasons that justify this strategy are: in a correct medium, a *dominant* bit transmission always overwrites a *recessive* value; physical disconnection from the network partition that includes a transmitter leads to a recessive idle bus; the frame bits where switching is allowed are the intervals, in the normal transmission of a frame, where several nodes may be transmitting simultaneously.

For the definition of an *error-based* media selection s-trategy, the CAN media redundancy entities must be able to identify the medium originating the error before the MAC layer performs error signaling to all media. Fault treatment procedures should: avoid switching to a medium exhibiting omission errors; declare failure when the allowed *omission degree*[4] is exceeded.

Though a solution integrating media redundancy mechanisms and MAC layer functionalities may exhibit a moderate level of complexity, such a specialized design will be too costly. On the other hand, the architecture of current CAN controllers does not favor the implementation of media switching strategies with off-the-shelf components (Figure 3). CAN controllers include a *bit synchronization* module, that internally recovers the receiving clock. To maintain synchronism on media switching, a smooth data signal transition would be required. Bus data would have to be delayed by one bit time, until a decision is available, but that prevents a transmitting node from correctly performing bus state monitoring. One possible solution would be to allow abrupt transitions without being concerned with a possible loss of synchronism, and rely on MAC level mechanisms to recover from the error. Thus, the fundamental obstacles to the implementation of CAN bus redundancy using media switching and off-the-shelf components do concern both complexity and effectiveness.

However, some questions remain: how much of the complexity associated with the architecture of Figure 3 would really be needed to ensure CAN non-stop operation? Would it be possible to provide an equivalent functionality with a simpler architecture?

The Columbus' egg idea

To answer those questions, let us analyze the problem under a slightly different perspective. Let us assume a simplified fault model, considering only the abrupt interruption of a transmission medium. When a given node transmits a frame, all the nodes located at the *in-partition*[5] receive a correct signal on all redundant media interfaces. On the other hand, nodes at the *out-partition* receive a recessive signal from the (idle) failed media.

As a consequence, we came up with this Columbus' egg idea of extending the bare properties of CAN bus operation to the media interface level. Assuming a common CAN implementation, where a *dominant* value is represented by a logical zero and a *recessive* value is represented by a logical one, all the media will operate in parallel, being seen at the channel interface, as an unique bus implementing a logical AND function.

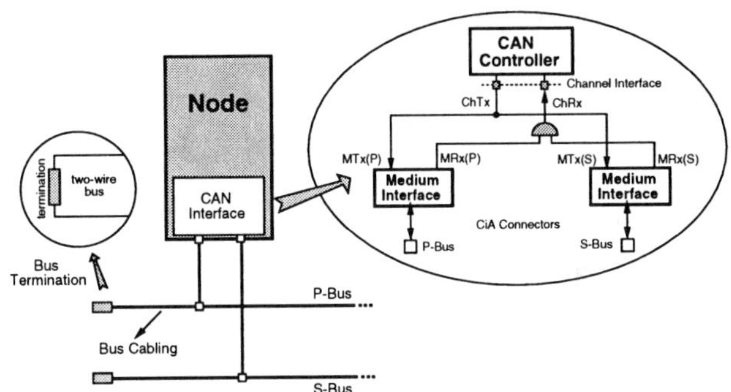

Figure 4. The Columbus' egg idea for bus media redundancy in CAN

This solution can be implemented by a conventional AND gate, to be inserted between the medium interfaces and the CAN controller, as exemplified in Figure 4 for a dual-media architecture. The complexity associated with media switching is avoided. The only disadvantage of this approach is that it is based on too restrictive a fault model. However, this basic architecture can be enhanced in order to support a less restrictive and thus more realistic fault model.

5 System Model

In this section we define a model for a redundant media network infrastructure, explain our fault assumptions and discuss a relevant set of CAN physical-level properties.

Let us assume a network composed of $\mathcal{N}$ nodes interconnected by a Channel. Each node $n \in \mathcal{N}$ connects to the Channel by a channel transmitter (outgoing bit stream) and a channel receiver (incoming bit stream). We denote the channel transmitter and the channel receiver of node n as Ch^n_{Tx} and Ch^n_{Rx}, respectively. If the Channel is composed of several media $m \in \mathcal{M}$, we use $M^n_{Tx}(m)$ and $M^n_{Rx}(m)$ to represent the Medium m transmitter and receiver interfaces, at node n. The node is connected by the Channel transmitter and receiver to a media selection module (as depicted

[3]The CAN protocol obliges a correct node to acknowledge the reception without errors of a frame, by asserting a *dominant* value at the *acknowledgment-slot* [5].

[4]Informally the *omission degree* is the number of consecutive omission errors of a component in an interval of reference [16].

[5]I.e., the partition that includes the transmitter.

in Figure 5), which internally connects to each Medium, accordingly to a given strategy.

For simplicity of exposition, we will omit the superscript identifying the node, whenever Channel and Medium refer to the same node. Medium is used to refer an instantiation of the Channel, comprising the network physical layer and the communication medium itself.

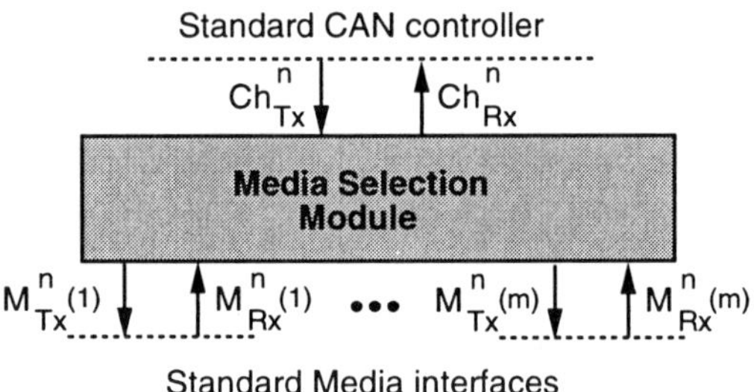

Figure 5. Channel and Media interfaces

Fault model

We introduce the following definition: a component is **weak-fail-silent** if it behaves correctly or crashes if it does more than a given number of omissions – called the component's *omission degree* – in an interval of reference.

In the context of CAN network components, an omission is an error that destroys a data or remote frame. It does not matter how many individual bits get corrupted: a single omission is accounted for each destroyed data/remote frame.

The fault assumptions are drawn from our previous works on CAN (e.g. [13]). The **CAN bus** is viewed as a single-channel broadcast local network with the following failure semantics for the network components:

- individual components are **weak-fail-silent** with *omission degree* f_o;
- failure bursts never affect more than f_o transmissions in an interval of reference[6];
- omission failures may be inconsistent (i.e., not observed by all recipients);
- there is no permanent failure of the Channel (e.g. the simultaneous partition of all media).

Establishing a bound for the omission degree ($Od = f_o$) of individual components provides a general method for the detection of failed components. If each omission is detected and accounted for, the component fails once it exceeds the omission degree bound. In particular, a Medium fails if it crashes (stuck-at or broken failures) or if it exceeds Od.

[6] For instance the duration of a broadcast round. Note that this assumption is concerned with the total number of failures of possibly different components.

PCAN1 - Bit **Simultaneity**: for any Bit p of any transmitter s starting at $t^s_B(p)$, if $t^r_B(p)$ is the start of Bit p as seen by receiver r, for any r, then in absence of faults, $t^s_B(p) = t^r_B(p)$.

PCAN2 - Wired-AND Multiple Access: for all transmitters s in $\mathcal{N}$, the value of any Bit p seen by the channel c is, in absence of faults, $v^c_B(p) = \prod_{s \in \mathcal{N}} v^s_B(p)$.

PCAN3 - Bit **Broadcast**: in absence of faults, for any Bit p on the channel c, and for any receiver r, $v^r_B(p) = v^c_B(p)$.

Figure 6. CAN physical level properties

The omission degree is also a general measure of the reliability of the CAN components to transient errors: failure bursts affect at most f_o transmissions in an interval of reference. However, for the particular set $\mathcal{M}$ of media, we make the additional fault assumptions:

- failures in different media are independent.
- permanent omission failures never affect more than $\#\mathcal{M} - 1$ media.

CAN physical-level properties

We define *logical bit slot*, that we denote Bit from now on, as the logical entity corresponding to a nominal bit time interval. A Bit occupies an interval of constant length T_B and $t^s_B(p)$ is the (unobservable) real time instant when Bit p starts at s (s is a transmitter, a receiver or the channel).

In absence of faults, a Bit p at s assumes one and only one logical value $v^s_B(p)$. Given the current CAN implementations, the logical value one represents the *recessive* state and the logical value zero represents the *dominant* state.

Figure 6 presents a relevant set of CAN physical layer properties. The PCAN1 property formalizes the *quasi-stationary* propagation of signals in CAN where, unlike longer and faster networks, a transmitted bit stream has the same phase along the bus. A single Bit is transmitted on the channel at a time. Property PCAN2 specifies the function that combines the signals from multiple simultaneous transmitters on the bus, into a single Bit value. A dominant value always overwrites a recessive state. The symbol $\prod$ is used to represent a logical AND function. Property PCAN3 is required by the CAN protocol for arbitrating accesses to the shared medium, bus state monitoring and data transfer.

Properties PCAN1 and PCAN2 are the foundation of CAN operation and are exploited in our method to implement bus-based media redundancy in CAN.

6 Media Redundancy Strategies

We now use the model defined in Section 5 to discuss our implementation of bus-based media redundancy in CAN.

Operational assumptions

Let us start with a description of some additional assumptions about the network infrastructure:

N1 - *channel redundancy is used, through replicated media (physical and medium layers), but only one MAC layer.*

However, apart from replication, standard CAN components are used. In particular, we do not exploit any of the fault-tolerant mechanisms of [10, 1]. Furthermore, we do not assume the use of any specific transmission medium. Hence, different solutions are allowed for the physical layer: inexpensive differential pair wiring and non fault-tolerant medium interfaces or fiber optics technology.

N2 - *each medium replica is routed differently.*

N3 - *all media are active, meaning every bit issued from the MAC layer is transmitted simultaneously on all media.*

Assumption N3 is simply enforced by logically connecting the Channel and all the Medium outgoing links together, thus implementing the function:

$$M_{Tx}(m) = Ch_{Tx} \qquad \forall\, m \in \mathcal{M} \tag{1}$$

The Columbus' egg strategy

The Columbus' egg strategy extends the PCAN2 wired-AND multiple access property to the Media interface level, taking into account the PCAN1 property: the receive signals of each Medium interface are combined in an AND function (equation 2), before interfacing the MAC layer.

$$Ch_{Rx} = \prod_{m \in \mathcal{M}} M_{Rx}(m) \tag{2}$$

where, $\mathcal{M}$ is the set of Medium interfaces. For example, in the dual-media architecture of Figure 4, $\mathcal{M} = \{P, S\}$.

This technique provides resilience to Medium partitions (e.g. A and B failures in Figure 2) and to stuck-at-recessive failures (e.g. failure D in Figure 2), without violating property PCAN3.

Handling stuck-at-dominant failures

A Medium stuck-at-dominant failure prevents equation (2) from delivering correct results. To detect these failures a special-purpose watchdog timer may be used. In CAN, a correct Medium is not allowed to be at a dominant state for more than a given number of bit times, that we denote $\mathcal{T}_{skd}$. This parameter is important because it provides an upper bound for the delay in the detection of a stuck-at-dominant Medium failure. We account for two different contributions:

$$\mathcal{T}_{skd} = (\mathcal{T}_{stuff} + 1) + 2\,.\mathcal{T}_{eflag} \tag{3}$$

The first term of equation (3) represents the minimum number of consecutive dominant bits violating the bit-stuffing coding rule, being $\mathcal{T}_{stuff}$ the bit-stuffing width. The second term of equation (3) represents the maximum duration of an error signaling action, being $\mathcal{T}_{eflag}$ the normalized duration of an error flag [5].

The state of each Medium is permanently monitored. Upon the detection of a stuck-at-dominant condition, an indication of Medium m failure is provided:

$$M_{skd}(m) = \begin{cases} true & \textbf{if } \mathcal{T}_D(m) > \mathcal{T}_{skd} \\ false & \textbf{if } \mathcal{T}_D(m) \leq \mathcal{T}_{skd} \vee M_{Rx}(m) = r \end{cases} \tag{4}$$

where, $\mathcal{T}_D(m) = \mathcal{T}(M_{Rx}(m) = d)$ represents the normalized time elapsed since Medium m is at a dominant state. If it exceeds $\mathcal{T}_{skd}$, the Medium has failed. The values *true* and *false* are represented by a logical one and a logical zero, respectively.

The M_{skd} failure indication can be used to directly request the disabling of the failed Medium, as follows:

$$M_d(m) = M_{skd}(m) \tag{5}$$

The receive signal – Ch_{Rx} – delivered at the channel interface is established by the receive signals of the non-failed media interfaces, as specified in equation (6), where the symbols $\prod$ and $+$ are used to denote the AND and the OR functions, respectively.

$$Ch_{Rx} = \prod_{m \in \mathcal{M}} (M_{Rx}(m) + M_d(m)) \tag{6}$$

With this technique we have made our architecture resilient to Medium stuck-at-dominant failures, such as failures C or G in Figure 2.

7 Omission Error Detection

In this section we extend the functionality of our architecture by introducing mechanisms able to detect and to account for omission errors. These errors may have their origin in subtle causes, such as a defective connector mount or a smashed cable, causing impedance mismatches that may introduce a reflection pattern which sporadically prevents communication. Another cause may be the incorrect dimensioning of CAN physical layer parameters.

Operational assumptions

We begin by making the following operational assumptions concerning the observable behavior of CAN at the PHY-MAC interface, as *per* the standard [5]:

N4 - *there is always a detectable minimum idle period preceding the start of every CAN data or remote frame transmission.*

N5 - *there is a detectable and unique fixed form sequence that identifies the correct reception of a CAN data or remote frame.*

N6 - *there is a detectable bit sequence that identifies the signaling of errors in the CAN bus.*

Let us shortly justify these assumptions. With regard N4, a Ch_{EFS} signal is asserted at the end of each frame transmission, when the minimum bus idle period that precedes the start of every data or remote frame transmission has elapsed. It is negated at the start of a frame transmission. The normalized duration of the *End of Frame Sequence* ($\mathcal{T}_{EFS}$) is equal for data/remote and for error/overload frames and includes the three bit intermission [5]. Equation (7) takes into account that a transmission may start at the last bit of the intermission, being $\mathcal{T}_L = \mathcal{T}_{EFS} - 1$.

$$Ch_{EFS} = \begin{cases} true & \textbf{if } \mathcal{T}(Ch_{Rx} = r) \geq \mathcal{T}_L \\ false & \textbf{if } \mathcal{T}(Ch_{Rx} = r) < \mathcal{T}_L \vee Ch_{Rx} = d \end{cases} \quad (7)$$

If a data or remote frame transmission ends without errors, a *Frame correct* signal (Ch_{Fok}) is asserted, changing of state accordingly to expression (8). The fixed form sequence of assumption N5 includes the recessive (r) CRC-delimiter, the dominant (d) acknowledgment-slot and the recessive acknowledgment-delimiter plus the first six recessive bits of the seven bit end of frame delimiter. The frame's last bit was not included because it is never considered by the recipients in the evaluation of frame correctness [5, 13].

$$Ch_{Fok} \mapsto \begin{cases} true & \textbf{if } Ch_{Rx} = rdrrrrrrr \\ false & \textbf{when } Ch_{EFS} \end{cases} \quad (8)$$

Conversely, when a frame transmission is aborted due to errors the Ch_{Err} signal, changes of state accordingly to expression (9). Errors are signaled on the bus through a detectable sequence of dominant bits (assumption N6), violating the bit-stuffing coding rule.

$$Ch_{Err} \mapsto \begin{cases} true & \textbf{if } \mathcal{T}(Ch_{Rx} = d) \geq \mathcal{T}_{stuff} + 1 \\ false & \textbf{when } Ch_{EFS} \end{cases} \quad (9)$$

Frame monitoring

In order to evaluate whether or not a given Medium is exhibiting omission errors, the reception of data and remote frames is continuously monitored. For every bit, the signal received from Medium m – $M_{Rx}(m)$ – is compared with the channel receive signal (Ch_{Rx}), until the frame transfer is successfully completed or aborted by errors. A *frame mismatch* signal – $M_{Fm}(m)$ – is asserted for Medium m, if the two signals do not exhibit the same value:

$$M_{Fm}(m) \mapsto \begin{cases} true & \textbf{if } M_{Rx}(m) \neq Ch_{Rx} \wedge Ch_{TiP} \\ false & \textbf{when } Ch_{EFS} \end{cases} \quad (10)$$

where, $Ch_{TiP} = \neg Ch_{Fok} \wedge \neg Ch_{Err}$ signals that a frame transfer is in progress. Once asserted, the $M_{Fm}(m)$ signal is kept in that state even if the two signals become equal again. It is negated only when Ch_{EFS} becomes true.

The Medium receive signals are not monitored in the interframe space, i.e. in the period between two consecutive data or remote frames. Network errors occuring in this period are not accounted as frame omissions.

Detecting Medium omissions

The $M_{Fm}(m)$ signal is used, together with the Ch_{Fok} and Ch_{Err} signals, in the update of the Medium omission degree. Let us define the following set of auxiliary functions:

$$\begin{aligned} M_{Fm-s} &= \sum_{m \in \mathcal{M}} M_{Fm}(m) \\ M_{Oer}(m) &= Ch_{Fok} \wedge M_{Fm}(m) \\ M_{Och}(m) &= Ch_{Err} \wedge \neg M_{Fm}(m) \wedge M_{Fm-s} \\ M_{Uer}(m) &= (Ch_{Err} \wedge \neg M_{Fm-s}) \vee (Ch_{Err} \wedge M_{Fm}(m)) \end{aligned}$$

that we use in the accounting of Medium m omission degree:

$$M_{Od}(m) = \begin{cases} M_{Od}(m) + 1 & \textbf{if } M_{Oer}(m) \vee M_{Och}(m) \\ M_{Od}(m) & \textbf{if } M_{Uer}(m) \\ 0 & \textbf{if } Ch_{Fok} \wedge \neg M_{Fm}(m) \end{cases} \quad (11)$$

If the $M_{Fm}(m)$ and the Ch_{Fok} signals are simultaneously asserted at the end of a frame transfer, that means: a correct data or remote frame has been successfully received; at least one bit in the stream received from Medium m did not have a correct value. Thus, the omission degree of Medium m should be incremented.

On the other hand, if the frame transfer is aborted due to errors, a Medium having its $M_{Fm}(m)$ signal negated can be made responsible for the errors and its omission degree count should be incremented.

However, we define one exception to this rule: the omission degree count should not be modified, despite the assertion of Ch_{Err}, when no Medium has the $M_{Fm}(m)$ signal asserted. The omission degree count of Medium m should also remain unchanged, when the Ch_{Err} and $M_{Fm}(m)$ signals are both asserted, because one cannot be sure Medium m has not exhibit omission errors[7].

For a Medium exhibiting a correct behavior, i.e. when a frame is correctly received and no *frame mismatches* have been reported for that Medium, the corresponding omission degree counter is set to zero.

Additional remarks on omission errors

As a general rule, a Medium that exceeds its omission degree bound should be declared failed and its contribution to equation (6) disabled. However, we have identified two situations where despite the occurrence of omission errors, those should not be accounted for in the omission degree:

- **common-mode errors**, with origin, for example, in a node with a failed transmitter or a failed receiver [17]. This scenario is easily detectable, because no media will report *frame mismatches*;
- **single Medium errors**, that nevertheless generate *frame mismatches* in all media. This scenario calls for fault treatment procedures where some "incorrect" media are temporarily disabled (*quarantined*), to allow operation to proceed with a "correct" set.

A detailed discussion of CAN-oriented *quarantine* techniques, similar to those introduced in [15] for LANs, is out of the scope of this paper and it will be reported in a future work.

8 Conclusions

There is an increasing demand for fault-tolerant and real-time distributed systems based on field-buses. Many of these systems are intended for critical control applications, where continuity of service is a strict requirement.

Network media redundancy is an effective solution for resilience against temporary medium faults and availability in the presence of permanent faults.

In this paper, we do a systemic analysis of how bus redundancy mechanisms can be implemented in CAN, the Controller Area Network, and we end-up with a Columbus' egg idea: an extremely simple mechanism that makes bus-based redundancy easy to implement in CAN using off-the-shelf components.

[7] One exception can be found in a dual-media architecture, when only one $M_{Fm}(m)$ signal is negated. Under a single-failure assumption the Medium not exhibiting omission errors will have its $M_{Fm}(m)$ signal asserted.

The simplest architecture just uses a conventional AND gate, together with the standard CAN components, to provide resilience to medium partitions and stuck-at-recessive failures in the network cabling. With some extra circuitry, of small complexity, we are able to ensure: resilience to stuck-at-dominant failures; omission failure detection and fault treatment; support to high-layer diagnose and distributed failure detection applications.

All the required functionality can be easily integrated in a single, medium capacity, Programmable Logic Device.

References

[1] Alcatel. *MTC-3054 CAN Interface Data Sheet*, Dec. 1995.

[2] J. Azevedo. *The WorldFIP protocol*. WorldFIP International Technical Center, Antony, France, Nov. 1996.

[3] CiA - CAN in Automation. *CAN Physical Layer for Industrial Applications - CiA/DS102-1*, Apr. 1994.

[4] F. Cristian, R. Dancey, and J. Dehn. High availability in the Advanced Automation System. In *Digest of Papers, The 20th International Symposium on Fault-Tolerant Computing*, Newcastle-UK, June 1990. IEEE.

[5] ISO. *International Standard 11898 - Road vehicles - Interchange of digital information - Controller Area Network (CAN) for high-speed communication*, Nov. 1993.

[6] H. Kopetz and G. Grunsteidl. TTP - a protocol for fault-tolerant real-time systems. *IEEE Computer*, 27(1):14–23, Jan. 1994.

[7] LONWORKS 78kbps self-healing ring architecture. Echelon Marketing Bulletin, Aug. 1993.

[8] C. Mateus. Design and implementation of a non-stop Ethernet with a redundant media interface. Graduation Project Final Report, IST, Lisboa, Portugal, Sept. 1993. (in portuguese).

[9] RED-CAN a fully redundant CAN-system. NOB Elektronik Product Note, Sweden. http://www.nob.se.

[10] Philips Semiconductors. *TJA1053 - Fault-tolerant CAN transceiver*, Oct. 1997.

[11] D. Powell, editor. *Delta-4 - A Generic Architecture for Dependable Distributed Computing*. ESPRIT Research Reports. Springer Verlag, Nov. 1991.

[12] L. Rodrigues, M. Guimarães, and J. Rufino. Fault-tolerant clock syncronization in CAN. In *Proc. of the 19th Real-Time Systems Symposium*, Madrid, Spain, Dec. 1998. IEEE.

[13] J. Rufino, P. Veríssimo, G. Arroz, C. Almeida, and L. Rodrigues. Fault-tolerant broadcasts in CAN. In *Digest of Papers, The 28th Int. Symp. on Fault-Tolerant Computing Systems*, pages 150–159, Munich, Germany, June 1998. IEEE.

[14] EN50170 - PROFIBUS. Presentation Slides - Siemens PROFIBUS Interface Center, Mar. 1998.

[15] P. Veríssimo. Redundant media mechanisms for dependable communication in Token-Bus LANs. In *Proceedings of the 13th Local Computer Network Conference*, Minneapolis-USA, Oct. 1988. IEEE.

[16] P. Veríssimo. Real-time Communication. In S. Mullender, editor, *Distributed Systems*, ACM-Press, chapter 17, pages 447–490. Addison-Wesley, 2nd edition, 1993.

[17] P. Veríssimo, J. Rufino, and L. Ming. How hard is hard real-time communication on field-buses? In *Digest of Papers, The 27th Int. Symposium on Fault-Tolerant Computing Systems*, pages 112–121, Washington - USA, June 1997. IEEE.

Message Logging in Mobile Computing

Bin Yao[†], Kuo-Feng Ssu[‡], and W. Kent Fuchs[†]

[†] School of Electrical and Computer Engineering, Purdue University
[‡] Coordinated Science Laboratory, University of Illinois

Abstract

Dependable mobile computing is enhanced by independent recovery, low power consumption and no dependence on stable storage at the mobile host. Existing recovery protocols proposed for mobile environments typically create consistent global checkpoints that do not guarantee independent recovery and low power consumption. This paper demonstrates the advantages of message logging by describing a receiver based logging protocol. Checkpointing is utilized to limit log size and recovery latency. We compare the performance of our approach with that of existing mobile checkpointing and recovery algorithms in terms of failure free overhead and recovery time. We also describe a stable storage management scheme for mobile support stations. Garbage collection is achieved without direct participation of mobile hosts.

1 Introduction

Mobile computing [1, 2] presents new challenges and requirements for checkpointing and recovery protocols [3]. Failures such as loss of connection or power outages that are rare in fixed networks can be common in mobile environments. Recovery algorithms are required to tolerate multiple simultaneous failures and failure during recovery, and it is desirable that processes be able to recover independently. Coordinated recovery among processes running on Mobile Hosts (MH) may slow down recovery [4] and increase the chance of having multiple rollbacks of the entire system in order to handle errors during recovery. Conserving battery power by means of limiting the number of extra messages during checkpointing and recovery is also important. Limiting additional transmitted messages has the added benefit of reducing contention on the wireless network.

As an MH may be lost or permanently damaged, hard drives on mobile hosts are not generally considered stable storage. Therefore they are not suitable as the only location for storing checkpoints or message logs. Traditional checkpointing and message logging algorithms [5–12] are not directly applicable under such conditions. Previous proposals have suggested that checkpoints be sent back to Home Agents (HA) [13]. Others have proposed that stable storage on Mobile Support Stations (MSS) be used for checkpoints and message logs [14–16]. Because checkpoints and/or message logs are stored on different MSSs as an MH moves from cell to cell, the organization of the distributed process state information is important for successful recovery. Several algorithms have been proposed to solve these problems [14, 17]. Garbage collection of stable storage on MSS is also of importance. When state information on MSS is no longer needed for recovery, it should be discarded to make room for new checkpoints and message logs. Most present schemes require cooperation from mobile hosts. If one participating MH fails, some stable storage may never be collected for reuse.

Checkpointing and recovery protocols previously proposed for mobile environments have typically saved consistent global checkpoints [13, 15, 18, 19]. This requires all participating mobile hosts to roll back during recovery, but some mobile hosts may not be able to rollback due to transient or permanent failures. This approach forces application messages to be resent over the slow wireless network during recovery, resulting in slow recovery and additional power usage at the MH. Recent work has shown through analytic modeling that message logging can be an attractive approach to recovery in mobile environments [14]. Another recent research project has derived mechanisms for managing stable storage on the MSS [20].

This paper describes a receiver-based pessimistic message logging protocol for MH, MSS and HA, and a distributed state organization scheme for mobile computing environments. Using our approach, processes running on mobile hosts are able to recover quickly and independently of other processes. The protocol is experimentally compared with an ideal consistent checkpoint protocol to demonstrate that message logging incurs similar failure free overhead and achieves much faster recovery in a wireless network implementation. This approach requires no extra control messages sent by the MH. Garbage collection

This research was supported in part by the Defense Advanced Research Projects Agency (DARPA) under contract DABT 63-96-C-0069, and in part by the Office of Naval Research under contract N00014-97-1-1013.

0-7695-0213-X/99 $10.00 © 1999 IEEE

is achieved without direct participation of the MH. Even if the MH permanently fails, state information left on MSSs can be identified and discarded.

2 The Mobile IP Environment

The mobile computing environment used in this paper is based on the Mobile IP architecture [2]. This environment, as illustrated in Figure 1, contains fixed hosts connected by a backbone network and mobile hosts that use a wireless interface to communicate with fixed hosts and other mobile hosts. Each MH is associated with a home network on which the MH receives packets like a normal fixed host. Each MH is also assigned a home address that has the subnet prefix of its home network. The home address never changes, regardless of the MH's movement. Mobile support stations (foreign agents) are those fixed hosts that have both a wireless interface and a fixed network (Ethernet, ATM, etc.) interface. They function as routers and provide connections for mobile hosts to the entire network. The area that a mobile support station's wireless interface serves is called a cell. As mobile hosts move from cell to cell, their IP addresses have to be changed to reflect the subnet mask of their new mobile support stations. This can cause difficulty in maintaining a connection as the MH traverses cells. Mobile IP solves this problem by providing both home agents and foreign agents.

When communicating with a mobile host, other hosts always send packets to the mobile host's home address. A home agent executes on the mobile host's home network. It maintains current location information of the mobile hosts. Packets destined for mobile hosts are intercepted by the home agent and then tunneled to the current foreign agent that is serving the mobile host. Packets are then delivered to the mobile host by the foreign agent. Packets sent by mobile hosts are generally delivered to their destination using standard IP routing mechanisms, not necessarily through the home agent. An example is illustrated in Figure 1. Packets from mobile host A follow the dotted line and pass an FA, a HA, and an FA, before reaching mobile host B.

One of the distinctive features of this architecture is the existence of home agents. When an MH switches cells, the home agent must know where the mobile host is located before any future packets can be delivered to the mobile host. This suggests that the home agent might be an attractive place to log messages for mobile hosts. However there are routing optimizations proposed in the literature [21] that route some packets directly to the foreign agent of the mobile host instead of through its home agent. On the other hand, we observe that all packets sent to mobile hosts must reach the mobile support station first before transmission through the wireless interface. In our approach stable storage at the MSS is used to store checkpoints and message

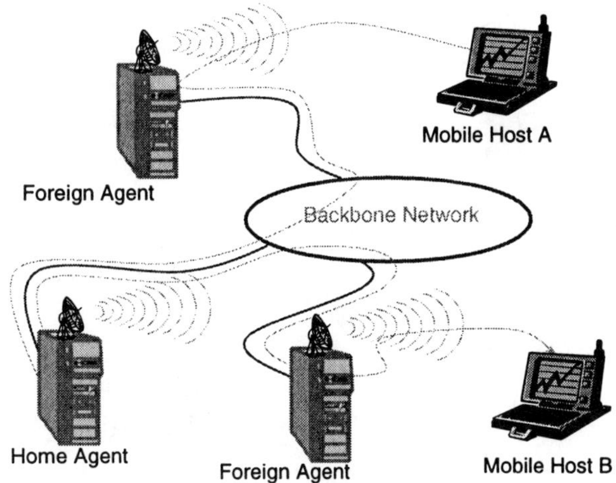

Figure 1: The mobile IP environment.

logs for mobile hosts.

We assume that the foreign agents and home agents do not fail when serving mobile hosts that are executing the checkpoint and roll-back recovery protocol. MSS and HA typically have a much smaller failure rate than that of MHs as they run on fixed networks. Even if they do fail, since HA and FA are processes that implement carefully defined state machines, checkpointing and message logging protocols can be designed relatively easily to tolerate those failures [22].

There can be multiple processes running on a single mobile host. They can have fail-stop failures independent of each other, or fail at the same time as the mobile host. Finally, we assume that MHs communicate with MSSs using a FIFO link level protocol, processes communicate with each other using TCP (or other reliable transport protocol) over Mobile IP, and processes execute according to the piece wise deterministic model.

3 Related Work

Elnozahy, Johnson, and Wang developed a general survey for checkpointing and message logging protocols in distributed systems [23]. Alvisi and Marzullo have provided an in-depth treatment of message logging [24]. Rao and Alvisi compared the cost of recovery for different message logging approaches [4], and Neves and Fuchs [25] compared recovery speed for a coordinated checkpoint protocol [13] and a sender based message logging protocol [8].

Acharya and Badrinath [15] introduced a two-phase method for taking global consistent checkpoints. They proposed that checkpoints be stored on the stable storage of mobile support stations instead of on mobile hosts. In their protocol, processes alternate between two states, SEND and RECV. If a process is in the SEND mode and receives a

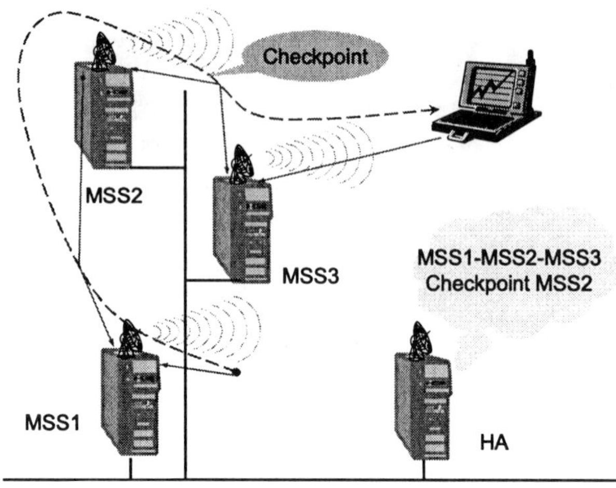

Figure 2: Message logging algorithm.

message, it is forced to take a checkpoint. During recovery, the global state is reconstructed from a set of checkpoints for each process.

Pradhan, et al. analytically evaluated the performance of different state saving protocols and hand off strategies [14]. They also suggested storing checkpoints and message logs at mobile support stations. Their result indicates that message logging is suitable for mobile environments except in cases where the mobile host has high mobility, wireless bandwidth is low, and failure rate is high.

A hybrid checkpoint-recovery protocol for mobile systems was proposed by Higake and Takizawa [17]. As a mobile host moves between cells, it leaves an agent process on each mobile support station on its itinerary. During recovery, processes on fixed hosts recover from consistent checkpoints and processes on mobile hosts restart from their own checkpoints and roll to a state that is consistent with those on fixed hosts with the help of agent processes.

Cao and Singhal proved that it is not possible for a checkpoint algorithm to preserve both non blocking and min process properties at the same time [18]. This work is based on an earlier work that tried to achieve non blocking and min processes at the same time [16]. They also proposed a non-blocking mobile checkpointing protocol [19]. Their scheme uses mutable checkpoints to avoid storing unnecessary checkpoints on mobile support stations.

Neves and Fuchs [13] developed an adaptive checkpointing scheme for mobile computing. Their protocol uses time to indirectly coordinate the creation of recoverable consistent checkpoints. Processes take hard checkpoints that are sent to home agents and soft checkpoints that are stored on the local disk of the mobile host.

4 Algorithm Description

4.1 Message Logging and Checkpointing

The message logging and checkpointing algorithm of this paper consists of three parts: one that executes on the MSS, one that executes at the HA, and one implemented by application processes on the mobile host. The protocol implemented by application processes on the mobile host is similar to existing message logging protocols. Processes tag every sent message and store a copy of the tag in memory. Upon receiving a message, a process also stores the tag of the received message in memory. The tag includes the message sequence number, a globally unique process identifier, and the tag of the last message received by the sending process. The process periodically writes checkpoints to the MSS that is currently serving as its foreign agent. Checkpoints are taken in a non-blocking fashion using copy on write [26]. The checkpoint includes not only the process state information necessary to recover the process, but also the tags of the last message it sent and received before the checkpoint.

Mobile IP maintains the TCP connection as the MH moves, thus switching cells when writing checkpoints does not create problems. Packets sent by the MH are routed as conventional IP, instead of having to go through the HA, thus not degrading performance on the MSS. When the MH switches cells, application processes are notified. Each process sends to the new MSS a *Report Message* that contains the tag of the last message it received from the old MSS. These messages can be piggybacked in the registration packet specified by the Mobile IP protocol.

Every time an MH enters a MSS's cell, the MSS assigns a unique id for the message log of each application process executing the message logging protocol on the MH. If the MH has visited this MSS before, the ids assigned are greater than those previous. Messages destined for mobile hosts in the MSS's cell are logged on the MSS before being forwarded. The sequence of messages seen by the mobile host are the same as seen and logged by the MSS due to the FIFO link-level wireless protocol. Some messages can be logged by the MSS and not yet delivered to the MH. This type of message is an *in transit message*. The new MSS forwards report messages sent to it from the MH at cell switch time to the old MSS of the MH. The old MSS can then use the last received message tag for each application process to detect in transit messages and can purge them from message logs. After each mobile host leaves a cell, the MSS that the MH just left sends a message to the MH's HA reporting the messages log ids for each application process on this MH. If an MH writes a checkpoint to an MSS, the MSS sends a *checkpoint message* to the MH's HA indicating that it has finished storing the checkpoint for the MH. In the event that a process failed on an MH, or the

MH failed, the MSS that was serving the MH detects the error and sends its home agent a *Failed Message* that contains message tags of the last sent message for each failed application to the MH's HA.

On the HA, a process keeps track of the location of an MH using the registration procedure specified by the Mobile IP protocol. It saves the whole itinerary taken by the mobile host into an array named *itinerary array*. Each element of the array is the address of an MSS on the MH's path. The HA waits for the checkpoint message from the MSS that contains the location of the last finished checkpoint of the mobile host. Upon receiving this message, the HA may begin the garbage collection procedure to reclaim stable storage on the MSSs.

The HA also serves as an MSS on the home network. It executes the protocol for MSSs in addition to HA protocols. If an MH does not use the wireless interface on its home network, its HA has to deviate from standard Mobile IP so that the HA can intercept and log messages destined for MHs that are "at home".

In our protocol, checkpoints are taken periodically and stored on MSSs. As one reviewer pointed out, using two kinds of checkpoints [13], one stored on the MH host's local disk and one on the MSSs can reduce power consumption of the mobile host even further (as a smaller number of checkpoints are sent through the wireless interface) and achieve even faster recovery if the local disk survives failure. The HA must be aware of these "possibly stable" checkpoints so that it can know which message logs should be sent to the MH. The associated cost is that larger message logs have to be stored at MSSs and extra processing performed at HAs. Also, if the local disk on the MH fails, recovery can take longer. Depending on the application, network characteristics and type of mobile hosts, this can serve as a viable alternative to saving all checkpoints on MSSs.

If processes running on mobile hosts maintain multiple TCP connections with other processes, they can see a different sequence of messages from those by the foreign agents due to scheduling in the thread library. During recovery they could take an execution path different from that before the failure. To ensure correctness, we limit applications running on the mobile hosts to be a single message queue shared by multiple processes, or a single process with one TCP connection.

Figure 2 illustrates the effects of the logging algorithm. As a mobile host moves along the dashed line, MSSs on its itinerary log messages for the mobile host. The mobile host takes a checkpoint while at MSS2. All this information is sent to the HA for further processing.

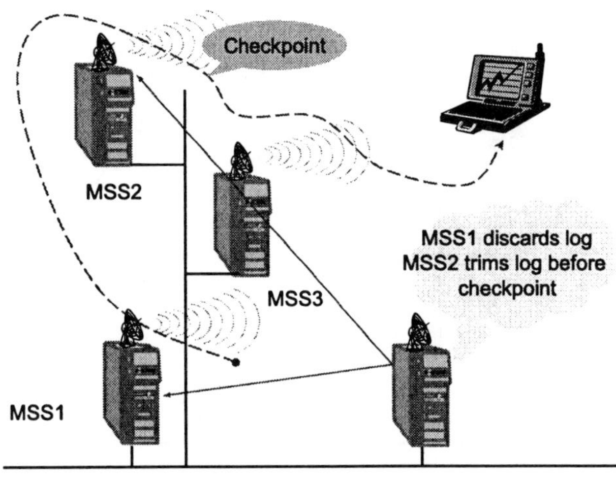

Figure 3: Garbage collection.

4.2 Distributed State Information and Garbage Collection

As the MH moves from cell to cell, it leaves message logs and checkpoints on the MSSs that are on its itinerary. Itinerary information kept at its HA is used to reconstruct a consistent state for the MH. The HA knows on which MSS the last checkpoints are stored for each application process on the MH by examining the checkpoint messages sent to it by MSSs. Messages logged after the checkpoint will have to be replayed in order for processes on the MH to recover. All other logged messages and previously stored checkpoints are no longer needed for recovery.

An example is sketched in Figure 3. Assume there is only one application process P executing on the MH. The MH moves from MSS1 to MSS3 and P takes a checkpoint on MSS2. HA has the MH's itinerary and the location of P's checkpoint stored in its memory. Since the HA knows that a checkpoint for P has been taken at MSS2, the HA can now ask MSS1 to delete message logs for process P, and ask MSS2 to delete messages logged prior to the checkpoint since they are no longer necessary for recovery.

Garbage collection is straight forward. After receiving a checkpoint message from an MSS, the HA examines its itinerary array and determines which message log is useful and which is rendered obsolete by the checkpoint. The HA sends out requests to those MSS with stale message logs and checkpoints so that they can garbage collect the stable storage. This request includes message log identifiers so that the MSS can distinguish among multiple logs in case the MH visits the MSS several times. Upon receiving the request, the MSS removes obsolete message logs and/or checkpoints, then sends back an ACK to HA. After receiving all the ACKs, the HA trims its itinerary array. The HA can also start the garbage collection either periodically to

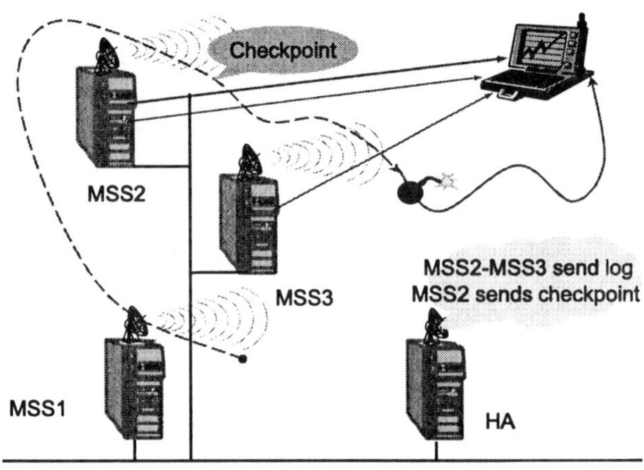

Figure 4: Recovery algorithm.

limit the length of the itinerary array or if stable storage at the MSS becomes depleted.

4.3 Recovery Algorithm

A mobile host restarts a failed process by sending to its HA a message containing the id of the process to be restarted. The HA responds by sending to the MH the message tag of the last message sent out by the process. The HA determines which MSS currently holds the latest checkpoint for this process and asks the MSS to send the checkpoint to the MH. Then the HA sends requests to MSSs that hold message logs for the process, which then in turn replay the log so that the process receives messages in the same order as before failure. When replaying the logged messages, the MSSs mark them as "replayed" so that they are not logged by the receiving MSS. If other processes continue to send messages to the recovering process, these messages will be logged and sent to the MH as normal messages, but they are not delivered to the application until after the recovery is complete. Figure 4 illustrates this procedure.

If an application attempts to send messages during recovery, the message tag is compared to the tag of the last message sent by the process before failure. If the tag indicates that the message has been sent before the failure, the message is not transmitted by the MH. This prevents the MH from re-transmitting application messages previously sent during recovery, thereby saving bandwidth and battery power. Failures during recovery are handled in the same way as failures during normal execution, since messages sent to the MH during recovery are logged on the MSS as normal messages.

4.4 Limited Stable Storage on Mobile Support Stations

If a mobile support station depletes its stable storage while trying to store checkpoints or message logs on behalf of mobile hosts, it has to either halt and perform garbage collection or find alternative storage. Halting an MSS effectively blocks every process on every mobile host in the MSS's cell. All incoming packets for mobile hosts are lost and must be resent later. Managing stable storage on the MSSs to reduce the frequency of blocking is therefore critical. Stable storage management is the focus of another recent project [20].

One way to reduce the possibility of halting an MSS is to use watermarks. When free stable storage on an MSS reaches a low watermark, that MSS selects a process as the target of garbage collection, forces it to take a checkpoint (maybe on another MSS), and discards previous message logs and checkpoints saved for that process.

Halting an MSS can also be avoided when storage is depleted by forwarding the logs and checkpoints to the mobile host's home agent, if there is enough bandwidth in the backbone network. The MSS can then execute the garbage collection algorithm. Another alternative is to have other MSSs or routers on the route of the packets store message logs. The MSS on the last hop can simply forward packets to the MH without logging them. This requires some signaling messages be sent to the HA so that the HA knows the exact locations of the logs.

5 Experimental Results

We compare the performance of our protocol with an ideal coordinated checkpoint protocol that takes periodic checkpoints without exchanging any messages. Failure free overhead and recovery time are evaluated.

5.1 Experiment

The specific environment used in the experiment is shown in Figure 5. A Sun Sparc 20 workstation running Solaris 2.6 with 320M memory and a Lucent Technology Wavepoint II [27] connected by 10M Ethernet served as the mobile support station. Checkpoints and message logs were stored on a dedicated file server that was connected to the workstation using a high speed ATM network. Two Pentium II 300MHz PCs equipped with Lucent Technology's Wavelan [27] wireless interface cards served as the mobile hosts. The PCs were running Windows NT 4.0 with 256M memory each. In our implementation, processes executed pre-generated traces that emulated WWW browsing behavior. The processes also functioned as servers and they read requests and generated replies in both sleep and request states. There were four client processes running, two on each PC. Each client was assigned a unique ID.

Table 1: Execution Time Overhead Comparison.

Trace	unmodified (seconds)	ckpt (seconds)	ckpt Overhead(%)	log with ckpt (seconds)	log with ckpt Overhead(%)
T1	1180.2	1243.6	5.3	1234.5	4.60
T2	869.1	9067.5	4.3	915.5	5.34
T3	1013.4	1060.1	4.6	1066.1	5.20
T4	871.5	898.1	3.0	905.6	3.92
T5	911.3	957.6	5.0	950.6	4.32
T6	866.7	910.0	4.9	913.1	5.35
T7	850.7	891.9	4.8	876.6	3.04

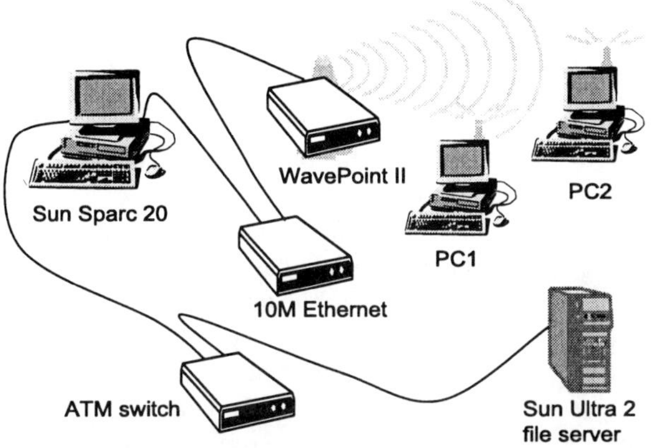

Figure 5: Experiment environment.

For routing and processing, a client attached to each message it transmitted a header that contained the destination ID, the type of message (request or reply), and the ID of the sender. Clients did not send messages directly to each other. Instead, they sent messages over the wireless network to a server process running on the Sun workstation. The server process was responsible for storing checkpoints and message logs as requested by the client processes. It also functioned as a router by examining the header field of each message and forwarding messages to their destination.

Checkpoints were not actual restartable process states, but were large messages intended to represent a range of reasonable state sizes for mobile hosts. Client processes had a separate thread that periodically sent checkpoints to a server. The server process also had separate threads that listened for checkpoints and wrote them to disk. Checkpointing was asynchronous.

5.2 Trace Generation

Request traces were generated from four individual traces to represent a variety of network load. These four individual traces represented the process sleep interval (SLEEP), number of requests sent during each active interval (NUMBER), the request packet distribution (RQ), and the reply packet distribution (RY). The request packet distribution was small as HTTP requests are typically less than several hundred bytes. Reply packets were large with a large variance to reflect the nature of a typical webservers' output. When accessing a web page, several requests are typically sent to the web server. We captured this behavior with the NUMBER trace.

A utility program read the first three traces and generated request traces used by each client. This program first read a value from the SLEEP trace and multiplied it by 1000 and a predefined coefficient to obtain the sleep time in milliseconds. The time value was written into the request trace file. The NUMBER trace was then read to determine how many request events were to be written out and the destination for these requests was randomly chosen. For every request event, the request length was read from the RQ trace. Seven traces (T1 ... T7) were generated, with coefficient of 1/2, 1/4, ... 1/128. By using several ratios, we obtained a variety of traces that represent distinct network loads.

5.3 Failure Free Overhead

The applications were first executed unmodified without message logging and checkpointing. They then ran with only periodic checkpointing enabled. Finally, the application executed with both checkpointing and message logging enabled. The checkpointing interval was five minutes. The execution times shown in the following figures and tables are the average of three runs. Total execution time of the three cases for different traces was measured and is shown in Table 1 and Figure 6. The overheads in-

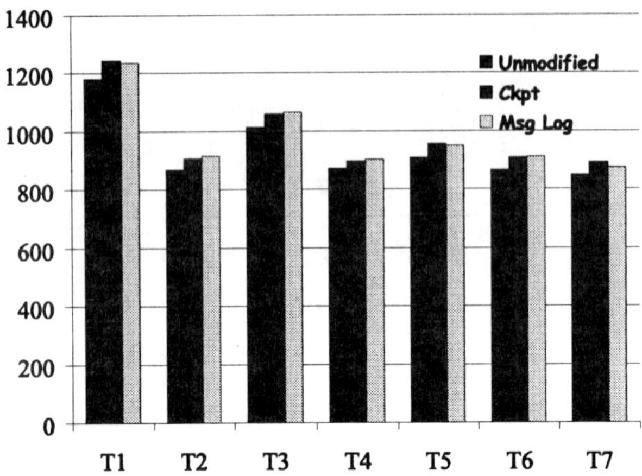

Figure 6: Normal execution overhead.

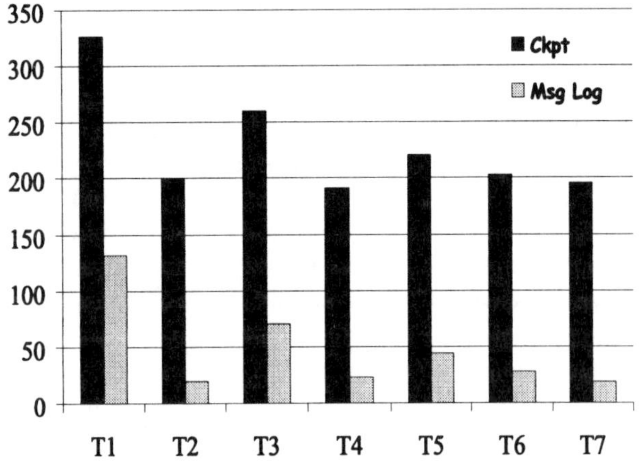

Figure 7: Recovery time.

curred by the coordinated checkpointing protocol and the message logging protocol are also shown.

5.4 Recovery Time

Recovery time is obtained by measuring the time for a process to read the checkpoint and proceed to a specific execution point. In our experiments, we chose that point to be after the 500th event in the request trace file. No checkpointing or message logging takes place during recovery. Recovery times for the consistent checkpointing protocol and the message logging protocol are measured and shown in Table 2 and Figure 7.

5.5 Discussion

From the failure free overhead data we see that for all of the traces message logging has similar performance to checkpointing without logging. The largest difference

Table 2: Recovery Time Comparison.

Trace	Using ckpts (seconds)	Using message logs (seconds)
T1	326.5	131.9
T2	200.4	19.82
T3	260.0	70.28
T4	191.00	23.16
T5	220.9	44.14
T6	202.6	27.67
T7	195.5	18.98

is less than 2 percent of the execution time without any checkpoints. When message logging is performed, the processes take checkpoints at the same frequency as the standard checkpointing protocol. The experiments illustrate that the overhead due to logging messages at the MSS is negligible. The reason is that messages are not written to disk before being forwarded to the MH.

As is known for fixed networks, recovery using message logging is often faster than that based on standard checkpoints. The processes recovered three to ten times faster using message logs than with checkpoints in our experiments with the Wavelan wireless network. Processes did not have to block and wait for other processes to transmit messages. Messages were also transmitted over the wireless link just once instead of twice, as in normal execution, resulting in less contention on the wireless network and lower latency for message transmission.

An interesting phenomenon is that for some traces the overhead due to message logging and checkpointing is actually less than that due to checkpointing. One explanation is that the action of logging message changed the timing of messages transmitted on the wireless network and thereby contentions were reduced.

6 Conclusions

This paper described a message logging protocol for mobile hosts, mobile support stations and home agents in a Mobile IP environment. An approach to organizing the distributed state information was also presented. The organizing scheme provides easy garbage collection without participation from mobile hosts and can tolerate the case where some mobile support stations do not have enough stable storage for mobile hosts to store state information.

Failure free overhead and recovery speed were compared between an ideal consistent checkpoint protocol and our message logging protocol. Message logging incurred only marginally larger overhead during failure free operation compared to the ideal consistent checkpointing protocol. Message logging has a decided advantage in recovery with mobile wireless networks.

Acknowledgment

We take this opportunity to thank the anonymous referees for their comments.

References

[1] C. Perkins, *Mobile IP Design Principles and Practices.* Addison-Wesley, 1997.

[2] C. P. (ed.), "IPv4 Mobility Support," *RFC 2002*, October 1996.

[3] B. R. Badrinath, A. Acharya, and T. Imielinski, "Impact of Mobility on Distributed Computations," *SIGOPS Review*, pp. 15–20, April 1993.

[4] L. A. S. Rao and H. Vin, "The Cost of Recovery in Message Logging Protocols," *Proceedings of the 17th Symposium on Reliable Distributed Systems*, pp. 10–18, October 1998.

[5] K. M. Chandy and L. Lamport, "Distributed snapshots: Determining global states of distributed systems," *ACM Transactions on Computer Systems*, vol. 3, no. 1, pp. 63–75, February 1985.

[6] R. Koo and S. Toueg, "Checkpointing and rollback-recovery for distributed systems," *IEEE Transactions on Software Engineering*, vol. SE-13, no. 1, pp. 23–31, January 1987.

[7] R. E. Strom and S. Yemini, "Optimistic recovery in distributed systems," *ACM Transactions on Computer Systems*, vol. 3, no. 3, pp. 204–226, August 1985.

[8] D. B. Johnson and W. Zwaenepoel, "Sender-based Message Logging," *Proceedings of the 17th International Symposium on Fault-Tolerant Computing*, pp. 14–19, July 1987.

[9] E. N. Elnozahy, D. B. Johnson, and W. Zwaenepoel, "The Performance of Consistent Checkpointing," *Proceedings of the 11th Symposium on Reliable Distributed Systems*, pp. 39–47, October 1992.

[10] L. M. Silva and J. G. Silva, "Global Checkpointing for Distributed Programs," *Proceedings of the 11th Symposium on Reliable Distributed Systems*, pp. 155–162, October 1992.

[11] J. Plank and K. Li, "Faster Checkpointing with N+1 Parity," *Proceedings of the 24th International Symposium on Fault-Tolerant Computing*, pp. 288–297, August 1994.

[12] Y.-M. Wang, Y. Huang, P. Vo, P.-Y. Chung, and C. Kintala, "Checkpointing and its Applications," *Proceedings of the 25th International Symposium on Fault-Tolerant Computing*, pp. 22–31, June 1995.

[13] N. Neves and W. K. Fuchs, "Adaptive Recovery for Mobile Environments," *Communications of the ACM*, vol. 40, no. 1, pp. 68–74, January 1997.

[14] D. K. Pradhan, P. Krishna, and N. H. Vaidya, "Recovery in Mobile Environments: Design and Trade-off Analysis," *Proceedings of the 26th International Symposium on Fault-Tolerant Computing*, pp. 16–25, June 1996.

[15] A. Acharya and B. Badrinath, "Checkpointing Distributed Applications on Mobile Computers," *Proceedings of the 3rd International Conference on Parallel and Distributed Information systems*, pp. 73–80, September 1994.

[16] R. Prakash and M. Singhal, "Low-Cost Checkpointing and Failure Recovery in Mobile Computing Systems," *IEEE Transactions on Parallel and Distributed Systems*, pp. 1035–1048, October 1996.

[17] H. Higaki and M. Takizawa, "Checkpoint-Recovery Protocol for Reliable Mobile Systems," *Proceedings of the 17th Symposium on Reliable Distributed Systems*, pp. 93–99, October 1998.

[18] G. Cao and M. Singhal, "On the Impossibility of Min-Process Non-Blocking Checkpointing and an Efficient Checkpointing Algorithm for Mobile Computing Systems," *Proceeding of the 27th International Conference on Parallel Processing*, pp. 37–44, August 1998.

[19] G. Cao and M. Singhal, "Low-Cost Checkpointing with Mutable Checkpoints in Mobile Computing Systems," *Proceedings of the 18th International Conference on Distributed Computing System*, pp. 462–471, May 1998.

[20] K. Ssu, W.K. Fuchs, and N. Neves, "Adaptive Checkpointing with Storage Management for Mobile Environments," *manuscript*, December 1998.

[21] D. B. Johnson, "Scalable and Robust Internetwork Routing for Mobile Hosts," *Proceedings of the 14th International Conference on Distributed Computing Systems*, pp. 2–11, June 1994.

[22] F. B. Schneider, "Implementing fault-tolerant services using the state machine approach: A tutorial," *ACM Computing Surveys*, vol. 22, no. 4, pp. 299–319, December 1990.

[23] E. Elnozahy, D. Johnson, and Y.-M. Wang, "A Survey of Rollback-Recovery Protocols in Message-Passing Systems," Tech. Rep. CMU-CS-96-181, School of Computer Science, Carnegie Mellon University, October 1996.

[24] L. Alvisi and K. Marzullo, "Message Logging: Pessimistic, Optmistic, Causal, and Optimal," *IEEE Transactions on Software Engineering*, pp. 149–159, February 1998.

[25] N. Neves and W. K. Fuchs, "RENEW: A Tool for Fast and Efficient Implementation of Checkpoint Protocols," *Proceedings of the 28th International Symposium on Fault-Tolerant Computing*, pp. 58–67, June 1998.

[26] J. Plank, M. Beck, G. Kingsley, and K. Li, "Libckpt: Transparent Checkpointing under Unix," *Usenix Winter 1995 Technical Conference*, pp. 213–233, January 1995.

[27] *http://www.wavelan.com.*

Session 10B

Student Papers II

Chair: Christian Landrault
LIRMM, France

Session 11A

Dependability Evaluation

Chair: Jean-Claude Laprie
LAAS-CNRS, France

Evaluating the Effectiveness of Fault Tolerance in Replicated Database Management Systems

Maitrayi Sabaratnam, Maitrayi.Sabaratnam@idi.ntnu.no
Norwegian University of Science & Technology(NTNU)

Øystein Torbjørnsen, ClustRa AS
Oystein.Torbjornsen@clustra.com

Svein-Olaf Hvasshovd, NTNU
Svein-Olaf.Hvasshovd@idi.ntnu.no

Abstract

Database management systems (DBMS) achieve high availability and fault tolerance usually by replication. However, fault tolerance does not come for free. Therefore, DBMSs serving critical applications with real time requirements must find a tradeoff between fault tolerance cost and performance. The purpose of this study is two-fold. It evaluates the effectiveness of DBMS fault tolerance in the presence of corruption in database buffer cache, which poses serious threat to the integrity requirement of the DBMSs.

The first experiment of this study evaluates the effectiveness of fault tolerance, and the fault impact on database integrity, performance, and availability on a replicated DBMS, ClustRa[6], in the presence of software faults that corrupt the volatile data buffer cache. The second experiment identify the weak data structure components in the data buffer cache that give fatal consequences when corrupted, and suggest the need for some form of guarding them individually or collectively.

1. Introduction

Increased global trade and travel demands that services provided by database applications, for example, in banking and telecommunication, are available 24x7x52 hours an year, in addition to the traditional requirement of preserving the integrity of the user data. In other words, the responsibility of masking both hardware and software failures, maintenance activities, and other natural or man-made catastrophes lies on the DBMS software.

These requirements are fulfilled to a great extent, by introducing fault tolerance. Fault tolerance can be achieved by redundancy, e.g., by a replicated DBMS. A replicated DBMS runs DBMS processes on different computers in a coordinated way. A computer running such a DBMS process is called a **node**. When a fault is detected in one node, the node is recovered. If this is not possible, the system will reconfigure such that the faulty node is excluded from the system configuration and its functionality is taken over by one of the replica nodes. Error detection, recovery, and reconfiguration must be done online automatically in order to achieve high availability .

Integrating fault tolerance in DBMSs as mentioned above need redundant hardware and enhanced software for effective fault detection, recovery, and reconfiguration. The enhanced software containing redundant execution of transactions and rigorous checks for error detection not only increases the software development cost, but also increases the DBMS's transaction response time. Therefore, the DBMS products serving critical applications with hard or soft real time requirements must find a tradeoff between fault tolerance and performance.

Though replication solves many problems regarding dependability, it is not a panacea. Replication enables controlled maintenance of hardware and software on a computer running a DBMS software, without compromising the DBMS availability. Further, replication limits the loss of data or DBMS unavailability due to some failures caused by operator errors or natural catastrophes. Still, it has some limitations. It is difficult to achieve complete error detection or fault-free software/hardware. Two situations that can give fatal consequences on availability and integrity are: 1) Simultaneous failure of all DBMS replicas, due to either fatal error propagation or accidental concurrent errors, making the system unavailable, 2) User data corruption (though the definition of fatal failure varies according to the requirements of the applications).

Software reliability has not kept pace with the hardware reliability over the past years. In the present systems, software is the bottleneck in achieving dependability, due to the complexity and the human factor involving in it. The software faults causing overlay errors are hard to trace and there impact are much higher than the regular errors [10].

The main goal of the DBMSs is to maintain the integrity

0-7695-0213-X/99 $10.00 © 1999 IEEE

of the database image. DBMSs cache parts (or whole) of the database image in data buffer area before processing, and later flush the processed data to a persistent medium in order to preserve the durability of the data. Residual hardware or software faults may result in corrupting the buffer area. In addition, DBMSs have increasingly started to integrate special-purpose application code in order to give extensibility and flexibility to applications. This application code is allowed to access data buffer area. This makes the buffer area vulnerable to get corrupted by unintentional application codes. Among the possible faults occur in a DBMS, one of the most interesting and important class of faults is the one that corrupt the buffer cache, since it is the one that could give a serious blow to the integrity requirement.

Gaining an insight in 1) situations that give fatal consequences, 2) how can they be masked, and 3) what is the overhead for such masking is valuable in building fault tolerant DBMSs.

Even though many DBMSs being built on shared-nothing architecture include fault tolerance by replication in their systems, e.g., Tandem Remote Duplicate Database Facility, Sybase Replication Server, Oracle7 Symmetric Replication Facility , IBM Remote Site Recovery, and Informix Online Server, there are very few studies highlighting the above mentioned aspects.

Ng and Chen [9] integrated reliable memory for caching data into Postgress DBMS in three different ways and used fault injection to evaluate them. Chillarege [2] studied the failure characteristics of the commercial transaction processing system, IBM's IMS, Version 1.3. These studies were performed on centralized database systems.

Our study improves the state of the art in the following ways:

It extends the idea of evaluating fault impact further to the next generation DBMSs, which are distributed, and replicated in order to achieve fault tolerance and thus, having increased complexity. Introduction of fault tolerance requires that the evaluation of fault impact incorporates the issues related to fault tolerance, such as, failure masking by replicas, error propagation to replicas, and so on. In addition, we concentrate on the effect of faults on the integrity of user data.

Our study reconciles concepts from separate research communities, fault tolerant computing systems and database systems. It applies fault injection to evaluate different coverage and performance parameters in a replicated DBMS context.

It introduces a generic fault injection method that can be adopted by any DBMS from the design/prototype phase throughout the development and testing phase to evaluate the effectiveness of the fault tolerance mechanisms and the performance tradeoff. This early evaluation enables the development team to improve design decisions as well as to detect and correct design faults at an earlier stage. Implementation of this method needs little effort since it exploits the existing client interface of a DBMS. Fault injection takes a few instructions and thus, the intrusion is minimal. In this experiment, this method is applied to the data structure in the data buffer area. This method can also be applied to other DBMS specific structures like log buffer, locks, message, etc. Data buffers are chosen because of their crucial role in DBMS integrity as mentioned earlier.

Different error scenarios are created by injecting errors into a test DBMS, ClustRa - version 1.1. The impact of these errors is analyzed and the performance degradation, the time the system is in reduced fault tolerance level, and coverage statistics are collected. Section 2 describes the testbed where the experiment was conducted. Section 3 describes the experiment setup and process. Section 4 analyzes the results. Section 5 contains a summary, conclusion, and future work.

2. The Testbed

ClustRa Architecture

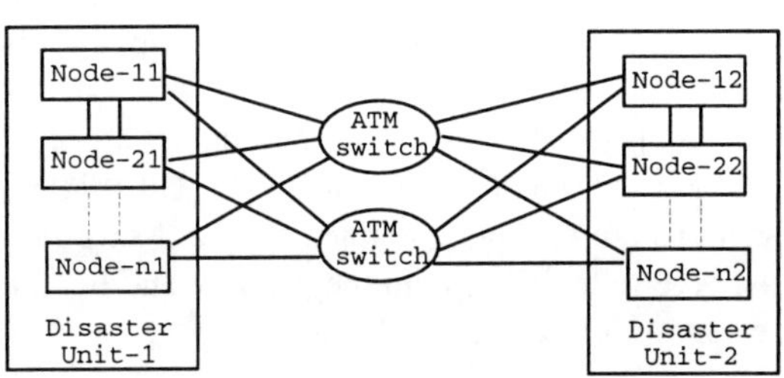

Figure 1. ClustRa architecture.

ClustRa provides a highly available, high performance, and fault tolerant DBMS platform for applications requiring soft real-time response time, e.g., applications in telecommunication. It is a replicated DBMS with a shared-nothing architecture, running on off-the-shelf UNIX work-stations. A **ClustRa node** is a work station running a ClustRa process. Nodes are grouped into different disaster units (having independent failure modes) connected by duplicated communication lines with high bandwidth. Duplication is used at process, data, and communication levels in order to minimize service unavailability and data loss, see Figure 1.

Data is partitioned into fragments and each fragment is replicated into **primary** and **hot standby** copies. They are placed in different nodes belonging to different disaster units, such that, the union of replicas in each disaster unit makes the whole database. Figure 2 shows how the data is partitioned and replicated among 4 nodes and 2 disaster units. Assume that the data is partitioned into 4 fragments, F_1, F_2, F_3, and F_4. Each fragment is replicated into two replicas, e.g., F_1 into R-111 and R-112 which are placed in Node-11 and Node-12 belonging to DisasterUnit-1 and DisasterUnit-2 respectively, and so on. **Counterpart nodes** are those nodes which contain the copies of the same data. E.g., in Figure 2, Node-11's counterpart is Node-12 and Node-21's counterpart is Node-22. Failures are handled at node granularity, i.e., a failure causes the ClustRa process to restart at that node it resides.

Active nodes contain data while **spare** nodes do not. Spare nodes are on-line, can serve as coordinators for client transactions. In case of an active node failure, a spare node from the same disaster unit can take over the failed node's role, if the failed node does not get repaired within a specified time. This reduces the time window the system functions without replication.

Each node runs a ClustRa process and a supervisor process. The latter manages (starts, stops, etc) the ClustRa process as well as sending heart beats to its neighbor nodes. A node is pronounced as dead by its neighbor nodes, if it does not send a heart beat within a timeout period. This message is spread to all nodes and a virtual partition management protocol is used to maintain a consistent set of available nodes and services[6]. A primary-hot standby coordinator process pair coordinates a transaction among primary-hot standby participant process pairs, using a 2-phase commit protocol [4]. Coordinator and participant processes are executed as light-weight threads within the ClustRa process. Transactions are executed atomically in a **2-safe manner**, i.e., they are reflected in both the primary and hot standby before commit or not reflected at all.

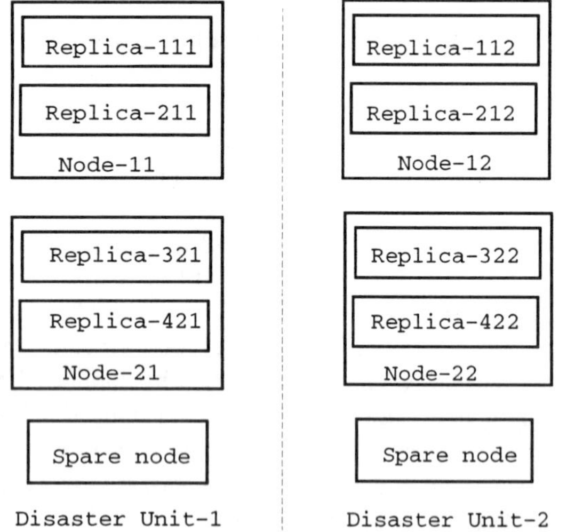

Figure 2. Data distribution in ClustRa.

ClustRa's Fault Tolerance Mechanisms: ClustRa masks all single node and single communication line failures. Different consistency checks are used to detect errors. Detected errors are categorized into three levels: normal, user, and serious. The first two error levels allow the system to continue functioning. User level errors do not harm the database integrity, therefore, the DBMS does not take any action other than informing the user about the error. Detection of serious errors makes ClustRa be fail silent [4].

A primary node failure is masked by its counterpart hot standby by **taking over** the primary role. The failure is detected by the missing heart-beat. During the takeover, some response to client transactions may time out for a fraction of a second, depending on the heart beat timeout. At the same time, the failed process is restarted by the supervisor process and an **online repair** is undertaken [1]. When the node (or eventually the spare) finishes repair, it **takes back** the primary role in order to balance the load.

3. Fault Injection Experiment

In complex systems like DBMSs, it is difficult to trace faults causing failures and system crashes. This is partly because the crash may leave incomplete or destroyed logs or the error has long latency. It is especially difficult in large, complex, parallel systems where the failure scenarios can not be reproducible since the order of the external events is not reproducible. Fault injection is used in order to identify and understand potential failures, their impact, and the system's ability to mask them, before the system is being operational, i.e., before the failure data from the field is available. Different hardware and software implemented fault injection (SWIFI) techniques are described in the literature. An overview of fault injection techniques and some tools is described in [5].

This section describes the experiment setup, underlying fault model used in the experiment, workload and fault injection process.

3.1. Testbed

A four-node ClustRa cluster is used in this experiment. Each disaster unit consists of one active and one spare node. A node is a Sun Ultra work station with a 200 MHz UltraSPARC processor, running ClustRa v.1.1, as illustrated in Figure 4.

3.2. Fault Model

Extensive field error reports and surveys are not available in young products like ClustRa, therefore we have to base our fault model on studies conducted in operating systems and databases [10, 11, 8]. Common software faults causing overlay errors are: assignment faults: e.g., code line *PreviousLog = tmp;* instead of *PreviousTrLog = tmp;* corrupts both PreviousLog and PreviousTrLog variables, initialization faults: wrong or forgotten initialization of variables, wild pointers: assignment or initialization faults to variables pointing memory locations, copy overflow: program copies bytes past end of buffer, type mismatch: a field is added to a structure, but all of the codes using that structure have not been modified to reflect the change, memory allocation: using a memory area after it has been freed, and undefined state: the system goes into a state unanticipated by the program may cause overlay errors since the invariant does not hold in this state.

The fault model that is relevant for our study is the software faults causing transient overlay errors that corrupt the data buffer area of the shared memory. Though overlay errors may corrupt any part of code or data, the ultimate (direct or propagated) corruption that affects the customers are those occur in database image. Since this corruption must be prevented in order to achieve the integrity goal of the DBMSs (see Sec. 1), the interest of this work lies in studying system behavior given that a corruption is occurred in the data buffer area. Since this corruption is a small subset of the errors resulting from the software faults causing overlays, we inject errors directly in the data buffer area in order to accelerate the database corruption, instead of injecting faults that result into direct or indirect corruption in data buffer area[1].

The question arises here is the validity of the mapping between the representative faults mentioned in the fault model and the errors being injected in this way. Christmansson and Chillarege [3] have proposed answers to the question of generating representative error sets that can be used in fault injection experiments, based on the field defect data for IBM OS. They address issues like what errors should be injected in which software module and when the injection should take place.

3.3. Workload Generator

The main purpose of the workload generator is to create an environment that can activate the error, i.e., it is accessed, propagated, or it crashes the system. The workload generator starts three parallel transaction clients (TC). Each TC sends single-tuple transactions to the DBMS, i.e., a transaction performs only one of the following operations on a single data record: insert, delete, update, or read. A TC is allowed to function 1) until it executes a maximum of 10,000 transactions sent in a back-to-back manner or 2) for a maximum of 300 seconds. 55% of the transactions are updates, 20% are read, and the rest is distributed among insert and delete such that at equilibrium, 75% of the inserted data exist. The size of the database is 4 MB at equilibrium. The data is divided into 3 tables, each is partitioned into 2 fragments, and each fragment is replicated. A data record consists of a primary key of type integer and a string type having variable length of maximum 512 bytes. Access to a data record is uniformly distributed, having no hot-spots. The workload is typical for telecommunication applications, for e.g., those setting up calls. Further, the transaction load is selected in order to exploit the system resources like CPU at the server to their maximum. The workload is designed to accelerate the access of a corrupted location by reducing the database size and increasing the number of transactions accessing the corrupted data.

[1] In [2], Chillarege inject overlay errors by overwriting a randomly chosen page of the real storage with hexadecimal 'FF's in order to accelerate an experiment studying the failure characteristics of the commercial transaction processing system, IBM's IMS, Version 1.3., instead of injecting faults.

3.4. Experiment Process

There are two experiments conducted. In the **first experiment**, errors are injected into a random area of the data buffer. This is referred to as error type *DBbuffer* in Sec.4. Start position for the corruption is uniformly distributed over the data buffer area. Number of bytes being corrupted is based on the study done by [10], but adjusted according to our software, platform, and experience. The distribution of number of bytes being corrupted is: 60% 1-4 bytes, 35% 5-1024 bytes, and 5% 1-9 KB.

This kind of general corruption does not give any specific information about 1) the data structure components lacking validity checks or 2) the causal relationship between the error source and the severity of the error impact, in other words, which particular component in the data buffer gives worst impact. If the answer to these questions are known, the weak component can be guarded with better detection techniques to limit the error impact. Therefore, we introduce specific errors in the **second experiment**. Here, we inject specific errors into particular components of the data structure covering the data buffer area.

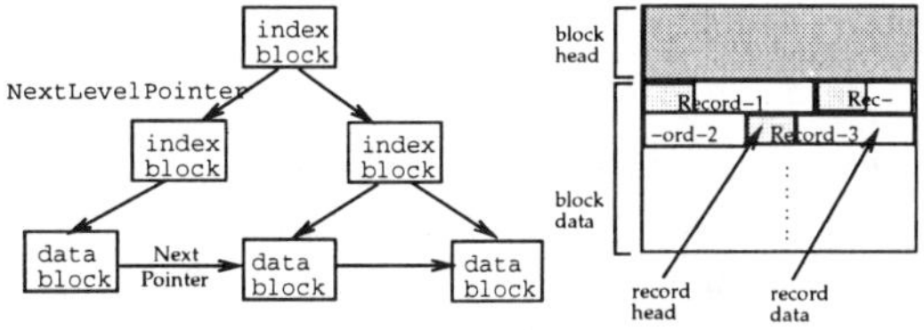

Figure 3. a) Structure of the data buffer area in use: index and data blocks are arranged in a tree structure. b) the layout of a block.

Data buffer area consists of used and unused data blocks. In order to accelerate the failures, we inject faults into the used area. Blocks in the used area are arranged in a B-tree structure, as shown in Figure 3. Each block has a header part and a data part. The data part consists of data records. The header part of a block consists of the following administrative data: block identifier, number of records in the block , number of free bytes in the block, high water mark - the position where a new record will be inserted, and a pointer to its next block (found in data blocks only). A record also has an administrative part and data part. Administrative part contains: a key descriptor describing the number of fields used to identify a record uniquely and an administrative descriptor stating whether a record has the knowledge about the log record that contains information about the last change a transaction made on the record. Data part of an index record contains access path to a block in next level. Data part of a data or leaf block contains user data. In the following sections, errors overlaid on these components are referred to as error types: *BlockId, NoOfRecords, NoOfBytesFree, HighWater, NextPointer, KeyDescriptor, AdmDescriptor, NextLevelPointer*, and *UserData*.

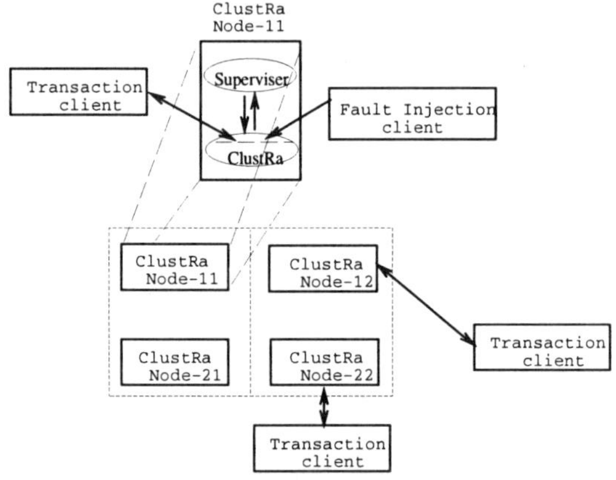

Figure 4. The experiment setup (ClustRa Node-11 is zoomed). Initially, Node-11 and Node-12 are active, and Node-21 and Node-22 are spare.

An experiment run consists of starting the DBMS and the workload generator, injecting an error, stopping the DBMS, and analyzing the logs, and is conducted by an experiment manager (EM). ClustRa processes are started on four ClustRa nodes as illustrated in Figure 4, two spare nodes and two active nodes. Active node-11 has primary data and node-12 has hot standby data. The workload generator is started 240 seconds after the DBMS is started, it is allowed to stabilize for 30 seconds, and then the fault injector is called with one of the error types mentioned above with relevant parameters. The workload is maintained for nearly 300 seconds. Then, the DBMS is requested to give the contents of the database. The DBMS is stopped after 300 seconds. In the analysis phase, the database content is compared with the database content maintained by the TC in order to see any discrepancy. Besides, each client checks each response delivered by the DBMS against its internal database for each transaction. The DBMS log containing repair information is also analyzed and the repair time is calculated.

There were 725 runs conducted in the first experiment, 50 runs for each specific error type in the second experiment, and 50 error-free or golden runs, totaling 1225 runs. The clock time used by each run is around fifteen minutes, giving a total of 306 hours. In order to create different fault scenarios as possible, each run was started with a different seed such that the choice of a block or position to be injected and the injection point in time varied. Therefore, the experiment did not evaluate the repeatability of the error impact.

The measures from the golden runs are used to evaluate the effects of fault tolerance mechanisms on performance in the presence of errors. In order to make the golden runs comparable to runs with fault injection, a golden run also executed the fault injection code, but overlaid an unused location instead.

3.5. Fault Injector

The fault injector (FI) injects error types mentioned in Section 3.4 into the data buffer area. The fault injector client (FIC) can also be started on a non-ClustRa node like a TC. FIC is started at a point in time distributed uniformly between 30-60 seconds after the workload generator is started. FIC is given the error type and the relevant parameters by the EM. For example, if the error type is BlockId, then the parameters will be a seed value used by EM to repeat the run if necessary, a data table identifier, and a flag saying whether the chosen buffer block is an index block, a data block, or any of them. FIC then sends a message containing the fault injection request together with the parameters. The DBMS server interface is extended to handle requests from a FIC. At the receipt of this message, this request is handled like the requests from the TCs. To process this request a small piece of software code is added to the DBMS server to access a memory address or data buffer component as specified by the parameters and overlay a random bit pattern accordingly. This takes very few machine instructions. In addition, comes one extra message-receiving cost per run. In order to enhance the analysis of the fault impact, ClustRa is run on trace-mode, i.e., it wrote information, such as, node crash detection time and the outcome of restart (success or not), and the restart finishing time to a trace file. This may result in some timing difference in the execution.

4. Analysis of Results

This section evaluates the fault tolerance of ClustRa from the experiment results. Two aspects of fault tolerance are

Error Type	# errors detected	# failures masked
Exp-1: DBbuffer	442(61%)	431 (97.5%)
Exp-2: NextLevelPointer	50	48
UserData	0	-
KeyDescriptor	48	47
AdmDescriptor	16	16
BlockId	50	50
NextPointer	25	24
NoOfRecords	50	49
NoOfBytesFree	1	1
HighWater	39	39
Total	279(62%)	274 (98%)

Table 1. Error coverage.

Error Type	# double failure	# data corruption
Exp-1: DBbuffer	11(1.5%)	11(1.5%)
Exp-2: NextLevelPointer	2	0
UserData	0	50
KeyDescriptor	1	0
AdmDescriptor	0	1
BlockId	0	0
NextPointer	1	0
NoOfRecords	1	1*
NoOfBytesFree	0	0
HighWater	0	7
Total	5(1%)	59(13%)

Table 2. Fatal failures. Data marked by '*' is explained in Fatal Failures section.

evaluated: effectiveness of error detection and efficiency of recovery.

4.1. Effectiveness of Error Detection

Effectiveness of error detection is measured by error coverage and fatal failures.

Error Coverage: Table 1 shows the coverage statistics. The first column shows the number of errors that are detected by the system and the error detection coverage - detected errors as a percentage of the total injected errors. Detection of an error causes the node to crash and a node failure is masked by a hot standby takeover. The second column shows the number of successful masking and coverage. In the first experiment, 61% of the 725 injected errors were detected. 97.5% of the detected failures were masked, except for the **double failures**, where both active nodes crashed almost simultaneously within a very short interval (see Table 2 for double failure statistics). The spare nodes cannot take over in this case because there is no available active node to copy data from online. In the second experiment, the corresponding figures were: 62% and 98%.

Locations *UserData* and *NoOfBytesFree* show very low detection, 0 and 1 cases respectively. Low error detection means that the erroneous locations were either not accessed, overwritten, or read without being tested. The experiment did not have enough instrumentation to verify whether an erroneous location is accessed or not, except from the failure manifestations and thus, cannot differentiate the errors overwritten and the dormant ones. However, the observed fatal failures of Table 2 shows clearly that the *UserData* is read without tested and contribute to severe integrity loss.

Fatal Failures: Double failures and user data corruption are defined as fatal failures from the severity of their consequences. The former makes the DBMS unavailable until the data is restored from a backup and also causes the recently committed transactions to be lost. The latter affects the integrity of DBMSs. Table 2 shows that there were 11 double failures in the first experiment (1.5%) and 5 double failures (1%) in the second one. Five of these 16 cases were traced to two design faults in the recovery mechanism, which were accidentally provoked on the recovering node and its counterpart almost simultaneously. The rest might be resulted from error propagation, but could not be verified.

User data corruption is detected by the client by comparing the DBMS reply with its internal database. In the first experiment, 11 runs shows user data corruption. In the second experiment, the corresponding figure was 59. In the second experiment, the majority (50) comes from the *UserData* corruption since *UserData* have no detection mechanism associated with it. Apart from that, there were only 9 runs found with data corruption for the rest of 400 runs (2%) in the second experiment. This figure corresponds to that of the first experiment (1.5%), where the choice of *UserData* for corruption was random, not as deterministic as 50 out 450 of the second experiment.

HighWater is very much vulnerable to data corruption (7 out of 50 runs). In 4 of the 9 runs, one or more committed transactions were missing. This can be the consequence of the design fault found in the double failure case or another design fault found in the checkpoint mechanism. One of these 4 cases show severe inconsistency in user data (marked by '*'). Further analysis shows that this case had consecutive node failures, i.e., after the first node crashed and repaired itself, the counterpart node crashed and re-

Error Type	Repair Time (sec)	Online repair	Rep.not finished
DBbuffer	124	315	116
NextLevelPointer	160	22	26
UserData	0	0	0
KeyDescriptor	147	42	5
AdmDescriptor	124	10	6
BlockId	110	40	10
NextPointer	143	19	5
NoOfRecords	134	43	6
NoOfBytesFree	66	1	0
HighWater	155	30	9

Table 3. Time taken to restore the replication level, number of cases where the online repair succeeded and not succeeded.

Error Type	**Performance Degradation**
DBbuffer	0.121019
NextLevelPointer	0.146497
UserData	0.0127389
KeyDescriptor	0.210191
AdmDescriptor	0.0764331
BlockId	0.146497
NextPointer	0.0764331
NoOfRecords	0.171975
NoOfBytesFree	0
HighWater	0.191083

Table 4. Performance degradation due to the errors.

paired itself, before the occurrence of double failure. Since this was the only case where consecutive node crash was found, it is difficult to draw any conclusions, but it may indicate an error propagation or some other design fault in the recovery mechanism. Due to the non-repeatable nature of the experiment, the fault could not be traced.

4.2. Efficiency of Recovery

Efficiency of recovery is characterized by the period of time the system is in reduced fault tolerance level and the performance degradation due to fault tolerance activities.

The period of time system is in reduced fault tolerance level: This is the time the system runs without replication after a node crash. It is calculated as the time between a node crash and a successful repair of it (or the spare). This period is very crucial because if the functioning replica node fails before the repair is finished, a double failure will occur. The longer the system is in a reduced fault tolerance level, the higher the danger to get a double failure. Column 1 of Table 3 shows the period of time the system was in a reduced fault tolerance level. *NextLevelPointer, HighWater, KeyDescriptor, NextPointer, NoOfRecords*, and *AdmDescriptor* show long repair time, and the double failures (Table 2) have occurred within these error types. The exceptions *HighWater* and *AdmDescriptor* indicate the non-deterministic nature of events causing double failure, depending on the transaction pattern and load, error propagation to the counterpart node, and the error detection mechanisms.

Columns 2 and 3 of Table 3 shows the node failure cases where the online repair was succeeded and not. The error type *NextLevelPointer* shows severe problems, having half of its runs unable to finish the repair. Further tracing shows that 80% of the repair-not-finished cases in the first experiment and 96% in the *NextLevelPointer* indicated a design fault in the repair mechanism. Due to this fault, the crashed node and the spare got into a deadlock situation such that none of them were able to complete the repair.

In two of the runs belonging to *NextPointer* error type, the failure was masked by recovery even though the error was not really removed. This dormant error had the potential to crash the process when being accessed next time. One of the runs showed a design fault in the repair algorithm, where the crashed and the spare node from the same disaster unit *both* repaired themselves successfully, which should not occur according to the replication semantics.

Performance degradation reflects the fault tolerance overhead. Performance degradation is measured from the clients' point of view. Each run measures the number of transactions succeeded per second (TPS). Average TPS for faulty runs is calculated for each error type. This average is compared with the average TPS of the 50 golden runs.

$$PerformanceDegradation_{ErrorType_i} = 1 - \frac{AverageTPS_{ErrorType_i}}{AverageTPS_{golden}}$$

The results are presented in Table 4. The repair activity generally has an adverse impact on performance. After a node crash, the active counterpart node must help the crashed node to recover in order to reestablish the fault tolerance level. In addition to serving the usual TCs, the active node must send the database image if necessary and the changes occurred in the database after the node crash, to the recovering node. This extra activity reduces the TC throughput. As shown in Table 4, this is evident in *UserData, NoOfBytesFree, AdmDescriptor*, and *NextPointer* which have less error detection coverage, and hence, less repair activity, and as a result, less throughput loss.

On the contrary, *KeyDescriptor, HighWater, NoOfRecords, NextLevelPointer*, and *BlockId* have high detection coverage and repair activity and show high performance degradation. Variations like *BlockId* having 50 error detection has 14% throughput loss while *KeyDescriptor* having 48 error detection has 21% throughput loss could have been caused by the factors such as, the size of the database and the period of time the crashed node was away at the time of the repair, which are not tracked in the experiment.

In order to get a real life statistics, the performance should be corrected to undermine the cost of fault injection and executing the DBMS in the trace-mode where it writes trace information regarding repair to a log file.

5. Summary, Conclusion, and Future Work

Fault tolerance ability of a replicated DBMS and fault impact are evaluated in the presence of software errors corrupting data buffer area in the DBMS process's shared memory. A generic fault injection method, extending the existing client interface, is used to inject errors in different data structures of a DBMS. Data buffer area is chosen in this experiment due to its crucial role in a DBMS.

Error detection and failure masking, together with the impact of faults on integrity, performance, and availability are evaluated. General corruption of the first experiment shows that 61% of the 725 errors are detected. All detected errors caused in node failures. All the node failures are masked by hot standby replica node taking over, except in the 1.5% double failure cases. The fault tolerance level is restored successfully in 71% of the failure cases, but in 26% of the failure cases, the repair was not finished. 91% of these repair-not-finished cases are caused by a design fault in the repair mechanism that put the repair in a deadlock situation. In 1.5% of the total runs show user data corruption. Two design faults in repair mechanism cause 2 double failures. A design fault in checkpoint mechanism and the one in repair mechanism (mentioned above) caused integrity problems. (Further, the study also identified another erroneous behavior of the system regarding to repair.) Performance degradation due to fault tolerance activities is 12%.

General corruption did not give enough feedback about 1) the weak components in the system, which have to be guarded in order to improve the fault detection and hence fault tolerance and 2) the causal relationship between the error source and the severity of the fault impact. Therefore, a second experiment was conducted by corrupting specific data components present in the data buffer area. We identified components which are very sensitive and affect database integrity (*UserData, HighWater*), availability (*NextLevelPointer*), and performance degradation (*KeyDescriptor*).

The results from the first experiment can be used to get an insight on fault tolerant DBMSs in general, while the results from the second experiment is more relevant to those DBMSs which arrange the data in a B-tree structure, which is the case with most of the traditional DBMSs. Further, fault injection proved to be an efficient complementary validation method. It provoked failure scenarios which other traditional testing methods did not do. In our case, this lead to trace 4 residual design faults in the recovery and checkpoint mechanisms.

The findings suggest that error detection mechanism connected to data buffer components needs an enhancement, such as, a checksum or some kind of memory scrubbing in order to guard the vulnerable components individually, or collectively at block level, or block head level together with record level.

A study similar to this is essential to evaluate the improvement on fault tolerance and tradeoff on performance by these proposed error detection methods. It would also be interesting to evaluate the dependability growth after the disclosed design faults being corrected. Further, Using standard workloads like TPC-C [7] will make the results of the study more interesting for a wider user community.

References

[1] S. Bratsberg, Ø. Grøvlen, S. Hvasshovd, B. Munch, and Ø. Torbjørnsen. Providing a Highly Available Database by Replication and Online Self-Repair. *International Journal of Engineering Intelligent Systems*, 4(3):131–139, 1996.

[2] R. Chillarege and N. Bowen. Understanding Large System Failures - A Fault Injection Experiment. *Proc. 19th. Ann. Int'l Symp. Fault Tolerant Computing*, pages 356–363, 1989.

[3] J. Christmansson and R. Chillarege. Generation of an error set that emulates software faults based on field data. In *Proc. 26th. Ann. Int'l Symp. on Fault Tolerant Computing*, 1996.

[4] J. Gray and A. Reuter. *"Transaction Processing: Concepts and Techniques"*. Morgan Kaufmann Publishers Inc., 1993.

[5] M.-C. Hsueh, T. Tsai, and R. Iyer. Fault Injection Techniques and Tools. *Computer*, April 1997.

[6] S. Hvasshovd, Ø. Torbjørnsen, S. E. Bratsberg, and P. Holager. The ClustRa Telecom Database: High Availability, High Throughput and Real Time Response. In *Proceedings of the 21st VLDB Conference, Zürich*, 1995.

[7] J.Gray, editor. *"The Benchmark Handbook for Database and Transaction Processing Systems"*. Morgan Kaufmann Publishers Inc., 1991.

[8] I. Lee and R. Iyer. Faults, Symtoms, and Software Fault Tolerance in the Tandem GUARDIAN Operating System. *Proc. FTCS-23*, pages 20–29, 1993.

[9] W. T. Ng and P. M. Chen. Integrating Reliable Memory in Databases. *Proc. of the 23rd VLDB Conference, 1997*, 1997.

[10] M. Sullivan and R. Chillarege. Software Defects and their Impact on System Availability- A Study of Field Failures in Operating Systems. *Proc. FTCS-21*, pages 2–9, 1991.

[11] M. Sullivan and R. Chillarege. A Comparison of Software Defects in Database Management Systems and Operating Systems. *Proc. FTCS-22*, pages 475–484, 1992.

Identification of Test Cases Using a Formal Approach*

Purnendu Sinha and Neeraj Suri
ECE Dept., Boston University, Boston, MA 02215
e-mail: {*sinha, suri*}*@bu.edu*

Abstract

A key feature in fault injection (FI) based validation is identifying the relevant test cases to inject. This problem is exacerbated at the protocol level where the lack of detailed fault distributions limits the use of statistical approaches in deriving and estimating the number of test cases to inject. In this paper we develop and demonstrate the capabilities of a formal approach to protocol validation, where the deductive and computational analysis capabilities of formal methods are shown to be able to identify very specific test cases, and analytically identify equivalence classes of test cases.

1 Introduction

Computers that support critical applications utilize composite dependable and real-time protocols to deliver reliable and timely services; the high (and often unacceptable) costs of incurring operational disruptions being a significant design consideration. Due to inherently large state-space covered by these protocols, the conventional verification and validation (V&V) techniques incur prohibitive costs in time needed for their testing. One commonly used validation technique is that of fault injection. Although a wide variety of techniques and tools exist for fault injection [9], the limitations are the actual coverage of the state space to be tested. In this respect, the challenges are to develop a comprehensive and complete suite of test cases over the large operational state space and be able to identify a limited number of specific and realizable tests. Thus, if mechanisms existed that could determine the specific set of conditions (cases) on which the protocol inherently depends, the effectiveness of the overall FI based validation would be significantly enhanced.

Towards these objectives, in [11] we had introduced the use of formal techniques for specification and V&V of dependable protocols, and the process of incorporating implementation information into formal verification. The intent was to utilize formal verification information to aid construct FI experiments for protocol validation. Particularly, we introduced two data structures, *Inference Tree* and *Dependency Tree*, to represent protocol verification information, with these structures having capabilities for symbolic execution and query processing, respectively.

*Supported in part by DARPA DABT63-96-C-0044 and NSF CAREER CCR 9896321

In this paper, we develop our formal approach introduced in [11]. Specifically, we **(a)** explore the deductive and computational analysis capabilities of our formal-method-based query processing mechanisms, **(b)** highlight the capabilities of our approach through a case study of a composite dependable, real-time protocol where we have been able to identify flaws in the analysis, and also ascertain specific test cases, and **(c)** analytically identify equivalence classes of test cases of infinite size.

The organization of the paper is as follows. Section 2 provides a background of our formal approach for pre-injection analysis introduced in [11]. Section 3 overviews the fault-tolerant real-time scheduling protocol that we utilize to demonstrate the effectiveness of our approach. Section 4 outlines our formal approach for identifying specific test cases to validate the protocol under consideration. We conclude with a discussion in Section 5.

2 Formal Pre-Injection Analysis

In [11] we introduced a formal approach for pre-injection analysis to determine fault and activation paths that would guide the FI-based validation of dependable protocols. In this paper, we develop the use of formal techniques identify test cases (pre-injection) to provide a FI toolset for it to construct a FI experiment, i.e., guide the selection and construction of specific FI experiments. We provide a brief review of our basic approach of [11] prior to detailing our test identification process in Sections 3 and 4. We also refer to [11] for a discussion on the impact of refs. [1-6] in the development of our formal approach.

In [11], we developed two novel data structures, *Inference Trees (IT)* and *Dependency Trees (DT)*, to encapsulate protocol attributes generated over the for-

0-7695-0213-X/99 $10.00

mal specification and verification process to identify system states and design/implementation parameters to construct test cases. For both IT and DT, we utilize the fact that fault tolerance protocols are invariably characterized by decision stages leading to branches processing specific fault-handling cases [1, 3, 5, 6, 12]. This is a key concept behind validation, which tries to investigate all the possible combinations of branching over time and with parametric information.

We review the basic features of IT and DT structures prior to discussing their use in identification of test cases in this paper. For a detailed discussion on the IT and DT, we refer the reader to [11].

2.1 Inference Trees: Symbolic Execution

The IT is developed to depict the inference (implication) space involved in a protocol. Each node of the tree represents a primitive *FUNCTION* of the protocol. Associated with each node is a set of *CONDITIONALS* which dictate the flow of operation to the subsequent *ACTION* as defined for the protocol, and the *INFERENCE* space which details the possibility of operations, assertions, and/or usage of event-conditional variables which can be inferred from the operation specification. Fig. 1 depicts an IT for a majority (2/3) voter. We emphasize that the generation of the IT is iterative (see block on top right in Fig. 1).

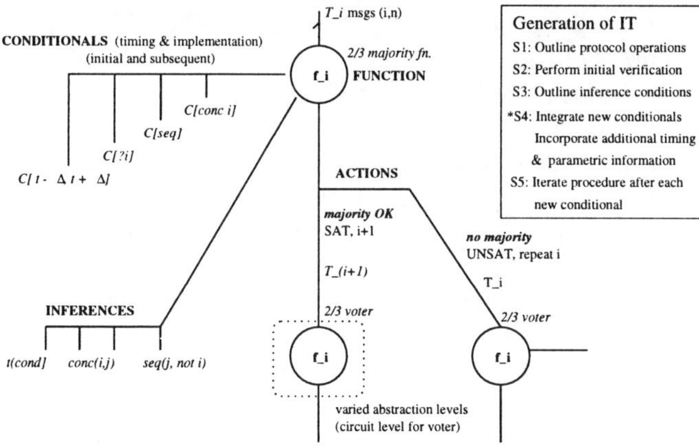

Figure 1: The Inference Tree for a 2/3 Voter Protocol

Although, the IT visually outlines the protocol operations, it does not in itself provide any FI information. The DT structure, described next, utilizes the IT generated inferences to facilitate query mechanisms that get used to identify test cases.

2.2 Dependency Tree: Query Engine

The DT is generated by identifying all functional blocks of a protocol, and ascertaining the set of variables that directly or indirectly influence the protocol operation. Deductive logic used by the verifier is applied to determine the actual dependency (or lack of it) of the function on each individual variable, thus determining the actual subset of variables that influence the protocol operation. Fig. 2 depicts the DT for a multiple round consensus protocol.

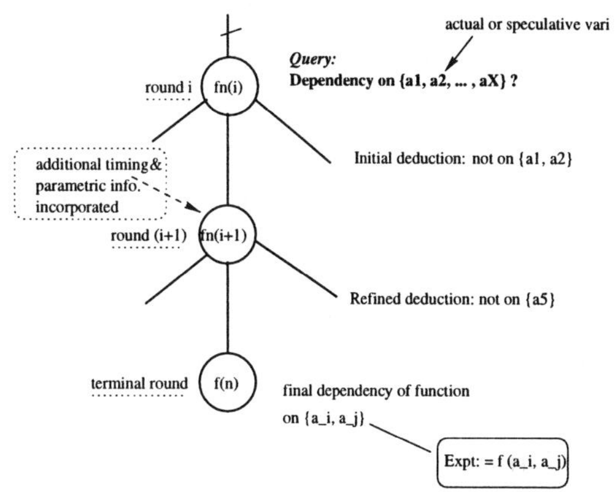

Figure 2: The Dependency Tree : Consensus Example

2.3 Nuances of the IT/DT Approach

The objective of our verification process is to guide the selection of appropriate queries to be posed in the DT. The set of conditionals in the IT are not fixed on *a priori* basis. Each round of iteration can generate constraining conditions which in turn get reflected as new conditionals. This initial set of conditionals serve as an actual (or speculative) list of variables for the DT. At each iteration, the dependency list is pruned as one progresses along a reachability path. In the absence of any new conditionals being added, the dependency list of the DT is monotonically decreasing. In case new conditionals are specified, variables which were pruned earlier from the dependency list may reappear in the next DT iteration.

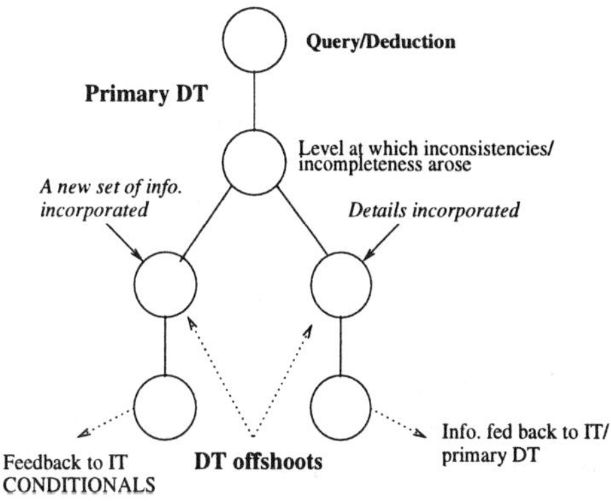

Figure 3: Spawning of the Primary DT

The primary DT represents a given level of specification detail incorporated in the IT. At any stage of query processing if an inconsistency arises, or an incompleteness is found, and accordingly a new set of information is added, the primary DT can have secondary DT offshoots as needed, as illustrated in Fig. 3. The deductions from the spawned DTs are then, as needed, fed back to the parent DT. The overall function dependencies can be used as feedback to specify conditionals in the IT. We emphasize that the DT may not fully represent all possible variable dependencies as it will always be limited to the amount of operational information actually modeled into the formal specification. At any desired level, the elements of the current dependency list provides us with a (possibly) minimal set of parameters which guides formulation of the FI experiments via all permutations and combinations, and *ideally* should generate specific (or a family of) test cases. We repeat that our intent is pre-injection analysis in identifying specific test cases. The actual FI experiments are implemented from these test cases based on the chosen FI toolset(s).

We stress that the IT/DT approach strengthens both verification and validation by making these two processes iterative (over varied implementation detail levels). Fig. 4 represents the general process of FI experimentation using the IT and DT approach.

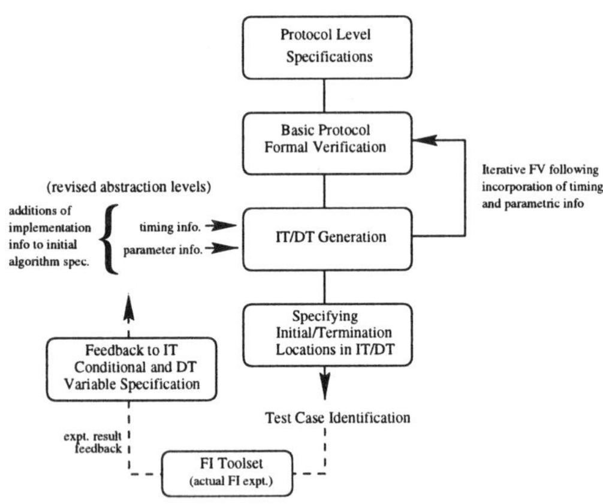

Figure 4: Generating the FI Experiments

The following steps are utilized in our approach to aid the FI process: **(a)** outline protocol operations and establish formal specification of the protocol, **(b)** perform initial verification to demonstrate that the specification conforms to the system requirements, following this, **(c)** generate the IT/DT utilizing the verification information to enumerate the execution paths and establish the dependency of the operations on the design variables, and **(d)** propagate through the DT to identify and select parameters and/or functional blocks to identify test cases for FI.

With this background, we now elaborate our IT/DT based process of ascertaining specific test cases through a case study.

3 A Case Study : FT-RT Scheduling

We have selected the fault-tolerant rate monotonic algorithms (FT-RMA) as they are representative of a large class of composite dependable, real-time protocols. FT-RMA was developed in DCCA [7] and a modified journal version in [8]. Over the process of using these protocols [7, 8] to show viability of our formal V&V approach, we have been able to identify test cases that actually make the FT-RMA protocols of [7, 8] fail. We first introduce the RMA [10] protocol on which FT-RMA [7, 8] is based. Given our space constraints, we refer the reader to [10, 7, 8] for details.

3.1 Rate Monotonic Algorithm

The *Rate Monotonic Algorithm* (RMA) [10] is a fundamental scheduling paradigm. Consider a set of n independent, periodic and preemptible tasks $\tau_1, \tau_2, \cdots, \tau_n$, with periods $T_1 \leq T_2 \leq \cdots \leq T_n$ and execution times $C_1, C_2, \cdots, C_n$, respectively, being executed on a uni-processor system where each task must be completed before the next request for it occurs, i.e., by its specified period. A task's utilization, U_i, is thus C_i/T_i. The processor utilization of n tasks is given by $U = \sum_{i=1}^{n} \frac{C_i}{T_i}$. The RMA is an optimal static priority algorithm for the described task model, in which *a task with shorter period is given higher priority than a task with longer period.* A schedule is called *feasible* if each task starts after its release time and completes before its deadline. A given set of tasks is said to be *RM-Schedulable* if RMA produces a feasible schedule.

A set of tasks is said to *fully utilize* the processor if (a) the RM-schedule meets all deadlines, and (b) if the execution time of any task is increased, the task set is no longer RM-schedulable. Given n tasks in the task set with execution times C_i for task τ_i; if $C_i = T_{i+1} - T_i \quad \forall i \in \{1, n-1\}$, and $C_n = 2T_1 - T_n$, then under the RM algorithm, the task set fully utilizes the processor. The following theorem provides a sufficient condition to check for RM-schedulability.

Theorem 1 (L&L Bound [10]) *Any set of n periodic tasks is RM-schedulable if the processor utilization is no greater than $U_{LL} = n(2^{\frac{1}{n}} - 1)$.* □

The classical RMA does not address the issues of fault tolerance. In the next section, we describe an approach proposed in [7] to provide for fault tolerance by incorporating temporal redundancy into RMA.

3.2 FT Rate Monotonic Algorithm

The FT-RMA approach [7] describes a recovery scheme for the re-execution of faulty tasks, including a scheme to distribute slack (i.e., idle time) in the schedule, and derives schedulability bounds for set of tasks considering fault-tolerance through re-execution of tasks. Cases with a single or multiple faults within an interval of length $T_n + T_{n-1}$ are considered. Faults are assumed to be transient such that a single identified faulty task can be re-executed by a backup task.

A recovery scheme that ensures re-execution of a task must satisfy the following conditions:

> **C[S1]:** There should be sufficient slack for any one instance of any given task to re-execute.
>
> **C[S2]:** When any instance of τ_i finishes executing, all slack distributed within its period should be available for the re-execution of τ_i in case a fault is detected.
>
> **C[S3]:** When a task re-executes, it should not cause any other task to miss its deadline.

The recovery scheme proposed in [7] being:
The faulty task should re-execute at its own priority.

The following lemmas show the proof of correctness of this approach.

Lemma 1 ([7]) *If backup task utilization* (U_B), $U_B \geq C_i/T_i$, $i = 1, \ldots, n$, *then* **[S1]** *is satisfied.* □

Lemma 2 ([7]) *If* **C[S1]** *is satisfied, and swapping*[1] *takes place, then* **C[S2]** *is satisfied.* □

Lemma 3 ([7]) *If* **C[S1]** *and* **C[S2]** *are satisfied, and the faulty task is re-executed at its own priority, then* **C[S3]** *is satisfied.* □

A FT-RMA utilization bound was computed to guarantee schedulability in the presence of a single fault. This schedulability bound was derived as: $U_{FT-RMA} = U_{LL}(1 - U_B)$, where U_B is equal to the maximum of all tasks utilizations ($U_B = \max U_i$).

However, this recovery scheme of [7] may fail in meeting a task's deadline, even though a given task set satisfies U_{FT-RMA} bound. A modified recovery scheme is presented in [8] as:
In the recovery mode, τ_r will re-execute at its own priority, except for the following case: *During recovery mode, any instance of task that has a priority higher than that of τ_r and a deadline greater than that of τ_r will be delayed until recovery is complete.*

After this brief introduction to FT-RMA, we now detail our IT/DT based process for identifying test cases for the V&V of FT-RMA.

[1]The slack is shifted in time by being swapped with the task's execution time if no fault occurs.

4 FT-RMA: The Formal V&V Process

We initiated the formal verification of FT-RMA to establish the correctness of the proposed solutions based on the assertions provided in the hand analysis of FT-RMA [7, 8]. It is important to note that the verification process only establishes the *correctness* of assertions, and does *not* by itself identify the explicit cause of a verification inconsistency.

4.1 Verification: Identification of Flaws in FT-Rate Monotonic Algorithm

Our initial step was to formally specify[2] and verify the FT-RMA protocols [7, 8]. Since in [8] the authors had modified the recovery scheme of [7] (see end of Section 3.2), our initial interest was to explore the capability of the formal process to identify a cause due to which a recovery task fails to meet its deadline. The main effort in formal specification was devoted in formalizing various assumptions on task and system models, system requirements, the scheduling policies, fault assumptions, and recovery schemes and associated conditions they must satisfy.

We initiated our efforts towards verification of FT-RMA (i.e., to ensure that conditions $C[S1]$, $C[S2]$ and $C[S3]$ in Section 3.2 are satisfied) by attempting to prove putative theorems reflecting expected behaviors of the protocol operations. With the initial verification and subsequent interactive usages of IT/DT (discussed in the next section), we found out that the scheme of [7] fails to ensure schedulability of lower priority tasks and thereby violates the $C[S3]$ stated in Section 3.2. This particular flaw was **not** discovered earlier by the authors of [7, 8]. With the same conditions being imposed on a task set and permitting changes in the priority of the recovery task, we were also able to discover that the modified recovery scheme [8] *also fails.* The process of identifying the causes behind these flaws appear in the subsequent sections, i.e., the test cases.

4.2 Visualization: IT/DT for FT-RMA

The objective of the formal verification and representation of verification information in the IT structure (Fig. 5) is to guide the selection of appropriate queries to be posed in the DT. It is important to note that the selection and formal representation of queries to be posed is still an interactive process. Automating this process is ongoing work.

The various assumptions on task characteristics, utilization bound, task ordering in the schedule, and the feasibility criteria for the task set are reflected

[2]The complete specifications, and issues pertaining to the automation of the formal processes, for RMA and FT-RMA are at http://eng.bu.edu/~suri/specs/specs.html.

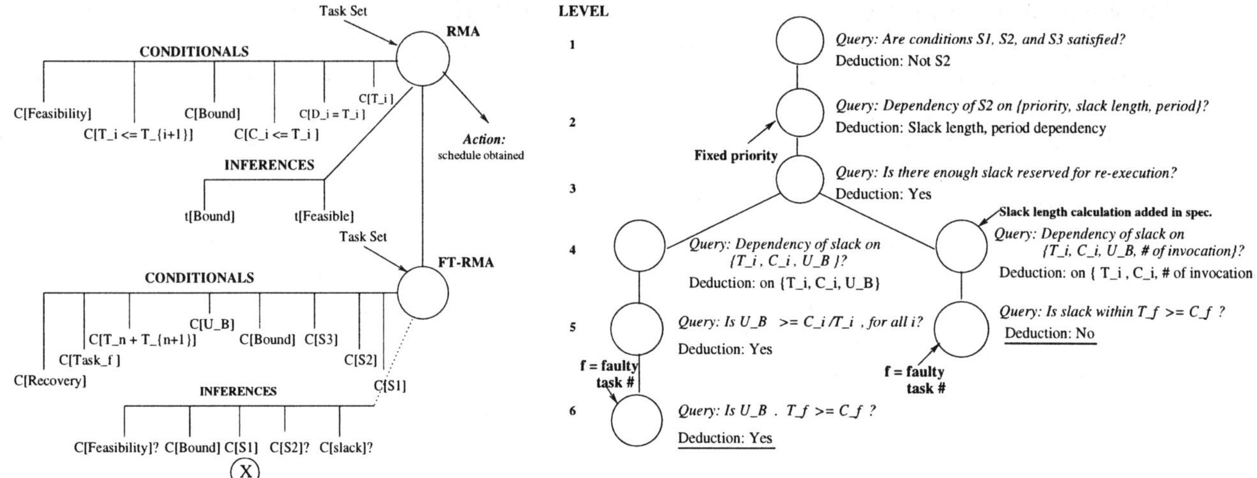

Figure 6: The DT for FT-RMA : Phase I

Figure 5: Inference Tree for RMA & FT-RMA

in the CONDITIONAL[3] space of RMA. Under a no-fault condition (for the given task set) the utilization bound and the feasibility conditions are satisfied, and are indicated in the INFERENCE space. The conditions for successful re-execution of a faulty task, namely, $C[S1], C[S2]$ and $C[S3]$ of Section 3.2, and various conditions on fault-tolerant schedulability bound, backup utilization, time between two faults, faulty task and recovery criteria are specified in the CONDITIONAL space of FT-RMA. The feasibility test under single fault case gets reflected in the INFERENCE space of FT-RMA indicating that the task set meets the U_{FT-RMA} bound but the schedule is not feasible. Based on the formal representation of backup utilization and backup slot distribution over a specified period, verification of recovery conditions also indicated that $C[S1]$ is satisfied but $C[S2]$ is not as indicated by *C[S2]?* in Fig. 5.

The above observation led us to pose queries in our query engine, the DT structure, to identify the exact dependencies of $C[S2]$. During the first phase of query processing in the DT (Fig. 6) at Level 1 we inferred that $C[S2]$ is not satisfied. Further we posed query (at Level 2) to determine the actual dependencies of $C[S2]$ on different parameters. With the priority of recovery task being fixed, the DT deduction declared dependencies on slack length and task's period (as deadline depends on task's period). Next, we posed the query to check whether there is enough slack reserved for the re-execution of the faulty task. Based on the definition of backup utilization and backup slots length calculation, the IT/DT confirmed that there was enough slack available in the schedule. These flagged discrepancies in Lemma 2 as $C[S2]$ should have been satisfied if there was enough slack reserved in the schedule and swapping had taken place. This observation led the primary DT to offshoot two DT's at Level 3 to identify the exact conditions on which satisfaction of $C[S2]$ depends on. The left branch of the DT basically went through the proof of Lemma 1, and as a final deduction indicated that there was enough slack reserved for re-execution of the faulty task. These conflicting observations revealed that the backup slots reserved for re-execution may not be available for that purpose, thereby contradicting the statement in Lemma 1. This information is then reflected in the IT (Fig. 5) as inference $C[S1]$ being marked as X, indicating that as per Lemma 1, $C[S1]$ may not be true. The right branch of the DT incorporated the specification for slack length calculation based on number of invocation of different tasks and their execution times. We next posed the query in the DT to determine whether backup utilization has any effect on the slack length calculation, and it turned out that there is none! We then posed the query, Level 5, to ascertain whether there is slack available in the schedule before the task's deadline. The DT deduced that there is not enough slack available for the faulty task to re-execute. This deduction confirmed that the claim in Lemma 2 is flawed. At this stage the inconsistency in the FT-RMA has been flagged, though the cause behind it is yet to be determined, i.e., the test cases.

4.3 Identification of Specific Test Cases

Observing these discrepancies highlighted by the DT, we started the second phase of the DT — Fig. 7. We incorporated the conditions in the DT to reflect full utilization of the processor by a task set. We

[3]Represented as $C[feasibility], C[Bound]$, etc. in Fig 5

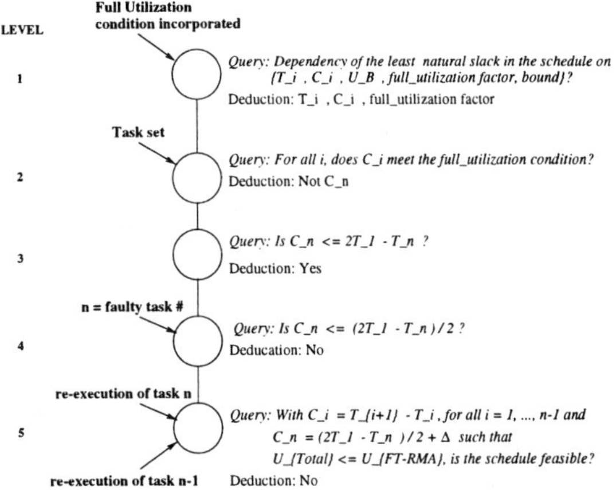

Figure 7: The DT for FT-RMA : Phase II

queried to determine the parameters on which the least natural slack length in the schedule depends on. Next, at Level 2, we posed a query to determine any correlation of the chosen task set to the definition of fully utilized task set. As it turned out that except for the lowest priority task, all other tasks in the set meet the criteria. We then confirmed whether the execution time of the lowest priority task is less than the maximum possible value of C_n. In case of the lowest priority task being faulty, to be able to re-execute successfully under full utilization condition, its execution time should not exceed $(2T_1 - T_n)/2$. At Level 4, the query deduced that this condition is not satisfied for the given task set. With the execution time of the lowest priority task, C_n, being $(2T_1 - T_n)/2 + \Delta$ ($\Delta > 0$ can be considered as small as possible) such that $\sum_i U_i \leq U_{FT-RMA}$, we next posed a query to determine whether such a task set is RM-schedulable under the following two fault conditions: (a) the lowest priority task n is faulty, and (b) the second lowest priority task $n-1$ is faulty. The faulty task is re-executed at its own priority while recovering. We inferred that for the first case the faulty task is not able to re-execute and complete successfully. For the second case, the lowest priority task cannot finish before its deadline due to the re-execution of the second lowest priority task. This led us to conclude that the proofs of Lemma 2 and also Lemma 3 in the hand-analysis failed to consider the case of full utilization of the processor by a task set.

We point out that with these set of conditionals and with the second lowest priority task, τ_{n-1}, being faulty, the modified recovery scheme of [8] fails to ensure schedulability of the lowest priority task, τ_n, as will be illustrated in Section 4.4.

We emphasize that cases to be tested are derived by queries related to discrepancies between the levels. In this case, the discrepancies arose in the first phase of the DT related to the availability of slack for re-execution. Phase II of the DT probed further into this issue. The propagation through the DT (phase II) outlines the set of conditionals those corresponding to full utilization of the processor by a task set which affected the availability of slacks for re-execution of the faulty task. Furthermore, these set of conditionals were enough to pinpoint the insufficiency of the U_{FT-RMA} bound (Level 5). Thus, the failure of query at Level 5 results in this query essentially being the test case, i.e., the test case is:

$$\begin{aligned} C_i &= T_{i+1} - T_i, \quad \forall\, i \;\; 1 \leq i \leq n-1, \\ C_n &= (2T_1 - T_n)/2 + \Delta, \\ & \quad \textit{such that} \sum_i U_i \leq U_{FT-RMA} \end{aligned} \tag{1}$$

We stress the fact that for validating scheduling protocols, identification of a fault case is similar to identifying a task set which would violate the basis of the protocol operations. We elaborate and illustrate these findings in the following section. Note that this test case will form the basis of constructing a FI experiment using a chosen FI toolset.

4.4 Identified Test Case Effectiveness

As discussed in the previous section, conditions for full utilization of the processor is a guiding factor to validate the proposed schemes of FT-RMA. Let us consider[4] a set of 4 periodic tasks, $\{\tau_1, \tau_2, \tau_3, \tau_4\}$, with their respective periods being 4, 4.5, 5 and 6, and the deadline of each task being equal to its period. Utilizing Eq. 1, the execution times are then computed as shown in Table 4.4. Thus, the values of U_B, U_{LL} and U_{FT-RMA}, as expressed in Sections 3.1 and 3.2, are 0.2, 0.7568 and 0.6054, respectively. Note that the value of C_4 is upper bounded by the execution time such that the corresponding total processor utilization is equal to U_{FT-RMA}. Thus, the execution time of τ_4, C_4, can have any numerical value[5] satisfying $1 < C_4 < 1.0158$. As a test case, we choose C_4 as 1.01. Thus, the total processor utilization by the task set is 0.6044. Since the total processor utilization by this task set is less than U_{FT-RMA} (0.6054),

[4]It is important to mention that any values for n and periods $T_1, \cdots T_n$ can be considered for illustration purposes, provided the resulting task set satisfies Eq. 1.

[5]The upper bound of C_4 is $\left(U_{FT-RMA} - \sum_{i=1}^{3} C_i/T_i\right) T_4$, which equals 1.0158.

with recovery schemes of [7, 8], a single fault should be tolerated by re-execution of the faulty task.

τ_i	C_i	T_i	$U_i = C_i/T_i$
τ_1	0.5	4	0.125
τ_2	0.5	4.5	0.1111
τ_3	1.0	5	0.2
τ_4	1.01	6	0.1683

Let us first consider the fault-free case. The resulting schedule without considering backup slots is depicted in Fig. 8. In subsequent timing diagrams of the RM-schedule of the task set, τ_i^j denotes the jth instance of task τ_i.

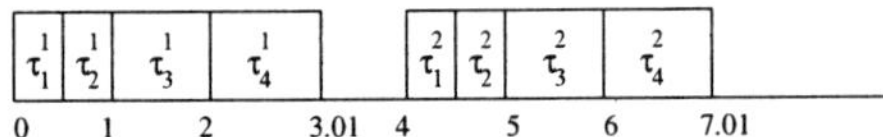

Figure 8: RM-Schedule of 4 tasks

We now illustrate the schemes [7, 8] to distribute slack to the schedule using FT-RMA. The backup task can be imagined to be occupying backup slots between every two consecutive period boundaries, where a period boundary is the beginning of any period. Thus, the length of backup slot between the kth period of τ_i and l^{th} period of τ_j is given by $U_B(lT_j - kT_i)$, where there is no intervening period boundary for any system task. For the given task set with $U_B = 0.2$, the lengths of backup from 0 to T_1 is 0.8, from T_1 to T_2 is 0.1, from T_2 to T_3 is 0.1, from T_3 to T_4 is 0.2, from T_4 to $2T_1$ is 0.4, and so on. The resulting schedule with inserted backup slots is depicted in Fig. 9.

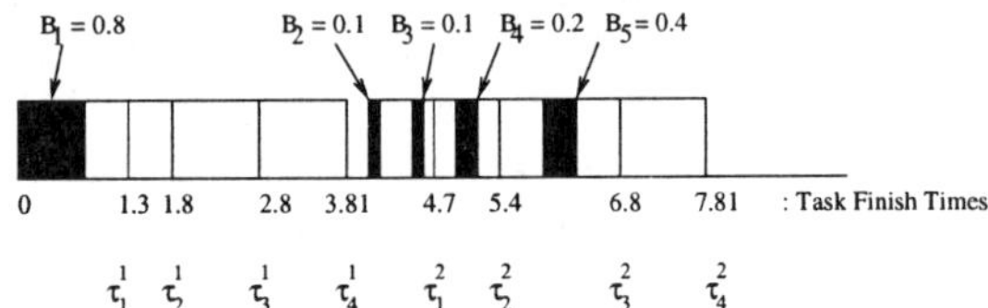

Figure 9: RM-Schedule of 4 tasks with backup slots

In the event when no fault has occurred, the backup slots are swapped with the computation time and the resulting schedule would be similar to Fig. 8.

Using the identified test case (Eq. 1) derived from the DT, we now illustrate the shortcomings in the recovery schemes of FT-RMA [7, 8]. The first example demonstrates two cases where the original recovery scheme [7] fails to guarantee the schedulability under fault condition, and then the second example highlights a flaw in the modified recovery scheme [8].

Note 1: Two cases where the original recovery scheme [7], the faulty tasks re-executes at its own priority, is found to be flawed.

Case (a) *The lowest priority task misses its deadline if a fault had occurred during its execution and it had re-executed.*

Let τ_4 be a faulty task. τ_1, τ_2, τ_3 and also τ_4 swapped their respective execution time slots with the backup slot B_1. τ_4 finishes at 3.01, and since no other higher priority tasks are ready, it is allowed to re-execute at its own priority. The recovery task τ_4^r only gets to execute for 0.99 time units utilizing backup slot B_1 of length 0.8 time units and a natural slack of length 0.19. During the time interval [4, 6], the execution of recovery task τ_4^r gets preempted by higher priority tasks and hence, never gets to complete its execution before time 6. Fig. 10 illustrates this fact.

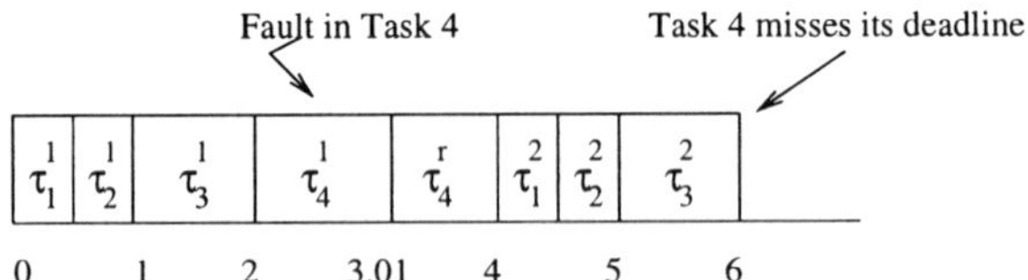

Figure 10: Task 4 misses its deadline

We now relate this to our findings through the IT/DT approach: as per Lemma 1, with backup utilization U_B being 0.2, there exist backup slots of total length 1.2 time units within τ_4's period. Also, per Lemma 2, with backup slots of length 1.2 time units being present and swapping being done, enough slack should have been available for successful re-execution of τ_4, which is not the case here. This is the discrepancy which was highlighted by DT queries in Phase I.

Case (b) *The lowest priority task misses its deadline due to re-execution of a faulty higher priority task.*

Let τ_3 be a faulty task. As per the recovery scheme, it re-executes at its own priority. The recovery task τ_3^r preempts τ_4, and causes the deadline of τ_4 to be missed. It can be observed from Fig. 11 that τ_4 executes for only 1.0 time units and still would be needing 0.01 time units to complete its execution.

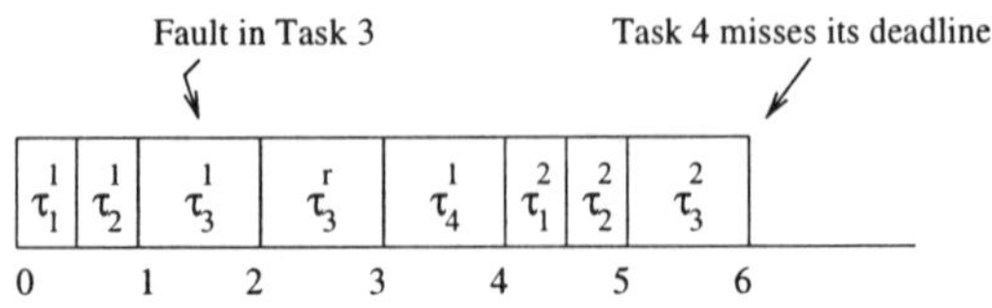

Figure 11: Task 4 misses its deadline

Case (b) highlights the flaw in Lemma 3 where it was proven that a lower priority task would not miss its deadline due to re-execution of a higher priority task. Moreover, as we will demonstrate next, the modified recovery scheme is flawed too.

Note 2: *A case where the lowest priority task misses its deadline if a fault had occurred in one of higher priority tasks, and the modified recovery scheme [8] has been used for re-execution.*

Consider the same task set as described above. Let τ_3 fail and re-execute at its own priority. This causes τ_4 to miss its deadline. Note that during τ_3's recovery, no other higher priority tasks are ready, therefore, τ_3 would maintain its priority and will complete successfully. As depicted in Fig. 11, τ_4 would utilize backups and execute for 1.0 time units and still would be needing 0.01 time units before time 6.

It is important to mention that the IT/DT based approach enabled us to identify and construct a *specific* case which highlights flaws and inconsistencies in both recovery schemes[7, 8] of FT-RMA.

4.5 Identification of Equivalence Classes

A key idea in FI-based experimental analysis of system dependability is to identify the equivalence class[6] in order to reduce the number of faults to be injected in the system. It was shown in [13] that when the fault population is infinite or extremely large and each fault equivalence class is of finite size, the usefulness of this concept is minimal and may not yield any benefit. In this study, we have identified two equivalence classes: (a) *the lowest priority task in the task set (constructed as per guidelines described in Section 4.3) is the faulty task*, and (b) *the second lowest priority task in the task set is the faulty task.* As shown in Section 4.4, with different values for C_4, we can have an infinite number of task sets generated. Thus, each of our equivalence class has (conceptually) infinite number of fault cases. Moreover, any periodic n-task set satisfying Eq. 1 suffices for any of these equivalence classes.

As a comparative analysis of our technique with conventional approaches, we would like to point out that FT-RMA protocols have been through extensive simulations and random FI, and still these fault cases were not identified. Typically, for simulations, task sets are randomly generated. The execution of all tasks in the set including re-execution of the faulty task is observed for a predetermined length of time (generally, it is taken to be a least common multiple (LCM) of tasks' period). Due to its obvious lacking in considering factors for the full utilization of the processor, a task set thus generated by this method has a low probability that it would belong to one of two equivalence classes. Even if we were able to generate a similar affecting task set, that would belong to one of our equivalence classes.

[6] Ascertaining if specific fault cases are equivalent in their capability of stimulating the system under test.

5 Conclusions and Future Work

We have established how formal techniques can be used to abstract large state space involved in protocols and to guide/supplement the conventional FI approaches. We have demonstrated the effectiveness and efficiency of our IT/DT based approach through an example of FT-RMA where we have been able to identify very specific test cases, and analytically identify equivalence classes of test cases.

A current limitation of our formal approach is the need of an interactive mechanism to effectively pose deductive queries in the DT to obtain a conclusive result. Currently, we are investigating the classes of protocols where the formal approach will be effective in identifying and selecting parameters to construct test cases. We are also automating and interfacing the IT/DT generation and iteration process to other existing FI toolsets [9]. Overall, we believe that we have shown the strength and viability of formal techniques for test case identification.

References

[1] D. Avresky, et al., "Fault Injection for the Formal Testing of Fault Tolerance," *IEEE Trans. on Reliability*, vol. 45, pp. 443–455, 1996.

[2] D.M. Blough, T. Torii, "Fault Injection Based Testing of Fault Tolerant Algorithms in Message Passing Parallel Computers," *Proc. of FTCS-27*, pp. 258–267, 1997.

[3] J. Boué, et al., "MEFISTO-L: A VHDL-Based Fault Injection Tool for the Experimental Assessment of Fault Tolerance," *Proc. of FTCS-28*, pp. 168–173, 1998.

[4] J. Christmansson, P. Santhaman, "Error Injection Aimed at Fault Removal in Fault Tolerance Mechanisms – Criteria for Error Selection Using Field Data on Software Faults," *Proc. of ISSRE*, pp. 175–184, 1996.

[5] K. Echtle, Y. Chen, "Evaluation of Deterministic Fault Injection for Fault-tolerant Protocol Testing," *Proc. of FTCS-21*, pp. 418–425, 1991.

[6] K. Echtle, et al., "Test of Fault Tolerant Systems by Fault Injection," *FTPDS, IEEE Press*, pp. 244–251, 1995.

[7] S. Ghosh, et al., "FT Rate Monotonic Scheduling." *Proc. of DCCA-6*, 1997.

[8] S. Ghosh, et al., "FT Rate Monotonic Scheduling." *Real-Time Systems*, vol. 15, no. 2, pp. 149-181, Sept. 1998.

[9] R. Iyer, and D. Tang, "Experimental Analysis of Computer System Dependability," *Chapter in 'Fault Tolerant Computer System Design'*, Prentice Hall, pp. 282–392, 1996.

[10] C.L. Liu, J.W. Layland, "Scheduling Algorithms for Multiprogramming in a Hard-Real-Time Environment." *Journal of the ACM*, 20(1), pp. 46–61, January 1973.

[11] N. Suri, P. Sinha, "On the Use of Formal Techniques for Validation." *Proc. of FTCS-28*, pp. 390–399, 1998.

[12] T. Tsai, et al., "Path-Based Fault Injection," *Proc. 3rd ISSAT Conf. on R&Q in Design*, pp. 121–125, 1997.

[13] W. Wang, et al., "The Impact of Fault Expansion on the Interval Estimate for Fault Detection Coverage," *Proc. of FTCS-24*, pp. 330–337, 1994.

Performance and Reliability Evaluation of Passive Replication Schemes in Application Level Fault Tolerance

Sachin Garg
Lucent Tech., Bell Labs
sgarg@research.bell-labs.com

Yennun Huang*
AT&T Labs
yen@research.att.com

Chandra M. R. Kintala
Lucent Tech., Bell Labs
cmk@research.bell-labs.com

Kishor S. Trivedi
Duke University
kst@ee.duke.edu

Shalini Yajnik
Lucent Tech., Bell Labs
shalini@research.bell-labs.com

Abstract

Process replication is provided as the central mechanism for application level software fault tolerance in SwiFT and DOORS. These technologies, implemented as reusable software modules, support cold and warm schemes of passive replication. The choice of a scheme for a particular application is based on its availability and performance requirements. In this paper, we analyze the performability of a server software which may potentially use these technologies. We derive closed form formulae for availability, throughput and probability of loss of a job. Six scenarios of loss are modeled and for each, these expressions are derived. The formulae can be used either offline or online to determine the optimal replication scheme.

1 Introduction

Replication has been proposed and used as a viable failure masking technique to improve reliability of software. Since software designers typically do not want to be burdened with implementing replication from scratch, tools that enable easy implementation are highly desirable. Work at Lucent Bell Labs has resulted in reusable software libraries and modules to facilitate embedding fault tolerance at the application layer [8, 11, 9]. These modules and libraries provide automated mechanisms for fault detection and recovery and are designed to work on a cluster of nodes connected via a LAN/WAN.

In the context of software server applications, the replicas of a server process can be configured in two ways, active or passive. In this paper, we focus on passive replication as provided in SwiFT and DOORS in two ways; cold and warm [8]. These two schemes result in different recovery time and runtime overhead. For instance, the cold replication scheme has a large recovery time because of the state transfer and initialization procedure required for recovery after a failure. In the case of warm replication, in contrast, periodic states updates are sent to the backup copy during normal execution. The time to switch the backup to primary is much smaller than the recovery time in the cold replication scheme. On the other hand, the run time overhead is larger. Since the choice of replication determines the performability characteristics of a server application, it is important to determine the right scheme which will meet the requirements.

Our contribution in this paper is to develop analytical models to study the performance and availability tradeoffs of these replication schemes for a software server application. We obtain closed form expressions for availability, throughput and the probability of loss of a request for a server application without any fault tolerance and with cold and warm replication. The models of replication schemes are specific to the implementations of these schemes in the technologies SwiFT and DOORS, developed at Lucent Bell Labs. The rest of the paper is organized as follows. In Section 2, we briefly describe the SwiFT and DOORS technologies. In Section 3, we describe the system model and list six possible cases of the loss behavior of a server. Section 4 describes the analysis methodology common to all replication schemes. In Sections 5, 6 and 7, we provide the Continuous Time Markov Chain (CTMC) models of server software without any fault tolerance, with cold replication and warm replication respectively. We also derive the expressions for availability, probability of loss and throughput for each of the six loss cases. Section 8 describes how the parameters in the expressions relate with controllable/monitorable parameters in the use of SwiFT or DOORS technologies. We conclude in Section 10.

*This work was done while the author was with Lucent Technologies

0-7695-0213-X/99 $10.00 © 1999 IEEE

2 SwiFT and DOORS

SwiFT (*Software Implemented Fault Tolerance*) is a collection of daemon processes and C/C++ libraries that together provide fault tolerance to applications on a cluster of Windows-NT nodes, logically configured as a ring. Each node runs a watchdog process `watchd` which detects the failure of its logical neighbor via polling. If the polling frequency is high, the detection time, and therefore the mean down time is reduced. The increase in the runtime overhead, however, reduces the service rate of the application. The models capture this tradeoff and can be used to determine the optimal polling interval. `watchd` is also detects the failures of locally running processes via either heartbeats or polling. The details of what happens when a node or a process failure occurs depend on the replication scheme and shall be explained with the description of the system models in Section 6 and Section 7 respectively. SwiFT also provides a set of APIs as a library module called `libft`. These may be used for checkpoint and rollback recovery, message logging, fault tolerant socket I/O etc. An application uses `libft` APIs and/or the utility programs along with `watchd` to implement cold or warm replication. We refer interested readers to [11, 9] for design and implementation details.

DOORS (*Distributed Object Oriented Reliable Service*) provides cold and warm replication support for CORBA based software applications on a cluster of UNIX or Windows-NT machines and also consists of a set of daemon CORBA processes and library APIs. Although some components are different than those of SwiFT, the recovery behavior is exactly the same for cold as well as warm replication. The reader is referred to [8] for further details. Cluster based fault tolerance solutions have been steadily gaining popularity in the commercial market with products such as Wolfpack [3], Firstwatch [6], Octopus Server [4], Vinca Corp's Standby Server for NT1.21 [7], MC/ServiceGuard [2], Tandem CAS [5] and Apcon Powerswitch [1]. Although the fundamental performance and availability tradeoffs remain the same, it is not clear if our models apply to any of these products. The methodology however is applicable, should the details of the implementation be known.

3 System Model

The server behavior is governed by two distinct phenomena. First, the failure/recovery phenomenon, which is directly determined by the nature of the replication technique (if any). Second, the arrival/service phenomenon. We assume that request arrival is modeled by a Poisson process with rate λ and is independent of the failure process. The service time of a request is modeled via an independent exponentially distributed random variable. μ, μ_c and μ_w are the service rates with no, cold and warm replication respectively. Server failure is caused by the application process failure or the node failure. Inter failure times of a process and a node are assumed to be exponentially distributed with parameters γ_p and γ_n respectively. We assume only single failures at any time in the system. For instance, if a process on a node has failed, the node itself is assumed not to fail until the process is recovery is complete.

We assume fail-silent behavior of the server. By the "loss behavior" of the server we mean the specific assumption on what happens to incoming requests when either the buffer, assumed to be of size K, is full or when the server fails. This of course depends on the server application itself. For instance, in the case of a WEB server, all jobs (requests for web pages) queued at the time the server failed are lost. Further, all new requests arriving while the server is down are lost as well and need to be manually resent by the clients. On the other hand, in the case of a database server, the jobs once accepted may not be lost upon server failure. In our analysis, we model the following six "loss scenarios". In all cases, an arriving request is lost if the buffer is full, regardless of the state of the server.

Case *I*. Jobs[1] already in the queue are never lost when the server fails and all jobs arriving while the server is down are queued. In this case, the only loss occurs when the buffer is full regardless of whether the server is up or down.

Case *II*. No jobs previously accepted in the queue are lost when the server fails but all jobs arriving while the server is down are lost.

Case *III*. The job currently in service, if any, is lost when the server module fails. Any requests arriving while it is down are also lost.

Case *IV*. The job currently in service (if any) is lost at the instant the server fails. Any request that arrives while the server is down is queued unless of course the buffer is full.

Case *V*. All jobs queued at the time the server fails are lost and any jobs arriving while it is unavailable are lost as well.

Case *VI*. All jobs queued at the time the server fails are lost but any jobs arriving while it is unavailable for service are queued.

4 Analysis Methodology

We use a hierarchical modeling framework to compute the closed form expressions for availability, loss probability and throughput. The system is modeled via a *lower* level (also called pure performance) model and a *higher* level (also called pure availability) model. This decomposition approach was proposed by Meyer [12, 13] and has since been extensively used in system's modeling.

[1]The word "job" is used interchangeably with the word "request" throughout the paper.

The higher level model, which in our case is a CTMC captures the failure, detection and recovery behavior of the server under a particular replication scheme. Let the underlying state space of this CTMC be Ω and the infinitesimal generator matrix be $\mathbf{Q}$. The steady state solution, denoted by vector π, is well known and is given by the solution of the following system of linear equations.

$$\pi\mathbf{Q} = 0, \quad \pi\mathbf{1} = 1, \text{where } \mathbf{1} \text{ is the column unit vector} \tag{1}$$

Availability is calculated simply by adding the steady state probabilities of those states in which the server is up.

The arrival and service behavior of the jobs at the server is modeled by an M/M/1/K queue. The steady state probability of i jobs in the queue denoted by p_i is well known [14] and is given by

$$p_i = \rho^i \frac{1-\rho}{1-\rho^{K+1}}, \quad 0 \leq i \leq K \tag{2}$$

The probability that an arriving request is lost due to buffer being full is equal to p_K. This M/M/1/K model constitutes the lower level model and is used to compute the expected rate of loss, $R(i)$, of incoming jobs conditioned on a specific state i of the higher level CTMC model. Expected rate of loss of incoming jobs conditioned on a transition i, j, denoted by $R(i,j)$ is also computed for each i, j transition in the higher level model. The expected unconditional rate of loss of incoming jobs, denoted by R, is then given by the following equation.

$$R = \sum_{i\in\Omega} \pi_i \left(R(i) + \sum_{j\in\Omega} R(i,j) \right) \tag{3}$$

Loss Probability, denoted by L, is calculated simply as:

$$L = \frac{R}{\lambda} \tag{4}$$

Throughput, denoted by T, is calculated via the following equation.

$$T = \lambda - R \tag{5}$$

$R(i)$, $R(i,j)$, R, L and T are appended with a subscript $_c$ or $_w$ and a superscript ^{I} through ^{VI} to denote the replication scheme and loss case respectively. The approximation made in the decomposition approach is due to the implicit assumption that the lower level model (M/M/1/K queue) reaches steady state in between the transitions from the "UP" states of the higher level CTMC. It is a reasonable approximation if the transition rates of the higher level CTMC models are much lower than the transition rates of the lower level M/M/1/K model and is typically true.

5 Server Software Without Fault Tolerance

Such a server needs to be restarted manually upon a failure. It is assumed that any state information, if needed for this restart is available. Both detection as well as recovery are done manually. Figure 1 shows the CTMC model with the state space $\Omega = \{0, 1, 2\}$. The server is available for service in state 0. The process itself or the node on which it is

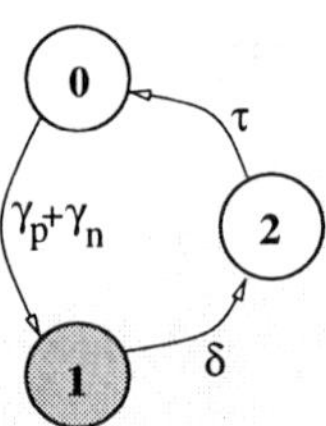

Figure 1. CTMC model for server with no replication

running may fail at a combined rate of $\gamma_p + \gamma_n$, upon which the system goes into state 1 in which the server becomes unavailable. The fact that the server is unavailable is not observed until the failure is not detected. This is represented in the figure by a dark shade filling the circle. After detection, which takes an exponentially distributed time with mean $\frac{1}{\delta}$, the system reaches state 2 in which recovery is initiated. Manual recovery takes an exponentially distributed time with mean $\frac{1}{\tau}$ after which the system is back in state 0. The states in which the service is stopped are indicated in the figure by a lighter shading around them.

Towards computing the output measures, the steady state probability vector π is derived using Equation 1 as following: $\pi_0 = \frac{\tau\delta}{\tau\delta+(\gamma_p+\gamma_n)(\tau+\delta)}$, $\pi_1 = \frac{(\gamma_p+\gamma_n)\tau}{\tau\delta+(\gamma_p+\gamma_n)(\tau+\delta)}$, $\pi_2 = \frac{(\gamma_p+\gamma_n)\delta}{\tau\delta+(\gamma_p+\gamma_n)(\tau+\delta)}$ The availability, A is constant across the six loss cases and is given simply by $A = \pi_0$.

Rate of loss: It varies with the particular loss scenario, so each case is solved individually. We provide the expressions for conditional rates of loss for each case in following subsections. The unconditional rate of loss R and the final measures L and T can then be computed via Equations 3, 4 and 5 respectively. Let $\phi_i(j)$ be the probability that there are i jobs in the queue when the system *enters* state j of the higher level CTMC. Further, let $g(x)$ denote the probability that an incoming job is lost in a state in which the exit rate is x.

Case *I* In state 0, loss occurs at the rate λ if the buffer is full. In state 1, the server has failed but the failure is undetected. Assume that when the server failed (and transited from state 0 to state 1), there were i jobs in the queue. Once in state 1, only one of two events can occur. Detection, which takes the system to state 2 or an arrival, which increases the number in the queue by one. An arriving job is lost only if the buffer is full. Therefore, in state 1, given that there are i jobs when the server went in state 1, the probability that an arriving job sees the buffer full is equal to the probability that $K - i$ arrivals occur before the system exits from state 1, i.e., before detection takes place. This conditional probability of loss is given by $\left(\frac{\lambda}{\lambda+\delta}\right)^{K-i}$, The unconditional probability of loss in state

1, therefore, is given by $g(\delta) = \sum_{i=0}^{K} \left(\frac{\lambda}{\lambda+\delta}\right)^{K-i} \phi_i(1)$. The probability that there are i jobs in the queue when a failure occurs is equal to the steady state probability that there are i jobs in the queue due to the PASTA property [14]. In other words, $\phi_i(1) = p_i, 0 \leq i \leq K$. Simple manipulation yields the following closed form expression. $L^I(1) = g(x) = \left(\frac{1-\rho}{1-\rho^{K+1}}\right)\left(\frac{\lambda}{\lambda+x}\right)^K \left[\frac{1-\left(\frac{\lambda+x}{\mu}\right)^{K+1}}{1-\left(\frac{\lambda+x}{\mu}\right)}\right]$ In state 2, the server is under manual recovery and the probability that an arriving request is lost is equal to the probability that the buffer is full. Assume that when the system entered state 2, there are i jobs in the buffer. Now, the conditional probability that the buffer is full is equal to the probability of $K-i$ arrivals before the system exits from state 2 and is given by $\left(\frac{\lambda}{\lambda+\tau}\right)^{K-i}$. The unconditional probability of buffer full, therefore, may be obtained as $L^I(2) = \sum_{i=0}^{K} \phi_i(2) \left(\frac{\lambda}{\lambda+\tau}\right)^{K-i}$. This leaves us to compute $\phi_i(2)$ and is done as follows. The presence of i jobs in the queue when the system entered state 2 is possible in many ways. The system may enter state 1 with empty buffer and then transit to state 2 exactly after i arrivals have occurred. Or the system may enter state 1 with only one job in the buffer and transits to state 2 after exactly $i-1$ arrivals have occurred and so on. Therefore $\phi_i(2) = \sum_{j=0}^{i} \phi_j(1) \left(\frac{\lambda}{\lambda+\delta}\right)^{i-j} \frac{\delta}{\lambda+\delta}$ which yields to $\phi_i(2) = p_0 \frac{\delta}{\lambda+\delta} \rho^i \left[\frac{1-\left(\frac{\mu}{\lambda+\delta}\right)^{i+1}}{1-\left(\frac{\mu}{\lambda+\delta}\right)}\right]$

In order to compute $L^I(2)$, let $N(j)$ denote the mean number of jobs in the queue when the system entered state j. Thus, the probability that an incoming job is lost in state 2 may be approximated by the probability that $K - N(2)$ arrivals occur before recovery occurs. That is $L^I(2) = \left(\frac{\lambda}{\lambda+\tau}\right)^{K-N(2)}$. $N(2)$, on the other hand, is the sum of the mean number of jobs in queue when the system entered state 1 and the mean number of arrivals before it exited state 1, provided this value is not greater than K. That is $N(2) = min\left(N(1) + \frac{\lambda}{\delta}, K\right)$. $N(1)$, in turn is the mean number of jobs in an M/M/1/K queue and is given by the closed form formula $\frac{\rho}{1-\rho}\left[\frac{1-\rho^K}{1-\rho^{K+1}} - \frac{K\rho^K(1-\rho)}{1-\rho^{K+1}}\right]$. Summarizing the rate of loss in various states,

$$R^I(0) = \lambda p_K, \quad R^I(1) = \lambda g(\delta)$$

$$R^I(2) = \lambda\left(\frac{\lambda}{\lambda+\tau}\right)^{K-N(2)}, \quad N(2) = \min\left(N + \frac{\lambda}{\delta}, K\right)$$

Equations 3, 4 and 5 may now be used to compute the desired measures L^I and T^I.

Case *II*: In this case, all requests arriving while the server is in either state 1 or 2 are lost. Therefore, the rate of loss in either of these states is λ. The rate of loss in state 0 is λ, only when the buffer is full. Thus

$$R^{II}(0) = \lambda p_K, \quad R^{II}(1) = \lambda, \quad R^{II}(2) = \lambda$$

Case *III*: In state 0, the rate of loss is λ only if the buffer is full. In state 1 and state 2, all arriving requests are lost as per this case. Therefore, the rate of loss in either is λ. Moreover, at the failure instant, the job under service is lost. The rate of loss is the product of the expected number lost (one in this case) and the rate at which the failure transition occurs, given by $(\gamma_p + \gamma_n)$. Of course, the queue has to be non-empty at the failure instant for the loss to occur.

$$R^{III}(0) = \lambda p_K, \quad R^{III}(0,1) = (\gamma_p + \gamma_n)(1 - p_0)$$

$$R^{III}(1) = \lambda, \quad R^{III}(2) = \lambda$$

Case *IV*: The rate of loss in state 0 and for transition $(0,1)$ is exactly the same (for the same reasons) as in case *III*. In state 1, however, the service is stopped and an arriving request is lost only when the buffer is full. Moreover, immediately after the transition to state 1, the queue can not be full as one job in service is lost. Therefore, the probability that an arriving request is lost given that there were i requests when the failure occurred is given by $\left(\frac{\lambda}{\lambda+\delta}\right)^{K-i}$ for $0 \leq i \leq (K-1)$. The unconditional probability, L^{IV} is given by $\sum_{i=0}^{K-1} \phi_i(1) \left(\frac{\lambda}{\lambda+\delta}\right)^{K-i}$. Moreover, $\phi_0(1) = p_0 + p_1$ and $\phi_i(1) = p_{i+1}, i = 1, ..., K-1$. Simplification yields the closed form expression. The probability of loss in state 2 is computed following the same arguments as given for state 2 in case *I*. The final expressions for the rate of loss are:

$$R^{IV}(0) = \lambda p_K, \quad R^{IV}(0,1) = (\gamma_p + \gamma_n)(1 - p_0)$$

$$R^{IV}(1) = \lambda\left[p_0\left(\frac{\lambda}{\lambda+\delta}\right)^K + p_K\frac{\lambda}{\lambda+\delta}\left[\frac{1-\left(\frac{\mu}{\lambda+\delta}\right)^K}{1-\left(\frac{\mu}{\lambda+\delta}\right)}\right]\right]$$

$$R^{IV}(2) = \lambda\left(\frac{\lambda}{\lambda+\tau}\right)^{K-N(2)}, N(2) = \min\left(N + \frac{\lambda}{\delta} - 1, K\right)$$

Case *V*: The rate of loss in state 0, as explained before, is λ only if the buffer is full. In case *V*, all the jobs queued at the time of failure are lost. That is, whenever the transition $(0,1)$ is taken, the rate of which is $\gamma_p + \gamma_n$, the expected number of jobs lost is given by the expected number in the M/M/1/K queue in steady state given by N. Further, any arriving requests while the server is down (in state 1 and 2) are also lost making the rate of loss in either state to be λ. Thus

$$R^V(0) = \lambda p_K, \quad R^V(0,1) = (\gamma_p + \gamma_n)N, \quad R^V(1) = R^V(2) = \lambda$$

Case *VI*: The rate of loss in state 0 and for transition $(0,1)$ is exactly the same as in case *V*. In case *VI*, when the system enters state 1, the queue is always empty as all the jobs in the queue are lost. Since in state 1, the service is stopped, an arriving job is lost only if K jobs have arrived before it. Therefore, the probability of loss of an arriving request in state 1 is $\left(\frac{\lambda}{\lambda+\delta}\right)^K$. The mean number of jobs in the buffer when the system entered state 2, $N(2) = \frac{\lambda}{\delta}$ as $N(1) = 0$. Following arguments explained earlier in the paper,

$$R^{VI}(0) = \lambda p_K, \quad R^{VI}(0,1) = (\gamma_p + \gamma_n)N, \quad R^{VI}(1) = \lambda\left(\frac{\lambda}{\lambda+\delta}\right)^K$$

$$R^{VI}(2) = \lambda\left(\frac{\lambda}{\lambda+\tau}\right)^{K-N(2)}, \quad N(2) = \min\left(\frac{\lambda}{\delta}, K\right)$$

6 Server Software with Cold Replication

Figure 2 shows the CTMC model for a server with cold replication as implemented in SwiFT and DOORS. The

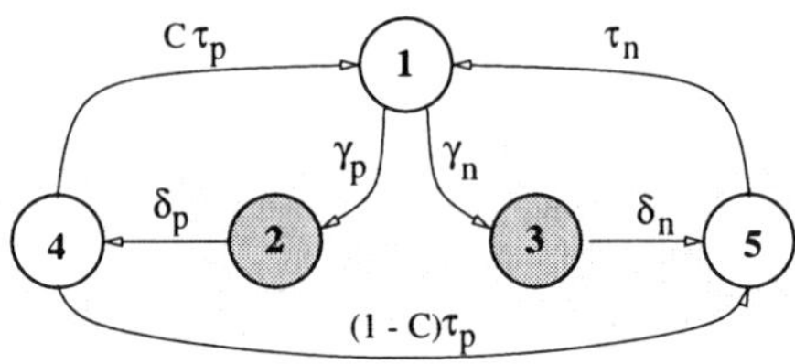

Figure 2. CTMC model for server with cold replication

state space is given by $\Omega = \{1, 2, 3, 4, 5\}$. The server process serves jobs only in state 1. It fails at the rate γ_p upon which the system goes to state 2. The node on which the server is executing also fails at the rate γ_n upon which the system goes to state 3. The unavailability in States 2 and 3 is not observable until the failure is detected. watchd detects a process failure via polling or heartbeats at the rate δ_p after which recovery is initiated. If the threshold of the number of failures within a certain interval has not been reached, the process is restarted on the same node. This takes an exponentially distributed time with mean $\frac{1}{\tau_p}$. If however, the threshold is exceeded, the process is failed over to a different node. Time to perform this failover is assumed to be exponentially distributed with mean $1/tau_n$. The threshold crossing behavior is captured by the use of a coverage parameter, denoted by c. The relation of c to measurable physical parameters of the system will be explained in Section 8

A node failure (system in State 3) is detected by the neighboring watchd at the rate δ_n. After detection, (system in State 5), the server process is restarted on another node possibly using some state transfer/checkpoint. After either the process restart from State 4 or failover from State 5, the system returns back to State 1.

The steady state probabilities $\pi_i, i = 1, ..., 5$ can be derived as:

$$\pi_1 = \left[1 + \gamma_p \left(\frac{1-C}{\tau_n} + \frac{1}{\delta_p} + \frac{1}{\tau_p}\right) + \gamma_n \left(\frac{1}{\tau_n} + \frac{1}{\delta_n}\right)\right]^{-1}$$

$$\pi_2 = \frac{\gamma_p}{\delta_p}\pi_1, \quad \pi_3 = \frac{\gamma_n}{\delta_n}\pi_1, \quad \pi_4 = \frac{\gamma_p}{\tau_p}\pi_1$$

$$\pi_5 = \frac{1}{\tau_n}\left(\gamma_n + \gamma_p(1-c)\right)\pi_1$$

Availability is given by $A = \pi_1$.

The rate of loss for all states and transitions for the six scenarios will be given next. Since the arguments for computing these closely mimic those for the server with no replication, we only provide the results.

Case *I*

$$R_c^I(1) = \lambda p_K, \; R_c^I(2) = \lambda g(\delta_p), \; R_c^I(3) = \lambda g(\delta_n)$$

$$R_c^I(4) = \lambda \left(\frac{\lambda}{\lambda + \tau_p}\right)^{K - \min\left(N + \frac{\lambda}{\delta_p}, K\right)}$$

$$R_c^I(5) = \lambda \left(\frac{\lambda}{\lambda + \tau_n}\right)^{K - \min\left(N + \frac{\lambda}{\delta_n}, K\right)}$$

Case *II*

$$R_c^{II}(1) = \lambda p_K, \; R_c^{II}(i) = \lambda \quad i = 2, 3, 4, 5$$

Case *III*

$$R_c^{III}(1) = \lambda p_K, \; R_c^{III}(i) = \lambda \quad i = 2, 3, 4, 5$$

$$R_c^{III}(1,2) = \gamma_p(1 - p_0), \; R_c^{III}(1,3) = \gamma_n(1 - p_0)$$

Case *IV*

$$R_c^{IV}(1) = \lambda p_K, \; R_c^{IV}(1,2) = \gamma_p(1 - p_0), \; R_c^{IV}(1,3) = \gamma_n(1 - p_0)$$

$$R_c^{IV}(2) = \lambda \left[p_0 \left(\frac{\lambda}{\lambda + \delta_p}\right)^K + p_K \frac{\lambda}{\lambda + \delta_p} \left[\frac{1 - \left(\frac{\mu_c}{\lambda + \delta_p}\right)^K}{1 - \left(\frac{\mu_c}{\lambda + \delta_p}\right)}\right]\right]$$

$$R_c^{IV}(3) = \lambda \left[p_0 \left(\frac{\lambda}{\lambda + \delta_n}\right)^K + p_K \frac{\lambda}{\lambda + \delta_n} \left[\frac{1 - \left(\frac{\mu_c}{\lambda + \delta_n}\right)^K}{1 - \left(\frac{\mu_c}{\lambda + \delta_n}\right)}\right]\right]$$

$$R_c^{IV}(4) = \lambda \left(\frac{\lambda}{\lambda + \tau_p}\right)^{K - \min\left(N + \frac{\lambda}{\delta_p} - 1, K\right)}$$

$$R_c^{IV}(5) = \lambda \left(\frac{\lambda}{\lambda + \tau_n}\right)^{K - \min\left(N + \frac{\lambda}{\delta_n} - 1, K\right)}$$

Case *V*

$$R_c^V(1) = \lambda p_K, \; R_c^V(1,2) = \gamma_p N, \; R_c^V(1,3) = \gamma_n N$$

$$R_c^V(i) = \lambda \quad i = 2, 3, 4, 5$$

Case *VI*

$$R_c^{VI}(1) = \lambda p_K, \; R_c^{VI}(1,2) = \gamma_p N, \; R_c^{VI}(1,3) = \gamma_n N$$

$$R_c^{VI}(2) = \lambda \left(\frac{\lambda}{\lambda + \delta_p}\right)^K, \; R_c^{VI}(3) = \lambda \left(\frac{\lambda}{\lambda + \delta_n}\right)^K$$

$$R_c^{VI}(4) = \lambda \left(\frac{\lambda}{\lambda + \tau_p}\right)^{K - \min\left(\frac{\lambda}{\delta_p}, K\right)}$$

$$R_c^{VI}(5) = \lambda \left(\frac{\lambda}{\lambda + \tau_n}\right)^{K - \min\left(\frac{\lambda}{\delta_n}, K\right)}$$

As before, Equations 3, 4 and 5 are used to compute the final measures of loss probability and throughput.

7 Server Software with Warm Replication

Figure 3 shows the CTMC model of the failure repair behavior of a server with warm replication as implemented via SwiFT and DOORS technologies. The state space is $\Omega = \{1, 2, 3, 4, 5, 6, 7, 8, 9\}$. In state 1, the primary and the standby process and the respective nodes are up. Any of the four may fail with rates of γ_p for process failures and γ_n for node failures. If the primary fails, the system

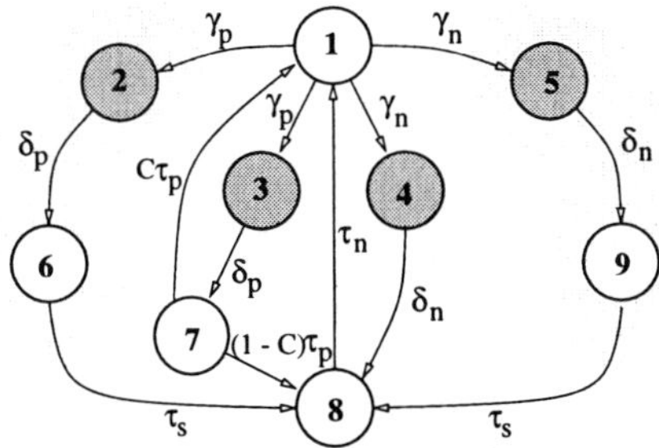

Figure 3. CTMC model for server with warm replication

goes to state 2, in which it is unavailable. The failure is detected by watchd at the rate δ_p upon which the system enters state 6. In this state, the standby assumes the role of primary (System enters state 8). The switching time is assumed to be exponentially distributed with mean $1/\tau_s$. A new backup process is started on another node at the rate τ_n and the system goes back to state 1. The node on which the primary is executing may fail at the rate γ_n upon which the server goes to state 5 and is unavailable. After detection by a neighboring watchd with rate δ_n, the system transits to state 9. As in the case of primary process failure, the backup is switched to primary bringing the server in state 8. A new backup is started on an available node to take the system back to state 1.

In the case of standby process failure, upon which the system is in state 3, the primary is still serving jobs. After the standby failure is detected by watchd (state 7), if the threshold of a predefined number of failures is not exceeded in a predefined interval due to the current process failure, it is simply restarted on the same node at the rate τ_p, after which the system is back in state 1. However, if the threshold is exceeded, the backup is started on a different node. In other words, failure of a standby is handled in exactly the same manner as the cold replication case, both with respect to the process as well as the node on which the standby exists and is reflected exactly in the model. The server is unavailable in states 2, 6, 5 and 9. Moreover, the fact that in states 2,3,4 and 5, the server is not available is not observable. The steady state probabilities of this CTMC are given as:

$$\pi_1 = \left[1 + \gamma_p\left(\frac{2}{\delta_p} + \frac{1}{\tau_s} + \frac{1}{\tau_p} + \frac{2-C}{\tau_n}\right) + \gamma_n\left(\frac{2}{\delta_n} + \frac{1}{\tau_s} + \frac{2}{\tau_n}\right)\right]^{-1}$$

$$\pi_2 = \pi_3 = \frac{\gamma_p}{\delta_p}\pi_1, \quad \pi_4 = \pi_5 = \frac{\gamma_n}{\delta_n}\pi_1, \quad \pi_6 = \frac{\gamma_p}{\tau_s}\pi_1$$

$$\pi_9 = \frac{\gamma_n}{\tau_s}\pi_1, \quad \pi_7 = \frac{\gamma_p}{\tau_p}\pi_1, \pi_8 = \left[\frac{(2-C)\gamma_p}{\tau_n} + \frac{2\gamma_n}{\tau_n}\right]\pi_1$$

The availability of the server is given by $A = \pi_1 + \pi_3 + \pi_4 + \pi_7 + \pi_8$. The rate of loss for the six loss cases are listed below. Once again, the arguments used to compute these expressions are exactly the same as given for server with no replication and therefore not repeated.

Case *I*

$$R_w^I(i) = \lambda p_K, \quad i = 1,3,4,7,8$$
$$R_w^I(2) = \lambda g(\delta_p), \; R_w^I(5) = \lambda g(\delta_n)$$
$$R_w^I(6) = \lambda\left(\frac{\lambda}{\lambda+\tau_s}\right)^{K-\min\left(N+\frac{\lambda}{\delta_p},K\right)}$$
$$R_w^I(9) = \lambda\left(\frac{\lambda}{\lambda+\tau_s}\right)^{K-\min\left(N+\frac{\lambda}{\delta_n},K\right)}$$

Case *II*

$$R_w^{II}(i) = \lambda p_K, \quad i = 1,3,4,7,8$$
$$R_w^{II}(i) = \lambda, \quad i = 2,5,6,9$$

Case *III*

$$R_w^{III}(i) = \lambda p_K, \quad i = 1,3,4,7,8$$
$$R_w^{III}(1,2) = \gamma_p(1-p_0)$$
$$R_w^{III}(1,5) = \gamma_n(1-p_0)$$
$$R_w^{III}(i) = \lambda, \quad i = 2,5,6,9$$

Case *IV*

$$R_w^{IV}(i) = \lambda p_K, \quad i = 1,3,4,7,8$$
$$R_w^{IV}(1,2) = \gamma_p(1-p_0), \; R_w^{IV}(1,5) = \gamma_n(1-p_0)$$
$$R_w^{IV}(2) = \lambda\left[p_0\left(\frac{\lambda}{\lambda+\delta_p}\right)^K + p_K\frac{\lambda}{\lambda+\delta_p}\left[\frac{1-\left(\frac{\mu_w}{\lambda+\delta_p}\right)^K}{1-\left(\frac{\mu_w}{\lambda+\delta_p}\right)}\right]\right]$$
$$R_w^{IV}(5) = \lambda\left[p_0\left(\frac{\lambda}{\lambda+\delta_n}\right)^K + p_K\frac{\lambda}{\lambda+\delta_n}\left[\frac{1-\left(\frac{\mu_w}{\lambda+\delta_n}\right)^K}{1-\left(\frac{\mu_w}{\lambda+\delta_n}\right)}\right]\right]$$
$$R_w^{IV}(6) = \lambda\left(\frac{\lambda}{\lambda+\tau_s}\right)^{K-\min\left(N+\frac{\lambda}{\delta_p}-1,K\right)}$$
$$R_w^{IV}(9) = \lambda\left(\frac{\lambda}{\lambda+\tau_s}\right)^{K-\min\left(N+\frac{\lambda}{\delta_n}-1,K\right)}$$

Case *V*

$$R_w^V(i) = \lambda p_K, \quad i = 1,3,4,7,8$$
$$R_w^V(1,2) = \gamma_p N, \; R_w^V(1,5) = \gamma_n N$$
$$R_w^{III}(i) = \lambda, \quad i = 2,5,6,9$$

Case *VI*

$$R_w^{VI}(i) = \lambda p_K, \quad i = 1,3,4,7,8$$
$$R_w^{VI}(1,2) = \gamma_p N, \; R_w^{VI}(1,5) = \gamma_n N$$
$$R_w^{VI}(2) = \lambda\left(\frac{\lambda}{\lambda+\delta_p}\right)^K, \; R_w^{VI}(5) = \lambda\left(\frac{\lambda}{\lambda+\delta_n}\right)^K$$
$$R_w^{VI}(6) = \lambda\left(\frac{\lambda}{\lambda+\tau_s}\right)^{K-\min\left(\frac{\lambda}{\delta_p},K\right)}$$
$$R_w^{VI}(9) = \lambda\left(\frac{\lambda}{\lambda+\tau_s}\right)^{K-\min\left(\frac{\lambda}{\delta_n},K\right)}$$

8 Model Parameterization

Failure rates used in the model may be obtained via two methods; measurement or numbers published in the literature. Failure rate of a node, γ_n, may be estimated via its system log where inter-failure times are recorded. γ_p is best known to the designer or developer. Software complexity metrics, such as the number of lines of code may be used together with fault density values to estimate the operational failure rate of the server software [10].

The polling and the heartbeat interval is explicitly configured in SwiFT and DOORS. Let this be D_p or D_n for a process and node respectively. The mean time between a process (node) failure and detection is $D_p/2$ ($D_n/2$). Therefore, $\delta_p = 2/D_p$ and $\delta_n = 2/D_n$ The rest of the parameters, $\tau, \tau_s, \tau_p, \tau_n$ need to be measured. As they are of the order of seconds, the measurement can provide very reliable estimates, possibly as a function of load. Typically, $\tau < \tau_p < \tau_n < \tau_s$. The arrival/service parameters are also to be determined via measurements. The arrival rate λ presumably will be same across different schemes. The service rate μ of the server without fault tolerance is known and the service rates μ_c and μ_w are also presumably measurable. In fact, fault free throughput can be measured and used to calculate these service rates. Note that this fault free throughput is not equal to T calculated in the equations. Huang et. al. [9] note that the polling mechanism of `watchd` results in approximately a 5% increase in the processor utilization for about 500 milliseconds on a Pentium-II based 200+ MHz machine. This can be extrapolated to estimate the service rate of a server in the design stage. The buffer size K is known exactly to the software designer. Typically, $\mu > \mu_c > \mu_w$.

The only parameter left in the models to be determined is c. It relates to two other parameters in the fault tolerance technologies, which are explicitly configured by the user. The first is a timeout interval, denoted by t_o, and the second is the number of retries, denoted by n_r. From the models in Figure 2 and 3, it can be seen that the c is the probability that the server is restarted on the same node while $(1 - c)$ is the probability that it is failed over to a different node. This happens only if at least n_r number of restart attempts have failed with in the time interval t_o. Thus, $c = 1 - \frac{(\gamma_p t_o)^M}{M!} e^{-\gamma_p t_o}$ We now provide a numerical example to illustrate the use of the models in evaluating the performance and reliability tradeoffs of the two schemes.

9 Numerical Illustration

We assume the following fixed parameters. The time unit is seconds. $\lambda = 10$. The mean process failure time is assumed to be 10 days, $\gamma_p = \frac{1}{10*24*3600}$. The mean node failure time is taken to be 20 days, $\gamma_n = \frac{1}{20*24*3600}$. The mean time to detect a process failure is 1 second, i.e., $\delta_p = 1.0$ In other words, the process polling/heartbeat interval in SwiFT is set at 2 seconds. The mean time to recover manually is assumed to be 2 minutes ($\tau = 1/120$). The mean time to restart a process on the same node is assumed to be 30 seconds and the mean time to failover a process to a different node is taken to be 2 minutes.

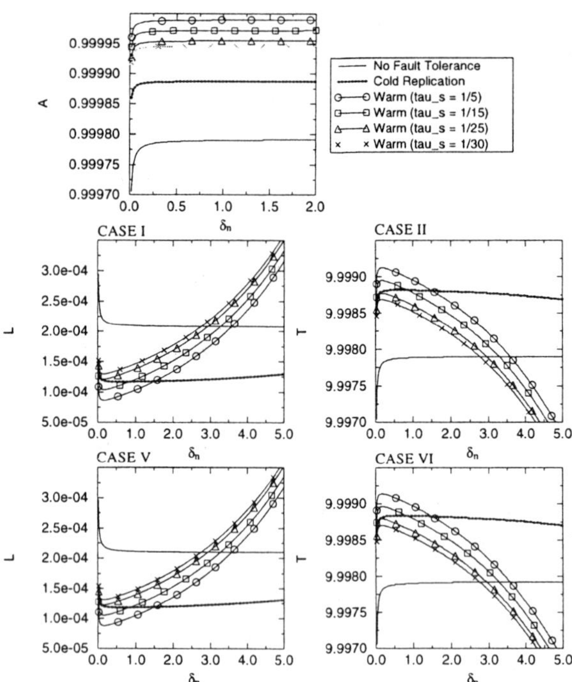

Figure 4. Effect of polling frequency, K = 12

In the first experiment, $K = 12$. The mean time to detect a node failure is varied from 0.04 to 5.0. The service rate without fault tolerance is assumed to be $\mu = 30$. When fault tolerance is used, either in cold or warm fashion, the service rate is affected in two ways. First, the server requires extra processing to implement checkpointing and recovery. The overhead is higher in warm than in cold. Second, the service rate is also a function of how often polling is done. To model this, we assume that the service rate with cold replication without any node polling overhead drops from 30 to 27, i.e., $\mu_c = 27$ and the service rate with warm replication further drops to $\mu_w = 21$. Experimentation has shown that single polling operation increases CPU utilization by about 5% for about half a second. Assuming proportional decrease in the service rate, it can be estimated as the function $\mu_c(40. - \delta_n/40)$ for cold replication and $\mu_w(40. - \delta_n/40)$ for warm replication. Alternatively, the exact function or its point values may be measured and plugged in the formulae. The time taken to switch the backup process to a primary is also varied to take values of 5, 15, 25 and 30 seconds in the warm replication scheme. Figure 4 shows the results obtained. In all of the five graphs, the X-axis is δ_n. The top graph plots Availability against δ_n and is the same for all the six cases of loss. As expected, server availability with warm replication is higher than that with cold replication. Further, within warm replication, higher the switching time, lower is the availability. The point to note, however is that in all three schemes, availability is a monotone increasing func-

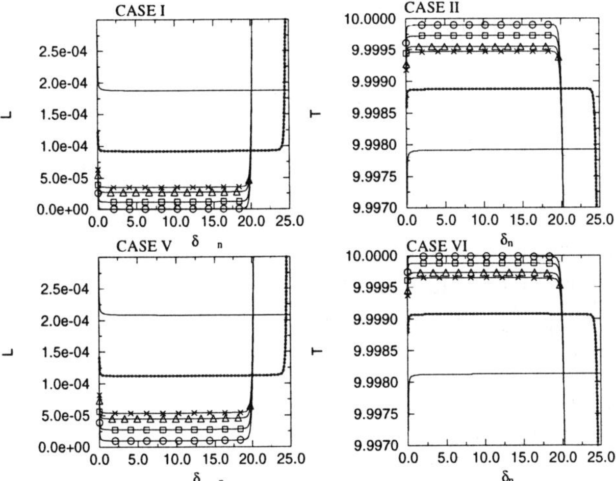

Figure 5. Effect of polling frequency, K = 128

tion of δ_n implying that if the objective is solely to maximize availability, the polling frequency should be arbitrarily high. The plots for the probability of loss (shown in the bottom left graphs for CASE I and V respectively) however suggest otherwise. These convex functions have a unique global minima. Therefore, if the objective is to minimize the probability of loss, the corresponding value of δ_n can be computed. For instance, for CASE I and cold replication, $\delta_n = 0.58$ corresponding to polling interval of 3.44 seconds whereas for warm replication the optimal $\delta_n = 0.16$ corresponding to a polling interval of 12.5 seconds. Since the throughput for the same case is only a constant factor of the loss probability, the maxima is achieved at the same δ_n. For a different case, however, it is different. The reliability objective may be to maintain a certain availability in which case the minimum value of δ_n that achieves that availability should be used. In this experiment, because of the low buffer size the loss is primarily due to buffer overflow and a small change in the service rate due to change in δ_n results in a relatively large change in the loss probability and throughput.

In the second experiment, we repeat the above with the same parameter values except that the buffer size is 128. Figure 5 shows the results for probability of loss and throughput for the same cases as before. The availability is not affected and hence not shown. The convexity of loss probability and the concavity of the throughput now shows a marked flatness implying that they remain roughly unchanged over a large range of δ_n values. The change occurs at very high polling frequencies when the service rate is substantially low and buffer overflow losses are high. However, if the recovery times $\frac{1}{\tau_p}$, $\frac{1}{\tau_n}$ were to be higher, the flatness will reduce.

10 Conclusion

We developed CTMC models of a server software under no replication, cold replication and warm replication. We modeled six scenarios of loss and computed closed form expressions for availability, throughput and loss probability for all the cases. The formulae may be used to determine the right replication scheme either offline or online. Higher detection rates imply lower down time for the server. However, they also take more CPU cycles and therefore decrease the throughput. These models enable us to evaluate these tradeoffs and determine optimal system parameters.

References

[1] *http://www.apcon.com.*

[2] *http://www.hp.com/gsy/high_availability/product_index.html.*

[3] *http://www.microsoft.com/NTServerEnterprise/.*

[4] *http://www.qualix.com/html/octopusha.html.*

[5] *http://www.tandem.com/brfs_wps/tdmtecbf/tdmtecbf.pdf.*

[6] *http://www.veritas.com.*

[7] *http://www.vinca.com/products/sbsnt.*

[8] P.Y. Chung, Y. Huang, S. Yajnik, D. Liang, and J. C. Shih. DOORS: Providing fault tolerance for corba applications. In *http://www.bell-labs.com/šhalini/doors.html*, Murray Hill, NJ, 1997.

[9] Y. Huang et.al. NT-SwiFT:Software implemented fault tolerance on Windows NT. In *Proc. of the 2nd USENIX NT Symposium*, Seattle, August 1998.

[10] S. Gokhale, W. E. Wong, K. S. Trivedi, and J. R. Horgan. An analytical approach to architecture based software reliability prediction. In *Proc. of Intnl. Performance and Dependability Symposium*, Durham, NC, August 1998.

[11] Y. Huang and C. M. R. Kintala. Software implemented fault tolerance: Technologies and experience. In *Proc. of 23rd Intl. Symposium on Fault-Tolerant Computing*, pages 2–9, Toulouse, France, June 1993.

[12] J.F. Meyer. On evaluating the performability of degradable computer systems. *IEEE Transactions on Computers*, C-29(8):720–731, 1980.

[13] J.F. Meyer. Closed-form solutions of performability. *IEEE Transactions on Computers*, C-31(7):648–657, 1982.

[14] K. S. Trivedi. *Probability and Statistics with reliability, queuing and computer science applications.* Prentice-Hall, 1982.

Dependability Analysis of Distributed Computer Systems with Imperfect Coverage*

Xinyu Zang, Hairong Sun and Kishor S. Trivedi
Center for Advanced Computing and Communications
Department of Electrical and Computer Engineering
Duke University
Durham, NC 27708
xzang, hairong, kst@ee.duke.edu

Abstract

In this paper, a new algorithm based on Binary Decision Diagrams (BDD) for dependability analysis of distributed computer systems (DCS) with imperfect coverage is proposed. Minimum file spanning trees (MFST) are generated and stored via BDD manipulation. By using the multistate concept, our algorithm can generate BDDs that can deal with imperfect coverage and obtain reliability expressions from these BDDs. Ordering strategies for variables are discussed in this paper as well. Due to the nature of the BDD, the sum of disjoint products (SDP) can be implicitly represented, which avoids huge storage and high computation complexity for large systems. Several examples are given to show the efficiency of this algorithm.

1 Introduction

With the rapid development of computer networking, distributed computer systems (DCS) have become an attractive and efficient way to share system resources, achieve fault-tolerance and obtain high extensibility and dependability. A successful execution of a distributed program usually requires one or more of the resources that reside on the hosts of the DCS, e.g., processing elements, memory modules, data files and so on. These hosts are interconnected via communication links that enable a running distributed program to access the resources on remote hosts.

In [1], Kumar et al. modeled a DCS as an undirected graph $G(v, e)$ in which the vertices represent the hosts and the edges represent the communication links. Fig. 1 shows an example of a four-node DCS. In the figure, *FA* represents the set of files; *PRG* represents the set of programs; and FN_i represents the set of files required by a program P_i. Both the vertices and the edges are in either operational or failed states and their behaviors are independent. The system resources (except for processing elements) required by a program are abstracted into files. A file spanning tree (FST) is defined as a spanning tree that connects the root node (the host that runs the program under consideration) to some other nodes such that its vertices hold all the required files for successful execution of the program. An FST is a minimal file spanning tree (MFST) if there exists no other FST that is a subset of this FST. For instance, program P_1 in Fig. 1 will function if it can run on node n_1 or n_4, and can access files $\{F_1, F_2, F_3\}$, the set of MFSTs of program P_1 in Fig. 1 are: $\{n_1, e_1, n_2\}$, $\{n_1, e_4, n_3, e_3, n_2\}$, $\{n_4, e_5, n_3\}$ and $\{n_4, e_2, n_2, e_3, n_3\}$.

Based on the definition of MFST, two reliability measures, i.e., distributed program reliability (DPR) and distributed system reliability (DSR), are defined as:

$$DPR = Pr\{\text{at least one MFST of a given program is operational}\} = Pr\{\bigcup_{j=1}^{n_{mfst}} \text{MFST}_j = 1\}$$

where n_{mfst} is the number of MFSTs that run the given program.

$$DSR = Pr\{\text{at least one MFST for all programs is operational}\} = Pr\{\bigcup_{i=1}^{m_{mfst}} \text{MFST}_i = 1\}$$

where m_{mfst} is the number of MFSTs over all programs, and where an MFST is said to be operational when all its elements are operational.

An algorithm to obtain the set of MFSTs is given in [1]. After obtaining the set of MFSTs, the sum of disjoint prod-

*This research was supported in part by the National Science Foundation under Grant No. EEC9418765, and by the Department of Defense as an enhancement project to the Center for Advanced Computing and Communications in Duke University.

0-7695-0213-X/99 $10.00 © 1999 IEEE

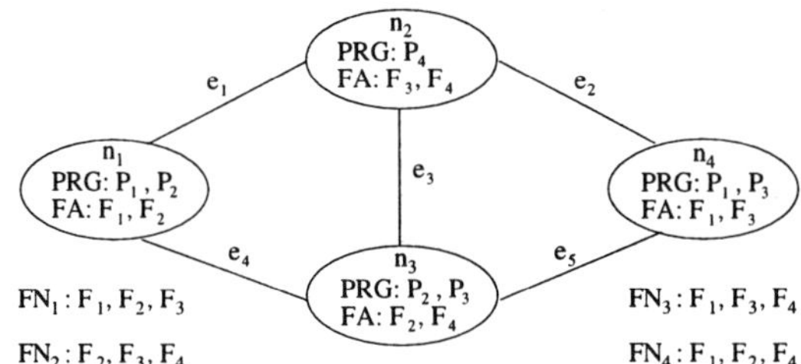

Figure 1. A four-node DCS

ucts (SDP) method is applied to obtain reliability expressions. To compute the DPR of a DCS efficiently, Kumar et al. [2] presented an algorithm that can obtain reliability expressions directly during the generation of the set of MFSTs. In [3], Kumar and Agrawal generalized this algorithm so that it can deal with the case in which one program can run on multiple nodes. Ke and Wang [4] gave an improved algorithm that addressed the possibility of imperfect nodes. The quoted algorithms except for [1], however, can not be used directly to obtain the DSR of a DCS.

Another issue that above algorithms did not consider is imperfect coverage. Generally, the hosts in a DCS can be located at different geographic sites. There exists a possibility that some faults of hosts and communication links may not be detected promptly and therefore the redundant units (the other hosts and links) can not be utilized, which cause the distributed program not to be carried out successfully. Markovian reliability models with imperfect coverage have been studied extensively [5]. Doyle et al. addressed imperfect coverage in fault-tree models [6], but they did not consider this problem in a DCS. To address the imperfect coverage in a DCS, Lopez-Benitez used stochastic Petri nets [7]. Like the other Markov chain based models, this method become impractical when the number of hosts and links in a DCS is large. In this paper, we use the multistate method developed in [8] to deal with imperfect coverage.

In this paper, a new algorithm based on BDD is proposed for dependability analysis of the DCS with imperfect coverage. Binary Decision Diagrams (BDD) have been used in VLSI design and verification as an efficient method to manipulate Boolean expressions [9–11]. Bryant [9] and other researches showed that, in most cases, BDDs use less memory in representing large Boolean expressions compared with a conventional representation. Because BDDs are based on Shannon decomposition, reliability of a system is very easily computed directly from the BDD format. Some researchers have used BDDs for the reliability analysis of fault trees [12–16]. The BDD for the structure function of a DPR can be generated via searching MFSTs of the given program. The BDD for the structure function of a DSR can be obtained by logic operations on the BDDs for its programs. In [6], imperfect coverage was accounted for in the computation of system unreliability from an ordinary BDD. By contrast, in this paper, the use of multistate BDDs allows us to incorporate the notion of imperfect coverage in the generation of the BDD, so the proof of correctness of our algorithm is straight. The final BDD for a given program or whole system can implicitly represent the SDPs, avoiding the huge storage for large number of disjoint products, and can be used to easily compute the system reliability. Ordering strategy in the BDD will be discussed in this paper as well, as the size of the BDD heavily depends on this order. Two ordering strategies will be presented and compared. To make the DCS model more pratical, we will consider the independent repair mechanisim for the hosts and the communication links in a DCS, i.e., each host or communication link can be repaired independently.

The paper is organized as follows. Section 2 reviews some preliminary concepts, such as the BDD and multistate model for imperfect coverage. Section 3 gives the details of our algorithm. Some examples are provided in Section 4 to show the efficiency of our algorithm. The last section gives the conclusion and future work.

2 Preliminary concepts

2.1 Binary Decision Diagrams (BDD)

In this section, we review the concept of BDDs as well as reduced ordered binary decision diagrams (ROBDD) which were introduced as efficient means to manipulate Boolean expressions [9]. Shannon decomposition is the basis for using BDD.

Shannon Decomposition: let f be a Boolean expression on $X = \{x_1, x_2, \ldots, x_n\}$, and x be a variable of X, then,

$$f = x \cdot f_{x=1} + \bar{x} \cdot f_{x=0} \tag{1}$$

where f evaluated with $x = v$ is denoted by $f_{x=v}$.

In order to express Shannon decomposition concisely, the If-Then-Else (*ite*) format is defined as:

$$f = ite(x, F_1, F_2) \equiv x \cdot F_1 + \bar{x} \cdot F_2 \tag{2}$$

where $F_1 = f_{x=1}$ and $F_2 = f_{x=0}$.

A BDD is a directed acyclic graph (DAG) that is based on Shannon decomposition. The graph has two sink nodes, labeled 0 and 1, representing the two corresponding constants 0 and 1. Each non-sink node is labeled with a Boolean variable x and has two outgoing edges that represent the two corresponding expressions in the Shannon decomposition. These two edges are called 0-edge (or *else*-edge) and 1-edge (or *then*-edge), respectively. The node linked by 1-edge represents the Boolean expression when $x = 1$, i.e., $f_{x=1}$ in Eqn. (1), while the node linked by 0-edge represents the Boolean expression when $x = 0$, i.e.,

$f_{x=0}$ in Eqn. (1). Thus, each non-sink node in the BDD encodes an *ite* format. Obviously, one of the key features of the BDD is the disjointness of the two subexpressions, $x \cdot f_{x=1}$ and $\bar{x} \cdot f_{x=0}$.

An ordered binary decision diagram (OBDD) is a BDD with the constraint that the variables are ordered and every source to sink path in the OBDD visits the variables in ascending order. A reduced ordered binary decision diagram (ROBDD) is an OBDD where each node represents a distinct Boolean expression.

ROBDDs are widely used in practice. To generate an ROBDD, the ordering of the variables has to be selected first, and this order of variables is not changed during the generation[1], i.e., there is an index assigned to each variable to indicate its position in the ordering. In this paper, we denote the fact that variable x_j is behind variable x_i in the order of variables as $x_i < x_j$.

2.2 Using multistate components to model imperfect coverage

In many combinatorial reliability models, components are assumed to be in one of two states: functioning or failed. However, in some applications, more than two states need to be considered. In a DCS, faults may occur at the hosts and the communication links. Some faults may not be detected promptly since the hosts and the communication links may be distributed in a wide area. These undetectable faults will cause the distributed program to fail. Hence, the imperfect coverage needs to be considered in a practical DCS. The components (hosts or links) in a DCS with imperfect coverage may exist in one of three states:

1. operational state;
2. undetectable failed state that will cause system failure;
3. detectable failed state that will not cause system failure.

Because the independent repair mechanisim for each host and communication link is considered, the behaivor of each component (host or link) can be modeled by a continuous-time Markov chain(CTMC) as shown in Fig. 2

In [8], we developed a BDD-based algorithm to solve multistate problems. Each state of the multistate component is represented by a Boolean variable. Because of the dependence among these Boolean variables, a Boolean algebra with restrictions on variables is used to address this dependence. In this paper, we will use the same concepts to deal with imperfect coverage in the DCS.

The three states, i.e., operational state, undetectable failed state and detectable failed state of component C_A can

[1] We do not consider the dynamic reordering of the BDD in this paper

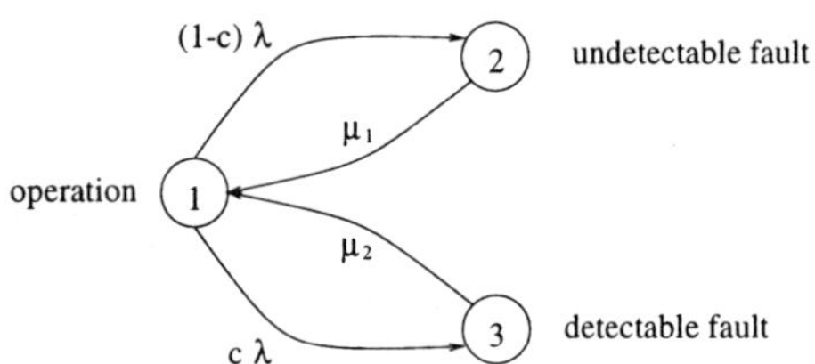

Figure 2. CTMC for a component (host or communication link)

be represented by three Boolean variables A_1, A_2 and A_3, respectively. Here, $A_i = 1, i = 1, 2, 3$, means that component C_A is in the corresponding state. These variables are related by:

$$A_1 = \overline{A_2 + A_3} = \bar{A}_2 \cdot \bar{A}_3 \quad (3)$$

This equivalence can be represented in the BDD format as in Fig. 3

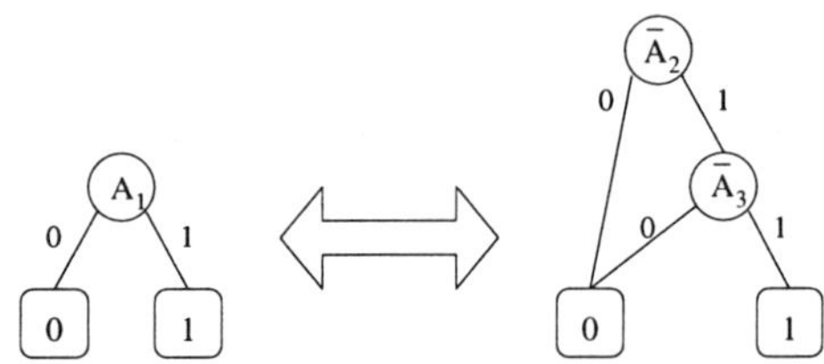

Figure 3. BDD format of the equivalence $A_1 = \bar{A}_2 \cdot \bar{A}_3$

3 BDD algorithm for DCS

3.1 Generation of BDD

The generation of a BDD for a DCS with imperfect coverage can be divided into two steps:

1. Generate ordinary BDDs by searching the set of MFSTs for each program, then use BDD operation *AND* to combine these BDDs into a BDD for the whole system.
2. Convert this BDD for the whole DCS to a multistate BDD that can reflect the imperfect coverage. If only the DPR is needed, this conversion may apply only to the BDD for a given program.

Fig. 4 shows the algorithm of generating a BDD for a given program. The function *bdd_gen_aux(p_id, node_i)* is used to search the set of MFSTs for a given program from a given node via a recursive method. The recursive method used here to search MFST set is adopted from [1], [3] and

```
bdd_gen(p_id) {
   mfst_bdd = 0
   for (node_i in the set of nodes at which p_id resides) {
      mfst_bdd = mfst_bdd OR bdd_gen_aux(p_id, node_i)
      disable all edges connected to node_i
   }
   enable back all edge_i that be disabled in above loop
}

bdd_gen_aux(p_id, node_i) {
   T_bdd = 0
   set node in this_mfst
   for (edge_i in the set of edges starting from all nodes in this_mfst) {
       disable edge_i
       next_node = the other end of edge_i
       if (next_node is already in this_mfst)
          continue;
       if (next_node and this_mfst contain all the required files)
          submfst_bdd = edge_i_bdd
       else
          submfst_bdd = bdd_gen_aux(p_id, next_node) AND edge_i_bdd
       T_bdd = T_bdd OR submfst_bdd
   }
   T_bdd = T_bdd AND node_i_bdd
   clear node in this_mfst
   enable back all edge_i that be disabled in above loop
   return T_bdd
}
```

Figure 4. Algorithm of generating a BDD for a given program

[4], however, we merge the search results into a BDD during the generation of MFSTs rather than store them separately. Boolean variables E_i amd N_i are used to represent edge e_i and node n_i, and their corresponding BDDs are *edge_i_bdd* and *node_i_bdd*. The structure function that program P_1 can successfully run on n_1 (in Fig. 1) can be represented by a Boolean expression:

$$\Phi_{P1n1} = N_1(E_1N_2 + E_4N_3(E_5N_4 + E_3N_2)) \quad (4)$$

Fig. 5 shows the BDD generated for distributed program P_1 in Fig. 1.

The BDD generated above is an ordinary BDD and does not contain coverage factor. To incorporate imperfect coverage, the following two steps are applied to the ordinary BDD:

1. Replace all nodes except sink nodes in ordinary BDD by their corresponding equivalent nodes shown in Fig. 3, i.e., for the node that represents component A, use $\bar{A}_2 \cdot \bar{A}_3$ to replace A_1. Then the structure function becomes:

$$\begin{aligned}\Phi_{P1n1} = \; & \bar{N}_{1,2}\bar{N}_{1,3}(\bar{E}_{1,2}\bar{E}_{1,3}\bar{N}_{2,2}\bar{N}_{2,3} + \\ & \bar{E}_{4,2}\bar{E}_{4,3}\bar{N}_{3,2}\bar{N}_{3,3}(\bar{E}_{5,2}\bar{E}_{5,3}\bar{N}_{4,2}\bar{N}_{4,3} \\ & +\bar{E}_{3,2}\bar{E}_{3,3}\bar{N}_{2,2}\bar{N}_{2,3}))\end{aligned} \quad (5)$$

2. Because any undetectable fault will cause system failure, the occurrence of these faults need to be considered separately in the structure function. Use BDD operation *AND* to merge the variables that represent the undetectable fault in components, i.e.

$$\Phi^c_{P1n1} = \Phi_{P1n1} \cdot (\bar{N}_{1,2}\bar{N}_{2,2}\bar{N}_{3,2}\bar{N}_{4,2}\bar{E}_{1,2}\bar{E}_{3,2}\bar{E}_{4,2}\bar{E}_{5,2}) \quad (6)$$

$(\bar{N}_{1,2}\bar{N}_{2,2}\bar{N}_{3,2}\bar{N}_{4,2}\bar{E}_{1,2}\bar{E}_{3,2}\bar{E}_{4,2}\bar{E}_{5,2}) = 1$ represents the condition that no undetectable fault has occured. Note that only the components that are contained in MFSTs will be considered, e.g., $\bar{E}_{2,2}$ is not included.

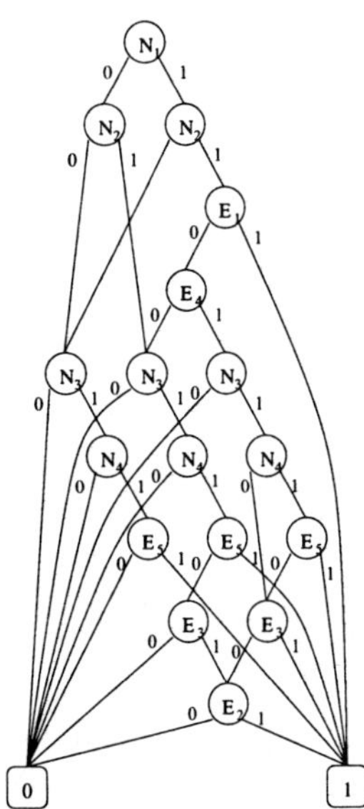

Figure 5. BDD for program P_1 in Fig. 1

After these two steps, the final BDD is able to deal with the imperfect coverage. Fig. 6 shows the final BDD that is obtained from Fig. 5.

Note that in Fig. 6,

- the nodes representing state 3 of the components have only one parent, i.e., the node representing state 2 of the same component.
- 0-edge of the nodes representing state 2 always connects to sink node 0 since the state 2 represents the undetectable fault that always leads to system failure.

Based on this fact, we can simplify the BDD representation by removing the nodes whose 1-edge connects to the variable for state 3 of components. Actually, in our implementation of the algorithm, step 1 of conversion is just to replace the nodes in the original BDD by nodes representing state 3 of components.

3.2 Reliability/Availability computation

Because the Boolean variables that represent the two failed states of the same component are not independent of each other, the algorithm for the ordinary BDD can not be

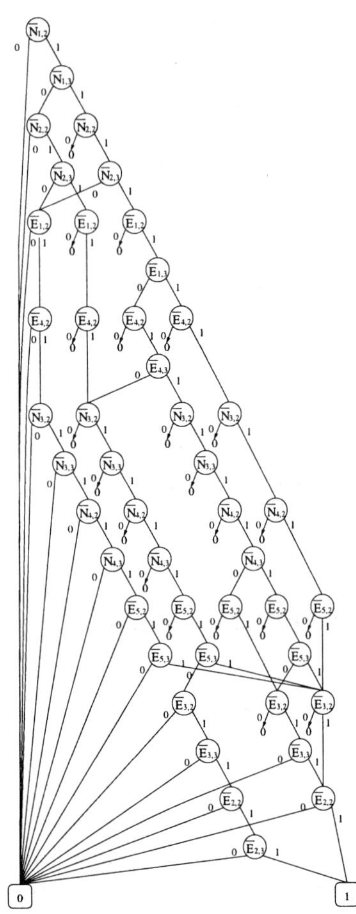

Figure 6. Final BDD for program P_1 in Fig. 1

used to compute the system reliability/availability from the BDD with dependence. In [8], we have developed an algorithm to deal with this dependence. This algorithm can be simplified here because there are only two Boolean variables for each component.

Observing the BDD in Fig. 6, we see that the 0-edge always links two variables that belong to different components. But for the 1-edge, there are two cases which need to be evaluated differently:

- the 1-edge linking the variables of different components;
- the 1-edge linking the variables of the same component.

To make the following expressions concise, the probability that a system is functioning or a component is in a specific state, i.e., $Pr\{\Phi = 1\}$, is denoted as $P(\Phi)$.

Lemma 1 *Let BDD G be*

$$G = ite(\bar{X}, G_1, G_2) = \bar{X} \cdot G_1 + X \cdot G_2$$

and

$$G_1 = ite(\bar{Y}, H_1, H_2) = \bar{Y} \cdot H_1 + Y \cdot H_2$$

then

$$P(G) = \begin{cases} P(G_1) - P(X)P(H_1) & X, Y \textit{ are diff. st. of the same comp.} \\ P(G_1) + P(X)(P(G_2) - P(G_1)) & \textit{otherwise} \end{cases} \quad (7)$$

Proof: Note that G_2 does not contain any variables that belong to component C_A, which implies that X and G_2 are independent, i.e. $P(X \cdot G_2) = P(X)P(G_2)$. So does G_1 in the case of the 1-edge linking the variables of different components.

The case in which the 1-edge is linking the variables of different components is the same as the ordinary BDD. Normal evaluation method for BDD can be used in this case:

$$\begin{aligned} P(G) &= P(ite(\bar{X}, G_1, G_2)) \\ &= P(\bar{X} \cdot G_1 + X \cdot G_2) \\ &= P(\bar{X})P(G_1) + P(X)P(G_2) \\ &= P(G_1) + P(X)(P(G_2) - P(G_1)) \end{aligned} \quad (8)$$

Next consider the case where the 1-edge is linking variables of the same component. Assume that X and Y represent the different states of component C_A, i.e., $X = A_2$, $Y = A_3$, then:

$$\begin{aligned} P(G) &= P(ite(\bar{X}, G_1, G_2)) \\ &= P(\bar{X} \cdot G_1 + X \cdot G_2) \\ &= P(\bar{X} \cdot (\bar{Y} \cdot H_1 + Y \cdot H_2)) + P(X)P(G_2) \\ &= P(\bar{X}\bar{Y}H_1 + \bar{X}YH_2) + P(X)P(G_2) \end{aligned} \quad (9)$$

According to the restriction relation among the variables associated with the same component,

$$\bar{X}Y = \bar{A}_2A_3 = A_3 = Y$$

$$\begin{aligned} \bar{Y} &= (\bar{X} + X)\bar{Y} \\ &= \bar{X}\bar{Y} + X \end{aligned}$$

Hence, we have:

$$\begin{aligned} P(G_1) &= P(\bar{Y} \cdot H_1 + Y \cdot H_2) \\ &= P((\bar{X} \cdot \bar{Y} + X) \cdot H_1 + \bar{X} \cdot Y \cdot H_2) \\ &= P(\bar{X}\bar{Y}H_1 + \bar{X}YH_2) + P(XH_1) \\ &= P(\bar{X}\bar{Y}H_1 + \bar{X}YH_2) + P(X)P(H_1) \end{aligned}$$

Because H_1 does not have variables that represent the states of the same component as X does, $P(XH_1) = P(X)P(H_1)$. Therefore,

$$P(\bar{X}\bar{Y}H_1 + \bar{X}YH_2) = P(G_1) - P(X)P(H_1) \quad (10)$$

In this case, since undetectable faults always cause system failure, $P(G_2) = 0$. This result can also be observed from Fig. 6, where all 0-edges of Boolean variables that represent the undetectable faults of components are connected to sink node 0. Substituting Exp. (10) in Exp. (9), we have

$$P(G) = P(G_1) - P(X)P(H_1) \quad (11)$$

□

Using recursive method, we can compute $P(G_1)$, $P(G_2)$ and $P(H_1)$ until reaching the sink node, i.e., $G_i = 1$ or $G_i = 0$:

- $G_i = 0$, implies the system or the subsystem represented by G_i is always down, hence $P(G_i) = 0$.
- $G_i = 1$, implies the system or the subsystem represented by G_i is always up, hence $P(G_i) = 1$.

In our implementation, all nodes whose 1-edge connects to variable representing state 3 of components are removed. Then, Lemma 1 can be changed to:

Lemma 2 *Let BDD G be*

$$G = ite(\bar{X}, G_1, G_2) = \bar{X} \cdot G_1 + X \cdot G_2$$

then

$$P(G) = \begin{cases} (1 - P(X_2) - P(X_3))P(G_1) + P(X_3)P(G_2) & X \text{ is variable for state 3} \\ (1 - P(X_2))P(G_1) & \text{otherwise} \end{cases} \quad (12)$$

where $P(X_2)$ is the probability of undetectable fault, and $P(X_3)$ is the probability of detectable fault.

Proof: In the simplified BDD, there are only two types of nodes:

- node for the variable that represent the component being in state 3;
- node for the variable that represent the component being in state 2;

In the first case, the node for state 3 is actually the combination of two nodes, the removed node $\bar{X}_2$ for state 2 and the node $\bar{X}_3$ for state 3. Because these two nodes represent the different states of the same component, the first formula in Eqn.(7), i.e., Eqn.(11), should be used. Let the removed node be

$$G' = ite(\bar{X}_2, G'_1, G'_2) = \bar{X}_2 \cdot G'_1 + X_2 \cdot G'_2$$

where

$$G'_1 = ite(\bar{X}_3, G_1, G_2) = \bar{X}_3 \cdot G_1 + X_3 \cdot G_2$$

Then,

$$\begin{aligned} P(G) &= P(G') \\ &= P(G'_1) - P(X_2)P(G_1) \\ &= P(G_1) + P(X_3)(P(G_2) - P(G_1)) - P(X_2)P(G_1) \\ &= (1 - P(X_2) - P(X_3))P(G_1) + P(X_3)P(G_2) \quad (13) \end{aligned}$$

where $P(X_2)$ and $P(X_3)$ can be obtained via solving the CTMC in Fig. 2.

In the second case, since the node $\bar{X}_2$ for state 2 always connects to the variables of different components and the sink node 0 ($P(G_2) = 0$), the second formula in Eqn.(7), i.e. Eqn.(8), should be used.

$$\begin{aligned} P(G) &= P(G_1) + P(X_2)(P(G_2) - P(G_1)) \\ &= (1 - P(X_2))P(G_1) \quad (14) \end{aligned}$$

□

Fig. 7 gives the algorithm for computing the reliability/availability of a DCS.

```
Prob(G) {
   if (G == 1)
      return 1
   else if (G == 0)
      return 0
   else if (computed-table has entry {G, P_G})
      return P_G
   else { /* G = ite(x, G1, G2) */
      P_G1 = Prob(G1), P_G2 = Prob(G2)
      if (x is variables for state 3 of component)
         P_G = (1 - P_X2 - P_X3) * P_G1 + P_X3 * P_G2
      else
         P_G = (1 - P_X2) * P_G1
   }
   insert_computed_table({G, P_G})
   return P_G
}
```

Figure 7. Algorithm for computing the reliability/availability of a DCS

3.3 Ordering strategies

The ordering of variables is very important for the generation of a BDD. The size of a BDD (the number of nodes in the BDD) heavily depends on the ordering. But the problem of computing an ordering that minimizes the size of a BDD is itself a co NP-complete problem [9]. Previous studies have shown that a set of heuristics may be used to select an adequate ordering [10, 17], however, these heuristics were proposed for the digital circuits that consist of logic gates and there is no similarity between the DCS and logic circuits. New ordering strategies are needed for the DCS.

Observing Eqn. 4, we see that a fault tree can be constructed from this structure function, so that some ordering heuristics developed for fault trees may be adopted for the DCS. Inspired by this relationship between fault trees and the DCS, we design the ordering strategies for the DCS. To avoid two traversal of the graph, we order the components (hosts or links) during which we use the algorithm shown in

Fig. 4 to generate a BDD, i.e., we put the components in the ordered list if we need a new variable to represent a component. There are two strategies for putting the variables in the ordered list.

- Strategy 1 (S1): always put the variables at the head of the list so that the list serves as a stack, i.e., we push the variable in the stack if we need this variable in BDD manipulation.
- Strategy 2 (S2): always put the variables at the end of the list so that the list serves as a queue, i.e., we add the variable at the end of the queue if this is a new variable.

For the example in Fig. 1, two orders are generated as:

- Strategy 1: $e_2 < n_1 < e_4 < n_3 < e_3 < n_4 < e_5 < n_2 < e_1$
- Strategy 2: $n_1 < n_2 < e_1 < e_4 < n_3 < n_4 < e_5 < e_3 < e_2$

The use of these two strategies is shown in Table 3.

4 Examples

4.1 Effect of coverage

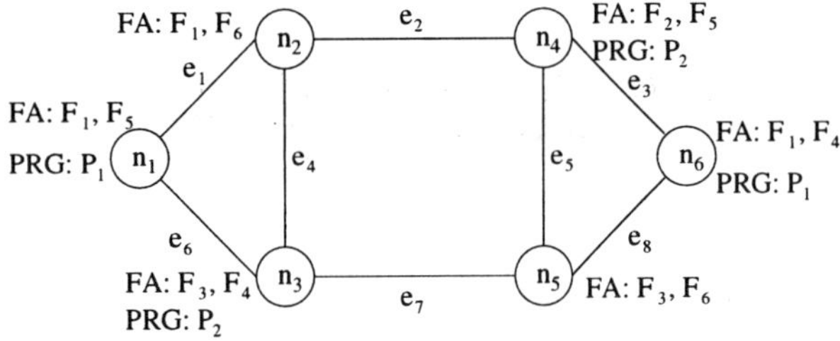

Figure 8. System topology of a DCS

Example: Fig. 8 shows the system topology of a DCS. The program P_1 needs files $\{F_1, F_2, F_3\}$ and P_2 needs files $\{F_4, F_5, F_6\}$. The failure rate of the hosts is 0.01/*hour*, and the both repair rates are 1/*hour*. The failure rate of the communication links is 0.015/*hour*, and the both repair rates are 0.5/*hour*. Fig. 9 shows the results of the DSR in the DCS with different coverage values.

4.2 Execution time

The execution time of our algorithm depends on system topology, the location of programs and files and the ordering of variables. We use the benchmarks $G_{i:j}$ given in [4], $j \leq i$, where i is the number of nodes in the network, and j means G with n_1 to n_j being completely connected. Fig. 10

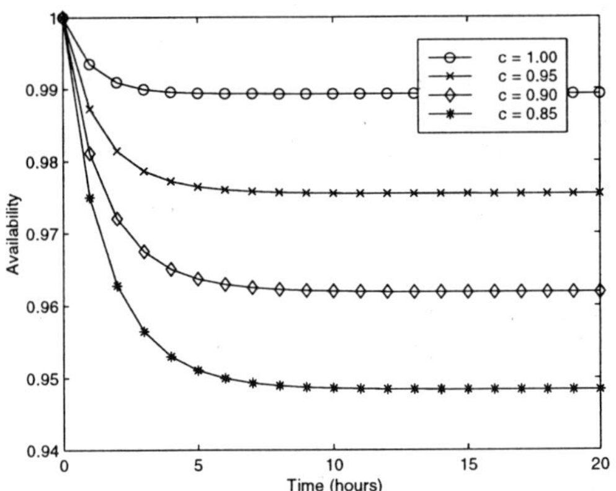

Figure 9. Availability of a DCS in Fig. 8

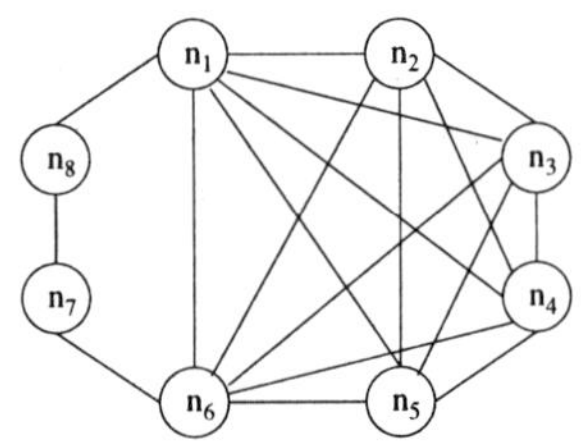

Figure 10. Benchmark network $G_{8:6}$

Node Name	Files
n_1	F_1, F_2, F_3
n_2	F_2, F_3, F_4
n_3	F_3, F_4, F_5
n_4	F_4, F_5, F_6
n_5	F_5, F_6, F_7
n_6	F_6, F_7, F_8
n_7	F_1, F_7, F_8
n_8	F_1, F_2, F_8
n_9	F_3, F_7, F_8
n_{10}	F_1, F_4, F_7

Table 1. File location

shows the benchmark network $G_{8:6}$. The program is located at n_1, and files F_1, F_3, F_5 are required to execute it. Table 1 gives the location of files.

Table 2 shows the experimental results with perfect coverage [2]. Table 3 shows the experimental results (BDD size and execution time) for computing DPR with imperfect coverage by using two ordering strategies: S1 and S2 that are described in Sec. 3.3. The execution times listed in tables are generated via *time* command on SUN Ultra 1.

From these results, we can observe some features of the BDD algorithm:

- The BDD algorithm is more efficient than KHR and ENR/KW [4] algorithms, because the reliability expression can be represented in format with much

[2]The experimental results for KHR and ENR/KW are obtained from [4].

Network	KHR [1]	ENR/KW [4]	BDD	
	# of subnets	# of subnets	# of Nodes	Time(s)
$G_{8:4}$	37	16	33	0.05
$G_{10:4}$	55	20	41	0.05
$G_{8:6}$	306	72	68	0.06
$G_{8:7}$	1159	289	141	0.07
$G_{10:7}$	3443	462	192	0.08
$G_{8:8}$	3225	1196	398	0.15
$G_{10:8}$	20464	2556	483	0.25
$G_{10:9}$	131899	17832	1500	1.83

Table 2. Experimental results with perfect coverage

Network	BDD (S1)		BDD (S2)	
	# of Nodes	Time(s)	# of Nodes	Time(s)
$G_{8:4}$	56	0.06	65	0.06
$G_{10:4}$	72	0.06	73	0.06
$G_{8:6}$	124	0.07	345	0.10
$G_{8:7}$	269	0.10	1433	0.25
$G_{10:7}$	309	0.12	1529	0.38
$G_{8:8}$	725	0.23	3952	0.74
$G_{10:8}$	891	0.36	6571	1.83
$G_{10:9}$	2503	2.10	28473	16.62

Table 3. Experimental results with imperfect coverage ($c = 0.95$)

smaller size (subnetworks in KHR and ENR/KW algorithm, BDD nodes in our algorithm) when the benchmarks become complex.

- BDD is very efficient for evaluating the dependability of a DCS with imperfect coverage.
- In most cases, the size of a BDD is not very large if an appropriate order is used.
- The size of a BDD heavily depends on the ordering of the variables.

5 Conclusion

In this paper, we presented a BDD-based algorithm for dependability analysis of distributed computer systems with imperfect coverage. Several related issues, such as generation of the BDD for a system or for a given program, computation of reliability and ordering strategies, were discussed. Due to the nature of the BDD, this algorithm is efficient in both computation time and storage, which makes it possible for us to study some practical and large distributed systems. As seen in Table 3, the size of a BDD heavily depends on the ordering of the variables. Our future work will focus on the search of an more appropriate ordering strategy or a set of ordering strategies based on features of different configurations in a DCS.

References

[1] V. Kumar, S. Hariri, and C. Raghavendra. Distributed program reliability analysis. *IEEE Transactions on Software Engineering*, SE-12(1):42–50, 1986.

[2] A. Kumar, S. Rai, and D. Agrawal. On computer communication network reliability under program execution constraints. *IEEE Journal on Selected Areas in Communications*, 6(8):1393–1399, 1988.

[3] A. Kumar and D. Agrawal. A generalized algorithm for evaluating distributed-program reliability. *IEEE Transactions on Reliability*, 42(3):416–426, 1993.

[4] W. Ke and S. Wang. Reliability evaluation for distributed computing networks with imperfect nodes. *IEEE Transactions on Reliability*, 46(3):342–349, 1997.

[5] J. Dugan and K. Trivedi. Coverage modeling for dependability analysis of fault-tolerant systems. *IEEE Transactions on Computers*, 38(6):775–787, 1989.

[6] S. Doyle, J. Dugan, and M. Boyd. Combinatorial-models and coverage: a binary decision diagram (BDD) approach. In *Proc. Annual Reliability and Maintainability Symposium*, pages 82–89, 1995.

[7] N. Lopez-Benitez. Dependability modeling and analysis of distributed programs. *IEEE Transactions on Software Engineering*, 20(5):345–352, 1994.

[8] X. Zang, H. Sun, and K. Trivedi. A bdd-based algorithm for analysis of multistate systems with multistate components. *Technical Report*, CACC, Duke University, 1998.

[9] R. Bryant. Graph based algorithms for boolean function manipulation. *IEEE Transactions on Computers*, C-35(8):677–691, 1986.

[10] S. Malik, A. Wang, R. Brayton, and A. Sangiovanni-Vincentelli. Logic verification using binary decision diagrams in a logic synthesis environment. In *Proc. IEEE International Conference on Computer-Aided Design (ICCAD-88)*, pages 6–9, Santa Clara, California, Nov. 1988.

[11] K. Brace, R. Rudell, and R. Bryant. Efficient implementation of a BDD package. In *Proc. 27th ACM/IEEE Design Automation Conference*, pages 40–45, 1990.

[12] A. Rauzy. New algorithms for fault tree analysis. *Reliability Engineering and System Safety*, 40:203–211, 1993.

[13] O. Coudert and J. Madre. Metaprime: An interactive fault-tree analyzer. *IEEE Transactions on Reliability*, 43(1):121–127, 1994.

[14] S. Doyle and J. Dugan. Dependability assessment using binary decision diagrams. *Proc. 25th International Symposium on Fault-Tolerant Computing*, pages 249–258, 1995.

[15] R. Sinnamon and J. Andrews. Improved accuracy in quantitative fault tree analysis. *Quality and Reliability Engineering International*, 13:285–292, 1997.

[16] R. Sinnamon and J. Andrews. Improved efficiency in qualitative fault tree analysis. *Quality and Reliability Engineering International*, 13:293–298, 1997.

[17] M. Bouissou. An ordering heuristic for building binary decision diagrams from fault-trees. *Proc. Annual Reliability and Maintainability Symposium*, pages 208–214, 1996.

Session 11B

Practical Experience Reports

Chair: Robert Horst
3ware, Inc., USA

Real Time Estimation for Usage-Dependent Reliability on a Dual-Backbone Network Subsystem

Meng-Lai Yin   Lawrence E. James   Rafael R. Arellano   Raymond V. Hettwer
Raytheon Systems Company

Abstract

This paper presents a method to efficiently estimate the network reliability, in support of the "real time" needs of a geographically diverse set of users. The network subsystem considered here is a ring-structured, dual-backbone network. The measurement is usage-dependent in terms of location and time. For users at different locations and/or different times, different requirements are applied to the network, thus different network reliabilities are expected. Our method applies the hierarchical decomposition principle and takes advantages of the graph similarities. The real-time estimation for all locations, at one time step, takes O(nmk) time, where n is the number of site nodes that need to be connected, m is the number of backbone nodes for one backbone network and k is the number of locations considered.

1. INTRODUCTION

For a wide area network, users at different locations usually have different network needs. Using a single reliability estimation to represent the network for all situations is unrealistic. For satellite navigation systems, "real-time" reliability assessment is inevitable since a user needs to determine, in real time, whether the service that the system provides is reliable enough. This "real-time" and "usage-dependent" reliability estimation is essential to demonstrate the suitability of such a satellite navigation system. In particular, a contour map of the U.S. showing areas that meet the reliability requirement is used to display the "real-time" and "usage-dependent" reliability estimation results. The computation complexity is a challenge for such a reliability measurement process. The efficiency issues of modeling such a usage-dependent network based on real time needs are the focuses of this paper.

The network subsystem considered here is a ring-structured, dual-backbone network. As shown in Figure 1, four backbone nodes form a backbone network that connects a large group of site nodes for the service area. Each site node is connected to the two backbone networks via two independent access networks[1]. For each site node and each backbone node, two independent sets of equipment are supported so that independence between the two networks can be assumed.

Considering the case where there are n different users, a naive approach would be to provide n different models for the n different users. This approach results in significant computation complexity and would require unrealistic computation times. Our strategy is to apply the hierarchical decomposition principle [9][10], recognize similarities in the network graphs [1][2][4][5] [6], and preprocess data that can be used (and reused).

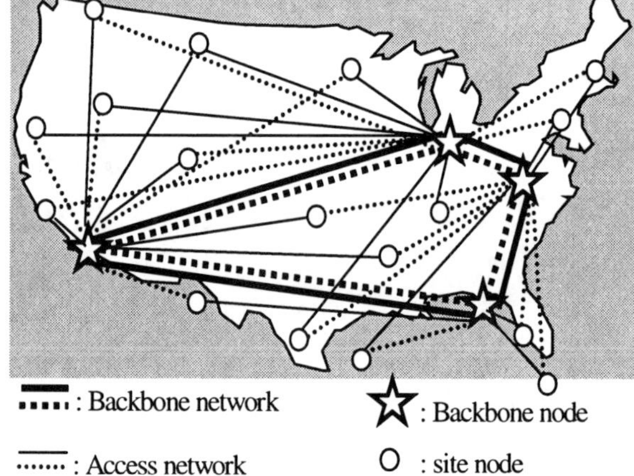

Figure 1. The Dual-Backbone Network Subsystem

2. BACKGROUND

The network is considered available if the network topology supports the required operation. The behaviors of components are assumed to be statistically independent, and only link failures are considered[2].

The topology of this network subsystem is shown in Figure 2. The network is considered operational as long as it provides the necessary connections for a user's needs. Note that a user at location A can have network needs differing from those of a user at location B. For example,

---

1 An access network connects a site node and a backbone node.

2 In [3], it was proved that the s,T-connectedness with node failures is polynomial time reducible to s,T-connectedness without node failures.

a user at location A requires that receiving stations 1, 2 and 5 connect to master station 1, and then connect to broadcast station A. Another user at location B requires receiving stations 17, 18 and 19 connect to master station 2, and then connect to broadcast station C.

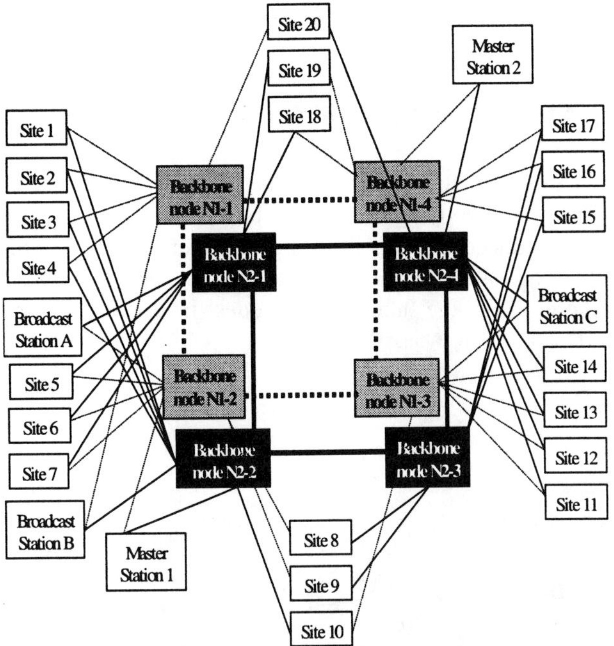

Figure 2. The Topology of the Network Subsystem

The complexity is a major concern for real-time estimation. The desire of high fidelity provided by the model makes the complexity problem even worse. One way to handle this is through the use of parallel processing, a topic that is not the focus of this paper. Here, we employ the "hierarchical decomposition" principle, a method that has been widely used in the field, to handle the largeness problem.

3. APPROACH

The largeness problem is one of the major challenges in the modeling field; considerable research has been pursued on this topic. The research falls into two categories: the largeness avoidance approach and the largeness tolerance approach [10]. The hierarchical decomposition method proposed by Sahner and Trivedi [9] falls into the largeness avoidance category. On the other hand, the largeness tolerance approach constructs and solves large models with special techniques tailored to the considered model [8]. Recognizing graphs similarities and reducing the size of the model are examples of the largeness tolerance techniques.

The hierarchy of the model is shown in Figure 3. The network subsystem is divided into the dual-backbone network segment and the access networks segment. The dual backbone network is further divided into the two independent backbone networks. Moreover, since each access network is independent from each other, they are also divided.

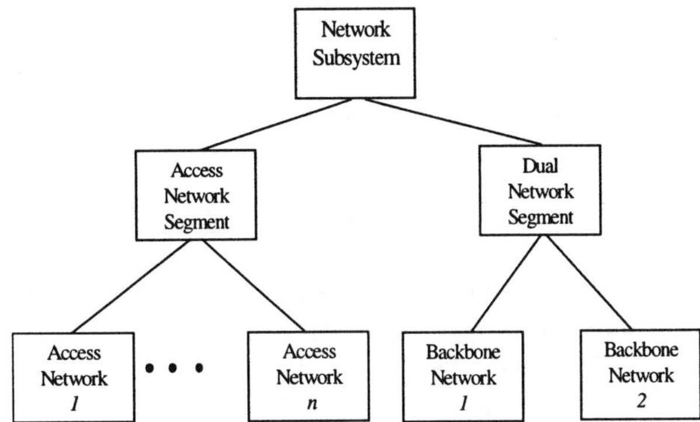

Figure 3. The Network Subsystem Hierarchy

For a specific user, certain site nodes will need to be connected, as explained before. This implies that the dual-backbone network needs to provide connections for those site nodes. Also, at least one of the 2 access networks for each site node needs to provide a connection between the site node and the dual-backbone network. Suppose at time t, an access network A_i has operational probability P_{Ai}, and the dual-backbone network has operational probability P_{dual}, then the probability that the network subsystem is operational at time t would be[3]

$$P_{\text{network subsystem}} = \Big(\prod_{\forall \text{required } Ai} P_{Ai} \Big) \times P_{dual} \qquad (1)$$

Note that P_{dual} is the probability that either network 1 is working (denoted as P_{N1}) or network 2 is working (denoted as P_{N2}). Therefore,

$$\begin{aligned} P_{dual} &= P(\text{N1 is operational} \cup \text{N2 is operational}) \\ &= P_{N1} + P_{N2} - P_{N1} \times P_{N2} \qquad (2) \end{aligned}$$

Also, note that P_{dual} varies for different users. Since different users may have different requirements on the dual backbone networks, different P_{N1} and P_{N2} (and so different P_{dual}) will be used. To access the values for $P_{N1}$and P_{N2}, a *mapping* process is used. For the example shown in Section 2, mapping the required site nodes for user A onto the backbone network N1, we obtain the requirement for network 1, e.g., backbone nodes N1-1 and N1-2 need to be connected. Similarly, mapping those nodes onto network N2, the requirement is that backbone node N2-1 needs to be connected to N2-2.

The problem of the above computation is that the mapping results can not be determined until runtime.

[3] For reliability, both P_{Ai} and P_{dual} are functions of time t.

Hence, it will be very time consuming (and unrealistic) to estimate the real-time reliability for all users, if we have to compute P_{N1} and P_{N2} in real time. Fortunately, in our case, the reliability feature of each individual network component is static. Therefore, preprocessing is possible. That means all possible combinations of P_{N1} and P_{N2} can be determined before the operation. Thus, all possible values of P_{dual} can be prepared beforehand. During the operation, once the mappings of all required sites on both backbone networks are known, the corresponding P_{dual} can be referenced efficiently. In other words, *preprocessing* is the key to efficiently estimating the network reliability in real time.

For a backbone network containing *m* backbone nodes, the total number of mapping types is on the order of 2^m. To see this, note that every backbone node is either mapped or unmapped. As described, during operation, the estimation process retrieves the corresponding mapping type's reliability and incorporates them into the formulas. In the following discussion, the site nodes that need to be connected are known[4]. The *preprocessing* of this method estimates the reliability for all access networks and the P_{N1} (and P_{N2}) for all mapping types. During operation, the required sites for a location are mapped onto the dual backbone networks and the corresponding P_{N1} and P_{N2} are obtained from the preprocessed data. Applying the values of P_{N1} and P_{N2} to formula (2) gives P_{dual}. Next, formula (1) is applied and the network subsystem's reliability is obtained.

In general, the estimation of P_{Ai} is a 2-terminal reliability analysis and the assessment of P_{N1} and P_{N2} is a *k*-terminal reliability analysis. The procedure is illustrated below.

```
Preprocessing:
for all A_i
        estimate P_Ai;
for all mapping types
        estimate P_N1 (P_N2);
Real-Time Processing:
for each user location
    mapping the required sites onto backbone network
                  N1 and N2;
    obtain the corresponding P_N1 and P_N2;
               (from the preprocessed data)
    calculate P_dual as P_N1 + P_N2 - P_N1 × P_N2;
    calculate P_network-subsystem using formula (1);
```

For real-time processing, the time to map a site node to the backbone network nodes is *O(m)*, *m* is the number of backbone nodes on a backbone network. The time to map all required *n* sites to the backbone network is then *O(nm)*. To reference the corresponding P_{N1} and P_{N2}, an efficient method which takes *O(m)* time is presented in [11]. The rest of the process takes *O(1)* time. Thus, the time complexity is *O(nm)* for a user at a particular location and at a particular time. If the number of locations to be considered is *k*, then the overall time complexity for real time estimation, for one time step, is *O(knm)*. Note that the time complexity for a complete state enumeration method with preprocessing is $O(k2^{n+m})$.

[4] The process described here is for runtime estimation. How to determine the necessary site nodes is beyond the discussion of this paper.

4. MODEL SIMPLIFICATION

Graph reduction techniques such as removing irrelevant edges and grouping nodes can be applied to our model and a reduced graph is illustrated in Figure 4. The number of groups after the *grouping* step is on the order of 2^m, where *m* is the number of nodes in each backbone network.

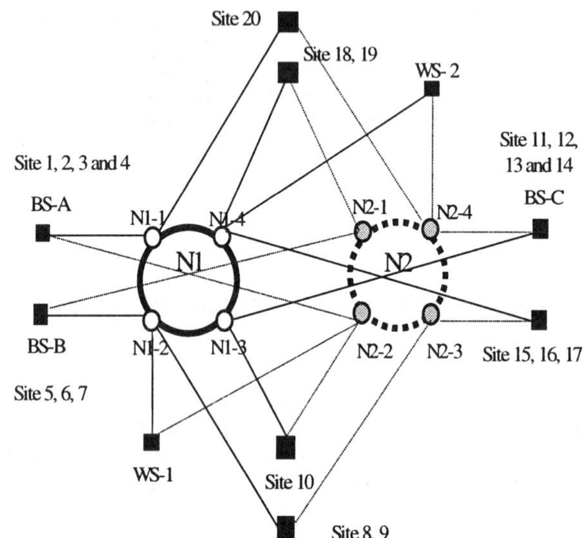

Figure 4. Reduced Graph from the Figure 2 Model

These 2^m cases can be further reduced, by recognizing the graph similarities. As shown in Figure 5, the number of mapping types for the dual 4-node ring-structured backbone network is reduced from *16* to *5*. For example, cases (2), (3), (4) and (5) are similar, since they all have 3 mapped nodes, and all mapped nodes are adjacent. When all links (nodes) have the same reliability, the similarity makes the operational probability the same. Also, case (10) and (11) are similar because they both have two mapped nodes that are not adjacent. This example demonstrates that graph similarities can be utilized in simplifying the analysis and reducing the complexity.

Based on the 5 types shown in Figure 5, detailed analyses were conducted [11] and the results are displayed in Table I. In Table I, the probability that a backbone node is operational is denoted as P_n, and the probability that a link is functioning is denoted as P_l. It is assumed in this analysis that all backbone nodes have the same failure rate and all links in the backbone network have the same failure rate.

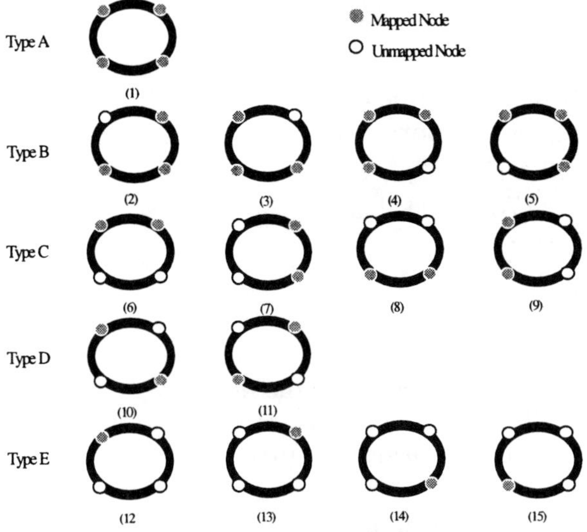

Figure 5. Mapping Cases

TABLE I. Network Reliability Summary

Type	**Network Reliability**
A	$P_n^4 \times P_l^4 + 4 \times P_n^4 \times P_l^3 \times (1-P_l)$
B	$P_n^3 \times (1-P_n) \times P_l^2 + P_n^4 \times P_l^4 + 4 \times P_n^4 \times P_l^3 \times (1-P_l) + P_n^4 \times P_l^2 \times (1-P_l)^2$
C	$P_n^4 \times P_l + P_n^4 \times P_l^3 \times (1-P_l) + 2 \times P_n^3 \times (1-P_n) \times P_l + P_n^2 \times (1-P_n)^2 \times P_l$
D	$P_n^4 \times P_l^4 + 4 \times P_n^4 \times P_l^3 \times (1-P_l) + 2 \times P_n^4 \times P_l^2 \times (1-P_l)^2 + 2 \times P_n^3 \times (1-P_n) \times P_l^2$
E	P_n

5. CONCLUSIONS AND FUTURE RESEACRH

An efficient method is presented here for real-time network reliability estimation on a ring-structured backbone network system. The reliability is user dependent in terms of locations and times. Reducing the complexity is the main purpose of this study. Note that a complete state diagram modeling approach for k different locations at one time step will take $O(k2^{m+n})$ time, where n is the number of site nodes and m is the number of backbone nodes in one backbone network. Our method takes advantages of the hierarchical decomposition method, and utilizes graph simplification techniques. The estimation based on this method for k locations takes $O(knm)$ time.

An interesting topic that follows from this study is to apply graph similarity to network reliability estimation. Ring-structured networks have a high degree of similarity due to their graph topology. There are other topologies where graph similarity can be recognized.

The case study presented in this paper is only a beginning of the whole area of "usage-dependent" reliability estimation. Today's advanced technology has led us to a new stage of reliability estimation, which requires high fidelity and high efficiency. How to provide users real-time estimation efficiently is a continuing challenge to this field.

6. REFERENCES

[1] M.O. Ball, C.J. Colbourn, J.S. Provan, "Network Reliability," in *Handbooks in Operations Research and Management Science, Vol. 7, Network Models*, Editors: M.O. Ball, T.L. Magnanti, C.L. Monma, G.L. Nemhauser, Publisher Elsevier Science B.V., The Netherlands, 1995.

[2] J.A. Bondy, U.S. R. Murty, *Graph Theory With Applications*, American Elsevier Publishing Co., INC. 1976.

[3] C.J. Colbourn, *The Combinatorics of Network Reliability*, Oxford University Press, 1987.

[4] H.M. AboElFotoh, C.J. Colbourn, "Computing 2-Terminal Reliability for Radio-Broadcast Networks," IEEE Transactions on Reliability, Vol. 38, No.5, Dec. 1989, pp 538-555.

[5] H. J. Strayer, C.J. Colbourn, "Consecutive Cuts and Paths, and Bounds on k-terminal Reliability," Networks, Vol.25, 1995, pp.165-175.

[6] B. Dengiz, F. Altiparmark, A.E. Smith, "Efficient Optimization of All-Terminal Reliable Networks, Using an Evolutionary Approach," *IEEE Transactions on Reliability, Vol. 46, No.1*, Mar. 1997, pp.18-26.

[7] J.F. Meyer, "Performability: a retrospective and some pointers to the future," Performace Evaluation 14(1992), pp. 139-156.

[8] D.R. Miller, "Reliability Calculation Using Randomization for Markovian Fault-Tolerant Computing Systems," *FTCS 1983*, pp. 284-289.

[9] R.A. Sahner and K.S. Trivedi, "A Hierarchical, Combinatorial-Markov Method of Solving Complex Reliability Models," *Proceedings of the 1986 Fall Joint Computer Conference, AFIPS*, pp.817-825.

[10] K.S. Trivedi, *lecture notes* on "Techniques and Tools for Performance and Reliability Analysis," *International Workshop on Modeling, Analysis and Simulation of Computer and Telecommunication Systems (MASCOTS'93)*, Jan. 1993.

[11] M.L. Yin, L.E. James, R.A. Arellano, R.V. Hettwer, "On Preprocessing Ring-Structured Network Reliability for Run-Time Estimation," submitted to 1999 SCS Symposium on Performance Evaluation of Computer and Telecommunication Systems, July 11-15, 1999, Chicago.

Wrapping Windows NT Software for Robustness*

Anup K. Ghosh†, Matt Schmid, & Frank Hill
Reliable Software Technologies Corporation
21515 Ridgetop Circle, #250, Sterling, VA 20166
phone: (703) 404-9293, fax: (703) 404-9295
email: aghosh@rstcorp.com
www.rstcorp.com

Abstract

As Windows NT workstations become more entrenched in enterprise-critical and even mission-critical applications, the dependability of the Windows 32-bit (Win32) platform is becoming critical. To date, studies on the robustness of system software have focused on Unix-based systems. This paper describes an approach to assessing the robustness for Win32 software and providing robustness wrappers for third party commercial off-the-shelf (COTS) software. The robustness of Win32 applications to failing operating system (OS) functions is assessed by using fault injection techniques at the interface between the application and the operating system. Finally, software wrappers are developed to handle OS failures gracefully in order to mitigate catastrophic application failures.

1 Introduction

Windows NT is rapidly becoming the development, engineering, and enterprise platform of choice. As more and more Windows NT workstations are employed in enterprise-critical and even mission-critical applications, the dependability of the Win32 platform is becoming increasingly important. For example, the U.S. Navy requires its ships to migrate to Windows NT workstations and servers under the Information Technology in the 21st century (IT-21) directive [3]. One casualty of this policy has been the USS Yorktown, a U.S. Navy Aegis missile cruiser, which suffered a significant software problem in the Windows NT systems that control the "smart ship". Reportedly, a database overflow error resulting from a divide by zero operation caused the ship's propulsion system to fail leaving the ship effectively dead in the water [13]. The ship had to be towed to the Norfolk Naval shipyard.

Despite the proliferation of NT Workstations in enterprise- and sometimes mission-critical environments, little analysis of the software that composes the NT platform has been performed. As a result, the decision to employ Win32-based systems (Windows 95/NT/2000/CE) in critical applications is based on anecdotal evidence or trust in the software vendor rather than based on scientific study.

To date, analysis on the reliability of operating systems has been performed for commercial and free software variants of Unix [7, 6, 10, 9]. The purpose for studying the reliability of the operating system (OS) and its associated software is to determine the extent to which confidence can be placed in the platform for running enterprise- and mission-critical applications. Once non-robustness in OS functions is identified, either the application software itself can be hardened, or software wrappers can be written for COTS software to gracefully handle non-robust OS failures. The latter approach is developed in this paper.

Robustness testing is now being recognized within the dependability research community as an important part of dependability assessment. Unlike traditional testing approaches [1, 2, 11, 8, 4] that either attempt to find errors through debugging tests, or show reliability through sampling the operational profile, robustness testing aims to show the ability, or conversely, the inability, of a program to continue to operate under anomalous input conditions. More formally, the IEEE Standard Glossary of Software Engineering Terminology states that robustness is "the degree to which a system or component can function correctly in the presence of invalid inputs or stressful environmental conditions". For the purposes of this work, an

*This work is sponsored under the Defense Advanced Research Projects Agency (DARPA) Contract F30602-97-C-0117. THE VIEWS AND CONCLUSIONS CONTAINED IN THIS DOCUMENT ARE THOSE OF THE AUTHORS AND SHOULD NOT BE INTERPRETED AS REPRESENTING THE OFFICIAL POLICIES, EITHER EXPRESSED OR IMPLIED, OF THE DEFENSE ADVANCED RESEARCH PROJECTS AGENCY OR THE U.S. GOVERNMENT.

†Ghosh is the correspondence author.

0-7695-0213-X/99 $10.00 © 1999 IEEE

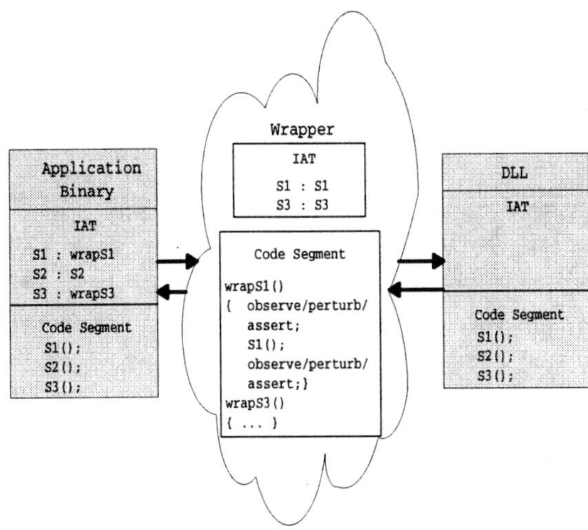

Figure 1: Wrapping Executable Binaries

application is robust when it does not hang, crash, or disrupt the system in the presence of anomalous or invalid inputs, or stressful environmental conditions.

In this paper we describe an approach for assessing then improving the robustness of the Win32 application software to anomalous and unexpected events. In our previous research on the Win32 platform, we identified a number of OS functions in the core dynamic link libraries (DLLs) of the Win32 API that throw exceptions when presented anomalous input [12]. Here, we use fault injection functions to artificially throw these exceptions in order to test the robustness of applications under these conditions. When applications fail to handle exceptions thrown by the operating system, they crash. In order to address this non-robustness, we developed a wrapping technology to handle anomalous behavior from the operating system on behalf of the application. These wrappers can be applied to COTS software applications that behave non-robustly to failing OS functions.

2 Fault Injection for Testing Application Robustness

From our previous studies of the Win32 platform [12, 5], we know not only which functions behave non-robustly, but also the specific input that results in exceptions being thrown by the operating system. This information can in turn be used to determine the robustness of software applications to exceptions thrown by these functions.

Rather than test the application until the unusual operating system condition occurs (an indefinite period of testing), our approach is to artificially inject anomalous behavior from an OS function and determine if the application is robust to the exception. The approach involves instrumenting the interface between the application executable and the DLL functions it imports such that all interactions between the application and the operating system can be captured and manipulated.

Figure 1 illustrates how program executables are wrapped. The application's Import Address Table (IAT), which is used to look up the address of imported DLL functions, is modified for functions that are wrapped to point to the wrapper DLL. For instance, in Figure 1, functions `S1` and `S3` are wrapped by modifying the IAT of the application. When functions `S1` and `S3` are called by the application, the wrapper DLL is called instead. The wrapper DLL, in turn, executes, providing the ability to modify, perturb, question or simply log the request to the target DLL.

A failure simulation tool has been written that modifies the executable program's import address table such that the address of imported DLL functions is replaced with the address to our wrapper functions. This modification occurs in memory rather than on disk, so the program is not changed permanently. The wrapper then makes the call to the intended OS function either with the program's data or with erroneous data. On the return from the OS function, the wrapper has the option to return the values unmodified, to return erroneous values, or to throw exceptions. We use this capability to throw exceptions from functions in the OS called by the program under analysis. If the application crashes due to these exceptions thrown by the operating system, then we know that the application is non-robust to exceptions thrown by OS func-

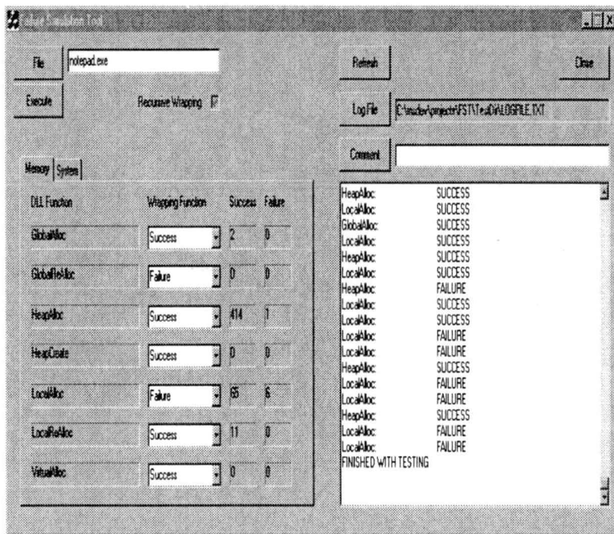

Figure 2: The graphical interface to the failure simulation tool that wraps Windows NT executable programs. The tool allows the user to interactively fail OS functions when they are called. The right panel shows a log of the calls made and the failures simulated if any for each call.

tions that we have shown capable of throwing exceptions. In addition, we can determine if the application is non-robust to error values returned from OS functions. This latter analysis is used for hardening the software described in Section 3.

Figure 2 shows the graphical interface to the failure simulation tool that allows selective failing of operating system resources. The window shows the memory functions that can be instrumented with failure or success functions. Other system functions such as file input/output functions are available for instrumentation via the `System` tab shown in the window in Figure 2.

The tool can be applied to any Win32 program. Testing of common desktop applications has already shown differences in robustness. For example, Microsoft's Powerpoint 97 is more robust to exceptions thrown by the `CreateFile()` function than Microsoft's Word 97. PowerPoint gives the user the opportunity to save work and exit when the `CreateFile()` function throws an exception. Word, on the other hand, immediately crashes when this function throws an exception. This capability can be applied to any number of applications to test the robustness to failing operating system functions.

3 Wrapping COTS Software for Robustness

In this section, we present a technique for making applications more robust to non-robust OS functions. In the preceding section, we described a tool that determines if a program is robust or not to exceptions generated by OS functions. In the case that an application is non-robust to an exception thrown by an OS function, the program can be wrapped to make it more robust.

The approach leverages the wrapping approach described in the preceding section. Instead of throwing exceptions to test robustness, the wrapper will catch any exceptions thrown by OS functions and return them as a specified error code. While many programmers will not handle exceptions (especially undocumented ones), the return value from a function is almost always checked for error values. Thus, handling an exception thrown by an OS function at the wrapper and returning a specified error value can be a robust way of dealing with a non-robust OS function. Using the wrapping approach to testing for robustness described in the preceding section, the robustness of an application to error values can be verified *a priori*.

Alternatively, the robustness wrapper can return an exception that is known to be handled robustly, instead of the unexpected exception that crashes the application. Therefore, the robustness of the wrapping approach to handling exceptions can be known before online deployment. Ideally the exception handler function that wraps the application would also provide a warning that an unhandled exception was thrown. This warning can be used by operation personnel, in turn, to gracefully degrade and restart the system.

The wrapper approach is particularly useful for mission-critical COTS software, where access to the source code is not available, but where robustness is important. The wrapper can be deployed with the application such that whenever the application is started, it is started with the wrapper in place. The degradation in performance due to the wrapper is not discernible from a user perspective. As a proof of concept, we wrapped Microsoft Word with a protective wrapper that converts exceptions to error codes. Using the wrapper, we sent in a zero as the first parameter to the `HeapAlloc()` function, which we know will cause an exception to be thrown. The protective wrapper trapped the exception thrown by `HeapAlloc()` and returned an error value (a null pointer). Rather than crashing, Word continued to function by attempting to allocate memory again. In our test case, we sent the erroneous parameter only once and Word recovered nicely.

4 Conclusions

This paper presented an approach to assessing the robustness of Win32 applications to non-robust OS functions, and an approach to hardening the application with a protective wrapper in order to provide application robustness.

The approach uses software wrappers to test robustness of applications in the presence of non-robust OS functions. A failure simulation tool was written to allow selective failures from OS functions in the form of thrown exceptions. If the program fails to handle the exception thrown by an OS function it will crash, rendering the system non-robust and unreliable.

The second part of this paper developed an approach to writing software robustness wrappers to protect applications from failing OS functions. The technique uses the software wrapping approach to handle exceptions thrown by the OS by returning specified error codes or other exceptions that are known *a priori* to be handled robustly. This technique is particularly useful for COTS software where access to source code is not made available and where robustness is critical.

References

[1] B. Beizer. *Software Testing Techniques.* Electrical Engineering/Computer Science and Engineering. Van Nostrand Reinhold, 1983.

[2] B. Beizer. *Black Box Testing.* Wiley, New York, 1995.

[3] M. Binderberger. Re: Navy turns to off-the-shelf pcs to power ships (risks-19.75). *RISKS Digest*, 19(76), May 25 1998.

[4] J. Duran and S. Ntafos. An evaluation of random testing. *IEEE Transactions on Software Engineering*, SE-10:438–444, July 1984.

[5] A. Ghosh, M. Schmid, and V. Shah. Testing the robustness of windows nt software. To appear, November 4-7 1998.

[6] P. Koopman, J. Sung, C. Dingman, D. Siewiorek, and T. Marz. Comparing operating systems using robustness benchmarks. In *Proceedings of the 16th IEEE Symposium on Reliable Distributed Systems*, pages 72–79, October 1997.

[7] N.P. Kropp, P.J. Koopman, and D.P. Siewiorek. Automated robustness testing of off-the-shelf software components. In *Proceedings of the Fault Tolerant Computing Symposium*, June 23-25 1998.

[8] B. Marick. *The Craft of Software Testing.* Prentice-Hall, 1995.

[9] B.P. Miller, L. Fredrikson, and B. So. An empirical study of the reliability of UNIX utilities. *Communications of the ACM*, 33(12):32–44, December 1990.

[10] B.P. Miller, D. Koski, C.P. Lee, V. Maganty, R. Murthy, A. Natarajan, and J. Steidl. Fuzz revisted: A re-examination of the reliability of UNIX utilities and services. Technical report, University of Wisconsin, Computer Sciences Dept, November 1995.

[11] G. Myers. *The Art of Software Testing.* Wiley, 1979.

[12] M. Schmid and F. Hill. Data generation techniques for automated software robustness testing. In *Proceedings of the International Conference on Testing Computer Software*, 1999. To appear.

[13] G. Slabodkin. Software glitches leave navy smart ship
dead in the water, July 13 1998. Available online: www.gcn.com/gcn/1998/July13/cov2.htm.

Functional and Faulty Behavior Analysis: Some experiments and Lessons Learnt

Yannick Le Guédart*, Luc Marneffe*, François Scheerens•, Jean-Paul Blanquart°, Thierry Boyer*
*LIS/Technicatome •LIS/SRTI SYSTEM °LIS/Matra Marconi Space France
LIS (Laboratory for Dependability Engineering)
LAAS-CNRS, 7 Avenue du Colonel Roche, 31077 Toulouse Cedex 4, France
{ylegued; marneffe; scheerens; blanquart; tboyer}@laas.fr

Abstract

The design of dependable systems requires that the assessment of fault tolerance solutions be carried out as early as possible. This paper addresses this issue by studying a framework aimed at analyzing the behavior of these systems in the presence of faults. The proposed approach combines functional and behavioral modeling, fault injection and simulation. The paper reports on the investigation of such an approach on four practical architectures derived from real-world industrial systems. In the experiments we used two design tools, namely: Statemate™ and RDD-100™. Finally, main results and lessons learnt are discussed, and subsequent directions to further exploit these results are proposed.

1. Introduction

Designing cost-effective fault-tolerant computer architectures is today one of the main concerns for the developers of dependable systems in a large segment of industrial control applications. However, besides evaluations carried out by means of probabilistic modeling studies or FMECA, the consideration of dependability issues encompassing detailed behavioral analysis in the early phases of the development process is still hardly supported in practice in industry, maybe with some exceptions such as studies reported in [1] and [9].

Accordingly, we are currently investigating a method to assist system designers in developing fault-tolerant systems by incorporating the explicit analysis of their behavior in the presence of fault in the early phases of the development process. The aim is to be able to support designers in making objective choices between different high-level architectural options and fault tolerance mechanisms. The proposed approach is based on the development of a functional and behavioral model of the system, and on the behavioral analysis of the model by means of simulation and fault injection. We are currently working on a way to insert the method in the current design process, without modifying or perturbing it. In order to gain credibility, we have to base the method on whatever already exists in industry, should it be current methods or tools.

This paper reports on a joint effort involving several industrial partners of the Laboratory for Dependability Engineering (LIS)[1]. Besides a general exploration of the techniques to be used and the feasibility of such an approach in the design process for dependable systems, we have carried out practical experiments on the basis of case studies provided by the industrial partners.

Several related studies were previously reported that are addressing the issue of supporting the design of dependable systems by means of simulation ([2, 3, 5, 6]). Although these approaches are generally supported by efficient tools, these tools are not designed to be included in the design process of systems. This is why we have tried to attack this issue from a different perspective, i.e., to study instead how several existing design tools can be enhanced to support such an early dependability validation analysis. In contrast to the work reported in [1], that dealt with formal techniques (in particular, SDL), we focus here on a more pragmatic approach aimed at elaborating on the modeling and simulation capabilities of two system engineering tools widely used in the industrial world by system designers: Statemate [7, 8] and RDD-100 [4, 11].

A set of target systems was selected to serve as a basis for preliminary investigations and experimentations of the approach. Although they originate from distinct fields (ground and on-board space, submarine nuclear propulsion), the target systems share the following two common characteristics: i) stringent dependability requirements, be they based on safety, availability, or reliability, ii) redundant architectures based on high-level fault tolerance mechanisms (voting, reconfigurations, etc.).

The rest of the paper is organized into three sections. Section 2 describes the main features of the target systems used as case studies, as well as objectives of the experiments. Section 3 describes the modeling and fault injection studies that were carried out. Finally, Section 4 summarizes the lessons learnt and sets some perspectives for further work.

---

[1] Hosted by LAAS-CNRS, LIS is a co-operative laboratory that gathers personnel from five French industrial companies, each designer of highly dependable systems (Aerospatiale, Electricité de France, Matra Marconi Space France, Technicatome and Thomson-CSF), and researchers from the Dependable Computing and Fault Tolerance group of LAAS-CNRS.

0-7695-0213-X/99 $10.00 © 1999 IEEE

2. The target systems

The target systems considered in our study are all related to critical applications. For confidentiality reasons, the actual names of these systems will not be quoted explicitly. They will be identified rather according to their application domains: submarine nuclear propulsion system (S1), ground-based space systems (S2 and S3), on-board space system (S4).

Table 1 summarizes the main particularities on the most important aspects with respect to the method.

3. System modeling and faults injection experiments

The method we want to develop is to be integrated into the industrial process for designing dependable systems in particular in the early phases dealing with the mapping of the functions with the computer architecture. The main goal is to help to make choices between architectures while focusing on dependability issues.

Figure 1 presents the principle of the approach. It is based on the construction of a nominal model of the system built by the designer himself. This nominal model is then modified so as to be able to inject faults, and the outputs of this simulation are compared with the output of the nominal model of the system. The main goal is to have the model evolve so as to have a description of fault tolerance mechanisms that fits with the system along with the design process.

The main idea is to inject faults in the model on a one-by-one basis, while modifying the model to include new fault tolerance mechanisms. Then, the model of system should be able to handle a multiple fault injection, and we should be able to verify whether its behavior is satisfactory or not.

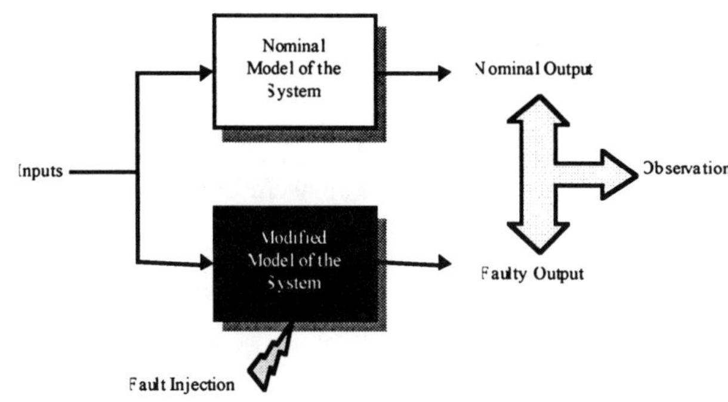

Figure 1

Several questions were raised during the elaboration and investigation of the method :

- Is it possible to use tools (and associated languages) already used in the engineering process (*i.e.* are they able to handle necessary modeling levels and observation of the results of the simulation, and do they support model validation)?
- How to modify the nominal model such that i) it is possible to inject faults, and ii) its behavior is identical to the nominal one when no fault is injected?

Target system	Dependability requirements	Main architectural features	Aim of the experiment
S1 (submarine nuclear propulsion system control)	Safety (nuclear nature of the system) and Availability (a submarine is considered lost should the propulsion system fails)	Recurrent architecture pattern consisting in an active triple modular redundant (TMR) architecture with majority voting (2/3) of the logical outputs.	Study to what extent the simulation approach could help system designers in tuning the functional and structural features of the architecture
S2 (ground-based space system aimed to transmit safety commands to a launcher)	Safety (protect populations that could be endangered by the launcher) and availability	A dual redundant architecture with two self controlled lanes operating in semi-active mode, and a TMR architecture implementing the configuration module aimed to switch between the two lanes.	Assess the ability of two considered tools (Statemate and RDD-100) in handling critical timing issues
S3 (ground-based space system aimed to help navigation among any kind of users: aircrafts, boats, cars,...)	Availability (in order to offer a continuous signal to the users)	Five identical processing units (active redundancy). Choice of the operational unit is made by another system using dual redundancy.	Model the algorithm for electing the master processing unit of the system, and observing model behavior upon the occurrence of faults
S4 (on-board space subsystem, devoted to the monitoring and management of reconfigurations for the restof the system)	Availability and Error confinement (no propagation of own errors to the rest of the system)	Four identical computing units (hot redundancy) and three identical I/O units (cold redundancy), N-version programming, executable assertion (on-line software error detection)	Analyze potential links, overlaps and complementarities between FMECA and the method. Assess the interest of the approach as a support to functional statistical testing of fault tolerance mechanisms

Table 1 : target systems and experiments

- What kind of faults should be injected in the modified model? Is there any interest in injecting faults identified by preliminary analyses like FMECA, or should we focus mainly on generic injectors and fault models?
- How can we easily observe the results of the simulation? What are the facilities provided by the tools to support this? How can we observe relevant behavioral differences between the nominal and the faulty simulations?

The experiments we present hereafter were aimed to help us answer these questions. They were conducted on the four systems we presented in Section 2. Both Statemate and RDD-100 have been used to model these systems. These two tools were chosen because they are widely used among industrial partners of LIS.

Modeling issues

The first experiments aimed to evaluate the capabilities of the method to facilitate the design process by defining and manipulating generic basic architectures, that can be instantiated at any abstraction level to meet the requirements of the considered application. Both architectural and application parts of the model make use of generic models. For example, in the system S1, at the bottom of the model hierarchy, each basic component (e.g. computer, voter) is described by such a model. At an upper level, the basic architecture pattern is that of a TMR model (three instances of a computer model and one instance of a voter). When the architecture was modeled, the application functions were mapped on it, once for each replicated component.

The incremental method used to build the model allowed us to separate the design of the architecture model on one side, and the design of the functional model of the application on the other side. This proved very useful to facilitate the integration of the method within the engineering process.

Another important point has to do with time related issues (response time, dynamic behavior, etc). Indeed, these issues are a real concern when designing computer architectures for dependable systems. This is particularly the case when dealing with switching among redundant lanes. Indeed, in such cases, the requirements to ensure the continuity of service delivery pose the most severe problem from a dependability viewpoint. The experiment that was conducted on system S2 focused precisely on this issue: it was developed to allow us to compare the ability of the modeling features of the two formalisms supported by Statemate and RDD-100, to handle such critical response times. Toward this end, we constructed two models (one with each tool), based on the same set of specifications. The main goal was to investigate to what extent these tools made it possible for a user to develop a model accounting for the underlying timing characteristics (and thus able to exhibit potential design deficiencies) during its normal design activity, or whether the modeling activity needed to be tailored to specifically address these issues. Whereas the Statemate model had to be modified many times to describe precisely the behavior we wanted to describe (due to the way the tools handle timing issues, using "step" as time unit), the model developed with RDD-100 allowed us to describe the considered temporal features without difficulty (this is mostly because the formalism used inherits largely from the SDL formalism). As a conclusion, modeling with RDD-100 was found to be more intuitive than with Statemate.

The modeling approach and the used formalism proved in these experiments their ability to master the complexity of such systems and fault propagation. However, constructing a detailed model of such systems is a very tedious task, and simulation time is often prohibitive (up to more than one hour for a 100ms cycle in the case of S4).

Though validation was not the prime objective of the study, the two tools allowed us to have a minimal validation of the models : with RDD-100, for system S3, the nominal model was validated by simulation and by controlling its SADT (Structured Analysis and Design Technics) representation. Equivalent results can be achieved with Statemate as it is reported in [13].

Fault injection issues

Depending on the validation objectives, two main forms of fault injection have been investigated: focused and statistical fault injection.

At first, for fault injection experiments, we selected faults that were identified in the FMECA studies. Their modeling was carried out independently from the construction of the functional model, in order to separate the elements of the nominal model on one side, and components added to support fault injection on the other side. These components that we called "saboteurs" were used to inject faults in the modified model. The models were based on the original specification and algorithms for the system, as well as timing data and FMECA studies. In S3 or S4, for example, both manual (which permits one activation at a time for a saboteur) and automatic (using simulation scenarios, which permits multiple and randomized fault injection) injection were implemented. From these experiments, the proposed approach proved useful both for validating static dependability analyses and for consolidating and enhancing them. Is this particular occurrence of fault injection, it is quite easy to observe the results of the simulation since we know precisely how the system should respond to any fault, thanks to the FMECA.

The injection of randomly selected faults permitted to assess the ability of the approach to reveal deficiencies in the design of fault tolerance mechanisms. This refers to the assessment of the techniques as a support to statistical testing (through fault injection since what is tested is the faults tolerance capability of the system). Statistical testing [12] is a promising approach for efficient software fault elimination, either in unit testing (based on a structural model of the software) or in integration or validation testing (based on a functional model). It is based on the application of test inputs following a distribution such that the probability of exercising any element of the model is (approximately) uniform. This is shown to minimize the test sequence length needed to achieve a given test quality.

On the basis of this experiment, the method appears as a very good complement to the FMECA analyses. This comes first from the ability to analyse thoroughly the behavior in the case of very specific faults conditions provided as inputs by the FMECA, and second from the application of statistical fault-injection aiming at identifying and testing potential faults conditions not taken into account by previous static analyses.

4. Lessons learnt and perspectives

Functional and faulty behavior analysis supports a dependability explicit development process. It allows to better support the early design decisions by focusing on critical issues (response time, reconfiguration management, etc...). It facilitates the validation of the considered solutions during the successive development phases.

Although the modeling features of each design tool, namely Statemate and RDD-100 led to different modeling strategies, both forms of fault injection (focused and statistical) could be quite easily integrated into the tools. Beside supporting the design phase by validating the adequacy of the fault tolerance mechanisms, fault injection was also used to elaborate and validate the functional test sets (unit, integration and validation tests).

In summary, the following major benefits could be identified during the experiments reported in this paper :

- Aid for the conduction of FMECA studies,
- Support and validation of classical dependability studies by establishing links between the specifications and the FMECA analyses,
- Verification and improvement of the observability at system level,
- Construction and validation of test scenarios.

Nevertheless, the observability of the results in the case of statistical or multiple fault injection is still subject to studies, since we were only able to compare the results of simulated modified model with the simulation results of the nominal model.

The wide range of target systems considered allowed us to investigate various issues : modeling features, support for fault injection, simulation. However, work is still to be carried out before we can propose to insert our approach in an actual development process. However, the insight we obtained comforts us in thinking that such an approach can actually be implemented to support the design process of fault-tolerant systems.

Although somewhat modest, the lessons learnt from these experiments allowed us to demonstrate to system designers the benefits of such a method in complement to their usual set of methods, design tools and dependability analyses. Accordingly, in addition to the problem of integration into the development process, which is more related to industrial concerns, further studies, carried out within LIS together with LAAS researchers, will address more extensively the fault modeling and hierarchical simulation issues. The elaboration of a consistent set of error models at the various levels of the model hierarchy, and at the various steps of the design process, is indeed a prerequisite for having a functional and faulty behavior analysis method actually used in practice, as recently identified in the work reported in [9] and [10].

Ackowledgements

The authors wish to thanks Neeraj Suri and the anonymous referees for their valuable comments and suggestions on earlier version of the paper. Special thanks go to Jean Arlat who provided helpful guidance all along the work reported here, and is at the origin of the paper.

References

[1] S. Ayache, P. Humbert, E. Conquet, C. Rodriguez, J. Sifakis and R. Gerlich, “Formal Methods for the Validation of Fault Tolerance in Autonomous Spacecraft”, *FTCS-26*, pp.353-7, 1996.

[2] J. Boué, P. Pétillon and Y. Crouzet, “MEFISTO-L: A VHDL-Based Fault Injection Tool for the Experimental Assessment of Fault Tolerance”, *FTCS-28*, pp.168-73, 1998.

[3] J.A. Clark and D.K. Pradhan, “REACT: A Synthesis and Evaluation Tool for Fault-Tolerant Microprocessor Architectures”, in *Proc. Annual Reliability & Maintainability Symp.*, pp.428-35, 1993.

[4] C. Fry, *“The RASSP Integrated Systems Tool Set Provides Better System Trade-off Studies”*, Lockheed Martin Advanced Technology Laboratories, Tech. Report, 1996.

[5] A. Ghosh, B. W. Johnson and J.A. Profeta III, “System-Level Modeling in the ADEPT Environment of a Distributed Computer System for Real-Time Applications”, *IPDS'95*, pp.194-203, 1995.

[6] K. K. Goswami, R. K. Iyer and L. Young, “DEPEND: A Simulation-Based Environment for System Level Dependability Analysis”, *IEEE Transactions on Computers*, 46 (1), pp.60-74, January 1997.

[7] D. Harel, H. Lachover, A. Naamad, A. Pnueli, M. Politi, R. Sherman, A. Stull-Trauring and M. Trakhtenbrot, “STATEMATE: A Working Environment for the Development of Complex Reactive Systems”, *IEEE Transactions on Software Engineering*, pp.403-14, 1990.

[8] D. Harel and A. Naamad, “The STATEMATE Semantics of Statecharts”, *ACM Transactions on Software Engineering and Methodology*, pp.294-333, 1996.

[9] M. Kaâniche, L. Romano, Z. Kalbarczyk, R. K. Iyer and R. Karcich, “A Hierarchical Approach for Dependability Analysis of a Commercial Cache-Based RAID Storage Architecture”, *FTCS-28*, 1998.

[10] Z. Kalbarczyk, G. Ries, M. S. Lee, Y. Xiao, J. Patel and R. K. Iyer, “Hierarchical Approach to Accurate Fault Modeling for System Evaluation”, *IPDS'98*, pp.249-58, 1998.

[11] N. Malcolm and M. Alford, *“System Engineering: Its Tool, its Future”*, Ascent Logic Corp., 1993.

[12] P. Thévenod-Fosse, H. Waeselynck and Y. Crouzet, “Software Statistical Testing”, in *Predictably Dependable Computing Systems*, pp.253-72, 1995.

[13] I. Traore, “Analyse dans l'Ingenierie des Systemes : Caractérisation et Multiformalisme”, Thèse LAAS n° 98214, 1998.

Programmable Memory BIST and a New Synthesis Framework

Kamran Zarrineh [1] Shambhu J. Upadhyaya [2]
[1] IBM Corporation, 1701 North Street, Endicott, NY 13760
[2] Department of Computer Science and Engineering, SUNY at Buffalo, Buffalo, NY 14260

Abstract

The development of two programmable memory BIST architectures is first reported. A memory synthesis framework which can automatically generate, verify and insert programmable as well as non-programmable BIST units is developed as a vehicle to efficiently integrate BIST architectures in today's memory-intensive systems. Custom memory test algorithms could be loaded in the developed programmable BIST unit and therefore any type of memory test algorithm could be realized. The flexibility and efficiency of the framework are demonstrated by showing that these memory BIST units could be generated, functionally verified and inserted in a short time.

1 Introduction

Memories are fabricated much denser than random logic and therefore are more prone to defects and failures. Defects in memories are due to shorts and opens in memory cells, address decoder and read/write logic. These defects are modeled as single and multi-cell memory faults and different classes of memory test algorithms have been proposed to detect these memory faults [1, 2]. The most popular and widely accepted deterministic test algorithm is the *march test*. A *march test* is a finite sequence of *march elements* applied to each memory cell in the memory in either ascending or descending order before proceeding to the next memory cell [3].

Application of test patterns using off-chip testers results in a high test time due to the large size of embedded memories. The computed test sequences are generated on-chip using a memory Built-In Self Test (BIST) unit.

A memory BIST unit consists of a controller to control the flow of test sequences and other modules to generate the necessary test data and control signals. A memory BIST controller could be designed as non-programmable or programmable. The non-programmable controllers are the hardware realization of a selected memory test algorithm and cannot be modified without changing the hardware realization of the memory BIST controller. Memories undergo different types of tests during their design and fabrication and therefore each memory BIST controller might have to generate different types of test patterns. Programmable memory BIST architectures could be used to generate different types of test patterns and might be an ideal solution to the problem of memory testing in memory-intensive designs.

The structure of a memory BIST unit depends on the characteristics of the memory-under-test, target fault model and the overall test strategy of the design. Memory BIST units could not be re-used from one design to the next unless they undergo a series of modifications and enhancements. This is time consuming and increases the design time-to-market. A memory test synthesis framework for automatic generation and insertion of memory BIST units would facilitate the task of memory testing and improves the time-to-market. The existing memory test synthesis frameworks do not have any support for programmable memory BIST architectures and generate memory BIST units as RT-level cores that could be processed only by specific logic synthesis frameworks [4]. Lack of support for verification of the generated and inserted memory BIST units is another shortcoming of the existing frameworks.

In this paper, we evaluate two programmable memory BIST architectures and provide insights on how well they scale with changes in the characteristics of the memory(s)-under-test, the flexibility of the architecture to realize different memory test algorithm, the impact of the memory BIST unit on the overall testability of the design and the test logic overhead of the memory BIST architecture. Furthermore, important practical issues related to generation, verification and insertion of programmable and non-programmable memory BIST units are also addressed.

This paper is organized as follows: the programmable memory BIST architectures are presented in Section 2. Section 3 contains the design and implementation of the proposed memory test synthesis framework and a discussion of the significance of the proposed BIST architectures and the framework. Section 4 concludes the paper.

2 Programmable BIST Architectures

The existing programmable memory BIST architectures [5, 6, 7] could not be used to test memories in different stages of their fabrication since they complicate the overall testing of the design and have high test logic overhead.

A *programmable FSM-based* memory BIST as an alternative and a microcode-based architecture as an enhancement to the previous programmable memory BIST architectures have been developed [8]. Here, we briefly describe these architectures.

The programmable FSM-based architecture consists of 2 sub-controllers: the top level controller is a 2-dimensional buffer to hold the test sequences while the lower level controller is a parameterized FSM that realizes the march test components of our design: $SM_0{=}\Updownarrow(w_d)$; $SM_1{=}\Updownarrow(r_{\bar{d}}\ w_d)$;$SM_2{=}\Updownarrow(r_{\bar{d}}\ w_d\ r_d\ w_{\bar{d}})$; $SM_3{=}\Updownarrow(r_{\bar{d}}\ w_d\ w_{\bar{d}})$;$SM_4{=}\Updownarrow(r_{\bar{d}}\ r_{\bar{d}}\ r_{\bar{d}})$;$SM_5{=}\Updownarrow(r_{\bar{d}})$;$SM_6{=}\Updownarrow(r_{\bar{d}}\ w_d\ w_{\bar{d}}\ w_d)$;$SM_7{=}\Updownarrow(r_{\bar{d}}\ w_d\ r_d)$ where r and w refer to read and write operations respectively while d is a binary pattern, based on the state of one of the fields in the loaded instruction. The address order and write/compare polarities of the realized march test are determined by other fields of the loaded instruction. A set of combinational logic and the control signals from different modules of the memory BIST unit are used to control the flow of the execution of the loaded instructions in the memory BIST unit. A combination of march test components is a march test. March C [1] is realized with SM_0, SM_1 with different address orders and values of d and SM_5 as shown in Fig. 1.

Instruction #	Cond. Test End	Up/Down Adrs Order	Hold/Inc. Data Gen.	True/Invtd. Test Data	Hold/Inc. Port	SM0 / SM1 / SM2 / SM3 / SM4 / SM5 / SM6 / SM7
	0/1	0/1	0/1	0/1	0/1	000 / 001 / 010 / 011 / 100 / 101 / 110 / 111
1	0	0	0	0	0	000
2	0	0	0	1	0	001
3	0	0	0	0	0	001
4	0	1	0	1	0	001
5	0	1	0	0	0	001
6	1	1	0	1	0	101
7	1	1	1	0	0	xxx
8	1	1	0	1	1	xxx

Figure 1. FSM-Based Instruction Definition

The instructions representing the selected memory test algorithm are loaded in the storage unit of the microcode-based memory BIST architecture and the instruction counter and selector determine which instruction should be executed. A branch register and an instruction decoder module use a field of the loaded instruction to control the flow of the execution of the loaded instructions. A reference module has also been added to allow re-execution of a group of the loaded instructions with different address order and write/compare polarities. A description of different fields and an example of memory test algorithm (March C) are shown in Fig. 2.

Instruction #	Hold/Increment	Up/Down Address Order	Hold/Inc. Data Gen.	True/Inverted Test Data	Compare Polarity	Hold / Read / Write	No Operation / Cond. Branch to branch reg. / Cond. Branch to specified inst. / Cond. Branch to top / Cond. hold / Cond. Inc. Port / Save Current Address / Unconditional terminate
	0/1	0/1	0/1	0/1	0/1	00 / 01 / 10	000 / 001 / 010 / 011 / 100 / 101 / 110 / 111
1	1	0	0	0	0	10	100
2	0	0	0	1	0	01	000
3	1	0	0	1	0	10	001
4	0	0	0	0	1	01	000
5	1	0	0	0	1	10	001
6	0	1	0	1	1	00	010
7	1	0	0	0	0	01	100
8	0	0	1	0	0	00	011
9	0	0	0	0	0	00	101

Figure 2. Microcode-Based Instruction Definition

3 Memory Test Synthesis Framework

A memory test synthesis framework for automatic generation, verification and insertion of programmable and non-programmable memory BIST units has been developed.

3.1 BIST Generation and Verification

The methodology flow of our proposed memory BIST generation framework is shown in Figure 3. Different design and implementations of memory BIST modules in Hardware Description Language (HDL) are developed to create a module library. The characteristics of the memory(s)-under-test and the requirements on the memory BIST unit are described in Memory BIST Description Language (MBDL). MBDL allows selection of different implementations as well as exclusion of different memory BIST modules and isolation logic from memory BIST unit. The top shell HDL is developed using sed/awk and UNIX shell programming to include the appropriate modules using component instantiation in the top shell design based on the information specified in the MBDL. A HDL verification and a timing file are also generated. The HDL verification file contains the patterns

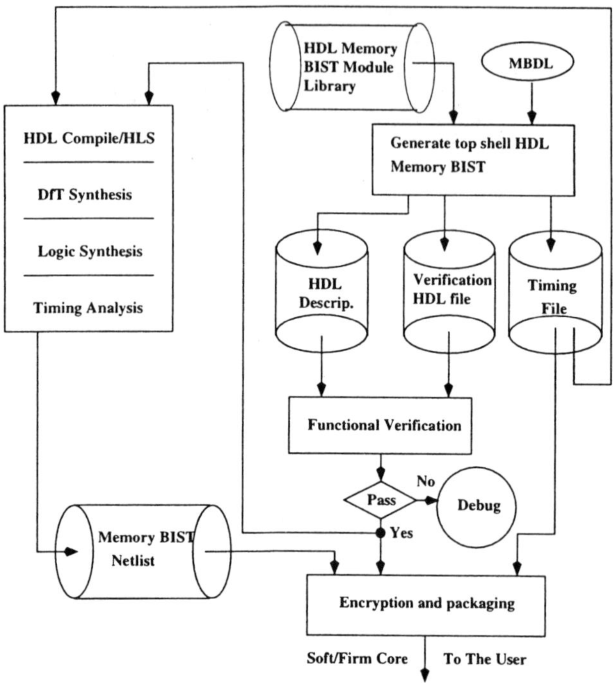

Figure 3. Memory BIST Generation Framework

to drive the generated memory BIST unit and the timing file has the timing constraints on the I/Os of the memory BIST unit. The top shell HDL and the verification files are loaded into a functional verification framework. The correct functioning of the memory BIST unit is verified by comparing the actual response of the memory BIST unit and the expected results derived from the selected memory test algorithm. The top shell HDL and the timing files could be packaged as a soft memory BIST core. To create a firm memory BIST core, the top shell HDL is first compiled into RT-level memory BIST design. This RT-level design and the timing file are loaded into a logic synthesis framework to generate a timed netlist of the memory BIST unit. This netlist is the firm memory BIST core.

3.2 Overhead and Performance Evaluation

The storage unit of the programmable memory BIST units has the highest contribution to the test logic overhead. Dynamic structures such as Random Access Memories (RAM) reduce the test logic overhead of the programmable memory BIST unit, however, they are hard to test and complicate the overall testing of the design. By using register files the testability of the memory BIST unit improves while the test logic overhead increases. Also, register files are random pattern resistant structures. Detailed analysis of the storage units of the two programmable architectures reveals that the functional paths of the storage elements in the register file of the microcode-based architecture are not used during functional operation of the memory BIST unit while the instructions have to be rotated and latched in the next row of the register file in the case of programmable FSM-based architecture. The storage unit of microcode-based architecture is re-designed using slower and smaller scan-only registers. The speed of the scan-only registers only affects the rate that the instructions are loaded in the memory BIST unit and not the operation speed of the unit.

An initialization module could load into the programmable memory BIST units different test algorithms that might be needed in different stages of design fabrication, without a hard coded memory test algorithm. The initialization module extends the usage of the memory BIST unit. The initialization of the scan-only registers is done in series through their scan-path and therefore other initialization module in the design such as the initialization module of the STUMPS channel random logic BIST architecture [9] could be used and further reduction in test logic overhead could be achieved.

The storage unit in the programmable FSM-based architecture requires addition of multiplexers to control the flow of the execution of the memory test algorithm for memories with more complex characteristics, eg. word-oriented, multiport, serial shared. Also, the programmable FSM-based architecture does not have the flexibility of the microcode-based architecture for the generation of different types of memory test algorithms which could become ineffective in the case of unknown defects of a new process or technology.

The memory BIST generation framework described in Figure 3 has been used to generate FSM-based ($prog._{cntrl}^{0}$) and two types of microcode-based controller with register file ($prog._{cntrl}^{1}$) and scan-only registers ($prog._{cntrl}^{2}$) storage units. A non-programmable realization of $March_C$ [1] memory test algorithm is also generated to evaluate the logic overhead of the programmable memory BIST units and the performance of the proposed memory BIST generation framework. The firm memory BIST controller cores are implemented in CMOS 0.35 μ technology running at 100Mhz. The results are summarized in Table 1. The first column specifies the architecture while the second and fourth columns contain the size as the number of 2-input NAND gates for single port Bit-Oriented, not shared and multiport Word-Oriented and serial shared of memory BIST controllers. The third and fifth columns specify the area overhead of the memory BIST architectures for a 16K×32 single and multiport memories. From the presented results in Table 1, re-designing the storage unit of the microcode-based architecture results in up to 60% reduction in the test logic overhead of the controller.

Table 1. Size and Overhead of Mem. BIST Cntrls.

Architecture	$BO^{sp.}_{nshrd.}$	% AO	$WO^{mp.}_{shrd.}$	% AO
$Prog.^{0}_{cntrl}$	449	0.94	630	0.66
$Prog.^{1}_{cntrl}$	461	0.97	641	0.67
$Prog.^{2}_{cntrl}$	203	0.42	263	0.27
March C_{cntrl}	135	0.28	166	0.17

The HDL verification file for the described memory BIST architectures was generated in 5-7 seconds compare to days for its manual generation. The experimental results show that the HDL simulation time (using MTI VHDL simulation framework) increases from 10 to 491 sec. as the complexity of the memory test algorithm increases. Our functional verification framework could reduce the number of sampling addresses and maintain the simulation time within acceptable level.

3.3 BIST Insertion and Verification

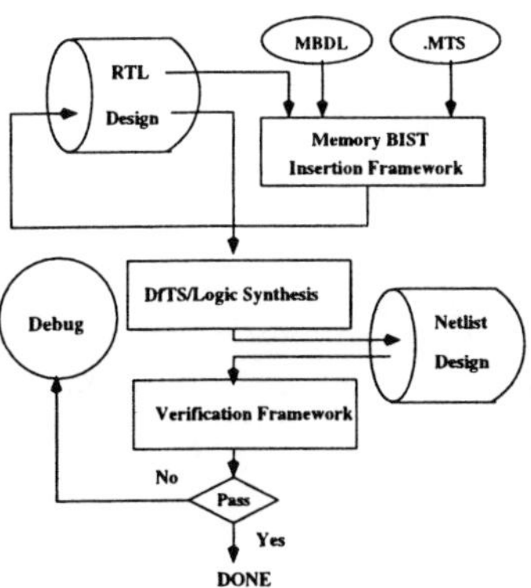

Figure 4. Memory BIST Insertion Framework

Once a memory BIST unit is generated, it has to be inserted in a design. An overview of the memory BIST insertion framework is shown in Figure 4. The functional design and the memory BIST unit are assumed to be in RT-level form. An extension to the MBDL file allows the design entity that the memory BIST unit has to be inserted in and the name of the memory(s)-under-test that will be tested by the same memory BIST unit. The description of the isolation logic could also be given in the MBDL. The user can specify a sub-pattern identifying different ports of the memory-under-test and memory BIST unit in the *.memory test synthesis* (*.mts*) file. The memory BIST insertion framework inserts the memory BIST in the specified design entity, creates and inserts the necessary isolation logic in the design and make the necessary interconnections. By performing the logic synthesis and timing correction, the functional design and the inserted memory BIST are compiled into a netlist. A gate-level structural verification framework has been developed to ensure correct functioning of the isolation logic and correct interconnection of the memory BIST unit in the design [10]. The longest time for generation and insertion of memory BIST units is 26 and 120 seconds while performing these tasks manually would take an experienced DfT designer days.

4 Conclusion

A programmable FSM-based and a microcode-based memory BIST architectures have been described. The two architectures have been evaluated based on their scalability, flexibility, impact on the overall testability of the design and test logic overhead. It has been shown that the microcode-based memory BIST architecture results in lower test logic overhead, is more testable, scales better for memory with different characteristics and has better flexibilities in realizing memory tests.

The details of an enhanced memory test synthesis framework has been described. The experimental results demonstrate that any style of memory BIST could be generated, verified and inserted in seconds and minutes compare to days and weeks if done manually and therefore huge reduction in time-to-market for designs could be achieved.

References

[1] A.J. van de Goor. *Testing Semiconductor Memories: Theory and Practice*. John Wiley and Sons, U.S.A, 1991.

[2] B. F. Cockburn and Y.-F. Nicole Sat. Synthesized Transparent BIST for Detecting Scrambled Pattern Sensitive Faults in RAM. In *Proc. Int. Test Conf.*, pages 23–32, 1995.

[3] M. Marinescu. Simple and efficient algorithms for functional RAM testing. In *Proc. Int. Test Conf.*, pages 572–576, 1982.

[4] LogicVision Web Page. http:www.lvision.com, 1998.

[5] H. Koike, T. Takeshima, and M. Takada. A BIST Scheme Using Microprogram ROM for Large Capacity Memories. *Proc. Int. Test Conf.*, pages 815–822, 1990.

[6] P. G. Shephard III, W. V. Huott, P. R. Turgeon, R. W. Berry Jr., G. Yasar, F. J. Cox, P. Patel, and J. B. Hanley III. Programmable built-in self test method and controller for arrays. *U. S. Patent No. 5,633,877*, May 1997.

[7] I. Schanstra, D. Lukita, A.J. van de Goor, K. Veelenturf, and P. J. van Wijnen. Semiconductor Manufacturing Process Monitoring Using BIST for Embedded Memories. In *Proc. Int. Test Conf.*, pages 872–881, 1998.

[8] K. Zarrineh and S. J. Upadhyaya. On Programmable Memory Built-In Self Test Architectures. *Design Automation and Test in Europe*, pages 708–713, March 1999.

[9] P. H. Bardell, W. H. McAnney, and J. Savir. *Built-In Test for VLSI: Pseudo random Techniques*. Wiley Interscience, 1987.

[10] K. Zarrineh and S. J. Upadhyaya. A New Framework For Automatic Generation, Insertion and Verification of Memory Built-In Self Test Units. *To appear in VLSI Test Symp.*, 1999.

Author Index

NOTES

NOTES

IEEE Computer Society Publications

The world-renowned IEEE Computer Society publishes, promotes, and distributes a wide variety of authoritative computer science and engineering texts. These books are available from most retail outlets. Visit the Online Catalog, *http://computer.org*, for a list of products.

IEEE Computer Society Proceedings

The IEEE Computer Society also produces and actively promotes the proceedings of more than 141 acclaimed international conferences each year in multimedia formats that include hard and softcover books, CD-ROMs, videos, and on-line publications.

For information on the IEEE Computer Society proceedings, send e-mail to cs.books@computer.org or write to Proceedings, IEEE Computer Society, P.O. Box 3014, 10662 Los Vaqueros Circle, Los Alamitos, CA 90720-1314. Telephone +1 714-821-8380. FAX +1 714-761-1784.

Additional information regarding the Computer Society, conferences and proceedings, CD-ROMs, videos, and books can also be accessed from our web site at *http://computer.org/cspress*

1/29/99